Taiwan

Taiwan

From Developing to Mature Economy

EDITED BY
Gustav Ranis

Westview Press
BOULDER • SAN FRANCISCO • OXFORD

All rights reserved. No part of this publication may be reproduced or transmitted in any form or by any means, electronic or mechanical, including photocopy, recording, or any information storage and retrieval system, without permission in writing from the publisher.

Copyright © 1992 by Westview Press, Inc.

Published in 1992 in the United States of America by Westview Press, Inc., 5500 Central Avenue, Boulder, Colorado 80301-2847, and in the United Kingdom by Westview Press, 36 Lonsdale Road, Summertown, Oxford OX2 7EW

Library of Congress Cataloging-in-Publication Data
Taiwan : from developing to mature economy / edited by Gustav Ranis.
  p. cm.
  Includes bibliographical references and index.
  ISBN 0-8133-8436-2
  1. Taiwan—Economic conditions—1945–   . 2. Taiwan—Economic policy—1945–   . I. Ranis, Gustav.
HC430.5.T338 1992
338.95124'9—dc20   91-44780
                                                                      CIP

Printed and bound in the United States of America

∞ The paper used in this publication meets the requirements of the American National Standard for Permanence of Paper for Printed Library Materials Z39.48-1984.

10 9 8 7 6 5 4 3 2 1

Contents

Preface vii

1 From Developing to Mature Economy: An Overview, *Gustav Ranis* 1

2 The Process of Agricultural Development in Taiwan, *Erik Thorbecke* 15

3 New Perspectives on Industrial Growth in Taiwan, *Howard Pack* 73

4 Money and Financial Markets: The Domestic Perspective, *Paul C. H. Chiu* 121

5 Money and Financial Markets: The International Perspective, *Christina Y. Liu* 195

6 Public Finance, *Ching-huei Chang* 223

7 International Trade in Taiwan's Transition from Developing to Mature Economy, *James Riedel* 253

8 Capital and Labor Mobility in Taiwan, *Joseph S. Lee* 305

9 Science, Technology and Human Capital Formation, *Paul K. C. Liu* 357

10 Living Standards, Labor Markets and Human Resources in Taiwan, *Gary S. Fields* 395

About the Contributors 435
About the Book and Editor 439
Index **441**

Preface

The developmental success story of Taiwan, once observed as an oddity and widely dismissed in the Third World as an irrelevant "special case," has drawn substantially increased attention in recent years. Undoubtedly, this is linked to the wave of structural adjustments the countries of Latin America, Asia and Africa have had to undergo in the wake of the deteriorating international environment of the 1980s. It is all the greater pity that Taiwan's relative isolation from the international agencies has prevented the global policy-making and academic communities from receiving the thorough and dispassionate examination the case so richly deserves.

Yet this volume is not simply focused on rehearsing once again the way in which public policy and markets interacted to bring Taiwan from its "basket case" status in the 1950s to the position of "the" leading NIC in the 1980s. Instead, it tries to build on that story and ask the additional, somewhat less conventional, question of what remains for that particular NIC to accomplish before it can fully join the charmed circle of the so-called developed or mature economies. This volume moreover does not claim to have provided a comprehensive, fully satisfactory answer to that intriguing question, but to have raised an issue -- hopefully in an intelligent and provocative fashion -- which should be of broad interest, not only to this and other NICs but also to the near-NICs and would-be NICs waiting in the wings.

The original idea behind this volume, like so many others dealing with various aspects of Taiwan's actual development over the decades, can be attributed to Ministers K.T. Li and Shirley W.Y. Kuo. The ROC Committee for Scientific and Scholarly Cooperation with the United States, Academia Sinica, provided financing and the Chung-Hua Institution for Economic Research, originally under the presidency of S.C. Tsiang and subsequently that of Tzong-shian Yu, overall coordination. The editor wishes to extend his thanks to all of the above. He also wants to express his appreciation to Sung Kang, Christopher Smith, Janet Tsai and Alexander Schrantz for their research assistance and especially to Setsu Essa for her editorial support and for shepherding the volume through its final stages. Glena Ames provided invaluable typing assistance.

Gustav Ranis
New Haven, Connecticut

1

From Developing to Mature Economy: An Overview

Gustav Ranis

1. Introduction

If one accepts Simon Kuznets' six stylized characteristics of modern economic growth, Taiwan seems close to being unambiguously classifiable as a mature industrial economy. Her per capita income in 1990 was just a bit under US$8,000, enough to place her in the World Bank's category of high-income countries. She long ago fully navigated her way through the necessary demographic transition, with population growth rates now so low that they are causing concern and per capita incomes soaring at sustained 6-8 percent annual rates over the past two decades. Kuznets' required structural transformation, in terms of a shift from agricultural to nonagricultural activities, has reached the point where only 4 percent of GDP and 13 percent of labor force employment are generated by agriculture. Taiwan's gross savings rate, at 30 percent, is easily two and a half times that of the minimum "take-off" savings rate stipulated by Arthur Lewis years ago and indeed has been maintained at these levels over the past decade. Proceeding beyond Kuznets, life expectancy at birth is currently about seventy-four years, higher than that of many developed countries. Even as a small island with a population of only 20 million people, Taiwan is today the twelfth largest trading country in the world and disposes over the world's second largest foreign exchange reserves (more than US$70 billion).

Along with the most rapid growth experienced anywhere in the third world, Taiwan has also achieved a persistent reduction in poverty and the most equitable distribution of income, in spite of some deterioration in recent years. It is also significant that her spectacular success in nontraditional export growth was achieved in the face of a marked deterioration in the international environment and accomplished without any special favors accorded by her advanced-country trading partners. Indeed, Taiwan has shown herself more than capable of overcoming the increased protectionism of recent years and absorbing the abrogation of GSP treatment by the United States without even a hiccup in the data. The island clearly seems to qualify, if not as a full-fledged member of the charmed circle of developed countries, at least to be within sight of the "promised land".

Nevertheless a few flies may still be spotted in the ointment. For one, the people of Taiwan, including its policy-makers, do not yet themselves believe that they have "arrived"; they are still "pinching" themselves and this continuing sense of insecurity does affect behavior. It is probably not an exaggeration to observe that even Japan, substantially ahead of Taiwan and certainly a full-fledged member of the mature economy club, frequently still behaves as if it were under threat of being pulled back into the ranks of aspiring developing countries. This may thus be part of an East Asian psychological syndrome.

There are, however, also some objective features of the landscape which provide a more substantive reason for holding up the initiation ceremony -- or at least lead one to acknowledge outstanding problems still in the way of mature economy status. In other words, while it may well be in the nature of so-called "follower countries" to experience a cultural lag between a changing reality and people's willingness to accept it, there also still exist some outstanding real problems which need to be addressed -- as well as some developed-country foibles which could possibly be avoided.

The contributors to this volume have endeavored to examine various major dimensions, sectors or markets descriptive of the economy's past performance and, in the process of venturing a gaze into the near-term future, point to what they believe to be still unresolved problems en route to full economic maturity. Since our profession is generally much better at predicting the past, the reader may note a certain preference for staying on terra firma in many of the chapter presentations which follow. But this is as it should be since one is really able to assess Taiwan's transition from successful developing to fully mature economy only by understanding where that system is coming from and how it is currently functioning -- perhaps with an occasional sideways glance at Japan which accomplished a similar transition some years ago.

In Section 2, I list some of the still unresolved or partially resolved issues or problems that loom ahead and the ways in which Taiwan's policy-makers are now preparing to address them, or, if not yet ready to do so, how they might well address them in the future. A few concluding observations are presented in Section 3.

2. The Final Mile to Economic Maturity: Problems and Solutions

One frequently encountered concern is whether Taiwan's spectacular success in raising her export/GDP ratio from 10 percent in the 1950s to 60 percent in recent years, has, in fact, resulted in exposing the economy excessively to external fluctuations, especially in a world of increased economic turbulence, including recession and neo-protectionist measures. Given that Taiwan is a relatively small economy, one would, of course, expect, *ceteris paribus*, that trade plays a relatively more dominant role than in most middle- or large-sized developing countries. Indeed, as Riedel points out, a 60 percent export/GDP ratio, instead of the 40 percent that might be expected from a multi-country regression, is not all that surprising, given the especially large potential gains from trade for a small natural-resource-poor economy. The issue, however, goes deeper than that, i.e., is the trade excessively focussed on one or two countries (e.g., 50 percent with the United States and Japan in 1988), and is the commodity composition too specialized in terms of the system's risk aversion if and when terms of trade and/or business cycle shocks are encountered?

These particular concerns seem to be substantially exaggerated. Taiwan has been able to dramatically change both the composition of her trade as well as her trading partners. Not only had her exports shifted from 10 percent non-agricultural in the 1950s to 95 percent by 1989 but also fully 50 percent of her exports are now in high technology areas, i.e., machinery and basic metals, transport equipment, and precision instruments, a marked change from the almost exclusive concentration on labor-intensive manufactured exports in the 1960s and the early 1970s. Table 1.1 illustrates her remarkable performance in increasing her overall share in world and total developing country manufactured exports. Also, by focussing on two specific major industries, it illustrates the shift in composition over time. Moreover, even within the loose category of so-called labor-intensive industries, as Riedel also emphasizes, there has been a continuous upgrading of product quality, partly in response to increased quantitative restrictions abroad, thus extending the lives of these industries beyond the end of the domestic cheap-labor phase in the early 1970s.

Similarly, with respect to Taiwan's trading partners, the United States, which was responsible for 34 percent of her total trade in 1985, only accounted for 20 percent five years later. As we would expect from Heckscher/Ohlin, with Taiwan's comparative advantage shifting away from cheap labor and towards technology- and skill-intensive goods, she can anticipate a relative increase in trade with other, mainly Asian, developing countries and away from her traditional advanced-country trading partners. Exports to the Mainland, for example, mainly finished consumer and

TABLE 1.1 Taiwan's Manufactured Exports

Year	Share of Manufactured Exports As % of world exports	As % of LDC exports
1970	0.50	8.8
1975	0.82	11.4
1980	1.54	14.9
1985	2.23	16.7
1988	2.66	17.4

Year	Industrial Export Structure (percent of total) Machinery & equipment	Textile fibers, yarn & clothing
1970	16.7	29.0
1975	19.6	29.3
1980	24.7	21.8
1985	27.8	20.4
1988	35.2	16.2

Source: *UNCTAD Commodity Yearbook*, 1990; *Handbook of International Trade and Development Statistics*, 1990.

technology-intensive goods, exchanging for raw materials and semi-finished goods, now amount to more than US$4 billion annually. Even though such trade remains largely indirect, i.e., via Hong Kong, it has been growing at a spectacular 40 percent annual rate recently and, barring unforeseen political developments, can be expected to continue to soar. Another dimension of this diversification of trade patterns has its roots in Taiwan's own outward DFI which has gained prominence in recent years. Investments motivated by the search for a continued cheap source of labor, "jumping over" actual or prospective LDC trade barriers, plus the circumvention of developed country quotas, have taken place in the ASEAN countries[1] and the Mainland, while more technology-sourcing related investments (see below) have been made in the advanced industrial countries.

A related "problem", also on the way to being at least partially resolved in the course of the normal processes of adjustment, is that of Taiwan's inordinately high savings rate which, in combination with still restricted capital markets and a still undervalued currency, has caused economic problems at home and trade friction abroad. As pointed out by a number of the authors in this volume, for some years now Taiwan has been accumulating foreign exchange reserves as a result of large export surpluses, also reflected in domestic savings substantially in excess of domestic investment. These persistent export surpluses, especially with the United States, culminating in excessively large foreign exchange reserves, have caused political friction and led to persistent U.S. efforts to get Taiwan to dismantle residual protectionism and permit a further appreciation of the currency. At home, the resulting excess liquidity -- further exacerbated by speculative capital inflows anticipating further revaluation of the currency (see Christina Liu) -- has fed stock market and land speculation booms and given rise to a so-called lotto mentality. Especially since Taiwan continues to hope for international support of its application for GATT membership, recent adjustments in the savings rate, the exchange rate and protection levels, as well as further steps toward the liberalization and internationalization of the capital market have been welcomed abroad. However, while the gross savings rate has declined from 38.5 percent in 1987 to about 30 percent in 1990, it is still substantially in excess of gross domestic investment, which is currently at about 20 percent. The current account surplus remains at over 8 percent of GNP and the policy-makers are apparently committed to keeping the currency from appreciating much beyond the NT$26/US$ rate.

The present-day policy response to the acknowledged need for further adjustment seems to be threefold: one, to increase domestic demand with the help of an ambitious (US$300 billion) Six-Year National Development Plan which proposes to help ensure a 7 percent annual GNP growth rate through 1996, permitting per capita income to rise from US$8,000 to $14,000. The macroeconomic intent here is to jack up domestic demand through substantial increases in infrastructural and other spending, to eliminate central government budget surpluses which have historically contributed approximately one-third of the inordinately high savings rate, and thereby to reduce the trade surplus from 8 percent to approximately 3 percent of GNP.

As both Chiu and Christina Liu point out, action on a second front, the complementary internationalization of the capital market, is also under way but still lagging behind. Currently, foreign exchange can be privately held but there are still strict limits on the levels of permitted annual inflows and outflows. Up to this point, traditional fiscal conservatism, traditional high private-saving habits and an equally traditional reluctance to disadvantage the export engine by revaluing the currency, while powerful, seem to be more easily overcome than the reluctance to further free up the capital accounts.

Private and public investment abroad has indeed increased substantially. DFI, as we have noted, has been driven partly by Taiwan's need to extend the life of some of her labor-intensive industries via investments in the

ASEAN countries and the Mainland, where wages continue to be relatively low, and partly by the desire to forge technological links with the frontier countries in the high-tech areas. Taiwan already is the second largest investor in the Philippines, Malaysia, Thailand and Indonesia and has a larger trade surplus with ASEAN than with the United States. Investments on the Mainland are, moreover, increasing rapidly, even though much of it is still indirect via Hong Kong. While the commercial ties between Taiwan and Fukien Province are by no means in the same league as Hong Kong's with Kuangdung Province, they are becoming increasingly important, even though there are still some official prohibitions against investing in a number of (mainly service) industries. As for public investments, in 1988 a US$1.1 billion government overseas aid program was initiated and indications are that this will be increased in the years ahead, for both economic and political reasons. But, as both Chiu and Christina Liu emphasize, Taiwan needs to take additional steps to further free up her capital accounts, permit foreigners to purchase domestic equities -- as well as vice versa -- and reduce central bank intervention in the foreign exchange markets, letting the forward exchange markets function as a hedging device.

A third, related, major dimension which can clearly be identified as "unfinished business" along Taiwan's road to economic maturity is represented by her still heavily segmented domestic financial markets. The fact is that, in spite of the increased reliance on market competition in the wake of the 1989 removal of controls on deposit and loan rates, the so-called commercial banking system remains largely in public sector hands, though a beginning to privatization has been made, with the government offering shares to the general public in some of the specialized banks. As Chiu points out, a national financial conference, convened in June, 1991 to address this very problem, recommended further privatization of the banking system, enhancement of the call loan market, more extensive access to a liberalized foreign exchange market, a widening of the spectrum of risk-return options through a broadened bond market and, perhaps most importantly, further diversification of the available financial instruments.

This lag in institutional change in the system's financial market is deeply rooted in Taiwan's particular development path. Industrialization throughout the past three decades occurred largely via the rapid expansion of small- and medium-scale firms, financed either through internal reinvestment or informal credit arrangements, including the so-called tsouh-wih family-based credit system. As the economy now increasingly moves into more capital- and technology-intensive activities, it requires a shift from extensive self and loan financing to equity financing and more effective intermediation channels between relatively small household and business savers and relatively large investors.

Deficient intermediation networks can also be expected to impact unfavorably on the prospects for a successful Six-Year National Development Plan. For one thing, that Plan calls for substantial increases in government investment, rising at a 15.5 percent annual rate through 1996, including a 9 percent annual increase in investments by public enterprises. Much of the proposed public sector investment is to take the form of public goods to cope with bottleneck problems in the realms of pollution, urban congestion, power, rapid transit and communication. There apparently are also plans, however, for a substantial volume of public investment in directly productive activities, including housing, telecommunications, shopping centers, information products, semi-conductors, petrochemicals, and steel. This should be seen against the backdrop of substantial past reductions in the public sector's role in manufacturing plus her announced intent to privatize such residual public sector enterprises as the tobacco and wine monopolies, China Steel, China Petrochemicals and Marine Transport, partially in response to U.S. pressure.

Overall, the net effect of implementing the proposed Six-Year National Development Plan will thus probably be to reverse past trends and increase the government's relative role as investor. One wonders, leaving overheads to one side, about the extent to which such decisions are being based on the inadequacy of the domestic financial intermediation network rather than on a consideration of cost effectiveness and externalities. If that suspicion is warranted, a superior choice might well be to tackle the inadequacies of the intermediation network head on as a way of aligning traditional small household and business savers with the non-traditional large investment requirements of any future program. Constructing a more competitive financial system, both in terms of admitting additional foreign banks and encouraging more branch banking, domestic and foreign, would contribute substantially to this objective.

The critical issue, of course, is whether or not the public investment program contemplated is likely to "crowd in" private investment or "crowd (it) out". This in turn depends very much on whether or not some of the lessons of the past experience with public and private sectors' relative contributions to development on Taiwan will be heeded. It would not seem to make sense to let the constraints of the existing financial markets carry public investment beyond the legitimate requirements of needed infrastructure -- quite aside from the legitimate need for increased public expenditures in health, education and other so-called social sectors.

It is worth noting at this point that fully half of the US$300 billion expenditure planned under the Six-Year Plan is intended to be borrowed from the non-bank public -- another way of trying to avoid addressing the underlying problem of inadequate domestic equity flows. As the recent experience of Pakistan has shown, while such a large expansion of domestic debt, simply by paying comparatively high interest rates to the non-bank public, is not inflationary in the short run, it can, in fact, become quite inflationary over time once the interest charges on the debt become deeply embedded in the national budget. As Chang points out, additional fiscal restructuring may be needed to broaden the income tax base, eliminate outdated tax preferences for interest income, and begin to deal with local government revenue sharing issues in the context of an increased public sector decentralization effort which is probably inevitable. One may also well ask whether the changed global environment does not entitle Taiwan to declare its own peace dividend via a reduction of its traditionally high defense expenditures.

The issue of locating the likely mainsprings of future growth in Taiwan goes, however, much deeper than to the relative size of the public and private sectors. It takes us to a consideration of the extent to which technology change on Taiwan has become truly endogenous and routinized, undoubtedly the most crucial of all of Kuznets' modern growth characteristics and one on which the jury is still out. As Pack points out, Taiwan's growth has from the beginning benefitted unusually -- certainly by LDC standards -- from a substantial contribution of technology change, as measured by total factor productivity growth. With most LDCs historically posting negligible or even negative total factor productivity growth, Taiwan's levels (in the 50 percent annual range) have persistently approached those of the developed countries, while at the same time accommodating spectacular increases in both physical capital and labor inputs. In the 1950s -- in spite of passing through an (albeit relatively mild) import-substitution phase -- Taiwan's extraordinary performance was undoubtedly due largely to the contribution of technology change in the agricultural sector (see Thorbecke). Thereafter, as the center of gravity of the economy began to shift, it can be increasingly laid at the doorstep of a unique combination of principally small- and medium-scale industrial enterprises interacting with a dynamic agriculture, on the one hand, and, at the same time, increasingly participating in international trade with the help of the selective assimilation of foreign technology.

Taiwan was thus both an early practitioner of the so-called Green Revolution in agricultural technology and subsequently eminently successful in adapting imported industrial technology to her labor surplus conditions. The big question which remains to be answered is whether, now that the reserves of agricultural productivity change have long ago disappeared and labor shortage is forcing the industrial output mix into more capital- and technology-intensive activities, Taiwan can continue to count on the sustained contribution of increasingly indigenous innovations.

Originally it was a combination of small traders and small-scale industrialists, partly Taiwanese ex-landlords and partly migrating Mainland entrepreneurs, who forged the tremendous industrial successes of the 1960s and 1970s, first in food processing, later in non-durables using imported inputs, successfully mopping up the system's surplus labor and simultaneously improving the distribution of income on the island. Small- and medium-scale (largely rural) enterprises not only were dominant from the outset but, even more startling, expanded more rapidly over time than large-scale enterprises. They moreover proved extremely flexible and adaptable in both the choice of output quality and the process dimensions of technology change.

As one tries to peer ahead, however, with the economy moving into the more capital- and technology-intensive range of industries sporting shorter product cycles, the question arises as to whether a shift to larger-scale enterprises is not now required, and relatedly, whether or not truly indigenous technology change must now increasingly take over as the Gerschenkronian late-comer benefits are exhausted. Clearly, more vertical rather than horizontal subcontracting lies in the future. Clearly as well, some loss in competitive pressure is likely as the exchange rate appreciates further, wages rise, and economies of scale become a larger factor in the output mix. But the most important issue will surely be from whence the needed new innovative response mechanisms will emanate. As Pack points out, the choice of imported technologies and their adaptation, with the help of domestic R&D enhancement, remains a crucial issue as Taiwan tries to develop new industrial niches for her exports. While, in the past, her small- and medium-sized firms have shown amazing adaptability with respect to the adoption and modification of newly imported technology, this challenge will undoubtedly be more difficult to meet in a world of shorter product cycles.

However, there are also clear indications that Taiwan's past adaptability in policy has not abandoned her. For example, while half of her recent overseas investments have been LDC- and cheap-labor-sourcing-oriented, the other half has been focussed on establishing technology channels with mature economy firms in the high-tech areas. While Lee suggests the relative encouragement of Western over Japanese firms since the latter tend to withhold technological information, the recent move by Sony and other Japanese firms to increase their presence on Taiwan indicates that they also are willing to contribute substantially to the technology transfer mechanism in these new areas. Clearly, as Lee also points out, when Taiwan has to cater more to specific customer designs and to innovate continuously herself at the cutting edge of technology, more investment in private domestic R&D will become essential for the maintenance of competitiveness. Indeed, according to Paul Liu, R&D expenditures have already increased from 0.7 percent in 1979 to 1.2 percent of GDP in 1988. Meanwhile, government R&D seems to be shifting towards more basic research, if the tripling of Taiwan's scientific citation index during the 1980s is any indication.

At the same time, in the complementary human capital arena, Taiwan's secondary education is now 70 percent vocational/technical and only 30 percent academic, in sharp contrast to the usual developing-country pattern. Taiwan's early emphasis on primary education was essential to the agricultural breakthroughs of the 1950s and 1960s and her shift to a focus on numeracy and general scientific education at the secondary level since have served to minimize frequently encountered screening and skills mismatch phenomena.

With respect to her high-level manpower, Taiwan has maintained the tradition of providing her population with competitive access to higher education via the merits-based imperial examinations system. As Paul Liu indicates, higher education's emphasis has gradually shifted from the humanities and the agricultural sciences towards engineering and the social sciences. Overall, educational expenditures, a non-negligible 1.7 percent of GNP in 1952, were raised to 5.2 percent by 1988. In addition, science parks have been established and other efforts expended to bring back to Taiwan Chinese scientists and entrepreneurs who had earlier emigrated to the various Silicon valleys of the industrial countries.

It is hard to see why the current educational structure, superimposed on underlying Confucian values, should not yield the kind of labor force which, together with imported technology and domestic R&D, would provide the necessary ingredients for the future routinization of technology change. The increased emphasis on applied science and technology certainly seems to have already paid off, judging by the jump in patents from 2,770 in 1980 to 7,450 in 1984, reported by Paul Liu. The tax code has been modified to encourage private risk-taking and, perhaps most telling, there has been a recent marked change in Taiwan's attitude towards intellectual property rights. In the past, Taiwan, along with other successful NICs, has been somewhat notorious as a pirater of Western technology; in fact, much of the recent friction between the United States and Taiwan has focussed on the protection of intellectual property rights, along with the exchange rate, capital and trade restriction issues. There is now clear evidence that Taiwan is beginning to consider intellectual property rights protection as important not only for the generation but also for the diffusion of new technology, and not only from the more advanced countries to Taiwan but also (and increasingly) from Taiwan to some of the countries to which she is now transferring capital and technology.

While, as we have seen, there is a clear-cut tendency for the industrial output mix to shift towards the high-tech, short-product-cycle end of the spectrum, Taiwan has wisely endeavored to maintain her competitiveness in some of the labor-intensive industrial sectors for as long as possible. Given her falling fertility rates,[2] an aging population and a levelling off of past increases in female participation rates, this combination has been achieved mainly by virtue of her overseas investments in the Mainland and ASEAN.

Another way of alleviating the current labor shortage problem would, of course, be via an inflow of permanent or guest workers. However, as Lee points out, such flows, if from ASEAN countries, have in the past caused social problems, while still "illegal" immigration from the Mainland might raise political tensions. Consequently, current official policy is that foreign workers may be recruited only when needs cannot be met by automation and that the outward-investment solution is clearly much preferred. Incidentally, this observed switch from importing capital and exporting labor to exporting capital and refusing to import labor represents one of the time-tested hallmarks of a successful transition to mature-economy status.

There are other dimensions of the changing labor market picture which probably have not yet been adequately addressed. The recent lifting of martial law has permitted the pressure for labor disputes, minimal before the advent of labor shortage and submerged thereafter, to exhibit itself, although labor militancy and associated political stirrings are still very mild on Taiwan by any international standard. Lee points out that Taiwan's unions were more or less the administrative arm of the ruling party until 1985 (*Industry of Free China*, April 1989), which made sense as long as markets remained workably competitive, as they have been in Taiwan. If there is to be a convergence to mature-economy status in this dimension as well, one would anticipate a movement from docile, government-supported and production-oriented unions towards more independent, pluralist, consumption-oriented union activity in the years ahead. However, one should probably not expect a really militant unionism to emerge on the island in the short run for a number of reasons. For one, in contrast to South Korea, where the large-scale chaebol-dominated industrial structure renders unionism as a plausible countervailing force, the prognosis for Taiwan is for a workably competitive industrial structure to be maintained even as the output mix continues to shift. For another, Taiwan is arriving on the mature-economy stage at a time when unionism is on the defensive in the West.

In addition to the ability to avoid the historical phase of a more militant unionism as experienced by earlier graduates to economic maturity, there are a number of other Gerschenkronian-type advantages which can accrue to the discriminating late-comer country. One such area is concerned with how much social welfare legislation how soon. Thus far, Taiwan has shown signs that she does not intend to precipitously eradicate traditional family protective schemes, preferring cost-sharing and supplementing such schemes to supplanting them quickly with Scandinavian-style modern welfare legislation. But there are contrary pressures, including those from protectionist-minded protagonists of globally applied welfare standards in the mature countries. Sometimes such pressures need to be manfully resisted since convergence to mature-economy status does not necessarily require converging to some of the now well-recognized excesses of the advanced countries.

A similar, perhaps even more critical, area in which Taiwan might do well to learn from the mistakes of the now-developed countries concerns the role of the agricultural sector. As is by now fully appreciated (see Thorbecke), agriculture played an important, indeed leading, role in Taiwan's early development, in terms of mobilizing domestic savings, generating the first non-traditional export surpluses via mushroom and asparagus production, and providing the basis for important rural linkages. Along that historical road, we have seen the major contributions made by land reform, by land-saving technology change, plus, early on, the avoidance of some of the excessive discrimination against agriculture that other developing countries have experienced. Consequently, the rapid reallocation of the labor force, in excess of 6 percent per annum during the 1960s, culminated in the exhaustion of the system's labor surplus by the end of the decade. It meant the gradual diminution of the "specialness" of the agricultural sector as it became just another fully-commercialized economic activity. In the course of this transition, agriculture in Taiwan has now been reduced to about 4 percent of GDP and to about 13 percent of the employed population. At the same time, a second agricultural reform has been under way since the 1980s, this one focussing on the consolidation of land, a shift in technology from the chemical/fertilizer type of innovation to the mechanical/tractor type and the appearance of new institutions, including the cultivating firm.

There has, however, also been in evidence a tendency towards increased agricultural protection in the mature-economy style, the most egregious examples of which are, of course, Western Europe and Japan, with the United States not far behind. In fact, according to Thorbecke, Taiwan's 1980 level of agricultural protection was higher than that of the European Economic Community. This problem is especially serious in food-stuffs which are the most protected and yet maintain the greatest competitive disadvantage. Currently there is a 30 percent subsidy on rice production, and Thorbecke estimates that the overall social cost of agricultural protection reduces annual GNP growth by 1 percent. While food, of course, is a very sensitive commodity, especially as long as there remains a state of tension in the Taiwan Straits, the current easing of the Cold War generally should also permit Taiwan to think increasingly in terms of international buffer stocks rather than price supports. Thorbecke suggests that agricultural R&D be increased to the level of middle-income industrialized countries, thus reducing the need for protectionism. This would also imply shifting to higher-valued commodities in place of rice and sugar and generally moving gradually, in the context of the current GATT negotiations, towards a more competitive agricultural sector.

3. Concluding Remarks

In spite of its well-deserved reputation as the most successful developing society to appear on the global stage since the end of World War II, Taiwan's policy-makers have continued to pinch themselves, i.e., they remain concerned about the durability or sustainability of their record of ensuring growth with equity in an increasingly unfriendly world. Such a reaction was perhaps justified in the past, given the continued tensions in the region, the small size of the island relative to the Mainland, and the increased political isolation in which Taiwan has found herself since the early 1970s. But, given her truly remarkable record during the turbulent 1980s in the face of increased protectionism by her major trading partners, Taiwan should by now be much more confident about the future, better able to take temporary setbacks in stride and more ready to heed the lessons of her own past ability to respond to crises. Whether we cite the famous 19 Points policy response to the announced end of foreign assistance in the early 1960s, the demonstrated capacity since to adjust to neo-protectionism, recession, inflation, and the end of preferences, or the ability to overcome continuous heavy defense expenditures, political ostracism and direct economic blackmail by Mainland China, Taiwan's sustained economic performance has been little short of extraordinary.

The current process of disintegration of socialism around the world, though still resisted on the Mainland, should provide additional encouragement. Certainly, economic blackmail will be much less effective in the future, while the Soviet Union and Eastern Europe are likely to become important additional markets for Taiwan's exports as well as for her investments. In the process of joining the advanced economies, Taiwan should, of course, not expect to continue to experience annual growth rates of exports in the 30 percent range or of GDP growth in the 8-10 percent range. Growth rates of 15 percent in exports and 6 percent in GDP, still substantially in excess of most mature economies, should not cause consternation or concern.

Taiwan has continuously demonstrated her pragmatism in policy over time, accommodating to a changing domestic and international environment and working through -- rather than attempting to replace -- markets. Persistently distancing herself from any type of central planning -- never even resorting to a strong planning commission as in South Korea -- she pioneered in "market-friendly" government interventions and an early version of indicative planning. It may be said that Taiwan's policy-makers have understood from the beginning that the ever-increasing complexity of development requires an ever-increasing reliance on indirect controls, with only highly-selective direct interventions by government. This recognition should not now be attenuated by the acknowledged need for long-term overhead and infrastructure investments in the future.

This observer, in other words, does not share Ian Little's fear that Taiwan might today be in danger of forgetting the lessons of her own prior successes (Little, 1979, p. 507). Pragmatism, translated into flexibility and the willingness to admit mistakes and correct them relatively quickly, has always won out thus far. Even if some aspects of the proposed Six-Year National Development Plan provide cause for concern (see above), its implementation, like that of all mixed economy plans, will undoubtedly turn out to be a more flexible year-to-year proposition. Societal turning points, like those in 1961 and 1970, always seem painful -- especially when the system is in the middle of a regime change. But there is no reason to expect a fundamentally different response by Taiwan's policy-makers in the future as they face up to the few remaining challenges en route to full-fledged mature-economy status.

Notes

1. Amounting to US$4.5 billion in 1990. Singapore is not a recipient, for obvious reasons.

2. In early 1991, public policy indeed shifted to providing incentives for larger families.

References

Handbook of International Trade and Development Statistics. 1990. United Nations Conference on Trade and Development. New York: United Nations.

Industry of Free China. April 1989. Taipei, Taiwan.

Little, Ian. 1979. "An Economic Reconnaissance," in Walter Galenson, ed., *Economic Growth and Structural Change in Taiwan.* Pp. 448-507. Ithaca: Cornell University Press.

UNCTAD Commodity Yearbook. 1990. United Nations Conference on Trade and Development. New York: United Nations.

2

The Process of Agricultural Development in Taiwan

Erik Thorbecke

1. STRUCTURAL TRANSFORMATION AND THE DECLINING ROLE OF AGRICULTURE

The process of economic development is characterized by a structural transformation which entails a continuous decline in the relative importance of agriculture in the economy. At an early stage of development the bulk of output originates in agriculture and the majority of the labor force is employed in that sector. As an economy grows, the relative importance of industry and services increases and gradually the center of gravity of the economy moves away from agriculture towards non-agricultural sectors. At some point the economy shifts from being considered underdeveloped (developing) to gaining a semi-industrialized status before, ultimately, reaching the stage of a developed and fully industrialized economy.

What is so remarkable about the recent economic history of Taiwan is not that it followed this typical pattern of development and went through the various stages -- as all presently developed countries had done previously -- but the incredible speed of its structural transformation. In the four decades following the end of the Second World War, *per capita* GNP in Taiwan rose from approximately US$150 to US$6,135.[1] The corresponding annual growth rate of per capita income of 9.72 percent throughout this period must be almost unique.

A strong case has been made by students of Taiwan's agricultural history, among which are P. S. Ho and its present President Teng-Hui Lee, that the relatively recent performance of agriculture in the post-World War II era can be understood only in the context of, and as a continuation of changes that occurred in the era of Japanese colonization.[2] In a nutshell, by the end of the colonial period a number of essential features were present which were conducive to a potential takeoff in the post-war era. These major elements were an appropriate labor-intensive technology relying on modern inputs, a physical infrastructure, particularly in terms of irrigation and drainage, which increased greatly the productivity of this technology, and, finally, a set of rural institutions that helped to disseminate knowledge, provide extension and credit services, and market both inputs and outputs.

Immediately following World War II, Taiwan was still a predominantly agricultural economy with well over half of its labor force employed in agriculture and about 44 percent of net domestic product (NDP) generated in that sector. The transformation of agriculture that had started in the colonial period had not altered significantly the agricultural shares in, respectively, NDP and the labor force.[3] In contrast, the decline in these two shares after the end of the war was dramatic. Clearly the preconditions for a takeoff were present.

As Table 2.1 reveals, the share of agriculture in NDP dropped from 33.7 percent in 1953-1956 to 6.1 percent in 1988, and the share of agricultural employment in total employment fell from 54.8 percent to 13.7 percent during the same period. While over half of the island's population in 1953-1956 still consisted of farm households, the latter made up less than one-fifth of the population by 1988. Another indicator of the structural shift away from agriculture is a major drop in the share of agricultural exports in total exports from over 90 percent in 1953-1956 to about 6 percent in 1988 (see col. 4, Table 2.1) and the decline in the relative importance of agricultural imports. Even as late as the middle 1960s agricultural exports had amounted to almost 45 percent of total exports.

TABLE 2.1 Relative Shares of Agriculture in Net Domestic Product, Employment, Population, Export and Imports, 1953-1988[a]

	Share of agriculture % of NDP	Agricultural workers as % of total employment	Farm household population as as % of total population	Agricultural exports as % of total total exports	Agricultural imports as % of total total imports
1953-1956	33.70	54.80	51.00	91.80	33.70
1957-1960	31.60	51.00	48.90	82.90	26.60
1961-1964	29.00	49.60	47.60	59.50	33.80
1965-1968	24.90	43.70	44.70	45.00	25.20
1969-1972	16.50	36.00	41.10	21.50	23.40
1973-1975	14.50	30.60	37.70	15.90	21.10
1976-1981	10.90	23.40	32.30	10.90	18.20
1982-1985	8.10	18.20	24.20	7.50	17.20
1988	6.10	13.70	19.20	6.10	11.80

[a]The percentage shares are computed as averages during the periods indicated, e.g., 1953-1956 as a four-year average.

Source: *Basic Agricultural Statistics, Republic of China* (1989 ed., Table 1).

In a sense, the agricultural sector was continuing until that time to perform its traditional role of transferring resources through exports, albeit in a more limited way than during the colonial period. In this connection, a comparison of total agricultural exports (including processed agricultural products) and total agricultural imports (including fertilizer inputs) shows, at first, an increase in the agricultural export surplus from approximately US$12 million in 1952 to US$120 million in 1965, to be subsequently transformed into an import surplus in the neighborhood of US$200 million in 1973-1975 which ballooned to US$2.611 billion in 1988.[4] Hence from the late 1960s on, agriculture as a sector had become a net drain on the economy from the standpoint of foreign resources.

A fundamental shift occurred, likewise, in the net flow of resources between agriculture and the rest of the economy. While until the late sixties agriculture provided a considerable net capital flow to non-agriculture, the direction of this flow was subsequently reversed and the agricultural sector became increasingly protected and subsidized.

What the above indicators suggest is that Taiwan moved from an agriculture-based economy in the late forties and fifties to a semi-industrialized one by the early seventies, and is presently reaching the stage of a full-fledged industrialized economy.

2. OVERALL AGRICULTURAL PERFORMANCE AND STAGES OF AGRICULTURAL DEVELOPMENT

Overview and Overall Agricultural Performance

Five fairly distinct stages of agricultural development can be identified in the post-World War II period:
1. 1947-1954: Post-war Recovery and Rehabilitation;
2. 1954-1967: Sustained Agricultural Growth;
3. 1967-1974: Slowdown;
4. 1974-1980: Government Support and Institutional Changes;
5. 1980-present: Agricultural Adjustment and Liberalization.

A general overview of the changing agricultural structure and performance during the last four decades is helpful before analyzing in more detail developments occurring in each of these five specific stages in the next two sections. In particular, it is important to examine: 1) the major trends in output growth; 2) the changing commodity composition of agricultural production (in terms of the changing relative importance of its major components); and, 3) the evolution in the use of major agricultural inputs (i.e., land, labor, intermediate inputs, and capital). The latter, in turn, reflects major changes in agricultural technology which took place over time.

Table 2.2 gives the growth rates of total agricultural production as well as that of its major components, i.e., farm crops (including rice), livestock, forestry, and fishery, for each of the above five stages.[5] The evidence relating to the changing commodity composition is given in Table 2.3, while Table 2.4 brings together information on a number of agricultural input indicators. In all three tables, data are shown for beginning and end years of the above five phases to illustrate discrete changes and key turning points which are used to identify and define these phases.

The main general observations which are suggested, at the outset, by Table 2.2 are: 1) the deceleration over time in the growth of overall agricultural output in each successive phase with the exception of a slight acceleration in the 1974-1980 phase as compared to the preceding period; 2) an even more pronounced deceleration in the growth rate of farm crops in each successive phase starting with a rate of 9.46 percent in the Recovery Period and ending with a negative rate of 0.7 percent in the Adjustment Period up to 1987 (rice output, which is included within the farm crops category, even fell by 2.68 percent annually during the Adjustment Period).

The same trends and changes are highlighted from a different perspective in Table 2.3. It shows that the relative share of farm crops in total agricultural production fell drastically from 76.6 percent in 1949 to 42.1 percent in 1986-1988. Within this group the big relative losers during the same timespan were rice, the share of which declined from 36.1 percent to 11.8 percent, and special crops (predominantly sugar) and "others" which together fell from one-third of the value of total agricultural output to less than one-tenth. In contrast, the relative performance of both fruits and vegetables improved significantly. Each of these categories increased its relative share from approximately 4 percent in 1949 to above 10 percent in 1986-1988. Table 2.3 also reveals the outstanding relative performance of the livestock and fishery sectors during the period under consideration. Together the value of their production is today significantly higher than the total value of farm crop production. Finally, it can be seen that forestry, after an upsurge in the late sixties and early seventies -- which went hand in hand with large scale deforestation and as a reaction triggered much stricter environmental controls -- has become a marginal activity.

The main message conveyed by Table 2.3 is that Taiwan, which had once been characterized as primarily a rice and sugar economy, became highly diversified during its structural transformation, with rice no longer playing a major role -- i.e., constituting less than 12 percent of the value of agricultural output in 1986-1988 and sugar having become a marginal crop.

Table 2.4 highlights interesting turning points for key agricultural inputs which help define and identify the distinct stages of agricultural development which have been adopted in this study. In Table 2.4 inputs are broken

TABLE 2.2 Stages of Agricultural Development: Growth Rates of Agricultural Output in Major Sectors, 1947-1987[a]

Stages of agricultural development		Total agricultural production (1)	Farm crops (2)	(Rice) (2a)	Livestock (3)	Forestry (4)	Fishery (5)
		I. Based on output indices using value added as weights					
Recovery	1947-1954	10.61	9.46	7.62	15.67	3.00	12.88
Growth	1954-1967	4.88	3.86	3.10	6.34	7.27	8.13
Slowdown	1967-1974	3.76	1.32	-0.21	6.74	-2.01	8.25
Government Support	1974-1980	4.15	0.77	0.00	8.83	-4.95	5.93
Adjustment	1980-1987	2.42	-0.71	-2.68	6.20	-1.25	4.23
	1947-1987	5.11	3.07	1.69	8.34	0.74	7.94

(continues)

TABLE 2.2 (continued)

Stages of agricultural development		Total agricultural production (1)	Farm crops (2)	(Rice) (2a)	Livestock (3)	Forestry (4)	Fishery (5)
		II. Based on output indices using quantities as weights					
Recovery	1947-1954	8.73	8.15	7.61	15.84	10.88	12.28
Growth	1954-1967	4.98	4.08	3.04	6.33	7.12	9.03
Slowdown	1967-1974	2.28	0.92	-0.22	6.49	-1.62	7.49
Government Support	1974-1980	2.76	1.11	0.00	8.82	-5.98	5.87
Adjustment	1980-1987[b]	1.33	-0.99	-2.00	6.57	-3.38	4.35
	1947-1987[c]	4.17	2.85	1.89	8.38	1.63	8.00

[a] Growth rates for above periods were computed on the basis of three-year averages between beginning and end of period, e.g. the growth rate between 1954 and 1967 is calculated as that between 1953-1955 (3-year average) and 1966-1968 (3-year average).
[b] Growth rate between 1979-1981 (3-year average) and 1987.
[c] Growth rate between 1946-1948 (3-year average) and 1987.

Source: Derived from data in *Taiwan Agricultural Yearbooks* and *Basic Agricultural Statistics*. (Note that the growth rates of agricultural output in Panel I are based on the indices appearing in Table 14 of the 1989 edition of BAS while the growth rates in Panel II are based on the indices appearing in BAS 1988.) The first set uses value added as weights, whereas the second set uses quantities.

TABLE 2.3 Commodity Composition of Agricultural Production (percentage shares based upon current prices)[a]

	Farm crops						Livestock	Forestry	Fishery	Total agriculture
	Rice	Special crops[b]	Fruits	Vege-tables	Others	Total				
1948[c]	36.1	10.2	3.9	4.1	22.3	76.6	14.3	2.3	6.8	100.0
1953-1955	40.5	14.2	2.0	3.1	8.5	68.3	16.9	6.0	8.8	100.0
1966-1968	30.1	9.4	7.4	6.2	9.1	62.2	22.1	5.8	9.9	100.0
1973-1975	26.1	9.1	5.2	8.2	5.9	54.5	26.0	4.5	14.9	100.0
1979-1981	19.8	6.1	7.0	10.8	3.4	47.1	29.2	2.4	21.4	100.0
1986-1988	11.8	5.3	10.6	10.3	4.1	42.1	29.2	1.1	27.5	100.0

[a]Percentage commodity composition is calculated on the basis of three-year averages, e.g. 1953-1955 means annual average of these three years.
[b]Predominantly sugar.
[c]The percentage breakdown within the farm crops group is based on the intragroup distribution for 1948 given in Thorbecke (1979), Table 2.6, p. 146.

Source: *Taiwan Agricultural Yearbook*, Department of Agriculture & Forestry, Taiwan Provincial Government, various issues.

TABLE 2.4 Selected Agricultural Input Indicators by Subperiods and Stages

	Cultivated area ×1000 ha (1)	Crop area ×1000 ha (2)	Multiple crop index (2)/(1) ×100 (3)	Agri- cultural workers ×1000 (4)	Total man-days ×1 mill (5)	Man-days per agricultural worker 5/4 (6)	Draft cattle ×1000 (7)	Chemical fertilizer NPK ×1000 MT (8)	Tractors units (9)	Fixed capital NT $ mill (10)
1946-1948[a]	843	1,202	143	1,331	169	127	286	na	--	--
1953-1955	873	1,499	172	1,541	245	159	401	117	--	8,401
1966-1968	899	1,691	188	1,602	306	191	341	230	474	11,909
1973-1975	910	1,623	178	1,506	285	189	198	285	988	15,067
1979-1981	908	1,431	158	1,194	210	176	84[b]	435[b]	3,565	22,871
1986-1988	890	1,248	140	1,094	193	176[c]	na	396[d]	10,152	31,882

Stage of agricultural development | | | | Corresponding growth rates | | | | | | |

Recovery	1947-1954[e]	0.50	3.20	2.67	2.11	5.45	3.26	4.95	na	--	na
Growth	1954-1967	0.22	0.93	0.69	0.29	1.72	1.42	-1.08	5.34	na	2.72
Slowdown	1967-1974	0.17	-0.56	-0.74	-0.83	-0.95	-0.02	-5.13	3.11	11.06	3.42
Govt support	1974-1980	-0.02	-1.88	-1.79	-3.19	-3.97	-1.11	-1.59	7.30	23.85	7.20

| Adjustment | 1980-1987 | -0.28 | -1.73 | -1.55 | -1.16 | -1.12 | 0.00 | na | -1.23 | 16.13 | 4.86 |
| | 1947-1987 | 0.14 | 0.09 | -0.18 | -0.18 | 0.35 | 0.81 | na | 4.01 | 14.94[f] | 4.12[g] |

[a] Three year average, except when specifically mentioned.
[b] 1980.
[c] It is assumed that average man-days per agricultural worker was 176 in 1986-1988 thus remaining at its 1979-1981 level.
[d] 1986.
[e] Growth rates are computed on the basis of three year averages for the beginning and the end of each phase.
[f] Growth rate 1966-1968 to 1986-1988.
[g] Growth rate 1953-1955 to 1986-1988.

Source: Thorbecke (1979, Table 2.7), Mao (1987, Tables 4 and 6), *Taiwan Agricultural Yearbook* (1989).

down into five major categories: land, human labor, animal labor, intermediate inputs (i.e., chemical fertilizer), and capital and mechanical implements (i.e., fixed capital and tractors). With respect to land, the key indicators are the amounts of cultivated and crop areas, respectively, and the multiple crop index which is the ratio of the latter to the former. An examination of the corresponding input columns in Table 2.4 reveals that the amount of cultivated area remained essentially constant over the period under consideration[6] and that the crop area increased significantly until the late sixties before declining sharply in the last two periods to reach a present level only marginally higher than that prevailing in 1946-1948. Likewise, the multiple crop index followed the same evolution as for crop area. It is interesting to note that all three land indicators reached a peak in the late sixties at the end of the second agricultural development phase.

The major indicators with respect to human labor shown in Table 2.4 are the total number of agricultural workers, the total number of man-days of agricultural labor, and the average number of man-days per agricultural worker. Again, all three of these indicators of labor inputs rose until the late sixties after which they started falling. However, in contrast with land inputs, the actual number of agricultural workers had declined absolutely by 18 percent in 1986-1988 as compared to its starting level in 1946-1948. The number of head of draft cattle (mainly water buffalo) -- reflecting animal labor -- rose during the first agricultural phase to decline very substantially thereafter and became marginal as a source of energy.

The major indicator of intermediate inputs is the consumption of chemical fertilizer which rose substantially until 1979-1981 to fall slightly in the last development phase.

The last category of inputs given in Table 2.4 is that of fixed capital and tractors. It can be seen that the amount of fixed capital (consisting of farm buildings, farm machinery, breeding livestock, and perennial crops and plants) continued to increase during the four decades under consideration but at an accelerated rate since the late sixties. Farm mechanization is a recent phenomenon which became important in Taiwan only from about the mid-1960s on. The number of tractors, starting from a very low base, rose at extremely high growth rates in the last two decades.

Thus, the major determinants of agricultural growth, in the first two stages, were the more intensive cultivation of land through a significant increase in the multiple crop index (MCI) together with rising labor inputs and increasing application of chemical fertilizer. Note that all labor and relevant land input indicators reached their peak by the end of the second period (i.e., in 1966-1968) to decline significantly in the subsequent periods which are characterized by a much greater use of capital inputs (fixed capital and tractors). After the late sixties both land and labor had become binding constraints and the technology had to become more capital-intensive.

To highlight the dramatic move away from a technology relying mainly on human and animal labor as major sources of energy until the mid-sixties to one gradually substituting mechanical power for human and animal power, an attempt was made to convert these sources of power to horsepower equivalents so as to make them comparable.[7] Whereas in 1952-1954, 67 percent of total energy used in agricultural crop production came from human labor and 33 percent from animal labor, by 1975, human labor represented only about 35 percent of total energy and animal labor 7 percent. On the other hand, mechanical energy, which was practically non-existent at the outset, appeared to contribute 58 percent of total energy in crop production in 1975. Since the total labor inputs have fallen significantly from 285 million man-days in 1973-1975 to about 193 million man-days in 1986-1988 and since animal labor has become marginal, the share of mechanical power in total energy used in crop production is bound to be even much higher today than in 1975.

We can now turn to a brief description of the first three phases of agricultural development before concentrating on analyzing in much more detail the performance of agriculture and the policy and institutional changes which occurred during the last two stages from 1973-1975 on.[8]

STAGES OF AGRICULTURAL DEVELOPMENT BEFORE 1973-1975

Post-war Recovery and Rehabilitation: 1946-1948 to 1953-1955

The exact determination of when a subperiod begins or ends is bound to be somewhat arbitrary. The major reason for ending this stage in 1953 is that it marks the completion of the institutional changes connected with the land reform process, that is, the enactment of the Land-to-the-Tiller Program.

This phase is marked by two essential developments: 1) the recovery of the agricultural sector from the disruption of the war which restored the level of total agricultural production to its pre-war level by the early 1950s; and 2) the set of land reform measures which were to have a crucial effect on the future agricultural development of Taiwan. This phase can be considered as establishing initial conditions conducive to an equitable growth path in Taiwan's agriculture.

The extremely high growth rate of agricultural output over this period of 10.6 percent annually (see Table 2.2) reflects the restoration of the level of capacity utilization more or less equivalent to the one that had prevailed before the war. Evidence that both land and labor were used at lower levels of intensity at the beginning of this phase is provided by the considerable jumps in, respectively, the multiple crop index from 143 to 170 and the average number of man-days per agricultural worker from 127 to 159 (see Table 2.4).

Three interrelated policy elements played a crucial role in this phase: 1) the establishment of the Chinese-American Joint Commission on Rural Reconstruction (JCRR) in 1948, which became the major institution -- comparable to a Ministry of Agriculture -- in planning and helping to carry out Taiwan's agricultural development; 2) US foreign aid, initiated in 1951, which was largely directed towards agriculture at the outset and provided the major resources to the JCRR; and 3) the set of land reform measures. Clearly, this last element had, by far, the greatest impact on the growth and distribution of output. Yet the close complementarity among these three elements made the land reform as successful as it was. The land reform process itself was undertaken in three steps: 1) the rent reduction program; 2) the sale of public land to cultivators and tenants; and 3) the Land-to-the-Tiller Program, which limited land ownership of current landlords.

Even though it is difficult to show unambiguously that land reform had a significant effect on static efficiency, its effect on income distribution was substantial. Samuel P. S. Ho (1978), in an excellent analysis of the impact of land reform on equity, calculated that the Tiller Act had a wealth redistribution effect, measured at 1952 prices, of NT$2.2 billion, or approximately 13 percent of Taiwan's GDP in 1952.

An interesting feature of this phase is that, notwithstanding the fact that this was a recovery period, there was a substantial net capital outflow from agriculture to non-agriculture amounting to about 22 percent of the total value of agricultural production.[9] It would thus appear that even in the recovery period (at least toward the end of it) the agricultural sector performed the crucial function of supplying the rest of the economy with capital resources.

Sustained Agricultural Growth: 1953-1955 to 1966-1968

At the outset of this period, the initial conditions were right for a sustained growth in agricultural output and a relatively equal distribution of value added generated in that sector. The extremely high growth of output achieved in the preceding period could not be maintained because agriculture was now working closer to full capacity. One remaining slack was seasonal underemployment of labor, which disappeared, to a large extent, over the course of this phase.

Agricultural output grew at an annual rate of about 4.9 percent during this period (see Table 2.2), with fruits, vegetables, and livestock acting as the most dynamic commodity groups. The major contributing factors to output growth were, as we have already seen, a somewhat more intensive use of land, a major increase in the use of current inputs, and the beginning of mechanization towards the end of this phase. Table 2.4 shows that the number of man-days per agricultural worker went from 159 at the beginning of the phase to 191 at the end of it, while the multiple crop index rose from 172 to 188.

The major factor that contributed to the substantial increase in output per worker during this phase was a continued sharp rise in the yield of land which was made possible through improved varieties and higher levels of application of intermediate inputs. From a technological standpoint, perhaps the most interesting changes are the substitution of chemical fertilizer for farm (organic) fertilizer, the substitution of human labor for animal labor, and the beginning of mechanization, particularly through the adoption of power tillers. During this stage of development, the transformation away from a system based mainly on tenants to one relying on owner-cultivators was completed. Taiwan's agriculture was in the hands of a large number of very small owners, the average size of a family farm having dropped from 1.29 ha. to 1.05 ha. (see Table 2.10).

The take-off of the industrial sector during this period -- particularly with the onset of the export-substitution phase at the beginning of the 1960s -- provided expanding working opportunities outside of agriculture. The appearance of new employment opportunities reflected itself not only in a leveling of agricultural employment, soon to be followed by a decline in the absolute labor force in agriculture, but also by a significant increase in the proportion of part-time farmers from approximately 60 percent in 1956 to about 68 percent in 1966. As the permanent migration rate out of the agricultural population in all farm activities was relatively low during this period, it appears that the great bulk of the farm family household members who engaged in off-farm activities were commuters and seasonal workers, who maintained their residence on the farm.[10]

Still another feature of this development is the beginning of a trend towards diversification on the output side. Tables 2.2 and 2.3 illustrate this shift in commodity composition towards livestock, fishery, and forestry activities as well as towards fruits and vegetables, and away from rice and other farm crops -- particularly sugar.

The most important policy measures affecting the agricultural growth process during this phase appear to have been 1) the set of rice policies and particularly the rice-fertilizer barter program; 2) the continued work of the JCRR in establishing a truly integrated rural development program based on farmers' associations and providing the whole gamut of services needed by farmers; 3) the various agricultural development plans which were largely formulated by and based on the programs of the JCRR, fitted within a national economic context; 4) the level and form of US foreign aid which continued to benefit agriculture; and 5) a very rapid rate of industrial development which was regionally decentralized.

The government control of rice was a large source of revenue for the public sector through such mechanisms as land taxes payable in rice, compulsory purchases, and the rice-fertilizer barter system. Since all rice collections were obtained at government purchasing prices, which were considerably lower than market prices, the government extracted through these various mechanisms an amount of taxes equivalent to the difference in these two prices multiplied by the total amount of rice purchased. Shirley W. Y. Kuo coined the term "hidden rice taxes" to embrace this form of taxation.[11]

The history of the JCRR has been well recorded and analyzed. The JCRR was actively engaged in a fully integrated program of rural development long before this concept became popular worldwide. Its activities included crop and livestock improvement, water resource development, soil conservation, agricultural organization and extension, agricultural financing, rural health improvement, and agricultural research. It was particularly successful in helping to organize and direct the activities of the farmers' associations.

The crucial role of foreign assistance in agriculture can be gathered from the fact that U.S. capital assistance to that sector represented nearly 60 percent of net domestic capital formation in agriculture up to 1965.

Agricultural Slowdown: 1966-1968 to 1973-1975

This phase was marked by a very significant deceleration of output growth. Depending on which weighting scheme is used, the annual growth in the index of overall agricultural production fell from 4.88 percent in the preceding phase to 3.76 percent during this phase, according to panel I of Table 2.2, and from 4.98 percent to 2.28 percent according to panel II of Table 2.2. The discrete structural break in the pattern of growth is even sharper if one focuses on farm crops. Based on the first index above, the annual growth rate of farm crops drops from 3.86 percent to 1.32 percent and from 4.08 percent to 0.98 percent according to the second index (see Table 2.2). Rice production and other farm crops fall absolutely in this slowdown stage while fishery and livestock continue to perform well.

From a technological standpoint, the binding constraint to further agricultural growth was clearly labor, which became superimposed upon the land constraint which had already become effective in the previous development stage. This phenomenon can be visualized from many angles. The first way is to go back to Table 2.4 and notice that all indicators of labor inputs -- total man-days, number of workers and man-days per average worker -- fell throughout this period, the former at almost 1 percent per year. Likewise, the crop area and the multiple crop index shrunk slightly as a direct consequence of labor shortages at peak times. Clearly an important turning point had been reached, as evidenced by the decline in the size of the absolute population in agriculture, which reached a peak of 6.15 million in 1969 and dropped sharply, particularly between 1974 and 1975, to a level of 5.6 million in that last year. Further evidence of the worsening labor shortage in agriculture is provided by the significant rise in the real agricultural wage rate compared to that of factory workers during this phase.[12] The rising labor cost relative to both the cost of capital and land induced a technological change.

In essence, the dual labor and land constraints could be relaxed only through mechanization, that is, the substitution of capital and mechanical energy for labor and human energy. Taiwan had reached the situation of having to switch from an agricultural development strategy based on a small scale, highly labor- and land-intensive pattern to one requiring mechanization and related changes in the scale and structure of production. Thus, for example, the number of power tillers almost tripled from about 17,000 in 1967 to over 45,000 in 1975, and the number of tractors went from fewer than 480 in 1966-1968 to almost 1,000 in 1973-1975 (see Table 2.4).[13]

The most dynamic activity during this slowdown period was the livestock sector which grew at 8.8 percent annually (see Table 2.2). Since the bulk of feedstuffs had to be imported, this was one of the major factors responsible for the reversal of the positive balance of agricultural trade in previous years.

During this phase, the rice-fertilizer barter ratio continued to be reduced before being eliminated in 1973. A major consequence of the elimination of the rice-fertilizer barter program was a substantial drop in the hidden rice tax.

There was perception during this phase that the relative income position of farmers vis-à-vis non-farmers was steadily deteriorating. Although the evidence is not clear-cut, some indicators would support this contention. Table 2.5 brings together a number of different indicators of the relative incomes of farmers versus non-farmers. Two of the three indicators in that table do not bear out this perception. Thus, farm family income as a percentage of non-farm family income remained at essentially its same level at the end of this phase (1973-1975) as at its outset (1966-1968) (see cols. 4-6 of Table 2.5). The same comparisons on a *per capita* basis even suggest that the income position of farmers improved slightly compared to, respectively, non-farmers, employees and laborers (see cols. 1-3, Table 2.5). By contrast -- and apparently inconsistent with the above trends -- the growth rate of farmers' per capita real income during this phase was substantially lower than that of average per capita real income for the population at large

TABLE 2.5 Relative Incomes of Farmers vs. Non-farmers and Terms-of-Trade of Prices Received by Farmers to Prices Paid by Farmers, 1952-1988

	Farm family per capita income as % of			Farm family income as % of			Index of prices		Terms of trade (7)/(8)×100 (9)
	Family income (1)	Employees' income (2)	Laborers' income (3)	Family income (4)	Employees' income (5)	Laborers' income (6)	received by farmers (7)	paid by farmers (8)	
1952-1954	na	na	na	na	na	na	12.96	13.02	99.6
1966-1968	63.9	66.7	77.1	79.6	81.5	94.1	29.13	27.78	104.9
1973-1975	65.2	70.1	80.0	79.2	82.8	93.3	58.7	52.68	111.4
1979-1981	65.9	71.6	80.5	73.0	76.9	83.9	85.79	85.66	100.2
1986-1988	72.9	78.6	87.4	72.9	74.9	80.9	101.71	99.44	102.3

	Farmers per capita income at current prices (10)	CPI (1986=100) (11)	Farmers' real per capita income at 1980 prices (10)/(11)×100 (12)	Annual growth rate of farmers per capita real income (13)	Annual growth rate of average per capita real income (14)
1966-1968	4,633	26.30	17,616		
1973-1975	11,996	48.10	24,940	5.09	7.82
1979-1981	35,947	82.05	43,811	9.85	7.51
1986-1988	69,378	100.77	68,848	6.67	6.41

Source: Basic Agricultural Statistics (1989): cols. 1-6 (p. 38); cols. 7-9 (p. 24); col. 10 (p. 38); col. 11 (p. 24); cols. 12-14 computed by author.

-- i.e., 5.09 percent vs. 7.82 percent between 1966-1968 and 1973-1975 (see cols. 13 and 14, Table 2.5).

Whether real or not, there is little doubt that this perception influenced policy. The elimination of the rice-fertilizer barter program was one measure among a number of others, undertaken to improve the relative standard of living of farmers, vis-à-vis non-farmers. Another related measure was a sharp increase in the official (current) price of rice, which more than tripled during this stage from approximately NT$3.50/kg to NT$11.50/kg in 1975.

The discrete jump in the government purchase price of rice in 1974-1975 converted a price policy that had been designed to extract a surplus out of farmers (in the form of the hidden rice tax) into a policy that amounted to a price-support program. The official price became the de facto market price. Whereas before 1973 the government purchased rice at an official price corresponding to only 70 to 80 percent of the prevailing market price, the subsequent jump in the official price transformed this policy from a tax measure into a subsidy benefitting farmers. As a result of this new policy, the stock of rice held by the government went up significantly -- an issue and problem which was to escalate in the two subsequent periods.

A major implication of the elimination of the rice-fertilizer barter program and the new price-support policy for rice is that their joint effect must have reduced substantially -- if not ended altogether -- the net capital outflow or squeeze out of agriculture that characterized the previous phases. The end of this development phase constitutes a crucial turning point away from an agricultural development strategy geared to generating a surplus to help capital formation outside of agriculture towards a strategy of protecting and increasingly subsidizing farmers' incomes.[14]

In a study that attempted to postulate the changes in the relative weight of rice policy objectives in Taiwan before and after 1970, it was argued convincingly that the three most important objectives before 1970 were consumers' welfare, government revenue, and economic stability. These objectives were judged to be equally important, each being given the weight of 0.3, and a final objective, foreign exchange, being given a weight of 0.1 so that the sum of the weights adds up to unity. After 1970, farmers' income and consumers' welfare were assigned weights of 0.3 each, while self-sufficiency and economic stability were assigned weights of 0.2 each. Thus, in fact, according to this subjective evaluation of experts, farmers' income after 1970 had replaced government revenue as a major policy objective.[15]

During this phase there was a continuation of the migration pattern previously mentioned. The bulk of the migration out of agriculture was not geographical but rather intersectoral in the sense that many members of farm families commuted daily from their residences on the farm to work and back. This intersectoral labor transfer without physical movement un-

TABLE 2.6a Sources of Farm Family Income (in percentages)

Source of income	1966-1968	1973-1975	1979-1981	1986-1988
Net agricultural income	59.3	46.7	30.9	37.8
Net non-agricultural income	40.7	53.3	69.1	62.2
Total income	100.0	100.0	100.0	100.0

Source: *Basic Agricultural Statistics*, 1989 ed., Table 29, p. 36.

TABLE 2.6b Changes in Farm Household Types in Taiwan, 1960-1988

Type of farm household	1960	1970	1980	1985	1988
Number of farm households					
Full-time farm household	384,501	276,959	79,757	115,164	75,839
Part-time farm household	241,060	371,434	316,584	168,447	662,903
Sideline farm household	182,039	267,573	494,774	496,367	
Total	807,600	915,966	891,115	779,978	738,742
Percentage of farm households					
Full time farm household	47.6	30.2	9.0	14.8	10.3
Part-time farm household	29.9	40.6	35.5	21.6	89.7
Sideline farm household	22.5	29.2	55.5	63.6	
Total	100.0	100.0	100.0	100.0	100.0

Source: *Agricultural Census*, Directorate-General of Budget, Accounting, and Statistics (DGBAS), Executive Yuan; various years.

TABLE 2.6c Rate of Average Annual Change for Different Types of Farm Household in Taiwan, 1960-1988

	1960-1970	1970-1980	1980-1985	1985-1988
Full-time farm household	-7.3	-24.9	18.4	-10.3
Full time farm household	10.5	-3.6	-25.2	0.0
Part-time farm household	9.3	15.2	0.2	

Source: Computed from Table 2.6a.

doubtedly contributed greatly to the developmental success of Taiwan. This process was crucial in raising significantly the share of farm family income originating outside of agriculture from 41 percent in 1966-1968 to 53 percent in 1973-1975 as Table 2.6a shows. This migration pattern is integrally related to the process of rural industrial decentralization as one transferable element of the Taiwan development strategy. As a corollary to the increasing off-farm job opportunities, the proportion of part-time farmers continued to increase substantially during this phase (see Tables 2.6b and 2.6c).

The superimposition of the labor constraint upon the already existing land constraint made further mechanization necessary as a condition to continued growth. At the same time, mechanizing a one-hectare farm (i.e., the average size of the farm in 1974) was an incredibly complex and difficult task. The continued existence and sustainability of small-scale farming was threatened. Consequently, the government, and more specifically the JCRR, encouraged some important institutional changes including joint decision making in specific operations, joint management and contract farming, and the promotion of specialized production areas. Whereas cooperatives to buy inputs and sell products existed on a large-scale basis, the establishment of cooperation in actual management of production activities to raise the efficiency of small farmers and to help introduce further mechanization was relatively unknown and very difficult to institute.

The implementation of these emerging new institutional forms as well as a number of additional ones (such as the Accelerated Rural Development Program which was initiated in 1973 and the Rice Stabilization Fund established in 1974), occurred on any significant scale only after 1973-1975 and will, therefore, be discussed within the context of the next two agricultural development phases. Even though these measures originated right at the end of one phase and at the beginning of another one, their impact was felt mainly in the subsequent phases.

Stages of Agricultural Development from 1973-1975 on

Government Support of Farmers: 1973-1975 to 1979-1981

Overview and Overall Agricultural Performance. A number of factors converged around the outset of this phase to engender major (almost fundamental) policy changes by the government in support of farmers. Most important among these factors were 1) the slowdown in agricultural production and particularly the virtual stagnation of the production of rice and special crops in the preceding period; 2) the perception that farmers' relative income was worsening relative to non-farmers; and 3) the increasingly binding nature of the land and labor constraints which endangered the future viability of small-scale farming in Taiwan unless massive mechanization were introduced. Although the evidence on the evolution of the relative income position of farmers vs. non-farmers in the prevailing phase is mixed, as was discussed previously,[16] the prevailing official view had become that it was no longer possible to maintain a decent level of living in Taiwan from income derived from a small farm.

The end of the preceding and the beginning of the present phase (1973-1975) marked a fundamental turning point in Taiwan's economic history. The major policy objective in this new phase was to shift from an agricultural development strategy which had been designed to capture an agricultural surplus providing the necessary capital for the industrial take-off process towards the opposite strategy of increasingly protecting and subsidizing agriculture. This shift is typical of a country joining the rank of developing countries as will be amply illustrated subsequently.

Before reviewing the major policy measures and institutional reforms which were implemented during this period, the agricultural performance is briefly scrutinized. Table 2.2 indicates that a slight acceleration in overall agricultural output occurred during this phase compared to the preceding one -- i.e., an annual growth rate of 4.15 percent vs. 3.76 percent according to the output indices in panel I and 2.76 percent vs. 2.28 percent according to panel II. The declining trend in rice production was stopped and, in fact, temporarily reversed. The rice crop reached an all-time peak of 2,713 thousand metric tons (mt) in 1976 to subsequently decline to a level in 1979-1981 equivalent to its level at the beginning of this phase (i.e., around 2,400 thousand mt). The diversification towards other grain crops, fruits and vegetables, as well as livestock, continued.

Table 2.4 shows that all land and labor input indicators declined absolutely during this phase. Most noteworthy were the drastic reduction in total man-days of labor from 285 million in 1973-1975 to 210 million in 1979-1981 (corresponding to a negative growth rate of almost 4 percent per annum) and the decline in the number of agricultural workers from 1.5 million to about 1.2 million over the same time span. In contrast, capital was increasingly substituted for labor and used in a land-augmenting sense; fixed capital grew at 7.2 percent per annum and tractors at a remarkable rate of 24 percent per annum.

The exodus out of farming went hand and hand with a significant growth in the share of part-time farm households which rose from about three-fourths of all farm households at the outset of this phase to 91 percent in 1980 (see Table 2.6b). This process contributed to a continuation of the trend towards a rising share of farm family income coming from non-agricultural sources. This share rose dramatically during this stage from 53 percent to 69 percent (see Table 2.6a).

On the whole, the various policy measures and reforms in support of farmers which are analyzed subsequently appear to have had some positive impact on the relative standard of living of farmers. Table 2.5 shows that the indicators of farm family *per capita* income as a percentage of per capita income of, respectively, average non-farm family, employees' family, and laborers' family rose marginally (see cols. 1-3). However, more dramatic evidence is provided by the acceleration in the growth rate of farmers' per capita real income from 5.09 percent in the preceding phase to 9.85 percent per annum during this phase which was significantly higher than the corresponding growth rate of 7.51 percent for the whole population (including farmers).[17]

Impact of Policy Measures and Reforms on Performance. We can now turn to a review and examination of the key policy measures and reforms which were implemented during this phase.[18] At the end of 1972, the Executive Yuan announced "The Accelerated Rural Development Program in Taiwan" (ARDP). The importance of this program was comparable to that of the land reform program of the 1950s.[19] The ARDP contained the following nine concrete measures: 1) abolition of the rice-fertilizer barter system, 2) abolition of the education surtax on farm land, 3) easing of the terms of agricultural credit, 4) improvements of agricultural marketing, 5) strengthening of the rural infrastructure, 6) acceleration of the extension of integrated use of improved cultural practices, 7) establishment of specialized agricultural areas, 8) strengthening of agricultural research and extension, and 9) encouragement of the establishment of new industries in rural areas. The implementation of this program, which had started in 1973 and was originally scheduled for only two years, was extended indefinitely.

In September 1973, the Agricultural Development Act was promulgated and made effective for a ten-year period, 1973-1983. Both the ARDP and the new Act spelled out the objectives of the Sixth Plan (1973-1976) which were 1) to change the agricultural production structure by enlarging the scale of farming operations; 2) to raise agricultural productivity by adopting capital-intensive technology; 3) to innovate agricultural marketing systems by adjusting agricultural prices; 4) to increase agricultural investment by improving agricultural credit systems; 5) to relieve the farmers' financial burden by reducing production costs; 6) to maximize the service functions by strengthening farmers' organizations; 7) to enhance rural welfare by improving farmers' livelihood; and 8) to strengthen agricultural administration by training more agricultural technicians.[20]

In a setting of miniature farms the successful implementation of the first two objectives above is an exceedingly difficult task. In the absence of an additional land base which could be converted into cultivatable land (the land frontier in terms of area of cultivated land having already been reached, as shown in Table 2.4, col. 1), the only alternative ways of enlarging the *operational* farm size which suggest themselves are, first, through land purchase-cum-sale (i.e., one neighbor buying land from another); or, secondly, through land rent, with again some farmers renting land from others who might be either short of labor to care for their farms or who intend to quit farming. Within the socioeconomic and cultural context prevailing in Taiwan in the mid-seventies, neither of these alternatives appeared viable. Under the family farm system, land has meant security to each of the farm families and, furthermore, a free land market did not exist. Neither was the second alternative above attractive given the institutional and legal framework of the time, which provided strong protection of tenancy rights and thereby could present serious obstacles to owners who wanted to reclaim land rented out on a long-term basis.[21]

The natural evolution -- without major institutional changes -- would have been a continuation and acceleration of a trend towards part-time farming on small farms and particularly towards sideline farm households (defined as part-time farmers whose off-farm income is greater than farm income). Over time such a group might become less professional in its approach to farming and less interested in pursuing this vocation with a resulting unfavorable impact on output and land productivity.

Consequently, given these major obstacles to expanding the physical size of individual family farms, the government had to come up with innovative schemes to enlarge the *operational* size without affecting the ownership pattern. This was absolutely essential to allow the *mechanization* process to continue. Since the land frontier had been reached and agriculture was shedding labor at a fast pace (4 percent per year during this phase), the adoption of an increasingly capital-intensive technology was the only way to increase agricultural output or even to prevent an absolute decline.

Once the mechanization process has gone beyond the stage of using small-scale implements and tools, such as power tillers, and has been extended to include tractors, combines and dryers, the issue of indivisibility has to be faced. When relatively indivisible capital equipment is substituted for highly divisible labor on small farms, a serious problem ensues. The great advantage of human labor, besides its divisibility, is that it works close to its capacity level, in contrast with machines, such as tractors and combines, which are much less divisible and which, even when in use in many agricultural tasks, require only a fraction of their total horsepower capacity. Clearly, a large tractor on a very small farm can only be used at a fraction of its capacity. Furthermore, even if this same tractor were to be rented out to many non-contiguous small farmers its contribution to output would be significantly less than if the same tractor were used on one large consolidated farm embracing the same total area as that of the small non-contiguous farms.[22] In other words, the other side of the coin reading indivisibility is the existence of increasing returns to scale.

In the final analysis, the only feasible way to expand the operational size of the farm without affecting the existing pattern of land ownership was to encourage group farming. The many potential advantages of group farming in the Taiwanese context are that it allows 1) the efficient introduction of mechanization to take advantage of increasing returns to scale, thereby reducing production costs per unit of output; 2) the continuing, largely intersectoral, migration of labor out of agriculture to contribute to farm household income; and 3) the maintenance of the value system inherent to small farm households.

The government encouraged many forms of group farming including joint operations, entrusted farming, and the joint management and promotion of specialized production areas.[23] The intent of joint operations was to organize farmers to manage jointly such specific operations as field preparation, transplanting, and harvesting, or a combination of operations, from land preparation to harvesting, on adjacent fields and thereby to be able to own and use jointly expensive machinery. This new form of farm management could best be implemented in practice by bringing together twenty to thirty farmers having an area of about fifteen ha. located in one block.[24] Such farmers, particularly if related by blood ties, could organize themselves more easily than when farm lands were fragmented and scattered, which, unfortunately, might well have been the rule rather than the exception.

Entrusted farming, in the Taiwan context, consists mainly of two types: entrusted cultivations and entrusted management. Under the first type, a farmer entrusts another farmer to carry out one or more farming operations on a part, or on all, of his farm land. The farm owner agrees to pay wages to the entrusted farmer for his services either before or after the operation. The farm owner remains the decision-maker while the entrusted farmer becomes a wage earner. Under the second type of entrusted farming, the farm owner entrusts another farmer to care for, manage, or carry out a series of farming operations on a part or all of his farm land for an agreed period of time (one year or longer) and for an agreed amount of income-sharing or produce-sharing. Under entrusted management, the entrusted farmer becomes the decision-maker. His status has been changed into that of owner of his own farm and operator-(tenant)-cum-manager of the rented farm.

A third new farm management form which the government tried to establish in 1973 under the ARDP consisted of joint management and promotion of specialized production areas. A number of specialized agricultural areas (SAAs) to promote mechanized group farming were established. Each SAA is supposed to produce a given farm product in which an integrated system of production, processing, storage, and marketing is practiced. Farmers are encouraged to form joint management groups by pooling their land, labor, and capital resources together under one management.[25]

The transition from participation in farmers' organizations (dealing mainly with off-farm services such as supply and purchases of inputs and marketing of output) to new institutional arrangements entailing joint actions and decisions directly related to farm activities was not an easy one.

Notwithstanding the obstacles which appear to stand in the way of expanding the scope and coverage of these new management forms, some progress was made. The most serious among the obstacles which had to be overcome were 1) the individualistic nature of the Taiwanese farmer, who is reluctant to give up even part of his decision-making authority over the use of his land; 2) the highly fragmented nature of land ownership, with even very small farmers owning non-contiguous sublots and the consequent problem of achieving true land consolidation; and 3) the difficulty in achieving an efficient division of labor, either on a geographical basis through an appropriate selection of specialized production areas or in terms of specific operations to be undertaken within the context of a consolidated set of individual farms.

The process of enlarging the operational farm size evolved slowly and only started to take off in the early eighties encouraged by additional institutional changes such as the Second Stage of the Land Reform Program, which provided the needed protection to owners who entrusted their farms by guaranteeing that the farms would not be considered as tenanted land. Gradually the emphasis shifted from joint operations to entrusted farming. Because group farming schemes became significant mainly in the last decade, they are discussed and evaluated critically within the context of the final Adjustment and Liberalization Phase (1979-1981 to 1986-1988) which follows in the next subsection.

The greatest impact on agriculture during the present phase came not from institutional reforms aimed at enlarging the operational size of the farm but rather from the various measures which reduced agricultural taxation and the costs of inputs, on the one hand, and the price support programs which subsidized the prices received by farmers, on the other hand. The elimination of the rice-fertilizer barter program (i.e., the hidden rice tax) and the educational surtax on farm land in 1973 -- combined with a revision of tax rates for farm buildings -- lessened considerably the farmers' tax burden. In turn, price stabilization and support of essential farm produce was very effective in raising farm income levels. The government used a combination of instruments such as guaranteed prices, deficiency payments, and import controls to protect domestic production, and enhance farm income. Stabilization funds were introduced not only for rice but also for sugar and hog production, and a Deficiency Payment Scheme was developed to encourage the production of small grains (including corn, soybean, wheat, barley, and sorghum).

The Rice Stabilization Fund, established in 1974, operates as a buffer stock scheme. The floor support price is, in principle, fixed so as to allow a 20 percent profit above production costs. A direct and integral part of the introduction of this new fund was a quantum jump in the official and producer rice prices from about NT$4.50/kg in 1972 to NT$11.00-11.50/kg in 1975. Furthermore, a successful undertaking at integrating biological, chemical, and mechanical innovations in the modernization of Taiwan's rice farming was the establishment of the Rice Nursery Centers (RNC).[26] As of 1981, 331 RNCs were in operation out of the 1,785 which are estimated to be needed to service the total paddy land base. Among the major functions of each RNC are the provision of seedlings, the regulation and coordination in the provision of farm machinery including heavy machinery, and the organization of farmers into joint operation teams operating on ten to twenty-five ha. of paddy land.

Table 2.7 brings together a series of key rice indicators which help unfold the dramatic changes which occurred in the rice economy of Taiwan during the last four decades. In particular, it can be seen that the new price support regime from 1973 on brought about a supply response with rice production reaching an all-time high of 2.71 million mt in 1976. To support the new price of rice, the government was forced to purchase far in excess of domestic commercial demand. The result was that large surpluses accumulated and government stocks went from 265 million mt in 1973-1975 to 914 million mt in 1977. This led to a change in the government procurement policy limiting purchases to 970 kg per ha. since 1977. This measure only had a limited effect as government stocks continued to grow until 1984, as can be seen from col. 6 of Table 2.7. Figure 2.1 shows the upward trend in the ratio of government rice stocks to rice production from 1973-1975 on.

The main observations suggested by Table 2.7 for the period under consideration (1973-1975 to 1979-1981) are 1) the support price (i.e., the so-called compulsory price), after having been about equal to the farm (producer) price at the beginning of this phase, diverged increasingly so that by 1981 the compulsory price was NT$3.48/kg higher than the farm price;[27] 2) the widening difference between the compulsory price and the farm price contributed significantly to raising the incomes of the farmers (see the estimated increase to farmers from the Rice Stabilization Board measures in column 7 of Table 2.7);[28] 3) rice production, after peaking in 1976, levelled off at a lower plateau around 2.4 million mt annually during 1978-1981; and 4) the level of public rice stocks, after reaching a peak in 1973, declined somewhat at least until 1981.

TABLE 2.7 Selected Rice Statistics, Selected Years 1946-1988

	Production 1000 MT (1)	Crop area 1000 ha (2)	Yield kg/ha (3)	Compulsory (support) price NT$/kg (4)	Farm price NT$/kg (5)	Government stocks 1000 MT (6)	Estimated increased income to farmers from RSB NT$ million (7)
1946-1948	987	653	1,516	0.70[a]	0.84[a]	na	--
1953-1955	1,651	769	2,148	1.56[b]	2.18[b]	na	--
1966-1968	2,437	789	3,091	3.17[c]	4.15[c]	na	--
1973-1975	2,400	764	3,141	8.85	9.00	265[d]	88[d]
1976	2,713	788	3,450	11.50	10.62	513	1,129
1977	2,649	779	3,406	11.50	8.91	914	2,179
1978	2,444	753	3,249	11.50	9.08	898	1,237
1979	2,450	722	3,400	12.50	10.99	799	1,372
1980	2,354	638	3,692	14.50	13.41	566	941
1981	2,375	669	3,560	17.60	14.12	812	3,172
1982	2,483	660	3,765	18.80	15.60	1,140	2,844
1983	2,485	646	3,850	18.80	14.14	1,025	4,812
1984	2,244	587	3,825	18.80	15.26	1,306	2,264
1985	2,174	564	3,856	18.80	14.04	1,256	3,343
1986	1,974	538	3,713	18.80	13.32	1,210	3,432
1987	1,900	502	3,790	18.80	12.76	1,104	3,788
1988	1,845	471	3,916	18.80	14.24	867[e]	1,841

[a] For 1951.
[b] For 1956.
[c] For 1966.
[d] Average 1974-1975.
[e] 730,000 MT in 1989.

Source: Columns 1-3: Mao (1990, Table 2.1); columns 4-7: Taiwan Food Bureau.

To understand the dynamics of rice stock formation, it is essential to identify the major components of, respectively, total government rice collection and total government rice disposal and see how these components varied over time. This information is gathered in Table 2.8 for the period 1974-1989. Total rice collection is broken down between the three support programs which have been dominant since 1975 (compulsory, planned, and supervised purchases) which are consolidated together in one category and "all others". In turn, public rice disposal is subdivided into "rations and market sales"; "exports"; "feed"; and "other". It can be seen that if total rice collection exceeds total rice disposal, the difference is the net addition to the

FIGURE 2.1 Ratio of Government Rice Stocks to Rice Production, 1973-1988

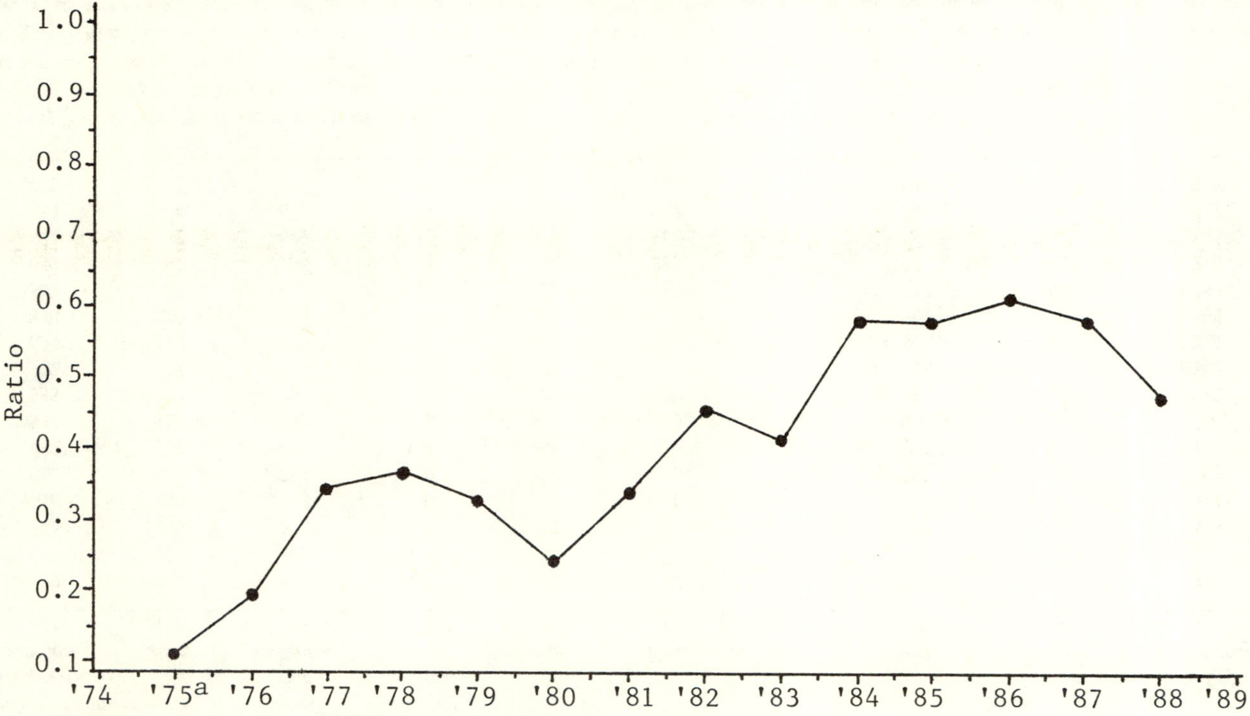

a1975 refers to a three-year average (1973-1975).

Source: Based on Table 2.7.

TABLE 2.8 Amount of Rice Collected and Disposed by Government and Changes in Stocks, 1974-1989 (thousand metric tons)

	Compulsory, planned & supervised purchases (1)	Other[a] (2)	Total rice collected (3)	Rations & market sales (4)	Export (5)	Feed (6)	Other[b] (7)	Total (8)	Net addition to or reduction from rice stocks (9)	Stocks at end of fiscal year (10)
1974	72	310	382	442	73	0	19	534	-152	211
1975	249	216	465	340	0	0	19	359	106	318
1976	346	209	575	358	0	0	22	380	195	513
1977	616	247	863	440	0	0	22	462	401	914
1978	560	221	781	440	324	0	33	797	-16	898
1979	412	208	620	437	264	0	18	719	-99	799
1980	534	169	703	395	505	0	36	936	-233	566
1981	555	172	727	347	127	0	7	481	246	812
1982	772	74	846	442	73	0	3	518	328	1,140
1983	674	113	787	245	649	0	9	903	-116	1,025
1984	870	120	990	255	395	0	59	709	290	1,306
1985	567	95	662	223	112	293	84	712	-50	1,257
1986	689	47	736	233	147	289	115	784	-48	1,210
1987	607	42	649	253	201	166	134	754	-105	1,105
1988	583	44	627	228	172	312	153	865	-238	867
1989	452	24	476	213	164	230	6	613	-137	730

[a] The category "Other" rice collection consists of i) farm land tax which remained around 100,000 mt until 1977 to fall between 24,000 and 30,000 in the 80's before disappearing in 1989; ii) rice production loans which, before being eliminated in 1986, ranged between 40,000 and 100,000 in most years; iii) import and others, only in 1974 were imports important (141,000 mt) in most other years there were no imports.

[b] The category "Other" rice disposal consists of i) rice field conversion: a program which started in 1984 and paid off in rice, farmers converting their rice fields to grow other crops (annually between 53,000 mt and 141,000 mt were disposed in this way between 1984 and 1988); ii) other marginal uses of rice which in total never amount to more than 34,000 mt annually.

rice stocks, or vice versa if total disposal exceeds total collection (see cols. 9 and 10 of Table 2.8). Thus, for example, Table 2.9 reveals that the quantum jump in the level of stocks from 513,000 mt in 1976 to 914,000 mt in 1977 was largely caused by an almost 80 percent increase in rice collection under the compulsory, planned, and supervised purchases. The reduction in the level of stocks which occurred between 1977 and 1980 was directly related to the large-scale disposal of stocks through exports -- amounting to a staggering (for Taiwan) half a million mt in 1980. Since the rice had been purchased at a high official support price and was resold at a much lower world price, the financial burden on the treasury was very large. This question is best discussed within the context of changes in nominal and effective protection, an issue which is analyzed subsequently.

As a means of encouraging -- or at least not discouraging -- a diversification away from rice production, the Small Grains Deficiency Payment Scheme was established at the end of 1971. The commodities covered by this scheme included corn, soybean, wheat, barley, and sorghum which are all essential raw materials for processing edible oils and animal feeds. The level of the deficiency payment for small grains was set in such a way as to yield an equivalent per-hectare profit as that of growing rice. This scheme did not have any impact on output during this phase but did encourage production of corn and sorghum significantly in the next phase. Finally, two other stabilization funds which might be mentioned are the Sugar Stabilization Fund and the Hog Stabilization Fund.

Changes in Nominal and Effective Protection. The rising government support to farmers during the phase under consideration led to fundamental changes in the level of nominal and effective protection. These changes can be clearly seen from Table 2.9 which provides estimates of the nominal protection coefficient (NPC), the effective protection coefficient (EPC), and the ratio of the wholesale (assumed to represent the consumer) price to the border price for a number of key commodities in selected years. The NPC -- i.e., the ratio of the producer price to the border (world) price -- increased drastically between 1974 and 1980 for most agricultural products shown in Table 2.9 (see top panel).[29] The sharpest increases were, respectively, rice from 0.86 to 2.35; wheat from 0.94 to 1.81; barley from 1.03 to 1.73; corn from 1.08 to 1.55 and finally, soybean from 0.95 to 1.31. Notice that the NPC was either slightly below unity or just above it in 1974 for each of the above products, implying that the producer price did not differ significantly from the border price. By 1980 the producer price exceeded very substantially the world price, reflecting Taiwan's transition from a regime of squeezing a surplus out of agriculture to one of increasingly protecting farmers.

Although the domestic price of beef in 1974 already exceeded the border price by about 70 percent, by 1980 it had grown to about 115 percent above the latter. The NPCs for the other two commodities shown in the top panel (pork and chicken) remained relatively stable at a level between 1.1 and 1.3 during this short period.

The estimates of effective protection in Table 2.9 (last panel) move, generally speaking, in parallel fashion with the NPCs. Between 1974 and 1980, the rise in the EPC[30] for the following commodities was, respectively, from 0.69 (an atypically low level as can be seen from the corresponding value of about 1.2 in both 1970 and 1972) to 1.38 for rice; 1.07 to 1.73 for corn; and from 0.90 to 1.52 for soybean. The same panel (last) also reveals the comparative advantage which Taiwan enjoyed in the production of bananas and

TABLE 2.9 Nominal and Effective Protection Coefficients and Ratio of Wholesale (consumer) Price to Border Price

	Nominal Protection Coefficient[a]								
	Rice	Wheat	Barley	Corn	Soybean	Beef	Pork	Chicken	Milk
1955	0.80	1.96	0.88	0.97	1.86	0.95	0.98	0.42	4.87
1967	0.87	1.36	1.55	1.31	1.34	1.14	1.29	1.18	2.40[d]
1974	0.86	0.94	1.03	1.08	0.95	1.70	1.22	1.22	1.63[e]
1976	1.41	1.29	1.17	1.25	1.29	2.60	1.10	1.20	
1978	1.64	1.90	1.58	1.70	1.34	2.69	1.04	1.34	
1980	2.35 (1.67)[b]	1.81	1.73	1.55	1.31 (1.40)	2.15	1.09 (0.65)	1.29 (1.13)	2.48
1982	2.70 (2.02)[c]	2.15	2.30	2.51 (−3.36)	1.96 (1.90)	2.84	1.02 (0.58)	1.37 (0.54)	
1984	2.06			2.20	1.53	2.26	0.45	0.77	
1986	3.38			3.54	2.39	2.65	0.36	0.96	
1988	2.14			3.72	2.69	2.65	0.42	1.09	

	Ratio of Wholesale Price to Border Price				
	Rice	Wheat	Barley	Corn	Soybean
1955	0.80	na	na	na	2.49
1967	0.89	1.29	na	na	1.38
1974	0.91	0.70	1.08	1.22	1.20
1976	1.57	1.00	1.01	1.03	0.98
1978	1.66	0.94	0.94	0.98	0.98
1980	2.53 (2.52)	1.06	1.10	1.02	0.99
1982	2.96 (2.93)	0.96	0.88	0.95	1.00
1984	3.04	1.12	na	0.95	0.95
1986	4.81	na	na	1.26	1.31
1988	3.76	na	na	1.21	1.31

(continues)

TABLE 2.9 (continued)

| | Effective Protection Coefficient[c] |||||||
	Rice	Sugarcane	Corn	Soybean	Pork	Banana	Orange
1970	1.22	1.51	1.23	1.19	na	0.51	na
1972	1.19	0.97	1.53	1.17	na	0.54	na
1974	0.69	0.33	1.07	0.90	na	1.00	na
1976	1.69	0.64	1.24	0.99	na	0.78	na
1978	1.02	na	1.86	1.40	na	1.03	na
1980	1.38	na	1.73	1.52	na	0.77	na
1982	2.39	2.49	3.50	2.32	0.32	0.60	0.46
1984	3.10	2.96	1.82	1.58	0.14	0.55	0.27
1986	4.56	na	3.37	2.85	0.17	0.74	0.70

[a]Source: 1) For 1955-1982: Anderson and Hayami (1986, Table A1.3, pp. 133-35). The nominal protection coefficient is defined as the ratio of the producer price to the border price of the commodity (either export or import). For beef, pork and chicken, the NPC is calculated as the ratio of the wholesale price to the border price. 2) For 1980-1988: author's computations; it should be noted that the producer price of rice was taken as the farm price as given by the Taiwan Food Bureau to which was added the government rice subsidy per unit equal to net farmers' increased income under the various programs of the Rice Stabilization Board divided by total rice output). This second time series (1980-1988) is not exactly comparable to the first one (1955-1980) computed by Anderson and Hayami (1986) as the estimates of the NPC for 1980 and 1982 under this method differ slightly from Anderson and Hayami's estimates for the same year.

[b]See footnote 29 in text. All figures in parentheses are computed by the author and differ somewhat from the Anderson-Hayami figures.

[c]Source: Cheng (1989). The effective protection coefficient (EPC) is defined as follows:

$$EPC = 1 + \frac{\left[t_j - \sum_{i=1}^{n} a_{ij} t_i\right]}{\left[1 - \sum_{i=1}^{n} a_{ij}\right]}$$

where t_j is the nominal rate of protection $t_j = (p_j^d - p_j^f)/p_j^f$; and p_j^d and p_j^f are, respectively, the domestic and foreign (border) prices of output j; it_j is the nominal rate of protection of input $it_j = (p_j^d - p_j^f)/p_j^f$; and p_j^d and p_j^f, respectively, are the domestic and world prices of i; and a_{ij} = (cost of i required to produce one unit of j)/(unit cost of j).

[d]1965.
[e]1975.

oranges. The fact that the EPCs are higher and have risen more rapidly than the corresponding NPCs reflects the growing importance of intermediate inputs in the value of farm output (at border prices) while price distortions for these inputs (including feedgrains) during this phase remained minor.

The middle panel of Table 2.9 gives estimates of the ratio of the domestic consumer price (as reflected by the wholesale price) to the border price. This ratio approximates the extent to which consumers are discriminated against by having to pay prices above import prices. It is interesting to note that in 1974 this ratio was either below unity (i.e., 0.91 for rice and 0.70 for wheat) or slightly above it (i.e., 1.08 for barley, 1.22 for corn and 1.20 for soybean), suggesting that consumers were either subsidized or charged prices close to border prices. This situation had been drastically altered by 1980 for rice -- the consumer being charged two and a half times the world price. On the other hand, the other grains listed in Table 2.9 continued to sell at prices around border prices.

By 1980, the NPCs had become substantially higher than the corresponding ratios of consumer to border prices. The difference between these two ratios provides a measure of the financial burden on the state. One interesting point from a political economy standpoint is that the increasing level of support received by farmers appears to have been funded indirectly through taxation rather than more directly, which would have been the case if consumer prices of small grains had been raised significantly above import prices. The Small Grains Deficiency Payment previously described allowed consumer prices to remain around world prices to the consumers' satisfaction. Of course, consumers had to pay for farm subsidies indirectly through taxation, but the fact that consumers were not charged higher prices for grains (except rice) blurred the link between consumer and producer prices. We return to this issue in a subsequent discussion of the political economy of protection in Section 3 where an attempt is made to estimate the costs of protection.

Adjustment and Liberalization Phase: 1978-1981 to 1988

Overview and Overall Agricultural Performance. The current phase of agricultural development in Taiwan is characterized by the implementation of institutional reforms and policies -- many of which had already been adopted in the preceding phase -- meant to speed up the structural adjustment process in agriculture. Structural adjustment, in the Taiwan context, is to be understood in terms of a number of interrelated but not necessarily mutually consistent objectives. The first one consists of enlarging the operational size of the farm to permit the adoption of more mechanized techniques to increase land and labor productivity, while simultaneously facilitating the migration out of agriculture.

A second objective was to encourage production diversification away from rice and towards higher-valued crops and products more consistent with the emerging consumer demand pattern. In particular, the production of commodities facing relatively high income elasticities of demand (such as pork, chicken, and feedstuffs) was promoted. Diversification went in two directions: 1) promotion of goods for the domestic market and for exports in which Taiwan enjoyed a comparative advantage, such as pork and some fruits and processed food; and 2) import substitution of goods in which Taiwan had a comparative disadvantage (e.g., corn, sorghum, and some dairy products). The first direction above was clearly desirable from an efficiency standpoint in contrast with the second one.

A third objective was to create a sustainable agricultural socioeconomic system. This entailed, among others, setting up a corps (nucleus) of better trained, more educated, and younger farmers with a permanent and vocational commitment to agriculture who could insure that a politically and militarily desirable level of food security prevailed, while maintaining a rural value orientation and system.

Still another objective during this phase was the so-called liberalization of agriculture. This concept, as used in Taiwan, is very broad and embraces many meanings, such as some degree of agricultural import liberalization (which the U.S. insisted on to reduce somewhat the enormous bilateral trade surplus of Taiwan), the reduction of at least some price distortions (particularly for rice), and the improvement in the functioning of product and factor markets -- particularly the labor market to encourage female participation.

Besides the fact that some of these objectives may be conflicting, their achievement entailed enormous financial burdens for the government as will be discussed subsequently.

Before analyzing the major policies and institutional reforms which were implemented since 1980, a brief overview of agricultural performance during this phase seems appropriate. The first observation is that by the end of the 1980s the structural transformation had evolved to the point that Taiwan was approaching the typical structure of a developed, industrialized country -- i.e., in 1988 only 6 percent of NDP originated in agriculture and 13.7 percent of the labor force was employed in agriculture (see Table 2.1). The overall growth of agricultural output decelerated markedly from the preceding phase (2.42 percent per annum between 1980 and 1987 as opposed to 4.15 percent in 1974-1980 as can be seen from Table 2.2).[31] Diversification away from rice production continued to the extent that for the first time in the post-World War II history of Taiwan rice production actually dropped significantly, by 2.68 percent per year (see Table 2.2). While rice production fell from 2.35 million mt in 1980 to 1.85 million mt in 1987, two other grain crops grew enormously during this same time span

-- i.e., the production of corn and sorghum rose from, respectively, 115,000 mt to 321,000 mt and from 9,000 to 118,000 mt (see Panel A, Table 2.12 on page 53). Notwithstanding this shift in commodity composition within the farm crops' category, its combined output also declined absolutely during the 1980s. In contrast, livestock products continue to grow -- particularly milk, the output of which rose 3.6 fold, chicken (84 percent) and hogs (51 percent).

Since corn and sorghum are used as feedstuff in the livestock (and dairy) industry, the diversification which occurred followed closely the pattern of consumer demand.[32] In relative terms, rice accounted for only 11.8 percent of the value of total agricultural output in 1986-1988 and all farm crops combined for 42.1 percent, while livestock and fishery accounted for 29.2 percent and 27.5 percent, respectively (see Table 2.3).

Table 2.4 reveals clearly the continuing process of substitution of capital for labor and land which occurred during this phase. Fixed capital went from NT$22.9 billion in 1979-1981 to NT$31.9 billion in 1986-1988 and tractors almost tripled in number from 3,565 to 10,152 while crop area and the number of agricultural workers shrank further. As Table 2.10 indicates, each agricultural worker possessed on average more land to cultivate (the land-man ratio having gone up from 1.02 ha. at the beginning of the phase to 1.21 ha. in 1987) and substantially more capital (NT$29,143 vs. $19,155 per worker).

TABLE 2.10 Selected Input Ratios in Key Years

	Total farm families (× 1000)	Total agricultural workers (× 1000)	Average cultivated area per farm household (ha)	Average cultivated area per agricultural worker (ha)	Fixed capital per agricultural worker NT$
1947	553	1,285	1.51	0.65	na
1954	717	1,548	1.22	0.56	6,312
1967	869	1,622	1.04	0.57	7,434
1974	916	1,542	1.00	0.59	10,005
1980	891	1,152	1.02	0.79	19,155
1987	739	991	1.21	0.90	29,143[a]

[a]Estimate.

Source: For 1947, Thorbecke (1979, p. 147, Table 2.7); for other years *Basic Agricultural Statistics, Republic of China* (1989 ed.), Table 10, p. 12.

The large scale support to agriculture combined with the diversification towards higher valued products (e.g., livestock) improved the relative income position of farmers compared to non-farmers. On a per capita basis, farm family income as a percentage of non-farm family income rose from 65.9 percent in 1979-1981 to 72.9 percent in 1986-88 (see Table 2.5, col. 1). Also during this phase, the increasing support received by farmers resulted in a reversal of the previous trend towards a declining share of farm family income originating from nonagricultural sources. This share dropped from 69.1 percent in 1979-1981 to 62.2 percent in 1986-1988.

Some interesting dynamic shifts occurred in the composition of different types of farm households as is highlighted in Table 2.6. Between 1980 and 1985, the number of full-time farm households actually increased substantially, from 80,000 to 115,000, while the number of part-time farm households dropped almost by half, from 317,000 to 168,000 (the number of sideline farm households remained more or less constant). However, somewhat paradoxically, the upward trend in full-time farm households was sharply reversed between 1985 and 1988, probably as the result of some of the liberalization measures.

During this phase the NT dollar was gradually appreciated vis-à-vis the U.S. dollar from about 40:1 in 1983 to 28:1 in 1988. The wholesale and retail prices of imported foodstuff and feedstuff (mainly from the U.S.) remained stable (e.g., the price of bread remained firm). The lack of "passing through" of exchange rate appreciation meant that consumers were deprived from the benefits of lower prices (in domestic currency). It has been suggested that middlemen in the distribution channels from farm gate to ultimate consumers absorbed the gains from currency appreciation. This would imply that the marketing and distribution sector is not competitive in Taiwan. A thorough analysis of the market structure of this industry is called for to determine whether the marketing margin is appropriate. We return to this issue in Section 3.

Finally, a crucial development during the present phase has been the large increase in total agricultural imports and to a lesser extent that of agricultural exports. One useful way of evaluating the relative magnitude of foreign trade in agricultural products is to compare it to the value of total agricultural production in Taiwan, as is shown in Table 2.11. Thus, it can be seen that the percentage ratio of the total value of agricultural imports to the total value of agricultural production went from 23.45 percent in 1954 to 74.26 percent in 1988, while the corresponding ratio for exports rose somewhat less from 28.73 percent to 46.97 percent during the same time span. Clearly some of the import liberalization measures must have contributed to the doubling of the value of agricultural imports and the emergence of an import surplus in agricultural trade of the order of US$2.15 billion in 1988.

TABLE 2.11 Total Value of Agricultural Imports and Exports and Total Value of Agricultural Production[a] and Percentage Shares, 1954-1988 (in millions US dollars and percentages)

	Total value			Percentage ratio to agricultural production	
	Imports (1)	Exports (2)	Production[b] (3)	Imports (4)	Exports (5)
1954	74.07	90.74	315.83	23.45	28.73
1967	199.64	260.31	930.23	21.46	27.98
1974	1,285.64	840.38	2,416.84	53.20	34.77
1980	3,090.03	1,876.53	4,514.08	68.45	41.57
1988	5,844.28	3,696.35	7,869.96	74.26	46.97

[a]Includes all agricultural products, i.e., crops, livestock, fishery and forestry.
[b]Computed from *Taiwan Agricultural Yearbook* (1989, Table 3) and converted at official exchange rates.

Impact of Policy Measures and Institutional Reforms on Performance. First, the impact of the Rice Stabilization Board (RSB) and other measures such as the Small Grains Deficiency Payment Scheme on the rice economy and on the diversification process towards other farm crops is analyzed. The official support price of rice (for compulsory and planned purchases which were the two key programs during this period) was raised from NT$14.50 per kg in 1980 to NT$18.80 per kg in 1982 and remained stable subsequently. This high support price translated to a producer price ranging from two to three and a half times the border price during the 1980s (see the NPC in Panel A of Table 2.9). The government purchases under the RSB peaked in 1984 at almost 1 million mt to fall subsequently to a level less than half that amount in 1989 (see col. 3 of Table 2.8). The gigantic level of government purchases (which constituted 44 percent of the total rice crop in 1984, for example) combined with a rapidly shrinking commercial demand led to drastic increases in government rice stocks.

Table 2.8 shows government rice collection and disposal, annually, and the resulting net additions to or reductions from stocks. A number of very interesting observations are suggested by this table. First, until 1984 the level of government purchases was such that, notwithstanding very large export sales, the stock of rice continued to rise to reach a peak of 1.3 million mt, corresponding to 58 percent of the annual production in that year, or approximately eight months' worth of commercial demand. Had it not been for the very expensive "safety valve" of exporting rice at a fraction of its official purchase price, the level of stocks would have become totally unmanageable. Thus, as Table 2.8 reveals, Taiwan exported over half a million mt in 1980 and 649 million mt in 1983.[33]

Secondly, after 1983 a number of measures such as the Small Grains Deficiency Payment Scheme and Planned Adjustment in Acreage Allocation between rice and three feedstuffs (i.e., corn, sorghum, and soybean) led to diversification away from rice production -- the output of which fell by 640,000 mt between 1983 and 1988 amounting to a reduction of one-fourth of total output (see col. 1 of Table 2.7). In contrast, the domestic production of both corn and sorghum rose significantly from, respectively, 115,000 mt in 1980 to 321,000 mt in 1988 and from 9,000 to 118,000 mt. Notwithstanding this diversification, the government was forced even after 1984 to continue to collect large quantities of rice in order to maintain the high support price, as can be seen from Table 2.8. These large surpluses were disposed of through exports and a new outlet, namely, feedstuff.[34] In any case, through the success of the diversification process and the massive surplus disposal of rice (through exports and feed), the level of the rice stock fell to 730,000 mt in 1988 -- representing over six months of commercial demand in that year.

The total public expenditures under the Food Stabilization Fund between its initiation in 1975 and 1989 amounted to almost NT$81 billion (i.e., about US$3.15 billion at the current exchange rate). The Taiwan Food Bureau estimated the increased farmers' incomes resulting from the operations of the RSB (according to the procedure explained in footnote 27). These estimates appear in col. 7 of Table 2.7. During 1974-1980 the estimated increased income to farmers amounted to almost NT$7 billion and to NT$25.5 billion between 1981 and 1988 (the sum of the above two figures is about US$1 billion). In fact, the actual social cost of protection is much higher. This cost can be estimated in any given year as the difference between the average price received by the farmer and the border price multiplied by the apparent total consumption in the same year. I estimated these total costs of protection to have amounted to almost US$3.7 billion for the decade preceding 1988 just to support the rice price.[35]

The accelerated level of protection during this phase comes out clearly from the estimates of nominal and effective protection coefficients in Table 2.9. The most noteworthy changes between 1980 and 1988 are: 1) the enormous increases in the NPC of sorghum from 1.83 to 4.35 and of corn from 1.55 to 3.72; 2) the quantum jump in the EPC for rice from 1.38 to 4.56; 3) the evidence of strong comparative advantage enjoyed by Taiwan in the production of pork, chicken, and some fruits; and finally, 4) the rise in the ratio of consumer prices to border prices for some feedstuff, suggesting that a part of the financial burden of protection was being shifted to consumers.

While the Taiwanese government encouraged diversification away from rice towards feedstuff and livestock production, it also liberalized imports by reducing a number of tariff rates and quantitative restrictions. The amazing jump in total agricultural imports from US$3.09 billion in 1980 to US$5.84 billion in 1988 has already been highlighted. Table 2.12 provides more specific information regarding the recent evolution of quantities and values of selected imported products. The table reveals the sharply upward trends in imports of wheat (from 686,000 mt to 935,000 mt), corn (from 2.60 million mt to 4.46 million mt), and soybeans (from 940,000 mt to 2.1 million

TABLE 2.12 Total Production and Imports of Selected Products, 1954-1988

	\multicolumn{8}{c}{Total production (100 metric tons)}							
	Rice	Wheat	Indian Corn	Sorghum	Soybean	Milk	Cattle	Hogs	Chicken 1000 heads
1954	1,695	15.5	11.1	1.4	20.3	1.7	2.6	130.6	12.9
1967	2,414	23.8	64.1	9.5	75.2	13.8	6.9	314.6	24.6
1974	2,452	0.7	107.1	21.9	66.9	41.9	4.8	462.5	50.0
1980	2,354	2.8	115.1	9.1	25.9	47.7	5.5	733.6	104.7
1982	2,483	2.3	118.4	13.2	12.0	55.9	5.7	753.9	122.4
1984	2,244	2.4	189.9	32.5	9.5	66.9	6.5	887.8	155.0
1986	1,974	3.7	271.7	97.0	14.9	109.7	3.9	1,053.8	155.9
1988	1,845	3.0	321.2	117.8	14.6	173.4	4.7	1,105.7	193.0

	\multicolumn{6}{c}{Selected Agricultural Imports}					
	Wheat	Corn	Sorghum	Soybean	Dairy products	Beef
Quantity (1000 metric tons)						
1980	685.7	2,603	429.3	939	59.8	10.9
1982	730.0	2,548	743.3	1,150	65.0	19.8
1984	669.1	2,960	596.9	1,345	76.9	24.1
1986	768.5	3,071	810.3	1,739	88.6	32.7
1988	934.7	4,457	97.9	2,099	92.1	38.3
Value (million US$)						
1980	146.4	437.6	68.5	30.9	292.3	110.1
1982	144.2	374.4	100.3	52.6	340.2	140.4
1984	125.0	475.8	85.6	65.8	438.1	147.1
1986	125.4	353.7	79.0	81.4	397.7	158.1
1988	160.2	548.4	11.2	129.8	552.0	179.4

Source: *Agricultural Production Statistics Abstract*, Statistics Office, Council of Agriculture, June 1989; *Agricultural Trade Statistics*, 1988.

mt), and the drastic curtailment of imports of sorghum which dropped from 810,000 mt in 1986 to 98,000 mt in 1988.[36] The apparent inconsistency between supporting small grains diversification, on the one hand, while liberalizing feedstuff imports (with the possible exception of sorghum in 1988), on the other hand, is explored subsequently.

In addition to the price support and stabilization measures discussed previously, the government committed itself to large-scale capital investments in order to vitalize the agricultural sector. Two programs were initiated during the current phase, namely the "Program on Enhancing Farm Income and Strengthening Rural Reconstruction" and the "Program on Basic Infrastructure Development" which were merged, in 1983, into a "Program on Strengthening Basic Infrastructure and Enhancing Farm Income."[37]

The crucial institutional development which was initiated during this phase was the Second Stage of the Agricultural Land Reform (SSALR) whose importance has been compared with that of the Land Reform Program of the 1950s. In particular, it recognized entrusted farming as a contract form which protected the rights of the farm-owners entrusting their farms to others and thereby removed the natural reluctance of owners to enter into an owner-tenant contractual relationship which up to that time had favored the rights of the latter. The door was open to a significant enlargement of the operational size of the farm.

The SSALR also included a detailed plan and target for the expansion of the scale of operation of different types of production. The common approach was to organize the small farms to participate in joint operations, entrusted farming, and cooperative farming.[38] In a nutshell, the following objectives were specified: 1) in farm crop production, priority should be given to rice production and the enlarged unit should cover an area between twenty and thirty hectares; the goal of the program was to cover 160,000 hectares between 1982 and 1986; 2) in livestock production, the program was to help each nucleus hog farm to raise between 200 and 500 head a season and to assist each beef cattle farm to raise at least 100 head in a grazing area of fifty hectares; 3) in fish production, the program was to organize small fish farms to participate in joint operations and cooperative marketing similar to the group action of rice farms; the scale of joint operations in each area varies from 200 to 4,000 hectares; and finally, 4) in upland utilization, the program emphasizes infrastructure improvement for larger areas with a minimum scale of 50 hectares.[39]

In 1983, the Council for Agricultural Planning and Development (CAPD) spelled out a detailed blueprint to guide and design the future development of the Taiwanese agricultural sector.[40] This blueprint contains twelve main objectives whose achievements are necessary to reach the desired state of rural villages by the turn of the century. The most important among these objectives are 1) to enlarge the scale of one-hectare small farms to more-than-10-hectares mechanized farms through arrangements for joint operations, entrusted farming, or cooperative farming on both irrigated and dry land, growing rice, other common crops, and sugarcane; 2) to organize small vegetable farms, flower farms, fruit farms, and special crop farms into large, several-hundred-hectare, specialized areas for individual crops; and 3) to shift from rice-dominated agriculture to profit-maximization-priority agriculture by growing rice only at the self-sufficiency level and developing other crops, livestock, and aquaculture, whichever enterprise appears to be the most profitable; moreover, to shift from diversified and scattered types of farm management to completely-planned specialized-area farm management according to the principle of comparative advantage.[41]

The realization of these objectives would require the training and establishment of a task force of 80,000 nucleus farmers. As Ong (1984) put it:

The forward thinking behind establishing such an "army" of nucleus farmers is based on their projection that over the next two decades more rural youth will seek employment in the non-farm sector and more senior farmers will retire from farming. When the national economy is further developed, Taiwan will need 80,000 modern farms to produce enough food to meet the country's requirements. On average, each nucleus farmer will operate a fully mechanized 10-ha. farm under group farming management (p. 63).

Each nucleus farmer is expected to be endowed with leadership capability and management ability and be able to organize joint operations, mainly through the process of farm entrustment. The resulting larger operational size of the farm unit would, in turn, allow the adoption of more productive and mechanized technology. The blueprint contains detailed plans and steps to select and train nucleus farmers and to coordinate auxiliary measures such as the availability of subsidized credit, the expansion of rural health services, the improvement of marketing channels, the building of better rural infrastructure, and the development of self-reliance among nucleus farmers.

In the absence of cost estimates of this extremely ambitious "Blueprint for the Outlook of New Rural Villages in Taiwan" and a clear vision of its anticipated impact on agricultural production and income, it is very difficult -- if not impossible -- to evaluate its desirability in terms of weighing the present discounted value of future streams of benefits against the present value of discounted streams of costs. In any case, it appears that progress with the implementation of the blueprint and, in particular, with the establishment of a large "army" of nucleus farmers has been slow and that the government might be exploring other alternatives.

3. THE POLITICAL ECONOMY OF PROTECTION AND CURRENT POLICY ISSUES AND RECOMMENDATIONS

The preceding sections describing the last four decades of the agricultural history of Taiwan illustrate clearly the remarkable speed of the structural transformation process from a very poor agrarian economy to a developed, industrialized country. The crucial turning point occurred around 1973-1975 when the government switched from a strategy of taxing agriculture to one of increasingly supporting it. This transition is typical of countries graduating from the status of developing to that of developed nation. In fact, the point when a country starts protecting its agricultural sector can be taken as a good approximation of the time it begins to join the ranks of the developed, industrialized economies.

In order to evaluate the last two phases of agricultural development in Taiwan and, in particular, the form and extent of agricultural protectionism, it is important to compare the Taiwanese experience with that of other developed countries. Such a comparison has recently been undertaken by Anderson and Hayami (1986) who contrasted the experience of East Asia (Japan, South Korea and Taiwan) to that of industrialized countries in Western Europe, North America and Oceania. Drawing on the new institutional economics (e.g., collective action) and public choice literature, they adopt a conceptual framework capable of explaining the causes of agricultural protectionism. In a nutshell, within the political market framework they explore how "the factors affecting the demand and supply curves for distortionary agricultural policies change over time with economic growth, how those factors might differ among countries with comparable per capita incomes, and how they might vary for different policy instruments" (p. 3).

In this political market, the potential benefits of the demanders of distortionary (protectionistic) policies have to be weighed against the political costs to the government (which is the supplier of these policies) of groups opposed to these policies. In theory, the political leadership attempts to introduce distortionary policies up to the point where the benefits (i.e., marginal revenue) to the groups supporting these policies equal the political cost (i.e., marginal costs) to the government of displeasing opponents of these policies.

Throughout the structural transformation which characterizes the process of growth, a number of fundamental changes occur in the intensity of, respectively, opposition to and support for protectionistic policies. The major factors affecting the degree of opposition and support over time, as identified by Anderson and Hayami (1986), are: 1) the decreasing importance of food prices and food shares in household budgets as income rises insures that political pressures from consumers and industrialists for lower food prices weakens; 2) the declining relative importance in the shares of agricultural output in total output and agricultural employment in total employment makes it less costly politically to succumb to farmers' demands for assistance measures helping them adjust to the declining role of agriculture; 3) furthermore, after an economy has reached the point where the absolute number of farmers declines, it becomes easier for the (smaller) number to form an effective lobby group to exert pressure on the government to implement distortionary policies through collective action. Conversely, as the size and number of non-agricultural interest groups increases so does the "free rider" problem so that collective action to oppose agricultural protectionism is weakened; and 4) there is a tendency for growing economies, particularly the densely populated ones, to lose their comparative advantage in agriculture and become net agricultural importers; this provides increasing scope to the government for assisting farmers through such instruments as import controls that do not require overt budgetary expenditures and for justifying agricultural protection on the grounds of food security.

It is clear that all the above factors occurred in Taiwan -- at least from the early seventies on -- so that it is hardly surprising that Taiwan conformed to the general pattern of advanced countries increasingly protecting their agricultural sector. What is perhaps more surprising is the degree and extent of protection as compared to many more developed countries and the rest of the world. Table 2.13 shows the nominal rates of agricultural protection in fifteen industrial countries between 1955 and 1980. It can be seen that the weighted average nominal rate of agricultural protection in Taiwan in 1980 was higher than in every member country of the EEC except Italy, while being below that of South Korea, Japan, Switzerland, and Sweden. Because feed grain prices paid by livestock producers in Taiwan are close to border prices (see panel C of Table 2.9) while in the EEC they are somewhat above border prices, it follows that a comparison based on nominal rather than effective protection rates underestimates the extent to which effective protection in Taiwan, in fact, exceeds that prevailing in the EEC.

Noting that the degree of agricultural protection is significantly more pronounced in East Asia (even more so in Japan and South Korea as compared to Taiwan) than in the more developed countries of Europe, Homma and Hayami (1986)[43] used multiple regression analysis to explore whether the high protection levels in East Asia resulted from a unique bias towards protecting agriculture relative to other industrialized countries. They concluded that no such bias existed but rather that the high level of protection

TABLE 2.13 Nominal Rates of Agricultural Protection in Fifteen Industrial Countries, 1955-1980 (percent)[a]

	1955	1960	1965	1970	1975	1980
East Asia						
Japan	18	41	69	74	76	85
Korea	-46	-15	-4	29	30	117
Taiwan	-17	-3	-1	2	20	52
Non-aligned Europe						
Sweden	34	44	50	65	43	59
Switzerland	60	64	73	96	96	126
European community						
Denmark	5	3	5	17	19	25
France	33	26	30	47	29	30
Germany FR	35	48	55	50	39	44
Italy	47	50	66	69	38	57
Netherlands	14	21	35	41	32	27
United Kingdom	40	37	20	27	6	35
Average[b]	35	37	45	52	29	38
Food exporters						
Australia	5	7	5	7	-5	-2
Canada	0	4	2	5	7	-3
New Zealand	na	2	0	-5	-4	2
United States	2	1	9	11	4	0

[a]Defined as the percentage by which the producer price exceeds the border price. The estimates shown are the weighted averages for twelve commodities, using production valued at border prices as weights.

[b]Weighted average for all six countries shown for 1975 and 1980, but excluding Denmark and the United Kingdom for earlier years.

[c]Not available.

Source: Reprinted with permission from K. Anderson and Y. Hayami, *The Political Economy of Agricultural Protection: East Asia in International Perspective*, Table 2.5, 1986, Allen and Unwin.

in East Asia could be explained by the extremely rapid development of a very strong comparative advantage in manufacturing. According to them:

> The social and political difficulties entailed in intersectoral resource adjustment might have become intolerable without protection growth. When this consideration is combined with the national security need

for maintaining political stability, which may only be achievable by effectively bribing farmers not to destabilize the polity, agricultural protection can rise to exceptionally high levels -- as in the case of Korea (p. 49).

A relevant question which suggests itself at this stage concerns the overall social costs of agricultural protectionism. Although it is extremely difficult to come up with any robust figure, these costs can be very roughly estimated. These costs include: 1) the excess producer prices over and above world prices for those commodities in which Taiwan has a comparative disadvantage multiplied by the corresponding domestic output of these products; 2) the public investment in agriculture to modernize rural infrastructure and create the necessary facilities for the new rural villages; 3) the public capital and current expenditures connected with all activities related to enlarging the operational size of farms -- such as the costs of land consolidation, organizing farmers for joint management, providing them with subsidized credit and additional extension services, and the training and selection of nucleus farmers; and 4) such intangible costs as reducing the outflow of labor to non-agricultural jobs and the consequent loss in labor productivity.

A very approximate order of magnitude for these social costs of agricultural protection might be around NT$30 to 40 billion annually, or about 1 percent of GNP (which amounted to NT$3,423 billion in 1988).[43] It could be argued, at first glance, that these social costs are, relatively speaking, fairly marginal. However, considering these costs from another vantage point in a dynamic sense -- i.e., as implying a reduction in the *growth rate* of GNP of say 1 percent annually over an extended transitional period -- puts them in their proper perspective.

On the other side of the ledger, one should also ask what Taiwan gets in return for these social costs in terms of social benefits and whether these benefits could have been obtained at lesser cost. Addressing, first, the former question, Taiwan obtains 1) a high level of food security (e.g., large stocks of rice) in addition to keeping alive a large domestic productive capability for rice and other grains; 2) a lessening of the political instability which could result from too rapid an agricultural adjustment process which would naturally occur in the absence of protection as farmers are pushed out of agriculture and pulled into other sectors; 3) the maintenance of traditional rural values and rural infrastructure -- including housing for household members of part-time and sideline farmers working outside agriculture;[44] and 4) the gradual rationalization of the structure of agricultural production towards larger, more mechanized, and more productive farm units managed by a cadre of better trained and more dynamic nucleus farmers.

These are substantial benefits which are, however, even more difficult to measure than the social costs. The crucial question is whether these benefits could have been obtained at lesser cost. This question can perhaps be better answered after reviewing and recalling very briefly the agricultural performance trends in the current liberalization phase.

The adjustment and liberalization process evolved rapidly in the 1980s as we have seen. The most noteworthy trends were the following. First, rice production fell and became more consistent with the changing demand pattern away from rice (which has become an inferior good in Taiwan). This was accompanied by a significant decline in government rice stocks which, however, still represent approximately six months of commercial demand. Even though the government rice collection in 1988 had fallen to their lowest levels since 1975, it amounted to almost half a million mt.

Secondly, the diversification process towards pork, chicken, and other commodities in which Taiwan possesses a comparative advantage proceeded in parallel fashion with diversification away from rice towards feedstuff in which Taiwan has a strong comparative disadvantage. This last shift can be explained by the limited scope for commercially warranted crop substitution on paddy land so that rice land released from rice production can mainly grow crops such as corn and sorghum at the present time. Clearly the substitution of the latter crops for rice, even though necessary in a transitional adjustment period (to maintain farmers' income), should be discouraged in the long-run. On the other hand, it behooves the authorities to help identify, through research, other non-grain products which could potentially be produced on rice land at a lesser comparative disadvantage -- admittedly an extremely difficult task.

Thirdly, a positive trend from a social welfare standpoint is the sharp rise in agricultural imports and the somewhat more limited rise in agricultural exports, during the current phase. However, this observation should be qualified to the extent that increasing feedstuff imports (amounting to about US$700 million in 1988)[45] contributes to the high effective protection enjoyed by the domestic beef and dairy industry. In contrast, the upward trend in the latter imports (from about US$400 million in 1980 to about US$731 million in 1988, as Table 2.12 shows) is a good sign.

Fourth, the agricultural adjustment process evolved -- although slowed down by distortionary support policies -- as revealed, for instance, by the continuing fall in the total number of farm households from about 890,000 in 1980 to about 739,000 in 1988, with only 10 percent of these households being full-time farm households (see Table 2.6). The key characteristics of the three types of farm households in Taiwan are shown in Table 2.14. In the recent past, sideline farm households (defined as part-time farm households earning less than half their total income from farming) enjoyed the highest income per employed person but, by far, the lowest land productivity (farm income per hectare of farm land). In contrast, part-time and full-time

TABLE 2.14 Labor and Land Productivity by Type of Farm Household in Taiwan and Share of Total Household Income from Farm Income

Type of farm household	Family income per employed person NT$ (1)	Farm income per hectare of farm land NT$ (2)	Share of Total household income from farm % (3)	Size of family (persons) (4)
1977				
Full-time	39,248	51,928	75.2	5.18
Part-time	37,945	51,160	54.9	6.05
Sideline	41,329	32,908	17.5	6.19
Average	38,009	44,035	34.5	5.99
1980				
Full-time	71,518	84,871	68.1	4.50
Part-time	65,567	70,821	46.3	5.40
Sideline	72,876	51,129	124.3	5.96
Average	71,574	62,839	24.5	5.69
1985				
Full-time	93,290	107,999	72.9	3.78
Part-time	107,473	114,540	50.7	5.15
Sideline	111,704	70,397	13.4	5.54
Average	109,016	103,286	28.7	5.21

Source: Mao (1988, Tables 3.2 and 3.3).

farm households enjoyed lower incomes per person employed but higher land productivity. It is also relevant to note that the average number of members in full-time farm households dropped drastically between 1977 and 1985 from 5.18 persons to 3.78 persons -- an average size substantially smaller than that of the other two types of households (see col. 4 of Table 2.14). Still another socioeconomic characteristic of full-time farm households is that they tend to be significantly older and less educated than the other two types of households.

We can now return to an evaluation of the likely future benefits of the present agricultural strategy in Taiwan and explore whether there might be alternative ways of obtaining these and other benefits at lower cost. The two fundamental objectives of the current agricultural strategy appear to be

1) the achievement of some degree of parity between farm incomes and rising non-farm incomes; and 2) food security, presumably implying self-sufficiency at least in rice.

What are the major means (policies and reforms) through which these objectives are to be achieved in the current agricultural strategy and how successful are these instruments likely to be? The various measures aimed at enlarging the operational size of the farm and encouraging the adoption of more mechanized technologies will undoubtedly increase both land and labor productivities. A whole set of studies conducted by researchers at different universities over the last twenty years concluded that farm incomes and yields would be significantly higher under joint operations and entrusted farming on larger farms than on individual small farms.[46] As progress is made through entrusted farming on larger operational farms towards reducing production costs and increasing farmers' incomes, the government can simultaneously reduce the extent of protection. However, there are clear limits, given present technology, to how far labor and land productivities can be pushed upward on a ten-to-twenty hectare enlarged-size farm. This suggests that Taiwan would be well served by investing more on agricultural research to help identify both improved technology and alternative products to rice and small grains which can be potentially grown on rice land at the least comparative disadvantage. In this context, international comparisons suggest that Taiwan spends much less on agricultural research per dollar of output than other middle income and industrial countries, as Figure 2.2 reveals. Granted that the payoff to agricultural research within the setting of labor and land constraints faced by Taiwan is uncertain, a greater level of research support financed through some reduction in protection may well prove to be a desirable alternative yielding higher potential social benefits.

In particular, the form which R&D takes is of crucial importance. It is not just a matter of increasing the level of support for R&D. It is just as important to identify clearly the agricultural commodities which have the greatest potential social productivity in the diversification process away from rice and feedstuff production. For example, it does not appear that specialized tropical fruits are aggressively marketed abroad. Other countries have had much success recently with the production and export of horticultural products, either in the form of flowers or bulbs. A concerted effort by the government to allocate more to agricultural R&D and focus it on potential export crops could have a high payoff.

A second important policy issue relates to the proposed land policy. The "Blueprint for the Outlook of New Villages in Taiwan" calls for the establishment of an "army" of 80,000 nucleus farmers operating, on average, fully-mechanized 10-ha. farms under group farming management. This means that it is anticipated that the total cultivated land area will remain at its present level of about 800,000 ha. Would it not be more reasonable to reduce some-

FIGURE 2.2 Agricultural Research Expenditure
Relative to Agricultural Output, 1959-1980

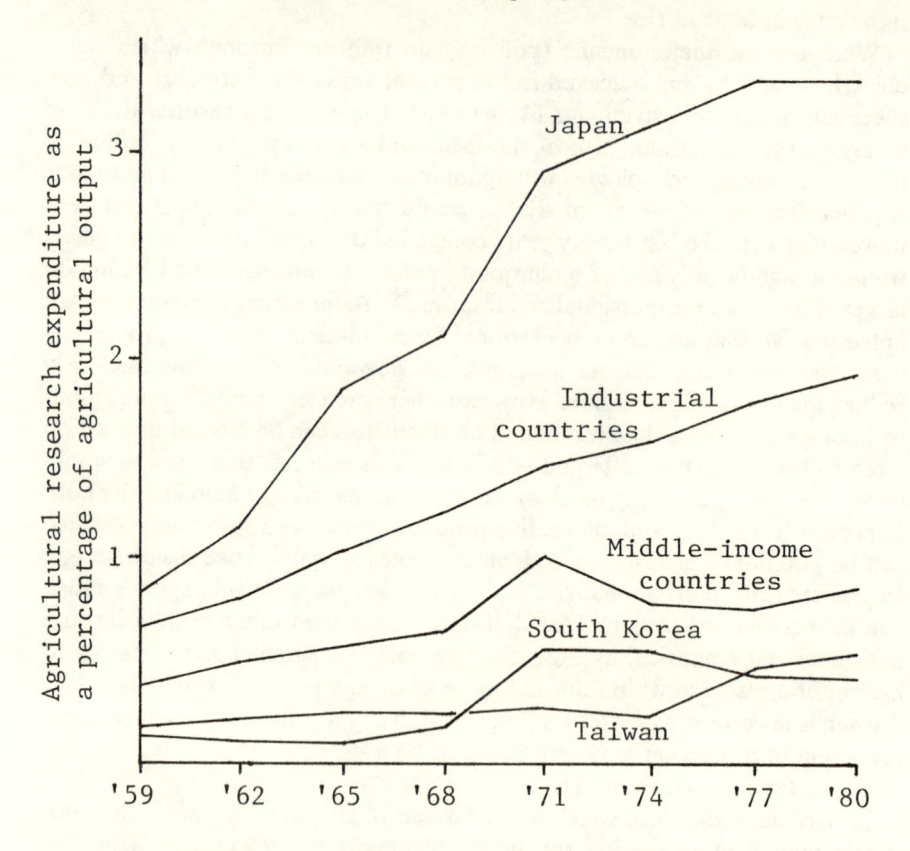

Agricultural research expenditure as a percentage of agricultural output

Japan
Industrial countries
Middle-income countries
South Korea
Taiwan

'59 '62 '65 '68 '71 '74 '77 '80

Source: K. Anderson and Y. Hayami, The Political Economy of Agricultural Protection: East Asia in International Perspective, Figure 9.1, 1986, reprinted with permission from Allen and Unwin.

what the land base and convert a part of it into a national land reserve? Before answering this question, it is useful to review briefly some very recent "land-aside" programs which are underway in both the U.S. and the U.K. and appear to have some relevance to the present Taiwanese conditions. In the U.S., the 1985 Food Security Act authorized a Conservation Reserve Program (CRP) with the multiple goals of 1) reducing erosion, 2) protecting soil productivity, 3) reducing sedimentation, 4) improving water quality, 5) improving fish and wildlife habitat, 6) curbing production of surplus commodities, and 7) providing income support to farmers. The objective is to remove from production 40-45 million acres of erodible cropland by 1990[47] and using it in ways that conserve the soil, such as planting trees or grasses for a contract period of ten years. An auction system is used to determine rental value of land under CRP. Even though it is too early to evaluate the benefit-cost ratio of this program ex post, estimates computed by the USDA are promising.[48]

In the U.K., it was estimated that 23 percent of the total agricultural land may no longer be needed for food production by the end of the century. The British Ministry of Agriculture is increasingly looking at alternative uses for farm land such as woodland management, recreational sites, and land diversification schemes (e.g., forests, wildlife reserves, and ponds). The Ministry put forward a land-aside scheme to the EEC which would appear to save money. Grain growers indicated that they would be willing to set aside land for an annual rental of £50-100 an acre, while buying surplus British grain costs the EEC £300 an acre and £40 a year to store. In land use allocation, planners will no longer have to take into account the productivity of farm land. Much of the demand for new homes and individual development should be met from agricultural land.[49]

In both the U.S. and the U.K., the value of agricultural land was artificially inflated by a succession of price support and other schemes which boosted land rent. As the level of agricultural protectionism is gradually reduced, so is the market value of land. This process reduces the cost of land-aside programs and facilitates their implementation.

Within the context of Taiwan, there may be lessons to be learned from the above experiences. Clearly, the extremely high level of protection enjoyed by farmers has drastically pushed up agricultural land values. The land market is further distorted by restrictions imposed on the sale of agricultural land. Indirectly, these distortions have contributed to the escalation of urban land prices. It is essential, at the present time, for the government to try to rationalize the whole process of land use allocation and planning and move towards a less distorted land market. A gradual reduction in the level of support enjoyed by farmers would contribute to a reduction in agricultural land prices and agricultural rental values. This would facilitate the implementation of a land-aside policy by the government by reducing its costs. The government should explore the transferability and adaptability of different land-aside schemes to the conditions prevailing in Taiwan.

In particular, two different variants suggest themselves: i) long-term rental contracts of the type described above with reference to the U.S. (CRP) and the U.K. which would convert farm land to alternative uses (such as forestry and fish ponds) and contribute to conservation; and ii) a more radical scheme of land purchase by the state into a national land reservation which could, for example, become a park area which in an emergency situation could be reconverted into cultivable land.

Furthermore, the government could gradually release some of this land reserve for non-agricultural uses which would relieve somewhat the urban housing and commercial land shortages which are presently plaguing Taiwan. Such a scheme would have the advantage of curtailing the costs of protecting the production of crops in which Taiwan possesses a strong comparative disadvantage while remunerating farmers for the fair value of their land, thereby providing them with capital which would presumably yield comparable returns. In addition, the government would be insured against external shocks which could cut off needed supplies of agricultural imports. Still another benefit of this scheme would be to improve the functioning of the land market which is now extremely imperfect. Clearly, the specifics of a land-aside policy can only be worked out by experts in Taiwan.

It might be mentioned, in passing, that the success of a land-aside policy would be enhanced if an international rice reserve program could be established -- an unlikely occurrence at the present time. Alternatively, the government could seek long-term commitments by rice exporting countries to supply Taiwan as it shifts gradually away from rice production.

A third current policy issue relates to which type of farm household the government should focus its attention on and support. Of the three types of farm households, sideline farm households enjoy the highest incomes per person employed (i.e., labor productivity) and the lowest land productivity and vice versa for full-time and part-time farm households. As Mao (1988) stated: "If our national policy goal is to increase farm family income in spite of agriculture, then it seems that the sideline farm household should be encouraged. But, if our policy goal is to develop a competitive agriculture, then the full-time farm household should be encouraged" (p. 516).

The government's plan to train 80,000 nucleus farmers and promote joint operations through entrusted farming suggests that the emphasis has been placed on favoring the full-time and part-time farmers. This may be an appropriate strategy as long as the government is prepared to simultaneously facilitate the move out of agriculture into services and industry by members of the rural population. If the effort at retaining workers in agriculture went too far, it would impede a continuation of the structural transformation and impose high efficiency costs. One can agree with the following evaluation by a keen student of Taiwan's agricultural history:

> It will be a truly unprecedented achievement if Taiwan as well as other small farm countries can create a dual structure with a small number of internationally competitive full-time farmers, with the rural majority consisting of part-time farmers who continue to hold titles to their land and to live in the villages as they earn the bulk of their income from non-farm occupations. Hence, this future farm income policy should focus mainly on full-time farmers, pay more attention to their income level and welfare, and help one improve their farm production and management. . . . Sideline farmers . . . should be encouraged to entrust their farms to the full-time farmers or the part-time farmers (Mao 1988, pp. 524-525).

The present government strategy is to raise farmers' incomes through a combination of measures: 1) enhancing the productivity of land and labor in agriculture; and 2) providing income transfers resulting from agricultural protection. One obvious alternative to the above measures is for the public sector to invest more heavily in the human capital of the rural population by educating and training the children of farmers to provide them the knowledge and skills required to qualify for productive employment opportunities outside of agriculture. It does not appear that this last alternative has been given a high enough priority in the present national agricultural policy package.

A final issue which ought to be studied thoroughly in an effort to increase the efficiency of the agro-business complex is the structure and competitiveness of the marketing and distributional network. If the evidence were to support the presumption that marketing margins by middlemen are unduly high, steps could be taken to improve the efficiency of the distribution channels by making them more competitive.

As with most instances of mutually conflicting objectives, it appears important to avoid extreme choices. The set of policy instruments and reforms constituting the present agricultural strategy is chosen so as to allow a level of achievement of these objectives based on the perceived welfare tradeoffs among them. Many components of the strategy are reasonable given the objectives and under the prevailing conditions. Thus, the major effort at rationalizing the structural agricultural production through enlarging the operational size of the farm, the training of nucleus farmers, and the encouragement of mechanization is entirely consistent with increased efficiency. However, greater investment in research to identify appropriate mechanized technologies and potential substitutes for rice and grains with higher value added and less comparative disadvantage appears indicated.

Agricultural protectionism of rice and small grains and the changing incentive system which has led to diversification away from rice and towards the production of feedstuff are measures which are consistent with both food security and the equity objectives. The issue which can be raised here is whether the target cultivated land base is not overly ambitious in the light of 1) the large government rice purchases, far in excess of commercial demand, which either have to be added to existing stockpiles or artificially disposed of as feedstuff or exports; and 2) the strong comparative disadvantage which Taiwan suffers from in the production of feedstuff crops which presently compete with rice. To bring domestic production more in line with commercial demand, while avoiding extreme protection rates, the establishment of a public land reserve should be seriously explored.

Finally, greater public spending on the education and skill formation of rural youth would contribute to a more efficient and equitable economy and thereby be a sound partial alternative to agricultural protectionism.

In summary, the path which Taiwan's agriculture has started on, although reasonable in the light of the mutually conflicting objectives and constraints, could lead to greater success if the proposed alternative measures above were seriously contemplated as substitutes for at least some reduction in the degree of agricultural protectionism.

Notes

I am grateful for all the help provided by my research assistant, Da-Nien Liu, particularly in gathering documents and data in Taiwan and Ithaca and providing me with translations and summaries of relevant Chinese texts. Dr. Yu-kang Mao of the Council of Agriculture, Executive Yuan helped us greatly with data and valuable source material. Finally, I want to acknowledge the many conversations which I have had with Henry Wan over the years regarding Taiwan. He contributed some useful insights, valuable comments, and a patient sounding board. I benefitted also from valuable comments by Gustav Ranis.

1. These figures are, respectively, for 1947 and 1988.

2. Three very good accounts of agricultural development during the colonial period are Lee and Chen (1975), Ho (1978), and Ho (1968). A very brief historical perspective of agricultural development in the colonial period (1885-1945) is contained in Thorbecke (1979, pp. 133-138).

3. The share of agricultural NDP in total NDP was around 42 percent in 1911-1920 and fell somewhat in the 1920s and 1930s to rise again in 1947 owing to war devastation. The share of the agricultural labor force in the total labor force did decline from about 73 percent in 1911-1920 to 66 per-

cent in 1931-1940. For more detailed information, see Thorbecke (1979, p. 134), Table 2.1.

4. The agricultural import surplus *per se* (total agricultural imports minus total agricultural exports) in that year amounted to US$2.148 billion, while fertilizer imports amounted to US$463 million, adding up to an overall import surplus of US$2.611 billion.

5. A perennial problem with time series of output indices is what weights should be used in computing them. The Basic Agricultural Statistics Yearbook for 1989 uses a weighting scheme for production indices based on value added, whereas the BAS for 1988 and prior years uses prices as weights. Hence Table 2.2 shows the growth rates corresponding to these two different weighting schemes. In general, the first set of output indices above are used in this study. Even though differences between the two sets are noticeable (compare Panels I and II of Table 2.2), both sets of growth rates move in parallel fashion.

6. It increased by about 8 percent between 1946-1948 and 1973-1975 to decline slightly subsequently.

7. See Thorbecke (1979, Table 2.11).

8. The first three phases prior to 1973-1975 are analyzed and described in detail in Thorbecke (1979) which provides the basis for the analysis which follows. It should be noted, however, that in the present study the most recent indices of output are used. The new statistical time series yield slightly different quantitative indicators than those appearing in the above referred source.

9. See Lee (1971). This percentage refers to the period 1950-1955, which does not correspond exactly to our first phase (1947-1954).

10. For evidence, see Thorbecke (1979, pp. 178-179).

11. See Kuo (1975, p. 150).

12. The ratio of the daily wage rate of farm workers deflated by the rural consumer price index to that of the daily wage rate of factory workers deflated by the urban consumer price index rose from a level of about 75 in 1966-1968 to 104 in 1975. See Thorbecke (1979, p. 187).

13. Other mechanical implements that were previously almost nonexistent, such as combines, rice dryers, and power sprayers, began to be used on an expanding scale.

14. Unfortunately, the excellent historical study by Lee (1971) on intersectoral capital flows has not been brought up to date after 1969.

15. See Chen, Hsu, and Mao (1974, p. 11).

16. Per capita relative indicators show an improvement while a comparison of the growth rates of per capita real incomes of farmers vis-à-vis non-farmers reveals a decline (see, respectively, cols. 1-3 and 13-14 of Table 2.5).

17. It can be noted from Table 5 that the relative income position of farm households to non-farm households worsens during this period (see

cols. 4-6 of Table 2.5). This appears to be inconsistent with the opposite trend on a per capita basis. Two phenomena may help explain these results: First, at the outset the size of farm households was significantly higher than that of non-farm households; and secondly, the average household size declined faster among the former than among the latter group of households.

18. Although, as was pointed out earlier, some of these measures were enacted during the transitional years between the end of the slowdown phase and the beginning of the phase presently under consideration.

19. See Yu (1978, p. 71).

20. For a good description of these measures see Ong (1984). This is a useful source which contains a thorough review of agricultural policies in Taiwan until the very early 1980s. It relies on a large set of references, mostly in Chinese.

21. It will be seen subsequently that an additional alternative tenure form resembling tenancy is that of an entrusted farmer. This form became popular later on, particularly after the Agricultural Development Act was amended in August 1983 to protect the rights of owners vis-à-vis the entrusted farmers and reduce the strict protection of tenancy rights which existed prior to this amendment. Politically, any suggestion on the part of the government that a reconcentration of landownership should occur was taboo in view of its consequences in alienating farmers and possible exploitation by the PRC or the separatists.

22. For example, if a tractor is used to service twenty individual non-contiguous one-hectare farms, its productivity would be significantly less than if the same tractor was used on one consolidated farm.

23. The present characterization of these different forms of group farming are based on Ong (1984, pp. 30-31) and Thorbecke (1979, pp. 191-92).

24. It has been argued that under the conditions prevailing in Taiwan, the ideal (optimal) size of an operational unit is between fifteen and twenty hectares, involving from twenty to twenty-five farms (see Ong 1984, p. 28).

25. The joint management system has had only limited success. The main exception is The Taiwan Sugar Corporation (TSC) which organized and provided technical assistance to a large number of small farms and helped them undertake a jointly managed "TSC Family Farm."

26. For a good description of RNCs, see Ong (1984, pp. 24-25).

27. The compulsory price is taken as reflecting the official support price. Other government rice collecting programs included planned purchases from 1974 on and supervised purchase from 1978 on. The price of planned purchases, in any given year, was either equal to or differed marginally from that of the compulsory price. The price of supervised purchase was consistently slightly below that of the compulsory price throughout the whole period of its existence from 1978 to the present.

28. These estimates of the contribution to farmers' incomes of the Rice Stabilization Board through its price support programs are arrived at by multiplying the quantities of rice collected by the government (under compulsory purchases, planned purchases, and supervised purchases) and multiplying these quantities by the corresponding difference between, respectively, each one of these three official prices and the farm price, which is assumed to reflect the average market price.

29. Two different sets of estimates of the NPC appear in Table 2.9, one by Anderson-Hayami (1986) for the years up to and including 1982, and another one by the author for the period from 1980 on. As can be seen from the two overlapping years (1980 and 1982), the two sets of estimates differ somewhat, although moving in the same direction over time. The reason for these discrepancies appears to be related to the somewhat different procedures used to estimate producer prices including imputed government subsidies.

30. The EPC takes into consideration the protection of inputs as well. For a definition of the EPC see footnote 3 of Table 2.9.

31. This deceleration is even more pronounced if one looks at the total agricultural production index using quantities as weights (panel II of Table 2.2). In this case, the annual growth rate dropped from 2.76 percent in the preceding phase to 1.33 percent in the current phase.

32. Per capita annual rice consumption during this phase dropped from 105 kg to 74 kg, while meat and milk consumption rose, respectively, from 43 kg to 58 kg and from 25 kg to 41 kg.

33. In 1980, the export price received by Taiwan was US$230 per mt while the government purchase price was US$403 per mt, so that the government was losing US$87 million on this transaction (i.e., (403 − 230) × 505,000). The corresponding loss in 1983 amounted to US$190 million.

34. Table 2.8 (col. 6) reveals that around 300,000 metric tons of rice were disposed of as feed in 1985, 1986, and 1988. Again, as in the case of exports, the government lost a large amount on these transactions. Assuming that rice is a substitute for sorghum as a feedstuff, the import price of the latter was US$97 per metric ton in 1986 and the official purchase price of rice was US$495.

35. Using the same estimation procedure, the costs of supporting the prices of rice, corn, sorghum, and soybean amounted to US$507 million in 1988 and US$467 million in 1986.

36. Some fairly significant cuts in ad valorem tariffs occurred in 1986-1987. Thus, for example, the ad valorem tariff on chickens declined from 65 percent to 40 percent, that on meat (presumably pork) from 65 to 45 percent and presently 20 percent, that on fresh milk from 75 to 50 percent, and that on butter from 50 to 30 percent.

37. It was calculated that, on average, public investment in vitalizing the

small farm economy between 1972 and 1981 amounted to about NT$84,000 per hectare cultivated land and NT$94,000 per farm family.

38. The following sources provide descriptions of these programs: a) CAPD, PDAF, PFA (1983); b) Chang (1982a); c) Chang (1982b); and d) Ong (1984, p. 59) which gives a good summary of these programs.

39. This summary is based on Ong (1984, p. 59).

40. See PDAF (1983). Ong (1984, in Appendix 1 entitled "A Blueprint for the Outlook of New Rural Villages") includes a detailed description of this blueprint. The summary which follows is based on his description.

41. Other objectives spelled out in the blueprint are i) to expand the scale of hog farms significantly; ii) to transform the small scale of cattle raising on individual farms to large-scale group cattle raising; iii) to replace fish raising in the small ponds amidst the rice fields with the newly developed aquaculture areas, each area covering from several hundred to more than 1,000 ha. equipped with fresh or saline water supply and drainage facilities; and iv) improvement in marketing procedures, reforming the management of farmers' and fishermen's organizations, modernizing rural village buildings and infrastructure, improvement in rural health services, and building a sense of self-reliance and self-esteem among farmers.

42. See Homma and Hayami (1986).

43. Some of the components of the social cost of agricultural protection can be better estimated than others. Thus, I estimated the cost of 1) above at around NT$20 billion (for rice and other grains the excess producer prices over and above the border prices times the corresponding quantities domestically produced amounted to about NT$14.3 billion; the remainder, i.e., NT$5.7 billion, reflects the cost of protecting domestic beef and dairy production). Public capital investment in agriculture might run as high as NT$10 billion a year, while the costs related to enlarging the operational size of the farms and training nucleus farmers could run another NT$5 to 10 billion a year.

44. A typical characteristic of Taiwan -- as we have seen before -- is a pattern of intersectoral as opposed to geographical migration. Farm household members commute back and forth from their farm residences to their outside jobs essentially on a daily basis. This commuting pattern reduces substantially the need for additional urban housing and infrastructure, which would have been required had the migration been of the more usual rural to urban type.

45. See Table 2.12.

46. These studies were conducted by researchers at, respectively, National Taiwan University, National Chung Hsin University, National Cheng Chi University, and the China Research Institute of Land Economics. Ong (1984, pp. 36-37) provides a summary of the results of these studies.

47. As of the present time, about thirty-five million acres had been enrolled.
48. For a description of the CRP see U.S.D.A. (1990).
49. The above is based on *Economist*, December 13, 1986, p. 63; January 17, 1987, pp. 47-48; and March 28, 1987, pp. 61-62.

References

Anderson, K. 1983. "Growth of Agricultural Protection in East Asia." *Food Policy* 8: 327-336
Anderson, Kym, and Yujiro Hayami. 1986. *The Political Economy of Agricultural Protection: East Asia in International Perspective*. Sydney: Allen & Unwin.
Basic Agricultural Statistics Yearbook for 1989. Taipei: Statistics Office, Council of Agriculture, Executive Yuan.
Boyce, J. K., N. A. Judd, and R. E. Evenson. 1982. "Intercountry and Interregional Comparisons of the Allocation of Resources to Agricultural Research and Extension," mimeo, Yale University, New Haven.
CAPD, PDAF, PFA. 1983. *A Handbook on Assisting Nucleus Farms to Promote Work Plans on Joint Management and Contract Management*. January. Taipei: Council for Agricultural Planning and Development, Executive Yuan, Taiwan Provincial Department of Agriculture and Forestry and Taiwan Provincial Farmers' Association. (in Chinese)
Chang, H. T. 1982a. "A Brief Report on the Draft Program for the Second State of Agricultural Land Reform." May. Taipei: Council for Agricultural Planning and Development, Executive Yuan. (in Chinese)
Chang, H. T. 1982a. "Adjustments on the Direction of Agricultural Development for the 1980's." May. Taipei: Council for Agricultural Planning and Development, Executive Yuan. (in Chinese)
Chen, H.-Y., Wen-fu Hsu, and Yu-kang Mao. 1974. "Rice Policies of Taiwan." Paper presented at the Workshop on Political Economy of Rice, July 1974, sponsored by Food Research Institute, Stanford University, Los Banos, Philippines.
Cheng, S. W. 1989. "The Impact of Economic Liberalization on the Adjustment of Agricultural Policies," in Paper and Proceedings of Conference on "The Impact of Economic Liberalization on Taiwanese Agriculture," May 5-6, 1989, Taipei, Taiwan. (mimeo)
Economist. December 13, 1986; January 17, 1987; March 28, 1987. London.
Ho, Samuel P. S. 1978. *Economic Development of Taiwan, 1860-1970*. New Haven: Yale University Press.
———. 1968. "Agricultural Transformation Under Colonialism: the Case of Taiwan." *Journal of Economic History* 28(3): 313-334.

Homma, M., and Y. Hayami. 1986. "The Determinants of Agricultural Protection Levels: An Econometric Analysis," Chapter 4 in Kym Anderson and Yujiro Hayami, eds., *The Political Economy of Agricultural Protection: East Asia in International Perspective*. Sydney: Allen & Unwin.

Kuo, Shirley W. Y. 1975. "Effects of Land Reform, Agricultural Pricing Policy and Economic Growth on Multiple Crop Diversification in Taiwan." *Philippine Economic Journal* 14(1&2): 149-174.

Lee, T. H. 1971. "Strategies for Transferring Agricultural Surplus under Different Agricultural Situations in Taiwan." JCRR, mimeo, July.

Lee, T. H. and Y. E. Chen. 1975. *Growth Rates of Taiwan Agriculture, 1911-1972*. Economic Digest Series No. 21. Taipei: Sino-American Joint Commission on Rural Reconstruction.

Mao, Yu-kang. 1988. "Analysis of Changes in the Type of Farm Households Under Rapid Economic Growth in Taiwan, R.O.C." Reprinted from Conference on Directions and Strategies of Agricultural Development in the Asia-Pacific Region, January 5-7, 1988. Taipei: The Institute of Economics, Academia Sinica.

_____. 1987. "Role of Agriculture in the Economic Development of Taiwan, R.O.C." Conference on Economic Development in the Republic of China on Taiwan, July 22-27. Taipei: Chung-Hua Institution for Economic Research,

_____. 1990. "Statistical Tables on the Rice Economy," unpublished.

Ong, Shao-Er. 1984. *Development of the Small Farm Economy in Taiwan, A Program of World Significance*. Taipei: The Council of Agriculture, The Executive Yuan.

PDAF. 1983. *A Program to Implement the Training and Servicing Plan for the Rural Reconstruction Army of 80,000 Nucleus Farmers in Taiwan*. Taiwan Provincial Department of Agriculture and Forestry, Taichung, Taiwan, November. (in Chinese)

Thorbecke, Erik. 1979. "Agricultural Development," Chapter 2 in W. Galenson, ed., *Economic Growth and Structural Change in Taiwan*. Pp. 133-138. Ithaca: Cornell University Press.

U.S.D.A. 1990. "Natural Resources and Users Benefit for the Conservation Reserve Program." January. Washington, D.C.

Yu, T. Y. H. 1978. "The Accelerated Rural Development Program in Taiwan." October. Agricultural Economic Research Papers, Economic Digest Series, No. 23. Taipei: Sino-American Joint Commission on Rural Reconstruction.

3

New Perspectives on Industrial Growth in Taiwan

Howard Pack

1. Introduction

In the general euphoria that has accompanied the extraordinary growth of the four East Asian export oriented countries, there has been only limited exploration of the sources of the growth of supply. The sustained growth in aggregate demand at 10 percent per year is less difficult to comprehend insofar as even a small increase in the share of worldwide exports generates very large increases in demand relative to the small domestic economy of a country like Taiwan. The possibilities offered by rapid growth in exports reduce the policy skills and consensus that would otherwise be required to pursue a fiscal-monetary mix that aims for such high growth in demand based largely on domestic components. On the other hand, the protracted growth in supply over a quarter-century that allows a country to achieve near-developed-country status requires careful attention.

Given a rapid growth in supply and per capita income, many structural changes that accompany such a development are set into motion: income elasticities partly determine that households will demand a changing set of goods; factor prices will be altered as employment growth leads to tighter labor markets; perhaps the size distribution of firms and their location will change. In the case of an open economy such as Taiwan, some of these effects will be attenuated as export earnings permit a looser connection between the growing sectoral demands for consumer and producer goods and local production of them.

In a well known and provocative analysis, Alexander Gerschenkron argued that latecomers to the development process, including presumably Taiwan of the 1950s, would be able to achieve rapid growth as they could take advantage of the benefits of "relative backwardness." Changing terminology, this hypothesis could be rephrased as implying that best practice technology in the developed countries (DCs) exhibited very high total factor productivity (TFP) while the actual technology employed in the LDCs generated lower TFP. Hence, obtaining command of both the hardware and "software" of advanced technology would enable the LDCs to generate rapid growth in TFP as they eliminated the gap between actual and best practice technologies. In effect, their capital accumulation and additions to the labor force would have a magnified growth impact. One implication of this view, not spelled out by Gerschenkron, was that once the gap was closed, it would be increasingly difficult to maintain rapid growth, an issue that Taiwan is likely to confront in the coming decade.

For most LDCs the opportunities offered by the highly productive technologies of the DCs have not been a source of rapid growth. For the industrial sector, with which this chapter is concerned, most LDCs encouraged excessively capital-intensive technology adoption. Even where modern technologies were efficiently absorbed,[1] they benefitted a small group of workers and plant owners. In contrast, in Taiwan there were limited factor price distortions (Little 1979; Ranis 1979; Fields 1985) and both the industry mix and technologies chosen within an industry were consonant with the country's factor endowments. The gains from closing the best practice gap were widely diffused, with many sectors, firms, and their employees benefiting. This undoubtedly helped the *aggregate* productivity performance in Taiwan whereas in most LDCs a handful of firms have experienced higher productivity over time which did not have a significant quantitative overall impact. This difference may go some way towards explaining the fact that Taiwan has experienced positive total factor productivity growth in the industrial sector whereas most LDCs have not (Pack 1988). Moreover, the diffusion of better practice partly explains the failure of significant income inequality to emerge during three decades of rapid growth (Fei, Ranis and Kuo 1979).

Kuznets (1979), using the Gerschenkronian framework in an analysis of Taiwan, noted that "the useful knowledge must be accessible -- through trade, capital flows, direct investment, and the like . . ." (p. 129). He then pointed out that such accessibility is far from sufficient -- both the institutional and policy framework conducive to fruitful deployment of these technologies must be set into place. Moreover, there will inevitably be severe costs imposed on some groups as a result of the rapid transformation of the economy implied by widespread adoption of newer technologies. Without considerable political skills being exercised by the government, the possible "losers" may oppose many of the potentially beneficial changes (p. 130). Analysis of the political and social requirements of successful development have now become the staple of the (non-Marxist) political economy approach to development (Deyo 1988).

In analyzing Taiwan's industrial development, I pursue several themes. First, what were the sources of the growth of supply? Can one identify the economic role of exports themselves as a contributor to the growth of total factor productivity; more broadly, did they somehow help strengthen the institutional and political framework that were conducive to growth? Within this framework more traditional concerns about the industrial sector will appear, such as the changing sectoral structure of production, the role of small scale enterprises, and so on. As will be clear, I do not think that exports were the sole source of the spectacular performance of Taiwan. Nevertheless, one is ignoring the obvious if no attempt is made to speculate on the impact of exports on the ability of Taiwan to close the best practice-actual practice gap and to facilitate the transformation of the economy. More precisely, one difference between Taiwan and some other countries that have saved almost as much and have had rapid labor force growth is that Taiwan has experienced a fairly high rate of growth of TFP, and part of this long-term TFP growth may be attributable to its export orientation.[2]

For expository purposes, much of the following assumes that the growth phenomena to be explained are those of the manufacturing sector. Insofar as manufacturing and its export growth were the primary determinants of Taiwan's aggregate growth, the exposition does not distinguish between the two. At points where this convenient didactic framework misses key phenomena, they will be explicitly discussed. The role of the service sector is considered separately. To understand past Taiwanese experience and the probable evolution of its growth in the future, a better understanding of the determinants of productivity growth is critical. In recent years the OECD countries have all undergone a considerable slowing in their overall growth rates. Much of this reflects lower rates of growth of total factor productivity since 1973 (Baily and Blair 1988). While the source of this slowdown has not been determined, and there is no inevitable contagion that will spread to Taiwan, setting out the issues in the context of TFP growth may allow policy-makers to consider the future in a broader context.

Under this wide umbrella that focuses on productivity growth, other aspects of Taiwanese growth that have been cited as critical can be placed within a more rigorous and comprehensive framework. For example, a few scholars, most notably Robert Wade (1990), have recently argued that Taiwan, far from being a *laissez-faire* economy, has seen considerable government intervention ranging from ownership of public enterprises to an extraordinarily sophisticated use of import-limiting measures, special credit facilities, and so on. It is maintained by these analysts, who have provided careful documentation supporting their views, that Taiwan, like Japan and Korea, followed a wide-ranging industrial policy that was an important component of its considerable success. These views contrast strongly with those scholars (Little 1979) who aver that the major sources of Taiwan's achievement were: (a) allowing exporting firms to obtain inputs at world prices; (b) low-cost labor, at least during the initial phases of industrialization; (c) high real rates of interest; and (d) a roughly balanced government budget. Interestingly, a re-examination of evidence presented by analysts who helped establish the conventional explanation partly supports the revisionist view. For example, Scott (1979), who largely agrees with Little, presents a number of tables showing the quite high nominal tariff rates and the importance of quantitative restrictions well into the 1970s, more than ten years after the initiation of the rapid growth rate of Taiwanese exports. While exporters may have faced international prices for both inputs and outputs, many producers were nevertheless protected and initiated production on the basis of protection in the domestic market, a phenomenon well documented by Wade.

The canonical analysis of development economists that Taiwan, like Korea, simply got the prices right may need some subtle modification. Nevertheless, the case that *selective* intervention was a critical component of the Taiwanese policy mix must demonstrate that intervention increased productivity growth rates.[3] Simply altering the sectoral structure will not confer beneficial effects unless productivity growth is increased. Industrial policy as used by Wade and others is a term employed to describe attempts to influence the structure of production through interventions that are not neutral across sectors: selective (among industries) credit policy, non-uniform protection whether in the form of tariffs or quantitative restrictions, research subsidies for specific products, and so on. Most analyses of efforts at industrialization of the LDCs during the last quarter-century have, of course, described industrial policy, though the term has emerged largely in recent discussion of manufacturing competitiveness among OECD countries.

One characteristic of Taiwan often noted is the greater importance of small-scale enterprises (SSEs) in manufacturing than in other developing countries. Static advantages may accrue in terms of employment generation if such firms choose socially appropriate lower capital-labor ratios in producing a given product than do larger firms (Ho 1980; Ranis 1979).[4] While correct factor choices may generate a greater output for a given commitment of capital and labor,[5] it is not easy to establish a link between the size distribution of firms and productivity growth rates. One possibility is that the greater flexibility of such enterprises allows them to adjust to changing markets more quickly than do their larger compatriots. The relation between total factor productivity growth and firm size will thus be considered.

The plan of this paper is as follows. Section 2 considers the determinants of intermediate-term growth in output. Section 3 briefly reviews Taiwan's export experience and suggests a new view of the overall strategy informing its policy. Section 4 considers the potential sources of technological change associated with exports. Section 5 investigates the probable impact of industrial policy on Taiwan's growth rate. Section 6 considers the evolving industrial structure and the size distribution of firms. Section 7 analyzes the evolution of the service sectors. Views about the future of Taiwanese growth are contained in Section 8.

2. Intermediate Term Growth Accounting

The Sources of Growth

A surprising omission in the literature analyzing development in outward oriented economies has been the failure to explain why export orientation will allow sustained growth in supply over a period as long as twenty to thirty years. Although the literature commending export orientation is quite good at delineating the short- and medium-term *level* effects to be derived from a switch to export promotion, it fails to set out the longer term growth *rate* augmenting effects. While a move from inefficient import substitution to neutrality in profitability between import substitutes and exports can generate once-and-for-all gains in allocative efficiency, perhaps spread over a number of years, such gains were presumably exhausted in Taiwan by 1970 or 1975, depending on one's preferred dating schema.[6] Not only were there intersectoral allocative benefits as the economy exploited its comparative advantage in particular sectors during the first decades of rapid export growth, but some gains in technical efficiency were obtained from greater capacity utilization and more product specialization. Moreover, new plants could be built on a large scale. But most of these benefits would presumably have been reaped by the early 1970s.[7] Yet Taiwan's TFP continued to grow with great rapidity after 1976.

The sources of growth equation for Taiwan has been calculated for several subperiods for 1951-1987 (Table 3.1). This equation is

$$Q^* = A^* + bK^* + (1-b)L^* \qquad (1)$$

where asterisks denote rates of growth, Q is constant price value added in manufacturing, K is the constant price fixed stock of capital, L is the number of workers in the manufacturing sector, and A is the unexplained growth of output. A^* is 5.3 percent per annum for 1961-1987 or about 40 percent of total growth (Table 3.1).[8] The figures for such a long period are unlikely to be affected by transitory phenomena such as changing rates of capacity utilization. The explanation of A^* implied by the trade and development literature suggests that it is due to learning effects and scale effects, greater utilization of capacity, growing education, and so on. But these lump together mechanisms that can work only in the long run (educa-

TABLE 3.1 Growth Rates of Input, Output and Total Factor Productivity in Manufacturing

Years	Value added	Labor	Capital	A	A/VA
1952-1961	12.1	2.7	8.7	6.8	.56
1961-1976	14.9	7.8	11.7	5.4	.36
1976-1987	10.7	5.1	6.6	5.0	.47
1961-1987	13.1	6.7	9.5	5.3	.40

Note: TFP is calculated using actual factor shares from national accounts for the subperiod.

Source: 1952-1961, Columns 1-3, Kuo (1983); columns 4 and 5 calculated by author using factor shares from *Statistical Yearbook of the Republic of China*, 1989, Table 45. 1961-1987, value added and capital stock from *Yearbook of Earnings and Productivity Statistics, Taiwan Area, Republic of China, 1988*, Table 92; labor from *Taiwan Statistical Yearbook, 1989*, Table 2-9a; factor shares from *Statistical Yearbook of the Republic of China*, 1989, Table 45.

tion) with those that exert a short- and medium-term effect (greater capacity utilization).

For the developed countries, a ratio of A^*/Q^* of .40 or .50 has been calculated for both the total economy and manufacturing. For most LDCs, this ratio has been zero or negative (Pack 1988). The latter has been attributed to import substitution policies though the usual calculation of the impact of ISI is one of static income loss rather than reduced A^*. Nevertheless, the standard for a successfully functioning economy has typically been the performance of the OECD countries over varying periods until 1973 in which TFP growth has been a major source of output growth. Normatively, output growth that is not attributable to that of primary inputs is critical insofar as growing labor and capital inputs have a welfare cost in terms of foregone leisure and current consumption. Taiwan has certainly done much better than other LDCs, roughly as well as the OECD norm (Baily and Blair 1988).

Table 3.1 also presents the growth rates for each of the variables contained in Equation 1. Growth in value added has been very high in the three periods shown, 1952-1961, 1961-1976 and 1976-1987. Between the first and second periods, the rate of absorption of factors into the manufacturing sector increased enormously yet TFP growth declined only slightly, an extremely impressive performance. The contribution of the residual to output growth declined from 56 percent of output growth in the 1952-1961 period, to 36 percent in 1961-1976. Nevertheless, it was the latter period that saw the transformation of Taiwan into a major exporter, a process begun roughly in the middle of the first period. This surprising result implies that even during its intensive import substitution phase the allocative inefficiency of ISI may have been offset by rapidly growing technical efficiency. If this tentative finding is correct, the factors that allowed the sector to perform well in contrast to other ISI regimes constitutes a fascinating area for additional research.

Taiwan's achievement in productivity is particularly impressive insofar as the A^*/Q^* figure in the OECD countries has been achieved with considerably lower growth rates of the primary inputs, typically capital growth rates of less than 4 percent and labor growth rates less than 2 percent. To me it appears that a signal achievement of the Taiwanese manufacturing sector has been to maintain positive TFP growth while absorbing enormous increases to its initial factor endowments. At the growth rates shown in Table 3.1, the capital stock doubles roughly every five years, the labor force every fourteen years. To deploy productively this many additional resources in so short a period is quite remarkable and a major characteristic of the economy to be explained. Thus, the productivity raising mechanisms to be discussed have to be viewed in a context of their ability to avoid diminishing returns to the rapid addition of factors to small existing stocks. An important question then is whether exports themselves helped to forestall the likely onset of diminishing returns. It will also be argued in Section 7 that the size structure of manufacturing may have been an important contributor to this performance.

The Import of New Technology

After 1965, it seems likely that some part of productivity growth was accounted for by the importation of new equipment which embodied productivity-increasing characteristics, the effect both Gerschenkron and Kuznets thought would be decisive.[9] One path of escape from relative backwardness is to be achieved by importing newer technology though, as I have shown elsewhere, realization of the promised productivity benefits is not automatic (Pack 1987).[10] Knowledge, particularly of production engineering, must also be obtained, a question to which I return below. To attach some magnitudes to the role of imported technical change, it is useful to expand upon the simple growth accounting formula contained in (1).

Nelson (1964) derived the following expression for the rate of growth of output in the presence of embodiment:

$$Q^* = A^* + (1-b)\lambda_k - (1-b)\lambda_k \Delta \bar{a} + (1-b)K^* + (1-b)L^* \qquad (2)$$

where $\Delta \bar{a} = 1 - (K^* + \delta)a_{t-1}$ is the rate of change of the average age of equipment, λ_k is the rate at which the productivity of equipment of new vintages increases, $\bar{a}$ is the average age of equipment, δ is the rate of depreciation, and b is the elasticity of output with respect to capital.

During most of the period under consideration Taiwan has imported a major fraction of its new machinery, though to be sure some was produced domestically. Moreover, a considerable percentage of investment in manufacturing has consisted of factory buildings for which it seems unlikely that embodied productivity growth is an important characteristic.[11] Assume that construction and locally produced equipment account for one half of total manufacturing investment. Then, λ_k should equal half of the rate of embodiment calculated for imported equipment. Recent estimates of Hulten (1989) suggest that the rate of improvement of equipment in the U.S. is about 5 percent per annum. Using one half of this figure plus the other appropriate numbers for equations (1) and (2), I calculate that of the TFP growth rate of 5.3 percent for 1961-1987, about 1.5 percentage points, or 29 percent, could plausibly be attributed to embodiment of more productive technologies in new equipment, leaving 3.8 points to be accounted for by other sources of productivity growth. This calculation suggests that the benefit from importing equipment containing new technology was a very important source of industrial growth in Taiwan, but it was only part of the story. Other sources of productivity growth must be analyzed.

It would be particularly useful to calculate the share of output growth accounted for by the changing quality of the labor force. As discussed below in Section 5, it is likely, given the aggregate changes in education levels, that it has had a major impact on the growth process. Unfortunately, as of now it is impossible to obtain employment in manufacturing by education and wages, thus precluding the standard calculation.

Clearly, all growth accounting should be taken as providing rough orders of magnitude and indications of where to search for explanations of growth rather than as precise measures (Nelson 1973, 1981). Nevertheless, several observations follow for the calculations for 1961-1987. First, the share of output growth accounted for by the residual was larger than in other LDCs, comparable to the now advanced countries at similar stages of development. The growth of total factor productivity was an important driving force behind Taiwanese industrial success. Second, the performance was in an important sense even better than a simple calculation of TFP growth rates suggests. In particular, the DCs in which TFP growth has accounted for a similar percentage of total output growth, had much slower growth rates for primary factors and much slower changes in industrial structure (examined below).[12] The ability to even maintain initial levels of TFP, let alone increase them in the face of the absorption of such massive amounts of factors, was an extremely impressive achievement implying considerable organizational ability at both the micro and national levels.

The continued rapid growth in TFP is intriguing, and absent any detailed microeconomic studies of the sources of this growth, several strands are worth pursuing. I consider in turn the possible role of exports in stimulating productivity growth, then, more conventionally, scale economies and learning by doing.

The Impact of Productivity on Export Growth Productivity

If exports are to explain long term *growth* rather than *level* effects, a link must exist between exports and productivity growth. Section 4 explores this question and attempts to set out the probable channels through which exports may affect productivity growth quite apart from those short- and intermediate-term benefits most often cited. Recent advances in the understanding of technological development are incorporated within the framework of growth accounting to explain the maintenance of output growth rates which are extraordinarily high by international standards. It is obviously a possibility that the causality works in another direction, namely, that productivity growth, originating in the local economy, reduces costs and generates exports if profitability of sales to the domestic and foreign markets are roughly kept at parity. However, as is often noted by analysts of the super-exporters, the sequence in which industries became exporters roughly conforms to their labor intensity, exports being based initially on low real wages rather than productivity growth.[13] Although it is possible that the initial export boom began as a result of initial productivity growth in the labor-intensive sectors based on accumulating production experience, this hypothesis is not testable with the data that are available. It is also not evident that the sectors which succeeded in increasing exports would have benefitted more from productivity growth than other sectors. For Taiwan, the Heckscher-Ohlin model works well in the early stages of development.[14]

3. The Export Experience of Taiwan

The Acquisition of Technology

The standard and probably most important explanation of Taiwan's spectacular growth in exports is that the foreign trade regime made exporting profitable (Lee and Liang 1982; Little 1979; Ranis 1979; Scott 1979). Early exports consisted mainly of labor intensive products (Ranis 1979; Scott 1979) such as clothing, textiles, athletic equipment, canned pineapple, and so on.

The technology underlying these products was mastered by three mechanisms: (a) experience during the Japanese colonial period; (b) knowledge brought to Taiwan from the mainland by industrialists fleeing the revolution; and (c) knowledge initially obtained from non-proprietary and inexpensively available sources on the world market, more recently from direct foreign investors, joint ventures, and licensing agreements. Ho (1978, Chapter 5) describes the growth of manufacturing, primarily food processing, until 1930 and then in a broader spectrum of industries during the 1930s. Although he does not discuss the extent of transfer of technical knowledge such as production engineering to the Taiwanese during this period, it is plausible to assume that many important production skills were learned by the indigenous residents. It seems unlikely that the rapid and broad growth of the 1930s could have been achieved simply by Japanese managers without some knowledge being appropriated by local employees. The fact that by 1951, despite the withdrawal of the Japanese and the devastation of World War II, industrial output had reached 1937 levels (Ranis 1979, p. 209) implies that considerable managerial and technological knowledge must have been absorbed during the colonial period, undoubtedly supplemented by the industrialists leaving the Mainland in the late 1940s.[15]

It seems probable that the huge number of small-scale enterprises (SSEs) characteristic of the 1950s and 1960s was made possible partly by skills acquired before 1949 both on the Mainland and under the Japanese. Unfortunately, the evidence collected on the small-scale sector (summarized by Ho 1980) does not report the background of small entrepreneurs. Although it may be conjectured that the initial conditions for industrial development were probably more favorable, just as they were in agriculture (Thorbecke 1979), than in many other LDCs, initial conditions are not automatically transmuted into good performance. Policy is important.

With respect to obtaining knowledge from external sources, as late as 1978, Taiwanese royalty payments were only US$52 million per year and remained below US$100 million through 1983 (Liang and Liang 1988). However, such formal methods of knowledge acquisition were undoubtedly dwarfed by the ability to absorb non-proprietary knowledge in the relatively uncomplicated sectors that formed the basis of the early industrialization drive. One benefit, often overlooked, of sectoral growth and technology choice that is consistent with relative factor prices is the greater availability of non-proprietary knowledge in simpler sectors and technology. It is not an accident that the most vocal criticism of the high cost of technology transfer (royalties or licensing fees) emanates from those countries following import substitution policies that lead to an early emphasis on capital- and technology-intensive production in which much of the knowledge is proprietary. As will be noted below, as Taiwan enters new technology-intensive areas, access to technology may become a major issue.

Given the relative ease of acquiring and mastering the relevant technology, the combination of low wages and a foreign exchange regime neutral between production for the domestic and foreign markets is probably a sufficient explanation of the early rapid growth in labor-intensive exports.[16]

In new products, the explanation for success is that substantial investment, made possible by the growing domestic saving rate and to a much lesser extent by foreign investment (Ranis and Schive 1985), was allocated according to comparative advantage. New investments were directed to sectors along the ladder of comparative advantage as measured by the domestic resource cost.[17] Additions to the labor force were similarly allocated as were those workers reallocated from agriculture and the informal urban sector to the industrial sector. An alternate interpretation is put forth by those who argue that some industries were established earlier than would have been "natural" according to the DRC ladder (Wade 1990).

The Structure of Incentives

I will return to an evaluation of these conflicting views in Section 5. The important issue here is that, whatever the investment allocation mechanism, much of the investment in new sectors resulted in exports, leading to a rapid change in the commodity composition of exports. Such exports may have been encouraged by a variety of government promotional measures, but the new sectors were not allowed simply to produce for the protected domestic market as in the import-substituting countries. Thus, old and new sectors grew because of relatively neutral incentive policies, new ones also benefiting from some promotional measures.

The growth in exports in turn was the primary source of growth in aggregate demand between 1956 and 1971 and was decisive in altering the structure of production as shown by the decomposition of deMelo (1985) presented in Table 3.2. This decomposition, following a method developed by Chenery and a variety of collaborators, divides the deviation of manufac-

TABLE 3.2 Decomposition of Sources of Growth of Taiwan's Gross Output

Deviation of manufacturing output from proportional growth	28.2
Percentage source of output deviation	
Domestic demand	2.5
Exports	71.3
Import substitution	10.6
Changes in input-output coefficients	15.6

Source: Calculated from deMelo (1985), Table 9.2.

turing's growth of gross output from that of the economy-wide average into four components, namely, the expansion of domestic demand, export expansion, import substitution, and a category attributable to changes in the input-output coefficients. Table 3.2 shows that roughly 71 percent of the disproportionate expansion in manufacturing gross output was attributable to the non-proportional growth of exports, the only remaining large source being the deepening of the input-output structure. While this calculation has not been updated, it is clear from successive input-output tables that exports have played a very large role as a source of demand for manufacturing in the ensuing period.[18]

Two aspects of the trade regime have been cited in Taiwan and other countries as important in generating allocative efficiency, namely, the low dispersion of rates of effective protection across production sectors and the neutrality of incentives as between exports and domestic sales. However, in the case of Taiwan these studies have largely been carried out for the early years of the industrialization process. For example, the analysis of Lee and Liang (1982) stops with 1970. Anecdotal evidence collected by Wade (1990) and often cited in journalistic accounts suggest that in some selected sectors effective rates of protection have continued to be very high up to the present time. The absence of systematic evidence precludes analyzing the possible anomaly of rapid and efficient growth in sectors that have continued to be protected,[19] though as noted in Section 2, the value of A^*/Q^* during the import-substituting 1950s was quite high.

Perhaps more important than the intersectoral variation in protection across manufacturing sectors is the fact that, with the exception of the post-oil-price-increase years of 1974 and 1975, Taiwan has exported more goods and services than it has imported in every year since 1971 (Table 3.3). The

TABLE 3.3 Export Surplus as a Percentage of Gross Domestic Product (current prices)

Year	Average of yearly figures
1952-1956	−6.2
1957-1961	−6.9
1962-1966	−1.7
1967-1971	0.6
1972-1976	0.5
1977-1981	2.7
1982-1986	12.1
1987-1988	14.4

Source: *Taiwan Statistical Data Book 1989*, Table 3.8b.

implied undervaluation of the currency must have contributed significantly to the continuing export surge across a broad spectrum of sectors.

The Role of Undervaluation

Undervaluation and the continuing surplus on goods and services account is often viewed as simply a misguided mercantilist policy. There is much merit to this view, known since Adam Smith. But it is possible to view it in a different light if exports are viewed as providing benefits, both economic and political. The economic externalities are discussed in detail in Section 5 and may provide some (limited) economic justification for the policy that was pursued. Politically, the accumulation of large foreign currency reserves and their potential use as a source of foreign aid and as an easy-to-assess measure of the government's intention of maintaining an environment conducive to business that would attract direct foreign investment would surely not go unnoticed in the world.

The increasing number of countries opening formal and informal relations with Taiwan is surely related to its economic strength, partly perceived as its GNP per capita, but partly reflecting its accumulated hard currency reserves and the potential for either Taiwan-based DFI or aid. As a means of preventing increasing political isolation given the sheer numbers and international strength of Mainland China, it would be difficult to design a better instrument of policy.

Exports and Aggregate Demand

Finally, the role of export growth in the maintenance of rapid growth in demand is often overlooked. Sustaining rapid growth in demand and incomes would have been extremely difficult without the contribution of exports. While it is theoretically possible to employ a monetary-fiscal policy that would sustain 10 percent per annum growth in GNP, it is likely that such a program, if dependent on domestic sales, would have been more susceptible to cycles that would have led investors to be more cautious and undermined the ability to maintain the requisite growth in domestic investment. I have argued elsewhere (Pack 1988) that the export orientation of the super-exporters allowed them to avoid the declining internal terms of trade that would have ensued had they accumulated factors as rapidly as they did but had to sell them to the more slowly growing domestic non-manufacturing sector. This would have led to declining profitability of investment and a slowing in its rate of growth. It is for this reason that the early closed economy, two-sector models of development such as Lewis and Fei-Ranis pay attention to the conditions for balanced growth, particularly the maintenance of a constant terms of trade between sectors. For the large, much less open economies which these models envisioned, internal balanced growth remains an important issue. For smaller, more open economies like Taiwan, exports reduce, to some extent, the overlapping issues of macroeconomic balance and micro-sectoral adjustment. As shown in Table 3.2, domestic demand was not an important source of non-proportional growth in manufacturing. However, the emphasis on non-proportional growth should not obscure the fact that as of 1986 the share of domestic absorption of manufactured gross output was 70 percent, exports being 30. The absolute size of domestic demand matters as well.[20]

4. Exports and Productivity Growth

Exports contribute to growing demand and to the reaping of the once-and-for-all gains from reallocation of resources from inefficient to efficient sectors. The major gains from greater utilization of capacity and scale economies are realized early in the process. Why then does the supply in Taiwan continue to grow at such rapid rates -- is there some characteristic of exports themselves that helps to increase TFP growth? It will be seen in Section 6 that I attribute part of the success of Taiwan's industrial growth to the structure of industry and other characteristics of the economy that are conducive to development. Nevertheless, consistency requires an attempt to answer the question of whether exports have a supply augmenting effect that contributes more to growth than would a comparable increase in domestic sales.

Reduction in Opposition to Structural Change

The changing structure of production resulting from the growth of manufactured exports, along with fast aggregate overall growth, was the source of an important benefit which might be described as an externality, namely, the reduction in opposition to a range of policies that were critical for Taiwan's continuing development. Mancur Olson (1982) has argued that a distinctive difference between high-growth countries (The Gang of Four, Japan and Germany) and other more slowly expanding countries is the absence of growth-obstructing interest groups. For Taiwan, this view would assert that land reform and the great upheavals accompanying the relocation of the Kuomintang government from the mainland in 1949 permitted the implementation of growth fostering policies without the need to overcome domestic resistance from groups that lost either relative income or power.[21]

As is usual in broad-brush views, there is some truth, but it is easy to neglect the possibility that, once growth begins, sectoral interests begin to emerge and may oppose growth-enhancing policies. In recent years the

Japanese government has had to design "exit" policies for no longer profitable industries, presumably because of the potential of these "sunset" sectors for disrupting the policies necessary to a continuing shift to more competitive sectors. The alleged "consensual" nature of Japan may be an endogenous outcome of specific policies rather than the result of socialization from the cradle.

In Taiwan, relatively low protection levels limited the rents accruing to factors employed in industrial sectors, hence limited their losses from policies that reduced rents (Lee and Liang 1982). Given the lower rewards from rent seeking, the resources devoted to such activities were presumably smaller. Equally important, the continuing extraordinary expansion of exports undoubtedly lessened the opposition to growth enhancing policies, as those engaged in relatively declining sectors such as food, beverages, and tobacco, non-metallic minerals, and chemical products (Table 3.4) under-

TABLE 3.4 Sectoral Structure of Employment and Value Added (percentage shares)

Sector	Share of value added current prices 1966	1986	Share of employment 1966	1986
Food, beverage, tobacco	.29	.11	.23	.06
Textiles	.12	.08	.17	.11
Cloth, leather, fur	.03	.08	.03	.08
Wood products	.04	.03	.06	.05
Paper, printing, publishing	.05	.04	.05	.04
Chemical, petroleum	.20	.15	.12	.05
Plastics	.00	.07	.00	.11
Rubber	.01	.01	.02	.02
Non-metallic minerals	.07	.03	.08	.04
Basic metals	.03	.06	.03	.03
Fabricated metals	.02	.05	.04	.08
Machinery	.03	.03	.05	.04
Electrical equipment & machinery	.05	.13	.06	.10
Transportation equipment	.04	.06	.04	.05
Precision instruments	{.02	.01	{.04	.01
Miscellaneous		.06		.06

Source: Value added, *National Income in Taiwan Area, the Republic of China*, 1989, Table 1. Employment, 1986, *The Report on 1986 Industrial and Commercial Census*, Table 3.8; 1966, Ho (1978, Table 10.9), based upon the 1966 industrial and commercial census.

stood that the rapid expansion in others would allow their absorption in newly profitable sectors. Not only does fast growth allow the sleeping dogs of class warfare to lie dormant, but it also reduces the anticipation of danger from the inevitable changes accompanying growing urbanization and industrialization.[22] This virtuous circle of growth-adjustment-growth may shed light on the inability of inward oriented countries to engage in the reforms necessary for more rapid growth. Fear of prolonged structural unemployment in these nations is not mitigated by the rapid growth in exporting sectors.

The shifting structure of production (Table 3.4), made possible by export growth, permitted a movement by factors from industrial sectors with low or declining marginal value productivity to those with higher or growing marginal value products. This was especially important in the early stages of growth, until the disguised and overt unemployment were eliminated. Although such a transformation would have occurred in any event, the time taken for it was probably compressed as the result of the large impact of exports on the production structure as shown in Table 3.2.[23] This change in structure must also have improved productivity growth in the intermediate term after 1975 given the continuing rapid change in the sectoral structure of employment and output, now in response to evolving profitability of various sectors and a rapidly changing constellation of products.

Knowledge Transfers from Foreign Purchasers

Research in Korea, as far as I know not replicated in Taiwan, suggests one mechanism through which productivity growth was probably enhanced in Taiwan as well. A study by Westphal, Rhee, and Pursell (1981) found that a considerable amount of the knowledge of production engineering possessed by Korean firms came from purchasers of Korean exports. Scott (1979, p. 367) reports some evidence of similar mechanisms in Taiwan. The continuing transfer of manufacturing "know-how," particularly in production engineering, to Taiwanese firms by importers desiring still lower cost, higher quality products must also have been an important feature of Taiwanese experience. A continuing flow of technical knowledge improves firms' total factor productivity and will have a larger impact insofar as firms are under competitive pressure to reduce costs and possess sufficient technical ability to effectively absorb this knowledge. Recent work by Lall (1987) demonstrates that Indian firms that were technically competent often did not translate new knowledge into cost reductions because of the absence of a competitive atmosphere.

Still another probable source of growth in TFP made possible by exports was knowledge obtained from purchasers of exports about both process and product *innovations* as opposed to better command of *existing* production engineering. The literature on diffusion of innovation suggests that process innovations are more appropriable and less easy to learn from the general knowledge pool. Nevertheless, it is likely that major importers of Taiwanese products were, in their own interest, quite willing to provide proprietary knowledge of processing improvements in order to obtain either lower prices or better quality from Taiwanese manufacturers, and hence increase their own competitiveness.

Product-specific knowledge conveyed by importers presumably allowed greater value added per unit of primary inputs as the price for final products would, on the average, be greater as Taiwan was enabled to shift among products, away from those whose price was declining (relatively) towards new products still in the early part of the product cycle.[24] A growth impact may also have been obtained insofar as advice about quality control increased value added per unit of combined inputs each year.

In all of these knowledge-transferring activities, growth rate-augmenting effects as compared to a once-and-for-all increase would have required continuing transfers. If, for example, the impact of advice from importers was merely to indicate quality requirements and to show how these could be met on a one-shot basis, there would have been a level effect but no growth rate impact from export orientation. In the context of a major exporter whose products were an important component of the ability of many importers to maintain profit margins, an ongoing transfer seems a more plausible specification, and the same would be true for other modes of knowledge transfer. There is no Taiwan-specific evidence on these issues and they constitute a fruitful area for further research.

Knowledge Transfers from Returning Nationals

In Korea, it has been documented that a large part of growing technical competence was obtained from returning nationals who had received American education and remained to work in the U.S. only temporarily (Westphal, Rhee, Pursell 1981). Korea, and presumably Taiwan, have experienced a much smaller brain drain than other developing countries as a result of rapidly rising income levels which enabled employers to offer salaries which, if not equal to those in the U.S., were close enough to induce a return home. Anecdotal journalistic evidence depicting this phenomenon is accumulating, many returning nationals having received education in the U.S. and then worked for an American firm.[25] Liu (1987, Tables 24 and 25) shows that more than 20 percent of executives in large Taiwanese firms had studied abroad, largely in Japan and the United States. One can speculate that the return of foreign-trained Taiwanese nationals helped provide part of the technical change that improved productivity and helped to avoid the slowdown inherent in an economy as diminishing returns set in to capital accumulation.

In contrast to Taiwan, nationals may fail to return to import-substituting countries insofar as the skills they have lead to employment in sectors in which exports rather than domestic sales are the natural outlet, yet these exports are discouraged by the international trade regime. Thus, the environment that is conducive to exports, if not the latter themselves, may induce the inflow of technology embodied in individuals; while not an externality, such an inflow may prove as important as more formally acquired technological knowledge.

The Purchase of Knowledge and the Location of MNCs

The hard currency earnings permitted by exports also enabled firms to purchase consulting services and engage in licensing agreements which required payment of royalties in hard currencies. This type of knowledge transfer must have been an important component in allowing some firms, particularly in newer sectors in which knowledge acquired under the Japanese or from mainland businesses did not suffice, to establish themselves and move towards world best practice. Although as noted earlier, royalty payments were relatively small until the late 1970s, even inexpensive technology licensing agreements can provide critically important knowledge for improving productivity and quality.

Unlike Japan and Korea, Taiwan's industrial development was characterized by a more substantial presence of MNCs whose willingness to locate was at least partly dependent on the stability implied by a growth commitment[26] which may also have been signaled by a growing level of exports. Insofar as the presence of MNCs enabled local firms to obtain knowledge, from emulation, from the movement of workers, and from the general atmosphere effects, they must have contributed to a continuing learning process.[27] Moreover, the small size of manufacturing firms in Taiwan probably enabled local employees of MNCs to leave and begin their own firms fairly easily.[28]

Ranis and Schive (1985) have shown that MNC activities accounted for less than 10 percent of manufacturing value added and employment through the late-70s. Nevertheless, the cumulative spillover effects can be quite substantial if even a small percentage of employees each year leave the firms and either go to existing locally owned ones or begin their own. Scott (1979, p. 339) cites anecdotal evidence that this occurred. Evidence from labor force surveys indicates quite substantial labor market turnover though separate data on MNCs, joint ventures, and local firms are not available. As can be seen in Table 3.5, the separation rates in manufacturing exceed 3 percent per year, few of these reflecting retirement or a move

TABLE 3.5 Separation Rates per 100 Employees

Industry	1978	1982	1986	1988
All manufacturing	3.43	3.77	3.55	3.69
Electric and electronic equipment	3.09	4.75	4.72	5.07

Source: *Yearbook of Earnings and Productivity Statistics, Taiwan Area, Republic of China, 1988*, Directorate-General of Budget, Accounting and Statistics, Executive Yuan, Republic of China, Tables 102, 103.

to unemployed status. While some of the same workers leave firms each year, the aggregate rates suggest that substantial knowledge must be transmitted from firm to firm as workers move. To the extent that MNCs bring in knowledge that is closer to the best practice frontier, some fraction must be diffused by employee mobility. Moreover, the separation rates are greater in newer higher technology sectors which Ranis and Schive find are often entered by non-Chinese owned MNCs.

Ranis and Schive (1985) provide a detailed account of the benefits conferred upon other firms of the interaction with the Singer Sewing Machine Company. The linkages described and the productivity gains obtained by other firms as a result constitute a good example of rarely documented real external economies. In the case of Singer, the external benefits arose at least partly as the firm attempted to satisfy local content requirements imposed by the government.[29]

In summary, the undervaluation that encourages exports confers an externality as the expansion of exports reduces the political opposition to rapid structural change and allows a more rapid transfer of resources, especially labor, to more (socially) profitable industries. More generally, exports generate knowledge transfers from potential purchasers, indirectly encourage the return of nationals residing abroad and their knowledge, provide the means to purchase knowledge that expands productivity still more, and may encourage the location of MNCs, the latter generating knowledge spillovers.

The above (non-exhaustive) list of the possible growth *rate* augmenting effects of exports runs the risk of attributing many features of a successful economy to exports excluding the purely domestic activities that contribute to a higher growth rate of TFP. Thus, the location of MNCs and the contribution at the margin of knowledge obtained from returning expatriates and consultants, would surely have been lower had there not been a high and growing level of education.[30] Similarly, fewer MNCs and Taiwanese trained abroad would have located there had there not been a reasonable level of social overhead ranging from communication to transportation services. Contrary to the provocative hypothesis of Hirschman that the absence of social overhead capital may serve as a catalyst to the breaking of bottlenecks, it seems more likely that the provision of communications, transport, and power ahead of demand was, as Ranis (1979) maintains, an important contributor to the successful initial industrialization effort.

In this sense, export growth may have been an important contributor, given the existence of a range of other conditions: it was, as Kravis would put it, a handmaiden to growth rather than the sole locomotive. Countries trying to emulate Taiwan by duplicating the trade regime but ignoring the many other policies, from education to the provision of social overhead capital, are likely to be disappointed. On the other hand, those providing critical nontradeable services but ignoring the benefits conferred by exports are unlikely to succeed in the same dramatic way. While the past quarter-century of export-propelled growth and its analysis have yielded many important lessons about the importance of trade regime, success in Taiwan was built on two foundations, the non-traded one having been subordinated in most analytic efforts to derive growth prescriptions from the East Asian experience.

5. The Role of Industrial Policy

As noted earlier, a number of scholars contend that Taiwan's success has been at least partly attributable to an intensive effort by the government to direct the sectoral evolution of the economy. To evaluate these views, it is necessary to briefly review the arguments most often made to support the potential beneficial effects of government intervention.

The Case for Industrial Policy

Consider the general case for government intervention in the manufacturing sector or industrial policy. Such activity can be welfare improving in the presence of real external economies or capital market imperfections. The latter can arise because of high failure rates by borrowers and the consequent need of financial institutions to charge high interest rates to insure acceptable rates of return. The externality is the loss in real income as some projects with high expected private and social rates of return are not financed. The imperfection here is the high cost of screening or asymmetric information between borrowers and lenders. Arguments about learning by doing and static scale economies, often invoked to justify intervention, are also encompassed under the capital market failure argument insofar as perfectly informed lenders would find it worthwhile to lend to projects whose present discounted value is positive. They do not lend because of risk aversion, an inability to lend the requisite minimum amount given the size of project required, or myopia.

The second valid argument for intervention stems from the possibility of real external economies conferred by a new firm or industry. In an open economy, such externalities must consist of allowing goods to be produced at less than the imported c.i.f. price.

In Taiwan there is reason to be skeptical of the quantitative importance of the impact of government intervention in the capital market. The view that government lending made a decisive difference in the sectoral *pattern* of investment is not very plausible in an economy in which domestic saving was at a high level (Table 3.6), rapidly growing, and the capital market closed for much of the period, making investment abroad difficult. Such conditions must have led to a growing and intense effort by private investors to identify high quality local projects. While the impact of asymmetric information would continue to be felt, the growing ratio of investment to GNP implies that an increasing number of projects with positive present discounted value at market rates would be financed. While it is possible that the sectoral structure of investment was affected, the overwhelming fact is the rapid growth of the capital stock for the entire manufacturing sector as was shown in Table 3.1.

As is well known, the first-best intervention in the case of either market failure is to direct policy to correct the specific failure. A second-best policy would subsidize industries during their learning period, provided that the Mill-Bastable criterion is satisfied. It is difficult to evaluate retrospectively whether these normative criteria were met by the policies that

TABLE 3.6 Gross Saving Rate

Year	Average of yearly figures
1952-1956	14.2
1957-1961	16.2
1962-1966	19.5
1967-1971	24.7
1972-1976	31.4
1977-1981	32.8
1982-1986	32.9
1987-1988	36.7

Source: Taiwan Statistical Data Book 1989, Council for Economic Planning and Development, Republic of China, Taipei, China, 1989, Table 3-11.

were followed, though in principle it could be done. It is not much less challenging to determine whether the various interventions[31] had a major quantitative impact as it is hard to construct a counterfactual scenario of growth without intervention. Nevertheless, it is possible to obtain some sense of the importance of industrial policy.

The Impact of Taiwan's Industrial Policy

Wade and others have vigorously argued that a critical component of Taiwan's success has been an industrial policy that: (1) established public enterprises when private initiative was not forthcoming or the capital market was reluctant or unable to fund very large projects; (2) extensively employed import restrictions; and (3) occasionally financed private enterprise. Although his evidence is anecdotal, I find Wade's case that wide intervention was employed to be persuasive. Such government direction raises two critical questions in terms of the preceding discussion: (a) did it matter -- was the sectoral structure of production affected with respect to the time at which various sectors were initiated or did its depth (the extent of forward and backward linkages) differ compared to what would have transpired in the absence of industrial policy; (b) was this intervention welfare enhancing? In both dimensions, Wade's view is affirmative -- government direction had decisive effects upon the structure of production and it improved welfare.

Before examining the impact of policy on structure and growth, it is worth noting that the role of government enterprises has declined continuously, their economy-wide value added share decreasing from 12.9 percent of domestic value added in 1951 to 11.6 in 1965 and 10.5 in 1988.[32] There was a corresponding decline in the current price economy-wide share of investment of these enterprises from 29 to 21 to 19 percent in these years.[33] Even more important is the decline in the share of constant price value added of government manufacturing enterprises, the figures for selected years being shown in Table 3.7. These shifts presumably reflected the increasing skill levels and capital available in the private sector. The decrease in the importance of government enterprises' share of value added from the early years occurred in the period of rapidly rising exports and changes in the structure of production toward more technologically complex activities. While it is possible that some important sub-sector activities were undertaken by such entities, it seems unlikely that they were critical to the growth of the entire sector. On the other hand, public enterprises may have been an important training ground for entrepreneurs: Liu (1987, Chapter 5) reports that, among executives in large companies, 30 percent of Mainland-born executives and 10 percent of Taiwan-born executives had earlier been employed in public enterprises.

TABLE 3.7 Share of Public Enterprise in Value Added in Manufacturing

1952	56.2	1975	14.2
1957	48.7	1980	14.5
1964	38.9	1984	14.2
1970	20.6	1988	11.1

Note: Share of 1981 constant price value added through 1980, share of 1986 constant price value added share afterwards.

Source: Taiwan Statistical Data Book, 1989, Council for Economic Planning and Development, Table 5-4.

Effects of Intervention on the Structure of Production. Are the views that contend that government intervention had important effects correct? First, the evolution of Taiwan's industrial structure can be compared with that of other developing countries. In particular, Taiwan's industrial structure can be compared to that of other countries of similar income undergoing a growth in income per capita employing the normal patterns calculated by Chenery and Syrquin (1986). A second, complementary method is to determine whether the industrial structure of Taiwan deepened more than other countries of similar income (and size), one goal of government direction being an increase in backward and forward linkages. There are well known problems with each method, for example, the intersectoral pattern of evolution of value added across nations includes the impact in all countries of changing levels of effective rates of protection as determined by government policy; hence in no sense can normal patterns be considered normative. Nor do linkages convey any information about social optimality unless direct measures of efficiency of the linked sectors are available. Nevertheless, to obtain a proximate insight into the impact of government intervention in the absence of a detailed computable general equilibrium model for Taiwan, such international comparisons provide a useful benchmark, keeping in mind their limitations.

The evolution of the sectoral structure of Taiwan has been compared to that of other developing countries in studies by Chenery and Syrquin (1986) and Kubo *et al.* (1986). Although their analysis ends in 1971, this is presumably the period in which the greatest quantitative impact of government policy would have been experienced as government enterprise was more important, savings rates were not as high, and the role of import restrictions loomed larger in the recently liberalized economy. Nevertheless, the evolution of the sectoral structure of manufacturing, at least at the two digit level, looks similar to that in the other countries contained in the study. Sectors promoted by the government, such as metals and chemicals, did not grow more rapidly than would have been expected from a typical country achieving Taiwan's level of income in successive years, although it could be conjectured that a comparable study over the succeeding fifteen years would demonstrate a growth in electronics that exceeded that attained in other countries.

Similarly, calculations that I have carried out (Table 3.8) show that while backward and forward linkages in Taiwan exceed those in other countries in an international sample, in most cases the differences are not statistically significant.[34] While it is possible that at a more detailed sectoral breakdown significant differences from international patterns would appear, it is not plausible to assert that for the entire manufacturing sector, government intervention had a decisive effect on economic structure.

It is possible, of course, that the other countries in the study were all pursuing policies to encourage a similar evolution. Hence, Taiwan's policy may have altered the "natural" pattern of its development but not have shown up in such comparisons. Other explanations can be offered given the limitations of cross-national comparisons. But I suspect that the broad conclusions would stand up to a more finely honed empirical analysis, namely, that at the two-digit level Taiwan's sectoral evolution appears similar to that of other countries.

Was industrial policy, in the sense of intentionally altering the sectoral composition of output, then largely irrelevant to Taiwan's development? To answer this question it is necessary to examine the major individual products whose growth has been large and to determine the importance of

TABLE 3.8 Linkages in Taiwan and Other Countries

Sectors	Taiwan Forward	Taiwan Backward	Other Forward	Other Backward
Food, beverage, tobacco	.36	.71	.26	.71
Textiles, clothing, leather	.52	.74	.36	.63
Wood, paper, printing, etc.	.53	.71	.57	.61
Rubber product, chemical	.78	.66	.64	.65
Non-metallic minerals	.77	.63	.81	.50
Metals and machinery	.63	.71	.46	.62

Note: Calculation for Taiwan is for 1984. Date of calculation for other countries varies.

Source: Taiwan, calculated from input-output table for 1984 reported in *Statistical Yearbook of the Republic of China*, 1988. Other countries from Syrquin (1989).

industrial policy, on the margin, in their development. However, a disaggregated breakdown of industrial production by value added, by units of production, and by major exports, shows any number of products exhibiting rapid growth in one or more of these dimensions. Many of them, particularly in electronics, would have been natural candidates for investment as Taiwan moved up the capital- and technology-intensive hierarchy. To separate "natural" sources of growth from those induced by government is probably impossible. Government encouragement may have led to a somewhat earlier initiation of production in some products or to slightly lower initial (private) costs, but hardly to the establishment of productive capacity in sectors that would not have been begun at all absent such efforts.

Table 3.4 presented evidence on the sectoral evolution of employment and value added, the point there being that considerable structural change did occur, my conjecture being that rapid aggregate growth and the promise of new opportunities reduced the political or social opposition to such changes on the part of those adversely affected. The implicit model of those who believe that industrial policy has had an important effect is that changes in the deployment of resources were not based on conventional comparative advantage but that the government created comparative advantage in new sectors. In the case of Taiwan, this implies that sectoral growth occurred in capital- or technology-intensive sectors rather than the more labor-intensive sectors which would have been "natural" for Taiwan given its initial resource endowment which was, of course, rapidly changing. While a rigorous test of this hypothesis is very difficult to construct, a simpler one is available.

Table 3.9 presents data on the ratio of value added and employment in 1986 relative to that in 1971 for each sector along with various characteristics of the sector, indexed to the sector-wide average for manufacturing. The characteristics include the ratio of fixed capital (at historic acquisition cost) to labor in 1986,[35] the average wage in 1986, and the ratio of value added to total employment in the sector.

Several results of analyzing these data are noteworthy. First, multiple regression analysis whose results are not shown does not find significant correlation between sector expansion, measured as either share of value added or employment, and the various sectoral characteristics. Second, the sectors that exhibited a large expansion in employment (or value added) -- clothing and footwear, plastics, electrical equipment, and metal products -- are all characterized by *below* average wages and value added per worker. Below average wages even at the end of the period in rapidly expanding sectors tends to confirm the standard view of the determinants of sectoral evolution. Lower than average value added per worker suggests no rents are being earned either by owners of capital or those who possess unusual skills. While it is possible that some of the development, for example, in

TABLE 3.9 The Evolution of Sectors and Their Characteristics

Sector	N_{86}/N_{71}	VA_{86}/VA_{71}	$\bar{W}$	VA/N	K/L
Food, beverages	.48	.38	1.07	1.91	1.64
Textiles	.56	.67	1.07	.76	1.05
Apparel	1.14	2.67	.90	1.00	.31
Wood products	.69	.75	.85	.63	.58
Paper and paper products	.95	.80	.99	.98	1.16
Chemical products	1.16	1.10	1.39	1.83	2.13
Petroleum products	.69	.63	1.43	7.95	7.85
Plastics	10.00	.98	.62	.52	⎰
Rubber	.92	1.00	1.05	.60	⎱ .68
Non-metallic minerals	.74	.43	.93	.76	1.46
Basic metals	1.16	2.00	1.28	2.07	3.99
Metal products	1.80	2.50	.86	.66	.65
Machinery	.84	1.00	.97	.70	.77
Electrical equipment	1.59	2.60	.87	.77	.75
Transportation equip.	1.59	1.50	1.13	1.30	1.23
Precision, misc.	1.63	1.40	.89	.98	.43

Definitions: N, employment; VA, value added; $\bar{W}$, average wage; K/L, fixed capital at historical cost/persons employed.

Source: Value added, employment, same as Table 3.4. Value added per employed person, wage per employed person, fixed capital stock per employed person, *The Report on 1986 Industrial and Commercial Census Taiwan-Fukien Area*, Table 19.

electronics would not have come about without specific efforts by the government to establish research institutes and industrial estates,[36] the main burden of the evidence is that even in the period of economic growth which saw the introduction of new technology-based products, the sectoral pattern of expansion is not consistent with assigning a major role to industrial policy. Indeed, the picture that emerges from Table 3.9 is very neoclassical. The cross-sector dispersion of wages is very small compared to other LDCs, comparable to that in the OECD countries, and is consistent with the hypothesis that labor markets are very competitive, it being likely that skill differentials account for the intersector variation that exists. While it is not possible to obtain rates of return on equity across sectors, it seems unlikely that these would vary greatly given the enormous pool of saving, seeking, at least initially, local reinvestment.

Effects on Growth. Given the difficulty of demonstrating any quantitatively unusual behavior in the growth of Taiwan's industrial structure as well as the complexity of demonstrating at the individual product level the contribution of industrial policy versus the natural evolution of industry, what may be concluded about the impact of industrial intervention by the government on growth rates? The major benefit of industrial policy would be to increase the rate of long-term productivity growth. But the view of Wade and others is that industrial policy induced individual sectors to emerge much earlier than they would have absent such a policy. It is not an argument about rates of productivity growth as much as about the timing of the changing industrial structure. Their view is implicitly that new sectors exhibit a higher level of total factor productivity, in which case initiation of production in new sectors does yield a greater level of total factor productivity for a given commitment of resources. As in the case of static international trade models, there is a level effect but no rate of growth impact. To obtain a conclusion that rates of TFP growth are increased, the introduction of new sectors with higher levels of TFP must occur on a continuous basis or the sectors introduced must themselves exhibit higher rates of TFP growth than older sectors.[37] However, no evidence has been adduced that such is the case.

Chen and Tang (1990) have calculated rates of TFP growth for two digit sectors for the period 1968-1982 (see Table 3.10). There is no systematic relation between the type or age of the sector and TFP growth rates. Thus, chemicals had a negative TFP growth rate for the period while that for textiles, an older sector, is quite high. While TFP growth in machinery is high, it is exceeded by that for leather and furs. TFP growth in electronic and electrical equipment is not much higher than that in apparel.

TABLE 3.10   Growth Rates of Total Factor Productivity by Sector, 1968-1982

Food processing	-.0015	Petroleum & coal	-.0063
Beverages & tobacco	.0088	Rubber	.0207
Textiles	.0346	Clay, stone, glass	.0099
Apparel	.0202	Basic metals	.0004
Leather & fur	.0413	Fabricated metals	.0142
Lumber & furniture	-.0076	Machinery	.0363
Paper & paper products	-.0001	Electronics & elec.	.0212
Chemicals	-.0067	Transportation equip.	.0226

Source: Chen and Tang (1990).

Contrary to the results of Chen and Tang obtained for two-digit branches, assume that for the period since 1982 each new sector has a higher value of A^* than the average earlier one. If this were the case, the need for government intervention to induce the establishment of the sector is not obvious, though one can postulate the existence of capital market failures or excessive risk aversion by private investors. While it is possible that the government's attention to a sector accelerated its introduction, to have an impact on measured TFP growth rates requires not an occasional success but a continuing stream of them. The existing evidence shown in Table 3.10 does not support this view.

Industrial Policy and the Sources of Growth

An alternative view of the contribution of industrial policy is possible, namely, that it increased the elasticity of substitution, slowing the decline in the marginal product of capital. The view behind such a formulation is that the government is more far-sighted than the private sector, anticipates changes in aggregate relative factor availability and relative factor prices, and initiates discussions and focuses attention on new industries (perhaps new technologies) before the private sector would have done so. The move to more capital-intensive sectors is faster and more efficient.

To ascertain whether such intervention could have increased the growth rate, an expanded form of the intermediate term growth equation, (1), the Nelson-Kmenta approximation, is useful.

$$Q^* = A^* + bK^* + (1-b)L^* + \frac{1}{2}b(1-b)[(\sigma-1)/\sigma][K^* - L^*]^2. \qquad (3)$$

This equation assumes that the underlying production function is a constant elasticity of substitution one, σ being the elasticity of substitution. The first three terms provide the conventional Cobb-Douglas explanation of output growth contained in (1) while the last term introduces a correction if σ, the elasticity of substitution, differs significantly from unity. When capital grows much more rapidly than natural units of labor, labor supply may constrain output growth rates as the sector encounters diminishing marginal rates of return to its fastest growing factor. Nevertheless, the greater the ease with which capital can be substituted for labor, the less is any such restrictive effect. A higher σ slows the onset of diminishing returns. Given the rapid increase in capital-labor ratios in Taiwan shown in Table 3.1, this explanation could be of considerable importance. Because of a high degree of collinearity, (3) cannot be estimated. But consider some hypothetical values. If the elasticity of substitution had in fact been 1.2, the unexplained residual for 1961-1987, A^*, declines from 5.25 to 5.09. For the period of the most rapid growth in the capital-labor ratio, 1961-

1976, the residual decreases from 5.39 to 5.09, hardly a significant fall. While some types of selective intervention were undoubtedly followed, it is very difficult to discern their impact either in terms of higher rates of growth of TFP in newer sectors or by positing that the government was more prescient in anticipating changes in the overall endowment of the manufacturing sector.

Such calculations do not preclude the possibility that industrial policy had a major effect on the growth path. It could be argued that the counterfactual scenario would have been an elasticity of substitution of 0.5 and that selective government intervention raised it to unity. The differences in realized growth rates would then have been much larger and industrial policy assumes a quantitatively significant role in the growth process. My own sense of the evidence is that if any one factor allowed the rapid changes in sectoral structure that permitted the staving off of the diminishing returns attributable to the growing capital-labor ratio, it is likely to have been the dramatic rise in education levels discussed below. At this point in our state of knowledge, it would be premature to isolate one aspect of the development process, whether learning derived from exports, selective industrial policy, or education. All had a role and these were surely mutually reinforcing. Without considerably more extensive and precise quantitative micro evidence, assigning priority to one aspect or another of the development process is impossible. With a particular choice of explanatory model and judiciously chosen parameters, any of these can be shown to be decisive.

Foreign Exchange and Education in the Intermediate Run

Within the intermediate-term framework and continuing to utilize equation (3), two other issues are relevant: the role of the availability of foreign exchange and the role of education.

To switch to more capital intensive industries (and technologies within existing sectors) as factor endowments changed often required the importation of new equipment and obtaining technical foreign production knowhow. As indicated in Section 4, some of this knowledge was probably transferred by importers and returning nationals. But some was also derived from technology licensing agreements and from imported new equipment. Given the imperative to alter the structure of the economy in response to the increasing capital-labor endowment, the availability of foreign exchange undoubtedly allowed a less difficult transition. Some countries have increased their saving rate but have been able to earn insufficient foreign exchange to allow such a transition, particularly the import of more modern capital equipment and intermediate inputs. Thus, export orientation and the foreign exchange it provides has a benefit of allowing the *de facto* production function along which the economy produces to avoid the onset of diminishing returns to its saving and investment effort. Again, the payoff to this capacity depends on the value that would have prevailed had the economy been dependent solely on its own capital goods sector, but the qualitative point is clear.

While those advocating the importance of industrial policy in facilitating a changing industrial structure focus on the government, an alternative complementary approach to the ability of Taiwan's industrial sector to evolve with continuing growth in TFP is the quality of its labor force. The growth of education levels in Taiwan has been striking (Table 3.11).

The growth in the capital-labor ratio shown in Table 3.1 along with the maintenance of very low unemployment rates required changes in the labor-intensive technology employed in existing sectors to a more capital-intensive one in response to changing relative factor prices. While the initial choice of appropriate labor-intensive technologies and sectors in response to undistorted price signals was important in achieving both output and employment growth (and an excellent income distribution) in the early decades of rapid growth, the ability to adjust to a rapidly growing capital-labor ratio, growing real wages, and changing international product markets, required considerable flexibility. The shift to new industries characterized by more capital- and technology-intensive processes and the adoption of new technologies such as shuttle-less looms within textiles, was facilitated by the simultaneous growth in the level of education.

Development as rapid as Taiwan's necessitates many types of technological development. Inevitably, much of the relevant technology is imported and successful absorption requires a large group of educated workers.

TABLE 3.11 Education Levels (percentage distribution)

Education level	1964	1987
Illiterate	22.9	5.1
Self-educated	4.3	2.1
Primary school	55.0	32.6
Junior high	8.0	19.8
Senior high	3.0	7.3
Vocational	3.8	19.2
Junior college	3.0	7.6
College & graduate school		6.2

Source: *Statistical Yearbook of the Republic of China,* 1989, p. 60.

Moreover, insofar as the product mix is changing quickly, the investigation of new products, market niches, and new export financing arrangements were required, all of these being skill-intensive activities. While industrial policy may somewhat accelerate the inter-industry and intra-industry shifts in technology, a key enabling factor is the high level of education which facilitates the efficient introduction of the requisite technologies. Without the corresponding growth in education, the economy would have been forced, despite its rapid capital accumulation, to remain with more traditional sectors and technologies, yielding a lower return on new investment than was in fact realized. Rather, the growing level of education altered the constellation of production possibilities. In terms of equation (3), with lower levels of education, the elasticity of substitution of the production function along which the manufacturing sector operated would have been lower than that which was realized. If education had been lower, the elasticity of substitution would itself have been lower, and the growth impact of the high national saving rate would have been considerably decreased insofar as capital would have encountered rapidly diminishing marginal returns. Unfortunately, as noted earlier, the data required to estimate the impact of the growing education levels of workers employed in the manufacturing sector are not yet available. If employment by education in the manufacturing sector even roughly resembles the overall trends shown in Table 3.11, the effect might be substantial.

Just as higher education is critical for permitting a shift in structure, so is new investment. Existing capital is not truly malleable. Sewing machines cannot, until replacement, become lathes. To take advantage of changing relative efficiency of a sector requires investment. Similarly, shifts of labor among sectors in accordance with changing social marginal product of labor requires investment.[38] Education and investment are thus complementary in permitting a shifting industrial structure, a characteristic feature of Taiwan's development. Assuming that these changes have been socially profitable, both were important.

6. Small-Scale Enterprises

Most analyses of the industrial development of Taiwan have noted the importance of small-scale enterprises (SSE) (Ho 1980; Levy 1988; Ranis 1979; Scitovsky 1985). Rather than repeat the comprehensive discussion in these studies, the following attempts to link the role of SSEs to total factor productivity growth discussed in Section 2.

Many inquiries into the sources of TFP growth assert the importance of scale economies.[39] This view is also maintained in the disaggregated two digit studies of TFP growth for 1968-1982 by Chen and Tang (1990) reported above. In particular, they find that the TFP growth rate across sectors is correlated with the rate of growth of output. For this explanation to carry a behavioral economic underpinning, the typical firm in each sector would have had to undergo an expansion in size to benefit from an increasing size of plant. While some growth in the average size of plant has occurred, available data suggest that the reaping of scale economies is not likely to have been a major source of productivity growth. Thus, Table 3.12 reports the average number of employees per establishment reported in the 1986 Census of Manufacturing. By international standards the typical size of firm in each sector is remarkably small. Although the measurement of

TABLE 3.12 The Size Structure of Taiwanese Manufacturing

Sector	Average number of persons engaged	Number of firms 1966-1970	1986
Food processing	17	1,129	217
Beverages, tobacco	160	13	9
Textiles	37	428	1,039
Clothing	44	112	417
Leather, fur	63	156	618
Wood products	15	505	760
Paper, printing, publishing	12	478	1,093
Chemical materials	67	70	73
Chemical products	25	265	113
Petroleum, chemicals	465	2	1
Plastic products	29	388	1,603
Rubber products	28	88	283
Non-metallic minerals	27	270	402
Basic metals	27	189	213
Fabricated metals	9	722	3,728
Machinery	11	504	1,091
Electrical equipment	61	274	1,010
Transportation equipment	30	209	445
Precision equipment	29	53	169
Miscellaneous	26	261	765

Source: Number of firms, *The Report on 1986 Industrial and Commercial Census Taiwan-Fukien Area*, General Report, Table 28; average firm size, ibid., Table 19.

firm size by employment can understate the ability to realize scale economies if each plant is very capital-intensive, it is extremely unlikely that firms at this level of employment are obtaining them.[40]

Table 3.12 also reports the growth in the number of firms operating between the period 1966-1970 and 1986. The absolute growth in the number of firms is extraordinary, especially in fast growing sectors such as plastics and electronics. While the expansion of firms is considerably less than that of the growth of output (the "elasticity" of the number of firms with respect to constant price value added being typically below 10 percent) it is nevertheless an important component in the explanation of the growth of TFP. In particular, small firms are likely to have: (1) exhibited great flexibility in movement among product lines; (2) managed employees more intensively to obtain high and growing productivity from a given set of factors; and (3) allowed the benefits of considerable subcontracting and the realization of economies of scope. While the average size of existing firms did increase given the slower growth of the number of firms compared to value added, the small average size and the limited size of even the largest one-fifth of firms relative to international competitors, suggests that scale economies were unlikely to have been a major source of growing total factor productivity.

The small average size of firms may have contributed to the growth of TFP. Levy (1988) documents the ability of relatively small Taiwanese firms to adjust to changing product markets in goods as diverse as athletic shoes, computer keyboards, and personal computers. Such firms have been able to move towards products which have just been developed or towards existing ones whose relative price has increased. For the same level of total factor productivity in purely physical terms, the ability to avoid declining prices clearly adds to the TFP of a sector as real value added will be greater. An important permissive factor that allows a rapid change in industrial structure is the large supply of trading firms which search for new product niches appropriate for Taiwan's smaller producers. The effect of this complex structure is to enable firms to begin production with small amounts of capital for both production facilities and for "the acquisition of specialized market information." While this is similar to the superior choice of technique emphasis of earlier discussions of Taiwanese industrial organization, it highlights two additional features: the ease of entry for new innovative participants and the ability to avoid large investment in informational requirements which is arguably more constraining, especially in the Taiwan context, than obtaining financing.

In addition, Levy maintains that Taiwanese firms have benefitted considerably from the ability to avoid complex organizational decisions about how to vertically organize large numbers of workers and departments. Setting adequate wage incentive systems when large numbers of employees are involved is one of the most difficult of management tasks and is best left to a later stage of development, as is organization of many "job-shops" within a large firm. The ability to maintain a small firm structure surely contributed to productivity growth over the first three decades of industrialization though some concerns about its implication for the future are surfacing (see section 8). The Taiwanese structure enabled firms to engage in considerable subcontracting, thus allowing supplier firms to realize economies of scope in the utilization of specialized capital and labor.[41]

What features contributed to the remarkable elasticity of entrepreneurs and the establishment of trading networks? Levy emphasizes the extremely high level of education of the population, contrasting it favorably with Korea, in which the supply of trading firms was quite low. I would argue that other factors were also at work, but they would take us beyond the scope of this paper. The critical point is that a plausible argument can be made that, given the enormously rapid increase in the capital stock and the labor force shown in Section 2, it seems unlikely that a more centralized form of economic organization would have been able to absorb such resources without much lower marginal returns. As noted in Section 2, although computed TFP growth rates were very impressive, it is even more remarkable in contrast to countries that have achieved similar ratios of A^*/Q^* only with much lower rates of factor accumulation. The smaller firm structure permitted more detailed supervision and the avoidance of principal-agent problems, flexibility in product niches, subcontracting and the exploitation of economies of scope, and the tapping of the ability of many innovative skillful entrepreneurs who would have been consigned to employee status in a larger industrial structure.

While the importance of competitive market pressure as a source of productivity growth is surely important, the size structure seems to me to have played an equally important role. Moreover, Chen and Tang (1990) do not find any evidence that intersectoral growth rates in exports, one measure of competitive pressure, are significantly correlated with TFP growth rates. It is likely that all the pieces contributing to Taiwan's performance were in fact interconnected. Even if it becomes possible to document the productivity-promoting effects of the discipline imposed by exporting, it is very likely that the size structure was an important complementary condition for such rapid industrial development, in particular, the high rates of TFP growth.

All of this is of more than just historical interest. A key question that often arises in the context of Taiwan's probable future performance is whether the emphasis on small-scale structure is likely to hurt it, an issue discussed in Section 8.

7. Services

In looking at cross-country patterns, Clark, Kuznets, Chenery, and others have noted that as per capita income grows, the share of the service sector in both employment and value added grows. This evolution reflects high income elasticities of demand for some household services (education, health, entertainment), growing demand for business services such as insurance and banking, and to some extent the fact that some services initially performed within other productive sectors, for example, accounting, become specialized and appear under the service rubric. Insofar as high income elasticities exist, and the services demanded are not tradeable, the share of services within Taiwan is likely to increase over time. During the 1980s the main growth in the share of services in GDP occurred in the business services such as finance, insurance, real estate, and banking (Table 3.13). Commerce (wholesale and retail trade, restaurants, and hotels) and transport (transport, storage, and communications) remained a roughly constant share of current price GDP. Nevertheless, despite its relative constancy, commerce required a significantly increased share of employment. This implies that the commerce sector had, on the margin, lower labor productivity compared with the rest of the economy.

For the first two service sectors, the share of value added is roughly similar to that of employment. Although marginal labor product may differ from average, it is likely that, in both sectors, marginal labor product is not far from the economy-wide average. In contrast, the average labor product

TABLE 3.13 The Share of the Service Sector in Value Added and Employment

Sector	VA_{1980}	VA_{1988}	N_{1980}	N_{1988}
Wholesale, retail, restaurants, hotels	.13	.14	.114	.154
Transport, storage, communications	.06	.06	.050	.045
Finance, insurance, real estate, business insurance	.13	.16	.020	.026

Source: Value added, *National Income in Taiwan Area of the Republic of China*, 1989, Table 1. Employment, *Statistical Yearbook of the Republic of China*, 1989, Table 9.

in business services (0.16/0.026) is about five times the economy-wide average, a level reflecting its higher capital-labor ratio rather than a higher level of total factor productivity. The greater capital-labor ratio reflects not fixed capital but working capital, presumably financial assets.[42]

To see the implications of the growth of the service sector, or some of its components, consider a simple transformation of equation (1), namely,

$$N^* = \{Q^* - A^* - bK^*\}/(1-b) \tag{4}$$

Assume that Q^* is set exogenously.[43] Then the absorption of labor in a given sector depends on the rate of growth of total factor productivity and the rate of growth of the capital stock in the sector. To obtain some insight on the evolution of Taiwan's service sector, consider the rates of growth of Q and N shown in Table 3.14 for the period 1980-1988.

For the two largest sectors, the growth rate of *labor* productivity shown in the last column is considerably less than that of *total factor productivity* for all manufacturing shown in Table 3.1, though for different periods. Moreover, the growth in labor productivity in these sectors reflects both the effect of capital deepening and growth in TFP. Assume that in Taiwan, as in other countries, A^* will be low or close to zero, in any case much lower than in manufacturing. Equation (4) implies that there will be a higher rate of growth of employment in services than in manufacturing. Moreover, one reason for the relatively high average product of labor in business services is the very high ratio of total assets per worker compared to other sectors. Thus, if the service sector grows, particularly its business service component as is widely forecast, it will require disproportionate shares of both labor and capital, reflecting both low values of A^* and high capital-labor ratios in the business service subsector. Given that the economy-wide value of total factor productivity growth rate is a weighted sector average, it seems likely that the changing structure will reduce the overall Taiwanese growth rate unless (1) the growth rate of TFP in manufacturing can be further increased or (2) TFP growth in services can be accelerated.

TABLE 3.14 Rates of Growth of Constant Price Value Added and Employment, 1980-1988

Sector	*Value added*	*Employment*	V^*-N^*
Commerce	9.6	6.6	3.0
Transport	9.1	1.4	7.7
Business	10.3	6.7	2.6

Source: Calculated from data underlying Table 3.13.

Greater productivity growth in the service sector is, however, likely to be difficult to achieve. TFP growth in this sector largely (but not completely) arises from entering service areas with high prices rather than improvement in physical productivity. Yet rents in this sector can be earned only from unusual knowledge including organizational ability, the devising of new financial services or software, and so on. While Taiwan may have the ability to obtain rents in some areas such as software development, it is likely to be difficult to generate such rents in most of these areas in competition with the huge financial service institutions that exist in the U.S., Japan, and a few of the European countries. As in manufacturing, the best promise (see below) is entry into niche markets.

8. Summary and Conclusions

It is perhaps inevitable, given Taiwan's remarkably successful growth, that some analysts will seek an Achilles heel in the process that may bring down a house of cards. Certainly, such a development would delight members of the "inward-orientation is best" chorus. Every time a transition point or a slowing of growth occurs, for example after the oil shocks, new variations on the "we told you so" theme are developed. Such well-wishers, having failed to see their dreams fulfilled in Japan, eagerly await the stagnation of Korea and Taiwan.

Even within Korea and Taiwan, analysts often maintain that the other country has chosen a better path. To evaluate the accuracy of such perceptions, a brief summary of the past decades and a broad view of likely evolution of the next two decades is necessary.

Both Korea and Taiwan entered world export markets by taking advantage of the relatively low wages of a fairly well educated labor force. In both countries, the quality of the labor force was continuously upgraded via high expenditures on education. The technology in the industries that formed the initial base of their export drives was relatively simple and was derived by obtaining non-proprietary information from machinery manufacturers and readily available trade literature, from returning nationals, from purchasers of exports, and so on. From the viewpoint of international trade theory, both countries were in a Hecksher-Ohlin world for much of the 1965-1980 period.

With the inevitable rise of unit labor costs, and the appearance of still lower wage countries seeking to export, Taiwan increased its share of more capital- and technology-intensive sectors in the 1980s, though many labor intensive activities continue to be of major importance. The latter have become more "technology"-intensive; for example, in athletic shoes the design component generates considerable product differentiation and they are no longer simple standardized goods. Both Korea and Taiwan entered the low end of the product spectrum of newer consumer goods such as microwave ovens, compact disc players, and color televisions. Often the technology was licensed from the Japanese. The overwhelming issue facing firms in Taiwan in the decade of the 1990s is their ability to identify new products that will enable them to maintain an inevitably slower but respectable rate of export growth. Services will play an increasing role but only a small fraction of them are likely to be characterized by high income per worker.

The critical export market will continue to be the U.S. While the European market offers potential for growth, the effort to integrate the East European countries into the planned 1992 unification will probably result in substantial investment to establish production in the Eastern European countries of many of the consumer products, from clothing to electronics, now produced in the Far East.

Given this tentative scenario, what are the prospects for the East Asian super-exporters and what conclusions may be reached about the appropriateness of their past evolution for addressing the next generation of problems? In particular, some analysts have argued that Korea's reliance on the chaebol confers an advantage that the smaller average size firms in Taiwan cannot match. Others have asserted that Taiwan's smaller firms are likely to be more nimble in responding to rapidly changing conditions.

There are two issues related to firm size. First, it is increasingly clear that the larger Korean firms provide an obvious target for extracting larger wage increases. Korea's unit labor costs are thus likely to rise more rapidly than those in Taiwan. Second, a new generation of products will require new technical knowledge, usually based on proprietary information. In both Korea and Taiwan, the era of low-cost acquisition of non-proprietary knowledge is coming to a close. While both countries have done brilliantly in many sectors at moving towards best world practice, the move into new product areas will be vigorously contested by OECD firms.

It is not clear *a priori* whether entry into new product markets will be better served by large or small firms. Insofar as there is a fixed cost component in licensing fees as well as largely fixed costs of absorbing the technology, firms that can allocate these over larger production runs will derive an advantage. Moreover, large firms with many products in their portfolio will have a lower firm-wide risk than smaller one or two product firms. However, the former may encounter reluctance to share new technology by the developers of the technology insofar as they present a threat in third markets given their size. In contrast, the smaller Taiwanese firms may encounter more willingness to license given the lesser threat they pose.

Other supposed differences between small and large firms are equally ambiguous. Thus, the many studies designed to investigate the Schumpeterian hypothesis about differential innovative success in large and small firms have been largely inconclusive. Moreover, there are no studies of which I am aware that investigate productivity growth by firm size. Hence, despite the fashionable trend asserting the probable superior performance of Korea given its industrial organization, the argument is far from compelling.

Taiwanese firms will undoubtedly face an increasingly difficult world in the 1990s. New product areas will have to be identified, their characteristics and production technology understood, and become the basis for another set of exports. This path is likely to be much more difficult than that of the past quarter-century. Moreover, the very success of the East Asian model has led to exporting becoming the goal of many countries, not least in some of the Latin American NICs whose debt service problems have led to new government policies that make exporting a more profitable activity compared to domestic sales.[45]

Although it is hard to document, it is fairly clear that product cycles are becoming increasingly short for many of the products in which Taiwanese firms are interested. When compact disk players were introduced in 1983, their price was about US$1,200 and they were largely produced by Japan and Holland. By 1990, retail prices for typical mass market players have declined to about US$200, with *ex factory* prices being less than half of this. Such rapid learning leaves very small profit margins in many newer consumer products after a very short period of production. Indeed, it seems likely that firms that were not producing CD players between 1983 and 1986 missed the bulk of profits. Yet, the technology in comparable new industries may become more difficult to acquire in the early period of production as developers try to recoup increasingly large research expenses. For example, in high density television, once a standard is adopted in the U.S., the bulk of profits are likely to accrue to the developers in the first few years of sales.

In view of this, the evolving comparative advantage of Taiwanese firms is likely to be in market niches that are being abandoned in the developed countries rather than in the newest consumer or producer products. In such markets, the relative smallness and the ability to act quickly of Taiwanese firms may confer an important advantage. With respect to new products, there is likely to be a temptation to try to compete in some of the advanced areas, such as the development of new chips. While this might be done as part of a technology sharing consortium, going it alone is likely to be exceptionally expensive. To take one example, IBM and Siemens have recently announced plans to undertake joint research on the production of 64 megabyte chips. Their combined annual sales are US$130 billion, yet neither is willing to undertake the new technology by itself.

The IBM-Siemens example is also instructive in another dimension. It is occasionally argued that a country must participate in the development of a current technology in order to keep its options open for the next generation. Yet the new x-ray lithography method being explored for the production of the 64 megabyte chip is totally different from that employed for the 256K and one megabyte chip. The losses incurred by latecomers to the latter market, particularly by Korean firms, cannot be viewed as an investment for the next stage. Their knowledge simply doesn't confer any advantage.

It seems unlikely that the growth rate of supply in Taiwanese manufacturing and services can be maintained at its rate of the past quarter-century. The likely shift to services will slow the rate of growth of capital given its higher capital-output ratio. The rapid growth rate of TFP in manufacturing is likely to slow because of the decline in rents accruing to the manufacturing sector. Moreover, part of TFP growth in manufacturing was attributable to the import of equipment embodying new technology, and some was ascribed to disembodied knowledge obtained from abroad. Given the relative modernity of its industrial equipment, the potential gains from importing new equipment are perforce more limited. Taiwan is in the enviable position of being relatively advanced. Hence, obtaining new equipment in existing industries is not likely to be a major source of productivity growth. While benefiting from new product research abroad will be possible, it will become increasingly expensive. Similarly, process research which is typically more easily appropriated by developers will become more expensive.

Joint ventures or technology agreements in which Taiwanese firms deploy their considerable production engineering skills combined with (still) relatively low-cost labor to produce products designed abroad is one possible direction. It avoids the pitfalls of entering product markets which experience rapid change as a result of intensive research, development, and design expenditures by major firms in the OECD countries. The great difficulties being encountered by Korea's huge Hyundai automobile manufacturing operation is instructive. After extraordinarily successful penetration of the U.S. market with a low-priced car, its sales have fallen precipitously as a result of the inability to introduce design changes. Although the possibility of increasing the size of the machinery sector is currently being discussed in Taiwan, the design issue suggests caution.[46]

A large literature attests to the slowdown in the rate of growth of total factor productivity in the OECD countries, including Japan, since 1973. Taiwan has averted this decrease through a variety of mechanisms discussed in this paper that allowed it to maintain high rates of TFP growth. But many of these are unlikely to be as important in the future as Taiwanese firms are already close to the best practice frontier in existing industries. In sum, the opportunities to increase productivity by inexpensive acquisition of external knowledge will inevitably decline. While a prospective decline in TFP growth rates could be offset by faster capital accumulation, it is not clear that the requisite decrease in consumption levels would be welfare enhancing at Taiwan's current levels of per capita income. As in Japan, increased levels of social satisfaction may militate in favor of a gradual shift towards the production of non-tradeable goods.

Taiwan in the 1990s thus faces difficult problems of competing in an increasingly complex world economy. Its problems now closely resemble those of the OECD countries in terms of where to fit into the evolving world economy. While there are dilemmas ahead, 140 governments surely wish they faced the future with the extraordinary achievements of Taiwan behind them.

Notes

1. In the sense that they exhibited similar TFP in their new locale as in the original one.
2. Pack (1988) reviews the available evidence on TFP growth for LDCs. For most LDCs for varying periods, TFP growth has been negligible.
3. An alternative is to examine the rates of return on investment in those sectors fostered by government policy, an empirically difficult path.
4. One obvious source of different factor choices is differential interest rates which result in differing user cost of capital and wages that differ by firm size.
5. Output will be larger, for a given capital stock, if the socially appropriate capital-labor ratio is chosen rather than if a higher capital-labor ratio is chosen.
6. Intersectoral variation in effective protection rates were already low by 1968 (Hsing 1970), corroborated by Lee and Liang (1982) for 1972. Different authors have varying views of the impact of reforms leading to rapid export growth. See, for example, Galenson (1979) and Kuo and Fei (1985).
7. There may be increases in technical efficiency if expansion in capacity is achieved with larger plant size relative to that which would have been built if sales were largely oriented to the domestic market. These gains will be particularly large if the initial structure is primarily small-scale and there is a substantial shift in typical plant size to one taking advantage of scale economies. As discussed in Section 7, the size of firms expanded over the period but the industrial structure does not imply that large gains from scale economies were obtained. Moreover, with respect to industrial sectors, Taiwan did not experience a large concentration of new production in those industries in which static scale economies are important, such as basic metals and chemicals.

8. The factor shares were obtained from *Statistical Yearbook of the Republic of China*, various years. Kuo also estimates the rate of technical change by estimating a Cobb-Douglas production function rather than weighting input growth rates by factor shares, assumed to reflect the elasticity of output with respect to each share. She finds lower values for A^* in the 1961-1980 period but a parallel decline from the earlier period.

9. In long term growth models capital embodiment does not affect the steady-state rate of growth, at least with a Cobb-Douglas production function (Phelps 1962). However, the intermediate-term growth rate will be affected by rates of embodiment.

10. Kuznets (1979, p. 97) explicitly drew attention to the fact that investment in equipment would be a major determinant of Taiwanese productivity growth though he did not distinguish between domestic and imported capital.

11. The breakdown of investment among equipment and structures is available for aggregate investment but not for investment by one digit sectors. See *National Income in Taiwan Area of the Republic of China*, 1989, Directorate-General of Budget, Accounting and Statistics, Executive Yuan, Republic of China, Table 15.

12. See, for example, Kuznets (1966).

13. See Ho (1978) and Kuo (1983) for evidence on the labor intensiveness of exports.

14. On the sources of success of the initial export drive see Fei and Kuo (1985), Ranis (1979), and Scott (1979).

15. Liu (1987, Chapter 5) presents data culled from biographical information of executives about the sectors in which they are engaged, though evidence on their earlier experience is not available.

16. Scott (1979, pp. 351-57) provides substantial evidence for this view for the period through 1975. He also examines (pp. 357-364) the cost structure of a number of major exporting sectors and shows the decisive role of low wages and the availability of intermediate inputs at international prices.

17. This is the thrust of Ranis' (1979) argument that the industrial sector succeeded because factor endowments were allowed to "speak."

18. Current price input-output tables are presented in various issues of *The Statistical Yearbook of the Republic of China*, an annual published by the Directorate-General of Budget, Accounting and Statistics.

19. The anomaly would disappear if an additional instrument of government policy such as explicit export targeting (as in Korea) were used systematically (Pack and Westphal 1986). However, I have found no evidence of such additional instruments in the existing literature though Wade (1990) reports some policies that might have such effects.

20. Little (1979) notes the income of domestic purchasers is affected to a considerable degree by income received from exporting, hence the

accounting partition between exports and domestic demand as a source of changing structure is somewhat arbitrary.

21. Little (1979) notes that the Mainland government, once established on Taiwan, owed no allegiance to *Taiwanese* landlords.

22. The undercutting of social and political opposition to industrialization may be the best defense of the "big push" argument of Rosenstein-Rodan and others. Whereas they were concerned with the ability to escape a low-level equilibrium trap, whether as a result of the growth of supply not conforming to existing income elasticities of demand or Malthusian concerns, three decades of additional observation suggest that overcoming the opposition of recipients of rents and those bearing the costs of transition from the current regime is more important.

23. Also see deMelo (1985) and Kuo (1983).

24. Levy (1988) provides evidence that Taiwanese export traders were also very important in this process. See also Section 6 below.

25. See, for example, the *Wall Street Journal*, June 1, 1990.

26. For an exhaustive study of the role of MNCs in Taiwan through the late 1970s and their motives for locating in Taiwan see Ranis and Schive (1985). Cohen (1975) provides case study material on MNCs in Taiwan and other Asian countries.

27. For a model of the potential beneficial impact of MNCs on local knowledge see Findlay (1974).

28. Scitovsky (1985) suggests that the small size structure of firms encouraged workers to begin their own firms and made it easier to accumulate enough capital through informal channels to finance the establishment of the firms. He also links this phenomenon to the rapid growth in the household saving rate.

29. Westphal and I (1986) have pointed out in the case of Korea that many of the policies pursued by the East Asian NICs are very similar to those pursued by the import substituting countries, in this case local content requirements. The difference in their success may be due to the more appropriate economic environment, for example, local suppliers in Taiwan being able to obtain specialized inputs without applying for licenses.

30. The role of education is discussed below.

31. For a very detailed list with large numbers of examples culled from government documents, newspapers, and periodicals see Wade (1990).

32. *National Income in Taiwan Area of the Republic of China, 1989*, Directorate-General of Budget, Accounting and Statistics, Executive Yuan, Republic of China, Table 3.

33. *Ibid.*, Table 14.

34. Significance tests have been carried out employing the standard deviations reported by Syrquin (1989). It is possible, of course, that the other countries in the study were all pursuing policies to encourage a simi-

lar evolution. Hence, Taiwan's policy may have altered the "natural" pattern of its development but not have shown up in such comparisons. Other explanations can be offered given the limitations of cross-national comparisons. But I suspect that the broad conclusions would stand up to a more finely honed empirical analysis, namely, that at the two-digit level Taiwan's sectoral evolution appears similar to that of other countries.

35. The value of all assets, rather than fixed assets per worker, could also be used, but the correlation is .99. The use of capital-labor ratios at historical cost is likely to be a fairly good indicator of true capital-labor ratios insofar as much of the equipment in each sector has been installed relatively recently and there is no reason to believe that machinery price inflation has differed significantly across various purchasing sectors. Nevertheless, in the absence of constant price estimates of capital stock, the comparisons in the text should be viewed as subject to some measure of error.

36. Some of these institutions are briefly described by Li (1988).

37. In an interesting paper analyzing the potential impact of industrial policy, Justman and Teubal argue that new sectors will exhibit higher *levels* of TFP.

38. Nelson (1964) emphasizes this important reallocative role of investment.

39. There is some inconsistency in the methodology employed. If indeed there are scale economies, observed factor shares do not necessarily equal elasticities of output with respect to each factor, hence the method for obtaining weighted factor growth is dubious.

40. For comparative international data and discussion see Berry (1990) and Lee (1990).

41. For examples of the costs in machinery production of the inability to engage in subcontracting and the consequent need to establish "captive" internal production facilities that are inadequately employed see Pack (1981).

42. *The Report on 1986 Industrial and Commercial Census, General Report*, Table 19 reports that net assets per person engaged in business services is roughly 34 fold that in all manufacturing.

43. In fact, Q^* is endogenous, depending on both income and price elasticities of demand.

44. I am not a partisan of the new export pessimism for all LDCs as a group. However, many of the specific industrial product markets, particularly the ones in which Taiwan has excelled, are attractive to many of the NICs and may become the arena for fierce competition.

45. See Pack (1981) for a discussion about the prospects of NICs, including Taiwan, in the machinery sector.

References

Baily, Martin Neal, and Margaret M. Blair. 1988. "Productivity and American Management," in Martin Neal Baily et al., *American Living Standards, Challenges and Threats*. Washington, D.C.: The Brookings Institution.

Behrman, Jere. 1990. "Thoughts on Human Resource Led Development Possibilities." Processed, University of Pennsylvania.

Berry, R. A. 1990. "Intra-industry Firm Heterogeneity in the Analysis of Trade and Development Allowing for Small and Medium Enterprises," in G. Helleiner, ed., *Trade Policies, Industrialization and Development: New Perspectives*. London: Oxford University Press.

Chen, Tain-Jy, and De-Piao Tang. 1990. "Export Performance and Productivity Growth: The Case of Taiwan." *Economic Development and Cultural Change* 38: 577-86.

Chenery, Hollis B., and Moshe Syrquin. 1986. "Typical Patterns of Transformation," in H. Chenery, S. Robinson, M. Syrquin, *Industrialization and Growth: A Comparative Study*. New York: Oxford University Press.

Cohen, Benjamin I. 1975. *Multinational Firms and Asian Exports*. New Haven: Yale University Press.

deMelo, Jaime. 1985. "Sources of Growth and Structural Change in the Republic of Korea and Taiwan: Some Comparisons," in V. Corbo, A. O. Krueger, and F. Ossa, eds., *Export-Oriented Development Strategies*. Boulder, CO: Westview Press.

Deyo, Frederic C. 1988. *The Political Economy of the New Asian Industrialism*. Ithaca: Cornell University Press.

Fei, John C. H., Gustav Ranis, and Shirley W. Kuo. 1979. *Growth With Equity: The Taiwan Case*. New York: Oxford University Press.

Fields, Gary. 1985. "Industrialization and Employment in Hong Kong, Korea, Singapore, and Taiwan," in Walter Galenson, ed., *Foreign Trade and Investment*. Madison: University of Wisconsin Press.

Hsing, Mo-Huan, John H. Power, and Gerardo P. Sicat. 1970. *Taiwan and the Philippines, Industrialization and Trade Policies*. London: Oxford University Press.

Ho, Samuel P. S. 1978. *Economic Development of Taiwan, 1860-1970*. New Haven: Yale University Press.

――――. 1980. "Small-Scale Enterprises in Korea and Taiwan." World Bank Staff Working Paper No. 384, The World Bank, Washington D.C.

Hulten, Charles, Jr. 1989. "The Embodiment Hypothesis Revisited." Processed, University of Maryland.

Justman, M., and Morris Teubal. 1990. "The Structuralist Perspective to Economic Growth and Development: Conceptual Foundations and Policy Implications," in R. Evenson and G. Ranis, eds., *Science and Technology in Developing Countries*. Boulder, CO: Westview Press.

Kubo, Yuji, Jaime deMelo, Sherman Robinson, and Moshe Syrquin. 1986. "Interdependence and Industrial Structure," in H. Chenery, S. Robinson, M. Syrquin, *Industrialization and Growth: A Comparative Study*. New York: Oxford University Press.

Kuo, Shirley W. Y. 1983. *The Taiwan Economy in Transition*. Boulder, CO: Westview Press.

Kuo, Shirley W. Y. and John C. H. Fei. 1985. "Causes and Roles of Export Expansion in the Republic of China," in Walter Galenson, ed., *Foreign Trade and Investment*. Madison: University of Wisconsin Press.

Kuznets, Paul. 1988. "An East Asian Model of Economic Development," Japan, Taiwan, and South Korea." *Economic Development and Cultural Change* 36: S11-S44.

Kuznets, Simon. 1966. *Modern Economic Growth*. New Haven: Yale University Press.

———. 1979. "Growth and Structural Shifts," in W. Galenson, ed., *Economic Growth and Structural Change in Taiwan*. Ithaca: Cornell University Press.

Lall, Sanjaya. 1987. *Learning to Industrialize*. London: Macmillan.

Lee, Norman. 1990. "Market Structure and Trade in Developing Countries," in G. Helleiner, ed., *Trade Policies, Industrialization and Development: New Perspectives*. London: Oxford University Press.

Lee, T. H. and Kuo-Shu Liang. 1982. "Taiwan," in B. Balassa and associates, *Development Strategies in Semi-industrial Countries*. Baltimore: Johns Hopkins.

Levy, Brian. 1988. "Korea and Taiwan as International Competitors." *The Columbia Journal of World Business*, Summer.

Li, K. T. 1988. *The Evolution of Policy Behind Taiwan's Development Success*. New Haven: Yale University Press.

Liang, Kuo-shu, and Ching-ing Hou Liang. 1988. "Development Policy Formation and Future Policy Priorities in the Republic of China." *Economic Development and Cultural Change* 36: S67-S102.

Little, I. M. D. 1979. "An Economic Reconnaissance," in W. Galenson, ed., *Economic Growth and Structural Change in Taiwan*. Ithaca: Cornell University Press.

Liu, Alan P. L. 1987. *Phoenix and the Lame Lion modernization in Taiwan and Mainland China 1950-80*. Stanford, CA: Hoover Institution Press.

National Income in Taiwan Area, the Republic of China. 1989. Taipei: Directorate-General of Budget, Accounting and Statistics, Executive Yuan.

Nelson, Richard R. 1964. "Aggregate Production Functions." *American Economic Review* 54: 575-606.
———. 1973. "Recent Exercises in Growth Accounting: New Understanding or Dead End." *American Economic Review* 73: 462-468.
———. 1981. "Research on Productivity Growth and Productivity Differences." *Journal of Economic Literature* 19: 1029-64.
Olson, Mancur. 1982. *The Rise and Decline of Nations*. New Haven: Yale University Press.
Pack, Howard. 1981. "Fostering the Capital-Goods Sector in LDCs." *World Development*. Pp. 227-250.
———. 1987. *Productivity, Technology, and Industrial Development*. New York: Oxford University Press.
———. 1988. "Industrialization and Trade," in Hollis B. Chenery and T. N. Srinivasan, eds., *Handbook of Development Economics*. Amsterdam: North-Holland.
Pack, Howard, and Larry E. Westphal. 1986. "Industrial Strategy and Technological Change: theory vs reality." *Journal of Development Economics* 22: 87-128.
Phelps, E. S. 1962. "The New View of Investment: A Neoclassical Analysis." *Quarterly Journal of Economics* 76: 548-567.
Ranis, Gustav. 1979. "Industrial Development," in W. Galenson, ed., *Economic Growth and Structural Change in Taiwan*. Ithaca: Cornell University Press.
Ranis, Gustav, and Chi Schive. 1985. "Direct Foreign Investment in Taiwan's Development," in Walter Galenson, ed., *Foreign Trade and Investment*. Madison: University of Wisconsin Press.
The Report on 1986 Industrial and Commercial Census of Taiwan. 1986. Taipei: Committee on Industrial and Commercial Census of Taiwan, Executive Yuan.
Scitovsky, Tibor. 1985. "Economic Development in Taiwan and South Korea." *Food Research Institute Studies* 19: 215-64.
Scott, Maurice. 1979. "Foreign Trade," in W. Galenson, ed., *Economic Growth and Structural Change in Taiwan*. Ithaca: Cornell University Press.
Statistical Yearbook of the Republic of China. 1989. Taipei: Directorate-General of Budget, Accounting and Statistics, Executive Yuan.
Syrquin, Moshe. 1989. "On Linkages." Discussion Paper 8925, Department of Economics and Business Administration, Bar Ilan University, Ramat Gan, Israel.
Taiwan Statistical Data Book. 1989. Taipei: Council for International Economic Cooperation and Development.
Thorbecke, Eric. 1979. "Agricultural Development," in W. Galenson, ed., *Economic Growth and Structural Change in Taiwan*. Ithaca: Cornell University Press.

Tsiang, S. C., and Rong-I Wu. 1985. "Foreign Trade and Investment as Boosters for Take Off: The Experiences of the Four Asian Newly Industrializing Countries," in Walter Galenson, ed., *Foreign Trade and Investment*. Madison: University of Wisconsin Press.

Wade, Robert. 1990. *Governing the Market: Economic Theory and Taiwan's Industrial Policies*. Princeton, NJ: Princeton University Press.

Wall Street Journal, June 1, 1990, "Taiwan, Long Noted for Cheap Imitations, Becomes an Innovator."

Westphal, Larry E., Yung Rhee, and Garry Pursell. 1981. "Korean Industrial Competence: Where it Came From." World Bank Staff Working Paper 469, Washington D.C.

Yearbook of Earnings and Productivity Statistics, Taiwan Area, Republic of China. 1988. Taipei: Directorate-General of Budget, Accounting and Statistics, Executive Yuan.

4

Money and Financial Markets: The Domestic Perspective

Paul C.H. Chiu

Over the past four decades, due to a combination of sound government macroeconomic policies, a cheap and hard-working semi-skilled labor force, and strong private entrepreneurship, the Republic of China on Taiwan has undergone a successful transformation from a poor, underdeveloped backwater to a newly industrialized country. Between 1952 and 1989, the island's per capita income at current prices has increased from US$187 to US$6,862, reflecting an average annual percentage increase in real per capita income of 6.3 percent. In addition, the Taiwan economy has rapidly evolved from being a closed, agricultural products-based economy into an export-oriented manufacturing products-based one. During this period, the total value of exports and imports as a percentage of gross national product has increased from 23 percent to 79 percent. Furthermore, Taiwan has transformed itself from a hyperinflation and low-savings economy to a low-inflation and high-savings one. The annual rate of inflation, measured in terms of the consumer price index, has declined from 4,680 percent in 1949 to an average of no more than 3 percent throughout the 1960s, 1970s and 1980s, except during the two major oil crises from 1973 to 1974 and 1979 to 1981. Taiwan's gross savings rate has also increased from 14 percent in 1952 to an average of more than 30 percent throughout the 1970s and 1980s. This is one of the highest rates recorded by international standards and to date is sufficiently high to finance the economy's high rate of investment.

With respect to the relationship that exists between economic and financial development in Taiwan, the rapid increases in income and savings, together with the huge increases in international trade, have, on the one hand, certainly shaped domestic price behavior and precipitated changes in the pattern of the financial system. On the other hand, the high economic growth rate and the high savings rate would not have been possible without the price stability brought about by appropriate monetary policies and changes that took place in the financial system.

Over the past decade, high economic growth and the rapid accumulation of financial wealth in Taiwan have made the financial system obsolete. In response, the government has adopted a series of liberalization and internationalization efforts aimed at modernizing the financial system. Since internationalization of the foreign exchange market and financial system will be discussed in another chapter of this book, I will discuss them briefly in this chapter only when they are deemed necessary. We will mainly focus on financial performance and financial liberalization in domestic markets.

This chapter is thus divided into five parts:

(1) Section 1 introduces the institutional settings of the financial system and its performance.

(2) In Section 2, an analytical framework depicting the money supply process is used to analyze the effect of high interest rate monetary policy on price stability in Taiwan. A price equation, derived from an open-economy quantity theory of money, is also estimated. The effect of changes in the import price index, in the interest rate, and in the interplay of the implicit demand for money and the supply of money on changes in the price level are explored as well.

(3) Section 3 examines the factors affecting high savings and high productivity in investment. Empirical studies that have sought to determine the long-run relationships deemed to exist between the money supply, increases in labor productivity and economic development in Taiwan are also presented. Furthermore, since the small- and medium-sized enterprise is a main pillar of the economy, its role in Taiwan's economic growth and its financing are also discussed.

(4) Section 4 explores the process of interest rate liberalization, deregulation of controls on international capital movements, and the role of financial markets in financing private enterprises and government.

(5) Section 5 presents concluding remarks and the prospects for further financial development.

Since I use the new Taiwan dollar as the currency unit throughout this chapter, those who are interested in their U.S. dollar equivalent may make use of the average exchange rates between these two currencies listed in Table 4.1. The time series data for price indices and interest rates are also given in Table 4.1 for general reference.

1. The Financial System: Classification and Performance of Financial Institutions

This section will give an overview of the structure of financial institutions in Taiwan and will briefly discuss their performance, also touching upon innovation in financial services and *de novo* entry into the financial market.

TABLE 4.1 Exchange Rates, Price Indices and Interest Rates

	Average exchange rates (NT$/US$) (1)	Rate of change in WPI (%) (2)	Rate of change in CPI (%) (3)	Interest rate on one-year savings deposits IR (%) (4)	Real interest rates IR−WPI (%) (5)=(4)−(2)	Real interest rates IR−CPI (%) (6)=(4)−(3)	Loan rates: secured-unsecured loans (1961-79) short- and long-term loans (1980-89) (%) (7)
1949	—	3405.73	4960.01	—	—	—	—
1950	—	305.54	383.68	83.87	−221.67	−299.81	—
1951	10.30	65.98	29.70	63.81	−2.17	34.11	—
1952	10.30	23.13	29.03	53.41	30.28	24.38	—
1953	15.55	8.79	18.27	26.82	18.03	8.55	—
1954	15.55	2.33	1.67	20.98	18.65	19.31	—
1955	15.55	14.07	9.90	20.98	6.91	11.08	—
1956	24.78	12.73	1.51	23.87	11.14	22.36	—
1957	24.78	7.22	7.53	21.70	14.48	14.17	—
1958	24.78	1.41	1.27	21.70	20.29	20.43	—
1959	36.38	10.26	10.57	18.43	8.17	7.86	—
1960	36.38	14.14	18.44	18.43	4.29	−0.01	—
1961	40.00	3.22	7.83	14.40	11.18	6.57	16.20 , 18.72
1962	40.00	3.03	2.34	13.32	10.29	10.98	15.84 , 18.72
1963	40.00	6.48	2.24	12.00	5.52	9.76	14.04 , 16.56
1964	40.00	2.48	−0.20	10.80	8.32	11.00	14.04 , 15.48
1965	40.00	−4.66	−0.08	10.80	15.46	10.88	14.04 , 15.48
1966	40.00	1.49	1.99	10.08	8.59	8.09	14.04 , 14.76
1967	40.00	2.53	3.35	9.72	7.19	6.37	13.32 , 14.04
1968	40.00	2.96	6.53	9.72	6.76	3.19	13.32 , 14.04
1969	40.00	−0.27	6.42	9.72	9.99	3.30	13.32 , 14.04
1970	40.00	2.73	3.58	9.72	6.99	6.14	12.60 , 13.20
1971	40.00	0.03	2.83	9.25	9.22	6.42	12.00 , 12.50
1972	40.00	4.45	3.01	8.75	4.30	5.74	11.25 , 11.75

(continues)

TABLE 4.1 (continued)

	Average exchange rates (NT$/US$) (1)	Rate of change in WPI (%) (2)	Rate of change in CPI (%) (3)	Interest rate on one-year savings deposits IR (%) (4)	Real interest rates IR−WPI (%) (5)=(4)−(2)	Real interest rates IR−CPI (%) (6)=(4)−(3)	Loan rates: secured-unsecured loans (1961-79) short- and long-term loans (1980-89) (%) (7)
1973	38.25	22.86	8.17	11.00	−11.86	2.83	13.25 , 13.75
1974	38.00	40.58	47.47	13.50	−27.08	−33.97	14.75 , 15.50
1975	38.00	−5.08	5.24	12.00	17.08	6.76	13.00 − 14.00
1976	38.00	2.76	2.50	10.75	7.99	8.25	11.75 − 12.75
1977	38.00	2.76	7.04	9.50	6.74	2.46	10.50 − 11.50
1978	36.95	3.54	5.77	9.50	5.96	3.73	10.50 − 11.50
1979	36.00	13.82	9.75	12.50	−1.32	2.75	14.00 − 15.25
1980	36.00	21.54	19.01	12.50	−9.04	−6.51	13.50 − 16.20
1981	36.79	7.62	16.34	13.00	5.38	−3.34	13.00 − 16.00
1982	39.12	−0.18	2.96	9.00	9.18	6.04	9.00 − 11.50
1983	40.06	−1.19	1.35	8.50	9.69	7.15	8.50 − 11.00
1984	39.62	0.48	−0.02	8.00	7.52	8.02	8.00 − 10.75
1985	39.86	−2.60	−0.17	7.75	10.35	7.92	6.25 − 10.25
1986	37.85	−3.34	0.70	5.00(6.25)[a]	8.34	4.30	5.00 − 9.75
1987	31.87	−3.25	0.52	5.00(6.25)[a]	8.25	4.48	5.00 − 9.75
1988	28.61	−1.56	1.28	5.25(6.25)[a]	6.81	3.97	5.00 − 9.75
1989	26.42	−0.38	4.41	9.50	9.88	5.09	6.50 − 13.00

Note: '-' denotes the data is omitted. [a]Figures in parentheses represent the ceiling rates.

Sources: The average exchange rates are taken from *National Income, Taiwan District, the ROC*, DGBAS, Executive Yuan, 1989, p. 27; rate of change in the wholesale price index (WPI) and consumer price index (CPI) for 1949-1959, from Chang (1967, p. 533) and for others from DGBAS, Executive Yuan; interest rates on one-year savings deposits for 1950-1960 (for 1950-1957, preferential interest rates were used), from Tsiang (1989, p. 121) and for others from the *Financial Statistics Monthly*, CBC; loan rates, from the *Financial Statistics Monthly*, CBC.

The financial system in Taiwan, R.O.C., is categorized in Table 4.2. Its individual components consist of monetary authorities, money deposit-taking institutions, savings deposit-taking institutions, medium- and long-term trust fund-taking institutions, and other financial institutions. These different entities may be briefly described as follows.

Monetary authorities: The monetary authority of the R.O.C. consist of the Ministry of Finance (MOF) and the Central Bank of China (CBC). The former is responsible for matters related to the administration of banks and the regulation of financial intermediaries, while the latter is in charge of matters related to the banking operations of financial intermediaries and the management of the nation's foreign exchange reserves.

Deposit money-taking banks: At the end of 1989, there were fifteen locally incorporated commercial banks, thirty-eight branches of foreign banks, eight medium business banks, and 381 credit cooperative associations, credit departments of farmers' associations, and credit departments of fishermen's associations. (Their shares of deposits are given in parentheses under the heading of "Financial Institutions" in Table 4.2.) Of these, the Cooperative Bank of Taiwan, a bank specializing in industrial and agricultural financing, had powers conferred on it by the Central Bank to conduct bank examinations of the operations of credit cooperative associations, the credit departments of farmers' associations, and the credit departments of fishermen's associations until the establishment of the Central Deposits Insurance Company (CDIC) in September 1986. Since then, only those cooperatives which have not participated in the CDIC are subject to bank examinations by the Cooperative Bank. With the exception of the Medium Business Bank of Taiwan, which operates under island-wide branching, other medium business banks operate under countywide branching, unless otherwise authorized by the MOF.

Of the fifteen locally incorporated banks, thirteen are either wholly owned or majority-owned by the government. These banks constitute the main pillar of the financial system. Table 4.3 shows that these banks together with the Export-Import Bank of China accounted for 56.68 percent and 40.62 percent of the total financial assets of financial institutions in 1961 and 1988, respectively, and that the annual growth rate of their assets ranged from 14 to 44 percent during this period.

In order to provide a financial environment conducive to internationalization and liberalization, the Banking Law was revised and promulgated in July 1989, incorporating the following features:
(i) Conferring greater authority on the MOF to broaden the scope of business in which banks can engage;
(ii) Prescribing a minimum 8 percent risk-based bank capital requirement;

TABLE 4.2 Monetary Authorities, Number of Financial Institutions and Branches, by Type, in Taiwan, R.O.C., 1953-1989

Monetary authorities	Financial institutions[a]			1953	1962	1966	1971	1976	1981	1986	1989
	General Domestic Banks (54%)		T[b] H B	201 6 195	261 10 251	331 11 320	412 13 399	479 14 465	557 14 543	615 15 600	706 15 691
	Local branches of foreign banks		T B T	-- -- 50	1 1 84	4 4 98	6 6 118	12 12 139	24 24 178	32 32 220	38 38 269
	Medium Business Banks (8%)		H B	7 43	8 76	8 90	8 110	8 131	8 170	8 212	8 261
Minister of finance (MOF)	Deposit money-taking institutions	Credit cooperative associations (12%)	T H B	71 -- --	150 81 69	208 82 126	228 78 150	263 75 188	286 75 211	378 75 303	432 74 358
		Credit department of Farmers' Associations	T H B	278 -- --	293 291 2	292 290 2	294 292 2	550 273 277	743 281 462	877 284 593	950 285 665
		Credit department of Fishermen's Associations (9%)	T H B	-- -- --	-- -- --	-- -- --	-- -- --	-- -- --	6 4 2	29 19 10	42 22 20
	Savings deposits-taking institutions	Postal savings system (16%)[c]	T H B	530 1 529	1,295 1 1,294	1,352 1 1,351	2,172 1 2,171	2,404 1 2,403	1,407 1 1,469	1,579 1 1,578	1,575 1 1,574

126

Central Bank of China (CBC)	Medium- and long-term trust funds-taking institutions	Investment and trust companies	T H B	— — —	1 1 —	1 1 —	6 6 —	8 8 —	28 8 20	35 8 27	52 8 44
		Life insurance companies	T H B	— 3 —	11 6 5	17 10 7	37 9 28	56 9 47	61 9 52	64 8 56	70 11 59
		Bills finance companies	T H B	— — —	— — —	— — —	— — —	1 1 —	9 3 6	14 3 11	18 3 15
	Other financial institutions	Securities finance company	T B	— —	— —	— —	— —	— —	1 —	1 —	1 —
		Specialized bank: Export-import bank	T H B	— — —	— — —	— — —	— — —	— — —	1 1 —	2 1 1	2 1 1

[a]Figures in parentheses under financial institutions are their shares of deposits as percentages of total deposits held by the deposits-taking institutions at the end of 1989. Property and casualty insurance company is not to be discussed in the text because it is not considered as a financial intermediary in the *Financial Statistical Monthly*, Economic Research Department, CBC. Its data is not available.

[b]T stands for total number of banking offices, 'H' stands for number of head offices, 'B' stands for number of branch offices.

[c]Prior to 1962, the Postal Savings System's function was conducted by the Post Offices. Prior to February 1979, Medium Business Banks were called Mutual Saving and Loans Associations.

Source: For 1962-1989 statistics, taken from Economic Research Department, CBC, *Financial Statistics Monthly*, various issues. For 1953 statistics, taken from Directorate General of Posts, *Statistical Abstract of Posts*, 1960; Research Department, Bank of Taiwan, *Finance Statistics Monthly*, January 1954, and Chang, 1957, pp. 541-552.

(iii) Strengthening the regulatory and supervisory system so that privately owned banks may be allowed to open in 1991;
(iv) Abolishing interest rate restrictions on deposits and loans.

Besides providing a more competitive financial environment by allowing *de novo* entry, more financial innovations, and completely free pricing of financial services, the newly revised Banking Law places more emphasis on banking discipline. In addition, as the first phase of the privatization of government-owned banks, the shares of government ownership in each of the three largest provincial commercial banks are expected to be reduced to 51 percent. These developments will surely enable the banking system to better meet more sophisticated demands for financial services beyond 1990.

Local branches of foreign banks: The presence of the first branch of a foreign bank in Taiwan (the Dai-Ichi Kangyo) dates back to September 1959. These banks are basically classified as banks specializing in foreign exchange and commercial banking. Their major sources of local currency funds are deposits, borrowings from the interbank call loan market and the temporary accommodation market, and swaps between foreign exchange and NT dollars. Due to their limited access to local currency, their main strengths are in export-import financing and foreign exchange lending. They also offer off-balance sheet services, including treasury operations regarding foreign exchange transactions, investment banking and private banking business. They have been active players in the short-term money markets by providing guarantees on commercial paper and on sellers' bankers' acceptances. Beginning in July 1989, the revised Banking Law has allowed the branches of foreign banks to enlarge the scope of their business to offer savings accounts, and to engage in consumer lending as well as medium- and long-term industrial loan and trust business. In addition, they are permitted to apply for licenses to operate as securities brokers, dealers, and underwriters.

Table 4.3a shows that the branches of foreign banks held between 0.86 and 3.96 percent of the total financial assets of financial institutions during the 1961-1988 period. Except for the years 1981-1985, the annual growth rate of these assets hovered between 79 and 22.6 percent (see Table 4.3b).

Medium business banks and credit cooperatives: In addition to locally incorporated banks, medium business banks and credit cooperatives constitute another type of money deposit-taking institution. Credit cooperatives consist of credit cooperative associations, credit departments of farmers' associations, and credit departments of fishermen's associations. The banking outlets of these financial institutions are located not only in small towns and rural areas throughout the island, but also in cities due to the urbanization of rural areas.

The medium business banks evolved from mutual savings and loan

TABLE 4.3 Growth Rate and Relative Percentage Share of Financial Assets of Financial Institutions[a]

	1961-1965	1966-1970	1971-1975	1976-1980	1981-1985	1986-1988
(a) Average of annual percentage share of total financial assets (%)						
Central Bank of China	23.90	23.29	22.61	20.58	20.65	27.15
Commercial banks, locally incorporated[b]	56.68	55.34	52.66	52.91	45.86	40.62
Branch offices of foreign banks in Taipei	0.86	1.73	3.93	3.96	3.48	2.38
Medium business banks (mutual savings & loan companies)	3.16	3.43	2.37	2.69	3.88	4.25
Credit cooperative associations	6.82	6.48	5.87	5.35	6.23	5.60
Credit department of farmers' & fishermen's associations	5.62	4.60	3.19	3.51	5.30	4.98
Investment & trust companies[c]	1.33	1.28	3.54	3.69	3.36	1.98
The postal savings system	1.35	2.90	4.91	6.37	9.74	11.00
Life insurance companies	0.65	0.95	0.93	0.94	1.50	2.04
Annual average of total financial assets (unit: NT$ million)	53,437	131,177	451,670	1,530,167	3,536,901	7,790,687

(continues)

TABLE 4.3 (continued)

	1961-1965	1966-1970	1971-1975	1976-1980	1981-1985	1986-1988
(b) Average of annual rate of increase in financial assets (%)						
Central Bank of China	35.07	16.73	39.50	20.00	18.84	34.49
Commercial banks, locally incorporated[b]	19.09	18.42	44.73	26.13	14.27	20.53
Branch offices of foreign banks in Taipei	79.65	42.55	84.08	26.20	4.75	22.60
Medium business banks (mutual savings & loan companies)	44.55	17.84	25.88	44.23	27.17	27.08
Credit cooperative associations	32.99	14.58	39.82	29.14	20.92	22.90
Credit department of farmers' & fishermen's associations	41.85	8.58	34.42	39.97	27.19	17.01
Investment & trust companies[c]	46.12	5.91	120.88	27.33	13.78	12.61
The postal savings system	124.38	66.57	45.68	36.42	32.03	18.55
Life insurance companies	207.19	20.80	41.77	35.70	31.30	35.56

[a]There are elements of double counting in this table. For example, before 1982 savings deposits collected by the postal savings system were redeposited with the Central Bank, which, in turn, used these redeposits as source of funds for its medium- and long-term lending to commercial banks.

[b]Commercial Banks locally incorporated as of the end of 1988, consistent of the Bank of Taiwan, the International Commercial Bank of China, the Bank of Communications, the Farmers' Bank of China, the Central Trust of China, the Land Bank of Taiwan, the Cooperative Bank of Taiwan, the City Bank of Taipei, First Commercial Bank, Hua Nan Commercial Bank Limited, the Chang Hua Commercial Bank, the Overseas Chinese Commercial Banking Corporation, the Shanghai Commercial and Savings Bank Limited, United World Chinese Commercial Bank, the Import-Export Bank of China and the City Bank of Kaohsiung.

[c]As of December 1988, financial assets of investment and trust companies included trust funds accepted by the Bank of Taiwan, the Central Trust of China and United World Chinese Commercial Bank.

Source: Economic Research Department, the Central Bank of China, *Financial Statistics Monthly*, Taiwan District, ROC.

companies when they were transformed into banks in 1976. During the period of 1986-1988, their assets accounted for 4.25 percent of the total financial assets of financial institutions (see Table 4.3a).

Credit cooperatives are financial intermediaries based on the support of members in the form of funds. Anyone can become a member of a credit cooperative association, but only farmers or fishermen can become members of their respective professional associations. Compared to other financial institutions, credit cooperatives have enjoyed the advantage of a 5 percent business tax exemption on their net income.

In 1986-1988, credit cooperatives, including both credit cooperative associations and credit departments of farmers' and of fishermen's associations, accounted for 10.58 percent of total financial assets (see Table 4.3a).

It is important to note that there have been only eleven failures in the credit cooperative associations and four failures in the credit departments of farmers' associations during the past forty years in Taiwan. The main reason for so few failures is that their surplus funds are allowed to be redeposited with the Cooperative Bank of Taiwan. The loans to deposits ratio in the case of credit cooperative associations decreased from 66.21 percent in 1966-1970 to 50.52 percent in 1986-1988. In addition, this ratio for the credit departments of farmers' associations decreased from 80.99 percent in 1966-1970 to 46.24 percent in 1986-1988. Except for extending low-risk loans, the credit cooperatives and farmers' associations have preferred to redeposit the passbook savings deposits they received with the Cooperative Bank of Taiwan in the form of time deposits. In this way, they could not only enjoy a high rate of return from a spread of about 3 or 4 percent per annum between these two kinds of deposit rates, but also could effectively avoid the possible interest rate risks should the economy take an abrupt turn.

Savings bank and the postal savings system: At present, there is no independent savings bank in Taiwan. However, as savings deposits constitute a main source of funds, commercial banks have established savings departments to receive time and savings deposits and to extend medium- and long-term loans. Furthermore, the postal savings system is an institution that specializes in accepting savings deposits. Its branches have accepted savings and time deposits from the general public in return for paying the interest rates set by the commercial banks. They are not allowed to extend loans. However, they enjoy a handsome interest rate premium above the cost rate when their deposits are redeposited with the Central Bank or other specialized banks. Table 4.3 shows that between 1961 and 1988, the share of the postal savings system as a percentage of total financial assets of financial institutions increased from 1.35 percent to 11 percent, although their annual growth rate decreased from 124 percent to 18.55 percent.

Investment and trust companies: At the end of 1989, there were eight such companies with forty-four branches, of which only the China Development Corporation was not authorized to accept trust funds. These companies are, however, quite unique in that they have seldom engaged in the management of trust funds on their clients' behalf; instead, they offer trust certificates with a minimum maturity of one month, guaranteeing a yield at a premium above the deposit rates of similar maturities offered by commercial banks. They assume the risks and responsibilities of managing funds received from such certificates. Their scope of business includes making both portfolio and direct investments, and extending consumer and business loans of various maturity lengths, but they are prohibited from making investments in unlisted stocks and in real estate other than for their own business use.

Tables 4.3a and 4.3b show that the investment and trust companies accounted for about 1.28-3.69 percent of the total assets of financial institutions, and their annual growth rate, with the exception of the years 1966-1970, was between 12 and 120 percent.

Life insurance companies: At the end of 1989, there were eleven life insurance companies, of which nine were locally incorporated and two owned by foreign companies. Table 4.3a shows that in 1961 and 1988 they held only 0.65 and 2.04 percent, respectively, of the financial assets of total financial institutions but that their annual growth rate ranged from 207 to 35 percent. Since August 1990, three to six new branches of U.S. life insurance companies may be established in Taiwan each year.

Bill financing companies: There are three such companies in Taiwan, and they are the only authorized dealers, underwriters, and brokers in the short-term money market.

Securities financing company: At the end of 1989, there was only one company authorized to extend securities financing according to the marginal requirement provisions.

In the United States and Japan, due to the increasing competition between the banking and securities industries, the barriers between these two industries have become increasingly blurred. In early 1991, there seems to be a consensus among monetary authorities and financial experts in the United States and Japan that banks should be permitted to operate securities and trust banking business.[1]

In the Republic of China on Taiwan, the problem of lifting barriers between the banking and securities industries has not become an issue of great concern since major banks already have securities powers. These include:

(i) The trust department of the bank may operate trust business and, especially beginning in April 1988, work as a securities broker, dealer, or underwriter.

(ii) Since October 1990, the licensed trust departments of banks and large securities companies with a paid-up capital equal to NT$2 billion or more have been permitted to provide financing to investors for the purchase of shares on the margin accounts.
(iii) According to Article 83 of the Banking Law, the savings departments of banks are permitted to invest in listed stocks up to 10 percent of the aggregate amount of the total balance of its deposits and debentures. However, investment in the stocks of any listed company cannot exceed 5 percent of the company's total capital.
(iv) According to the revised Banking Law of 1989, the MOF may grant the trust departments of banks permission to engage in other kinds of securities business, as deemed necessary.

Evidently, the revised Banking Law has advanced the institutional environment to encourage the development of local banks into a limited universal banking system.

2. Interest Rate Policy, Control over the Money Supply, and Price Stabilization Policy in Taiwan: 1950-1989

Over the past four decades, the monetary policy in Taiwan has been characterized by the achievement of economic development with price stability. Contrary to Lundberg's (1979, p. 271) assertion that there appeared to be no clear relation between the rate of growth of narrow money supply (M_1) and the rate of inflation in Taiwan in 1952-1976, I will show that there was a close relationship between these two variables. The narrow money supply has appeared to be a critical policy indicator and has received constant attention from the Central Bank of China on Taiwan. Furthermore, the high nominal interest rate (positive real interest rate) policy has served as an important policy instrument in enhancing monetary savings. I will discuss these policies in turn below.

The Roles of the Preferential Interest Rate Deposit
(PIRD) Scheme and Base Money in Combating
Inflation and Enhancing Savings: 1949-1953

During the late 1940s, the continued influx of civilian and military personnel from Mainland China into Taiwan precipitated a rapid increase in the money supply which led to rampant inflation. The extremely excessive demand for goods and their corresponding shortage then caused prices to increase by an average of 1,400 percent per annum. Interest rates in the curb money market moved upwards in response to changes in prices, and the average annual interest rate charged by private moneylenders in 1947-

1949 was 206 percent (Liu 1970, p. 100). However, the interest rates offered by the government-owned commercial banks remained at a relatively low level. For example, at the end of 1949, the interest rate on one-year deposits posted by the Bank of Taiwan was 18 percent per annum. Households consequently lost confidence in banks as places to entrust their savings. Instead, they raised the specter of capital flight, whether in the form of cash, precious metals, foreign exchange, or goods. The economy was under a severe threat of collapse.

One of the government's top priorities was thus to try to bring the hyperinflation under control. Monetary policy subsequently sought to combat inflation in two key areas. The first was to promote saving. Based on the recommendations of a group of scholars led by Tsiang, a Preferential Interest Rate Deposits scheme (hereafter referred to as the PIRD scheme) was initiated in March 1950 in order to encourage the public to deposit their savings into the banking system. The one-month PIRD paid an interest rate of 7 percent per month, which, when compounded, was equivalent to 125 percent per annum. This approximated the curb market interest rates at that time and also during the period that immediately followed.

The second area in which monetary policy sought to overcome the problem of inflation was that of currency reform and controlling the money stock. This reform was promulgated in June 1949 in order to restore the public's confidence in the currency, with the result that the old Taiwan dollar was replaced by the New Taiwan dollar as the new currency unit. In addition, and perhaps even more important, ceilings were imposed on the maximum amount of currency that could be issued. These ceilings were adjusted from time to time in order to meet transaction needs. It was through the combined effects of the above measures that, by the end of 1957 when the PIRD scheme was phased out, public confidence in the currency and banking system was fully restored.

As the high interest rate policy was quite unique in those days, the relationship between the PIRD scheme and price stability has been a subject of considerable interest to many economists who have studied monetary policy in Taiwan (Tsiang 1989, Ch. 5; Kohsaka 1984; and Lundberg 1979). However, while Tsiang emphasized the importance of the PIRD scheme in curbing expansion in the money supply and encouraging savings, Lundberg argued that "to what extent such a policy effectively contributed to the dampening of demand and the increase in monetary savings is an open question" (1979, p. 292). These two findings seem to be contradictory. Since the policy implication of the PIRD scheme has had a long-lasting effect on the shaping of monetary policy in Taiwan over the past four decades, this issue deserves careful reexamination.

Since money stock was closely related to the price level in Taiwan during the period from 1946 to 1951 as shown in Figure 4.1, this sub-section

FIGURE 4.1 Money and Price, 1946-1951
(Log-linear form)

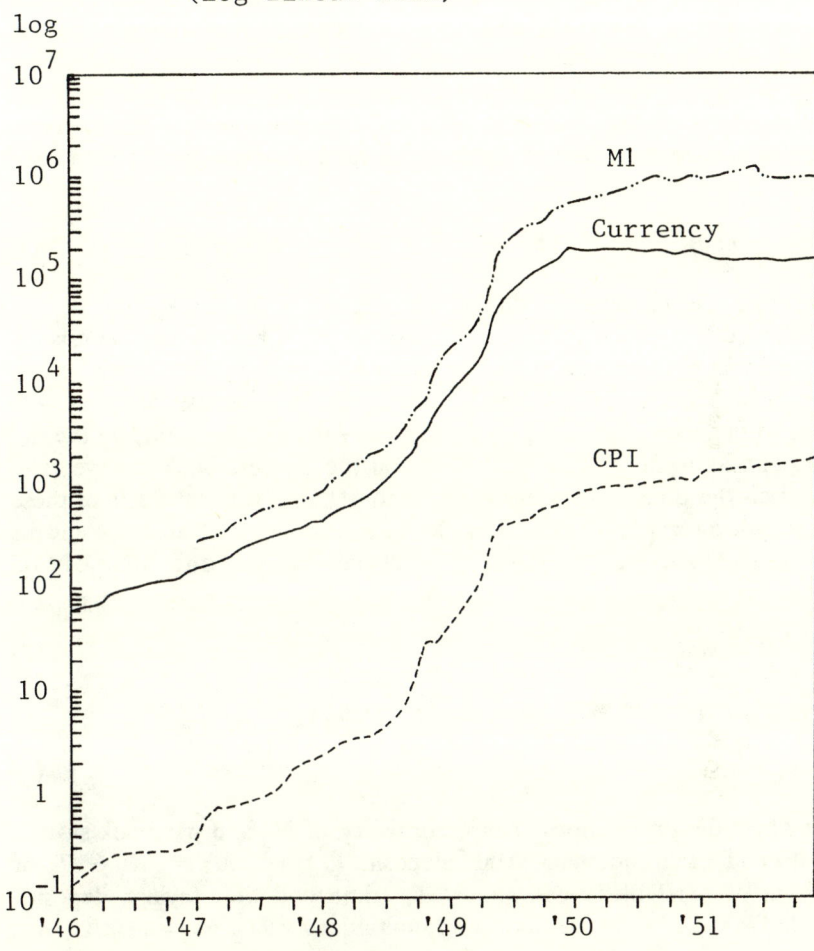

Note: units: NT$1,000
CPI = 100/40,000, first half of 1937

Source: Lin and Wu (1989 p. 919). Reprinted with permission from the Institute of Economics, Academia Sinica, Taipei, Taiwan.

develops an analytical money supply framework to quantitatively assess the roles of the PIRD scheme, control of money stock and other policy measures in enhancing savings and curbing inflation from 1949 to 1953.

Narrow money stock M_1 consists of currency in circulation, checking accounts, and passbook demand deposits -- M_1 is also referred to as $M1A$; narrow money stock $M1B$ consists of $M1A$ and passbook savings deposits; broad money stock M_2 consists of $M1B$ and time and time-savings deposits. For ease of exposition, let us assume that money stocks can be expressed as follows:

$$M_1 = m_1 B \tag{1}$$

where m_1 is the monetary multiplier for M_1, $m_1 = M_1/B$; M_1 and m_1 are also referred to as $M1A$ and m_{1A} respectively. B is base money, consisting of currency in circulation and total reserves against deposits. Multiplier m_1 (or m_{1A}) depends on both the public's and bank's allocative behavior with respect to financial assets, i.e., on the currency to $M1A$ ratio (c), on the demand deposits to $M1A$ ratio ($d = 1-c$), on the average bank reserve ratio (k), and on the time and savings deposits to $M1A$ ratio (t). Effects of these components on m_1 in 1943-1953 could be inferred from Table 4.4 and its footnote a. However, for simplicity, I will only focus on the effect of t on m_1 below.

$$M1B = m_{1B} B, \tag{2}$$

where m_{1B} is the monetary multiplier for $M1B$, $m_{1B} = M1B/B$.

$$M_2 = m_2 B, \tag{3}$$

where M_2 is the broad money stock, consisting of M_1 and passbook savings deposits and time and time-savings deposits (T), i.e., $M_2 = M_1 + T$, or consisting of $M1B$ plus quasi-money T_b (time and time-savings deposit), $M_2 = M1B + T_b$, m_2 is the monetary multiplier for M_2, $m_2 = M_2/B$.

$$m_2 = m_1(1+t), \text{ where } t = T/M_1 \tag{4}$$

$$m_2 = m_{1B}(1+t_b), \text{ where } t_b = T_b/M_{1B} \tag{5}$$

$$M_2/M_1 = 1+t \tag{6}$$

$$M_2/M_{1B} = 1 + t_b \tag{7}$$

The rate of change forms of equations (1), (2) and (3) are respectively as follows:

TABLE 4.4 Components of Money Supply Functions 1949-1953[a]
(unit: NT$ million)

	Currency in circulation C Amount (1)	Growth rate (%)	Narrow money stock M1A Amount (2)	Growth rate (%)	Time and time-savings deposits T Amount (3)	Growth rate (%)	Time deposits to M1A ratio $t=T/M1A$ (4)=(3)/(2)
1949	192	--	293	130	6(0)[b]	--	0.02
1950	365	90	584	99	26(19)	333	0.04
1951	559	53	940	63	161(158)	519	0.17
1952	762	36	1,336	42	446(436)	177	0.33
1953	918	20	1,683	26	579(565)	30	0.34
Annual average 1950-53	651		1,136		303 (295)		0.22

	Broad money stock M2 Amount (5)=(2)+(3)	Growth rate (%)	Total reserves against deposits R Amount (6)	Base money B Amount (7)=(1)+(6)	Growth rate (%)	Money multiplier m_{1A} =M1A/B (8)	m_2 =M2/B (9)
1949	299	--	13	205	--	1.43	1.46
1950	610	104	40	405	98	1.44	1.50
1951	1,101	80	129	688	70	1.36	1.60
1952	1,782	62	221	983	43	1.34	1.81
1953	2,262	27	188	1,106	13	1.58	2.04
Annual average 1950-53	1,439		135	796		1.43	1.74

[a]Money supply functions: (i) $M1A = m_{1A}B$, where $M1A = C+D$, $m_{1A} = (C+D)/B = 1/[c + k(1-c+t)]$, $c = C/M1A$, $k = R/(D+T)$, $(1-c) = D/M1A$, $t = T/M1A$; (ii) $M2 = mB$, where $M2 = M1A+T$, $m_2 = M2/B = (1+t)m_{1A}$; M1A: Narrow money supply; M2: Broad money supply; B: Base money.

[b]Figures in parentheses are balances of the preferential interest rate time deposits. There was no passbook savings account in 1949-1953.

Sources: (i) Columns (1) and (2) of the table are drawn from Liu, 1970, pp. 165, 168); (ii) column (3) from *Taiwan Financial Statistics Monthly*, 1954, p. 10; (iii) column (6), 1949-1951 figures, vault cash (VC) from *TFSM*, 1954, p. 4. Reserve deposits (RD) from *Taiwan Financial Statistical Annual Report*, 1954, p. 22, where TR = VC + RD. Figures for 1952-1953, from Liu, 1970, pp. 165, 169.

$$\dot{M}1A = \dot{m}_{1A} + \dot{B} + (\dot{m}_{1A})(\dot{B}) \qquad (8)$$

$$\dot{M}1B = \dot{m}_{1B} + \dot{B} + (\dot{m}_{1B})(\dot{B}) \qquad (9)$$

$$\dot{M}_2 = \dot{M}_2 + \dot{m}_2 + (\dot{m}_2)(\dot{B}) \qquad (10)$$

As m_1 (or m_{1A}) is a negative function of t (see footnote a of Table 4.4) and m_2 is a positive function of t (see equation (4)), this simple multiplier approach is useful in giving insights into the role of the PIRD scheme in mobilizing financial savings into the banking system. Also, it can be used to explain the role of measures to control the money stock, such as ceilings imposed on the currency issues, in tackling the rampant inflation.

To examine the role of the PIRD scheme in enhancing monetary savings, it can be seen from Figure 4.2, for example, that monthly changes in the balances of PIRD were positively correlated with levels of the Preferential Interest Rates (hereafter called PIR) and negatively correlated with monthly rates of inflation. Firstly, with a one-month PIR of 7 percent (compounded to 123 percent per annum) between March and June 1950, the monthly rate of increase in PIRD balances remained positive and the monthly rate of inflation decreased to −10 percent in June 1950.

Secondly, this decline in the rate of inflation induced the government to cut the one-month PIR by half to 3.5 percent (or 52 percent per annum) on July 1, 1950 and to even 3.0 percent (or 44 percent per annum) on October 1, 1950. As a result, between July 1950 and January 1951, due to the lowered PIR together with an average rate of inflation of about 8.25 percent per month, the monthly balances of PIRD declined.

Subsequently, in order to enhance savings and curb inflation, the one-month PIR was raised to 4.2 percent (or 64 percent per annum) on March 26, 1951, and with the exception of seasonal decline in December 1951 and December 1952, monthly balances of PIRD continued to increase.

Furthermore, in order to explore the role of the PIRD scheme in enhancing savings more concretely, we may look into the effect of PIRD on M_2. Prior to the adoption of the PIRD scheme, the average annual interest rate charged by private money market lenders between 1947 and 1949 was 206 percent. At that time, the ratio of time and savings deposits to money stock (the t ratio, where $t = T/M_1$) was only 2 percent, and the curb money market was the only major conduit for channelling savings into productive uses. After the adoption of the PIRD scheme, between 1949 and 1953, the t ratio increased from 2 percent to 34 percent (see Table 4.4, column (4)). This also resulted in an increase in the broad money multiplier m_2 from 1.46 to 2.04, or a 40 percent increase. Between 1949 and 1953, although the narrow money supply still dominated the behavior of the broad money supply, monetary stability was greatly improved by the in-

139

FIGURE 4.2 Monthly Rate of Changes in Balance of the Preferential Interest Rates Deposit (PIRD) and in Price Level, and the Level of the Annualized One-Month Preferential Interest Rates (PIR)

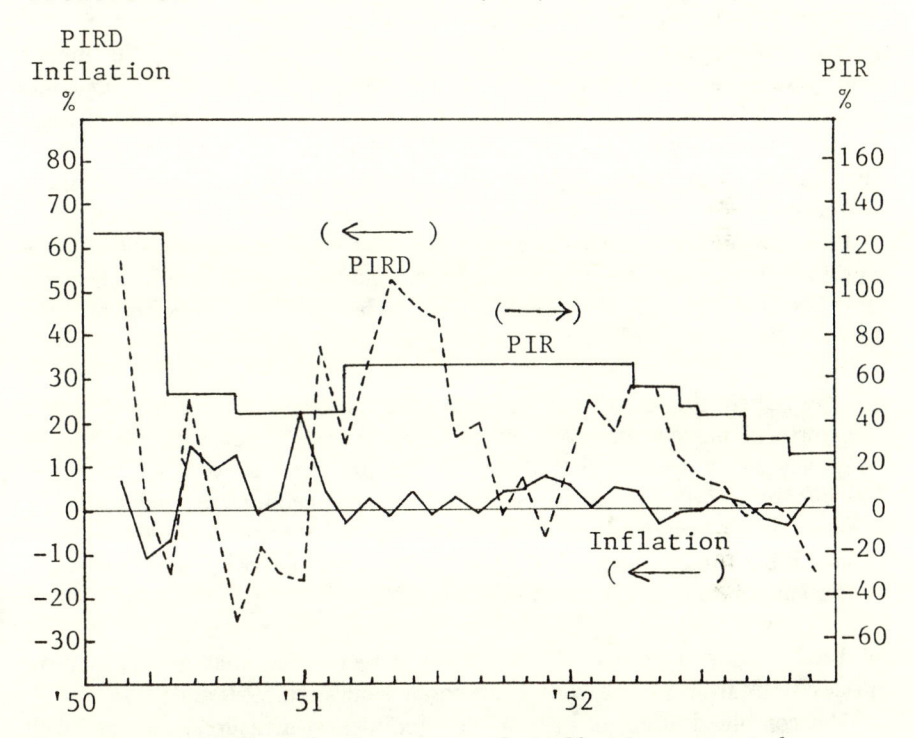

Sources: PIRD and the rate of inflation are taken from Hsu, 1989, p. 120. The PIR is taken from Taiwan Financial Statistics Monthly.

creased time and savings deposits of the banking system, as evidenced by an increase in the ratio of M_2 to M_1 (equation (6)) from 1.02 to 1.34. As capital was a scarce resource during that period of time, the increase in financial savings in the banking system allowed the banks to effectively channel funds into productive uses. The PIRD scheme served as a catalyst in making the financial system more efficient and laid the foundation for a stable economy conducive to further economic growth.[2]

Since the narrow money supply constituted the major portion of the broad money supply, we may explore roles of PIRD and other monetary measures in curbing the narrow money stock and combating inflation. The narrow money stock can be decomposed into two parts, i.e., the money multiplier m_1 and the base money, on the assumption that the former could be affected by the Preferential Interest Rates and the latter mainly affected by other monetary measures. Table 4.4 shows that between 1949 and 1953, the narrow money stock M_1 increased by 474 percent, its money multiplier increased by 10.5 percent and base money increased by 439.5 percent.

It is obvious that the behavior of the narrow money stock during that period was overwhelmingly affected by the increase in the base money, and only slightly affected by its multiplier. The PIRD scheme might have effectively

> ... halted the growth of the multiplier, lessening its effect on the growth of narrow money; however, contractive measures on the base money stock were most likely the major force in controlling the rampant growth of narrow money. Both the ceiling imposed on the maximum amount of currency issued and the contraction effect of absorbing funds into the U.S. Aid's counterpart deposits helped lower the annual growth rate... (Lundberg, 1979)

of base money from 98 percent to 13 percent, and that of the narrow money stock from 910 percent to 20 percent between 1950 and 1953.

The combined effect of base money contraction measures, together with the introduction of the PIRD scheme in enhancing savings, effectively restrained excess demand for goods and generated a deflationary impact on the price level. The inflation rate decreased from 197 percent in 1950 to 9.7 percent in 1953.

The effectiveness of the PIRD scheme and the money control measures in the early 1950s implied certain policy choices for price stability in the 1960s, 1970s, and 1980s. When there has been inflation or inflationary expectation, the Central Bank has exhibited a penchant for using a mix of high interest rates and restrictive control over the supply of money to combat inflation and encourage savings. When there is no inflationary pressure, positive real interest rates alone have been used as the principal policy indicator to ensure a smooth flow of savings into the banking system through a steady increase in the t ratio. These policy implications will be discussed in detail below.

The Role of Monetary Policy in the Pursuit of Price Stability: 1960s-1980s

It is interesting to note that between 1960 and 1972, the money supply (*M1A*) grew on average by 20 percent per annum and real GNP by 10 percent, whereas the price level only increased by an average of 2 percent per annum. This seems to contradict the simple concept that the growth rate of the money supply should be roughly equal to the sum of the rate of economic growth and the rate of inflation. Furthermore, a similar paradox existed between 1985 and 1986, in which the narrow money supply *M1B* grew by an average of 36 percent, but with an inflation rate of almost zero (see Figure 4.3). What explains the coexistence of the high growth rate of the money supply and the low rate of inflation?

In a small, open economy like Taiwan's, the inflation rate is affected by many factors such as (1) the interaction of demand for and supply of money; (2) the growth of production and productivity; (3) the effects of foreign commodity prices, especially oil, and the exchange rate through their impacts on import prices; and (4) the balance of payments, fiscal policy, and interest rate policy. In order to give an efficient description of the effects of these factors on prices, let us work on a reduced form of a money stock equation.

Money Stock, Demand for Money, Import Price, Interest Rates, and Their Effects on Prices. Based on a quantity theory of money model for a small open economy (Chen and Chen 1989; P. Chiu 1989), I used quarterly data (reflecting the rate of changes from the same quarters in the previous years) to estimate a price equation for the period between the first quarter of 1967 and the last quarter of 1989 as follows:[3]

$$\dot{p} = 3.449 + 0.194(\dot{q}-\dot{M}) + 0.339\dot{M} - 0.244\dot{y} + 0.085\dot{i} \qquad (11)$$
$$\phantom{\dot{p} = }(1.67) \quad (4.22) \qquad\quad (4.65) \quad\;\; (-1.76) \quad\; (3.98)$$

$$\bar{R}^2 = 0.867, \; SEE = 2.824, \; Rao = 0.787, \; D.W. = 1.52$$

where $\dot{p}$ = rate of change in the GNP deflator; $\dot{q}$ = rate of change in import prices; $\dot{M}$ = rate of change in the money supply *M1B*; $\dot{y}$ = rate of change in the real GDP, also representing changes in production and productivity; $\dot{i}$ = rate of change in the interest rate on a one-month time deposit; and figures in parentheses represent t statistics.

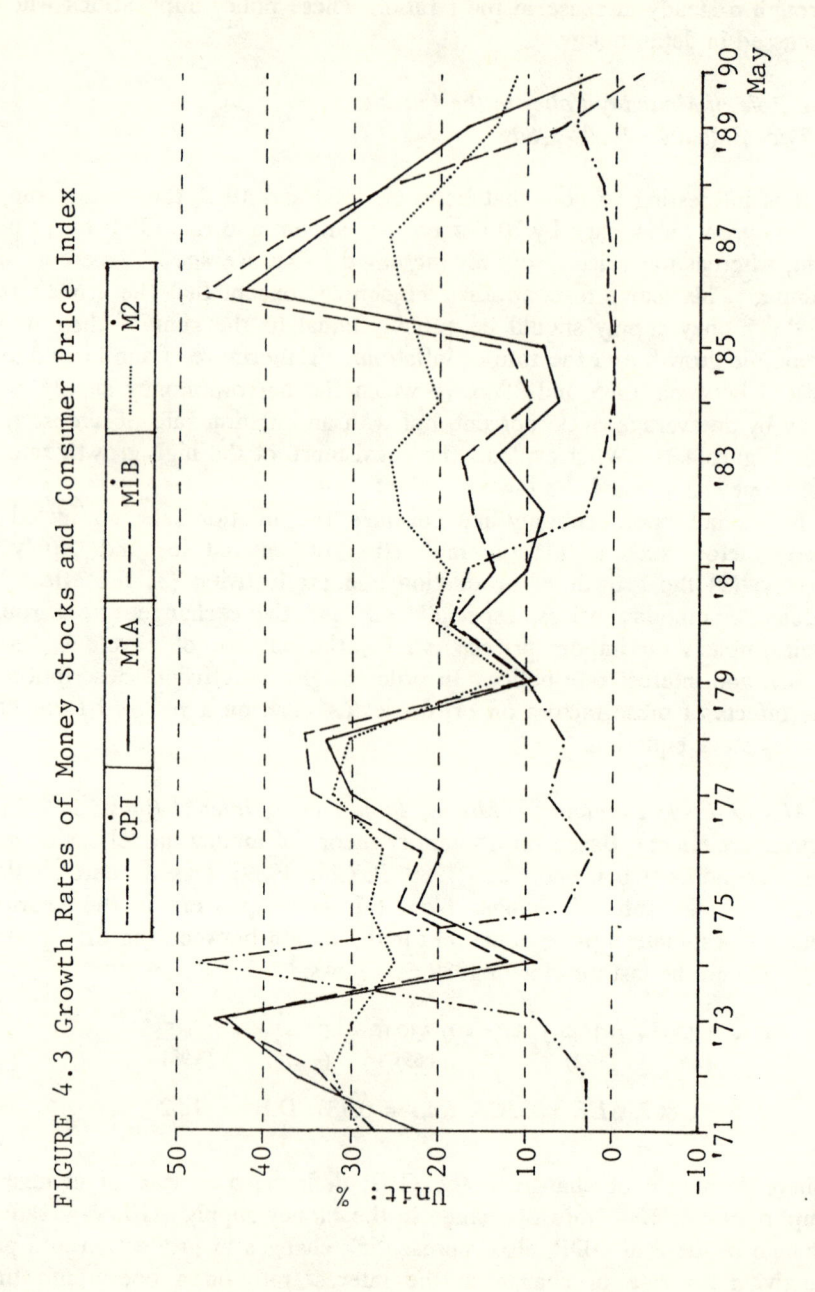

FIGURE 4.3 Growth Rates of Money Stocks and Consumer Price Index

The effects of the money supply items in equation (7) can be combined and rewritten as:

$$\dot{p} = 3.449 + 0.194\dot{q} + 0.145\dot{M} - 0.244\dot{y} + 0.085\dot{i}. \tag{12}$$

With respect to the effect of import prices ($\dot{q}$) on the general price level, equation (12) implies that a 1 percent increase in import prices will result in a 0.194 percent increase in the price level. Import prices are mainly affected by international commodity prices, especially oil prices, exchange rates, and import duties. One major factor offsetting the inflationary effect of the sharp increase in money supply was the decrease in import prices, which in turn was affected by the following two factors. Firstly, as a result of the internationalization and trade liberalization policies, tariff rates on 1,714 imported items were either reduced to zero or adjusted downwards in 1987. Another sweeping reduction on more than 4,700 items, or 61 percent of all items subject to tariffs, resulted in a further average tariff reduction of 23 percent in 1989. The net effective tariff rate was reduced from 11.7 percent in 1974 to 7.9 percent in 1985 and to 5.9 percent in 1990. It is expected that the rate will fall further in the future in order to conform with the rates in OECD countries. Secondly, the appreciation by nearly 50 percent of the new Taiwan dollar against the U.S. dollar between 1985 and 1988, together with the declining oil prices in the late 1980s, greatly helped to pull down import costs, contributing to price stability.

Furthermore, as regards the income effect ($\dot{y}$) and the money supply effect ($\dot{M}$) on the price level in equation (12), let us first digress slightly to a simple quantity theory of money. The traditional form of its equation of exchange is:

$$MV = Py \tag{13}$$

where V is the income velocity, M is money stock, P is price and y is real GNP.

Next, as according to Milton Friedman's celebrated theory that the income velocity can be interpreted as a reciprocal form of the real demand for money function, the relationship between the velocity and the real demand for money function may be written as follows:

$$V^{-1} = (M/P)^d / y = y^a i^{-b} \tag{14}$$

where the real demand for money function is $(M/P)^d = y^{(1+a)} i^{-b}$, $(1+a)$ is the income elasticity of the real demand for money and $(-b)$ is the interest rate elasticity of the real demand for money.

Then, by substituting V^{-1} from equation (14) into equation (13) and rearranging the resulting terms, we obtain:

$$P = My^{-(1+a)}i^b \tag{15}$$

This expression's rate of change form is:

$$\dot{P} = \dot{M} - (1+a)\dot{y} + b\dot{i} \tag{16}$$

Equation (16) implies that an increase in M and i has a positive impact on P and an increase in y has a negative impact. It is thus a prototype of equation (12).

In the real world, an empirical study by Shih (1988) found that in Taiwan, from the last quarter of 1968 to the last quarter of 1987, the long-run real GNP elasticity of the real demand for money, i.e., $(1+a)$ in equation (16), was 1.65. Interestingly, our equation (12) also implies the same long-run interest elasticity of demand for money. This can be seen from the ratio of the regression coefficient for y to that for M, i.e., 0.244/0.145 = 1.68. To see how this elasticity is used to interpret price changes in the real world, let us consider the above-mentioned stable growth period from 1960 to 1972. Since the average growth rate of real GNP was 10 percent per annum, the transactions demand for money was therefore 16.5 percent per annum, this being the product of the long-term elasticity and the real GNP growth rate. Therefore, if the nominal money supply grew by 16.5 percent per annum, it would satisfy the 16.5 percent growth rate of the demand for money, and other things being equal, the price would not change. This result is confirmed by equation (12), in which the effect of $\dot{M}$ ($\dot{M}$ = 16.5 percent) on price would be nullified by the effect of $\dot{y}$ ($\dot{y}$ = 10 percent). The actual average growth rate of the money supply during that period was 20 percent per annum, higher than that implied by the non-inflationary demand for money, and therefore resulted in a 2 percent annual rate of inflation. The high income elasticity of the demand for money was mainly due to the need for money to facilitate increasingly international trade activities and other monetization processes. It is also noteworthy that from 1985 to 1986, due to the impact of the huge trade surplus and the influx of short-term private capital, foreign exchange reserves continued to increase, and as a result, $M1B$ grew by an average of 36 percent each year. However, due to the high income velocity of demand for money, decreases in import prices and the high interest rate policy, the WPI decreased by an average of 2.7 percent and the CPI increased by less than 1 percent.

Equation (12) also reveals that in the long run there exists a positive procyclical relationship between interest rate changes and price changes. A 1 percent rise in the interest rate has been associated with a 0.085 percent increase in the price level. One should not assume, however, that the interest rate could only have procyclical movement with price changes. In fact, during the boom period, the price dampening effect of the interest rate through the money stock was predominantly countercyclical. In other words, interest rates affect prices through both interest rate and money stock variables in equation (12).

A rise in the interest rate would lower inflationary pressures through its contractive impact on the narrow money stock by shifting the transaction balances (*M1A* or *M1B*) to the time and savings deposits (increasing t or t_b ratio), lowering the money multiplier (m_{1A} or m_{1B}), enhancing savings, and restraining effective demand for goods and services, thus lowering the rate of inflation. In the year preceding the oil crisis in 1973-1974, the growth rate in the money supply (*M1B*) jumped from about 37 to about 49 percent per annum, while the average economic growth rate was 13 percent per annum. The excess demand created by the expanded supply of money together with the increase in the oil price in 1973 resulted in an WPI inflation rate of 22.86 percent during that year. The mounting inflationary pressures in 1973 prompted the Central Bank to raise the interest rate on one-year deposits several times, first to 9.5 percent on July 26, 1973, and finally to 15 percent on January 27, 1974. As a result, the t ratio increased from 149 percent in 1973 to 190 percent in 1974 (see Table 4.5a). Since the money multiplier m_{1A} is a negative function of time deposit ratio t, this induced a dampening effect on *M1A*, which only grew by 7 percent in 1974. This increase in *M1A* could be ascribed to an increase in base money by 24.77 percent, a decrease of m_{1A} by 20.05 percent, and their cross product term during 1990 (see equation (8)). However, the tight monetary policy had little effect on the availability of total funds; M_2 increased by 24 percent in 1974. Finally, although the WPI increased by 40.58 percent in 1974, it decreased by 5 percent in 1975, and the CPI increased by 5 percent in 1975 (see Table 4.5a).

Furthermore, the CBC has changed its intermediate monetary policy indicator to *M1B* from *M1A* since June 1982. The CBC adopted contractive measures in April 1989 in order to restrain the high growth rate of narrow money supply. High interest rates generated a tightening effect on money supply (*M1B*) again in 1989 and 1990. The interest rate on one-year time and savings deposits increased from 5.25 percent per annum in 1988 to 9.5 percent per annum in 1989. The rising interest rates prompted a massive shift of funds from low-interest-rate passbook deposits to high-interest-rate time deposits. The t_b ratio rose from 152 percent in 1988 to 174 percent in 1989 and to 222 percent in 1990 (see Table 4.5b). As a result, *M1B* decreased at an annual rate of 6.62 percent in 1990, which, according to equation (9), could be accounted by a decrease of its money multiplier by 6.81 percent and by an increase of base money by 0.61 percent in 1990. By contrast M_2 increased by an annual rate of 9.8 percent in 1990.

TABLE 4.5a Money Supply, Savings and Time Deposits and Prices 1960-1982 (unit: NT$ million, %)

Year	Money supply M1A Amount (1)	Changes % p.a. (2)	Quasi money T[b] (3)	(3)/(1)×100% t ratio (4)	Interest rate on one-year time deposits (% p.a.)[c] (5)	Price changes WPI % p.a.	Price changes CPI % p.a. (6)
1960	6,757	8.09	5,705	84	18.43	14.14	18.44
1961	7,699	13.94	9,019	117	14.40	3.22	7.83
1962	8,086	5.03	10,955	135	13.32	3.03	2.34
1963	10,355	28.06	14,488	140	12.00	6.48	2.24
1964	13,979	35.00	18,362	131	10.80	2.48	-0.20
1965	16,194	15.85	21,156	131	10.80	-4.66	-0.08
1966	16,814	3.83	25,240	150	10.08	1.49	1.99
1967	23,637	40.58	31,238	132	9.72	2.53	3.35
1968	25,907	9.60	35,799	138	9.72	2.96	6.53
1969	28,772	11.06	46,296	160	9.72	-0.27	6.42
1970	32,035	11.34	60,553	189	9.72	2.73	3.58
1971	39,980	24.80	79,351	198	9.25	0.03	2.83
1972	55,126	37.88	102,986	187	8.75	4.45	3.01
1973	82,310	49.31	122,847	149	11.00	22.86	8.17
1974	88,079	7.01	167,905	190	13.50	40.58	47.47
1975	111,780	26.91	215,931	193	12.00	-5.08	5.24
1976	137,560	23.06	275,479	200	10.75	2.76	2.50
1977	177,575	29.09	367,638	207	9.50	2.76	7.04
1978	238,079	34.07	476,052	199	9.50	3.54	5.77
1979	254,703	6.98	527,582	207	12.50	13.82	9.75
1980	305,444	19.92	648,169	212	12.50	21.54	19.01
1981	339,465	11.14	791,936	233	13.00	7.62	16.34
1982	366,925	8.09	1,038,363	282	9.00	-0.18	2.96

TABLE 4.5b Money Supply, Savings and Time Deposits and Changes in Wholesale Prices and Consumer Prices 1982-1990 (unit: NT$ million, %)

Year	Money supply (M1B)[a] Amount (1)	Money supply (M1B)[a] Changes % p.a. (2)	Quasi Money Tb[b] (Time and time-savings deposits) (3)	(3)/(1)×100% t_b ratio (4)	Interest rate on one-year time deposits (% p.a.)[c] (5)	Price changes WPI % p.a.	Price changes CPI % p.a. (6)
1982	517,480	16.43	888,709	171.7	9.00	-0.18	2.96
1983	612,902	17.57	1,164,706	190.0	8.50	-1.19	1.35
1984	669,619	9.44	1,464,601	218.7	8.00	0.48	-0.02
1985	751,469	11.85	1,881,673	250.4	7.75	-2.60	-0.17
1986	1,137,863	47.36	2,160,999	190.0	5.00	-3.34	0.70
1987	1,568,225	37.66	2,606,796	166.2	5.00	-3.25	0.52
1988	1,950,472	25.05	1,970,331	152.3	5.25	-1.56	1.28
1989	2,068,759	6.41	3,603,182	174.2	9.50	-0.38	4.41
1990	1,931,897	-6.62	4,298,072	222.4	9.50	3.20	3.14

[a]$M1B$ is defined as $M1A$ plus pass book savings deposits, i.e., the sum of currency in circulation, checking account, passbook demand deposits and passbook savings deposits. Its rate of change is computed from seasonally adjusted figures for the current month (December) and compared with an annual average centered on the same month last year.

[b]Quasi money T: in Table 4.5a consists of passbook savings deposits, time deposits and time-savings deposits, whereas quasi money Tb: in Table 4.5b consists of only time deposits and time-savings deposits, $t_b = Tb/M1B$.

[c]Year-end figures.

Source: *Taiwan Financial Statistics Monthly*, The Central Bank of China, and *Monthly Statistics of the Republic of China*, Directorate-General of Budget, Accounting and Statistics.

Taiwan's monetary experience indicates that the narrow money supply $M1B$ maintains a stronger correlation with price movements than the broad money supply M_2, while increases in M_2 are more apt to explain the increase in real GNP (see Figure 4.3, equations (d) and (g) of Table 4.9 in Section 3 below, and Table 4.14 in the Notes section). The monetary policy in 1973-1974 and in 1989-1990 therefore reflects a unique philosophy of encouraging saving and ensuring the availability of production funds to the enterprises in the midst of an attack on inflation, through keeping a high growth rate in M_2 but a low (or negative) growth rate in $M1B$.

It may be safe to say that, in general, except during the two oil crises (1973-1974 and 1979-1981) and the late 1980s, the positive real interest rate alone was adopted as the principal monetary policy indicator for pursuing financial and price stability throughout the 1960s-1980s. For example, due to the high real interest rate policy, during the periods 1961-1972 and 1975-1978, the t ratio measured by the quasi-money (T) to $M1A$ ratio increased from 117 percentage points to 199 percentage points (see Table 4.5a). Also, between 1982 and 1989, the t_b ratio measured by the quasi-money (T_b) to $M1B$ ratio increased from 171 percentage points to 174 percentage points (see Table 4.5b). And prices have remained stable during these subperiods (see Tables 4.5a, 4.5b).

Control of Base Money (Reserve Money). Besides the use of interest rates as an important monetary policy instrument, the CBC has also effectively used other domestic policy instruments to control base money in order to achieve economic stability.

Table 4.6 reveals that the long-run elasticity of $M1B$ with respect to base money was 0.9959 between the first quarter, 1970 and the last quarter, 1988, and was 0.7767 between the first quarter, 1970 and the last quarter, 1990. This implies that, for example, between 1970:QI and 1988:QIV, a 1 percent increase in base money resulted in a 1 percent increase in money supply $M1B$. Also, the long-run elasticities of $M1B$ with respect to the interest rate on one-year deposits were -0.066 and -0.1286 for 1970:QI – 1988:QIV and 1970:QI – 1990:QIV, respectively. Lower base money elasticity and higher interest rate elasticity in 1970:QI – 1990:QIV was largely due to the contractive effect of interest rates on the monetary multiplier m_{1B} in 1989-1990.

The above empirical evidence suggests that base money is a major determinant of money supply $M1B$ and is a key control variable through which the effect of monetary policy is transmitted. From the demand side, base money is defined as currency in circulation plus both the required and the excess reserves held by banks. From the supply side, base money is affected by its external components such as foreign assets held by the central bank, and its net domestic components such as balances of open market

TABLE 4.6 Regression Results for the Money Supply (M1B) Function, 1971:QI – 1990:QIV (quarterly data)[a]

Dependent variable Ln M1B[a]	Independent variables				R^2-Adj.	S.E.E.	D.W.
	Constant	Ln B	Ln B_{-1}	i	Ln M1B_{-1}			

Sample period

(a) 1971:QI – 1988:QIV	0.1635 (2.5720)	0.3767 (6.0505)	−0.2787 (−4.2069)	−0.0065 (−4.5727)	0.9017 (17.8581)	0.9993	0.0274	1.3457
(b) 1971:QI – 1990:QIV	0.2924 (4.7976)	0.3476 (4.7972)	−0.3032 (−4.1675)	−0.0074 (−4.2272)	0.9427 (18.7076)	0.9991	0.0334	1.3890

Long-run elasticities of M1B with respect to base money B and interest rates i, $\varepsilon(M1B, B)$ and $\varepsilon(M1B, i)$[b]

(c) Based on equation (a) $\varepsilon(M1B, B) = 0.9959$, $\varepsilon(M1B, i) = -0.066$

(d) Based on equation (b) $\varepsilon(M1B, B) = 0.7767$, $\varepsilon(M1B, i) = -0.1286$

[a]Figures in parentheses are t statistics. S.E.E. is standard error of regression; D.W. is Durbin-Watson statistic; Ln M_{-1} and Ln B_{-1} are natural log of one quarter lagged money supply and base money respectively.
[b]Long-run elasticities are derived from equations (a) and (b) by assuming Ln M1B = Ln M1B_{-1} and Ln B = Ln B_{-1}.

operation conducted by the central bank and rediscounts and accommodations extended to banks by the central bank.

In a small open economy like Taiwan, the behavior of base money has been dominated by changes in foreign assets, which are affected by the balance of payments situation and therefore cannot be effectively controlled by the central bank. Table 4.7a shows that over the twenty-six years between 1962 and 1987, the increase in net foreign assets has been the dominant factor affecting increases in base money, amounting to 93 percent of the increase in 1962-1970, 198 percent in 1981-1985, and 668 percent in 1986-1987. Only during 1988-1989, when net capital outflow outweighed the current account surplus, did net foreign assets show a negative contribution of 41 percent to changes in base money.

It is in this sense that the monetary instruments and institutional settings to be discussed below have been designed to sterilize the balance of payments effect on the money supply in order to promote financial stability and maintain the stability of both the internal and external value of the new Taiwan dollar.

In contrast to the net foreign assets, Table 4.7a shows that changes in net domestic assets (the net domestic factors) sterilized 98 percent of the increase in base money during 1981-1985, and 568 percent in 1986-1987, but contributed 141 percent to changes in base money during 1988-1989.

Major policy instruments affecting the changes in the net domestic assets component of base money are: (i) adjustment of rediscount rates and the management of rediscount and refinancing facilities; (ii) open-market operations; and (iii) accepting redeposits from the postal savings system.

(i) The Central Bank's rediscount and refinancing facilities. The CBC's rediscount facility is related to the traditional function of the Central Bank as the lender of last resort. However, it also provides a set of selective accommodations, such as the accommodation to imported capital goods through banks, export credit, etc. to help the country's economic development. The rediscount and refinancing facilities (the column entitled "Claims on financial institutions" in column (2) of Table 4.7b) contributed between 53 and 85 percent of the annual increase in base money in during 1962-1980 and worked as a sterilization factor between 1981-1989; they sterilized about 46 percent of the increase in base money between 1981-1985, and between 2 and 8 percent in 1986-1987 and 1988-1989.

(ii) Open-market operations. The open-market operation is one of the most important instruments through which the central banks of developed countries affect money supply and the amount of bank credit. Due to the lack of short-term financial instruments and the absence of an official money

TABLE 4.7a Factors Affecting Changes in Base (or Reserve) Money B ('+' ('–') Contributing to Increase (Decrease) in Money Base) (unit: NT $100 million or percent)

Period	Base money (B) (also called reserve money) B	% of B	Net foreign assets (NFA) NFA	% of B	Net domestic assets (NDA) NDA	% of B
1962-70	155	100.00	145	93.55	10	6.45
1971-75	546	100.00	408	74.73	138	25.27
1976-80	1,209	100.00	1,104	91.32	105	8.68
1981-85	1,969	100.00	3,909	198.53	-1,940	-98.53
1986-87	2,509	100.00	16,769	668.35	-14,260	-568.35
1988-89	4,348	100.00	-1,788	-41.12	6,136	141.12

TABLE 4.7b Factors Contributing to Changes in Net Domestic Assets ('+' ('−') Contributing to Increase (Decrease) in Base Money) (unit: NT $100 million or percent)

Period	Net domestic assets (1)=(2)+(3)+(4)+(5)	Claims on financial institutions (AC) AC	% of B (2)	Treasury bills, certificates of deposits and savings certificates issued by CBC (TB&CD) TB & CD	% of B (3)	Postal savings deposits replaced with CBC (PSDR) PSDR	% of B (4)	Treasury deposits placed with CBC and other items (GD&O) GD & O	% of B (5)
1962-1970	10	133	85.81	6	3.87	−73	−47.10	−56	−36.13
1971-1975	138	487	89.19	−26	−4.76	−289	−52.93	−34	−6.23
1976-1980	105	644	53.27	148	12.24	−989	−81.80	302	24.98
1981-1985	−1,940	−904	−45.91	−1,155	−58.66	−1,502	−76.28	1,621	82.33
1986-1987	−14,260	−63	−2.51	−10,839	−432.00	−3,767	−150.14	409	16.30
1988-1989	6,136	−358	−8.23	7,722	177.60	−1,287	−29.60	59	1.36

Note: A part of foreign exchange claims on financial institutions during 1974-1984 period was in fact CBC's own foreign exchange assets and under CBC's own management. This part has been adjusted from claims on financial institutions to the net foreign assets.

Source: *Financial Statistics Monthly*, the Central Bank of China.

market before May 1976, the Central Bank first started with only the sales side of open-market operations in the early 1970s. For example, the Central Bank issued the CBC Certificate of Time Deposit to commercial banks in August 1972 in order to reduce the high excess reserves of commercial banks and to cope with inflationary pressures. In January 1979, two and a half years after the establishment of the official money market (short-term bills market), the Central Bank started purchasing treasury bills and commercial papers for the first time -- about NT$4 billion worth -- to accommodate the liquidity needs of the lunar new year at that time. Another notable example occurred during 1986-1987, when the current account surplus and capital inflows were together pouring US$36.6 billion into the economy. Massive open-market operations were conducted through the issue of short-term type-B treasury bills, short-term and two-year CBC certificates of deposits, and six-month to three-year CBC savings bonds. These operations sterilized an amount equivalent to 432 percent of the net increase in base money (see Table 4.7b, column (3)) or 65 percent of the increase in net foreign assets. Conversely, in 1988-1989, when the net foreign assets dropped by an equivalent of a -41 percent of the base money during that period, the open market contributed to 177 percent of the base money and therefore provided the necessary liquidity to the economy.

(iii) The postal savings system. Although it has been prohibited from lending, the postal savings system has been very effective in mobilizing savings in the rural and newly developed areas. At the end of 1989, about 80 percent of its NT$857 billion postal savings deposits were redeposited with the Central Bank, while the remaining 20 percent were redeposited with four specialized banks.

Besides using a part of the postal savings as an important source of funds for medium- and long-term loans (until 1982), the Central Bank effectively used the redeposits as a contractive monetary instrument to achieve economic stability. The postal savings system's redeposits sterilized an amount equivalent to 47 percent of the net increase in base money in 1962-1970, and 150 percent in 1986-1987 (see Table 4.7b, column (4)). Without the postal savings system's redeposit scheme with the CBC and the CBC's open-market operations, the average annual growth rate of the money supply ($M1B$) and inflation in 1986-1987 would have been much higher than the actual average of 42 percent and 1 percent, respectively.

Figure 4.4 summarizes the control of base money (reserve money) during the period between 1981 and 1989, and shows that a large part of increases in money stock resulting from trade surplus and capital inflow during the period between 1986 and 1987 was effectively sterilized by the Central Bank.

FIGURE 4.4 Factors Affecting Changes in the Reserve Money, 1981-1989
("+") Contributing to an Increase in Reserve Money;
("−") Contributing to a Decrease in Reserve Money

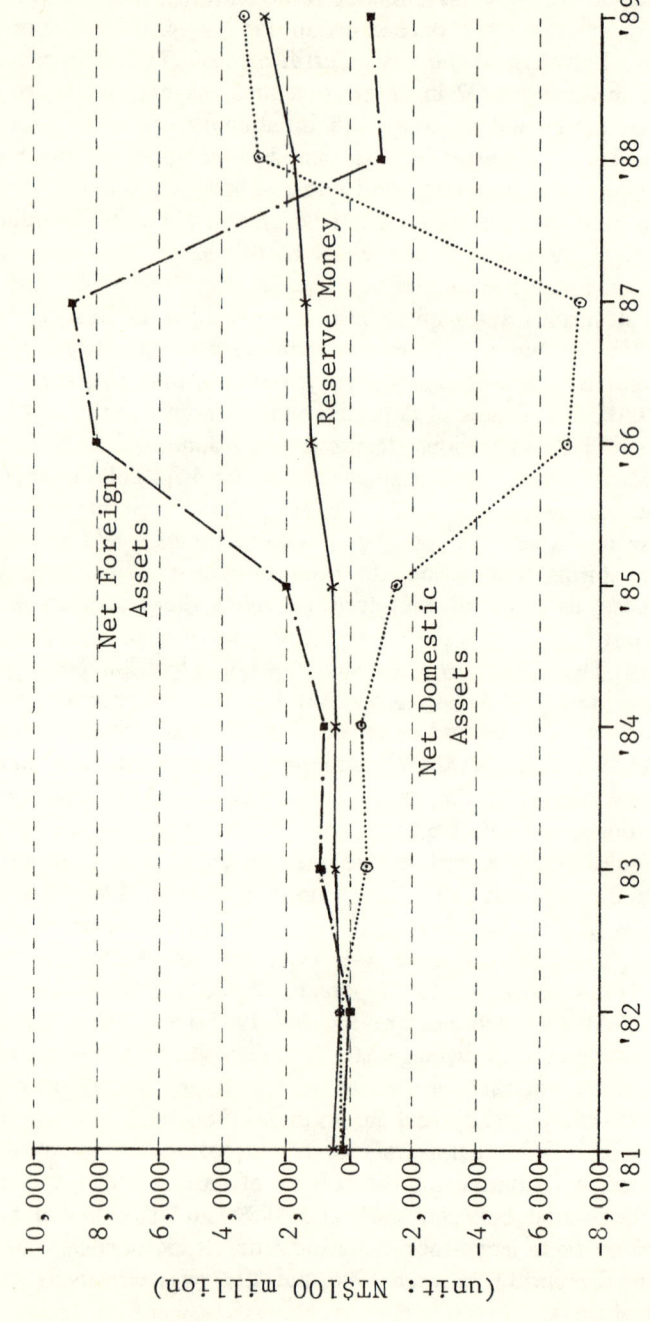

3. Money, Bank Credit, Savings, Investment, and Economic Growth

Since one of the main purposes of this chapter is to focus on the relationship between financial intermediaries and economic growth, it is helpful at the outset to discuss the major factors that have affected investment and savings activities. From there, a discussion follows as to how financial intermediaries channel savings into productive use and the relationship between money, bank credit, and economic growth.

Savings, Investment, and Economic Growth

Factors Contributing to High Investment Rate: An Export-Oriented Policy and High Capital and Labor Productivities before 1988. Between 1950 and 1954, the government smoothly carried out a land reform program which consisted of three projects: the 37.5 percent reduction in farm land rents, the release of public land for farming, and the transfer of farm land ownership to the tiller. The land reform program achieved the goal of building up industry through agriculture and using industry to develop agriculture. Furthermore, even in the agriculturally dominated decade of the 1950s, processed agricultural products accounted for more than 50 percent of total exports, signifying a close relationship between agriculture and industry in producing export commodities.

From the early 1960s onwards, Taiwan gradually turned away from an agriculturally-dominated economy and moved towards an export-oriented and more open, liberalized one. The value of total trade (exports plus imports) as a percentage of GNP increased from 23 percent in 1962 to 77.51 percent in 1973 (the year of the first oil crisis), and to 95 percent in 1980. It then tapered off to 88 percent in 1987.

Many studies show that developing countries that have experienced rapid export growth tend to have higher rates of economic growth (Balassa 1981; Feder 1982). Furthermore, Fry (1989) has shown that due to the combination of domestic development and export promotion, the annual average rate of return on Taiwan's capital stock, as measured by the annual average of the net productivity of capital, was 25 percent in the 1960s, 20 percent in the 1970s, and 15 percent between 1981 and 1987. In addition, Hsing (1986, p. 23) has shown that between the years 1973 and 1984, technological innovation and progress in the manufacturing industry was mostly labor-augmenting. The growth of exports in Taiwan has mainly been promoted by many nimble and energetic small- and medium-sized enterprises (hereafter referred to as SMEs). It can be inferred that the substantial increases in labor productivity are to be related to the growth of SMEs and the associated growth of exports. Officially, a firm with a paid-up capital equal to or less than NT$40 million (equivalent to US$1 million, according to the exchange rate in 1982) is defined as a small- or medium-sized firm. SMEs accounted for 95 percent of all firms and employed about 70 percent of industrial workers in 1982. Furthermore, if we take the manufacturing industry, which contributed 36 percent of GDP in 1986, as an example, 48.2 percent of the manufacturing output was produced by SMEs. Lastly, the value of SME exports totalled 61.2 percent of total export value while 93.8 percent of export value came from the manufacturing industry as a whole.

In conclusion, the above analysis implies that Taiwan's highly productive sectors could afford to pay high interest rates as a price for the use of savings in Taiwan's economic development process.

Factors Contributing to the High Savings Rate. Figure 4.5 shows that the ratio of gross savings to GNP increased from 14 percent in 1953 to 32 percent in 1980, and that the ratio of gross investments to GNP rose hand in hand with the increase in the savings ratio. However, these two ratios have tended to diverge from each other since 1981, signifying a slowdown in investment momentum. By 1989, the ratio of gross savings to GNP was 31 percent whereas the ratio of investments to GNP had declined to 21 percent.

Furthermore, Table 4.8 shows that the high gross savings to GNP ratio mainly came from households and private non-profit organizations and from a combination of government institutions and government-owned enterprises. The former sectors, for example, accounted for about 27 percent of gross national saving in 1960, 43 percent in 1970, 36 percent in 1980, and 45 percent in 1988. The latter combination accounted for about 32 percent of gross national savings in 1960, 22 percent in 1970, 31 percent in 1980, and 26 percent in 1988. The savings ratio for private enterprises remained less than 2.75 percent, and the savings ratio represented by reserves and depreciation remained basically unchanged, ranging from 6.75 percent in 1965 to 8.82 percent in 1988.

Sun and Liang (1982), in their study on savings in Taiwan for the period 1953-1980, concluded that high interest rates and low inflation, together with income level, the growth rate of income and income distribution, had statistically significant effects on savings, but that none of these alone provided a satisfactory explanation for the high savings ratio. Then, in view of the fact that the high savings ratio was partly due to the practices of government institutions and government-owned enterprises, they further concluded that the high ratio in Taiwan could be attributed to high government saving, the public's saving against uncertainty under a relatively underdeveloped social security system, and frugality stemming from Chinese culture and tradition.

There can be no doubt that the high savings rates could also be ascribed

FIGURE 4.5 Saving to GNP Ratios (S/GNP) and Investment to GNP Ratios (I/GNP)

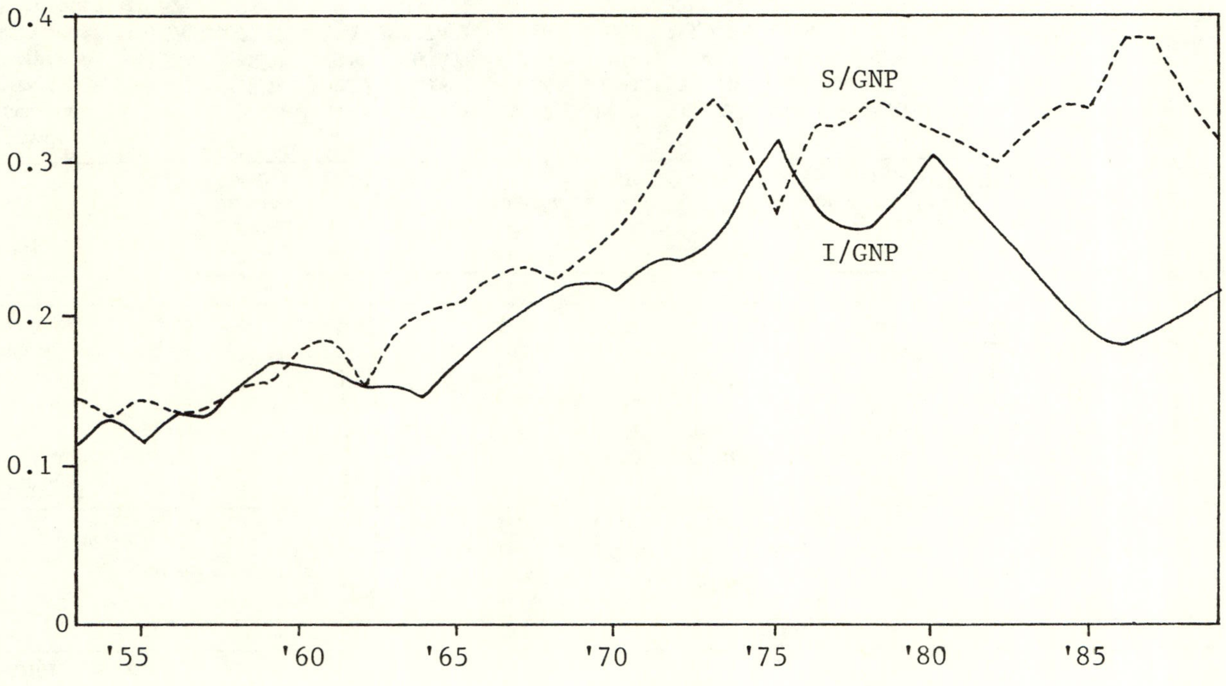

TABLE 4.8 Composition of Saving as a Percentage of Gross National Savings and of GNP (at Current Value) (unit: NT$ million, percent)

	1960			1965			1970			1975		
Sector	Saving	As % of gross national savings	As % of GNP	Saving	As % of gross national savings	As % of GNP	Saving	As % of gross national savings	As % of GNP	Saving	As % of Gross national savings	As % of GNP
Households & private non-profit organizations	2,995	26.98	4.79	9,220	39.58	8.20	25,010	43.18	11.05	64,756	41.33	11.04
Private enterprises	421	3.79	0.67	2,149	9.23	1.91	3,764	6.50	1.66	-2,966	-1.89	-0.51
Government enterprises	1,155	10.41	1.85	1,929	8.28	1.72	5,770	9.96	2.55	12,404	7.92	2.12
Government institutions	2,155	19.41	3.45	2,407	10.33	2.14	6,965	12.03	3.08	37,195	23.74	6.34
Reserves for Depreciation	4,374	39.41	7.00	7,589	32.58	6.75	16,480	28.45	7.25	45,296	28.91	7.73
Gross national savings	11,100	100.00	10.76	23,294	100.00	20.72	57,917	100.00	18.34	156,685	100.00	26.72

	1980			1985			1988		
Sector	Saving	As % of gross national savings	As % of GNP	Saving	As % of gross national savings	As % of GNP	Saving	As % of gross national savings	As % of GNP
Households & private non-profit organizations	170,906	35.56	11.48	365,155	46.00	15.00	533,432	45.03	15.63
Private enterprises	40,940	8.52	2.75	22,692	2.86	0.93	31,203	2.63	0.91
Government enterprises	41,727	8.68	2.80	60,339	7.60	2.48	63,443	5.36	1.86
Government institutions	106,676	22.20	7.16	117,472	14.80	4.83	255,643	21.58	7.49
Reserves for Depreciation	120,379	25.05	8.08	228,197	28.75	9.37	301,016	25.41	8.82
Gross national savings	480,628	100.00	32.27	793,855	100.00	32.61	1,184,737	100.00	34.71

Source: DGBAS: *National Income of the Republic of China*, 1988, pp. 122-124.

to the tax and banking policies aimed at giving the public incentive to save. Between 1960 and 1980, the Statute for the Encouragement of Investment prescribed income tax exemption for interest from two-year or longer term deposits. In addition, since 1965, the interest income from the postal passbook accounts has been exempted from income tax, provided that the amount of postal savings deposits per person is under the ceiling of NT$1 million (NT$700,000 prior to March 1990). Between 1981 and 1990, combined interest and dividend income up to a limit of NT$360,000 was exempted from income tax. Furthermore, locally incorporated banks have provided attractive financial services in order to encourage the public to deposit their savings with banks. For example, until May 1990, depositors were able to lock their funds into high interest rate long-term savings deposits and were subject to no loss of interest if they canceled the accounts before maturity.

Finally, it must not be overlooked that a considerable portion of households' savings is "forced" savings contributed by the owners of SMEs. Since the majority of the SMEs are family-owned, owners have to save funds to meet the working and investment needs of their enterprises. Further discussion on this issue will be given in the sub-section on curb-market lending in Section 4.

The high savings ratio has caused the M_2 velocity, measured by the ratio of GNP to M_2, to decrease from 3.18 in the first quarter, 1966 to 0.73 in the last quarter, 1990, and the $M1B$ velocity, in the same respective quarters, to decrease from 7.73 to 2.43, greatly contributing to Taiwan's price stability and productivity.[4]

The Relationship Between Capital Formation and Economic Growth. One important implication of the high gross savings and investment ratios shown in Figure 4.5 is that the increase in the ratio of net savings to GNP can represent a net increase in capital formation, and that the depreciation element of gross savings and investment can embody an advance in technological improvement in the production process.

Table 4.9 presents a regression analysis on a production function in Taiwan for 1966-1989 (annual data). Due to economies of scale, the Cobb-Douglas equation shown in equation (a) of Table 4.9 is unrealistic, because it gives an unacceptably high value (0.91) for the coefficient of the labor to capital ratio, $ln(K/L)$. Thus, we follow Feder (1982) and Fry (1989) by adding an export to real GNP ratio as an additional explanatory variable to equation (a) to explain the economies of scale. As shown in equation (b), both $ln(K/L)$ and the export variable show statistical significance in explaining the growth of the real GNP to labor ratio, and $ln(K/L)$ is 0.74, still too high when compared with the values of the same coefficient in other countries. Finally, I estimate a constant elasticity of substitution

TABLE 4.9 Regression Results for the Finance Demand for Money and the Broadly-defined Money Stock in Production Functions in Taiwan, 1966-1989 (annual data)

Dependent variable	Constant	ℓn(K/L)	ℓn(x/gnp)	ℓn L	R²-Adj.	S.E.E.	Rao	D.W.
		Independent variables[a]						
(a) ℓn(gnp/L)	0.027 (0.14)	0.91 (28.15)			0.973	0.060		0.44
(b) Ln(gnp/L)	3.048 (1.24)	0.748 (4.13)	0.403 (4.29)		0.995	0.026	0.89 (9.22)	0.78
(c) ℓn gnp	3.900 (2.54)	0.555 (3.83)		1.728 (5.61)	0.997	0.034	0.84 (5.14)	0.96

Equation (c) can be rearranged as below:

| (d) ℓn(gnp/L) | 3.900 | 0.555 | | 0.728 | | | | |

Dependent variable	Constant	ℓn(K/L)	ℓn(m/L)₋₁	(Mₜ−Mₜ₋₁)/Mₜ₋₁	d74	R²-Adj.	S.E.E.	Rao	D.W.
		Independent variables							
A. When narrowly-defined money stock M1A is used									
(e) ℓn(gnp/L)	0.440 (1.49)	0.729 (12.91)	0.185 (4.80)	0.113 (2.81)	−0.082 (−3.14)	0.997	0.020	0.72 (3.52)	1.55
B. When narrowly-defined money stock M1B is used									
(f) ℓn(gnp/L)	0.890 (3.59)	0.639 (11.56)	0.196 (6.61)	0.108 (3.25)	−0.081 (−3.66)	0.998	0.018	0.65 (3.44)	1.82

C. When broadly-defined money supply M2 is used

(g) $\ell n(gnp/L)$	1.113 (4.23)	0.533 (8.34)	0.239 (8.15)	0.100 (1.64)	−0.080 (−4.13)	0.998 0.017 0.65 2.19 (3.92)

[a]$(\ln(K/L))^2$ term in Kmenta's formula (1967) is dropped because of statistical insignificance. Figures in parentheses are t-values. For degrees of freedom d.f. = 20, the level of significance $t_{0.1}$ = 1.325, $t_{0.05}$ = 1.725 and $t_{0.025}$ = 2.086 for one-tailed test. Variable K is the real capital stock (unit: NT $ million); L, labor force (unit: one thousand persons); x, real export; gnp, real gnp; m, real money stock, deflated by the consumer price index; M, nominal money stock, definitions for M1A, M1B and M2 see Tables 4.1 and 4.2; d74, dummy variable representing the year of the first oil crisis; R²-adj is the adjusted R-squared; SEE, the standard error of estimate. A Cochrane-Orcutt procedure was used to estimate the first-order autoregressive parameter Rao; D.W., the Durbin-Watson statistic.

Sources: Data for capital stock is taken from the Council for Economic Planning and Development, others from the Central Bank of China and DGBAS, Executive Yuan.

(CES) production function advanced by Kmenta (1967), the results of which are given in equation (c) and are rearranged as equation (d) in Table 4.9. Equation (d) shows that the elasticity of the real GNP to labor ratio with respect to the capital to labor ratio is 0.555. Although this value is still higher than a ratio of approximately 0.35 for most industrial countries (Maddison 1987; Munnell 1990), it is explainable in that it may reflect the above-mentioned high rate of return on capital stock in Taiwan. Furthermore, the elasticity of GNP with respect to the labor force in equation (c) is 1.728, which also confirms Hsing's observation that, between 1973 and 1984, technological innovation in Taiwan was mostly labor-augmenting.

The Relationship Between Money, Bank Credit, and Economic Growth

As Tsiang (1989, Ch. 7) argues, in Taiwan a considerable portion of M_1 ($M1A$) has been used to finance export and import activities.[5] I will first explore the role of M_1 in financing the export sector's productivity in the production function. Furthermore, in light of the fact that deposits have been the major source of finance to industry, I will also explore the statistical relationship between the broad money stock and economic growth. I will then investigate the role of M_2 in financing the increase in labor productivity. My approach will not follow the conventional analysis of the effect of M_2 on aggregate demand. Rather, it will analyze the effect of financial constraints on output growth and economic growth discussed in the structuralist macroeconomics literature (Blinder 1987; Taylor 1981).

Let us reexamine the production function shown in Table 4.9 with financial variables. It is noteworthy that in equation (e) of Table 4.9, where we use the real narrowly defined money supply ($M1A$) to labor ratio and the growth rate of $M1A$ to replace the exports to GNP ratio in equation (b), we find that both the coefficients of $\ln(K/L)$ and the money variables are statistically significant and that the coefficient of $\ln(K/L)$ remains almost unchanged (0.7), just as in equation (b). Thus, despite the effect of $\ln(K/L)$ on $\ln(gnp/L)$, the monetary effect of equation (e) reaffirms the hypothesis advanced by Tsiang that a part of $M1A$ was used to facilitate foreign trade transactions implied in equation (b), thereby enhancing labor productivity.

Furthermore, in equation (g) of Table 4.9 we use the one-period lagged real broad money supply (M_2 deflated by CPI) to labor ratio, $\ln(m/L)^{-1}$ and the growth rate of M_2 as a substitute for the variable $\ln L$ in equation (d) of Table 4.9. Again it is most striking to note that the coefficient of the variable $\ln(K/L)$ remains about 0.5, approximately the same as in equation (d). This signifies that, given the unchanged effect of $\ln(K/L)$ on

$\ell n(gnp/L)$ in both equations (d) and (g), a significant part of $\ell n(gnp/L)$ can be explained by M_2 in equation (g) through its relationship with scale economies in labor productivity in equation (d). It appears that the supply of funds, supported by increases in M_2, necessary for capital formation, for technological innovation, and for working capital needs was adequate and therefore resulted in an increase in labor productivity.

To further explore the relationship between bank financing and economic development, we may look into the relationship between loan structures and sectoral contributions to GNP in Taiwan. Table 4.10 presents an interesting feature of this relationship. The domestic output shares generated by government-owned enterprises as a percentage of total domestic output were 15.20 percent in 1966-1970, 13.44 percent in 1971-1975, 15.01 percent in 1976-1980, and 15.01 percent in 1981-1985, whereas shares of loans and

TABLE 4.10 Percentage Share of Government Enterprises in Total Output, Bank Loans and the Maturity Structure of Bank Loans

	1961-1965	1966-1970	1971-1975	1976-1980	1981-1985	1986-1988
Domestic output generated by government enterprises as percentage of total domestic output (%)	17.75	15.20	13.44	15.01	15.01	11.65[c]
Demand deposit taking banks:[a] Loans outstanding extended to government enterprises as percentage of total loans outstanding (%)	23.48	14.40	14.27	16.52	16.95	8.63
Commercial bank locally incorporated:[b] Medium- and long-term loans as percentage of total loans and discounts (%)	28.93	29.04	29.82	34.92	50.15	61.39

Notes: a. 'Demand deposit-taking banks' is also called 'deposit money banks'. b. 'Commercial banks, locally incorporated' is also called 'domestic banks'. c. 1986-1987.

Source: DGBAS: *National Income of the Republic of China*, 1988, pp. 72-76, Economic Research Department, CBC: *Financial Statistics Monthly*, June 1989, pp. 17, 79.

discounts extended to them by banks were 14.40 percent, 14.27 percent, 16.52 percent, and 16.95 percent, respectively. While these ratios were closely correlated, the relationship did not hold for 1986-1988 because of the relative decrease in borrowing from government-owned enterprises. During that period, the world price of crude oil declined and the New Taiwan dollar appreciated about 50 percent against the U.S. dollar, both of which significantly reduced the costs of imported oil to government monopoly enterprises, e.g., China Petroleum Corporation and Taiwan Power Company, thus reducing their borrowing needs. Government-owned enterprises contributed 11.65 percent of the nation's total domestic product, but accounted for only 8.67 percent of total bank loans.

In order to gain a deeper insight into the above relationship between loans and economic activity, we will look further into the details of the changes in loan financing. As shown in Table 4.10, the locally incorporated commercial banks have functioned positively in providing a stable source of funds for the investment and working capital needs of industry and for the mortgage loan needs of the public. Between 1961 and 1988, their medium- and long-term loans as a percentage of total loans and discounts increased from an average annual ratio of 28.93 percent in 1961-1965 to 61.31 percent in 1986-1988. These statistics were not available for branches of foreign banks in Taipei, but it is reasonable to expect that they too moved towards a longer-term maturity loan structure as they were generally even more successful than domestic banks in extending medium- and long-term loans.

It is important to note that the above asset transformation (from short-term loans to medium- and long-term loans) was possible because the banks did not have to assume more interest rate risk in extending more medium- and long-term loans. Since 1979, the local banks have gradually adopted a financial innovation introduced by branches of foreign banks in Taiwan, i.e., an adjustable-variable interest rate scheme, which has replaced the then prevailing fixed interest rate scheme on medium- and long-term loans. The transformation was also due to the huge increase in long-term mortgage loans since 1985. At the end of 1988, fixed interest rate loan contracts accounted for only a small portion of total loans outstanding.

4. Liberalization of Interest Rates and Capital Movements, and the Changing Role of Financial Markets in Business and Government Financing

This section will discuss the process of interest rate liberalization from both the internal and external perspectives. Furthermore, the changing roles of money, bond, stock and curb markets in financing private enterprise and the government will be discussed.

The Interest Rate Liberalization Process

Interest Rate Liberalization Efforts and Evaluation – The Internal Perspective. Efforts have been made to introduce more flexibility into the process of interest rate determination in Taiwan since 1975 (Kuo 1989; Shieh 1989). From a broad perspective, the most important catalyst of interest rate liberalization efforts in Taiwan was the interplay between inflation, real economic problems, and regulated interest rates. Efforts to liberalize the interest rate since 1975 in Taiwan may be divided into three phases. The resulting movements of interest rates on loans and deposits are shown in Figures 4.6a and 4.6b.[6]

(1) The first phase, 1975-1981: As Taiwan did not suffer from pressures of high inflation and low real economic growth problems between 1975 and 1979, the aim of interest rate liberalization during this phase was to allow the banks more flexibility in their loan pricing and to establish a money market (short-term bills market) as an additional conduit of funds to private enterprises. Major developments in interest rate liberalization during this stage were as follows:

(i) In July 1975, spread-bands of 0.25 percent on unsecured loans and 0.75 percent on secured loans were introduced to provide flexibility for borrowers and lenders.

(ii) In May 1976, the short-term bills market was established. The instruments introduced were commercial paper and bankers' acceptances guaranteed by banks and investment and trust companies, as well as treasury bills and negotiable certificates of deposits.

However, in 1980-1981, the second oil crisis and global stagflation resulted in a nearly 18 percent inflation rate in Taiwan, leading the money market rate to rise to a level higher than that of the regulated deposits rates, as shown in Figure 4.6a. In response to this, the "Essentials of Interest Rate Adjustment" was promulgated and implemented in November 1980. The purpose of these guidelines was to allow banks to have more flexibility in the determination of interest rates when there were changes in money market conditions. The following types of interest rates on bank deposits and loans were liberalized:

(i) negotiable certificates of deposit and bank debentures;
(ii) discounts on bills of exchange; and
(iii) on-lending foreign currency loans and foreign currency accommodation for negotiations of usance letters of credit.

Interest rates on the first two types were allowed to gear towards liberalized interest rates on open-market financial instruments. Liberalization of the last type allowed foreign loans to compete with local funds.

(2) The second phase, 1982-1984: The prime mover of interest rate liberalization in this phase was the Central Bank's revision of the postal savings

FIGURE 4.6a Actual and Ceiling Interest Rates on Deposits and Spread Bands Between the Maximum Unsecured and Minimum Secured Loan Rates, 1961-1974

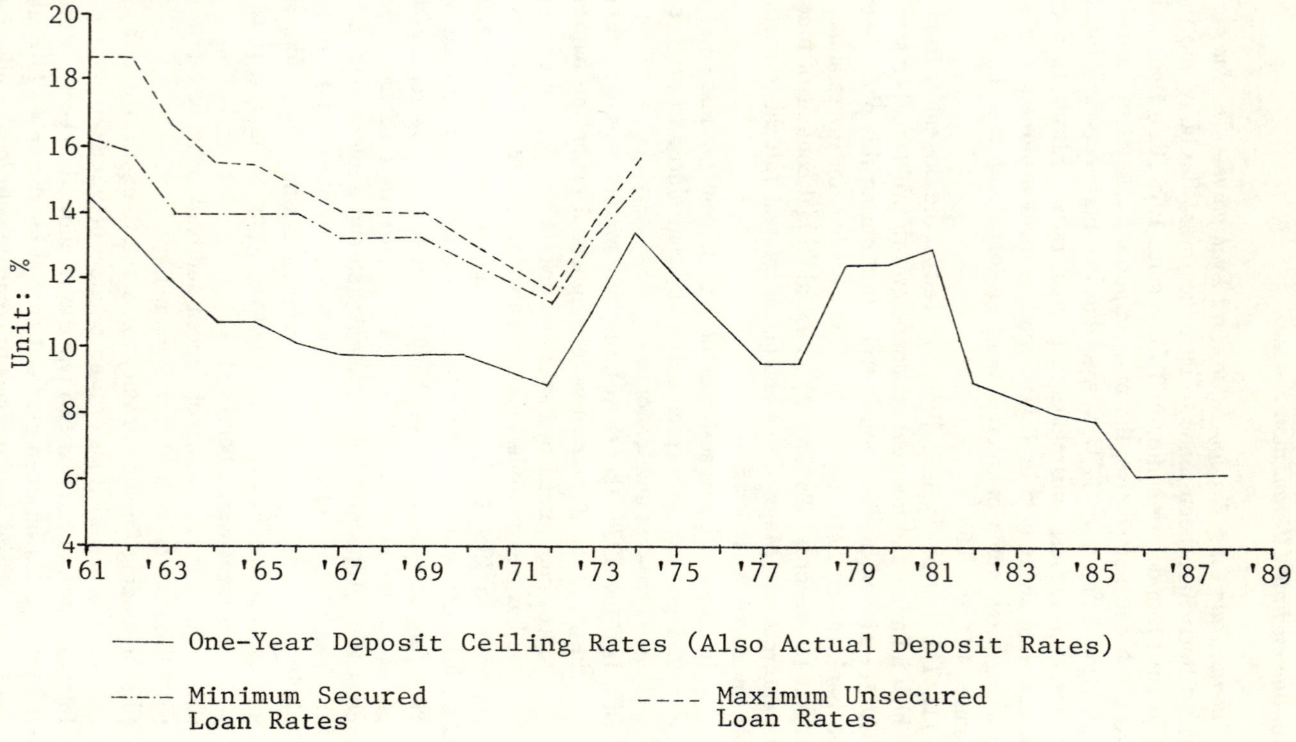

——— One-Year Deposit Ceiling Rates (Also Actual Deposit Rates)
----- Maximum Unsecured Loan Rates
—·—·— Minimum Secured Loan Rates

FIGURE 4.6b Actual and Ceiling Interest Rates on Deposits, Prime Rates and Spread Bands Between the Maximum Long-Term and Minimum Short-Term Loan Rates, 1975-1989

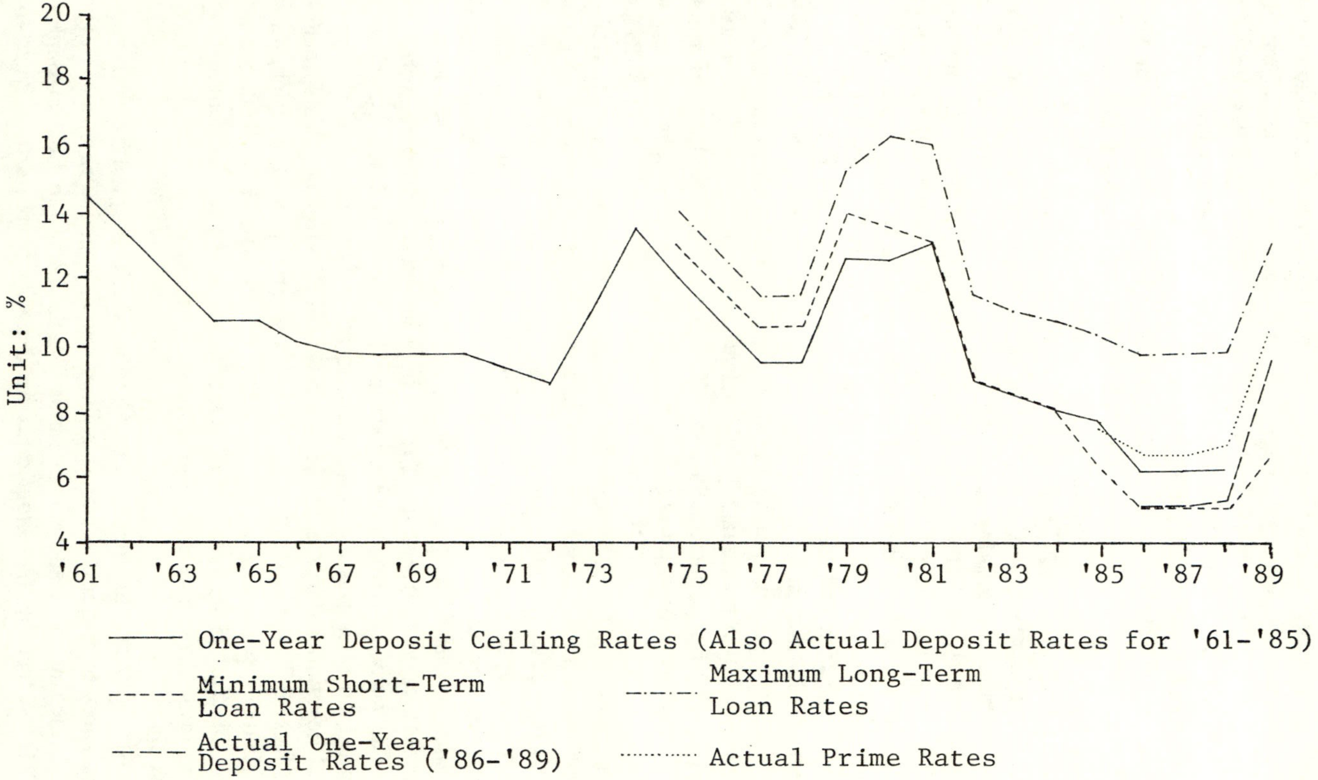

———— One-Year Deposit Ceiling Rates (Also Actual Deposit Rates for '61-'85)
---- Minimum Short-Term Loan Rates
–·–·– Maximum Long-Term Loan Rates
——— Actual One-Year ('86-'89) Deposit Rates
········ Actual Prime Rates

system redeposit scheme. In response to the double-digit inflation rate and the low economic growth rate of 5.8 percent in 1981, the Central Bank announced in March 1982 that the new increment in the postal savings deposits from April 1982 onwards should be redeposited with the four designated specialized banks rather than with the Central Bank. This measure reflects an important deregulation of the supply of market funds. The impact on market liquidity was tremendous and long-lasting. The new increment of postal savings funds redeposited with the four specialized banks amounted to NT$67 billion in 1982 and accounted for 18 percent of the total increase in the broadly defined money supply during that year. The increase in liquidity resulted in a downward slide in short-term money market rates, and the Central Bank responded to them by lowering the ceiling rate on one-year deposits from 13 percent per annum in 1981 to 9 percent per annum in 1982. Furthermore, due to the favorable economic environment in 1982-1984, including the low average annual inflation rate of 1.43 percent and the increasing excess saving to GNP ratio from 13 percent to 20 percent, the ceiling rate on one-year deposits declined still further to 8 percent per annum in 1984. The loan rates were also adjusted downward by 5 percentage points between 1981 and 1984 (see Figure 4.6b).

(3) The final phase, 1985-1989: The continuously stable performance of the macroeconomy during this period, with a 9 percent average annual growth rate of the GNP, a 1.3 percent inflation rate, and a 16 percent excess savings to GNP ratio (see Figure 4.5), again created an economic environment conducive to further interest rate liberalization.

A loan rate liberalization policy was implemented in March 1985. Banks were required to set their own prime rates and use them to replace the minimum or maximum loan rates set by the Central Bank in the loan documents, so that when the Central Bank abolished its approved loan rates in the future, no quarrels would result between banks and borrowers.

The spread between the maximum long-term and the minimum short-term loan rates was also broadened to allow for more flexible loan pricing and negotiation. For example, as shown in Figure 4.6b, this spread widened from 2.75 percent at the end of 1984, when the maximum long-term rate was 10.75 percent and the minimum short-term rate 8.00 percent per annum, to 4.75 percent at the end of 1988, when the maximum long-term rate was 9.75 and the minimum short-term rate was 5 percent per annum.

Also during this phase, the Central Bank adopted several important measures to further liberalize ceilings on deposit interest rates. The first such measure was adopted in January 1986, when the Central Bank reduced the categories of ceiling rates on deposits from thirteen types to four, namely, passbook demand deposits, passbook savings deposits, time deposits with maturities of one year or less, and time and savings deposits with maturities over one year. The second measure was that the ceiling rates on these four simplified categories of deposits were kept at relatively high levels (6.25 percent) between 1986 and 1988, irrespective of the continued decline in the market rates and the actual deposit rates since 1986 (see Table 4.1, column (4)). As the ceiling rates were not binding, there was a *de facto* liberalization of interest rates on deposits. The final measure was adopted in July 1989. Based on the Banking Law, which was revised at that time, the Central Bank abolished all interest rate regulations on bank deposits and loans, except for the requirement that no interest could be paid on checking accounts due to their money-like qualities.

The effect of interest rate liberalization on the efficiency of the financial system in Taiwan can be evaluated from two perspectives. The first concerns the movement of the interest rate spread between deposit and loan rates in response to changes in market rates. Figures 4.8a and 4.8b show that the differential between the weighted average loan rates and the weighted average deposit rates of locally incorporated banks continued to decline from 1982 onwards, falling from 5 percent in January 1982 to less than 2.5 percent in March 1989, which signified the success of the efforts for interest rate liberalization.

Furthermore, there can be little doubt that adjustments in deposit rates were very flexible with respect to changes in money market conditions. Figure 4.7 shows that since the change in the redeposit scheme of the postal savings system in April 1982, the actual interest rate on one-month deposits moved very closely in line with that on 30-day commercial papers. The correlation coefficient for the monthly data of these two rates was as high as 0.91 during the whole of the 1980-1989 period.

However, these achievements should not lead one to conclude that the interest rate structure is sufficiently sophisticated to meet the economy's need for an efficient trade-off between liquidity, return, and risk. For example, as explicitly indicated in Table 4.12, the volume of government bonds outstanding was too small to create market-determined medium- and long-term interest rates. The lack of these rates reflects a serious missing link in the interest rate structure.

Liberalization of Control on Capital Movements and the Interest Rate – The External Perspective. Due to Taiwan's frequent annual current account deficit prior to 1976, capital, especially foreign exchange, was quite scarce. Also, prior to 1978, in order to encourage domestic savings, Taiwan's interest rates were higher than U.S. interest rates (see Table 4.1 for NT$ interest rates and Wood and Wood (1985, p. 207) for U.S. interest rates). Under these circumstances, the CBC adopted, until June 1987, the following foreign exchange system to aid national economic stability and growth:
(i) There were no restrictions on trade-related capital transactions.

FIGURE 4.7 One-Month Time Deposit Rate, 30-day Commercial Paper Rate, 1981–1990

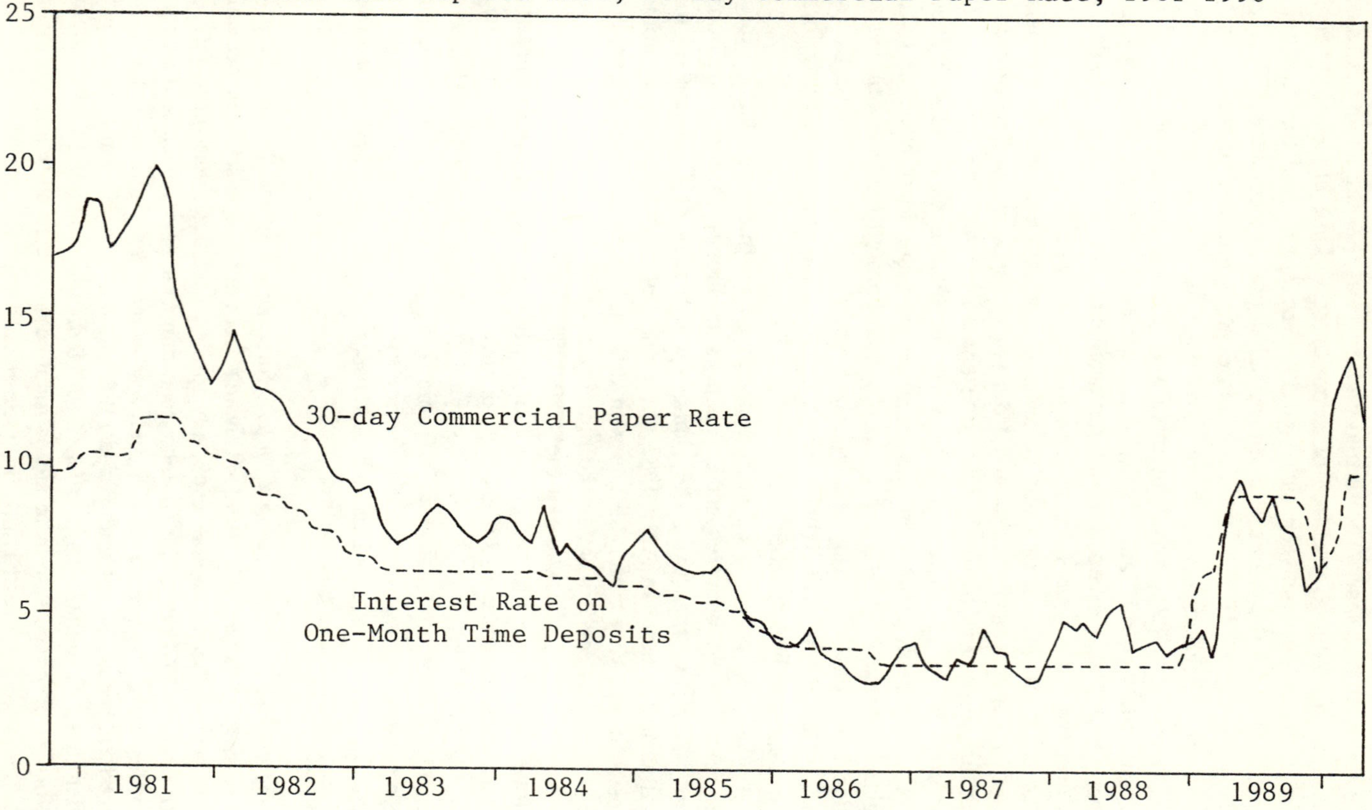

FIGURE 4.8a Weighted Average Loan Rates and Deposit Rates of Domestically Incorporated Banks
Unit: % p.a.

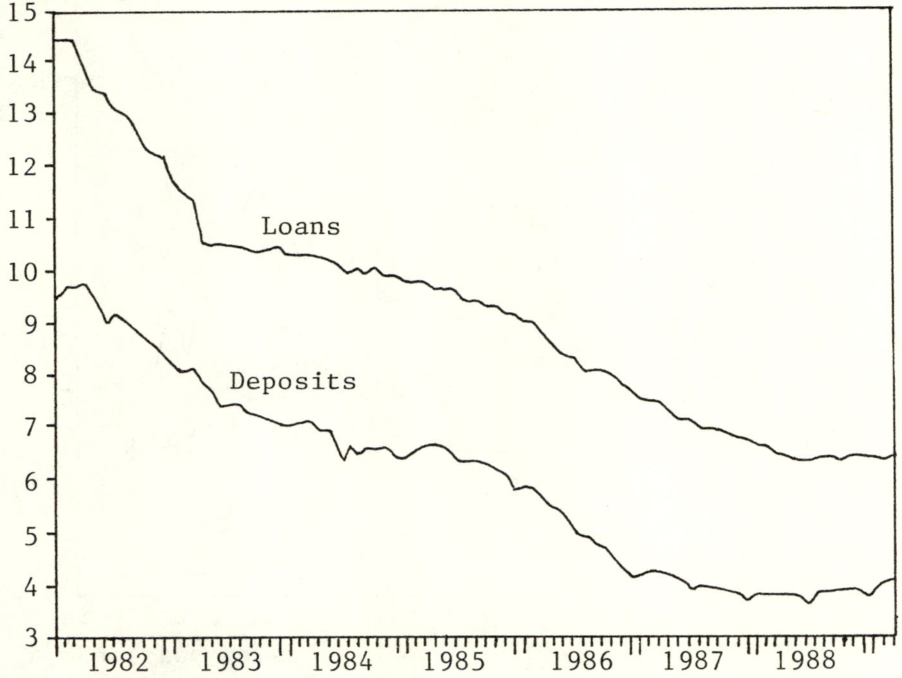

Source: Economic Research Department, Central Bank of China

FIGURE 4.8b Interest Rate Differentials Between Weighted Average Loan Rates and Deposit Rates of Domestically Incorporated Banks

Unit: % p.a.

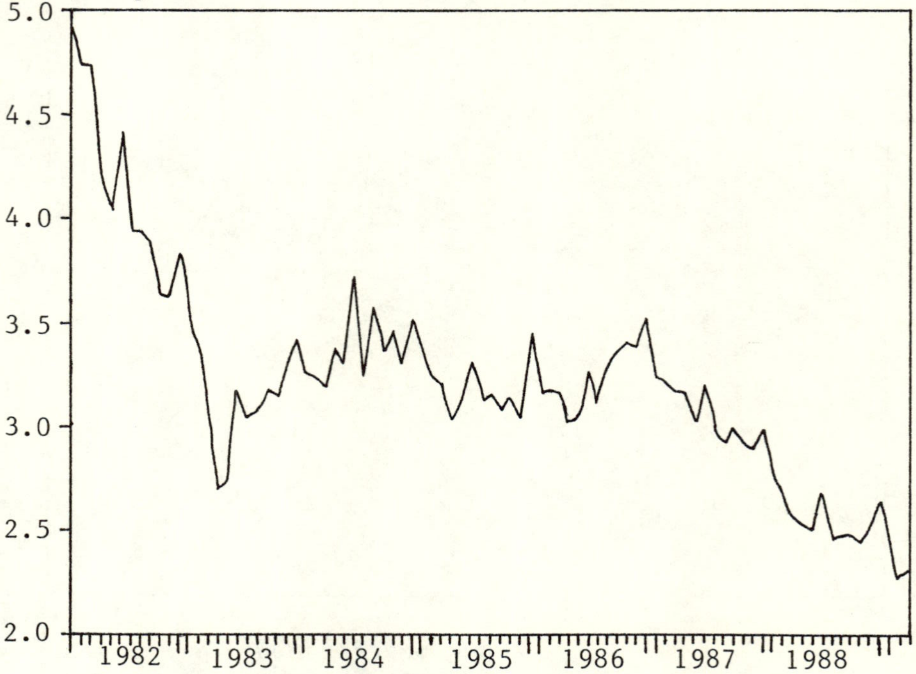

Source: Economic Research Department, Central Bank of China

(ii) There were no controls on the inward remittance of foreign exchange until June, 1987. However, non-trade-related outward remittance by local residents was subject to a strict ceiling imposed by the CBC.
(iii) Both outward and inward remittances of direct capital investment were subject to the approval by the Investment Commission of the Ministry of Economic Affairs.

Although all three types of capital movements might affect the behavior of domestic interest rates, I will focus on the first two as they are more related to business financing and the associated short-term movement of domestic interest rates.

As regards the relationship between trade-related capital transactions and domestic interest rates, it is important to note that Taiwan is a small, open economy, highly dependent on trade activities. Trade-financing has therefore been an important source of funds to both exporters and importers. Prior to 1978, the absence of controls on trade-related capital movements permitted traders access to low-cost foreign funds, making part of their interest costs internationally competitive. Furthermore, it also ensured traders the availability of trade-related foreign funds during periods of domestic credit crunch. While foreign funds could be borrowed for the importation of capital goods, they were limited to foreign exchange uses and were prohibited from conversion into local currency. The policy of control-free trade-rated capital transactions continued to be effective after June 1987.

Prior to 1976, foreign exchange controls in general had effectively insulated domestic interest rates from external influences. However, between 1976 and 1986, persistent current account surpluses, accompanied by more active bank and private non-bank short-term capital movements and other domestic factors, made domestic interest rate adjustments more responsive to market forces. The interest rate was adjusted downward towards the level of international standards between 1975 and 1979, and then it generally tended to vary in accordance with international standards between 1978 and 1986 (see Figure 4.9). Furthermore, the economic upturn in 1985-1987, accompanied by huge increases in both the current account surplus and short-term capital inflow caused the government to take steps toward foreign exchange liberalization. "Foreign Exchange Trust Funds" and "investment fund beneficiary certificates" were created in late 1986 to enable local residents to invest in foreign securities. The most important single foreign exchange liberalization was certainly the removal of foreign exchange controls in July 1987. The amendment allowed each person or company to make outward remittance up to US$5 million a year and inward remittance up to US$50,000 a year. The ceilings have repeatedly been changed since then and both have been adjusted to US$3 million since July 1990. The effects of these measures on the demand for and the supply

FIGURE 4.9 Taiwan's Interest Rate on One-Year Savings Deposits and the U.S. Three-Month Treasury Bill Rate, 1971-1990 (Quarterly Data)

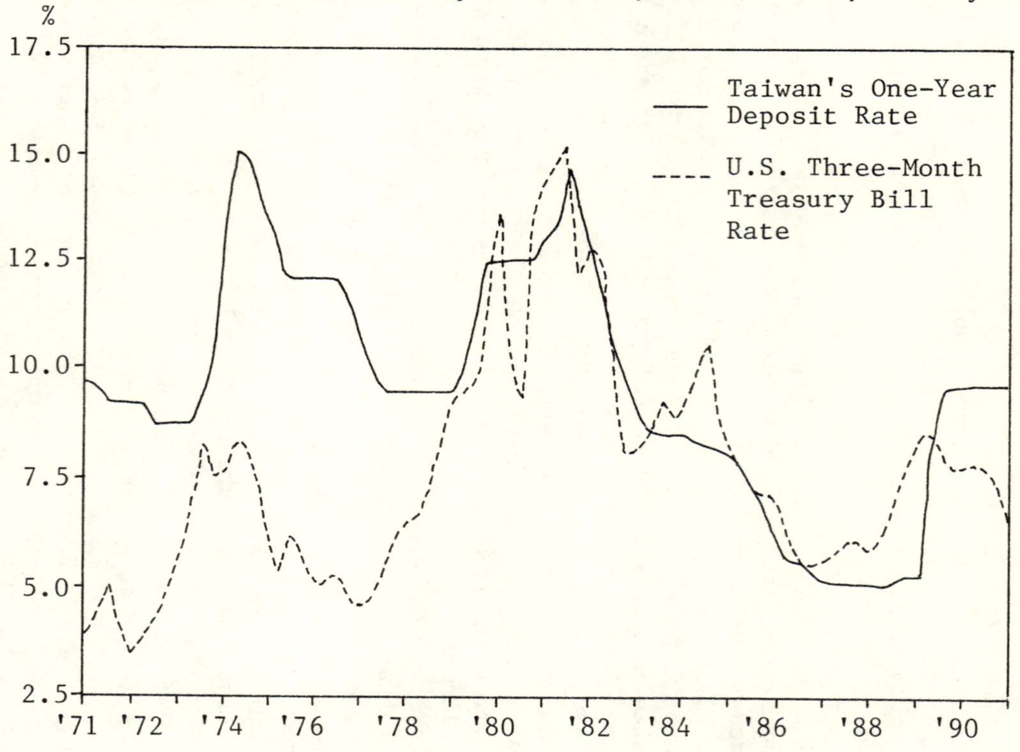

of funds and on domestic interest rates have increased since 1988. The interplay of the competitive supply and demand forces of domestic and international markets resulted in a non-bank private capital outflow (both long-term and short-term) of US$7.4 billion in 1988, US$8.2 billion in 1989, and US$10.7 billion in 1990, and an average annual bank capital outflow (mostly trade-related financing) of about US$3.9 billion during 1988-1990. International interest rate differentials, combined with exchange rate expectations, have become an important determinant of domestic interest rates, as in the typical mature economy.

The Financial Market and Its Role in Financing Private Enterprises and Government

Up until 1976, capital was relatively scarce and the most important source of capital for private enterprises was the banking system. However, since then, there has been a surplus of capital. This development resulted in foreign exchange liberalization and the creation of active money, bond and stock markets in order to meet the needs of savers and investors. The curb-lending market has also played an important role in providing financing to SMEs.

Short-term Bills Market (money market) between 1985 and 1989. In the case of the primary money market, issuances of short-term bills, including treasury bills, commercial paper, bankers' acceptances, and negotiable certificates of deposit (CDs), increased from NT$826 billion in 1985 to NT$2,782 billion in 1989, an increase of 236 percent in this short period of time. The volume of transactions in the secondary market increased from NT$3,441 billion in 1985 to NT$8,195 billion in 1989, reflecting an increase of 138 percent (see Table 4.11). The volume of transactions was greatly affected by the phase of the business cycle, the interest rate, and liquidity conditions of the market. In 1985, when the economy was beginning its recovery phase, loan demand was sluggish. With excess liquidity in the financial system, total issues of negotiable CDs by financial institutions in the primary market were low. The purchase and sale of short-term bills, mostly commercial paper and bankers acceptances in the secondary market, by financial institutions accounted for about 68 percent of the total volume of transactions, whereas government-owned and privately-owned enterprises together only accounted for about 26 percent of total transactions. In contrast, during 1987-1988, when financial institutions were relatively tight, as evidenced by an increase in their issuance of negotiable CDs in the primary market, both the government-owned and privately-owned enterprises were very liquid due to the wealth and liquidity they had rapidly accumulated since export boom in 1985-1986. The purchase and sale of short-term bills by

TABLE 4.11 Money Market Instrument Issues, Outstandings and Transactions (NT $ billion)

	1985	1986	1987	1988	1989
Short-term bill markets:					
Issues	826	910	724	1,394	2,782
Outstandings	310	253	230	480	580
	(3,441)	(3,466)	(3,510)	(4,648)	(8,195)
Treasury bills:					
Issues	107	99	66	283	99
Outstandings	78	80	66	197	34
	(29)	(76)	(253)	(571)	(323)
Commercial papers:					
Issues	330	442	375	441	863
Outstandings	85	83	79	86	135
	(2,054)	(2,173)	(2,269)	(2,437)	(3,282)
Bankers' acceptances:					
Issues	298	304	204	215	377
Outstandings	110	72	59	43	57
	(1,093)	(1,033)	(836)	(601)	(748)
Negotiable CDs:					
Issues	91	65	79	455	1,443
Outstandings	36	18	26	154	355
	(265)	(184)	(152)	(1,039)	(3,842)
Interbank call loans market	2,054	956	1,554	2,925	2,798
Temporary accommodation market	1,930	1,822	2,495	2,819	7,019

Note: Issues represent total issues during a year. Outstandings represent the year-end figures. Figures in parentheses represent transactions through bills finance companies, and include buying and selling figures, and the first issuance balances.

Sources: Research Department, CBC: *Financial Statistics Monthly*, April 1990, pp. 97-98, 103-105; Hendrie, 1990, Table 11.6.

enterprises accounted for about 55 percent of the total volume of transactions, whereas those by financial institutions accounted for only about 30 percent of transactions. The tight monetary policy after April 1, 1989 caused shortages in banks' reserve positions and resulted in a dramatic increase in issuances of commercial paper and negotiable CDs, respectively, by enterprises and financial institutions (see Table 4.11). As a result, in 1989, the short-term bills purchase and sale by enterprises accounted for about 40 percent and that by financial institutions accounted for about 45 percent.

Bond Market. Table 4.12 shows that at the end of 1989, the outstanding amount of government bonds was NT$209 billion, equivalent to only about 5.3 percent of GNP. The outstanding amount of corporate bonds in the same year was only NT$45 billion, or less than 1.1 percent of GNP. However, the ROC government will launch a new initiative, The Six-Year National Development Plan (1991-96), which will involve spending as much as NT$8.2 trillion (about US$300 billion) over the next six years. Since this proposed spending is so large, much greater than the total balance of the broad money supply of NT$5.8 trillion at the end of 1989, it is expected that about NT$1.1 trillion (US$40 billion) in new government bond issues and other forms of financing will be needed to compensate for the shortfall in fiscal revenue. Therefore, a more broadly based government bond market will be necessary in order to meet these new economic challenges.

On the corporate bond side, the restrictive provisions of Articles 247, 249, and 250 of the Company Law have been a hindrance to the development of a viable corporate bond market. For example, Article 247 stipulates that the total amount of corporate bonds outstanding must not exceed the difference between the total amount of assets and the sum of total liabilities and intangible assets (goodwill). Thus, total bonds outstanding can never be greater than the net worth of the company. Furthermore, Article 250 stipulates that a company cannot issue bonds if the average after-tax profit rate for the last three years is lower than the interest rate for the proposed bond issues. The Securities and Exchange Commission has seriously considered removing these restrictive provisions in order to create a viable corporate bond market.

Table 4.12 shows that the outstanding and trading volumes of both corporate and government bond markets were very small compared to the market value and trading volume of the listed stocks.

Stock Market (Equity Market). Due to an economic upturn in the second half of 1985, the Taiwan Stock Exchange (TSE) price index rose from 477 to 745 between 1982 and 1985, an increase of 56 percent. In addition, due to the huge foreign trade surplus, the index increased 10.5 times from 745 to 8,616 between 1985 and 1989. In 1989, the average stock price to its after-tax net earnings ratio (the P/E ratio) rose as high as 55.91. Also the

TABLE 4.12 Bond and Stock Markets (NT $ billion)

	1985	1986	1987	1988	1989
Number of listed corporations	127	130	141	163	181
Number of public unlisted corporations	169	182	198	226	319
Number of dealers, brokers & underwriters	71	74	79	187	372
Taiwan Stock Exchange (TSE) price index (monthly average)	745	944	2,135	5,202	8,616
Annual growth rate of TSE price index (%)	-14.54	26.71	125.99	143.66	65.62
A. Corporate bonds outstanding	39.1 (3.5)	46.6 (21.5)	51.6 (6.3)	52.0 (8.1)	45.4 (15.0)
Government bonds outstanding	66.4 (23.4)	92.1 (105.4)	130.7 (210.9)	184.0 (404.6)	209.4 (890.4)
Beneficiary certificates	--	--	--	--	--
(closed-end mutual funds)	--	--	--	(51.7)	(264.8)
Listed stocks (par value)	213.4	240.8	287.3	343.6	421.3
(market value)	415.7 (195.2)	548.4 (675.7)	1,386.1 (266.6)	3,383.3 (7,868.0)	6,174.2 (25,408.0)
B. The ratio of the market value of listed stocks to GNP (%)	16.5	18.7	42	94	155.8
As a comparison, the ratio of broadly defined money supply (M2) (daily average) to GNP (%)	93.7	99.2	111.9	125.3	132.3
C. Bank debentures	(21.8)	(13.8)	(4.2)	(1.2)	(0.3)

Note: Figures in parentheses represent total trading amount. For bonds, including trading amounts in both centralized and over-the-counter markets.

Sources: *Financial Statistics Monthly*, April 1990, pp. 100-107. Research Department, Central Bank of China; *Major Indicators of Securities Market*. Securities and Exchange Commission.

market value of the listed stocks to GNP ratio rose from 16.5 percent in 1985 to 155.8 percent in 1989, outweighing the broad money supply to GNP ratio of 132.3 percent in 1989 (see Table 4.12). It seems natural to ask to what degree the rapidly rising stock prices between 1985 and 1989 caused private enterprises to turn from the banking system to the capital market for their funds. The answer depends on the size of private enterprises in question and the stipulations of corporate and securities laws governing the issuance of stock.

According to the practice and regulations of the corporate and securities laws, only a company with a paid-up capital equal to NT$100 million or more could apply for the issuance of shares through public offering and negotiation in the open market. As a result, only large companies were able to take advantage of the rapid rise in stock prices by raising funds through the issuance of shares.

Since flow of funds data for the stratum of such narrowly defined large companies is not available, a broadly defined large enterprise is used instead in this study. For example, in the case of the manufacturing industry, the enterprise with total assets of NT$70 million or more will be classified as a large enterprise, as shown in the definition given below in Table 4.13. To illustrate the changing role of the banking system and the securities market in financing private enterprises, it may be observed from Table 4.13 that for broadly defined large enterprises, internal financing grew by 11 percent in 1986. However, between the end of 1987 and June 1989, internal financing rose from NT$602 billion to NT$1,072 billion, an increase of 78 percent, or an average annual growth rate of 23.7 percent. The rapid increase in the internal financing of large enterprises was primarily due to two factors. The first was the moderate increase in new issues (at par value) from NT$432 billion in December 1986 to NT$608 billion in June 1989, an increase of only 40 percent in an era of big increases in stock prices. The second was the rapid increase in reserves and retained earnings, from NT$170 billion in December 1986 to NT$462 billion in June 1989, an increase of 171 percent. The moderate increase in the former mainly reflected the reluctance on the part of stockholders to lose their control over management to new investors and, consequently, the market demand for shares was still higher than the market supply. Therefore, stock prices remained high during that period. The rapid increase in the latter reflected the fact that a large part of the increase in net worth came from nonoperational profits, which were mostly realized profit derived from the excess of market prices over par prices of new shares issued, and from the sale of existing shares during that period. In contrast, in the case of the small- and medium-sized enterprises (SMEs), internal financing increased by 21 percent from 1986 to 1987, and by an annual average rate of about 27 percent from the end of 1987 to June 1989. Since the SMEs could

TABLE 4.13 Liabilities and Net Worth of Private Enterprises, 1985-1989 (as of the end of year) (unit: NT $ billion)

	1985 Amount	1985 % of total	1986 Amount	1986 Annual growth rate	1987 Amount	1987 Annual growth rate	1988 Amount	1988 Annual growth rate	1989 (June)[b] Amount	1989 (June)[b] Annual growth rate[b]
I. External financing	2,028	59.66	2,625	29.44	3,170	20.76	3,592	13.31	3,905	17.43
(i) Large enterprises[a]	851	25.03	1,057	24.21	1,155	9.27	1,285	11.26	1,399	17.74
(ii) Small & medium sized enterprises	1,177	34.63	1,568	33.22	2,015	28.51	2,307	14.49	2,506	17.25
1. Loans from financial institutions	670	19.70	826	23.28	1,017	23.12	1,294	27.24	1,403	16.85
(i) Large enterprises[a]	358	10.53	433	20.95	494	14.09	585	18.42	640	18.80
(ii) Small & medium sized enterprises	312	9.17	393	25.96	523	33.08	709	35.56	763	15.23
2. Curb market	530	15.59	667	25.85	735	10.19	671	-8.71	715	13.11
Borrowing from other enterprises	40	1.18	55	37.50	65	18.18	77	18.46	83	15.58
Borrowing from households	490	14.41	612	24.90	670	9.48	594	-11.34	632	12.79
(i) Large enterprises[a]	62	1.82	95	53.23	92	-3.16	96	4.35	93	-6.25
(ii) Small & medium sized enterprises	428	12.59	517	20.79	578	11.80	498	-13.84	539	16.47
3. Loans from government agencies	2	0.05	1	-50.00	1	0.00	1	0.00	1	0.00
4. Borrowing from abroad	26	0.78	26	0.00	19	-26.92	24	26.32	22	-16.67
5. Money market	84	2.47	75	-10.71	60	-20.00	63	5.00	61	-6.35
(i) Large enterprises[a]	82	2.41	70	-14.63	52	-25.71	55	5.77	52	-10.91
(ii) Small & medium sized enterprises	2	0.06	5	150.00	8	60.00	8	0.00	9	25.00
6. Corporate bonds	11	0.34	11	0.00	11	0.00	11	0.00	11	0.00
7. Bills & accounts payable	705	20.73	1,019	44.54	1,327	30.23	1,528	15.15	1,692	21.47
(i) Large enterprises[a]	280	8.23	395	41.07	453	14.68	490	8.17	558	27.76
(ii) Small & medium sized enterprises	425	12.50	624	46.82	874	40.06	1,038	18.76	1,134	18.50
II. Internal financing (net worth)	1,371	40.34	1,607	17.21	2,033	26.51	2,648	30.25	2,870	16.77
(i) Large enterprises[a]	542	15.95	602	11.07	815	35.38	1,010	23.93	1,070	11.88
(ii) Small & medium sized enterprises	829	24.39	1,005	21.23	1,218	21.19	1,638	34.48	1,800	19.78
8. Stockholders' equity (par value)	1,190	35.02	1,382	16.13	1,680	21.56	2,143	27.56	2,318	16.33

(i) Large enterprises[a]	339	9.98	432	27.43	491	13.66	586	19.35	608	7.51
(ii) Small & medium sized enterprises	851	25.04	950	11.63	1,189	25.16	1,557	30.95	1,710	19.65
9. Reserves & retained earnings	181	5.31	225	24.31	353	56.89	505	43.06	552	18.61
(i) Large enterprises[a]	203	5.97	170	−16.26	324	90.59	424	30.86	462	17.92
(ii) Small & medium sized enterprises	−22	−0.66	55	350.00	29	−47.27	81	179.31	90	22.22
III. Total	3,399	100.00	4,232	24.51	5,203	22.94	6,240	19.93	6,775	17.15
(i) Large enterprises[a]	1,394	41.01	1,658	18.94	1,971	18.88	2,295	16.44	2,469	15.16
(ii) Small & medium sized enterprises	2,005	58.99	2,574	28.38	3,232	25.56	3,945	22.06	4,306	18.30

[a]Classification of enterprises: For this table only, enterprises which satisfy the following minimum standards are classified as large enterprises. Otherwise, as small and medium-sized enterprises (SME).

Minimum Standards of Large Enterprises

service	Mining	Manufacturing	Electricity gas and water	Construction of buildings	Commerce	Transportation & communications	Other enterprises
Total assets, 1987-89	25	70	10	60	25	55	30
Annual sales, 1985-86	30	50	50	30	30	30	50

[a]Minimum standards for 1987-89 are slightly higher than for 1985-86. Nevertheless, these two standards are quite close in order to keep the splicing dicrepancy of these two periods to the minimum. The official definition of SME for manufacturing includes the enterprise with registered capital of NT$40 million or less. Therefore, its size is larger than our SME definition here. However this difference does not affect our conclusions in this chapter.

[b]As of the end of June, 1989; growth rate is annualized.

Source: *Data for Flow of Funds in Taiwan District, ROC.* Economic Research Department, Central Bank of China.

not take advantage of the increases in stock prices through the issuance of shares in the open market, the increase in their internal financing mainly came from the increase in the new issue of capital subscribed by their share holders, and increases in their reserves and retained earnings.

In the case of large enterprises, the increases in their fundings from the stock market have resulted in decreases in the growth rates of their demand for bank loans and money market funds. The latter two sources of funds, when combined, rose from NT$503 billion at the end of 1986 to NT$692 billion in June 1989, an increase of 37 percent or an average annual growth rate of about 14 percent. This growth rate was not only less than the growth rate of their internal financing but also much lower than the increase in bank loans and money market funds to SMEs, which increased from NT$398 billion at the end of 1986 to NT$772 billion in June 1989, reflecting an average annual growth rate of 27.87 percent. In addition, as Table 4.13 indicates, the share of bank loans to large enterprises was higher than that of bank loans to SMEs in 1985-1986. But in 1987, the rapid rise in stock prices marked a reversal of the high loan share of large enterprises, and since then the loan share held by SMEs has become higher than that held by the large enterprises.

Furthermore, as shown in Table 4.13, SMEs are characterized by their low-debt and high-equity based financial structure. For example, in 1985, their borrowings from financial institutions and internal financing were NT$312 billion and NT$829 billion, respectively, or 27 percent vis-à-vis 73 percent. However, it should be cautioned that the statistics used to calculate the amount of equity contains a serious problem of double counting. Many SMEs are in fact subsidiaries of other SMEs and large enterprises. When the parent company uses its own paid-up capital for new investment in SMEs, its original paid-up capital will remain unchanged according to accounting practice, while the paid-up capital of the new subsidiary will be registered as a net increase in paid-up capital at the aggregate level. Caution should therefore be exercised when inferring that, since the equity of SMEs outweighs their borrowings from banking institutions, the banking institutions are not important sources of funds to SMEs.

Evidently, in 1986-1989, while the SMEs still relied on banking institutions as an important source of financing, the large enterprises turned to some extent from the banks to the capital market in their search for cheaper funds.

It is also worth noting that households have played a very important role in equity financing. In 1988, of the total listed shares outstanding, 46.7 percent were held by local households and 9.6 percent by overseas Chinese and foreigners, as compared with 21.6 percent held by the government and 22.1 percent by financial and non-financial corporations and other institutional investors. These small investors from the local households sectors have accounted for more than 80 percent of active stock market players. Their market assessments are not carefully drawn, and their responses to market price changes have generally been to jump on the bandwagon, which has been one of the major contributing factors to the speculative element in the movement of stock prices since 1986. Although the total turnover volume of shares on Taiwan's stock market reached 220.56 billion shares in 1989 (NT$25,408 billion, or about US$960 billion, see Table 4.12), which was only surpassed by the New York and Tokyo stock exchanges, these sales were mainly financed by investors' own funds; the amount of stock purchases financed by margin accounts only represented 4.58 percent of total stock purchases in 1989 and 10.29 percent of the total during the first half of 1990. In other words, the purchase of shares was mainly financed by investors' own savings, not by borrowing funds from banks. This practice might be the most important factor which prevented a crisis in the payment system between February 12, 1990 and July 5, 1990, when the Taiwan Stock Exchange (TSE) stock price index plummeted about 65 percent from its peak of 12,682 points to 4,524.55 points.

Finally, it is noteworthy that prior to January 1991, except for foreign direct investment in Taiwan and the channel that foreigners could invest in Taiwan stocks through the purchase of four overseas funds, including Taiwan Fund, etc., there was no other channel through which foreign investors could invest in Taiwan's stock market. Since January 1991, the government has adopted the following measures to internationalize the local stock market and to encourage foreign institutions to participate in the Taiwan stock market:

(i) Granting permission for the establishment of branches of foreign securities companies in Taiwan through which local investors can invest in listed stocks on the New York, Tokyo, and London stock exchanges.
(ii) Allowing foreign institutional investors to invest in the listed stocks in Taiwan. About fifty overseas institutions will be permitted to make such investments, but tentatively with a total limit of no more than US$2.5 billion during the initial phase. This foreign investment will be in addition to the already permitted channel of foreign direct investment in Taiwan.

Curb Market Lending. Table 4.13 indicates that loans by households to SMEs (curb market lending) accounted for 12.59 percent of the total funding to both large enterprises and SMEs in 1985, or 21.35 percent (dividing 12.59 percent by 58.99 percent at the bottom line of Table 4.13) of the total funding to SMEs during that year. This high percentage of curb market financing to SMEs is not necessarily a reflection of the inefficiency of the financial system, since much of this financing represents shareholders financing their own enterprises. First, as mentioned above, the SMEs are mostly export-oriented enterprises, and their shareholders may prefer to use their earnings from their business as loans to their SMEs rather than as deposits with banks and then to borrow funds from banks to finance their SMEs. The former kind of financing is more direct and efficient than the latter. As evidence, a survey conducted by the Bank of Taiwan in 1988 on the manufacturing industry indicated that about 82 percent of the households' financing to SMEs consisted of loans by shareholders to their own enterprises. Secondly, there are also tax-saving considerations. During 1990, for instance, the corporate profit tax rate was 25 percent, the personal income tax rate was, say, 30 percent (the maximum rate is 40 percent), and interest expenses were tax-deductible up to a maximum interest rate of 20 percent per annum on the borrowings from households. Given these circumstances, if the interest income tax rate is 20 percent and interest rates on curb lending are equal to or less than 20 percent per annum, the net income would be higher if the shareholders in the SMEs chose to lend to SMEs instead of investing in the SMEs' equities. If the before-tax interest income is the same as the before-tax dividend income, the net after-tax income per dollar of loan is (1−0.2), since interest payments are tax-deductible at the enterprise level; the net after-tax income per dollar of investment is (1−0.25)(1−0.30). The former is thus better than the latter. Although borrowings from households by SMEs merely increased from NT$428 billion at the end of 1985 to NT$539 billion in June 1989, only a 26 percent increase in three and a half years, as shown in Table 4.13, it remains an important source of financing for SMEs. Borrowings from households have never been an important source of funds in the case of large enterprises.

5. Concluding Remarks and Prospects for the Financial System

Over the past four decades, the Republic of China on Taiwan has achieved a remarkable degree of success in its economic development. It has witnessed a high growth rate and low inflation, which suggests that the measures adopted to promote financial deepening were appropriate. In retrospect, major monetary policy and financial liberalization measures can be summarized as follows:

(1) High interest rate policy and the dominant indirect financing to achieve economic development with price stability: The government has effectively used a policy mix of high interest rates and control over the narrowly defined money supply ($M1A$ and $M1B$) to combat inflation and encourage savings.

(2) Sequence-specific liberalization: Before 1982, when capital was relatively scarce, indirect financing was promoted to support both large and

export-oriented small- and medium-sized enterprises, while bond and equity markets were underdeveloped. However, since 1982, there has been a surplus of capital, and thus liberalization measures have been adopted to promote the competitiveness and efficiency of banking institutions and equity markets. The main measures in this regard have included:
(i) Liberalization of the foreign exchange market in July 1987.
(ii) Interest rate liberalization beginning in 1980 and the removal of interest rate controls in July 1989.
(iii) The broadening of the business scope of the banking industry to encompass the securities business in April 1988.

It is also important to note that the process of financial liberalization has not been carried out without certain problems. The sequence of events in the financial liberalization process in Taiwan has shown that money market and interest liberalization came first and the removal of foreign exchange controls came second. However, it should be pointed out that the latter was accompanied by the liberalization of the labor market at the same time (through the lifting of Martial Law in July 1987). The higher wage rates together with the sharp appreciation of the NT dollar since the end of 1987 have caused Taiwan's labor-intensive enterprises to relocate their manufacturing facilities abroad, especially in Southeast Asian countries, and have led to a huge capital outflow since 1988. Furthermore, there have been cases of huge short-term capital movements, both in terms of outflows and inflows, which have caused volatile changes in the money supply during 1986-1990. The above development, in conjunction with the deteriorating business climate, such as labor shortage, high land prices, environmental concerns, etc., resulted in a 8.88 percent decline in domestic private investment and a low economic growth rate of 5.29 percent in 1990. One may question whether Taiwan's economic miracle is over.

The government is concerned about this development and has created the Six-year National Development Plan (1991-1996) aimed at transforming Taiwan into a fully modernized nation by the end of this century. It will improve infrastructure in order to try to maintain a 7 percent economic growth rate per year during this period and try to control inflation so that consumer prices will rise by no more than 5 percent in 1991 and by no more than 3.5 percent years between 1992 and 1996. Furthermore, in view of Taiwan's recent achievements in financial liberalization and national economic strength, the government also includes in the Plan the project of developing Taipei into an Asian financial center. Indeed, the government has done much in the way of liberalizing the financial system to meet the increasingly sophisticated needs of savers and investors. In addition, Taiwan is the world's fifteenth largest trading nation, and as the world's highest or second highest official foreign reserve holder, it has US$72 billion in foreign exchange reserves. Finally, Taiwan reached a level of

US$8,000 per capita GNP in 1990 and expects to reach US$14,000 per capita GNP by 1996 when the Six-Year National Development Plan is completed. These factors will contribute greatly to broadening Taipei's base as a regional financial center. Nonetheless, as the existence of sound and competitive financial intermediaries and markets is a prerequisite to the success of a regional financial center, more financial liberalization and internationalization are needed in Taiwan in order to meet that target.

In this regard, the government gave licenses for fifteen new private commercial banks in June, 1991. As their size is large, each with the required minimum paid-up capital of NT$10 billion (about US$370 million), these new banks will bring about unprecedented competition in the financial service industry and will upgrade banking services. More private domestic bank and foreign bank licenses will be awarded in the future. In addition, the Asian Development Bank will issue at least US$100 million in bonds in Taipei at the end of 1991. The issue will certainly help the development of the bond market in Taipei.[7]

The Ministry of Finance and the Central Bank of China jointly sponsored the National Financial Conference in June 1991, designed to upgrade the financial system. The Conference reached 255 items of recommendations for financial reforms. Major proposed reforms include the following:

(1) Financial Structure: (a) Enacting legislation to remove government restrictions on the management and control of government-owned specialized banks so that they may be allowed to compete with other privately owned banks on an equal footing.

(b) Expediting the privatization of the three largest government-owned commercial banks, Taiwan Medium Business Bank, and government-owned life and property insurance companies.

(c) Revising the Banking Law to allow investment and trust companies to do commercial banking business or to convert them to commercial banks, subject to terms and conditions set by the Ministry of Finance.

(d) Establishing an *ad hoc* Committee for Financial Reform to study the possibility of developing practical proposals to modernize the existing specialized banking system into a universal banking system.

(2) Foreign Exchange Market and Foreign Exchange Regulations: (a) Reactivating the forward exchange market through relaxation of restrictions on a bank's foreign exchange position, encouraging the introduction of foreign financial innovations into local markets and enhancing the Taipei-foreign currency call loan market to be more closely integrated with world financial markets.

(b) Expediting the revision of the Statute for Foreign Exchange Control, permitting Taiwan residents more general access to foreign exchange activities, while clarifying individual exceptions.

(c) Conferring responsibility for reimposing foreign exchange controls under emergency circumstances on the Executive Yuan (cabinet).

(d) Establishing a formal reporting system of foreign exchange activities for statistical purposes.

(3) Money and Bond Markets: (a) Introducing new instruments, such as money market mutual funds, etc. to compete with deposit accounts when deemed necessary.

(b) Removing entry barriers to the money market by allowing more bill financing companies and/or commercial banks to engage in money market activities.

(c) Establishing active and liquid primary and secondary government-bond and corporate-bond markets, which could not only provide high-quality open-market instruments but could also generate market-determined medium- and long-term interest rates. A complete spectrum of interest rates could therefore be established and serve as a useful channel through which monetary policy could effectively influence the equity market and the economy.

(d) Introducing more innovative financial instruments such as convertible bonds, floating rate notes, securities futures and options, when deemed necessary.

(4) Developing Taipei to become an Asian Financial Center: (a) Improving the free entry and exit of capital, information and personnel.

(b) Changing the tax codes to lower tax rates on international banking activities so as to make foreign exchange business internationally competitive.

(c) Upgrading international telecommunications facilities and lowering their rates to make them internationally competitive.

(d) Introducing internationally well-known money market brokers to participate in the local markets, enhancing OBU (off-shore banking unit) activities and building an international financial trading center to economize the use of telecommunications facilities.

As regards the stock market, the entry barrier to margin financing will be further liberalized. One more securities financing company may be established, and more investment trust funds are expected to be established. The stock market will also be opened to foreigners.

Of course, the Conference also recommended that financial laws and regulations be further streamlined and enforced to maintain a safe and sound financial system.

As the broad purpose of these recommendations is to develop practical proposals to promote a more competitive and internationalized financial system, it is expected that the Government will schedule a timetable of financial reforms to implement these recommendations as far as possible.

Notes

The views expressed here are mine alone and do not necessarily represent those of the Central Bank of China on Taiwan, the Republic of China. I am grateful to Gustav Ranis, Ghon Rhee and Rosita P. Chang for constructive suggestions and Chao-Kai Chen, Teh-Chian Hou, Chai-Chiu Hsu, Yi-Hsiung Hsu, Bruce S. Stewart, Ching-Hsiang Su, Huey-Mei Tsay, Rong-Tzaw Yeh, and Duh-Yuan Yuan of the Central Bank of China for their helpful comments.

1. See the Secretary of the Treasury: *Modernizing the Financial System -- Recommendations for Safer, More Competitive Banks* (February, 1991), and "Japanese Financial Reforms: Encourage Free Competition," an editorial (*Kinzai Financial Briefing*, September 10, 1990).

2. It can be seen from equation (g) of Table 4.9 in Section 3 that the broad money supply is a significant variable in explaining the real GNP to labor ratio and therefore has contributed to sustained economic growth.

3. In the case of alternative estimates in the Table 4.14 it can be seen that, while the rates of change in the narrow money supply $M1A$ and $M1B$, respectively, are significant variables in explaining the rate of change in prices during the 1967:QI - 1989:QIV period (see equations (a), (b), (d), (e), (g), and (h) of Table 4.14), the rate of change in the broad money supply M_2 is not significant (see equations (c), (f), and (i) of Table 4.14). However, this result does not necessarily imply that the broad money supply cannot be used as an ideal monetary indicator beyond the sample period. As a matter of fact, the rate of change in $M1B$ became very volatile in 1990, and the Central Bank of China has instead used M_2 as the major monetary policy indicator since July 1990.

4. For the contribution of M_2 to economic stability, see footnote 2.

5. Tsiang (1989, p. 161) has presented a simple estimate of the demand function for real money balances in Taiwan, 1953-1972, as follows:

$$\ln m = 0.1037 + 0.8311(\ln y) + 0.6965(\ln T/Y) - 0.3219(\ln r)$$
$$(t = 3.3349) \quad (t = 3.1430) \quad (t = -1.8080)$$

$$\bar{R}^3 = 0.9950, \ SEE = 0.0036, \ D.W. = 1.8925$$

where m is the real money balances (currency plus demand deposits), y is the GDP in real terms, T/Y is the ratio of the volume of trade to GDP (i.e., exports plus imports to GDP ratio), both in their nominal values, and r is the average market rate of interest.

TABLE 4.14 Regression Results of the Rates of Changes in Price Equations (1967:QI - 1989:QIV)

Dependent variable	Constant	$\dot{q}-\dot{M}$	$\dot{M}$	$\dot{y}$	$\dot{i}$	R^2-Adj.	SEE	Rao	D.W.
(a) PD	4.470 (2.19)	0.198 (4.27)	0.300[a] (4.04)	-0.218 (-1.53)	0.072 (3.58)	0.863	2.860	0.790	0.73
(b) PD	3.449 (1.67)	0.194 (4.22)	0.339[b] (4.65)	-0.244 (-1.76)	0.085 (3.98)	0.867	2.824	0.787	1.52
(c) PD	11.487 (3.11)	0.170 (3.65)	-0.083[c] (-0.62)	-0.078 (-0.60)	0.036 (1.56)	0.865	2.844	0.870	1.25
(d) CPI	6.978 (2.49)	0.268 (3.83)	0.376[a] (3.43)	-0.540 (-2.49)	0.105 (3.54)	0.829	4.378	0.747	1.56
(e) CPI	5.738 (1.98)	0.260 (3.74)	0.426[b] (3.96)	-0.583 (2.75)	0.122 (3.81)	0.832	4.336	0.738	1.58
(f) CPI	14.239 (2.81)	0.247 (3.48)	-0.019[c] (-0.10)	-0.369 (-1.85)	0.069 (1.98)	0.830	4.368	0.801	1.45
(g) WPI	-3.656 (-1.29)	0.362 (5.31)	0.601[a] (5.58)	-0.01 (0.05)	0.109 (3.74)	0.867	4.229	0.772	1.71
(h) WPI	-5.689 (-1.95)	0.344 (5.16)	0.662[b] (6.30)	-0.031 (-0.15)	0.139 (4.46)	0.874	4.119	0.771	1.74
(i) WPI	2.150 (0.41)	0.345 (4.82)	0.220[c] (1.09)	0.271 (1.35)	0.073 (2.07)	0.857	4.396	0.816	1.57

Note: Figures in parentheses are t statistics. Dependent variables: PD: Annual rate of change in GDP deflator from the same quarter in the previous year; CPI: Annual rate of change in the consumer price index from the same quarter in the previous year; WPI: Annual rate of change in the wholesale price index from the same quarter in the previous year. Independent variables: Definitions of $\dot{y}$, $\dot{q}$, $\dot{M}$ and $\dot{i}$ see equation (11) in the text.

[a] Represents $M1A$.

[b] Represents $M1B$.

[c] Represents $M2$.

6. In 1975-1978, there were spreads for the interest rates on both unsecured loans and secured loans. However, for the sake of simplicity and without a loss of generality, only the upper limit (i.e., the maximum loan rates) of the unsecured loans and the lower-limit (i.e., the minimum loan rates) of the secured loans are shown in Figure 4.6. Likewise, from 1976 to June 1989, although there were spreads for the interest rates in the case of the short-term loans (one year or less) and the medium- and long-term loans, respectively, only the upper limit of the latter loans and the lower limit of the former loans are shown in Figure 4.6.

7. See "Central Bank Calls for Tax Exemption for Bond Buyers," *The China Post*, July 20, 1991.

References

Balassa, Bela. 1981. "Incentives for Economic Growth in Taiwan," in Bela Balassa, ed., *The Newly Industrializing Countries in the World Economy*. Pp. 407-422. Oxford: Pergamon Press, Pergamon Policy Studies on International Development.

Blinder, Alan S. 1987. "Credit Rationing and Effective Supply Failures." *The Economic Journal* 97: 327-352.

Borio, C. E. V. 1990. *Leverage and Financing of Non-financial Companies: An International Perspective*. Basel: Bank for International Settlements.

Brunner, K., and A. H. Meltzer. 1989. "An Aggregate Theory for a Closed Economy," in K. Brunner and A. H. Meltzer, eds., *Monetary Economics*. Pp. 159-192. Oxford: Basil Blackwell.

———. 1981. "Time Deposits in the Brunner-Meltzer Model of Asset Markets." *Journal of Monetary Economics* 7: 129-139.

———. 1988. "Money and Credit in the Monetary Transmission Process." *American Economic Review* 78(2): 446-451.

Burger, Albert E. 1971. *The Money Supply Process*. Belmont, CA: Wadsworth.

Cargill, Thomas. 1990. "Korean Financial Liberalization, Lessons from the Japanese Experience." *Japan and World Economy* 2: 71-89.

"Central Bank Calls for Tax Exemption for Bond Buyers." *China Post*, July 20, 1991, p. 12. Taipei, Taiwan.

Chang, Kowie, ed. 1967. *Taiwan's Economic Development*, 2 volumes. Taipei: Cheng Chung Books. (in Chinese)

Chen, Shih-meng. 1990. *Macroeconomics*. Taipei: Department of Economics, National Taiwan University. (in Chinese)

Chen, C. N., and S. K. Chen. 1989. "Quantity Theory of Prices under the Open Economy: The Case of Taiwan." *Taiwan Economic Review* 17(2): 189-196. (in Chinese)

Chirinko, Robert S. 1987. "Tobin's Q and Financial Policy." *Journal of Monetary Economics* 19: 69-87.

Chiu, Cheng-hsiung. 1989. "Comment on Chau-Nan Chen and S. K. Chen: Quantity Theory of Prices under the Open Economy: The Case of Taiwan." *Taiwan Economic Review*, 197-202. (in Chinese)

Committee for Economic Revitalization. 1985. *Report: Volume III: Finance Section*. Taipei: Executive Yuan. (in Chinese)

Corrigan, E. Gerald. 1990. "Reforming the U.S. Financial System: An International Perspective," Statement before the United States Senate Committee on Housing and Urban Affairs (with Appendices). *Quarterly Review* 15(1): 1-14. Federal Reserve Bank of New York.

———. 1987. "Financial Market Structure: A Longer View." *Seventy-second Annual Report*, Federal Reserve Bank of New York.

Dornbusch, Rudiger. 1976. "Comments on Brunner and Meltzer," in J. L. Stein, ed., *Monetarism*. Pp. 104-125. New York: American Elsevier Publishing Co.
Fama, Eugene. 1985. "What's Different about Banks?" *Journal of Monetary Economics* 15: 29-40.
Feder, Gershon. 1982. "On Exports and Economic Growth." *Journal of Development Economics* 12(1): 59-73.
Friedman, Milton. 1959. "The Demand for Money: Some Theoretical and Empirical Results." *Journal of Political Economy* 67: 327-351.
Fry, Maxwell J. 1988. *Money, Interest, and Banking in Economic Development*. Baltimore: The Johns Hopkins University Press.
_____. 1989. "The Rate of Return to Taiwan's Capital Stock, 1961-1987." University of Birmingham (unpublished).
Gertler, Mark. 1988. "Financial Structure and Aggregate Economic Activity: An Overview." *Journal of Money, Credit and Banking* 20(3): 559-588.
Hanke, Steve H., and Alan A. Walters. 1989-90. "Confidence and the Sequencing Problem." *Journal of Economic Growth* 4: 18-19.
Hess, Alan C. 1984. "Variable Rate Mortgages: Confusion of Means and Ends." *Financial Analysts Journal* 40: 67-70.
Hsing, Mo-huan. 1986. "Further Observations on the Growth and Structural Shifts of the Taiwan Economy -- A Re-examination and Extension of Professor Simon Kuznets' Studies." *Economic Papers No. 104*. Taiwan: Chung-Hua Institution for Economic Research. (in Chinese)
Hsu, Z. C. 1953. "Studies on Taiwan's Preferential Interest Rate Deposits." *Quarterly Review*, March 1953. Taipei: Bank of Taiwan.
"Japanese Financial Reforms: Encourage Free Competition," an editorial. *Kinzai Financial Briefing: A Bi-Weekly Newsletter on Japanese Finance and Economics*. September 10, 1990. Bethesda, Maryland.
Kmenta, J. 1967. "On Estimation of the CES Production Function." *International Economic Review* 8(2): 180-189.
Kohsaka, A. 1984. "The High Interest Rate Policy under Financial Repression," in *The Developing Economies*. Pp. 453-475. Tokyo: Institute of Developing Economics.
Kuo, Shirley W. Y. 1989. "Liberalization of the Financial Market in Taiwan in the 1980s." *Economic Review*, No. 250. Taipei: International Commercial Bank of China.
_____. 1983. *The Taiwan Economy in Transition*. Boulder: Westview Press.
Li, K. T. 1989. "Sources of Rapid Economic Growth: The Case of Taiwan." *Journal of Economic Growth* 3: 4-13.
Liang, K. S., and Hou Liang Ching-ing. 1988. *The Financial System and Financial Policy*. Taipei: Council for Economic Planning and Development. (in Chinese)

Lin, K. S., and T. M. Wu. 1989. "Taiwan's Big Inflation: 1946-1949," in *The Second Conference on Modern Chinese Economic History*. Taipei: Institute of Economics, Academia Sinica.

Liu, Fu-Chi. 1970. *Essays on Monetary Development in Taiwan*. Taipei: China Committee for Publication Aid and Prize Awards.

Lundberg, Erik. 1979. "Fiscal and Monetary Policy," in Walter Galenson, ed., *Economic Growth and Structural Change in Taiwan: The Postwar Experience of the Republic of China*. Pp. 263-307. Ithaca: Cornell University Press.

Maddison, Angus. 1987. "Growth and Slowdown in Advanced Capitalist Economies: Techniques of Quantitative Assessment." *Journal of Economic Literature* 25(2): 649-698.

Mckinnon, R. 1973. *Money and Capital in Economic Development*. Washington, D.C.: Brookings Institution.

Munnell, Alicia H. 1990. "Why Has Productivity Growth Declined? Productivity and Public Investment." *New England Economic Review*, Jan/Feb 1990, 1-22.

Ranis, G. 1977. "Economic Development and Financial Institutions," in B. Balassa and R. Nelson, eds., *Private Value and Public Policy*. Pp. 27-55. Amsterdam: North Holland.

Secretary of the Treasury. 1991. *Modernizing the Financial System -- Recommendations for Safer, More Competitive Banks*. Taipei: Department of Treasury.

Shea, Jia-Dong. 1990. "Financial Development in Taiwan: A Macro Analysis." Presented at the Conference on Financial Development in Japan, Korea and Taiwan. The Institute of Economics, Academia Sinica, Taipei, Taiwan.

Shieh, Samuel C. 1989. "Financial Liberalization and Internationalization in the Republic of China -- Current Status and Future Policy Directions." *Economic Review*, No. 254. Taipei: International Commercial Bank of China.

Shih, Yen. 1988. "A Re-examination of Short-run Demand for Money in Taiwan." *Quarterly Review* 10: 21-49. Taipei: Economic Research Department, The Central Bank of China. (in Chinese)

Sun, Chen, and Ming-yi Liang. 1982. "Savings in Taiwan, 1953-1980," in Kwoh-ting Li and Tzong-shian Yu, eds., *Experiences and Lessons of Economic Development in Taiwan*. Pp. 295-312. Taipei: Institute of Economics, Academia Sinica.

Taylor, Lance. 1981. *Structuralist Macroeconomics: Applicable Models for the Third World*. New York: Basic Books.

Townsend, Robert M. 1983. "Financial Structure and Economic Activity." *American Economic Review* 73: 895-911.

Tsiang, S. C. 1989. *Finance Constraints and the Theory of Money*, Meir Kohn, ed. Boston: Academic Press.
Wood, John H., and Norma L. Wood. 1985. *Financial Markets*. New York: McGraw Hill.
Yu, Kuo-Hwa. 1982. "How to Promote Interest Rate Liberalization." *Quarterly Review* 4: 7-18. Taipei: The Central Bank of China. (in Chinese)

5

Money and Financial Markets: The International Perspective

Christina Y. Liu

1. Introduction

Since economic liberalization and internationalization were adopted as national policies in Taiwan in the early 1980s, the international financial market has become an increasingly important sector. The recent development of Taiwan's international financial market has not only generated strong effects on its macroeconomy but also induced a much tighter link between the capital market in Taiwan and the international capital market.

This chapter presents an analysis of the past, present, and future development of Taiwan's international financial market. The effects of the recent liberalization of both domestic and foreign capital markets are examined, and the opportunities and pitfalls that lie ahead for Taiwan as it endeavors to join the circle of the mature economies are discussed from an international financial point of view.

The organization of this chapter is as follows: Section 2 provides a general background for our discussion. Section 3 examines the domestic financial liberalization program implemented in Taiwan in the 1980s, focusing particularly on deregulation of the domestic money market. Section 4 presents some of the most recent institutional changes in the international financial market, including restrictions and relaxations on capital flows in and out of the country and current developments in the foreign exchange market. Section 5 discusses issues of the internationalization of the financial market, covering globalization of the banking system and the securities and insurance markets. The establishment and development of the "Foreign Currency Call Loan Market" in Taipei in the 1989-1991 period is also elaborated in this section. Lastly, to provide a perspective on the future, Section 6 summarizes and outlines the opportunities and difficulties that lie ahead for Taiwan as it tries to join the circle of the mature economies.

2. General Background of Financial Liberalization in Taiwan

In the past four decades, Taiwan has successfully made the transition from a developing to a newly industrialized country. Over the past forty years, the real GNP grew at an average rate of 9 percent per year, and the real per capita GNP grew at an average rate of 6.4 percent per year, increasing from US$70 at the end of World War II to US$8,000 at the end of 1990. The success was characterized not only by rapid growth but also by expansion in exports and the achievement of stable prices, full employment, and a relatively equitable distribution of income.[1]

In this successful development process, the adoption of a relatively free economic system has played a crucial role. For example, liberalization of the trade sector has been emphasized since the 1960s, helping Taiwan make a smooth transition from the import-substitution policies of the 1950s to the export-expansion policies of the 1960s. In contrast to the liberalization of the trade sector, financial liberalization did not take place until a later date. Before the 1980s, restrictions on the interest rate, exchange rate, capital flows, and foreign investment were all quite severe. However, starting in the early 1980s, there was an increasing demand in Taiwan for adjustment to the new circumstances of global financial deregulation. As a result, liberalization and internationalization of the financial sector were adopted as national policies in Taiwan in the 1980s.

In general, the primary objective of a financial market is the efficient allocation of capital in production and investment opportunities, and increasing efficiency in the capital markets requires continued deregulation to promote competition. However, while it is essential for a mature economy to have a liberalized financial market, there are usually a number of problems that have to be faced during the course of liberalization. The order and speed of liberalization have hence received a great deal of attention in both academic and policy-making circles in recent years.

There is no general agreement in the existing literature regarding the order and speed of liberalization. Nevertheless, it is now fully recognized that liberalization of any single market will not only affect that particular market but also create externalities by inducing reactions from a large number of other markets which may sometimes be harmful enough to force the abandonment of the liberalization program. It is therefore usually not feasible or desirable to adopt a liberalization program which lifts controls on all markets at the same time.

Regarding the timing and sequence of liberalization, it is now also widely accepted in the literature that both stable prices and a balanced fiscal budget are essential prerequisites for financial liberalization. In addition, it has increasingly been suggested that a country's domestic financial market should be liberalized prior to its international capital market, and that the international trade sector should be liberalized prior to its international capital sector.[2]

Based on the above suggestions, it is clear that the timing of Taiwan's financial liberalization programs in the 1980s was very favorable. As shown in Table 5.1, in the early 1980s the island recorded a massive export surplus, a high savings rate, a sound government budget, an increase in the real wage rate, a low inflation rate and low tax rates. The necessary preconditions for financial liberalization were hence satisfied. In addition, since the liberalization of the international trade sector had been continuously emphasized long before the 1980s, the economy was ready in every respect for financial liberalization at the beginning of the 1980s.

3. Domestic Financial Market Liberalization

There were two stages of domestic financial liberalization in Taiwan, one starting in the early 1980s and the other beginning in 1985. The first stage of liberalization was in response to the oil crisis and the resulting international financial disorder. The second stage of liberalization was prompted by massive foreign reserves and a rapid growth in the money supply which were induced by a huge trade surplus. The basic aim of both stages of liberalization was the same: to implement liberalization programs such that the price mechanism could adjust for any imbalances.

The First Stage of Interest Rate Liberalization

The official money market in Taiwan was established in 1976. The main objectives were to pave the way for flexible interest rate movements and to channel financial savings from the unorganized private money market to enterprises. The money market instruments consist of commercial paper, bankers' acceptances, negotiable certificates of deposits, and treasury bills. When the market was first established, interest rates in the money market were not subject to the standard ceiling regulation. However, according to the Banking Law effective at that time, the maximum rates for different kinds of deposits were prescribed by the Central Bank of China. In addition, the ranges of interest rates on different kinds of loans were proposed by the Bankers' Association and submitted to the Central Bank of China for confirmation and enforcement, and the minimum loan rate was not allowed to exceed the maximum deposit rate. Due to these restrictions, the money market was not able to perform its function actively in the 1970s.

Deregulation of the money market was the first step in interest rate liberalization in Taiwan. In November, 1980 the Central Bank of China promulgated the "Essentials of Interest Rate Adjustment," which permitted

TABLE 5.1 Characteristics of the Taiwan Economy (1961-1988) (in percentages)

Item	1961-71	1971-81	1981-86	1987	1988
Production					
1. GNP (% real change)	10.0	9.5	7.4	11.9	7.1
2. Unemployment Rate (%)	2.9	1.5	2.4	2.0	1.7
3. Gross Domestic Investment Rate (% GNP)	22.3	30.4	21.9	19.3	23.6
4. Gross National Savings Rate (% GNP)	21.8	31.8	32.6	38.5	34.7
Balance of Payments					
5. Exports (% GNP)	18.4	42.0	49.5	53.8	50.7
6. Imports (% GNP)	21.0	40.0	37.6	34.8	41.7
7. Current Account Balance (% GNP)	-0.5	1.4	10.7	19.2	11.1
8. Debt Service Ratio	-	3.8[a]	4.4	3.1	
Fiscal Surplus					
9. Public Sector Expenditures (% GNP)	23.7	24.3	24.9	22.1	26.5
10. Fiscal Surplus (% GDP)	2.4	6.7	4.9	6.1	7.7
11. Total Change in Monetary Base (% GDP)	1.4[b]	2.5	2.3	4.4	5.1
Money Prices					
12. M_2/GDP (%)	34.1	57.9	91.3	134.8	148.2
13. Annual Change in CPI (%)	3.3	11.6	3.5	0.5	1.4
14. Annual Change in WPI (%)	1.9	10.4	0.1	-3.2	-1.5
15. Annual Change in Real Wage					
Rate of Manufacturing	6.2	8.0	6.1	9.1	9.3
Staff	1.3[c]	5.6	7.4	6.1	7.3
Workers	11.9[c]	9.7	5.6	9.4	8.8
16. Exchange Rate (NT$/US$1)	40.0	37.8	38.9	31.8	28.6
17. Real Effective Exchange Rate Index (Trade weighted, 1979=100)	108.9	104.0	100.1	98.5	101.0

[a]1974-81. [b]1962-71. [c]1969-71.

Note: Figures are period averages given in percentages.

Source: Liu (1992).

a wider range of loan rates and also allowed for the free setting of interest rates on CDs and on some other money market instruments. One of the most important effects of this first-step liberalization program was the expansion of the money market. For example, within a period of only one and a half years (from the end of 1980 to May 1982), the ratio of the money market outstanding loans to the total banking loans doubled from 8.6 percent to 15.6 percent. Among all money market instruments, bankers' acceptances had the fastest growth, increasing by 5.4 times; CDs came second, increasing by 2.4 times; and the commercial paper increased by 40 percent.

At the same time, to move closer to the market-determined money market rate, official interest rates were adjusted much more frequently than before. From November 1980 to September 1982, the official interest rates were adjusted to be close to the movement of money market rates and inter-bank call rates and there were as many as ten adjustments during this period. However, the implementation of first-stage interest rate liberalization was only partially successful because it failed to widen the range of loan rates.

The Second Stage of Interest Rate Liberalization

One of the obstacles to widening the range of loan rates in the early 1980s came from the "Regulations for Interest Rate Management," which stipulated that the maximum deposit rate should not exceed the minimum loan rate. In September, 1985 this regulation was abolished and, beginning in March 1985, each depository bank was asked to make a daily announcement of its "prime rate" which was then adopted as its own minimum loan rate. Differences in prime rates among banks were not only officially recognized but also encouraged. At the same time, the "Central Inter-bank Call Rate System" was abolished to give each bank complete freedom in the determination of its own call rate. In addition, in January 1986, deposit categories were reduced from thirteen to four, greatly expanding the free zone of banking activities.[3]

Another factor which contributed to the success of the second stage in interest rate liberalization was the timing of its implementation. Since interest rates in a controlled economy are often repressed at artificially low levels, a common concern is that financial liberalization will lead to an increase in interest rates which is normally painful for an economy to adjust to. From this point of view, the timing of the second stage of interest rate liberalization in Taiwan was very favorable. While the huge trade surplus in the early 1980s generated excess liquidity in the economy, domestic financial liberalization provided an opportunity for the market interest rate to *decrease* rather than *increase* to reflect that excess liquidity. The interest rate liberalization program has thus been implemented smoothly and successfully and, as a result, the market interest rate is now mostly determined by market forces. Revision of the Banking Law in 1989 also removed controls on all deposit and loan rates.[4]

4. International Capital Market Liberalization

This section analyzes recent international capital market liberalization in Taiwan, focusing particularly on the background of international financial liberalization, restrictions and relaxations on capital flows in and out of the country, and on the current development of the foreign exchange market.

Background of International Financial Liberalization

The foreign exchange system in Taiwan was officially changed from a fixed exchange rate regime to a flexible rate regime in February 1979. As shown in Figure 5.1, the currency value remained quite stable during the 1981-1985 period but appreciated by more than 40 percent relative to the US dollar during the 1986-1988 period.

Extensive central bank intervention during the late 1980s induced Taiwan to hold the second largest amount of foreign reserves in the world. Foreign reserves held by the central bank in Taiwan increased from US$23.7 billion in early 1986 to US$76 billion by the end of 1987. That is, the central bank had purchased US$52.3 billion in foreign exchange in only a two-year period. This level of foreign reserves was sufficient to cover nearly three years' worth of imports, in contrast to the three-month coverage most major countries have as central bank reserves. The sharp increase in foreign reserves is shown in Figure 5.2.

The continuous appreciation of the NT dollar and the accumulation of foreign reserves in the late 1980s were initiated by the large trade-surplus in Taiwan during that period. Since 1985, the current account balance in Taiwan has increased dramatically. As presented in Table 5.2, the current account balance accounted for 15.5 percent of GNP in 1985, and this share increased to 22.4 percent and 20.7 percent of GNP in 1986 and 1987, respectively. During the same period, since the G-5 meeting in September 1985, the US dollar continuously depreciated against most of the major currencies in the world. Both of the above factors created a natural tendency for the NT dollar to appreciate against the US dollar.

However, the NT dollar did not appreciate to its full extent due to the central bank's intervention. Even though the general public believed that the appreciation of the NT dollar was eventually inevitable, there was still strong pressure on the central bank to intervene in the exchange market.

FIGURE 5.1 Unit Value of the NT Dollar (in terms of the US Dollar)

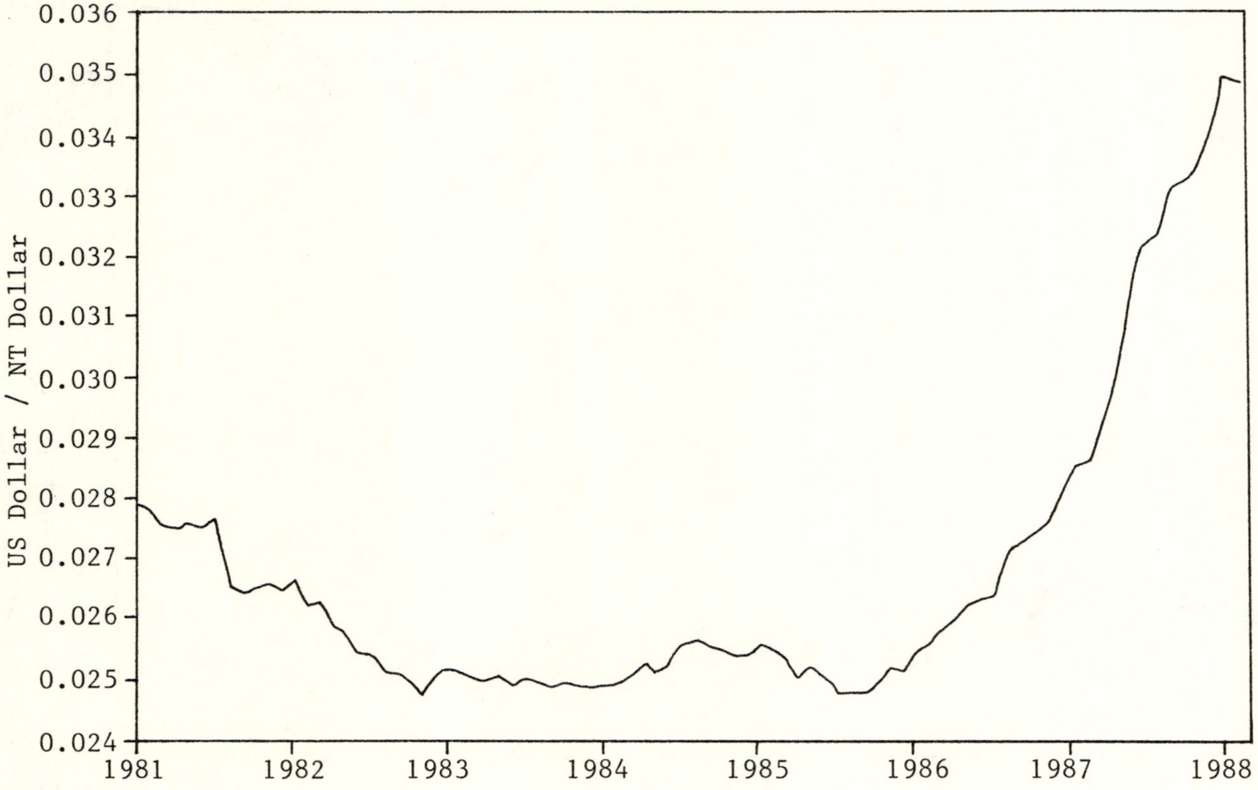

202

FIGURE 5.2 Foreign Reserves in the Central Bank

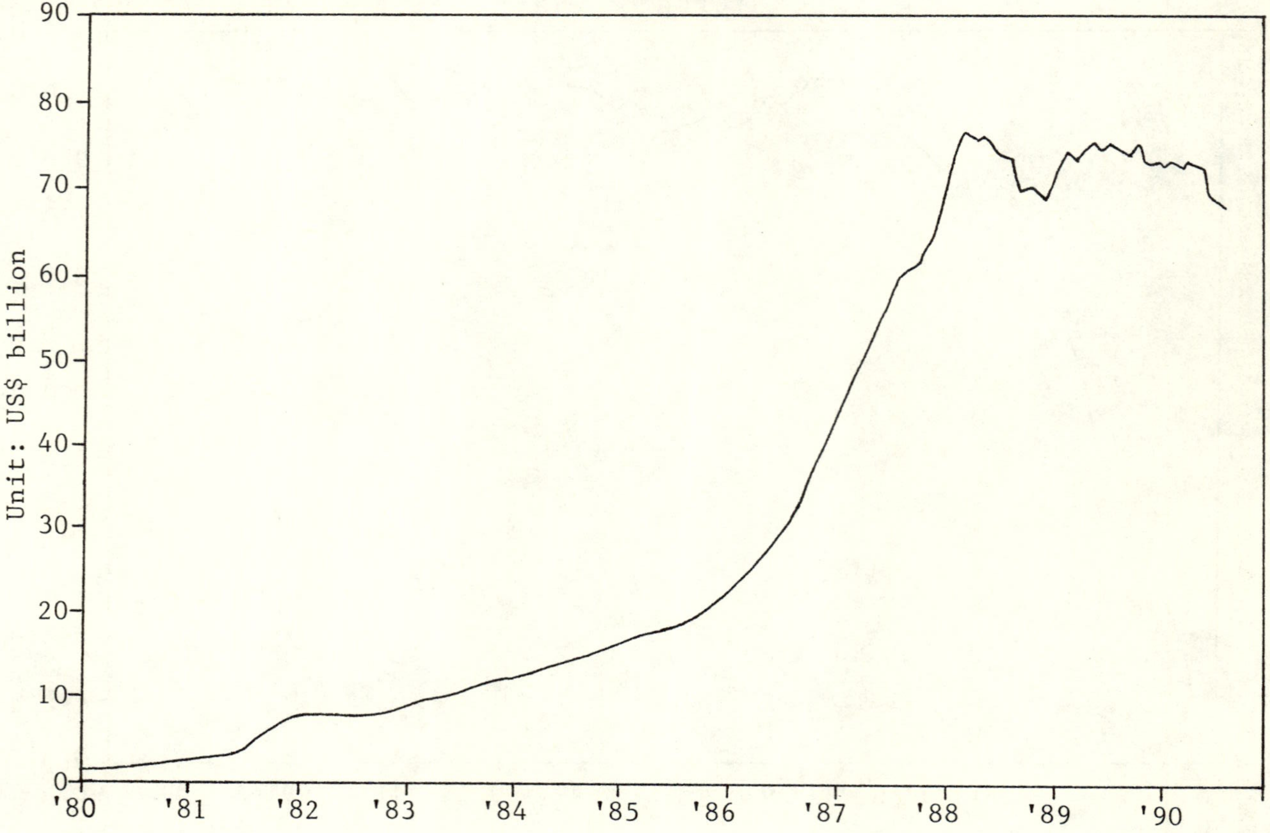

Unit: US$ billion

TABLE 5.2 Current Account Balance and Excess Savings as Percentage of GNP (in percentages)

Year	Gross National Product GNP	Exports of Goods and Services X	Imports of Goods and Services M	Current Account Balance X-M	Gross Savings S	Gross Investment I	Excess Savings S-I
1971	100.0	37.3	34.7	2.6	28.8	26.2	2.6
1972	100.0	43.9	37.4	6.5	32.1	25.6	6.5
1973	100.0	48.9	43.6	5.3	34.4	29.1	5.3
1974	100.0	45.7	53.4	-7.7	31.5	39.2	-7.7
1975	100.0	41.6	45.4	-3.8	26.7	30.5	-3.8
1976	100.0	49.4	47.8	1.6	32.4	30.8	1.6
1977	100.0	50.9	46.6	4.3	32.6	28.3	4.3
1978	100.0	54.6	48.5	6.1	34.4	28.3	6.1
1979	100.0	56.1	55.6	0.5	33.4	32.9	0.5
1980	100.0	55.3	56.8	-1.5	32.3	33.8	-1.5
1981	100.0	55.0	53.7	1.3	31.3	30.0	1.3
1982	100.0	53.9	49.0	4.9	29.7	24.8	4.9
1983	100.0	56.7	47.8	8.9	31.5	22.6	8.9
1984	100.0	60.4	48.4	12.0	32.9	20.9	12.0
1985	100.0	58.9	43.6	15.3	32.6	17.3	15.3
1986	100.0	63.1	41.0	22.1	37.7	15.6	22.1
1987	100.0	63.2	44.0	19.2	38.5	19.3	19.2
1988	100.0	60.8	49.3	11.5	34.9	23.4	11.5

The general concern of the community and of the government sector was that any drastic appreciation of the NT dollar would involve high adjustment costs which might be too painful for both the export and import-competing sectors to bear. Reflecting this philosophy, the central bank frequently intervened and sterilized the foreign exchange market to absorb the excess supply of US dollars, leading to the huge foreign exchange reserves held in the central bank in Taiwan.[5]

While central bank intervention is common in most countries,[6] the particular central bank intervention in Taiwan during the 1986-1988 period induced a serious violation of a fundamental international capital market equilibrium condition. That is, the interest rate parity condition was continuously violated during this period. Since the central bank intervened in such a way that the NT dollar was appreciated "gradually" and "smoothly," the extent of appreciation never fully satisfied market expectations. This partial liberalization situation hence induced an expectation of further appreciation of the NT dollar. As a result, from 1986 to 1988, the expected forward premium of the NT dollar strongly outweighed the domestic and foreign interest rate differential and the interest rate parity condition was strongly violated.[7] Discussion of the parity condition in greater detail and formal empirical evidence of the deviations during the 1986-1988 period are presented in Appendix A.

The violation of the interest rate parity condition induced a huge speculative capital inflow into the economy, which in turn generated an even greater excess supply of US dollars in the foreign exchange market and further fueled the initial problem created by the trade surplus. Besides inducing the huge foreign reserves held by the central bank, this overall imbalance in the international capital account generated two other serious adverse effects on the economy.

The first was a drastic increase in the money supply (Figure 5.3) which was a direct result of intervention in the foreign exchange market. Figure 5.3 shows that while the monetary growth rate was quite stable in the early 1980s, it increased drastically in the 1986-1989 period. Actually, since the intervention implemented was partially "sterilized" through open market operations, the effect on the money supply was not as obvious as it otherwise would have been. However, the increase in the money supply was still quite large, leaving the local capital markets awash in liquidity and generating a second problem -- "inflation" in the stock market and the overheated real estate market.

Since 1987, prices in the stock market and in the real estate market have both skyrocketed. For example, from January 1987 to September 1987, the level of the weighted stock index in Taiwan increased from 1150 to 4459, a more than 300 percent increase. On average, this yielded a 33 percent return per month, or a 400 percent return per year. It can be seen in Figure 5.4 that the stock index reached the 8000 level in September 1988, and later a record-high level of 12,054 by January 1990. Due to this abnormally high return in the stock market, resource allocation in the economy was greatly distorted, adding further to the adjustment costs the economy had to pay for its trade imbalance problem.

Capital Flows in and out of the Country

Direct capital movement by the general public was severely restricted in Taiwan before July 1987. However, there were other official channels for capital flows long before that time. According to the foreign exchange regulations, commercial banks were allowed to borrow foreign exchange

FIGURE 5.3 Money Supply (M1B)

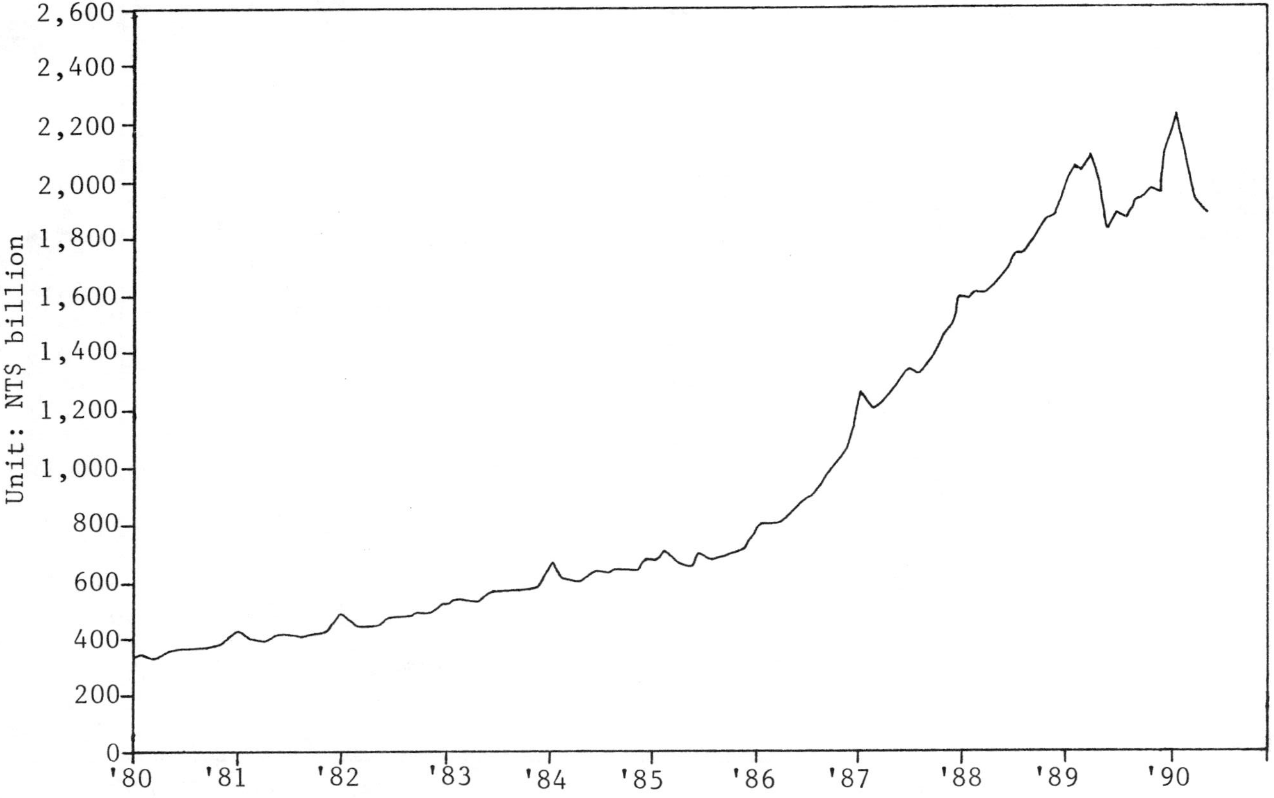

Unit: NT$ billion

FIGURE 5.4 Taiwan Stock Exchange Weighted Stock Index (end of month)

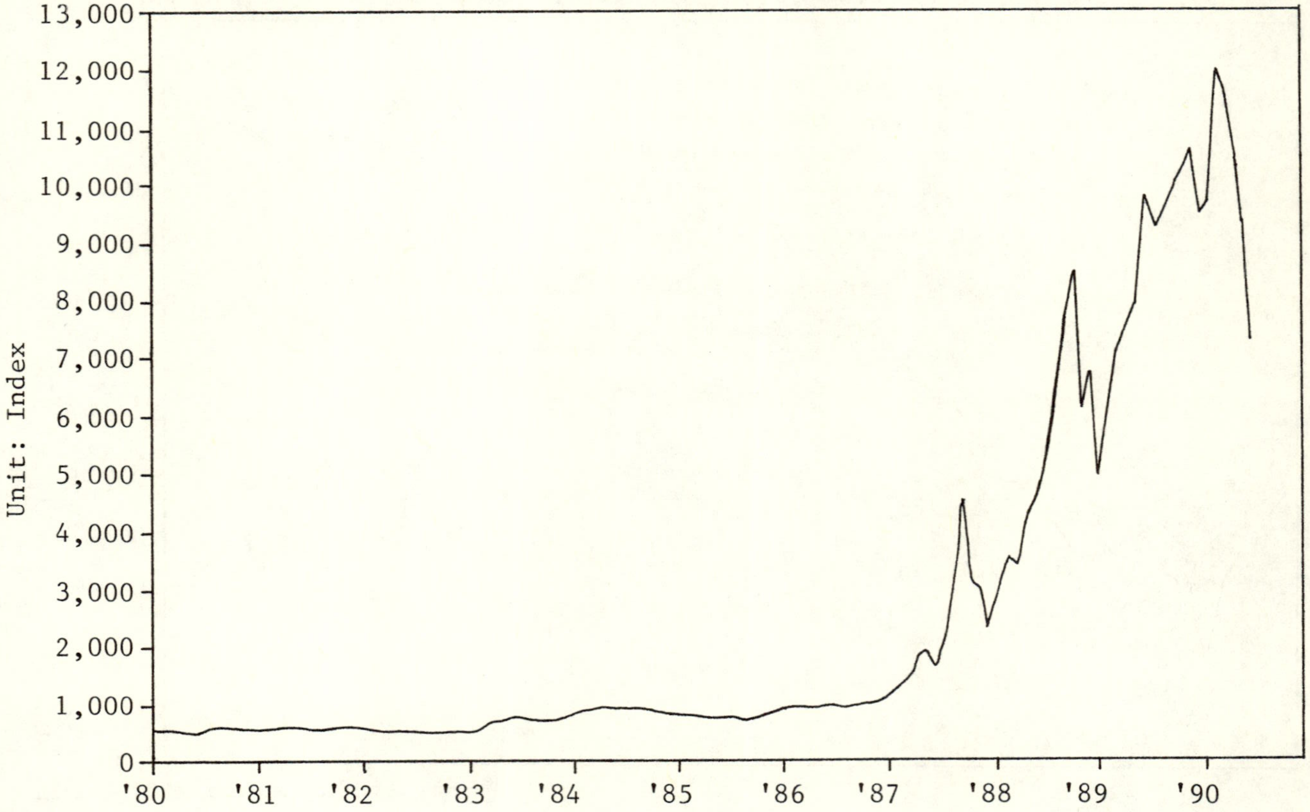

from abroad, and any importer/exporter was eligible to borrow foreign exchange through commercial banks and sell it in the foreign exchange market for the NT dollar.

Figure 5.5 presents clear evidence of the capital inflows through commercial banks. It can be easily seen from Figure 5.5 that the foreign liabilities outstanding in commercial banks increased drastically starting in 1986, especially between the last quarter of 1986 and the first quarter of 1987. Within that short six-month period, the foreign liabilities outstanding in commercial banks went up from just a little over US$5 billion to US$13.8 billion. These huge capital inflows were mainly speculative and, as mentioned earlier, were induced due to violations of the interest rate parity condition. Rigorous empirical evidence of the connection between the foreign liabilities of commercial banks and the expectation of currency appreciation is provided in Appendix B.

Towards the end of May 1987, market expectations for further appreciation of the NT dollar remained very strong, attracting even larger capital inflows than before. To put a stop to this continuing capital inflow, on May 31, 1987, the central bank of Taiwan announced a freeze on the level of foreign liabilities outstanding at the then existing level of US$13.8 billion (see the first peak in Figure 5.5). With the freeze on the foreign debt of commercial banks, the link between capital inflow and the expectation of currency appreciation was broken. Termination of the continuous huge capital inflow helped to moderate further currency appreciation and to reduce the current account surplus for the following reasons.

While there existed a speculative profit opportunity during the 1986-1987 period, capital movement was not officially permitted for the general public until July 1987. The exporters in Taiwan, however, had official channels for capital flows, and therefore took the most advantage of that speculative opportunity. In fact, since many exporters charged their foreign customers the same foreign currency price as before the NT dollar was appreciated and covered the trade loss with their speculative profits, the trade surplus remained high even after the NT dollar had greatly appreciated. After the central bank imposed controls on foreign liabilities, the exporters in Taiwan lost this speculative profit opportunity, forcing them to charge prices which truly reflected their rising costs. As a result, the trade surplus declined, reducing the pressure for a further appreciation of the NT dollar.

On October 1, 1987, the central bank tried to lift the restrictions on foreign liabilities outstanding in commercial banks. However, the amount of capital inflow on that day alone exceeded US$3 billion, which prompted the central bank to announce another freeze. This time the freeze was set at the October 2, 1987 level of US$16.2 billion (see the second peak in Figure 5.5). Since then, the NT dollar has been relatively stable, and central bank intervention has also been relatively mild.

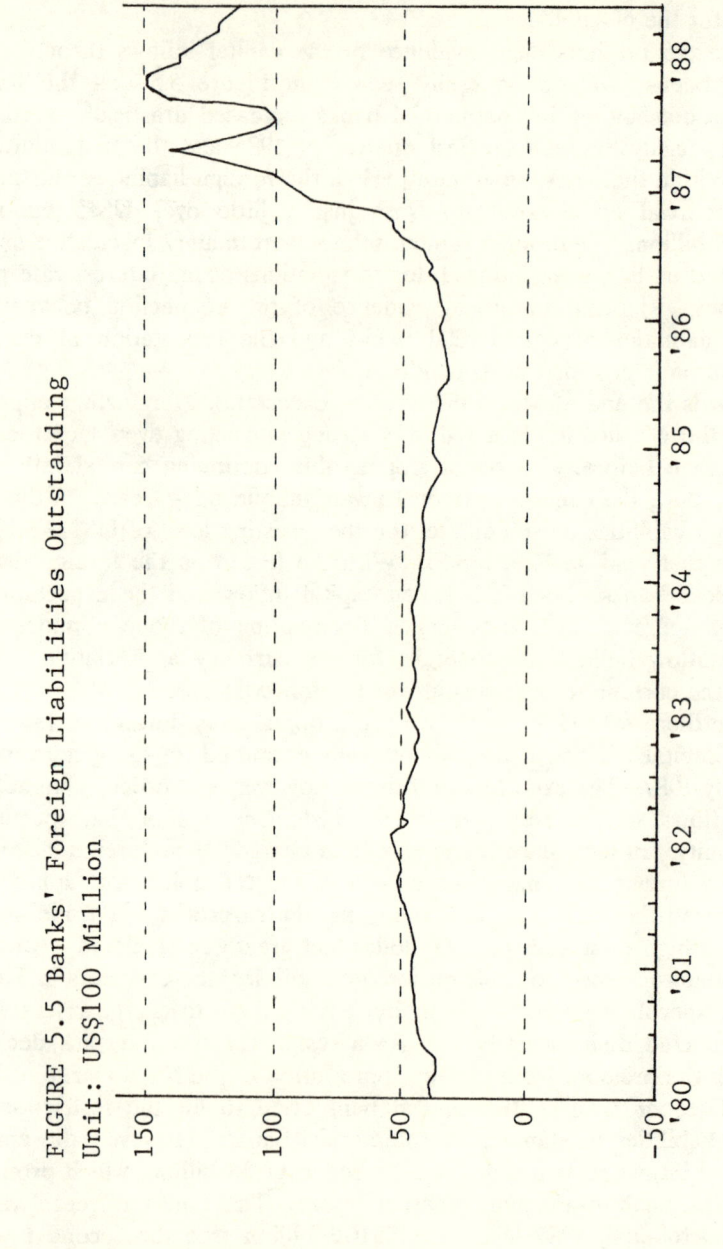

FIGURE 5.5 Banks' Foreign Liabilities Outstanding
Unit: US$100 Million

Institutionally, foreign exchange controls, other than restrictions on the level of foreign liabilities, were largely relaxed to allow direct capital outflow by the non-bank private sector. Specifically, on May 31, 1987, the maximum amount of annual outward remittance for each adult was expanded to US$5 million, while the maximum amount of annual inward remittance for each adult was only increased to US$50,000. This was a significant step towards liberalization in the direction of capital outflow. However, no immediate net capital outflow was observed in the wake of this capital movement liberalization program because of the continued expectation of an appreciation of the NT dollar.

During the 1989-1991 period, since the pressure for the appreciation of the NT dollar was reduced, the capital inflow restrictions were also greatly relaxed. The permitted maximum annual capital inflow for each adult was first increased from US$50,000 to US$200,000 in June 1989, to US$500,000 in September 1989, to US$1,000,000 in November 1989, to US$2,000,000 in July 1990, and most recently, to US$3,000,000 in March 1991. Therefore, each adult in Taiwan is now allowed to annually invest up to US$3,000,000 abroad and is allowed to annually transfer up to US$3,000,000 from a foreign country back to Taiwan. These relaxations on capital movement will encourage individuals in Taiwan to invest in foreign financial assets and also enhance internationalization of the securities market in Taiwan.

Foreign Exchange Market

Even though the exchange rate system in Taiwan was officially changed to a floating rate regime in February 1979, the foreign exchange market today, based on the following two observations, is still only a partially liberalized market.

First, the spot exchange rate has often been affected by central bank intervention and hence cannot fluctuate to respond to market forces fully or immediately. As mentioned earlier, the particular way in which the central bank intervened in the 1986-1988 period generated an obvious gap between the market expectation of the future NT dollar and the market spot rate, which induced huge capital inflows into the economy and made adjustment of the current account surplus even harder. In the 1989-1991 period, the central bank still intervened in the spot market frequently. However, since the trade surplus had been reduced substantially, the magnitude of intervention was much smaller than during the 1986-1988 period.

Second, due to the central bank's extensive intervention in the forward foreign exchange market in the 1986-1988 period, the forward exchange rate was greatly distorted and the forward market was almost closed. Even now, the forward foreign exchange market in Taiwan is not active, which makes it almost impossible for exporters and importers in Taiwan to hedge their exchange rate risk. This, of course, makes it more difficult for the economy to adjust to a flexible exchange rate system and hence harder to have a successful liberalization of the foreign exchange market.

5. Internationalization of Financial Markets

Internationalization of financial markets has been one of the major goals in Taiwan in recent years. This section covers globalization of the banking system and of the securities and insurance markets. The establishment and development of the "Foreign Currency Call Loan Market" is also introduced.[8]

Banking System

To encourage more competition and enhance the efficiency in the banking industry, privatization and internationalization of the banking system have been greatly emphasized in recent years. Under the revision of the Banking Law in 1989, the banking industry is now open to the private sector. There are currently sixteen applications for establishing private banks in Taiwan, and the application results were to be revealed in June 1991. An effort has also been made to privatize the originally government-owned banks. However, this issue is politically sensitive and the timing of this privatization remains unclear.

The globalization of the banking industry has advanced quite rapidly in the past two years (1988-1990) both in terms of the number of foreign bank branch offices set up in Taiwan and in terms of the number of domestic commercial banks' branch offices set up in foreign countries. For example, there were thirty-two foreign commercial banks which had branch offices in Taiwan at the end of 1988. At the end of 1990, this number had increased to thirty-five, and among these thirty-five banks eight had two branch offices each, bringing the total number of foreign commercial bank branch offices to forty-three. The increased number of foreign banks will induce more competition among domestic banks, which will be helpful for the development of the banking industry. However, in view of the number of foreign branch offices set up in Korea and in Japan (sixty-six and 200, respectively), the pace of internationalization of Taiwan's banking industry probably needs to be increased.

The establishment of foreign branch offices by domestic commercial banks has, by comparison, advanced more rapidly during the 1988-1990 period. At the end of 1988, there were only three domestic banks which had set up fifteen branch offices abroad, and the ICBC was the only domestic bank with a branch office in the United States. By the end of

1990, six domestic banks had established twenty-three branch offices and eight subsidiary companies in more than eleven foreign countries, and each of these six banks had established branch offices in the United States.

Securities and Insurance Markets

The basic idea of the internationalization of the Taiwan securities market is to allow for participation of foreign nationals in this market. According to the "Plan for Introduction of Foreign and Overseas Chinese Capital into Securities" approved by the Executive Yuan in 1983, this internationalization program was to be implemented in three phases.

The first phase was to allow foreign investors to make indirect investments through the purchase of mutual funds. By the end of 1990, there were four investment trust companies in Taiwan which managed their own Taiwan fund for foreign investors. The "Taiwan Fund" has been listed on the New York Stock Exchange since December 1986, and the "ROC Taiwan Fund" has been listed on the American Stock Exchange since 1988. Through these two listings, foreign residents could easily invest indirectly in Taiwan securities.

The second phase permitted foreign institutional investors to invest directly in the Taiwan securities market. Under the Securities and Exchange Law, as revised in January 1988, foreign investors could participate in Taiwan's securities business by investing in or by managing local securities firms. However, to facilitate technology transfer and to improve the quality of local securities firms, the total amount of investment by any individual foreign national was limited to ten percent of the amount of the total issued shares of any securities firm, and each securities firm was allowed to have up to 40 percent of its investment from foreign nationals.

This revision of the Securities and Exchange Law further enhanced technology transfers by lifting restrictions on foreign investment in securities investment consulting enterprises (SICE). Among the seventy-six SICEs currently in operation, many are joint ventures between local and foreign funds, and ten of them are more than ninety percent foreign-owned.

The revised Securities and Exchange Law also allowed foreign securities firms to establish branch offices in Taiwan. Recently, Merrill Lynch and Shearson Lehman opened branch offices in Taiwan.

Compared with the world's major securities markets, the participation of institutional investors in the Taiwan securities markets has been small. One important purpose of phase two has therefore been to introduce more institutional and mature investment behavior into this market. In the third phase, foreign individuals and overseas Chinese will be allowed to invest in the Taiwan securities market directly.

Another internationalization program regards foreign insurance firms.

Starting in 1986, U.S. insurance firms were conditionally allowed to enter the Taiwan insurance market. In February 1989, the "Regulations Governing Securities Investment by Overseas Chinese and Foreign Investors, and Procedures for Remittance" were revised. Under the new revision, branches of foreign insurance companies were allowed to invest up to 35 percent of their capital and reserves in the Taiwan securities market.

Due to these recent internationalization programs, the link between the domestic and world financial markets has become much stronger. Through these programs, international financial know-how was also introduced, which will aid the further development of the international financial market in Taiwan.

The "Foreign Currency Call Loan Market" in Taipei

The "Foreign Currency Call Loan Market" was established in Taipei in August 1989 as an expansion of the "offshore banking unit" established in Taiwan in June 1984. While the short-term goal was to provide an efficient mechanism for banks to borrow foreign currencies, the long-term goal was to promote Taipei as a regional financial center in the future. Even though the size of the market is still relatively small compared to that of the offshore markets in Tokyo and in Singapore,[9] the government has formulated aggressive strategies to facilitate the future growth of this market.[10]

When the market was first established, the US dollar was the only foreign currency transacted. The market has been expanding over time and, as of October 1990, included transactions in the West German mark, the Japanese yen, and the Hong Kong dollar, with an average daily turnover of US$800 million. Since the market is essentially an extension of a "Eurocurrency" market, the interest rates in this market, the TIBOR (Taipei inter-bank offer rate), closely follows the LIBOR (London inter-bank offer rate) and the SIBOR (Singapore inter-bank offer rate). Since February 1991, the Taipei Eurocurrency inter-bank market has also been linked with the market in Singapore through Astley & Pearce, Inc. in Singapore which also connects the Eurocurrency market in Taipei to the inter-bank markets in Japan and Hong Kong.

6. The Prospect for the Future and Conclusions

During the past decade, there has been explosive growth in international capital markets. This growth has been fueled in part by a trend towards liberalizing securities markets in the most important world capital markets. The United States was the first to liberalize, followed by the European Common Market countries and then by Japan. As the world capital markets become more and more integrated, it is extremely important for

Taiwan to establish a liberalized international capital market in order to join the circle of the mature economies.

Overall financial liberalization has received much attention in Taiwan since the 1980s. In the past few years, deregulation of the domestic money market and capital movements has been quite successful, and the internationalization of the securities market and the banking system has advanced smoothly. Since floating interest rates and free capital movements are essential preconditions for a liberalized international capital market, the recent success of interest rate liberalization and of relaxation on international capital flows have paved the way for further development of the international financial market.

Currently, liberalization of the international capital market continues to be greatly emphasized by the government in Taiwan. The specific programs include privatization and internationalization of the banking system, encouraging the issuance of "Eurobonds" abroad, permitting foreign institutional investors to invest directly in the Taiwan securities market, and the establishment of the "Foreign Currency Call Loan Market" in Taipei. Due to these programs, the link between the domestic and international capital markets has become much stronger. Moreover, international financial know-how has been introduced through these programs which will aid in the further development of the international capital market in Taiwan.

However, there is still a long way to go towards establishing a "complete" international capital market. From a functional point of view, a complete international capital market should be able to provide various financial instruments to facilitate any international financial transaction. For example, a multinational firm should be able to use currency futures or options to hedge its foreign exchange risk, or to use the Eurocurrency deposits or Eurobonds to avoid interest rate risk. A complete international capital market therefore usually includes spot and forward foreign exchange markets, currency futures and options markets, and a Eurocurrency market. As mentioned before, the foreign exchange market in Taiwan is still only partially liberalized and is thus an obstacle to the further development of the international capital market. It is extremely important for Taiwan to reestablish its forward market and to rely even more on the free-market mechanism in its spot market. Lastly, to enhance various interbank activities, it is important to expand the domestic bond market and foster more competition among the domestic banks.

Appendix A: Violations of an International Equilibrium Condition

The interest parity condition is a fundamental international capital equilibrium condition. A violation of this condition will create speculative profit opportunities, which will then induce large capital movements between countries. A continuous violation of this capital equilibrium condition occurred in Taiwan in the 1986-1987 period.

The Interest Rate Parity Condition and Capital Inflows

The conventional uncovered interest rate parity condition is a condition in which the interest rate differential between domestic and foreign countries roughly equals the expected rate of depreciation of the domestic currency. For example, if the annual domestic interest rate is 10 percent and the foreign interest rate is 3 percent, then the interest rate parity condition holds if the domestic currency is expected to depreciate by 7 percent by the end of next year. Under this equilibrium condition, since it does not pay to borrow from one country to invest in another country, no speculative movements would be induced between countries.

In contrast, a violation of the parity condition will induce speculative capital movements. Specifically, if the expected net return from holding domestic assets is higher than that of foreign assets, the speculator would expect to make a profit by borrowing from the foreign country and investing domestically. This expected speculative profit would thus lead to a capital inflow. Similarly, a reverse situation would induce the speculator to borrow from domestic sources and invest in foreign assets, which would result in a capital outflow.

The uncovered interest rate parity condition is presented in equation (1):

$$\frac{i_t - i_t^*}{1 + i_t^*} = E_t(S_{t+1}) - S_t \tag{1}$$

where i_t and i_t^* are domestic and foreign interest rates, respectively, at time t; S_t and S_{t+1} are the logs of the spot exchange rate, defined as the unit price of foreign currency in terms of domestic currency, at times t and $t+1$, respectively; and E_t denotes the expectation based on the information set at time t. Since the right-hand side of equation (1) denotes the expected percentage change in the spot rate, equation (1) implies that the interest rate differential between domestic and foreign countries is roughly equal to the expected rate of depreciation of domestic currency. Under this condition, the *ex ante* expected return of borrowing from one country and investing in another country would be zero. In contrast, if the parity condition is violated, the *ex ante* expected return would not be zero. That is:

$$E_t(y_{t+1}) = 0, \text{ if the parity condition holds} \tag{2}$$

and

$$E_t(y_{t+1}) \neq 0, \text{ if the parity condition is violated} \tag{3}$$

where $E_t(y_{t+1})$ denotes the expected excess return per dollar borrowed from abroad and invested domestically and is defined as:

$$E_t(y_{t+1}) = \frac{i_t - i_t^*}{1 + i_t^*} - [E_t(S_{t+1}) - S_t]. \quad (4)$$

Now, note that a violation of the interest rate parity (equation (3)) further implies either one of the following conditions:

$$E_t(y_{t+1}) > 0 \quad (5)$$

or

$$E_t(y_{t+1}) < 0. \quad (6)$$

Equation (5) indicates a situation in which the expected return from a speculative activity of borrowing abroad and investing domestically is greater than zero, which therefore induces capital inflow. On the other hand, equation (6) describes a situation where a speculator can make a profit by borrowing domestically and investing in foreign assets, which induces capital outflow.

An Empirical Test of the Interest Rate Parity Condition

To present statistical evidence of violations of the parity condition for the case of Taiwan during the 1986-1988 period, the following two procedures are adopted. First, to test the parity condition from an *ex ante* point of view, a proxy for the market expectation term $(E_t(e_{t+1}))$ is adopted. Second, by inserting this proxy into equation (4), an unconditional mean of the expected excess return is estimated.[11] This unconditional mean will then provide a statistical test which will show that the parity condition was seriously violated, and that the situation described in equation (5) occurred in Taiwan over this particular period.

By adopting the Box-Jenkins time-series analysis, the spot exchange rate S_t is identified as following a random walk process with a drift, as given in equation (7):

$$\log S_t = -0.13 + \underset{(0.03)}{1.03} \log S_{t-1}, \text{ adjusted } R^2 = 0.99 \quad (7)$$

where the standard error of the estimated coefficient is in parentheses.

Expectation is assumed to be formed based on the expected value of the model. That is, it is assumed that, over this period, the market predicted the exchange rate level based on the model presented in equation (7), which yields:

$$E_t(S_{t+1}) = -0.13 + 1.03 \, S_t. \quad (8)$$

TABLE 5A.1 Estimated Expected Speculative Return $E_t(y_{t+1})$
(from borrowing US$ and investing in the NT dollar asset)

	Mean	Standard Deviation	t-Value
1981.01-1985.12	-0.00263	0.00214	-1.23
1986.01-1988.03	0.00944	0.00062	15.29

Based on the forecasting equation (8), a proxy for market expectations is first obtained. Then, by inserting this proxy for market expectations into equation (4), the expected excess return $E_t(y_{t+1})$, is estimated. To contrast the 1986-1988 period with an earlier period, the interest rate parity condition is tested for each of the two sub-periods: from 1981.01 to 1985.12, and from 1986.01 to 1988.03.[12] It is expected that the parity condition was violated for the second sub-period, but not for the first sub-period. Following equations (2) and (3), the interest rate parity condition holds if the expected excess return is estimated to be zero, and is violated if the expected excess return is statistically different from zero. The test results are presented in Table 5A.1

The results in Table 5A.1 support our hypothesis that, while the interest rate parity condition holds for the first sub-period (1981.01-1985.12), it is violated for the second sub-period (1986.01-1988.03). In particular, for the first sub-period, the mean of the expected return is estimated to be -0.00263, with a t-statistic of -1.23. This indicates that the expected speculative return is not statistically different from zero at any conventional significance level. The parity condition hence holds for this first sub-period.

In contrast, for the second sub-period, the mean of the expected speculative return is estimated to be 0.00944, with a t-value of 15.29. The test result for the 1986-1988 period hence provides statistically significant evidence of positive expected speculative returns, which is consistent with the situation described in equation (5). This positive expected return induced capital inflows which added to the problem of the huge excess supply of US dollars in Taiwan during the 1986-1988 period.

Appendix B: Borrowed Foreign Exchange and Expectations

This appendix provides empirical evidence of the connection between borrowed foreign exchange and the expectation of appreciation in the NT dollar. In particular, it is shown in this appendix that the banks' borrowing of foreign exchange was closely dependent on the expectation of currency appreciation before May 31, 1987, the date of the freeze; and the link was much looser after May 31, 1987.

To obtain a proxy for market expectation, a time-series model of the exchange rate is first estimated, using monthly data from January 1983 to April 1988. The exchange rate series is identified as a random walk process with a drift, as given in equation (1) with t-statistics in parentheses:[13]

$$e_t = -1.35 + 1.03\ e_{t-1}, \text{Adjusted } R^2 = 0.99 \qquad (1)$$
$$(-3.13)\quad (89.53)$$

where e_t is the exchange rate at time t, e_{t-1} is the exchange rate at time $t-1$, and both stand for the value of one US dollar in terms of the NT dollar.

Then, by assuming rational expectations, the market expectation is assumed to be equivalent to the expectation formed by the model. That is, we assume that over the period 1983-1988, the market was forecasting the exchange rate based on the model presented in equation (1). This is represented in equation (2):

$$E_t(e_{t+1}) = -1.35 + 1.03 e_t \qquad (2)$$

where $E_t(e_{t+1})$ is the market expectation of the exchange rate at time $t+1$ formed at time t. A proxy for expectation can be obtained from equation (2).

After obtaining the proxy for expectation, the net foreign debt of the commercial banks is regressed on the expected exchange rate. Equation (3) presents the regression results for the period from January 1984 to May 1987, and equation (4) presents the results for the period from April 1987 to June 1988, with t-statistics in parentheses.

$$\text{NFL} = 600126.90 - 16399.43\ \text{EXP},\ R^2 = 0.96 \qquad (3)$$
$$(3.13)\qquad (-3.17)$$

$$\text{NFL} = 10210.33.81 - 27480.33\ \text{EXP},\ R^2 = 0.55. \qquad (4)$$
$$(1.36)\qquad (-1.08)$$

where NFL is the net foreign debt of commercial banks and EXP is the expectation of future exchange rates.

Note that in equation (3), the coefficient associated with the variable EXP has a negative sign and is statistically significant at the 1 percent level, indicating that the expectation of the future exchange rate had a negative effect on bank's foreign debt. That is, a market expectation of appreciation of the NT dollar (i.e., a lower exchange rate) would lead to an increased foreign debt.

In contrast, the coefficient associated with the variable EXP in equation (4) is not statistically significant even at the 10 percent level. These results support our hypothesis that the close link between foreign debt and exchange rate expectation was loosened after May 31, 1987.

On the part of the nonbank private sector, the situation was somewhat different. The relationship between foreign debt by the nonbank private sector and the expected exchange rate for the period before and after May 31, 1987 are provided in equations (5) and (6), respectively.

$$\text{LFC} = 23517.86 - 509.96 \text{ EXP}, R^2 = 0.98 \qquad (5)$$
$$\phantom{\text{LFC} = }(15.28) (-12.04)$$

$$\text{LFC} = 36898.28 - 951.67 \text{ EXP}, R^2 = 0.98 \qquad (6)$$
$$\phantom{\text{LFC} = }(8.45) (-6.41)$$

where LFC is the outstanding amount of liabilities in foreign currencies held by the nonbank private sector, and t-statistics are in parentheses.

Note that in both equations (5) and (6), the coefficients associated with the variable EXP are negative and are statistically significant at the 1 percent level. Again, this association indicates that the expectation of an appreciation of the NT dollar induced an increase in foreign exchange borrowing by the nonbank private sector. In addition, equation (5) shows a strong link between capital flows by the nonbank private sector and expectations of currency appreciation even before the capital account was officially partially liberalized on May 31, 1987. Moreover, equation (6) provides an interesting contrast with equation (4). Equation (6) shows that the central bank freeze on the foreign debt of commercial banks did not hinder bank borrowing by the nonbank private sector because the latter were exempt from the freeze. Therefore, the gradual decline in the outstanding amount of foreign exchange borrowing by the nonbank private sector in the 1988-1989 period was largely due to the relatively stable NT dollar rather than to the freeze by the central bank.

Notes

1. For an extensive study of the Taiwan economy, see Kuo (1983).
2. For the order and speed of liberalization, see Balassa (1982), McKinnon (1982), Frenkel (1982), Krueger (1984), and Harberger (1984), among others.
3. According to the Banking Law, the central bank determines the maximum interest rate for each kind of deposit. The thirteen categories of deposits led to the restriction of thirteen different maximum rates. Reclassifying deposits into only four categories therefore reduced the number of restrictions.
4. For more details on the process and effects of interest rate liberalization in Taiwan, see Kuo (1990).

5. Another reason for the public to pressure the central bank was the concern about the shift from a short-run to a long-run equilibrium. In particular, after the NT dollar had appreciated by some 20 percent in early 1987, the currency level did not seem too far away from its long-run level, which was indicated by the real effective exchange rate. Based on this real effective exchange rate indicator, some believed that the NT dollar was already "overshooting" its long-run level. That is, the NT dollar had probably appreciated by more than enough based on the real exchange rate indicator. For a formal empirical examination of this, see Liu and He (1991a) and Liu and He (1991b). For a theoretical model of overshooting, see Dornbusch (1976) and Frenkel and Rodriguez (1982).

6. For official intervention in the foreign exchange market in the industrialized countries, see Taylor (1982) and Beenstock and Dadashi (1986).

7. In general, there are various explanations for the failure of the parity condition. For example, it may be due to transaction costs (Frenkel and Levich 1975, 1977), capital and exchange controls (Dooley and Isard 1980), political risks (Aliber 1973), or risk premia (Frenkel and Razin 1980; Hansen and Hodrick 1983; and Liu 1986).

8. For a more extensive study of the globalization of the financial industry in Taiwan, see Liu (1992).

9. While the value of the total assets in the offshore market in Taipei was US$15.9 billion by May 1990, it was US$338.6 billion in Singapore and US$565 billion in Japan.

10. See Liu (1992) for more details.

11. Alternatively, one can estimate the conditional mean instead of the unconditional mean. However, that requires a more complicated analysis while yielding a similar result for this particular case. See Liu (1989) for more details.

12. For the first sub-period, the proxy for the expectation term was separately obtained. While the spot exchange rate for this first sub-period is also identified to follow a random walk process, it has different estimated coefficients from those obtained for the second sub-period (which is given in equation (7)).

13. For random walks in foreign exchange rates, see Mussa (1979) and Liu and He (1991c).

References

Aliber, Robert. 1973. "The Interest Rate Parity Theorem: A Reinterpretation." *Journal of Political Economy* 81: 1451-1459.

Balassa, Bela. 1982. *Development Strategies in Semi-Industrial Economies*. Baltimore: Johns Hopkins University Press.

Beenstock, Michael, and Saiid Dadashi. 1986. "The Profitability of Forward Currency Speculation by Central Banks." *European Economic Review* 30: 449-456.

Dooley, M. P., and Peter Isard. 1980. "Capital Controls, Political Risk and Deviation from Interest Rate Parity Condition, a Test of the Fisher Hypothesis." *Journal of Finance* 36: 697-703.

Dornbusch, Rudiger. 1976. "Expectation and Exchange Rate Dynamics." *Journal of Political Economy* 84(6): 1161-1176.

Edwards, S. 1984. "The Order of Liberalization of the External Sector in Developing Countries." *Princeton University, Essays in International Finance*, No. 156.

Frenkel, Jacob A., and Richard M. Levich. 1975. "Covered Interest Arbitrage: Unexploited Profits?" *Journal of Political Economy* 83: 325-338.

Frenkel, Jacob A., and Assaf Razin. 1980. "Stochastic Prices and Tests of Efficiency of Foreign Exchange Markets." *Economics Letters* 6(2): 165-170.

Frenkel, Jacob A. 1982. "The Order of Economic Liberalization: Discussion," in K. Brunner and A. H. Meltzer, eds., *Economic Policy in a World of Change*. Amsterdam: North-Holland.

Frenkel, Jacob A., and Richard M. Levich. 1977. "Transaction Costs and Interest Arbitrage: Tranquil Versus Turbulent Periods." *Journal of Political Economy* 86: 1209-1226.

Frenkel, Jacob A., and Carlos A. Rodriguez. 1982. "Exchange Rate Dynamics and the Overshooting Hypothesis." *I.M.F. Staff Papers* 29: 1-30.

Hansen, Lars Peter, and Robert J. Hodrick. 1980. "Forward Exchange Rates as Optimal Predictors of Future Spot Rates: An Econometric Analysis." *Journal of Political Economy* 88: 829-853.

Harberger, Arnold C. 1984. "Welfare Consequences of Capital Inflows." Paper presented at World Bank Conference.

Krueger, A. O. 1984. "Problems of Liberalization," in A. C. Harberger, ed., *World Economic Growth*. San Francisco: Institute for Contemporary Studies.

Kuo, Shirley W. Y. 1983. *The Taiwan Economy in Transition*. Boulder: Westview Press.

_____. 1990. "Liberalization of the Financial Market in Taiwan in the 1980s," in S. Ghon Rhee and Rosita P. Chang, eds., *Pacific-Basin Capital Market Research*, Vol. 1. New York: Elsevier Science Publishing Co.

Liu, Christina Y. 1986. "Tests of Expected Real Profits in the Forward Foreign Exchange Market." *Economics Letters* 21: 57-60.

_____. 1989. "Expected Excess Returns Under a Managed-Floating Exchange Rate Regime." Paper presented at the First Annual Pacific-Basin Finance Conference, Taipei, Taiwan.

_____. 1992. "Liberalization and Globalization of the Financial Market in Taiwan," in N. T. Wang, ed., *Taiwan's Enterprises in Global Perspective*, forthcoming. Armonk, NY: M. E. Sharpe.

Liu, Christina Y., and Shirley W. Y. Kuo. 1990. "Interest Rate and Foreign Exchange Liberalization in Taiwan in the 1980's," in Seiji Naya and Akira Takayama, eds., *Essays on Economic Development in Asia*. Honolulu: University of Hawaii Press.

Liu, Christina Y., and Jia He. 1991a. "Permanent or Transitory Deviations from Purchasing Power Parity: An Examination of Eight Pacific-Basic Countries," in S. Ghon Rhee and Rosita P. Chang, eds., *Pacific-Basin Capital Market Research*, 2: 413-436. New York: Elsevier Science Publishing Co.

_____. 1991b. "Do Real Exchange Rates Follow Random Walks? A Heteroscedasticity-Robust Autocorrelation Test." *International Economic Journal*, September 1991.

_____. 1991c. "A Variance-Ratio Test of Random Walks in Foreign Exchange Rates." *The Journal of Finance*, 46(2): 773-785.

McKinnon, R. I. 1982. "The Order of Economic Liberalization: Lessons from Chile and Argentina," in K. Brunner and A. H. Meltzer, eds., *Economic Policy in a World of Change*. Amsterdam: North-Holland.

Mussa, M. L. 1979. "Empirical Regularities in the Behavior of Exchange Rates and Theories of the Foreign Exchange Market," in Karl Brunner and Allan Meltzer, eds., *Policies for Employment, Prices, and Exchange Rates*, Vol. 11. Carnegie-Rochester Conferences on Public Policy, *Journal of Monetary Economics*, Supplement: 9-57.

_____. 1986. "Financial Liberalization in Retrospect: Interest Rate Policies in LDCs." Policy Paper, Center for Policy Research.

Taylor, Dean. 1982. "Official Intervention in the Foreign Exchange Market, or, Bet Against the Central Bank." *Journal of Political Economy* 90: 356-368.

6

Public Finance

Ching-huei Chang

1. Introduction

During the past few decades, Taiwan's economic performance has often been described as "miraculous." Not only has growth in per capita gross national product (GNP) reached and sustained an impressively high rate but also income size distribution has become more equitable (see Table 6.1). The economy has also exhibited considerable stability, even in the face of major external shocks. Despite limited natural resources and the unfavorable blows of various diplomatic shocks, Taiwan's economy has successfully transformed itself from backwardness and poverty to modernity and prosperity.

TABLE 6.1 The Performance of the Taiwan Economy: Selected Indicators, 1965-1988

	Annual growth rate (%) GNP (1)	GNP per capita (2)	CPI (3)	Unemployment rate (%) (4)	Gini coefficient (5)
1965-70	10.02	7.35	3.63	2.32	0.347
1971-75	8.95	6.92	13.34	1.67	0.319
1976-80	10.70	8.56	8.82	1.54	0.283
1981-85	7.12	5.39	4.10	2.31	0.286
1986-88	10.76	9.53	0.83	2.11	0.299

Sources: Directorate-General of Budget, Accounting and Statistics, Executive Yuan, *National Income of the Republic of China, 1989*; DGBAS, *Taiwan Statistics Data Book, 1989*; DGBAS, *Report on the Survey of Personal Income Distribution in Taiwan Area, Republic of China, 1990*.

Taiwan's economic success has been attributed to many factors, including a high rate of savings, an export-oriented development strategy, and large investments in both physical and human capitals.[1] This chapter focuses on the role government fiscal policy may have played in Taiwan's economic growth process. Important questions addressed include the following: apart from the "high interest rate policy" which is often credited for Taiwan's savings performance, have there been any concerted fiscal policy efforts to promote domestic savings? How has the rapid expansion of capital stock been influenced by tax policy? How has the government, confronted with the burden of excessive defense expenditures, generated sufficient revenue to finance public investment in education and infrastructure?

Impressive past performance notwithstanding, Taiwan's economy now faces several serious difficulties, including losing competitive advantage (to emerging developing countries), urban pollution and traffic congestion (especially in the capital city), a phenomenal surge in urban land and housing prices, and a worsening income distribution. These problems represent great challenges to the island's people, especially as Taiwan aspires to join the ranks of industrially developed nations by the year 2000. It is of interest to speculate about how Taiwan's government will be able to maintain the high rate of economic growth attained in the past and, at the same time, meet these challenges. Of equal importance, at least for the purposes of this chapter, is how the government can finance anticipated increases in public outlays and, simultaneously, maintain an annual budgetary surplus. In addition to reviewing Taiwan's use of fiscal policy as a development strategy in the past, this chapter will attempt to describe current problems and prospective opportunities facing Taiwan's economy as it makes the final transition to mature status.

2. An Overview

It is remarkable that though government expenditures have increased substantially over the past three decades, they have remained more or less constant as a percentage of GNP. Measured at a constant price (taking 1986 as the base year), outlays for all government organizations as a whole (national and subnational) were around NT$797 billion (nearly US$30 billion) in fiscal year 1988, which was about twelve times as much as the average level in 1960-1965.[2] Per capita government expenditures also exhibited a similar upward trend, though at a more modest rate. In fiscal 1988, per capita outlays were NT$40,500, compared to an average of NT$5,300 in 1960-1965. However, since Taiwan's economy grew at a very high rate (about 8-13 percent each year) during this period, total govern-

Public Finance

ment expenditures expressed as a percentage of GNP rose only slightly from 21 percent in 1960-1965 to 23 percent in 1988. Table 6.2 summarizes the distribution of government expenditures.

Before explaining the content of this table, it should be noted that some items of public spending which are closely related to national defense have been erroneously included in other categories. For example, expenditures for veteran's programs, which can be thought of as payments for previous services provided by retired soldiers, have been erroneously placed under the heading of "expenditures for social security." Similarly, expenditures for military education and training are classified as spending for education. Obviously, then, total defense expenditures have been understated and expenditures for education and social security overstated.

As Table 6.2 shows, expenditures for general administration have experienced a downward trend in relation to total government expenditures. The percentage of total expenditures devoted to administrative spending was 14 percent during 1965-1970; it dropped to 10 percent during 1976-1980 and remained at that level thereafter. The biggest loser in sharing the "fruit" of government outlays has been national defense, however. Defense expenditures accounted for almost 40 percent of total public spending during 1965-1970. Since then, this ratio has declined steadily and significantly. It was merely 23 percent during 1986-1988, which was even lower than the share of expenditures for economic development.

Expenditures for education, science and culture have increased substantially relative to total public spending. Their share rose gradually from 15 percent during 1965-1970 to 20 percent during 1986-1988. Growth in expenditures for social security has taken up much of the increase in public spending. During 1965-1970, welfare expenditures constituted only a trivial

TABLE 6.2 Distribution of Gross Expenditures (percentage of total)

Fiscal years	1965-70	1971-75	1976-80	1981-85	1986-88
General administration	14.05	13.00	10.44	10.42	10.90
National defense	38.85	29.54	26.84	24.62	22.67
Education, science & culture	14.58	16.98	15.86	18.68	20.17
Economic development	17.83	22.32	31.96	27.78	25.27
Social security	7.63	10.96	11.04	14.60	16.20
Other	6.96	7.20	3.86	3.90	4.79

Source: Department of Statistics, Ministry of Finance. *Yearbook of Financial Statistics of the Republic of China.*

proportion of total government outlays; by Western standards, they were unbelievably low. Welfare spending jumped to 11 percent of total expenditures in the 1970s and has since climbed to 16 percent.

Expenditures for economic development have taken up the largest share of government outlays since fiscal 1980. As Table 6.2 shows, development expenditures accounted for only 18 percent of total outlays during 1965-1970, far below the share devoted to defense. After the government's "Ten Big Construction Projects" got underway in 1975, development spending increased substantially in both absolute and relative terms. It reached a record high (32 percent) during 1976-1980. However, due to a slowdown in public investment, development expenditures as a percentage of total public spending have decreased steadily in the 1990s.

Table 6.3 displays the structure of tax revenues for various periods of time. The share of total revenue accounted for by taxes, the government's main revenue source, has varied from 70 to 75 percent over the past three decades. It is also noteworthy that taxes take up only 15 to 19 percent of GNP. Compared with Western countries, it is remarkable how low the tax burden has been kept.[3]

Like any other developing country, Taiwan's main source of revenue is indirect taxes, though their relative importance has declined rapidly over time. As Table 6.3 shows, indirect taxes accounted for 78.4 percent of total tax and monopoly revenues in 1966-1970, decreasing to 60 percent in 1986-1988. While the revenue generated from taxation on domestic products (mainly commodity taxes and business taxes) has remained more or less constant (at 30 percent), revenue from customs duties has fallen markedly since 1976, due to several large-scale and widespread reductions of tariffs and liberalization of import restrictions. In essence, monopoly revenue is generally considered to be commodity tax plus excess profit collected from tobacco and liquor which are produced and supplied by a government monopoly. This was one of the major sources of government revenue in the past. However, because of severe competition from imported tobaccos, beers, wines, and liquors (especially from the US), monopoly revenue has dwindled substantially. Its contribution to total revenue has remained constant at about 11 percent since 1976.

With respect to direct taxes, the percentage of total revenue originating from property-related taxes (including house tax, land value tax, and deed tax) has remained at a modest level (about 10 percent), except during 1976-1980 when it dropped to 4 percent. On the other hand, taxes on income (individual income tax (IIT), business income tax, and land value increment tax (LVIT))[4] generated only a minor share (less than 10 percent) of total tax and monopoly revenues during 1966-1970. Due to rapid growth of IIT and LVIT revenues in recent years, however, the share of total revenues derived from income taxes rose to 30 percent during 1986-1988.

TABLE 6.3 Structure of Tax Revenues (percentage of total taxes)

Fiscal year	Direct taxes			Indirect taxes				Total taxes as % of GNP
	Total	Income	Property	Total	Monopoly revenue	Domestic products	Imports	
1966-70	21.64	9.28	12.36	78.36	19.14	32.84	26.38	16.10
1971-75	26.56	16.44	10.12	73.44	13.04	31.80	28.60	17.30
1976-80	25.68	21.66	4.02	68.78	10.84	30.10	27.84	19.38
1981-85	37.14	27.30	9.84	62.86	10.92	31.00	20.94	18.12
1986-88	40.23	30.07	10.16	59.77	10.50	29.93	19.33	15.10

Source: Department of Statistics, Ministry of Finance. *Yearbook of Financial Statistics of The Republic of China, 1987.*

Finally, except for fiscal 1982, the budget for the public sector has been kept in surplus throughout the 1960-1988 period. On average, the surplus was NT$1.4 billion annually for the years 1960-1969, expanding to NT$176 billion over the next decade, and increasing further in the 1980s. This sound budgetary position primarily reflects policy-makers' efforts to pursue a year-to-year balance in government expenditures and revenues. However, it should be noted that though the central government continues to enjoy a large budget surplus each year, the subnational governments, especially the Taiwan provincial government and some of the poorer counties, have long been confronted with serious fiscal difficulties.

3. Fiscal Policy and National Savings

It is widely held among economists that one of the most important determinants of economic growth is capital formation, and apparently the primary source of capital formation is domestic savings. During the past few decades, the government on Taiwan has employed a wide variety of fiscal policy measures aimed at stimulating the level of savings. As mentioned above, the public sector budget has always been in surplus. In addition, the government confers various tax preferences on earnings from savings. For example, up to NT$360,000 of dividends and interest from savings and investment is exempt from IIT. Interest income from small-size and compulsory savings accounts is not subject to tax and realized capital gains from security-related (i.e., bonds and stock) transactions are completely excluded from income taxation.

How has the level of savings responded to these fiscal stimuli? As Table 6.4 illustrates, ever since the Taiwan economy first took off in 1961-1963, the ratio of domestic savings to GNP has remained fairly high (over 22 percent). This ratio has also increased steadily and significantly, except for the years 1981-1985, when the economy was in a mild recession due to the 1982-1983 oil shock, and the so-called "Tenth Trust Cooperative (financial) scandal" in 1985. The savings ratio reached an unprecedented high of 38 percent during 1986-1988. Equally noteworthy is that up to 1980, domestic savings had been almost completely channeled into domestic investment, thereby further supporting economic growth. However, as a result of a slowdown in domestic investment, an excess of savings over investment began to appear in 1980 and the gap became even bigger during 1986-1988.

Savings performance in recent years has been closely related to the rapid growth of Taiwan's foreign trade surplus. According to the national income identity, trade surplus (or deficit) necessarily implies an excess (or shortage) of gross domestic savings over domestic investment.[5] Rapid trade expansion resulted in large surplus in the current account of Taiwan's

TABLE 6.4 Ratios of Domestic Savings and Investment (in percentages)

Year	Ratio of domestic savings to GNP	Ratio of domestic investment to GNP
1965-70	22.40	23.98
1971-75	30.60	30.14
1976-80	33.17	30.81
1981-85	32.43	23.87
1986-88	37.99	19.98

Source: Directorate-General of Budget, Accounting and Statistics, Executive Yuan. *National Income of the Republic of China, 1989*.

balance of payments after 1981. Consequently, domestic savings were kept at a level substantially greater than that of gross domestic investment.

Table 6.5 shows the sources of domestic savings. In Taiwan the profits of public utilities and corporations are generally considered as part of government revenue. Calculated in this way, government savings amounted to 32 percent of domestic savings in 1965-1970, rose to 39 percent in 1976-1980, and dropped to 27 percent in 1986-1988. As pointed out above, to some extent general government savings or budgetary surplus reflects a restraint on the growth of public expenditures. Compared with Western countries, it is astonishing how low the social and health budget and pension payments have been kept. In addition, public spending on traffic improvement, garbage collection, noise or pollution prevention, etc. has

TABLE 6.5 Sources of Domestic Savings (percentage of total)

Year	General government	Public enterprises	Private enterprises	Households and private non-profit institutions	Total
1965-70	13.93	18.60	27.27	40.21	100.00
1971-75	21.16	12.45	22.81	43.58	100.00
1976-80	25.28	13.49	22.88	38.35	100.00
1981-85	17.52	16.48	19.96	46.04	100.00
1986-88	15.78	11.88	21.70	50.63	100.00

Source: Directorate-General of Budget, Accounting and Statistics, Executive Yuan. *National Income of The Republic of China, 1989*.

been limited. As a result, the quality of life in Taiwan, especially in the capital city, has actually declined in recent years.

More than 60 percent of domestic savings since 1965 comprised private savings, the sum of household and business savings. Though the relative importance of business savings has decreased gradually with time, in 1986-1988 it still constituted almost one-third of private savings. On the other hand, the rapidly increasing amount of household savings has more than compensated for the decrease in business savings and, to some extent, government savings as well.

An important question that naturally arises is whether and to what extent government fiscal policy may have encouraged this increase in the level of private savings. On the surface, it might be argued that the favorable tax treatment of earnings from savings, together with the high interest rate policy, could be credited for the high savings rate. However, the suggestion lacks both theoretical and empirical support. Theoretically, in the familiar life-cycle model, a rise in the after-tax rate of interest, brought about by an increase in the market rate of interest or a decrease in the effective rate of income tax, exerts a substitution effect and an offsetting income effect on the level of household savings. A priori it cannot be argued that a change in the after-tax interest rate will necessarily lead to an increase in the supply of household savings. However, the influence of taxation on business savings is somewhat different. First, the double taxation of business profits under the "classical" income tax system, which exists in Taiwan now, is believed to induce corporations to retain and accumulate earnings rather than distribute them as dividends. Second, a reduction in the business income tax (BIT) rate, or the adoption of any special tax preference (such as tax holidays or investment tax credits) that lowers the effective BIT rate, tends to raise after-tax profits, thereby increasing the funds available for business savings.

Empirical findings seem quite consistent with these theoretical reasonings. For example, the results obtained by applying the ordinary least square (OLS) approach to a set of time-series data from 1960-1983 by Tzeng (1985) indicate that the supply of household savings is very inelastic with respect to interest rates, but quite responsive to changes in income level. This of course implies that the marked increase in household savings, especially after 1986, may well be explained by the rapid growth of GNP rather than by the high interest rate policy or favorable tax measures given to savings and financial investments, as postulated by some previous studies (Ho 1978; Kuo 1983). On the other hand, a study of corporate savings behavior by Li (1990) found that discrimination inherent in the present income tax system, which favors capital gains over dividends, causes most corporations in Taiwan to accumulate their after-tax profits.

Another important question, closely related to the previous one, is whether the growth of household savings may have depressed or replaced business savings. This problem is important because one of the tax reforms proposed by the Ministry of Finance is to integrate completely business and individual income taxes. Though a policy change would solve the aforementioned double-taxation problem, as some economists here correctly predict, it might also lead to a significant reduction in corporate savings as most corporations increase their payout ratios. Of course, if these companies' stockholders can completely "pierce through the corporate veil," as von Furstenberg (1981), Poterba (1987) and others postulate, then the gains in household savings would completely offset the loss in corporate savings, thereby leaving the total amount of private savings unchanged.

Apparently, to what extent household savings can substitute for corporate retained earnings, or vice versa, is an empirical question. As pointed out above, since 1981 the increase in household savings has more than compensated for the decrease in corporate savings. However, this evidence cannot very well be used as an argument for the "perfect substitution" case. Too many other factors (like the growth of GNP, the unemployment rate, the business cycle, etc.) are at work here. Only after these variables are isolated will the correct relationship between household and corporate savings be ascertained. An empirical study by Li (1990) that approached this problem in exactly this way found no systematic or close relationship between the two savings figures. From this it may be inferred that the proposed integration of individual and business income taxes, if actually carried out, might have a seriously adverse impact on the savings of the private sector in Taiwan.

The remaining question is whether or not private savings should be reduced to a lower level. During 1986-1988, domestic savings amounted to 38 percent of GNP and over 70 percent of domestic savings was from the private sector. The accumulated wealth from these savings, with no proper outlet for real investment, has flooded into the financial sector of the Taiwan economy resulting in skyrocketing urban land prices and severe instability in the stock market. However, as was hinted at above, this excess saving may only be a transitory phenomenon, owing to an abnormally low level of domestic investment and an unusually strong performance in foreign trade in 1981-1988. The problem may soon disappear when the economy, and thus domestic investment, returns to the normal, pre-1981 level, and the massive trade surplus falls to a more modest level.

The above viewpoint, however, should not be used as an argument against the income-tax integration. Too many factors are involved in this complicated issue. For instance, in deciding for or against integration, the detrimental impact on private savings must be weighed against the potential benefits of improving resource allocation, which arise mainly from treating similarly or equally retention and payout or debt-financing and equity-issuing. However, a reform of the individual income tax by abolishing all tax preferences to savings would not entail any great hardship. As stated above, the favorable treatment of interest income was found not to be very effective in increasing private savings. The resulting loss in tax revenue, however, is of sizable magnitude. For example, during 1982-1987, at least NT$23 billion in individual income tax revenue was lost due to these preferential devices (Chang 1989). In addition, they may have created a serious "horizontal inequity" problem since they discriminate against wages and other income. They may have also resulted in vertical inequity if the wealthy save more than the poor.

4. Fiscal Policy and Capital Formation

It was shown in Table 6.4 that the ratio of domestic investment to GNP had been pretty high up until 1980 and fell steadily thereafter. During 1986-1988 it dropped to the abnormally low level of 20 percent. To understand further the composition of capital formation, in Table 6.6 we have listed the levels of public and private investment for selected years.

Public investment, or the investment undertaken by general government and public enterprises as a whole, accounted for almost one-half of gross domestic investment from 1971 to 1985. Due to the rapid growth of private investment since 1976 (except in the recessed 1981-1985 period), the relative importance of public investment has declined substantially in recent years. Yet public investment still accounted for as much as 36 percent of all investment in 1986-1988. It is worth noting that while investment by public enterprises, as a percentage of domestic investment, dropped markedly

TABLE 6.6 Gross Investment in Private and Public Sectors

Year	Percentage distribution				Growth rate	
	Private sector	Public sector	Public enterprises	Government	Private sector	Public sector
1966-70	61.37	38.63	28.19	10.44	10.34	19.13
1971-75	56.84	43.16	32.76	10.40	9.57	20.40
1976-80	53.36	46.64	32.35	14.29	19.10	10.02
1981-85	53.88	46.12	29.70	16.42	−1.78	−7.60
1986-88	64.26	35.74	18.65	17.09	25.87	9.71

Source: Department of Statistics Ministry of Finance. *Yearbook of Financial Statistics of The Republic of China, 1987.*

after 1981, the share of direct government investment has increased steadily though slowly since 1971. This may imply that investment in infrastructure, upon which the continued growth of the economy depends, has gradually taken the place of expansion of production equipment, plants and factories which public enterprises use in their daily operations. In addition, the government also enacted a Statute for the Encouragement of Investment (SEI) aimed at speeding up capital formation in the private sector. This statute has since been amended several times, with articles added and more favorable terms offered to more industries or activities which are considered to be eligible for tax preferences. Major devices applied in the SEI include (not exhaustively) the following:

(1) Productive enterprises (PEs) that are newly established or that undertake capacity expansion with additional paid-in capital, are given an option of a five- or four-year tax holiday (from BIT) or an accelerated depreciation allowance. If the firm opts for the latter, the stipulated service life of an eligible asset (machinery, equipment, buildings, or other structures) is reduced by at least one-third.

(2) For "important productive enterprises," which include PEs in basic metals, heavy machinery, petrochemical industries, and all PEs classified as capital- or technology-intensive, the amount of the BIT should not exceed 20 percent of taxable income.

(3) Those PEs designated as "strategic (critical)" by the government are granted an investment tax credit of 5 to 20 percent of the sum invested in machinery and equipment against the BIT payable for the current and ensuing five years.

(4) For a PE, total research and development expenditures are deductible from taxable income for the current year. Where R&D expenses in a tax year exceed the highest annual amount in the five preceding years, 20 percent of the expenses in excess thereof may be deducted from the BIT payable in that year. The amount of this tax credit cannot exceed 50 percent of the BIT payable; however, unused credit can be carried forward over the ensuing five years.[6]

It is remarkable that the preferred productive enterprises under BIT are so broadly defined. Equally striking is the variety of measures in the incentive system, which includes tax holidays, accelerated depreciation or depletion allowances, limited tax liability, investment tax credits, and special tax credit (for R&D expenditures) (Riew 1988). In fact, apart from BIT provisions, IIT, custom duties, commodity taxes, business (value-added) taxes, and property-related taxes are also used to stimulate private investment. It is estimated that in 1982-1987 the loss of BIT revenue from these preferences was over NT$46.1 billion, which was about 20 percent of total BIT revenue collected in the same period (Chang 1989).[7]

An important but complicated question is whether and to what extent investment in the private sector has been influenced by these tax incentives.[8] Though more research may be needed to provide a correct answer to this problem, most, if not all, empirical studies undertaken in Taiwan (for example, Kiang 1982; Hsu and Chen 1988) have found that tax holidays and accelerated depreciation have only a marginal impact on business investment. The intuition underlying this result can be easily explained by using the familiar neoclassical equation of the demand for capital, taken from Hall and Jorgenson's paper, 1967:

$$F_k = c = q[(1-u)i + \delta](1-k)(1-uz)/(1-u),$$

where F_k denotes marginal product of capital, c the user cost of capital, q the price of capital goods, u the marginal rate of BIT, i the before-tax rate of interest, δ the economic depreciation rate, k the investment tax credit rate, and z the present value of the one-dollar statutory depreciation allowance. This equation states simply that at equilibrium the marginal product of capital equals the user cost, the latter being a function of q, i, u, k, and so forth.

A reduction in u resulting from a tax holiday increases the after-tax marginal product of capital $(1-u)F_k$ but also raises the cost of capital as it reduces the tax savings from depreciation and interest deduction. Therefore, the net impact on the desired level of capital, and hence investment, is insignificant. On the surface, one might argue that accelerated depreciation could raise the present value of the statutory depreciation, z, thereby causing the user cost to fall and the demand for capital to increase. However, this is not the case. With perfect foresight, accelerated depreciation does not affect z in a significant way since the tax saving from over-depreciation (i.e., the excess of statutory depreciation over true depreciation) at present will be offset almost completely by the tax dissaving from under-depreciation in the future. As z remains constant, the level of investment will also stay unchanged (Boadway and Bruce 1979).

The investment tax credit is different. In the above equation an increase in k reduces unambiguously the user cost of capital and thus increases a firm's demand for capital if i, q, and other variables remain unchanged. Some empirical research (Chang and Riew 1990; Hsu and Chen 1988) has confirmed that investment tax credit has a significant effect on business investment. Moreover, as one would expect, a temporary credit is more powerful in the short run than a permanent one (Chang 1985). Intuitively, with q, i and other variables fixed, business investment can be expected to increase substantially in response to an anticipated temporary rise in the value of k as most firms attempt to expedite investment projects that might otherwise be left for the future (Abel 1982).

A permanent system does, however, have its drawbacks. Though a permanent tax credit may be effective in stimulating capital formation, it is also distortionary to the extent that it affects a firm's long-run capital-labor ratio. This allocative inefficiency must be weighed against the expansion of potential GNP brought about by the tax credit in order to determine whether the tax measure will be beneficial or detrimental to the economy. In contrast, a temporary investment credit has no effect on a firm's capital-labor ratio, thus avoiding the problem of excess tax burden. Moreover, temporary investment credit can be used as an effective fiscal instrument to counter cyclical fluctuations in macro-economic variables. That is, when an economy faces (for example) the threat of recession, a temporary credit policy can be used to stimulate business investment and thus the level of aggregate demand.

It seems clear from the discussion above that aside from investment tax credits, special incentive schemes such as tax holidays and accelerated depreciation allowances have little, if any, impact on private investment. Public investment in infrastructure, however, has added greatly to domestic capital formation in the past few decades. Indeed, as Table 6.6 shows, the recent decrease in domestic investment can largely be attributed to the retardation of public investments, especially those undertaken by state-owned enterprises.

5. Fiscal Policy and Human Capital

In addition to the expansion of physical capital, government spending on human capital has continued to increase.[9] As Table 6.2 shows, public outlays on education, sciences, and cultural services (of which investment in education is the main part) have increased from 14.6 percent of total government expenditures in 1965-1970 to 18.7 percent in 1981-1985 and 20.2 percent in 1986-1988, respectively. To a great extent the increased spending on education reflects the increase in schooling costs at all levels of education. For example, in 1981 the average expenditure was NT$10,075 for each elementary school student, $14,986 for junior high, $41,606 for senior high, $41,017 for college, and $79,942 for each university student. In 1987, the corresponding figures were NT$13,765, $21,360, $51,286, $52,840, and $19,284, respectively.[10]

In Taiwan it is generally thought that a large part of the benefits arising from education accrue to society as a whole in the form of external economies. Thus most educational services are provided directly, or supported indirectly, by the public sector and their costs are financed by tax revenue. The nine-year compulsory, elementary education is supplied completely free of charge to students and their families. Publicly funded senior high schools, colleges, and universities, which are widespread on the island, collect only a small amount of tuition and fees from students. Even private schools receive large subsidies or grants from the government. Therefore, a very low proportion of the cost of education is born by students and their families.

As a result of increasing investment, education in Taiwan has grown rapidly. Total student enrollment for all age groups grew at a rate of 4.9 percent annually from 1950 to 1975, which was substantially higher than the rate of increase in the school-age population. The enrollment rate (number of students as a percentage of school-age population) went from 36 percent during 1951-1955 to 57 percent during 1976-1979. It is worth noting that the growth rate of higher education (in terms of total enrollment) has been higher than that of secondary education, which has in turn been higher than that of primary education. Equally noteworthy is the structural change in the types of education demanded, with vocational and technical types of education (engineering and natural sciences) gaining increasing importance relative to the humanities and social sciences.

How has education contributed to economic growth? Advocates of the "screening hypothesis" (such as Arrow and Stiglitz) argue that the educational system does no more than screen students on the basis of skills and attitudes they already possessed before entering a particular type of education. Thus only a small part of the wage differential between various levels of education can actually be attributed to education; most of the differential arises simply because lack of education is a barrier to entry into high-paying jobs. However, considerable evidence in Taiwan supports the human capital approach, developed mainly by Schultz, Becker, and others, which argues that education increases knowledge and skills, improves productivity and thus contributes greatly to economic growth.[11]

First, available evidence indicates that the private rate of return on investment in higher education was about 15 percent in 1973,[12] which compares well with returns on other types of investment. Other findings suggest that earnings of employees and workers are positively correlated in a significant way with their educational achievement. For example, data from a large labor force survey in 1978 showed that taking all age groups as a whole, the earnings of those with a college education or higher were 2.3 times as much as that of those who were illiterate. As Hou and Hsu, 1975, correctly argue, such differences can be taken to imply that the marginal productivity of the more educated is higher, for otherwise it is hard to imagine that businesses would pay higher wages to the more educated.

Second, available data shows that the mobility of the labor force is closely related to levels of educational achievement. According to a labor force survey undertaken in 1976 and 1978, the mobility rates of the illiterate or those without formal schooling were the lowest. Individuals with secondary education had a mobility rate higher than those with primary education.

However, those with higher education had a slightly lower mobility than those with secondary education, probably because they were largely employed in professions demanding special technical skills in which turnover rates tended to be small (Hou and Chang 1983).

In theory, efficient allocation of human resources requires that the marginal productivity of labor of the same quality be the same among industries or localities. A high degree of labor mobility is especially necessary when new technologies and industries are continually introduced, as economic development calls for laborers to move away from low to high productivity sectors.

Finally, changes in the participation rate of the labor force were found to exhibit an interesting pattern among different levels of educational achievement. From 1966 to 1977 the total participation rate remained quite stable (around 58 percent), as the increase in female participation just offset the decrease in male participation. While participation for both sexes declined modestly for those who were illiterate or had only elementary schooling, this rate went up substantially for those with an education at the secondary or college level (Hou and Chang 1983). The intuition underlying this finding seems quite straightforward. As potential earnings rise with educational level, the opportunity cost of having leisure (i.e., not working) is higher for those who are more educated.

Using the approach developed by Solow, Hou and Chang estimated the contribution of education to economic growth in Taiwan. From 1953 to 1979, total employment grew at an average annual rate of 3.2 percent, but GDP grew at 9.1 percent, implying an increase of average labor productivity of nearly 6 percent per year. Total capital stock grew at 5.5 percent and the average productivity of capital grew at 3.4 percent each year. It may be computed that 54 percent of the GDP growth was due to technological improvement, 29 percent to labor growth and 18 percent to capital accumulation (Hou and Chang 1983). A considerable part of the technological improvement is believed to be attributable to educational development growth.

It is also widely held that education has contributed to equitable distribution of income in Taiwan. As mentioned above, the cost of education to students and their families is relatively low. On the other hand, rewards from receiving education, especially at the higher levels, are very attractive. A well-educated person has the potential to earn a handsome income, and the social status he or she can attain is also very high. Therefore, almost all parents, particularly poorer ones, have a great incentive to send their sons or daughters to school. Because even higher-level education is equally accessible to every youth, any able hard-working student has the chance to pursue advanced study in a university. After graduation he or she can enter a well-paying occupation (such as law, accounting, medicine, architecture, etc.). Indeed, in Taiwan many high-ranking government officials and university presidents are from very poor families.

To illustrate the above reasoning, imagine what might happen were there no readily accessible, low-cost education. Children from poor families would not be able to afford senior high or college education, though they would still be able to complete junior high school, which is almost completely free to students of all ages. They could only get low-level, low-paying jobs with little prospect of future promotion and poor job security. With the meager income they would make from this type of work, they could hardly expect to have sufficient savings to send their own children to university. Thus their sons and daughters might just repeat what happened to them. Here we have another type of "poverty cycle." Though somewhat over-exaggerated, this phenomenon did characterize the situation prior to, and immediately after, Taiwan's retrocession in 1945. At that time a doctor's son had on average a good chance of becoming a doctor, while a farmer's was destined to be a farmer too.

6. Problems and Prospects

As mentioned in the introductory section, Taiwan's economy is now confronting some difficult problems. Despite a slow-down in economic growth and hence an increase in unemployment, money wages and the general price level have crept upward gradually. Income distribution has worsened as a boost in the prices of securities, land and housing has substantially increased the income and wealth of owners of these assets. The "stagflation" which the market experienced this past year can be attributed mainly to supply shocks such as the oil crisis and crop failures and can be viewed as a transitory phenomenon by which the economy is adjusting itself back into long-term equilibrium. However, there are some more fundamental problems embedded in the budget of the public sector that deserve careful scrutiny.

The Budgetary Surplus Problem

It is true that the budget surplus has largely added to domestic savings and contributed to rapid economic growth in the past. It is also doubtless that, as documented by Kuo (1983), the decision to maintain a balanced budget in the 1950s helped to bring down the runaway inflation that occurred during the early years of that decade. What is false, however, is that keeping the government budget in balance or even with surplus every year has in effect stabilized the economy, which was constantly subject to external shocks. It is absurd to assume that the continued growth of Taiwan's economy in the future is contingent on the public sector maintaining an annual budget surplus.

It is quite straightforward that a year-to-year balanced budget tends to aggravate the business cycle. Consider, for example, a situation in which the economy is facing a mild recession, with income and employment declining and hence tax revenue contracting. The government budget can be kept in balance by cutting down on current expenditures or enhancing taxation efforts. No matter which method is adopted, however, the level of aggregate demand will fall even further and consequently the recession will worsen. Indeed, Taiwan's recession of 1982-1985 might have been shortened if the China Petroleum Company, a state-owned enterprise, had left domestic oil prices unchanged and reduced its profit level. Similarly, to some extent the recession of this past year (1990) can be attributed to the relatively slow growth of public investment since 1981, though, without a doubt, the main cause for this bad situation was the worldwide recession.

Apparently, the annual budget surplus has been made possible by, at least partially, holding back the growth of public spending on current consumption (social welfare programs and law enforcement) and infrastructure (urban traffic facilities). Some public goods, which are pertinent to human rights, are either undersupplied or provided inefficiently. The safety of human life and property has been challenged by increases in violent crime such as kidnapping, murder, and arson. For example, the number of criminals who were jailed for committing robbery, murder and kidnapping was 11,021 in 1987, 40 percent more than the number (7,892) in 1978.[13]

It is astonishing that while the government budget has been in surplus for decades, its expenditures on pension plans, unemployment relief and disability and welfare benefits continue to be minuscule. Equally ridiculous is that while the Central Bank has accumulated the world's largest foreign reserves, most public works have lagged far behind schedule simply because of lack of money. With more than two million people living in a small valley-like area, Taipei is probably the only major modern city in the world without a subway system (which is now under construction). Traffic jams and accompanying problems such as noise and air pollution have made the capital city one of the worst places to live in the world.

The decline in public investment has placed a brake on the further growth of Taiwan's economy. For years the incentive for firms to undertake domestic investment has been negligible, while direct foreign investment by Taiwan's businessmen and corporations has increased almost nine-fold from 1987 (US$103 million) to 1989 (US$931 million).[14] Accompanying this foreign investment abroad, some important firms have moved out to Mainland China and Southeast-Asian countries. The annual growth rate of Taiwan's GNP this year has been adjusted downward to 4.5 percent, which is substantially lower than the originally projected level of 8 percent.

It seems clear that the so-called "sound budgetary policy" (i.e., always maintaining the budget in balance or with surplus) is not necessarily harmonious with growth objectives. Recognizing the importance of public investment in facilitating or accommodating private economic activity, the Council for Economic Planning and Development (CEPD) of the Executive Yuan has recently released a "Six-Year National Construction Program" (SYNCP). The main objectives of the program will be to increase national income, lay a solid foundation for modern industrial development, balance regional growth, and improve the standard of living of the 20 million people in Taiwan. To achieve these objectives the government will increase public investment to stimulate domestic economic demand and growth. As Dr. Shirley Kuo, the chairman of the CEPD, has remarked, such public investment will be a major driving force behind future development.

In addition to maintaining a higher rate of economic growth, the ambitious six-year plan aims at implementing a comprehensive national insurance program, extending the nine-year compulsory education to twelve years, and improving the political and economic relationship between Taiwan and Mainland China, among other objectives. If the plan is successful, Taiwan will no doubt enter into a new era of prosperity and equality. It is beyond the scope of this chapter to assess and evaluate the content of this plan. Rather, what concerns us is how the government can raise sufficient revenue to meet the increased public expenditures called for by the plan.

Among the three major financing methods, issuing money is probably out of consideration because of its tendency to kindle inflation. It is very difficult, if not impossible, to impose a new tax or even to raise current taxes. (As will be discussed below, a reform of the existing income tax system may be able to increase government revenue.) It seems inevitable that these public expenditures must be financed by new issues of government bonds.

In Taiwan the amount of public bonds outstanding is quite small, compared with that in the United States and most Western countries. For example, the central government's outstanding (domestic and foreign) debt in fiscal 1988 was NT$157 billion (at the current price), which amounted to only 3.6 percent of the GNP for that year. Additional issues of a reasonable amount of bonds should not affect the government's ability to pay off the interest and principal on these debts. A change in the price-setting policy may also give rise to some other beneficial effects. At present, both the selling price and the interest earnings are fixed, the former being fixed by law, which requires public bonds to be sold at its face value only (with no premium or discount). Since the coupon rate of earnings is higher than the market rate of interest, public bonds are purchased almost wholly by the banks which are consigned to issue them; only a small proportion are held by non-financial firms and households. Obviously, allowing the price of the bonds to vary (i.e., selling them at a discount or premium), in accordance with the underlying demand and supply conditions, would help to promote the circulation of public bonds in the private sector. Most importantly, this would also provide the Central Bank with a means of influencing the operation of the open market; the Bank can influence private consumption and investment by buying or selling government bonds and other securities, thus affecting the market interest rates.[15]

The Central and Local Government Budget Problem

While the national government has for years enjoyed a large budget surplus, most of the subnational governments are now confronting very serious fiscal crises. As Table 6.7 shows, the size of the central government's budget surplus, at constant price, increased steadily and markedly between 1980-1988. The local government (counties and municipalities) as a whole incurred a deficit every year since fiscal 1960 and the size of these deficits has increased over time. Except for incurring deficits in 1981 and 1982, Taiwan Province and two special cities (Taipei and Kaoshiung) have maintained a long-term budget surplus.

Behind these aggregate data lies the unequal distribution of revenues and expenditures between the national and subnational governments, between provincial and city governments, and among counties and municipalities. The central government squanders taxpayers' money on, for example, "buying" friendship from some countries with which Taiwan has no formal relation. Taiwan Province and most prefectures (such as Penghu, Yuanlin and Taitung) have long relied heavily on aids from the central government or other localities' cross-subsidies to keep their governments in daily operation. Indeed, some counties (such as Taipei, Taichung, and Kaoshiung) are so poor that they could not pay wages and salaries to their employees in 1990.

The relationship between the national and subnational governments is complicated. First, the central government gives direct grants, and it uses the province or special cities and counties to administer national programs. Such expenditures thus may be reported as both national and subnational expenditures. Second, there exist serious overlaps between the expenditures of national and subnational governments and also between those of provinces and counties (or municipalities). Among the twenty-seven kinds of government functions listed in the Demarcation Law of the Central and Local Governments' Revenues and Expenditures (DLCLGRE), eighteen functions are performed by almost all levels of government. Because of these complications, a dividing line can hardly be drawn. Speaking roughly, the national government takes primary responsibility for national defense, foreign affairs, legislation and law enforcement, sciences and cultures,

TABLE 6.7 Decomposition of the Public Budget by Levels of Government (at constant price)

Fiscal year	Revenue	Expenditure	Surplus (+) or deficit (−)
Central government			
1966-1970	65,828	61,322	+4,506
1971-1975	122,208	103,656	+18,552
1976-1980	215,270	186,094	+29,176
1981-1985	>95,570	274,786	+20,784
1986-1988	467,966	412,970	+54,996
Subnational government			
Provincial government & municipalities			
1966-1970	22,270	17,418	+4,582
1971-1975	39,715	31,878	+7,837
1976-1980	73,945	69,454	+4,491
1981-1985	133,721	128,956	+4,765
1986-1988	193,259	176,339	+16,920
Prefectuates and cities			
1966-1970	15,662	19,660	−3,998
1971-1975	23,613	31,657	−8,044
1976-1980	44,791	57,290	−12,499
1981-1985	60,323	79,692	−19,369
1986-1988	96,015	111,976	−15,961

Source: Department of Statistics Ministry of Finance. *Yearbook of Financial Statistics of The Republic of China, 1989.*

economic development, communication facilities, and social welfare. The subnational governments, on the other hand, provide police and fire protection, compulsory education, medical care, and environmental protection. In terms of economic functions, the central government is responsible for maintaining economic stability and equitable income distribution, while the subnational governments are obligated to provide local public services to their residents.

Since demands for various (pure or impure) public services, in general, change with rising income, there have been marked changes in the relative expenditure pattern at different levels of government. According to the empirical research by Hsu *et al.*, 1989, the income elasticity of subnational expenditures is slightly higher than that of national spending (1.12 and 1.03, respectively). Though expenditures by national and subnational governments have increased substantially over the past few decades, the national government's expenditures have exhibited a slight decrease compared to subnational governments' expenditures.

Although subnational governments perform most of the same functions as the central government, they have access to limited revenue sources only. Income from the four major taxes (custom duties, commodity taxes, BIT and IIT) and 65 percent of monopoly revenue go to the central government. Together, these accounted for about 55 percent of total tax and monopoly revenues in fiscal 1988. On the other hand, the provincial government is restricted to using business tax, harbor use taxes, license taxes, stamp taxes, and 35 percent of monopoly revenue. In addition to the above four taxes, the special cities of Taipei and Kaoshiung are also authorized to use those taxes which counties and other municipal governments are empowered to levy. They are land value taxes, LVIT, house taxes, deed taxes, and some other miscellaneous taxes.

It has been found that tax revenues (except for business taxes and LVIT) used by subnational governments are income inelastic. As GNP grows, these tax revenues tend to increase by a smaller percentage than does income. As shown above, the share of local expenditures (in total public expenditures) has remained relatively stable or has even increased in recent years. Inevitably, as national income grows, the budget deficit of the local governments will become larger. This bad situation is aggravated by the abolition of some of the taxes upon which the local governments rely heavily. For example, the slaughter taxes and duty on farmland were repealed for their adverse effect on resource allocation. No compensation was made and losses to counties and municipalities were enormous.

Apparently, to achieve balanced development between the central and local governments, DLCLGRE must be revised thoroughly and significantly. On the expenditure side, the responsibilities assumed by all levels of government should be succinctly and clearly redefined to avoid unnecessary overlapping. Exactly which public services are to be provided by the central and local governments must be determined by some acceptable criteria set forth by public-finance economists (such as the degree of spillover effect, the relative cost of production, difference in preferences, etc.). On the revenue side, allotting a fixed proportion (say, 20 percent) of revenues from IIT and BIT to local governments (including the province and counties) would add substantial revenues to their treasuries. What is most important is that the present business, land value, and housing taxes should be allowed to rise. The statutory rate structures which apply uniformly to all local jurisdictions are not desirable. The tax rates, and even the kind of taxes used and public services supplied, should be allowed to vary between different localities according to the needs and capabilities of their residents.

The Income-Tax Problem

As pointed out above, taxes on income (IIT, BIT, and LVIT) account for only a small proportion of total government tax and monopoly revenues (for example, one-fifth in 1980). LVIT is a tax levied on the capital gains realized from land transactions. It uses a progressive rate structure which is markedly different from that which IIT adopts. In essence, however, it is an income tax. LVIT accounted for only a minor share of total revenues (5.85 percent) in 1980. Due to skyrocketing land values (especially in urban areas), it was one of the most important revenue sources in Taiwan in 1988, second only to custom duties (13.76 vs. 14.08 percent). BIT, which once generated more revenue than did IIT, has been lagging behind the latter in recent years. This tax is unique in that it is imposed on all businesses, incorporated and unincorporated, and uses a progressive rate structure as well. The revenue from IIT has increased steadily and gradually since 1980. For example, it accounted for only 7.01 percent of tax and monopoly revenues in that year but moved up to 11.12 percent by 1988.

BIT and IIT have long been subject to severe attacks by both the general public and public-finance economists. Among other things, the double taxation of business profits is criticized as discriminating in favor of debt leverage and retention of earnings in a firm's financial decisions. The serious erosion of both tax bases through numerous exclusions, exemptions and provision of tax holidays or special incentives for savings and investment is said to distort in a significant way the economic behavior of the private sector, thus causing inefficiency in allocation and/or inequity in distribution. In view of these drawbacks, some economists and government officials even question the theoretical appeal of the current income tax system.

In theory, a taxpayer's income should be defined as the amount he spends on consumption plus the increment to his wealth (i.e., savings). However, because the concept of income has to be interpreted by tax officials on a case-by-case basis, many important items (such as owner-occupied housing) that are qualified as realized income are omitted from the tax base. Moreover, numerous types of income are explicitly exempt from taxation. They include: (1) wages and salaries of primary school and kindergarten teachers; (2) pensions and annuities, and in-kind income, dividends and interest from savings and investments (up to NT$360,000 per tax unit per year), and realized capital gains from security transactions; (3) royalties or receipts from sales of inventions or patents by an individual to a firm; and (4) free lunches or lunch subsidies (up to NT$21,600 annually per person) and other fringe benefits provided by an employer to employees.

Another major source of IIT erosion is the failure to collect taxes from income produced in the underground economy. A crude estimate indicates that in 1985, taxable gross income amounted to only 53 percent of personal income, while nontaxable income and tax-evaded income were 16.90 percent and 20.59 percent, respectively. After allowing for personal exemptions, dependent allowances, and standard or itemized deductions, taxable net income amounted to 19.52 percent of personal income (Chang 1989). It is this serious erosion of the tax base which has retarded the normal growth of IIT revenue.

The adverse effects of this erosion in the tax base are numerous. First, to the extent that labor and capital are perfectly mobile among occupations or activities so that after-tax rates of return are equalized everywhere, the tax preference for certain types of income may result in an excess tax burden. Though there is no reliable estimate of the efficiency loss, its magnitude is certainly not negligible because of the serious base erosion and the highly graduated marginal tax rate. Second, even if the tax arbitrage above is incomplete, there exists an inequality or inequity between tax-preferred and ordinary activities. Finally, tax preferences may aggravate the tax avoidance or evasion situation. High-income taxpayers, for example, have actually been found transferring part of their property income to their relatives or friends to take advantage of the interest income deduction.

Apparently, there are no convincing reasons for exempting from taxation most of the items listed above. Some legislators, especially those elected by educational associations, think that compulsory education is of paramount importance to the economic and social development of a country, and that a tax preference should therefore be granted to primary school teachers. This reasoning, if justified, can also be applied to soldiers' wage income, since the output of military services is national defense, which is a pure public good.

However, the argument is far from convincing. It is true that primary education and national defense confer external benefits to society as a whole or to some members of it. To attain Pareto optimum, a subsidy should be given to the suppliers of education or defense. But teachers' or soldiers' labor services are merely one input into the production of these public goods. Since defense and basic education are publicly funded or have already received direct subsidies from the government, there is no reason for giving special preference to a soldier's or teacher's wage income.

Itemized deductions have continually been subject to scrutiny. Among these, contributions to education, charitable, and cultural institutions of up to 20 percent of a taxpayer's taxable gross income (TGI) and an unlimited amount of donations to national defense have been most controversial. Feldstein, 1980, argued that when public and private actions are close substitutes in consumption, a wide range of circumstances exists in which a tax subsidy on charitable contributions is generally more efficient than direct government spending in achieving a particular goal. However, against this efficiency gain is the fact that some high-income taxpayers often use charitable contributions as a loophole to evade high-rate taxes imposed on their incomes.

Another group of itemized deductions is, in effect, a subsidy to personal consumption expenditures. For instance, deductions of property taxes and interest on home mortgages provide an incentive for purchasing and owning houses. Since the implicit rent of owner-occupied housing is not imputed and included in the owner's taxable income, the deduction of expenses (including taxes and interest) associated with the house is not warranted.

The above discussion seems to lead to an obvious conclusion: the IIT base must be broadened by taxing soldiers' and teachers' wage income, eliminating tax preferences to income from savings and investment, retaxing capital gains from security transactions, and excluding from itemized deductions payments of property tax and interest on home mortgages. Moreover, converting charitable contributions and some other deductions into tax credits can solve, or at least relieve, the so-called "upside-down subsidy" problem of tax expenditures in the existing income tax system.

Future Prospects

Several major changes in government expenditures and taxes have been taking place. The most conspicuous is income tax reform, which is an attempt to broaden the tax base by eliminating unreasonable preferences given to specific industries, economic activities, or special interest groups. For example, soldiers' and teachers' wage income will soon be subject to taxation, and special deductions for income from savings and investments will be gradually repealed in the near future. Accompanying these changes will be a restructuring of IIT rates by reducing the number of tax brackets, widening the difference between the upper and lower limits, and lowering the nominal tax rate applied to income in each bracket. Obviously, in addition to relieving the taxpayers' burden, income tax reform should be able to mitigate tax-induced distortions resulting from the severe base erosion in the existing systems. It is also believed that this reform will generate a substantial amount of additional tax revenue because improvements in resource allocation, together with a reduction of the overall tax burden, should stimulate work and investment incentives and thus lead to further economic growth.

Government expenditures will increase tremendously after SYNCP is implemented. The biggest increase should be toward the National Health Insurance Program (NHIP) which will be put into effect in 1994. Basically, this program will unify the existing health plans for laborers, public employees, and farmers and extend its coverage to all of the 20 million people living on the island. In addition to providing medical care benefits that cover illness, injury, and maternity, NHIP contains a pension plan for the retired, aged, and disabled. It uses a cost-sharing scheme to reduce waste of medical services that might arise from "moral hazards"; yet each insuree's share will be quite small (20-30 percent of out-of-patient charges and 10-15 percent of hospitalization expenses). This program will be financed primarily by the revenue collected from a payroll tax, which will be introduced after the program is implemented, with the deficit being met by government subsidies. Apart from being regressive with respect to income level, a payroll tax has a base much narrower than an income tax. It is therefore conceivable that unless the tax rate is quite high, the payroll tax will not be able to generate a sufficient amount of revenue to cover the required insurance payments, and a substantial amount of government subsidy is inevitable.

Another large expenditure will be for public investment in transportation and communication, water resource development, environmental protection, construction of low-cost housing for the poor, and other public works projects. It is estimated by CEPD that total government expenditures on these public projects will be about NT$6.2 trillion (equivalent to US$230 billion). To finance these expenditures the government plans to borrow NT$4.6 trillion (about US$165 billion) from the private sector (households, firms, and commercial banks). According to CEPD, after these public investments are implemented, national income will be able to maintain a growth rate of 6 percent each year. However, since the annual rate of interest on public debts is about 9.5 percent, the additional interest payment on public debt each year will total NT$161 billion ($4.6 trillion × 0.35). The government's debt burden will be quite heavy in the future.

From the discussions above, we can easily infer that government expenditures will increase substantially, both in absolute amount and as a percentage of GNP. The proportion of public expenditures for general administration should remain unchanged or decrease slightly, while that for national defense will be kept at a level of 20 percent as long as tensions between mainland China and Taiwan continue to exist. Expenditures for social security will account for the largest increase in public outlay after the NHIP is implemented. As the island's population ages, pension benefits will become a major expenditure for the government as well. The proportion of public expenditures allotted to economic development will decline significantly in the future, for as the economy matures, the role of the public sector in promoting export expansion, stimulating investment in R&D, exploring trade opportunities, and sharing or pooling private risks will become much smaller. On the other hand, expenditures for education, science and culture will probably increase, if, as SYNCP proposes, more than 25 new universities and colleges are established throughout the island in the near future. Finally, as was mentioned above, interest payments on public debt and redemption of the principal when these bonds mature will account for a large proportion of government expenditures.

On the revenue side, income taxes (IIT and BIT) will no doubt become the major source of government revenue. Economic growth and a broadening tax base will increase revenue tremendously, though falling tax rates may have a slightly adverse effect on tax revenue. Indirect tax revenues from domestic products (mainly business tax and commodity taxes) will probably remain unchanged (at about 30 percent of total revenue) unless there are big changes in these taxes (which seems very unlikely in the near future). However, the share from monopoly revenue will certainly become smaller, or even be absorbed into direct tax revenue, as state-owned enterprises become gradually privatized. Similarly, the relative contribution of import revenue will continue to fall as the economy becomes more liberal with respect to foreign trade. It is conceivable that after Taiwan's economy joins the ranks of developed nations in the year 2000, direct taxes will account for more than 50 percent of government revenue.

7. Conclusion

This chapter has reviewed the use of fiscal policy as a keen development strategy in the past and highlighted both the current problems and future prospects facing the Taiwan economy. From the analyses above it is clear that the special tax preferences for income from private savings and investment have actually contributed little, if anything, to the high savings and investment trend that has existed since 1970. In other words, these preferences might merely have resulted in enormous revenue losses, misallocation of resources, and inequitable distribution of income among taxpayers. However, public investment in physical and human capital is different. Expansion of important infrastructure (such as transportation and communication, airports and harbors) increases the productivity and output of the private sector and also stimulates business investment. Public investment in education, on the other hand, increases the supply of human capital and thus greatly benefits potential and actual growth.

Despite its impressive past performance, Taiwan's economy is now facing several serious problems, including urban pollution and traffic congestion, and an unprecedented surge in urban land and housing prices. To solve these problems, and also to maintain a high economic growth rate, the government must undertake many public investment projects. These projects will probably be financed by issues of public bonds rather than by creation of money. Compared to most Western countries, Taiwan still has a low ratio of public debt to GNP (about 3.6 percent in 1988). New bond issues should not affect the government's capacity or credibility in meeting its debt obligation. However, the bond prices should be variable so as to reflect the underlying supply and demand conditions.

In addition, restructuring government revenues and expenditures among different levels of government may help solve the fiscal crises of most subnational governments. The present income tax system must be reformed to reduce inefficiency in allocation and inequity in distribution caused by serious erosion of the tax base.

Finally, based on past and current developments, it can be inferred that once Taiwan joins the company of developed nations in the year 2000, income taxes will become the major source of government revenue. Both income growth and broadening tax bases will contribute greatly to the rapid increase in income tax revenue. On the other hand, expenditures for social security and welfare and for education, science, and culture will account for larger portions of total government spending, and there will be quite a heavy debt burden on the public sector as well.

Notes

The author wishes to express his gratitude to Professor Gustav Ranis for his valuable comments on earlier drafts of this paper.

1. See Kuo (1987) and Hou (1987) for details.
2. Data are taken from Ministry of Finance, 1988.
3. For example, in 1983 the ratio of taxes (excluding social security tax) to gross domestic product was 17.6 percent in Taiwan, 20.7 percent in the United States, 28.8 percent in Canada, 45.1 percent in Switzerland, 23.5 percent in W. Germany, 26.2 percent in France, 19.0 percent in Japan, and 31 percent in the UK. These figures are taken from Hsu et al. (1989), Table 1.
4. LVIT should be treated as an income tax here because it is imposed on capital gains resulting from land transactions.
5. Specifically, the identity states that $S = I + (G-T) + (X-M)$, where S is private savings, I domestic investment, G government expenditures, T government tax revenues, X exports, and M imports. Thus, $S + (T-G) - I = X - M$; that is, trade surplus equals the excess of domestic savings, the sum of private and public savings, over domestic investment.

6. In addition, income from invention or innovation of new products, designs or processes is exempt from IIT.

7. This estimate may be biased because it does not take into account the second-round effect on tax revenue of the changes in capital stock that result from these tax incentives.

8. It might be argued that tax incentives can reduce the effective rates of taxes on capital and thus may create a supply-side effect. However, this is not the case. Statistical data show that these tax preferences are mostly enjoyed by a small number of firms in some stipulated industries (mainly manufacturing). They actually create inequality in tax treatment among industries and between large-size and small- or medium-scale firms, thus aggravating misallocation of resources. It is widely believed among economists that abolition of these preferences accompanied by a reduction in the BIT rates would lead to an increase in private investment.

9. This section draws heavily on Hou and Chang (1983).

10. These values are calculated from Ministry of Education, *Education Statistics of the Republic of China*, 1988, pp. 21, 39.

11. For a review of the literature, see Bowman (1980).

12. For the estimated rate of return on investment in education, see Gannicott (1973).

13. These figures are taken from Table 1-1-6, Ministry of Judicial Affairs, 1987.

14. Data are taken from Table 2, Chen and Chang (1990).

15. The main reason the Central Bank has never used an open market policy is simply that the purchasing or selling price of a bond is fixed. This can be easily illustrated as follows: assuming the bond to be a consol, its market value is $P = R/i$, where R is the coupon earning and i the (average) market interest rate. At present, both P and R are fixed, and thus purchases or sales of the bond by the Central Bank cannot affect the market rate, i.

References

Abel, A. 1982. "Dynamic Effects of Permanent and Temporary Tax Policies in a q Model of Investment." *Journal of Monetary Economics* 9: 353-373.

Boadway, R., and N. Bruce. 1979. "Depreciation and Interest Deductions and the Effects of the Corporation Income Tax on Investment." *Journal of Public Economics* 11: 93-105.

Bowman, M. 1980. "Education and Economic Growth: An Overview," in *Education and Income*. World Bank Staff Working Paper No. 402.

Chang, C. 1985. "The Revenue and Economic Effects of Investment Tax Credit" (in Chinese). *Public Finance Review* 17: 32-52.

Chang, C. 1989. "Income Taxes in Taiwan: Issues and Possible Solutions." *Industry of Free China* 72: 9-22.

Chang, C., and J. Riew. 1990. "Tax Policy and Business Investment -- The Case of Taiwan's Manufacturing Industry." Presented at the Conference of Tax Policy and Economic Development among Pacific Asian Countries held in Taipei, January 5-7, 1990.

Chen, T., and P. Cheng. 1990. "International Aspects of Taiwan's Income Taxation." Presented at the Conference of Tax Policy and Economic Development among Pacific Asian Countries held in Taipei, January 5-7, 1990.

Feldstein, M. 1980. "A Contribution to the Theory of Tax Expenditure: The Case of Charitable Giving," in H. Aaron and M. Boskin, eds., *The Economics of Taxation*. Pp. 97-122. Washington, D.C.: Brookings Institution.

Gannicott, K. 1973. *Rates of Return to Education in Taiwan, Republic of China*. Unpublished.

Hall, R., and K. Jorgenson. 1967. "Tax Policy and Investment Behavior." *American Economic Review* 57: 391-414.

Ho, S. 1978. *Economic Development of Taiwan, 1960-70*. New Haven, CT: Yale University Press.

Hou, C. 1987. "Strategy for Industrial Development." *The Proceedings from the Conference on Economic Development in the Republic of China on Taiwan*, Conference Series No. 7, pp. 245-273. Taipei: Chung-Hua Institute of Economic Research.

Hou, C., and C. Chang. 1983. "Education and Economic Growth in Taiwan: The Mechanism of Adjustment," in K. Li and T. Yu, eds., *Experiences and Lessons of Economic Development in Taiwan*. Pp. 337-390. Taipei: Academia Sinica.

Hou, C., and Y. Hsu. 1975. *Manpower Utilization and Labor Mobility in Taiwan*. Taipei: Economic Planning Council.

Hsu, S., and Y. Chen. 1988. "The Statute for the Encouragement of Investment and Fixed Capital Formation" (in Chinese). *Taiwan Economic Review* 17(1): 77-120.

Hsu, W. et al. 1989. *A Comparative Study of Tax Burdens among Countries* (in Chinese). Technical Report 2. Taipei: Tax Reform Commission, Ministry of Finance.

Kiang, L. 1982. *A Research into the Investment Function of Industries in Taiwan* (in Chinese). Taipei: Taiwan Institute of Economic Research Press.

Kuo, S. 1983. *The Taiwan Economy in Transition*. Boulder: Westview Press.

Kuo, S. 1987. "Economic Development in the Republic of China." *The Proceedings from the Conference on Economic Development in the Republic of China on Taiwan*, Conference Series No. 7, pp. 21-61. Taipei: Chung-Hua Institute of Economic Research.

Li, I. 1990. *Income Taxes and Corporate Saving* (in Chinese). Unpublished Master's Thesis. Taipei: National Chengchi University.

Ministry of Education. 1988. *Education Statistics of the Republic of China*. Taipei.

Ministry of Judicial Affairs. 1987. *Crimes: Situations and Analyses* (in Chinese). Taipei.

Poterba, J. 1987. "Tax Policy and Corporate Saving." *Brookings Papers on Economic Activity* 2: 455-503.

Riew, J. 1988. "Taxation and Development: The Taiwan Model." Presented at the American Economic Association Annual Conference in New York, December, 1988.

Tzeng, Y. 1985. *Taxes and Household Saving* (in Chinese). Unpublished Master's Thesis. Taipei: National Chengchi University.

von Furstenberg, G. 1981. "Saving," in H. Aaron and J. Pechman, eds., *How Taxes Affect Economic Behavior*. Pp. 327-396. Washington, D.C.: The Brookings Institution.

Yearbook of Financial Statistics of the Republic of China. 1988. Taipei: Department of Statistics, Ministry of Finance.

7
International Trade in Taiwan's Transition from Developing to Mature Economy

James Riedel

1. Introduction

Over the past twenty-five years, the Republic of China (hereafter Taiwan) and its neighbors -- South Korea, Hong Kong and Singapore -- have been the most successful of the developing countries by almost any standard one might choose to consider. Hong Kong and Singapore, as a result of their rapid growth, have reached per capita income levels comparable to the lower tier of OECD countries. They were the first of the contemporary developing countries to "graduate," though the significance of their achievement is diminished by the fact that, as city-states, they are a rather special kind of economy. Taiwan, the next in line to enter the per capita income range of the OECD countries, is a more interesting case. Taiwan has been a path breaker among developing countries for three decades. It was the first to demonstrate the relative merits of the outward-oriented development strategy which, due in large measure to Taiwan's success, has achieved the status of orthodoxy in development economics. Taiwan is again breaking new ground as it attempts to take the final step in the transition from a developing to a developed economy, and again those who follow behind will find useful lessons in Taiwan's experience.

This chapter examines the role of international trade in Taiwan's transition from developing to developed economy. Trade has been important and still is, but will it continue to be as important as Taiwan takes its place among the developed countries? Much of Taiwan's past success has been attributed to its ability to exploit its comparative advantage in relatively labor-intensive manufactures, but how will it fare as it loses this advantage as a consequence of rapidly rising real wages? Will Taiwan be as adept at exploiting its emerging comparative advantage in more capital- and skill-intensive products? How will the role of direct foreign investment and the transfer of technology via direct investment change? Will changes in comparative advantage and patterns of trade ease or intensify the pressure Taiwan's exports place on its competitors in world markets? Will Taiwan's graduation lessen tensions with its principal trade partners, especially the United States, or will it come to be regarded as another Japan, a country that enjoys the benefits of the liberal international trading system but does not, or so it is alleged, play by its rules. Finally, what changes in trade policy will be required of Taiwan to avoid allegations of that kind and to fulfill the responsibilities of a developed country within the international trading system?

2. The Importance of Trade

It is commonplace to suggest that trade, more precisely exporting, is the engine of Taiwan's growth. Yet, it is not obvious what this means. Certainly exports (and imports) account for a large proportion of GDP (as shown in Figure 7.1). If resources were idle, and as a consequence aggregate output were strictly determined by demand, then exports, as the most dynamic component of aggregate demand, could reasonably be considered the engine of GDP growth. However, in Taiwan resources are not idle, nor have they been for more than three decades. The unemployment rate in Taiwan has been on average less than one percent of the labor force over the past twenty-five years. In these circumstances, it is not clear whether export growth drives GDP growth, or vice versa. Indeed, both GDP and export growth are more likely driven by common forces that govern the long-term rate of capital accumulation and technical change.

Trade certainly plays a role in these processes. International trade following the principle of comparative advantage allows a country to achieve a higher income than is possible otherwise, thereby raising the capacity to save and invest and hence to accumulate capital. Trade also makes foreign technologies and technological changes available through the import of capital goods and through other channels, such as production licensing. In addition, it is often suggested that international trade raises economic efficiency through the force of foreign competition and leads to various positive demonstration effects as a result of exposure to world markets (Krueger 1985).

Certainly, for a country like Taiwan, which is relatively small and not particularly well endowed with a range of natural resources, the gains from trade (i.e., the opportunity cost of autarky) must be enormous. Needless to say, without trade Taiwan could never have generated the income to allow saving and investment on the scale required to raise per capita income sixfold in twenty-five years, as it did. For Taiwan, trade was essential for growth, if not the engine *per se*.

FIGURE 7.1 Exports and Imports of Goods and NFS as a Percent of GDP

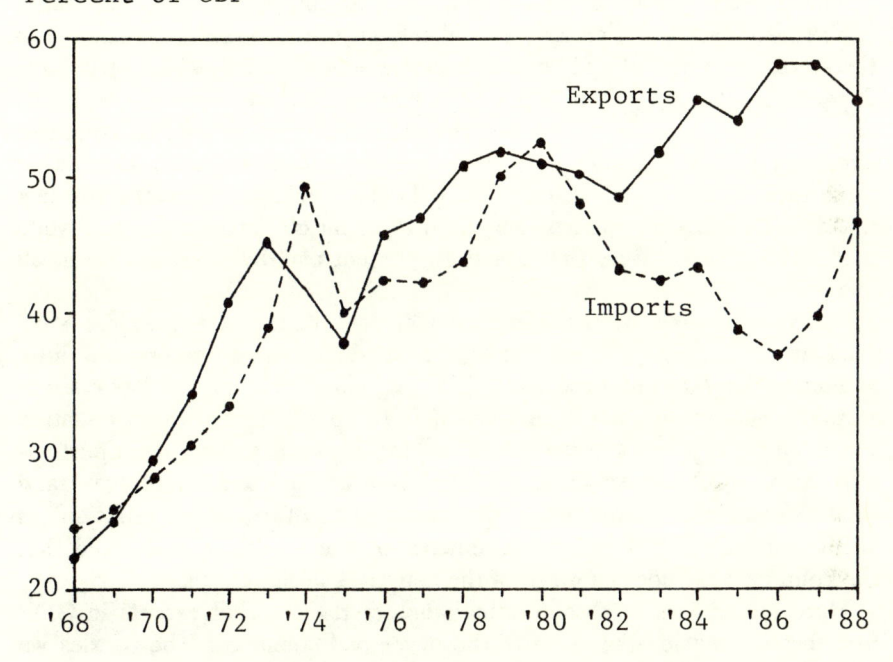

Source: <u>Taiwan Statistical Data Book</u>, 1989.

Will trade continue to be as important for economic growth once Taiwan takes its place among the developed economies? It is sometimes alleged that, even as a developing economy, Taiwan relies too much on exports, as evidenced by Taiwan's large trade surplus and the strong pressure Taiwan's exports place on import-competing industries in the developed countries, the United States in particular. As a consequence, Taiwan, like Japan, is a favorite target of protectionism and is frequently exhorted to rely for growth more on domestic aggregate demand than on exports. But, does Taiwan export too much?

The problem, of course, is knowing what is "too much." Certainly there is no reason why every country should rely on trade to the same extent. In theory, there is an optimal level of trade relative to GDP, which essentially depends on the strength of a country's *comparative* advantages (and hence disadvantages) vis-à-vis the rest of the world. Normally, smaller countries and those with a relatively poor endowment of natural resources depend on trade more than others, which is what theory predicts. Therefore, the fact that in 1986 Taiwan's exports amounted to about 60 percent of GDP, while in the U.S. exports were only about 10 percent of GDP, may not be at all exceptional.

There is a large literature which addresses issues of this kind. Most recently it has focused on the question: does Japan import too little (Takeuchi 1989)? The procedure, following Chenery's (1960) cross-country study of patterns of industrial growth, is to specify a regression equation which purports to explain the "norm" of, for example, exports or imports as a share of GDP. Proxy variables are chosen to represent country size and relative resource endowment. If the actual share of exports in GDP differs significantly from that which is predicted by the model, it is inferred that the country is outside the norm of the countries in the sample.

Here our interest is to determine whether the share of exports in GDP in Taiwan is outside the norm of the developed countries. The proxies we use for country size and relative resource endowment are population (POP) and land area per capita (*LPC*), respectively. The "normal" or predicted share of exports in GDP (*XS*) in 1986 is given by the following double logarithmic regression equation (*t*-statistics in parentheses):[1]

$$\log XS = 4.86 - \underset{(-5.73)}{0.35 \log POP} - \underset{(-3.69)}{0.17 \log LPC} \tag{1}$$

$R^2 = 0.71$, $\bar{R}^2 = 0.67$, $SEE = 0.32$, $n = 19$

These results confirm the hypothesis that the smaller and the less well endowed with natural resources a country is, the more it relies on trade. The variables which proxy for country size and resource endowment account for about 70 percent of the cross-country variation in export shares,

International Trade   257

TABLE 7.1 Actual and Predicted Export Share in GDP (in percentages)

Country	Actual	Predicted
Taiwan	60	40
Spain	20	22
Ireland	57	49
New Zealand	29	39
Italy	20	22
United Kingdom	26	23
Belgium	69	46
Austria	37	41
Netherlands	54	41
France	22	20
Australia	16	16
Germany, Federal Republic of	30	23
Finland	27	34
Denmark	32	49
Japan	12	19
Sweden	33	30
Canada	27	14
United States	7	9
Switzerland	37	47

Source: I.B.R.D., *World Development Report: 1988*, appendix tables.

the standard deviation of which is 16 percent around a mean value of 32 percent for the sample of eighteen developed countries and Taiwan. Although this is a remarkably good fit for cross-country data, a cautionary note is in order. The results are undoubtedly sensitive to the choice of explanatory variables, which is somewhat arbitrary. The findings should therefore be considered as only indicative.

The actual and predicted values of *XS* for Taiwan and the developed countries are shown in Table 7.1. The data suggest that, on the basis of size and resource endowment, Taiwan is expected to have a higher than average export share (i.e., 40 percent). However, the difference between actual and predicted values (i.e., 20 percent) falls outside the standard error of the estimate. It would appear, therefore, that Taiwan in 1986 deviated from the norm of the developed countries and in some sense exported "too much."

Taiwan's exceptionally high share of exports in GDP could be explained by either structural or cyclical factors. In looking for the most important, however, there is one obvious place to start -- that is, with the real exchange rate. A change in the real exchange rate alters two relative prices: first, it alters the price of a country's traded goods relative to the prices of comparable goods in world markets; secondly, it alters the price of traded goods relative to domestically produced non-traded goods. For example, a real devaluation, which is sustainable (i.e., accompanied by the appropriate absorption adjustment policies) (1) raises international competitiveness and (2) provides an incentive for a transfer of resources from the non-traded to the traded goods sector, which together are necessary conditions for raising the share of exports in GDP. If a country's real exchange rate should deviate from its long-run equilibrium, it is likely therefore that the share of exports in GDP would also deviate from the long-run average.

In order to examine this hypothesis empirically it is necessary to reach some judgment about the long-run equilibrium exchange rate. One approach, probably the most common, is to consider the long-run equilibrium exchange rate as that which balances the current account. The idea of "stages in the balance of payments," according to which a country's current account balance depends on its level of economic development, is not well supported. Evidence seems to suggest that in the developed countries, at least, the current account normally balances out over about a decade or so (Feldstein and Horioka 1980). This suggests that a rise in the share of exports in GDP which accompanies the emergence of a current account surplus will eventually be reversed as the real exchange rate converges to the long-run equilibrium.

Taiwan has recorded exceptionally large current account surpluses since 1982. As Figure 7.2 shows, however, during the decade or so prior to 1982 the current account exhibited the normal behavior, with a trend around zero. It is further apparent in Figure 7.2 that the movement of the current account in Taiwan is closely associated with movement in the real exchange rate.[2,3] The rise in the current account surplus from one percent of GNP to 21 percent between 1981 and 1986 was accompanied by a 24 percent real depreciation of the NT dollar. Since 1986, the currency has appreciated in real terms, and the current account surplus has come down accordingly.

Given that Taiwan had a large current account surplus in 1986, the 60 percent share of exports in GNP in 1986 may be exceptional only because of a large but temporary deviation of the real exchange rate from its long-run equilibrium. This issue can be examined by re-estimating the export share equation (1) with the current account balance (expressed as a percent of GNP) included as an additional explanatory variable. The result is:

$$\log XS = 4.67 - 0.37 \log POP - 0.11 \log LPC + 0.03 \, CAY \quad (2)$$
$$ (18.9) \quad (-6.52) \quad\quad (-2.19) \quad\quad (2.07)$$

$$R^2 = 0.78, \, \bar{R}^2 = 0.74, \, SEE = 0.29, \, F = 17.8$$

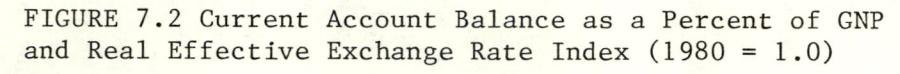

FIGURE 7.2 Current Account Balance as a Percent of GNP and Real Effective Exchange Rate Index (1980 = 1.0)

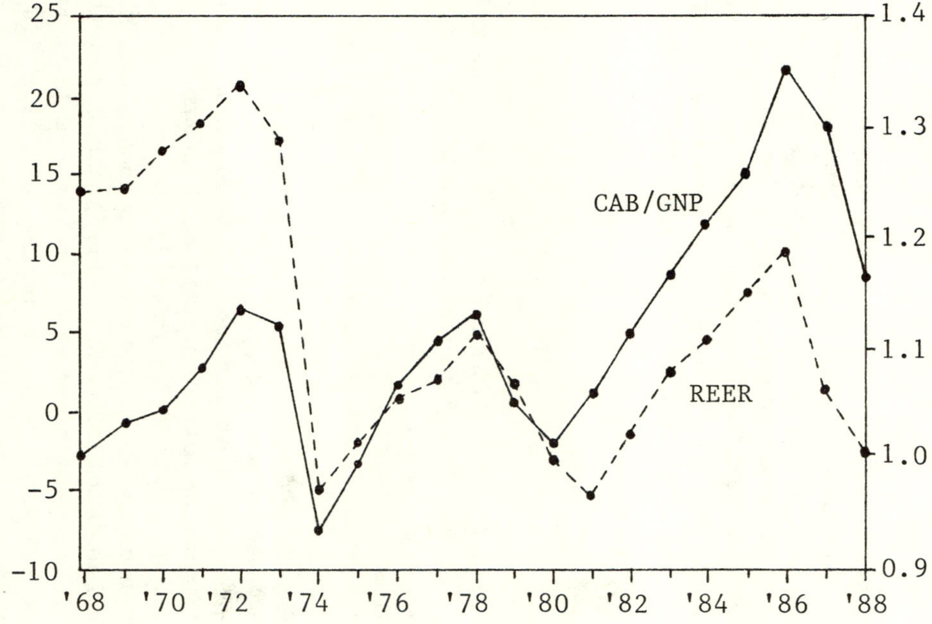

The hypothesis that the share of exports in GDP is influenced by deviations of the real exchange rate from long-run equilibrium, as represented by the current account as a percent of GNP, is given support by these results. Equation (2) can be used to obtain the predicted or "normal" share of exports for a country of Taiwan's size, resource endowment and current account balance. The value obtained is 64 percent, which is somewhat higher, but not significantly higher, than the actual value for Taiwan in 1986. From this we reach the tentative conclusion that the importance of exports in Taiwan was outside the norm of the developed countries in 1986 principally because the real exchange rate deviated from its long-run equilibrium, a cause which is temporary and indeed is already being corrected. However, when the real exchange rate is fully corrected, the export share in GDP for Taiwan will still be relatively high, around 40 percent, simply because Taiwan is relatively small and rather poorly endowed with natural resources.

3. The Pattern of Trade

The transformation of Taiwan from a predominantly agricultural economy to an industrial powerhouse is vividly revealed by the commodity composition of Taiwan's trade. As shown in Figure 7.3, agricultural products and processed agricultural products, which in the mid-1950s accounted for as much as 90 percent of exports, currently account for no more than about five percent. Taiwan's comparative advantage, once in agriculture, is today almost exclusively in industry.

The commodity composition of imports, on the other hand, is rather more stable. As shown in Figure 7.4, capital goods and agricultural and industrial raw materials make up the bulk of imports, with consumer goods accounting for only about 8 percent. The disproportionate share of intermediate inputs and capital goods is not as anomalous as it might appear, since such goods account for about 80 to 85 percent of world trade (GATT 1988). A somewhat higher share for Taiwan is to be expected, given Taiwan's relatively poor natural resource endowment. Nonetheless, the share of consumer goods in imports has been rising since the late 1960s, albeit from a small base. Furthermore, it is likely that this trend will continue as barriers to consumer goods imports continue to come down in Taiwan and as real income continues to rise, since consumer goods imports typically exhibit relatively high income elasticities of demand (Goldstein and Khan 1985).

The geographic pattern of exports and imports is shown in Figures 7.5 and 7.6, respectively. The most striking aspect of the geographic pattern of Taiwan's trade is the overwhelming predominance of two countries, Japan

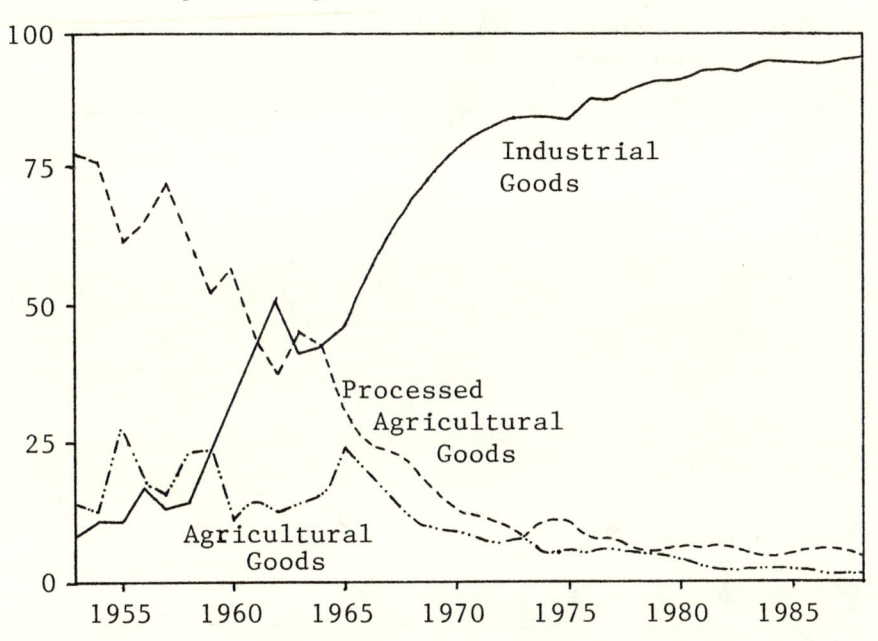

FIGURE 7.3 Commodity Composition of Exports, 1952-1988 (percentages)

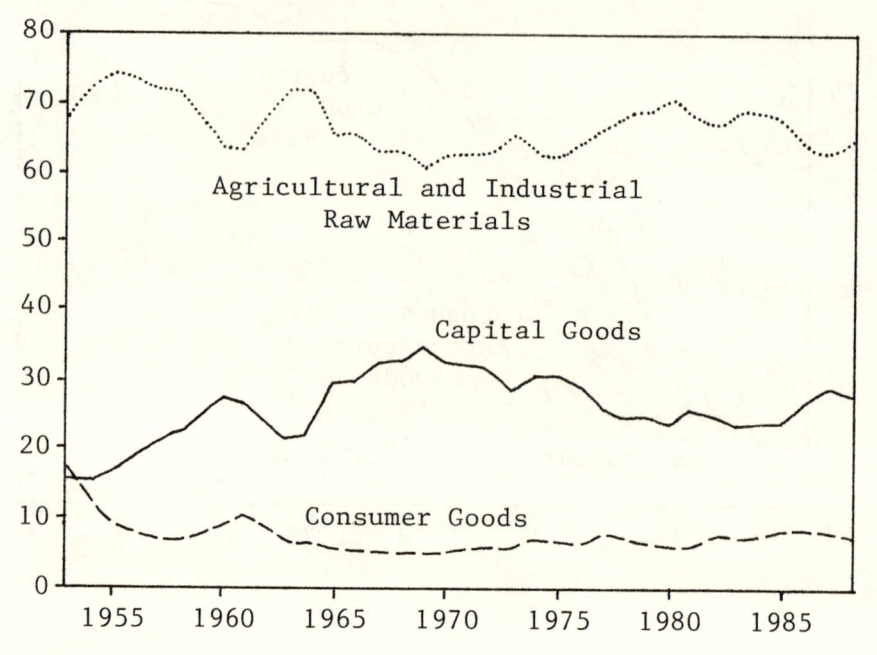

FIGURE 7.4 Commodity Composition of Imports, 1952-1988 (percentages)

263

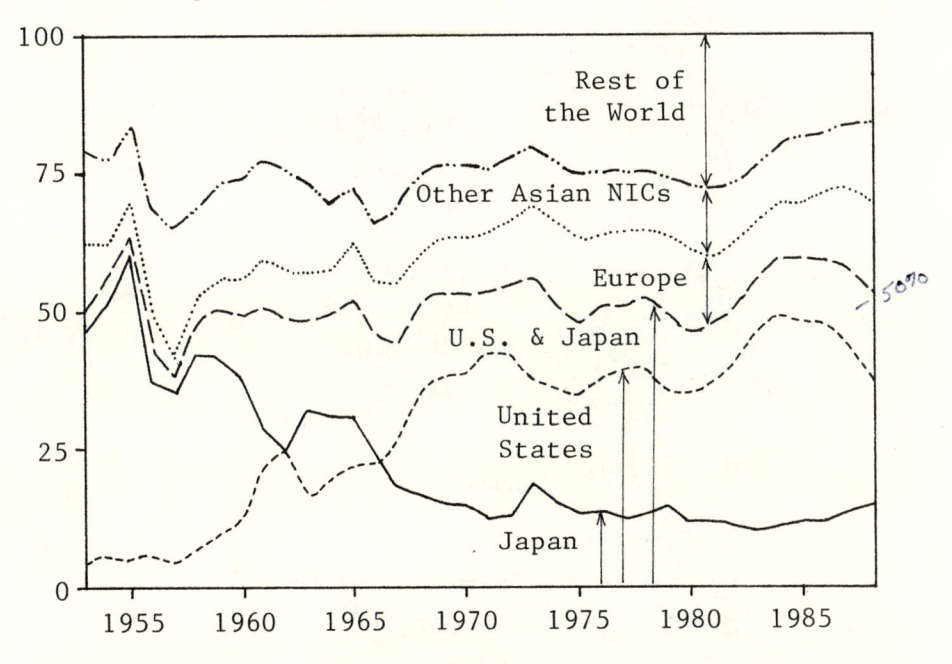

FIGURE 7.5 Geographic Pattern of Exports, 1952-1988 (percentages)

FIGURE 7.6 Geographic Pattern of Imports, 1952-1988 (percentages)

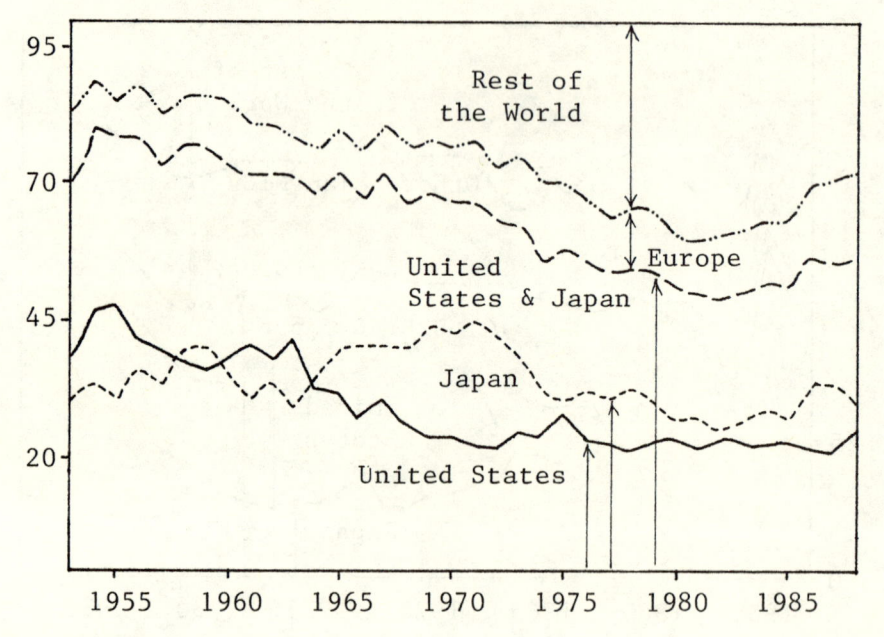

and the United States. Interestingly, the two countries traded places in terms of relative importance as both a source of imports and a destination for exports in the mid-1960s. In the 1950s, Japan was the principal market for Taiwan's exports and the United States was the principal source of imports, a pattern which reflected the legacy of Taiwan as a prewar colony of Japan and the dominance of production capacity in the United States in the immediate postwar period. By the mid-1960s, however, Japan had accomplished reconstruction from the devastation of war and had greatly expanded its industrial base, and as a consequence was in a position to supply Taiwan with the capital goods and industrial raw materials it required for its own industrialization. At the same time, Taiwan was undergoing a major change in economic policy favoring production and export of manufactured goods, for which the United States provided the largest and most accessible market in the world.

In spite of the lowering of tariffs and the relatively rapid growth of income in Western Europe and Japan, the United States has remained, by a large margin, the single largest market for Taiwan's exports. Indeed, as shown in Figure 7.5, the United States' share increased sharply in the early 1980s, a fact which did not go unnoticed by protectionists in the United States. A great deal of noise has been made about the "un-level playing field" on which the United States and Taiwan allegedly compete; however, as shown in Figure 7.7, the increasing proportion of exports destined for the United States in the first half of the 1980s was closely associated with the real appreciation of the US dollar against all the major currencies as well as the NT dollar.[4] The appreciation of the U.S. dollar naturally made the U.S. market relatively attractive to Taiwan exporters, who in six years, from 1980 to 1986, raised the U.S. share from 34 to 48 percent of exports, a 40 percent increase. Since 1985, the US dollar has fallen against the NT dollar, the yen and other major currencies, and not surprisingly the United States share in Taiwan's exports has declined.

Given the geographic pattern of Taiwan's trade, the US dollar-yen exchange rate is a matter of considerable importance to Taiwan. Since Taiwan is a heavy net importer from Japan and a heavy net exporter to the United States, a realignment of the *real* US dollar-yen exchange rate can have a significant effect on Taiwan's terms of trade. A real depreciation (appreciation) of the dollar against the yen lowers (raises) the price Taiwan gets for its exports relative to the price it pays for imports, when both prices are expressed in a common currency.

In the 1970s, the dollar-yen realignment worked decidedly against Taiwan, as shown in Figure 7.8. There is, of course, no escape from this dilemma other than to attempt to change the direction of trade, shifting exports toward the strong-currency country and imports toward the weak-currency country, which Taiwan attempted to do in the 1970s with some

FIGURE 7.7 Share of Exports to the U.S. (SXUS) and
Real Exchange Rate (RER)

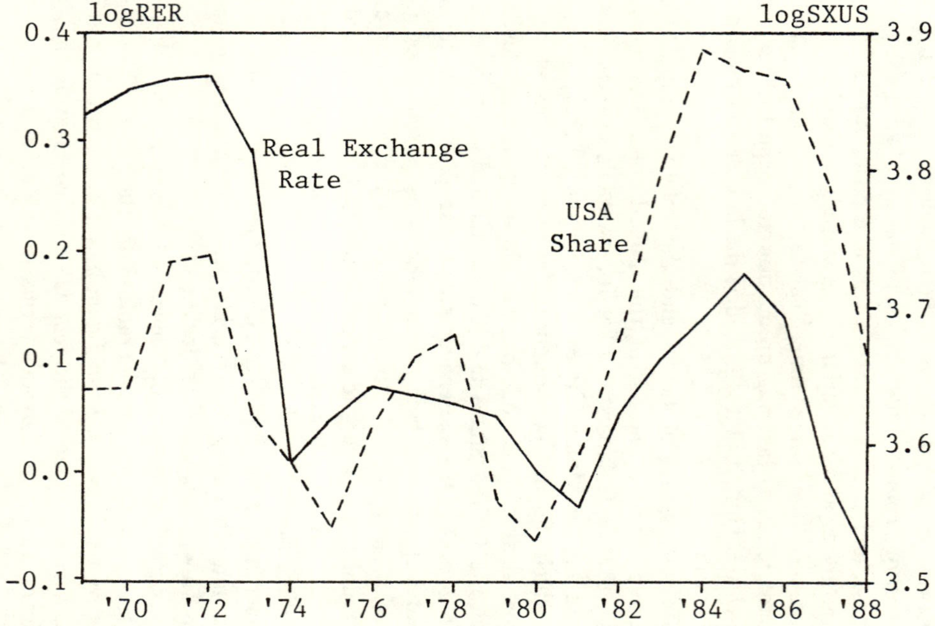

Source: Monthly Statistics of Exports and Imports, Taiwan Area, R.O.C.; I.M.F. International Financial Statistics, various issues

FIGURE 7.8 Nominal and Real U.S.-Japan Exchange Rate

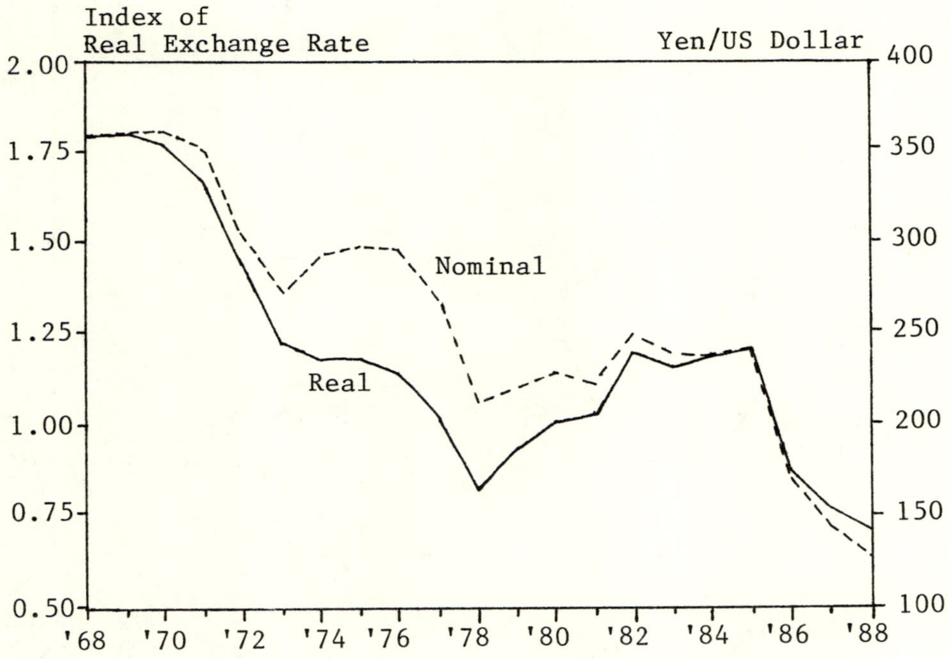

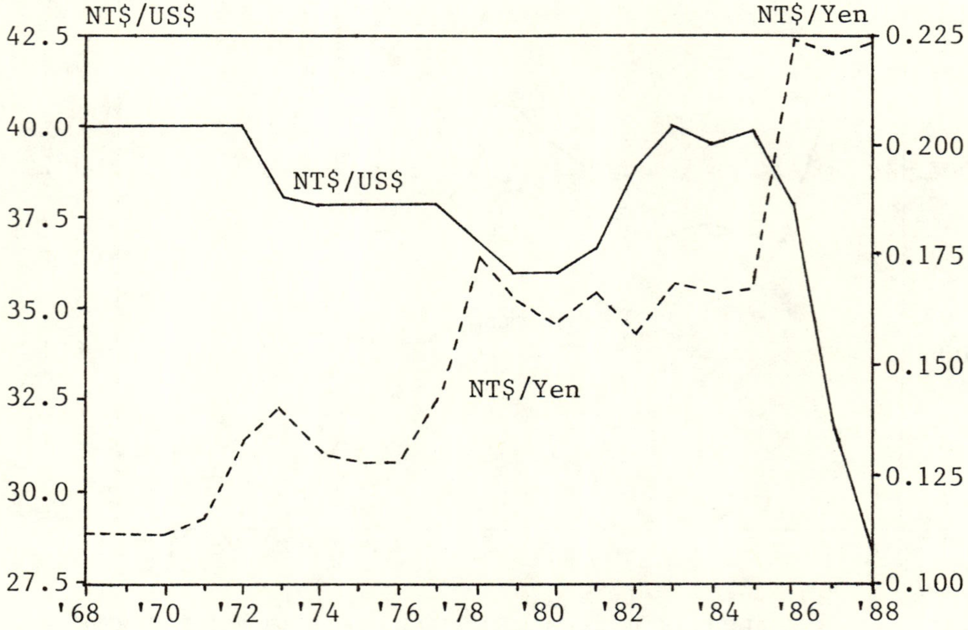

FIGURE 7.9 Exchange Rates Against the U.S. Dollar and Japanese Yen

success (Figures 7.5 and 7.6). In addition, exchange rate policy has an important effect on how the burden of the US dollar-yen realignment is distributed between importers and exporters. As Figure 7.9 shows, Taiwan chose a not quite middle course in the 1970s, with some appreciation against the US dollar, but significantly more depreciation against the yen, thereby favoring exporters over importers.

Just when the downward movement of the US dollar against the yen became an inexorable fact of life, however, the direction of this exchange rate realignment was reversed, and for seven years, from 1978 to 1985, the US dollar rose against the yen. This shift undoubtedly benefitted Taiwan, whose net barter terms of trade rose 20 percent from 1980 to 1986.

In 1985, however, the movement of the US dollar-yen exchange rate reversed direction once again, placing Taiwan in the same predicament it faced in the 1970s. In the recent period, however, the exchange rate policy response in Taiwan has been very different from that during the 1970s. Authorities have held the NT dollar steady against the yen, and allowed it to appreciate against the US dollar, putting the full burden on exporters. It is not difficult to understand the reasons behind this approach to the dilemma in the 1980s, given the pressure and the threats of protectionism Taiwan faces because of its large overall trade surplus and its bilateral surplus with the United States in particular.

4. Revealed Comparative Advantage

With hindsight it is obvious that resource-poor Taiwan would find its comparative advantage in industry, but precisely where within the industrial sector is the strength of Taiwan's comparative advantage, how has it changed and how is it likely to change? We begin an examination of these questions with a more detailed look at the commodity composition of exports.

The strength of comparative advantage (and disadvantage) according to trade theory is measured by differences in *pre-trade* relative prices. Unfortunately, the data available for analyzing comparative advantages are generated in *post-trade* equilibria. Therefore, we can only observe comparative advantage as it is "revealed" in trade flow data. Of course, if markets are reasonably free and efficient, there should be a close correspondence between the pattern of trade and true comparative advantage; maximizing behavior would lead to the export of goods whose pre-trade relative prices are low and the import of goods whose pre-trade relative prices are high. When one looks at the data, however, one finds that most countries export and import some amount in virtually every commodity category, even when the aggregation is relatively low. For example, at the three-digit SITC level of aggregation, there are some 129 categories of manufactured and processed primary commodities; Taiwan in 1987 had exports in every single category. Obviously it did not have a comparative advantage in everything; that is a logical impossibility.

For empirical purposes, therefore, we require some criterion by which to determine whether a given level of exports reveals a strong or a weak comparative advantage or disadvantage. There are different criteria one could choose, but by far the most common is one introduced by Bela Balassa (1965) known as the "revealed comparative advantage" (RCA) index, which for commodity i, country j, is defined as:

$$RCA_{ij} = (X_{ij}/\sum_i X_{ij})/(\sum_i X_{ij}/\sum_j \sum_i X_{ij}).$$

By convention, if $RCA_{ij} > 1.0$, in which case the share of commodity i in country j's exports is greater than the share of that commodity in world trade, country j is revealed to have a comparative advantage in commodity i. It is also suggested that the higher the RCA index the stronger the comparative advantage, though in recent years it has been questioned whether the RCA index can be interpreted as a cardinal measure (Hillman 1980; Yeats 1985).

Tables 7.2 and 7.3 show period average values and the rank order (out of 129 three-digit SITC categories) of RCA indexes and export shares (the numerator of the RCA index) for the 40 categories for which the RCA index for 1986-1987 was greater than unity.[5]

It is worth noting that these forty categories accounted for between 80 to 84 percent of total exports in each of the four periods; in other words, as an aggregate these forty commodities were as important in 1970-1972 as they were in 1986-1987. Within the group of commodities, however, there have been some significant changes in values and rank orders of both RCA indexes and export shares.

An indication of the magnitude of the changes in the ranking of these commodities by RCA index and export share is given in Table 7.4 which contains a matrix of Spearman's rank correlation coefficients between the two variables in each of the four periods. The rank correlations reveal two interesting findings: first, that changes over time in RCA index rankings have been greater than in export share rankings and, second, that the correspondence between RCA index ranking and export share ranking has diminished to the point where, by 1986-1987, there was in fact only a weak correlation (i.e., $r_s = 0.362$) between the two rankings.

These findings would seem to indicate that the commodity composition of exports has more inertia than revealed comparative advantage. For example, clothing, which ranked number one in export volume in every period, declined in RCA rank from 4 to 20 between 1970-1972 and 1986-1987. However, while Taiwan's comparative advantage in clothing has

TABLE 7.2 The Value and Rank Order of Top 40 RCA Indexes

Commodity	RCA 1970-1972 Value	Rank	RCA 1976-1977 Value	Rank	RCA 1983-1985 Value	Rank	RCA 1986-1987 Value	Rank
831 Travel goods, handbags	4.928	8	9.004	2	10.478	1	7.064	1
984 Toys, sporting goods, etc.	3.519	11	5.230	5	7.232	3	6.646	2
851 Footwear	6.330	5	8.056	3	7.426	2	6.412	3
666 Pottery	0.447	53	2.420	18	5.194	5	5.354	4
632 Wood manufactures, n.e.s.	6.784	3	7.654	4	6.338	4	5.176	5
733 Road vehicles, non-motorized	1.905	22	2.124	22	4.896	7	5.009	6
697 Base metal household equipment	2.859	15	4.120	9	5.069	6	4.596	7
899 Other manufactured goods	2.899	14	4.402	8	4.660	8	4.361	8
812 Plumbing, heating, lighting equipment	0.387	58	0.674	45	2.876	16	3.398	9
821 Furniture	1.178	29	1.673	29	3.494	11	3.382	10
696 Cutlery	2.586	17	2.185	19	2.812	17	3.105	11
893 Articles of plastic, n.e.s.	3.667	10	3.348	12	3.050	14	3.105	12
055 Vegetables, etc., preserved, prepared	18.023	1	11.237	1	4.450	9	3.041	13
612 Leather manufactures, etc.	0.851	38	1.949	24	3.581	10	3.009	14
694 Steel, copper nails, nuts, etc.	0.316	61	1.178	35	2.447	21	2.913	15
032 Fish, etc, tinned, prepared	0.919	35	3.066	15	2.936	15	2.733	16
653 Woven textiles noncotton	1.936	21	2.662	16	2.320	23	2.610	17
723 Electrical distributing machinery	3.314	12	2.023	23	2.640	19	2.549	18
724 Telecommunications equipment	5.314	6	4.074	10	3.134	13	2.511	19
841 Clothing, not of fur	6.573	4	4.855	6	3.445	12	2.477	20

(continues)

271

TABLE 7.2 (continued)

Commodity	RCA 1970-1972 Value	Rank	RCA 1976-1977 Value	Rank	RCA 1983-1985 Value	Rank	RCA 1986-1987 Value	Rank
695 Tools	0.466	50	1.168	36	2.722	18	2.456	21
656 Textile, etc., products, n.e.s.	1.590	24	2.166	21	2.520	20	2.424	22
698 Metal manufactures, n.e.s.	0.453	52	0.819	40	2.083	24	2.110	23
654 Lace, ribbons, tulle, etc.	0.970	32	1.197	34	1.735	27	2.051	24
655 Special textile, etc., products	1.257	28	1.760	27	1.698	28	1.835	25
714 Office machines	0.297	62	0.503	54	1.087	41	1.609	26
651 Textile yarn and thread	2.278	19	3.319	13	1.963	25	1.593	27
895 Office supplies, n.e.s.	1.021	31	0.931	38	1.525	30	1.407	28
266 Synthetic, regenerated fiber	0.111	88	0.663	46	1.461	32	1.402	29
722 Electrical power machinery, switchgear	0.609	44	0.595	49	1.336	36	1.374	30
631 Veneers, plywood, etc.	8.825	2	4.502	7	2.429	22	1.370	31
717 Textile, leather machinery	0.548	48	0.848	39	1.410	33	1.241	32
652 Cotton fabrics, woven	5.190	7	3.373	11	1.510	31	1.226	33
725 Domestic electric equipment	0.261	64	0.377	62	1.395	34	1.209	34
897 Gold, silverware, jewelry	0.592	45	1.238	33	1.248	38	1.145	35
729 Electrical machinery, n.e.s.	1.346	27	1.578	31	1.151	40	1.130	36
891 Sound recorders, producers	0.868	37	1.784	26	0.864	43	1.056	37
629 Rubber articles, n.e.s.	0.365	59	0.754	42	1.211	39	1.052	38
665 Glassware	0.641	43	1.147	37	0.982	42	1.016	39
661 Cement, etc, building products	1.681	23	1.324	32	1.573	29	1.002	40

TABLE 7.3 The Value and Rank Order of Top 40 of Export Categories

Commodity	Share 1970-1972 Value	Rank	Share 1976-1977 Value	Rank	Share 1983-1985 Value	Rank	Share 1986-1987 Value	Rank
831 Travel goods, handbags	0.853	21	2.029	14	3.074	8	2.465	12
984 Toys, sporting goods, etc.	2.586	11	3.482	8	5.671	4	6.099	5
851 Footwear	5.659	4	7.455	3	8.051	2	7.564	2
666 Pottery	0.090	71	0.486	41	1.040	25	1.110	24
632 Wood manufactures, n.e.s.	1.576	14	2.100	13	1.499	17	1.279	21
733 Road vehicles, non-motorized	0.612	28	0.720	31	1.512	16	1.626	16
697 Base metal household equipment	0.668	26	0.998	22	1.213	22	1.038	26
899 Other manufactured goods	1.511	15	1.942	15	1.918	13	1.945	13
812 Plumbing, heating, lighting equipment	0.133	62	0.204	59	0.769	33	1.078	25
821 Furniture	0.796	23	1.402	18	3.263	7	3.759	7
696 Cutlery	0.399	37	0.284	53	0.308	52	0.341	44
893 Articles of plastic, n.e.s.	2.024	12	2.122	12	2.205	12	2.703	11
055 Vegetables, etc, preserved, prepared	6.191	3	3.812	5	1.174	23	0.740	32
612 Leather manufactures, etc.	0.055	83	0.129	64	0.314	50	0.298	49
694 Steel, copper nails, nuts, etc.	0.098	69	0.378	46	0.697	36	0.833	30
032 Fish, etc., tinned, prepared	0.264	46	0.762	27	0.655	38	0.682	37
653 Woven textiles noncotton	3.528	8	3.603	7	2.503	11	3.089	9
723 Electrical distributing machinery	1.129	17	0.710	32	1.147	24	1.160	22
724 Telecommunications equipment	11.289	2	9.770	2	7.962	3	6.748	4
841 Clothing, not of fur	19.325	1	15.891	1	12.307	1	10.644	1

(continues)

TABLE 7.3 (continued)

Commodity	Share 1970-1972 Value	Rank	Share 1976-1977 Value	Rank	Share 1983-1985 Value	Rank	Share 1986-1987 Value	Rank
695 Tools	0.236	52	0.575	37	1.214	21	1.129	23
656 Textile, etc, products, n.e.s.	0.449	35	0.654	35	0.710	35	0.724	35
698 Metal manufactures, n.e.s.	0.388	38	0.691	33	1.673	15	1.785	15
654 Lace, ribbons, tulle, etc.	0.121	66	0.113	69	0.145	67	0.185	60
655 Special textile, etc., products	0.610	29	0.730	30	0.626	40	0.722	36
714 Office machines	0.638	27	0.940	23	3.971	6	6.886	3
651 Textile yarn and thread	3.356	10	3.770	6	1.914	14	1.626	17
895 Office supplies, n.e.s.	0.129	64	0.110	71	0.206	58	0.211	56
266 Synthetic, regenerated fiber	0.046	86	0.207	57	0.358	48	0.326	45
722 Electrical power machinery, switchgear	1.009	20	1.076	21	2.631	10	2.842	10
631 Veneers, plywood, etc.	5.477	5	2.518	10	1.034	26	0.604	38
717 Textile, leather machinery	0.691	25	0.735	29	0.819	30	0.865	28
652 Cotton fabrics, woven	3.763	6	2.335	11	0.859	29	0.737	33
725 Domestic electric equipment	0.177	56	0.281	54	0.994	27	0.957	27
897 Gold, silverware, jewelry	0.126	65	0.336	49	0.540	43	0.533	39
729 Electrical machinery, n.e.s.	3.635	7	4.739	4	4.927	5	5.100	6
891 Sound recorders, producers	0.775	24	1.519	17	1.260	20	1.799	14
629 Rubber articles, n.e.s.	0.271	44	0.634	36	0.918	28	0.848	29
665 Glassware	0.175	58	0.297	51	0.238	55	0.255	53
661 Cement, etc., building products	0.426	36	0.394	43	0.518	44	0.299	48

TABLE 7.4 Spearman's Rank Correlation Coefficients

	RCA 1970-1972	RCA 1986-1987	Share 1970-1972	Share 1986-1987
RCA 1970-1972	1.000			
RCA 1986-1987	0.379	1.000		
Share 1970-1972	0.800	0.150	1.000	
Share 1986-1987	0.265	0.362	0.631	1.000

$r_s = 1 - 6\Sigma D^2/n(n^2 - 1)$, where D = (Rank Var 1 - Rank Var 2).

clearly slipped since the early 1970s, it remains positive (i.e., RCA > 1), and because of the predominance of the sector in the earlier period it has remained the single largest export, albeit by a diminishing margin. On the other hand, the second largest export category, footwear, has maintained a steady share of total exports since the mid-1970s and a relatively constant RCA, while the third most important export in 1986-1987, office machinery, ranked 27th in the early 1970s with an RCA of only 0.64. Clearly, comparative advantage in Taiwan has been subject to change, the basis of which we consider in the next section.

Before proceeding, however, it is worth noting another interesting development highlighted by the RCA indexes and exports shares, which is a diversification of exports and broadening of the categories in which a comparative advantage is revealed. This is illustrated in Figure 7.10, which shows the distribution of RCA indexes greater than unity in descending order for 1970-1972 and 1986-1987. In the earlier period, revealed comparative advantage was stronger (as indicated by a higher RCA) and more concentrated in a fewer number of categories. Over time the strength of comparative advantage at the high end of the range weakened, but was spread more broadly over a larger number of categories, from thirty to forty between 1970-1972 and 1986-1987.

As these data reveal, comparative advantage is subject to change. In the process of economic development, comparative advantage rises in some sectors and declines in others. At the stage of development through which Taiwan has recently passed, it would appear that comparative advantage in manufacturing has broadened and exports have become somewhat more diversified. This is to be expected in a maturing economy that is expanding rapidly, and no doubt lessens the pain of structural adjustment which accompanies changes in comparative advantage. As Taiwan comes to resemble more closely the economies of higher-income developed countries it may find changes in comparative advantage more difficult to absorb.

FIGURE 7.10 The Distribution of the Top Forty RCA Indexes for 1970-1972 and 1986-1987

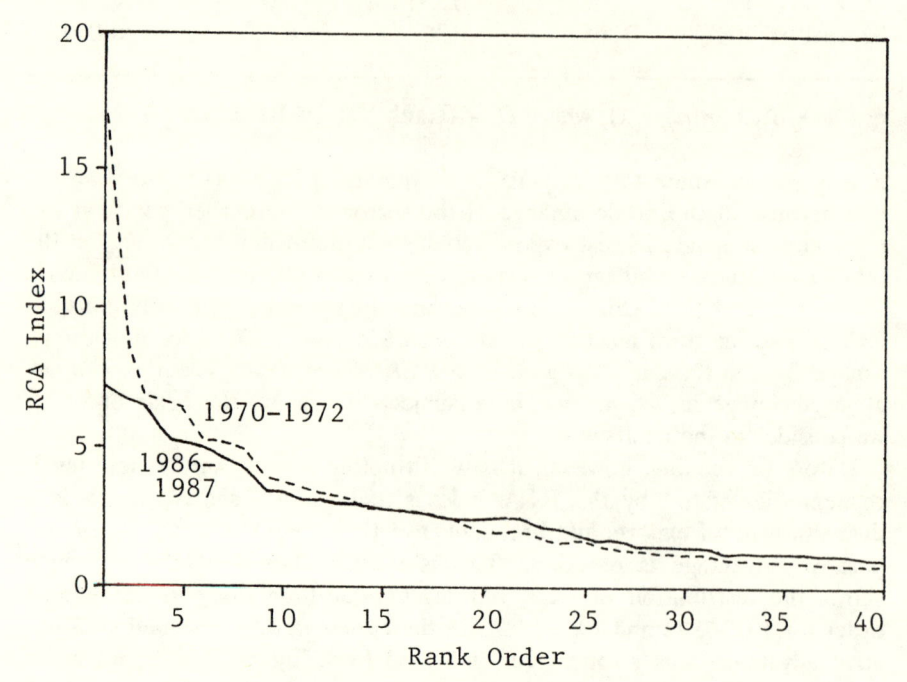

Source: Data provided by Dr. Alexander Yeats.

5. Factor Proportions and Changing Comparative Advantage

In looking for the source of change in comparative advantage in Taiwan, the obvious place to begin is with the Heckscher-Ohlin factor proportions theory. The bedrock of international trade theory for many decades, the Heckscher-Ohlin theory, has recently been called into question by the recognition that a large proportion of international trade is between countries at similar levels of income, with similar relative endowments of resources, and often involving the simultaneous export and import of similar goods, i.e., intra- as opposed to inter-industry trade. Nonetheless, rumors of its demise are greatly exaggerated (Krugman 1987). There are, in fact, explanations of intra-industry trade based on international differences in relative factor abundance that are as plausible and convincing as those which stress imperfect competition (Kierzkowski 1984). Furthermore, for many countries, especially developing countries, the bulk of trade is with countries whose incomes and relative factor endowments are vastly different from their own. Taiwan is such a country, though it is closing the per capita income gap with its principal trade partners. The rapid rise of per capita income in Taiwan is a product of the change in Taiwan's relative factor endowment, and so too are the changes in Taiwan's comparative advantage. In the previous section we described the changes in comparative advantage; in this section we examine their basis in terms of changing factor endowment.

Measuring the factor content of exports and imports is more complicated than is generally recognized. Leontief's (1953) pioneering work showed that in measuring the factor intensity of production it was necessary to consider not just the direct factor requirements at the last stage of production, but also the indirect factor requirements for producing the intermediate inputs used at the final stage of production. His method for calculating the total, direct plus indirect, requirement of kth factor in producing the jth good (f_{kj}), and the method used in most studies of the factor content of international trade, is:

$$f_{kj} = \sum_i f_{ki} r_{ij}$$

where f_{ki} is the direct requirement of kth factor in ith industry and r_{ij} are elements of the inverse Leontief matrix, $[I-A]^{-1}$, where $[A]$ is a matrix of input-output coefficients.

The problem with this method is that it is appropriate only if all intermediate inputs are produced domestically; if instead some are imported, then the factor requirements of the imported inputs are not those of producing the inputs themselves, but rather the factor requirements of producing the exports which exchange for imported intermediate inputs (Riedel 1975). For example, if Taiwan imports capital-intensive steel in exchange for relatively labor-intensive cloth, it is the factor intensity of cloth, not steel, that is relevant in measuring the total, direct plus indirect, factor requirements of goods which use imported steel as an input.

The total factor requirements in an economy like Taiwan's, which imports a significant proportion of intermediate inputs, consist therefore of two parts: first, the factor requirements at the last stage of production and in producing domestic intermediate inputs, which is calculated by:

$$f'_{kj} = \sum_i f_{ki} s_{ij}$$

where s_{ij} are elements of the matrix $[I - (A-M)]^{-1}$, where M is a matrix of imported input-output coefficients; and, second, the direct and indirect factor requirements of the exports which exchange for the imported intermediate inputs required, directly and indirectly, to produce a unit of good j:

$$f''_{kj} = m_j[f_x/(1 - m_x)]$$

where m_j is the direct and indirect per unit imported input, f_x is the direct and indirect factor requirement of one unit of a representative export, and where m_x is the direct and indirect import requirement per unit of the representative export, which takes into account that imports are required to produce exports, which in turn requires more exports and hence more imports, and so on.[6] Thus, the total requirement of the kth factor in the jth industry, in which both domestic and imported intermediate inputs are used, is:

$$\tilde{f}_{kj} = f'_{kj} + f''_{kj}.$$

There are two different approaches to analyzing the changing factor content of international trade. One approach is to compute the factor requirements of representative bundles of exports and import-competing goods to determine whether exports require relatively more of the relatively abundant factor and import-competing goods relatively more of the relatively scarce factor. This was the approach of Leontief in discovering his famous paradox. The other approach, which is purportedly superior if the aim is to test the Heckscher-Ohlin hypothesis, is to compute the factor content of net exports, the hypothesis being that countries will be net exporters of relatively abundant factors and net importers of relatively scarce factors

(Leamer 1980). Unfortunately, the latter approach runs into problems when applied to an economy like Taiwan's which has a very large trade surplus, in which case the country may be found to be a net exporter of all factors, both scarce and abundant. Since our purpose is not to test the theory *per se*, we take the former approach, computing the factor requirements of representative bundles of exports (X) and import-competing goods (M) in years t (t = 1978 to 1988):

$$f_{kXt} = \sum_j f_{kj} e_{jt}, \quad e_{jt} = X_{jt}/\sum_j X_{jt}, \quad \sum_j e_{jt} = 1$$

$$f_{kMt} = \sum_j f_{kj} m_{jt}, \quad m_{jt} = M_{jt}/\sum_j M_{jt}, \quad \sum_j m_{jt} = 1.$$

Total, direct and indirect, requirements of labor, fixed capital, industrial land and agricultural land of representative bundles of manufactured exports and import-competing goods for the years 1978 to 1988 are shown in Figures 7.11 to 7.14.[7] The analysis is confined to trade in manufactures since factor proportions theory is not applicable to trade in natural resources.

Figures 7.11 and 7.12 indicate that, as expected, Taiwan's manufactured exports embody more labor and less capital than import-competing goods. Furthermore, while the differences in labor and capital requirements of the two bundles of goods are substantial, they have diminished. This, too, is to be expected, given the substantial increase in the capital stock per employee in manufacturing and the rise in real wages of almost 7 percent per annum from 1974 to 1988 (see Figure 7.15).[8] Indeed, given the change in relative factor endowment, it is surprising that the differences in the relative requirements of labor and capital in export and import-competing goods did not diminish by more than they did.

The industrial and agricultural land requirements of representative bundles of export and import-competing goods are shown in Figures 7.13 and 7.14. As expected, the industrial land requirement of a representative bundle of import-competing goods is significantly higher than that for exports. Moreover, it appears that the increasing relative scarcity of industrial land has led to changes in the composition of exports toward less industrial land-intensive goods. Changes in the composition of exports have also significantly lessened demand for agricultural land, which was substantial in the early phase of export-led growth.

Numerous studies have suggested that the one factor of production whose relative abundance, more than any other, determines the pattern of comparative advantage (and disadvantage) in manufacturing is human capital (Keesing 1968; Baldwin 1971). Moreover, human capital accumulation is

FIGURE 7.11 Total Labor Requirement for Representative Bundles of Export and Import-Competing Goods (persons/NT$million)

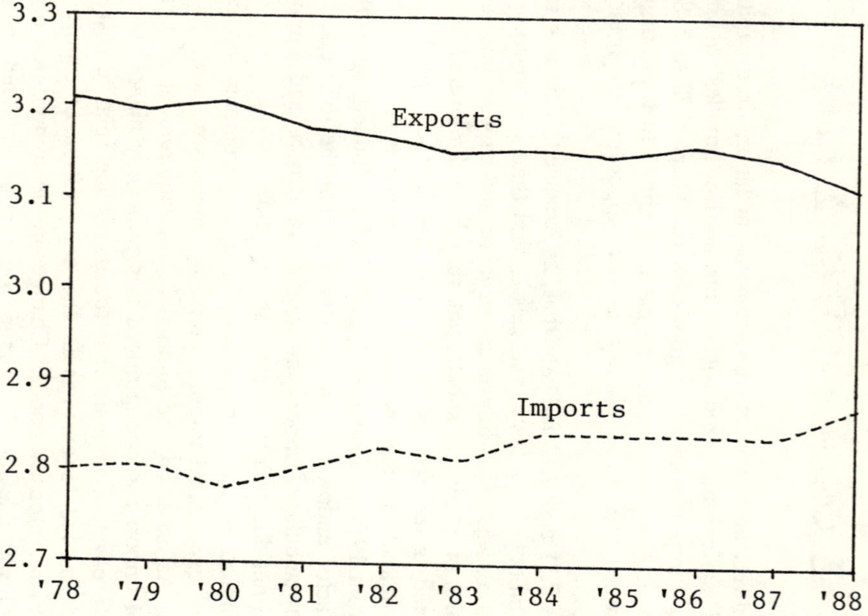

FIGURE 7.12 Total Per Unit Requirement for Representative Export and Import-Competing Goods (NT$)

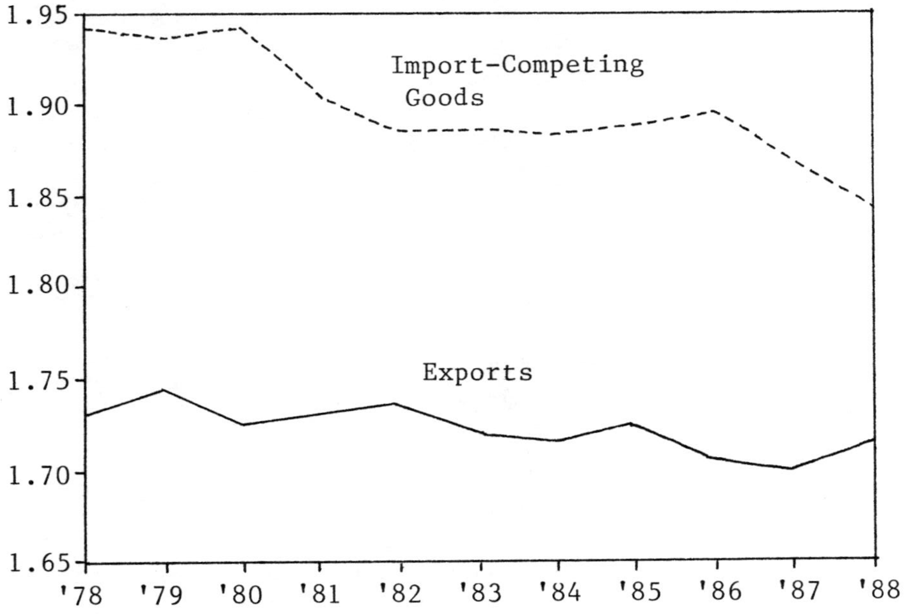

FIGURE 7.13 Total Industrial Land Requirement for Representative Export and Import Competing Goods (m^2/NT$million)

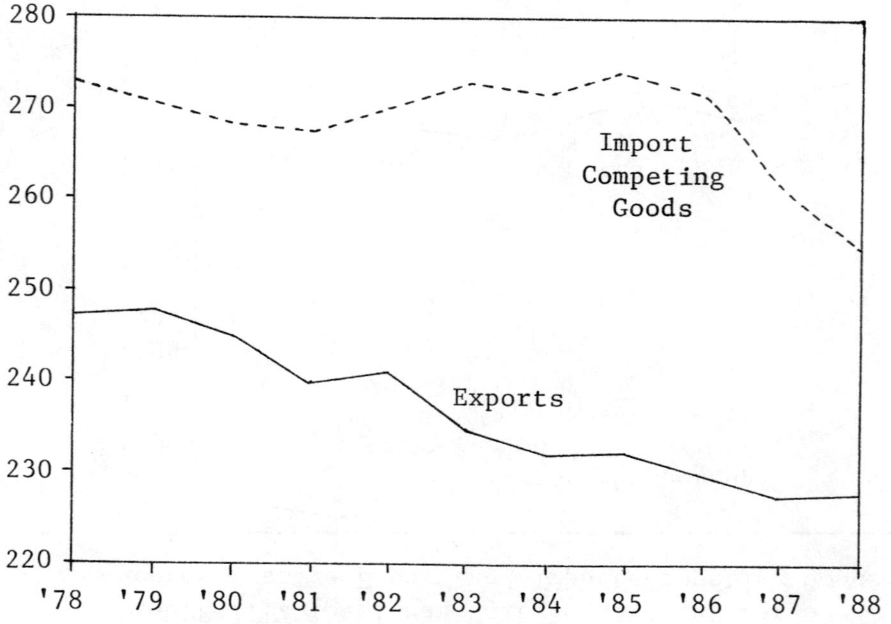

FIGURE 7.14 Total Agricultural Land Requirement for Representative Export and Import Competing Goods (m^2/NT\$million)

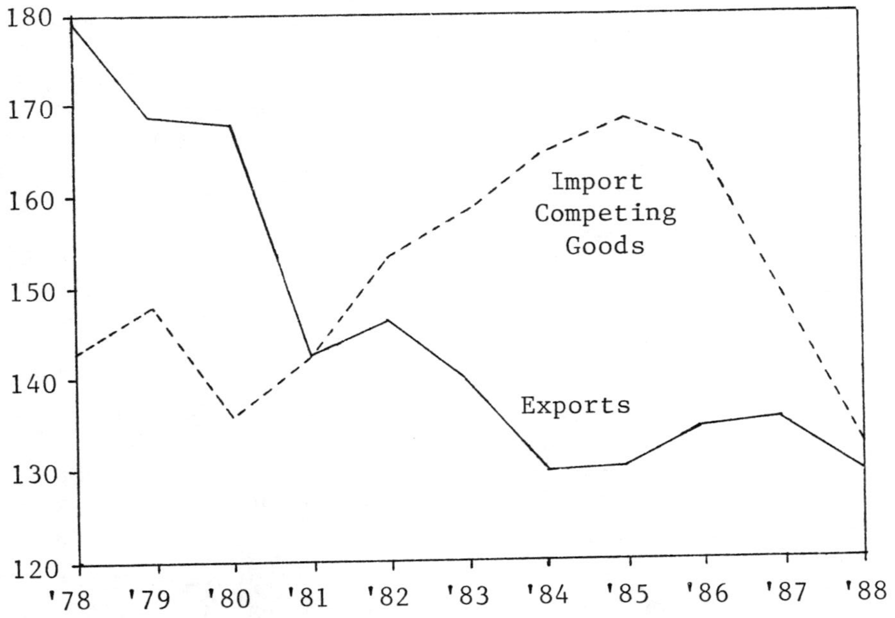

FIGURE 7.15 Real Capital Stock/Employee and Real Wage in Manufacturing

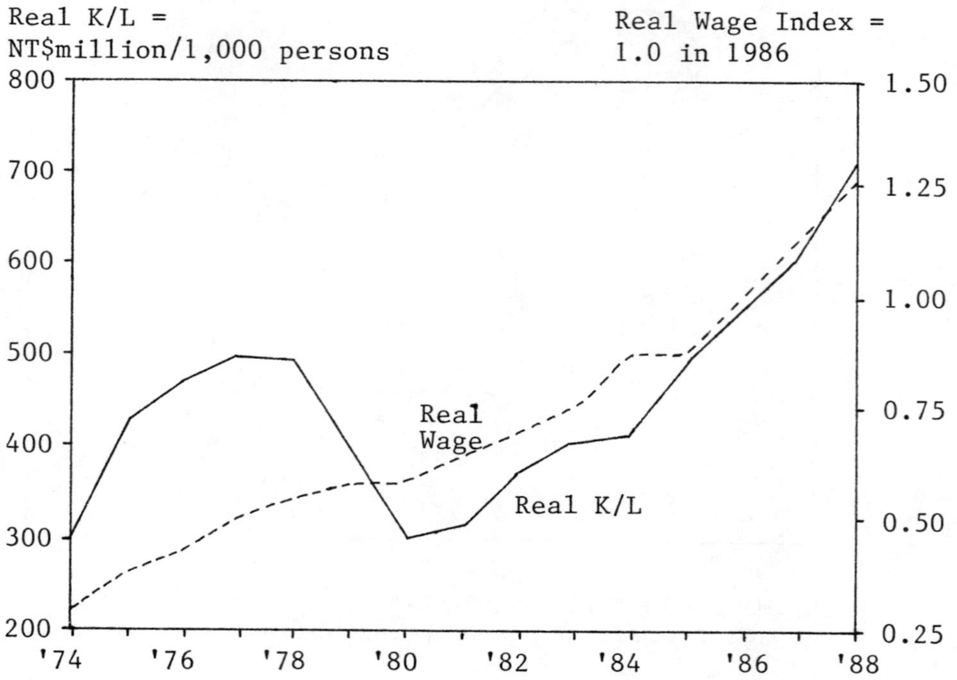

Real K/L = NT$million/1,000 persons

Real Wage Index = 1.0 in 1986

generally regarded as the single most important source of growth in developed and high-income developing countries. Taiwan certainly has emphasized human capital formation. Government spending on education rose at 12.4 percent per annum in constant prices from 1968 to 1988. In 1988, Taiwan sent over 7,000 students abroad and had almost 500,000 enrolled in higher education at home.[9] The numbers of students in higher education at home and abroad have increased at 5 percent per annum, at which rate the stock of graduates doubles every fourteen years.

Unfortunately, human capital is as difficult to measure as it is important. While industrial census data reveal employment, fixed capital and land use by sector, no comparable figures are available on human capital. There are, however, variables which can be used to proxy human capital. One is the average wage of a sector. If labor markets are reasonably efficient, differences across industries in average wage should be associated with differences in the skill level of the work force in different sectors. Therefore, a finding that the average wage in import-competing industries is higher than in export industries would indicate that the former are more skill-intensive than the latter. As Figure 7.16 shows, this is precisely what is observed in Taiwan. Moreover, while imports have become less skill-intensive over time, the composition of exports does not appear to have responded to the increased abundance of labor skills in Taiwan.

A similar conclusion is reached in a recent study which uses the venerable NBER-Hal Lary measure of labor intensity to analyze shifts in comparative advantage in developing countries (Yeats 1989). Lary's index of sectoral labor intensity, which is simply the ratio of value-added to employment by sector, is intended to stand as a proxy for the ratio of both human and physical capital to labor. For an economy like Taiwan's, in which the stock of physical and human capital is rapidly expanding, one would expect a decline in the relative importance of labor-intensive exports. This, however, is not what the data indicate. As shown in Table 7.5, the share of labor-intensive products in total manufactured exports in Taiwan is very high (85 percent) and does not appear to be declining, either in Taiwan or the other Asian NICs which, like Taiwan, have experienced rising real wages. Even Hong Kong, which is perhaps a decade ahead of Taiwan in the level of real wages, exports primarily (i.e., 94 percent) labor-intensive manufactures. In terms of the overall importance of labor-intensive goods in manufactured exports, Taiwan is second only to Hong Kong. However, as a supplier to world markets, Taiwan is second to no developing country and, as Table 7.5 shows, occupies the number one position by a wide margin.

FIGURE 7.16 Index of Labor Skill Intensity of Manufactured Export and Import-Competing Goods (NT$)

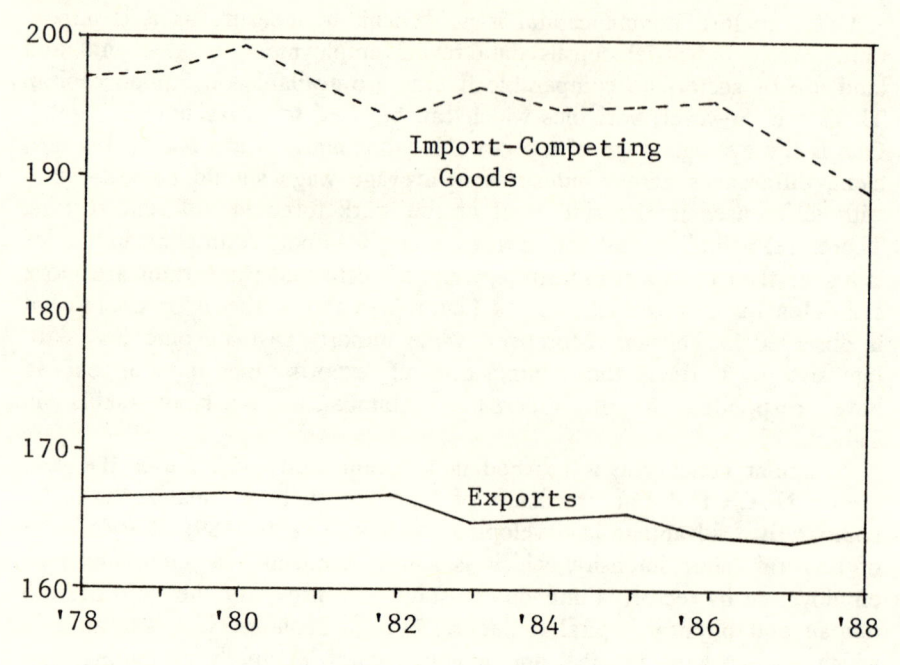

TABLE 7.5 Labor-Intensive Manufactured Exports in Selected Countries[a] (in percentages)

	Share of L-I exports in total manufactured exports			Share of L-I exports in LDC L-I exports		
	1965	1975	1986	1965	1975	1986
Taiwan	45.5	78.9	85.0	4.3	14.5	22.3
Korea	51.1	79.2	78.2	1.8	13.8	15.3
Hong Kong	89.9	94.2	93.6	22.8	18.9	13.5
Brazil	6.2	16.7	29.7	2.5	4.7	4.0
India	44.3	65.2	63.1	15.8	4.5	3.1

[a]Yeats defines labor-intensive products as those which meet two conditions: "(1) value added per employee did not exceed the national average for all United States manufacturing by more than 10 percent, and (2) imports by developed from developing countries total at least $100,000 at the three-digit level of the SITC system in 1965" (p. 4).

Source: Yeats (1989, p. 16).

6. Product Quality and the Dynamics of Comparative Advantage

The foregoing analysis of the relative factor intensity of Taiwan's exports presents a paradox akin to Leontief's own. Although Taiwan has increased substantially its relative endowment of physical and human capital, its exports remain concentrated in relatively labor-intensive product categories. The paradox, however, is perhaps more apparent than real and may simply be the result of the classic problem of aggregation, in this case the lumping together of similar products of different quality. If higher quality products require more physical and human capital per worker than lower quality products, a change in the relative endowment of capital and skills would lead to both intra- and inter-sectoral shifts in the composition of exports. The standard analysis of the factor content of trade captures only the inter-sectoral shifts. However, intra-sectoral shifts may well be more important if there are substantial fixed start-up costs to getting established in a new industry. In these circumstances, firms would normally exploit the advantage of a greater relative abundance of capital and skills by upgrading to higher quality products within an industry before shifting to a different industry in which they lack experience and the know-how that comes from experience.

Product quality is not an easy concept to quantify, but some indication of change in product quality within export categories can be gleaned by comparing export price and unit-value indexes. Unit-values are derived by dividing export values by some physical quantity measure, either weight or the number of units, and as such make no allowance for change in quality. Price indexes, on the other hand, are derived by taking weighted averages of price indexes of specific commodities, and therefore control for shifts in product quality to a greater degree (Leamer and Stern 1965). A comparison of export unit-value and price indexes gives an indication of the change in product quality.

Figure 7.17 shows the ratios of the export unit-value index to export price index for two major export categories, machinery and electrical equipment. These ratios, which we interpret as indexes of product grading, rise at an annual rate of 6.9 percent for machinery and 4.5 percent for electrical equipment. The phenomenon is illustrated at a more disaggregated level in Table 7.6 which shows the rate of increase in unit values from 1983 to 1988 of the three largest export items within these categories: sewing machines, machine tools and automated data processing equipment. Since the export price index for machinery and electrical equipment was virtually constant over the period, it would appear that substantial product up-grading took place in these important sub-categories.

Similar evidence of upgrading has been found for Taiwan footwear exports. Aw and Roberts (1988) construct translog price indexes for the three-digit SITC category of footwear for Taiwan and other major exporters based on twenty-seven seven-digit SITC footwear categories for the period 1974 to 1982. Since the translog price indexes correct for cross-section and time-series changes in the mix of footwear exports between the twenty-seven seven-digit categories, while the unit-value index does not, the ratio of the latter to the former yields an index of product quality. As shown in Figure 7.18, the quality of Taiwan's footwear appears to be rising,

TABLE 7.6 Unit-values of Selected Electrical Machinery Exports

	Unit Values 1983	Unit Values 1985	Annual rate of increase (%)
Sewing Machines (NT$/set)	2,296	3,342	7.7
Machine Tools (NT$/tonne)	0.085	0.121	7.3
Data processing equipment (NT$/set)	3,817	19,067	38.9

Source: Ministry of Finance, *Monthly Statistics of Exports and Imports*, May 1989.

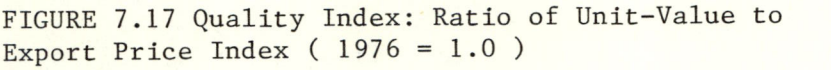

FIGURE 7.17 Quality Index: Ratio of Unit-Value to Export Price Index (1976 = 1.0)

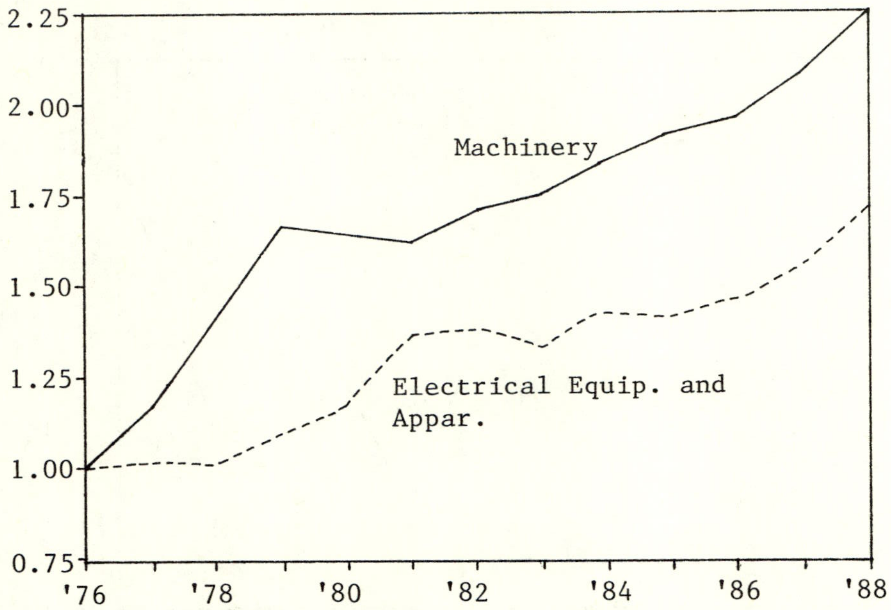

Source: Monthly Statistics of Imports and Exports, May 1989, Ministry of Finance; Taiwan Statistical Data Book, 1989.

FIGURE 7.18 Quality Index of Taiwan's Footwear Exports, 1974–1988 (1974 = 1.0)

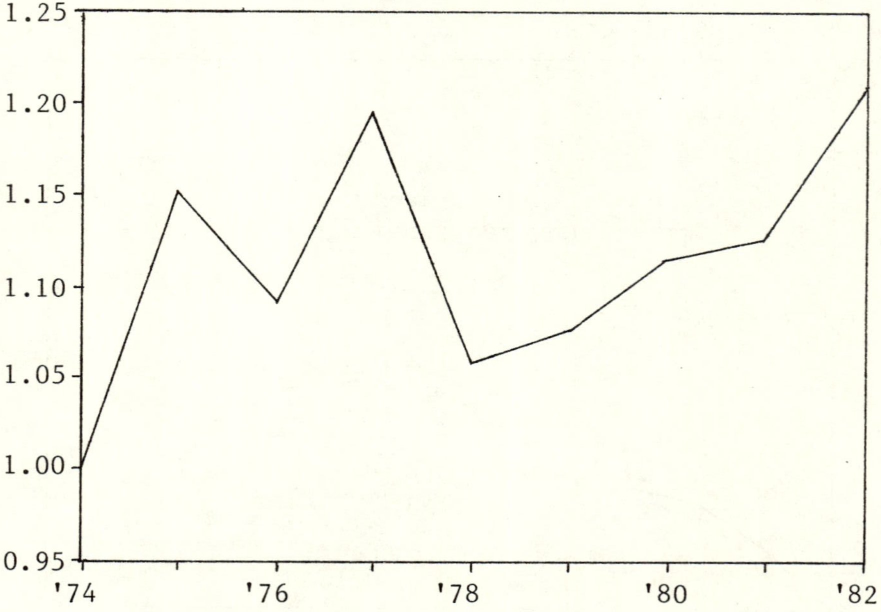

Source: Aw and Roberts (1988)

albeit at a somewhat slower rate than for machinery and electrical equipment. A similar rate of increase in product quality was observed in Korean footwear exports (i.e., 3.0 percent annually), while for the three major non-Asian footwear exporters, Brazil, Spain and Italy, quality increased at only 0.7, 0.5 and 1.2 percent per year, respectively.

The cross-country differences in both the level and rate of change of the quality of footwear exports are consistent with the hypothesis that quality upgrading occurs in response to a change in factor endowment. A clear relation was found between the level of real wages and the average unit-value of footwear exports, with relatively high-wage countries exporting predominantly high-quality products. A similar relationship was observed between the rate of change in real wages and the rate of change in quality, with quality rising more rapidly in countries like Korea and Taiwan whose real wages were rising relatively rapidly. However, a caveat is in order. Since Taiwan and Korea were both subject to orderly marketing agreements in footwear during the period of this analysis, it is quite possible that at least part of the upgrading of footwear exports was in response to these quantitative restrictions.

Although the evidence presented here on the relation between changing factor endowment and quality upgrading of exports is rather circumstantial, it meets the test of common sense. The main implication of it is that Taiwan, like Hong Kong and even Japan earlier on, will retain a strong comparative advantage in traditional export categories, such as clothing, footwear and consumer electronics, for some time to come. Competitors in the developed countries cannot count on rising real wages in Taiwan to lessen the competitive pressure they face from Taiwan. On the contrary, as Taiwan moves up the quality ladder, and its exports become closer and closer substitutes for domestic products in the developed countries, competitive pressure will only intensify. Furthermore, attempts by the developed countries to relieve the pressure by restraining Taiwan's exports may only exacerbate their problem by encouraging even more quality upgrading than would occur in the absence of quantitative restraints on exports.

7. DFI and Technology Transfer

An important contributor to changing comparative advantage and product-quality upgrading in Taiwan is direct foreign investment, both inward and outward bound. The contribution of inward direct foreign investment in Taiwan has not been great in terms of financing investment to which it has contributed only about 2 percent of total domestic investment. Rather the main contribution has been to provide manufacturing technology and international marketing know-how. The direct contributions of foreign-owned firms to manufacturing output and exports are shown in Table 7.7 and appear to be declining from peak levels in the mid-1970s.

The decline in the relative importance of foreign direct investment in Taiwan is a consequence mainly of its own success. The rapid growth of direct investment in Taiwan began in 1966 with the establishment of export processing zones around the city of Kaoshiung, Taiwan's largest harbor. The export processing zone provided adequate infrastructure, access to intermediate and capital goods at world prices, and a stable economic and political environment. But the main attraction to foreign firms was the ready availability of motivated workers at relatively low wages (Riedel 1975). The ensuing growth in the demand for labor both by foreign and domestic manufacturers led to rising real wages and a diminution in the incentive to invest in labor-intensive manufacturing activities.

Government authorities recognized the imperative of changing comparative advantage and in the 1970s adopted measures to encourage direct foreign investment in more capital- and technology-intensive industries. Perhaps the most important such measure was the establishment in 1980 of the Hsinchu Science-based Industrial Park, which has attracted foreign and domestic firms engaged mainly in electronics manufacturing.

The electronics industry in Taiwan illustrates most vividly the interaction between foreign investment, technology diffusion and changing comparative advantage. The forerunners of the electronics industry in Taiwan were the transistor radio and television producers. Over the years, these firms extended their activities from televisions to microcomputers, disk drives, printers, terminals and monitors, which are produced in Taiwan almost exclusively for export (Liu *et al.* 1989). As Figure 7.19 shows, exports of information hardware have increased five-fold, from US$1 billion in 1984 to

TABLE 7.7 Contribution of DFI to Income, Employment and Exports

	GNP	Employment	Exports
1974	21.4	15.8	21.8
1977	24.3	16.3	20.9
1979	28.0	16.6	20.4
1982	19.1	14.6	19.7
1985	13.0	8.8	15.8

Source: Schive (1988) from *An Analysis of the Operations of Foreign Enterprises*, various issues (Investment Commission, MOEA).

293

FIGURE 7.19 Information Hardware Exports

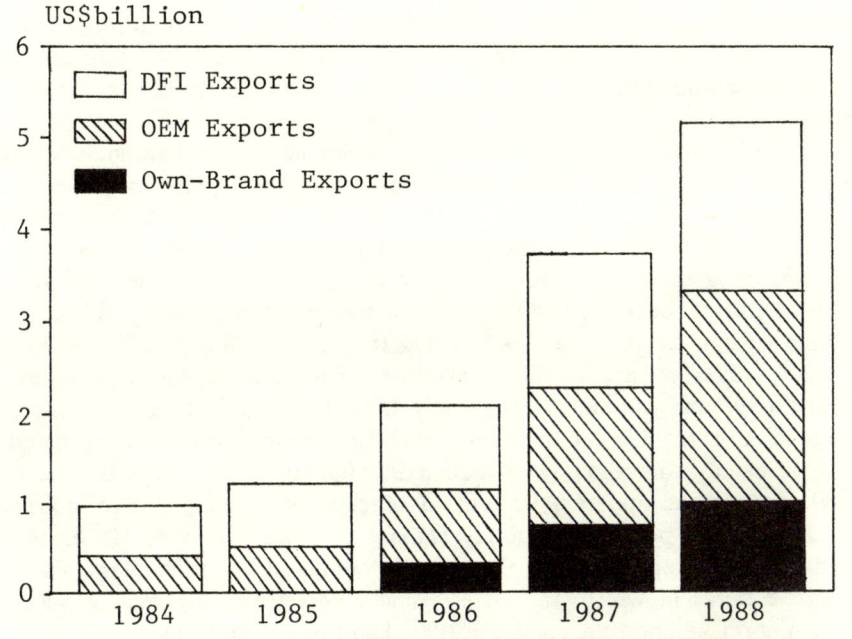

US$billion

[Bar chart showing stacked bars for 1984-1988 with DFI Exports, OEM Exports, and Own-Brand Exports categories]

Sources: Liu et al. (1989); *Information Industry Yearbook*, 1989, Institute for Information Industry.

over US$5 billion in 1988. As is further illustrated in Figure 7.19, only a few years ago production was dominated by foreign-owned firms, and that which was produced by local firms was exported almost exclusively under foreign brand names, what is called "original equipment manufacturers" (OEM). However, since 1984 exports of information hardware by Taiwanese firms of own-brand products have more than doubled every year, and by 1988 accounted for 20 percent of the total. The experience of the electronics industry illustrates clearly that the contribution of foreign direct investment is not limited to the production and exports of foreign firms themselves, and that even more important perhaps is the diffusion of foreign technology to domestic firms which emulate their foreign counterparts.

At the bottom end of the technology spectrum where Taiwan is losing comparative advantage, direct foreign investment also plays an important role, but it is direct investment in the opposite direction. Rising relative labor costs in Taiwan have induced both foreign and domestic firms to begin relocating their more labor-intensive manufacturing activities in lower-wage countries, in particular the ASEAN countries and, since 1985, in the People's Republic of China. According to Schive (1988, p. 372), by 1985 US$214 billion of outward direct investment had been approved by authorities, though his estimate is that only US$60 billion had been remitted. Meanwhile, since 1985, more than 1,000 Taiwanese firms, it is estimated, have invested more than US$1 billion in Mainland China (by the end of 1989) despite the apparent hazards of official bans on direct and indirect investment and political instability (*Financial Times*, June 6, 1990). According to this report, "Most of the funds went into low technology, labor-intensive fields in which Taiwan is losing competitiveness, such as shoes, toys, umbrellas, sporting goods, textiles, handbags, simple electronic hardware and furniture." Moreover, Taiwanese authorities intend to keep it that way, having recently drafted a provision as part of a bill which will govern relations with the Mainland to ban investment in high technology and capital-intensive industries. As further evidence of the complementarity of direct investment and international trade, it is worth noting that some 20 percent of Taiwan's indirect exports to the Mainland (estimated at US$3.1 billion in 1989) are related to direct investment there (Schive 1988).

8. Trade Policy and the International Environment

It is a widely held view that the economic prospects of developing countries depend in large measure on what goes on in developed countries, which is the source of much pessimism. If it is not the dismal outlook for growth in the developed countries, it is the threat of a rising tide of protectionism which is seen to stand in the way of LDCs' progress, and by some leap in logic to justify all sorts of illiberal economic policies in developing countries. Taiwan rejected this viewpoint long ago, and in the meantime has demonstrated the relative merits of an outward-looking policy under conditions both of solid growth and stability in developed countries (e.g., from 1960 to 1973) and of economic slowdown and instability (e.g., from 1974 to 1982). Moreover, Taiwan has shown that protectionism in developed countries, of which it is a target more often than any other country, except possibly Japan, is not insurmountable. Protectionism is, nonetheless, an obstacle, and one which promises to get more difficult as Taiwan becomes bigger and richer and more competitive in capital- and skill-intensive products; at least that is what the Japanese experience would suggest. What then can, and should, Taiwan do by way of trade policy and through international diplomacy to improve access to world markets and secure, stable trade relations?

What Taiwan's trade partners increasingly demand is that Taiwan lower its trade barriers. Fortunately, this demand is in accordance with Taiwan's own self-interest, since lower trade barriers generally mean higher economic efficiency. Trade liberalization also has important distributional consequences which generate political resistance to liberalization even when it is clearly in the nation's interest. Certainly there is, and always has been, political resistance to trade liberalization in Taiwan. Nevertheless, trade barriers have been coming down in Taiwan since the mid-1950s, and with the fall in barriers have come all the benefits to the country which trade theory promises.

Trade liberalization in Taiwan has occurred in three distinct phases. The first phase culminated in 1958 with a 250 percent nominal devaluation of the NT dollar and the removal of quantitative restrictions on permissible imports (i.e., non-prohibited and non-controlled imports), which at the time constituted about 50 percent of all importable items. The devaluation and unification of the exchange rate, together with the system of export incentives, including import duty rebates for exporters, were the key elements in what became known as the "export promotion strategy," emulated with success in many countries (Hsing 1971; Kuo 1983). The essence of the strategy was to make the incentive to export equal, *on average*, to the incentive to produce import-competing goods, which Bhagwati (1988) terms the "trade-neutral or bias-free strategy." This, however, did not imply free trade, since within the average effective exchange rate for export and import-competing sectors there were very substantial variations between different industries (Liang and Liang 1982).

The second phase of trade liberalization occurred in the 1970s as policymakers came to the realization that foreign exchange was no longer the binding constraint on growth it was thought to have been. After three years of surplus in the trade account, which in 1973 reached 6.2 percent of GDP, the Ministry of Economic Affairs, in 1974, drastically cut the number of controlled and prohibited imports, reducing their number from 42 percent to only 2 percent of all importable items (Tu and Wang 1988). However, although almost all imports became "permissible," licensing continued for the ostensible purpose of protecting the national security and maintaining health and safety standards. It is well known, however, that licensing procedures were employed for purely protectionist purposes, especially for the benefit of public enterprises (Tu and Wang 1988).

The third phase of import liberalization began in the late 1970s and was accelerated in the 1980s, again in response to growing trade surpluses, especially bilaterally with the United States. As shown in Figure 7.20, since 1974 Taiwan has reduced the average tariff rate by about 84 percent. The average tax on imports, defined as tariff revenue as a percent of the value of imports, has fallen from 18 percent in 1968 to only 6 percent in 1988. In 1984, the Ministry of Economic Affairs declared its intention to bring Taiwan's tariff schedule into line with those of the OECD countries within six years. However, as shown in Table 7.8, Taiwan still has some distance to go toward meeting this objective. Nonetheless, the government is committed to this goal and has included it as a formal offer of concession in its January, 1990 application for membership in the GATT.

In recent years Taiwan has also lowered numerous non-tariff barriers, including the lifting of bans on importation of some agricultural products, relaxing import procedures for steel products, eliminating local content requirements for VCRs and color TVs. However, perhaps the thorniest of all non-tariff trade issues has been intellectual property rights, of which Taiwan had earned a reputation as one of the world's most flagrant violators. As a result of a series of bilateral negotiations with the United States

TABLE 7.8 Distribution of Tariffs on Industrial Products in Taiwan (1988), USA, EEC and Japan (in percentages)

	Taiwan	USA	EEC	Japan
Free	8.7	31.1	37.9	56.3
0.1 to 5.0	20.6	44.1	19.0	25.2
5.1 to 10.0	33.0	17.1	32.5	14.6
10.1 to 15.0	22.7	1.9	9.1	2.9
15.1 to 20.0	9.6	2.2	1.3	0.8
20.1 to 25.0	3.8	0.8	0.2	0.1
Over 25.0	1.6	2.8	0.0	0.1

Source: Balassa and Balassa (1984) and Tu and Wang (1988) p. 84.

FIGURE 7.20 Average Nominal Tariff Rate and Average Tax on Imports

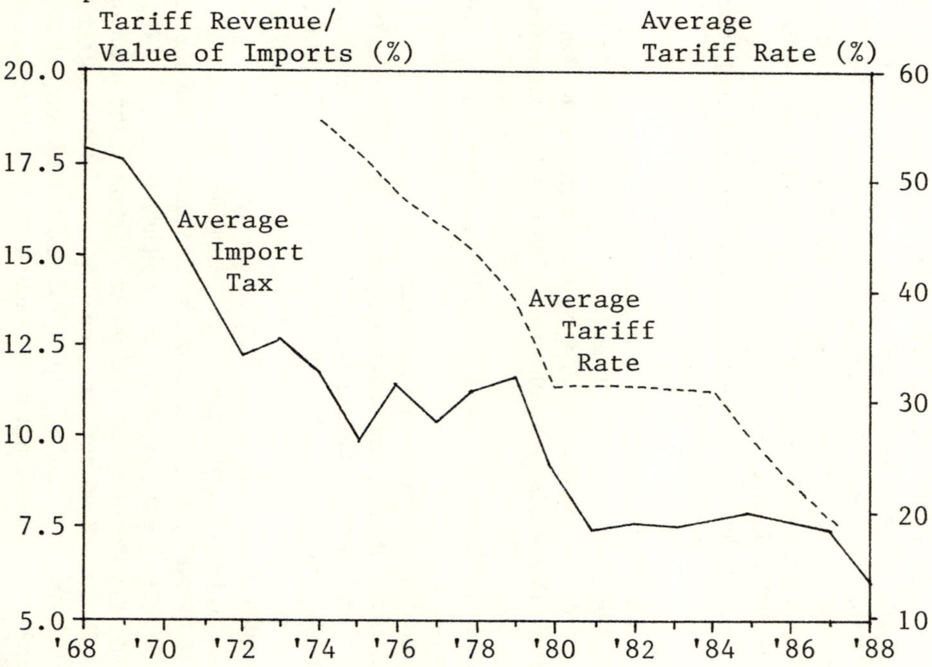

Sources: Ministry of Finance, R.O.C.; Tu and Wang (1988, p. 67).

in the early 1980s, Taiwan undertook in 1984 to completely rewrite its copyright, patent and trademark laws. Since then the point of contention has shifted from the nature of the laws to Taiwan's enforcement of the law, which the United States alleges is inadequate. A study by the U.S. International Trade Commission, for example, estimated that losses to U.S. firms from inadequate enforcement of property rights laws in Taiwan exceed US$750 million in 1986 (Liebeler 1990, p.15). In retaliation for not vigorously enforcing property rights, the United States placed Taiwan on the "priority watch list" under the "special 301" provision of the 1988 Trade Act. However, with presentation of an "accelerated plan of action" to improve enforcement, Taiwan was downgraded to the "watch list" on November 1, 1989 (USTR 1990).[11]

After about a decade of trade surpluses and mounting international reserves, and under intense pressure from the United States, Taiwan has made major "concessions" in trade policy and it promises to make even more. No doubt these changes will improve economic efficiency and yield a higher national income, but will they achieve the purpose for which they were intended -- namely, forestalling protectionism in the United States and securing more stable trade relations? Unfortunately, there is not much ground for optimism.

The dominant theme of United States trade policy over the last decade or so has been "fair trade, not free trade." In pursuit of this undefinable concept, the United States has increasingly used unilateral and bilateral policy initiatives, forsaking the principle of multilateralism which the United States itself enshrined as the fundamental principle of the GATT. As a natural consequence of its retreat from multilateralism, the United States has increasingly resorted to country-specific, non-tariff measures to achieve its trade policy objectives. Over the past twenty years, the United States has imposed country-specific quantitative restrictions in steel, automobiles, non-rubber footwear, color televisions, semiconductors and machine tools (Baldwin 1990a). These measures clearly violate the spirit of the GATT, and only by circumventing it do they avoid violation of the letter of GATT law. GATT law allows for discriminatory quantitative restrictions only when there is an injury-causing import increase due to dumping or subsidization which in the GATT are deemed unfair trade practices. The United States, however, is attempting to extend the concept of unfair trade to include the practice of successfully raising one's market share (Baldwin 1990a). At the Uruguay Round it has joined with the European Community in attempting to have this concept incorporated into the GATT by amending Article XIX (the safeguard provision) to allow for country-specific restrictions on imports in industries injured by import increases even when there is no allegation of unfair practices (Baldwin 1990a). Clearly, this poses a serious threat to the more successful exporters, especially those which are relatively small and lack a credible threat of retaliation, such as Taiwan.

Is there any reason to believe that the liberal trading system which existed from the late 1940s to mid-1960s will reemerge? Baldwin (1990b) suggests not, following his argument that the liberal trading system requires a world hegemon to establish and protect it, a role the United States played at the end of World War II, but one it is supposedly no longer capable of performing, having lost its hegemonic position. Bhagwati (1988), on the other hand, offers grounds for optimism based on what he calls the "spider's web" phenomenon -- the globalization of production through "a web of criss-crossing DFIs (direct foreign investments) and lesser relationships," which in his view creates "an increasingly important, pro-trade interest and voice in the arena where protectionist forces seek to triumph" (p. 75). The spider's web phenomenon may well be a mitigating force, but can it halt the drift toward managed trade in which powerful bureaucracies and important political constituencies have strong vested interests?

In these circumstances, what can a country like Taiwan do? Reducing and even eliminating its own trade barriers may divert protectionist pressure temporarily, but it will not forestall it entirely. Even free-trade Hong Kong is not exempt from allegations of unfair trade and the imposition of discriminatory restrictions against it.[12] However, the best reason for liberalizing trade is that it raises economic efficiency, the benefits from which accrue to the country whether or not these measures influence trade policy in other countries.

Aside from lowering its own trade barriers, Taiwan should do its part to try to strengthen the multilateral trading system, which at present is best represented by the GATT. Taiwan's January 1990 application for accession to GATT as a developed country, promising to bring its tariff and non-tariff trade policies into conformity with GATT principles and the practices in other developed countries, is clear evidence that Taiwan is prepared to do its part. If political obstacles to Taiwan's accession to GATT can be overcome, Taiwan will provide an important model of successful graduation which other developing countries following behind can emulate, just as they emulated the development strategy which transformed Taiwan from a developing into a mature economy.

Notes

I wish to thank the Chung-Hua Institution for Economic Research for its hospitality and especially Dr. Tzong-shian Yu and Dr. Po-kuei Chen for their help and cooperation. I am indebted to Morris Morkre, Richard Pomfret and Gustav Ranis for comments on an earlier draft, and to

Patricia Calvano, Rodney Chun and especially Jamil Mubarek for assistance in preparing this paper.

1. The sources of the data are: IBRD, *World Development Report, 1988* and *Taiwan Statistical Data Book*, 1989.

2. The real effective exchange rate (RER) in Figure 7.2 is a weighted average of the consumer price adjusted real exchange rate for the United States and Japan, Taiwan's two principal trade partners. RER is defined as the ratio of foreign to domestic prices in a common currency, and thus a rise in RER indicates a real devaluation.

3. The close relationship between the current account as a percent of GNP (CAY) and the real exchange (RER) is shown by the following regression, where D1 and D2 are shift dummy variables for 1974 and 1981, respectively (t-statistics in parentheses):

$$CAY = \underset{(-7.2)}{-87.6} + \underset{(7.5)}{69.6\ RER} + \underset{(5.6)}{14.7\ D1} + \underset{(5.0)}{6.5\ D2} + \underset{(3.40)}{0.29\ CAY_{-1}}$$

$$\bar{R}^2 = 0.91,\ D.W. = 1.93,\ F = 54.4.$$

The lagged dependent variable is included to allow for lags in the adjustment of *CAY* to changes in *RER*. The coefficient on CAY_{-1} indicates that 71 percent of the adjustment occurs within one year.

4. The relation between the real exchange rate and share of exports going to the United States is described by the following regression equation in which about 90 percent of the annual variation in the logarithm of the share of exports to the U.S. (*SXUS*) for the period 1968 to 1988 is explained by the logarithm of the real exchange rate (*RER*), the two shift dummy variables used in previous regressions, and a lagged dependent variable which is included to capture lags in the response of the export share to changes in the real exchange rate (t-statistics in parentheses):

$$\log SXUS = \underset{(5.66)}{2.04} + \underset{(5.56)}{0.89\ \log RER} + \underset{(3.96)}{0.20\ DUM1} + \underset{(4.19)}{0.10\ DUM2}$$

$$+ \underset{(3.52)}{0.36\ \log SXUS_{-1}}$$

$$R^2 = 0.89,\ \bar{R}^2 = 0.87,\ SEE = 0.04,\ D.W. = 2.42.$$

Note: the coefficient on the lagged dependent variable suggests that 64 percent of the adjustment in *SXUS* occurs within one year.

5. The revealed comparative advantage indexes were generously provided by Alexander Yeats of the World Bank.

6. For the full derivation of this algorithm, see Riedel, 1975.

7. The factor requirements are derived using the 1984 forty-nine sector

input-output tables and labor-output, capital-output and land-output ratios from the *Report on 1986 Industrial and Commercial Census*, DGBAS, Executive Yuan, October 1988.

8. The capital stock in manufacturing is derived by subtracting and adding, backward and forward, net investment from the fixed capital stock reported in the *Report on 1986 Industrial and Commercial Census*, i.e. $K_{t+1} = K_t(1-d) + I_t$, where d = depreciation rate.

9. Approximately 50 percent of high school graduates, who in turn number about 80 percent of the high school age cohort of the population (DGBAS, *Taiwan Statistical Data Book, 1989*).

10. In 1980 Taiwan enacted a "two-column" tariff, the second column being a preferential tariff which in fact applies to almost all of Taiwan's trade partners. The average tariff shown in Figure 7.20 is the column-two rate.

11. On August 31, 1989, the Executive Yuan announced that statistics would be compiled on enforcement of intellectual property rights by the fifteenth of each month and forwarded to the United States. Moreover, beginning in January 1990, textbooks for elementary and junior high schools are to contain lessons on the importance of intellectual property rights (Liu 1989).

12. In 1989, the E.C. Commission alleged that Hong Kong was dumping products as diverse as video cassettes, color TVs, photo albums and denim cloth, even though there is no significant home market price on which to base a dumping case (*FEER*, 19/1/89, p. 53).

References

Aw, Bee Yan, and Mark J. Roberts. 1988. "Price and Quality Level Comparisons for U.S. Footwear Imports: An Application of Multilateral Index Numbers," in Robert Feenstra, ed., *Empirical Methods for International Trade*. Pp. 257-275. Cambridge, MA: M.I.T. Press.

Balassa, Bela. 1965. "Trade Liberalization and 'Revealed' Comparative Advantage." *The Manchester School of Economic and Social Science* 33: 99-124.

Balassa, B., and C. Balassa. 1984. "Industrial Protection in the Developed Countries." *World Economy*, June 7, 1984, pp. 179-196.

Baldwin, Robert E. 1971. "Determinants of the Commodity Structure of U.S. Trade." *American Economic Review* 51: 126-136.

_____. 1990a. "Recent Changes in U.S. Trade Policy Toward The Republic of China and Other Newly Industrializing Nations." Presented at Conference on *U.S.-R.O.C Relations Since 1979: Review and Prospects*, Taipei, January.

———. 1990b. "U.S. Trade Policy, 1945-1988, from Foreign Policy to Domestic Policy," in Charles S. Pearson and James Riedel, eds., *The Direction of Trade Policy*. Pp. 9-23. Oxford: Basil Blackwell Inc.

Bhagwati, Jagdish. 1988a. *Protectionism*. Cambridge, MA: M.I.T. Press.

———. 1988b. "Export-Promoting Trade Strategy: Issues and Evidence." *World Bank Research Observer* 3: 27-57.

Chen, Pochih. 1989. "Policies and Structural Adjustment in Taiwan in the 1980s." Presented at the FAIR Conference on Asia Pacific Development, Taipei, July.

Chenery, Hollis B. 1960. "Patterns of Industrial Growth." *American Economic Review* 50(4): 624-654.

Fei, John C. H., Gustav Ranis, and Shirley W.Y. Kuo. 1979. *Growth with Equity: The Taiwan Case*. London: Oxford University Press.

Feldstein, Martin S., and Charles Morioka. 1980. "Domestic Saving and International Capital Flows." *Economic Journal* 90: 314-329.

Financial Times, June 6, 1990. London.

Galenson, Walter, ed. 1979. *Economic Growth and Structural Change in Taiwan: The Postwar Experience of the Republic of China*. Ithaca: Cornell University Press.

G.A.T.T. 1989. *International Trade: 1988-89*, Vol. II.

Goldstein, Morris, and Mohsin Khan. 1985. "Income and Price Effects in Foreign Trade," in Ronald W. Jones and Peter B. Kenen, eds., *Handbook of International Economics*. Pp. 1041-1106. Amsterdam: North-Holland.

Hillman, Arye L. 1980. "Observations on the Relation Between 'Reveal Comparative Advantage' and Comparative Advantage as Indicated by Pre-Trade Relative Prices." *Weltwirtschaftliches Archiv* 116(2): 315-321.

Hsing, Mo-huan. 1971. *Taiwan: Industrialization and Trade Policies*. London: Oxford University Press.

Keesing, D. B. 1968. "Labor Skills and the Structure of Trade in Manufactures," in Peter B. Kenen and R. Lawrence, eds., *The Open Economy: Essays on International Trade and Finance*. New York: Columbia University Press.

Kierzkowski, H. 1984. *Monopolistic Competition and International Trade*. Oxford: Oxford University Press.

Krueger, Anne O. 1985. "Trade Policies in Developing Countries," in Ronald W. Jones and Peter B. Kenen, eds., *Handbook of International Economics*. Pp. 519-570. Amsterdam: North-Holland.

Krugman, Paul R. 1987. "Is Free Trade Passé?" *The Journal of Economic Perspectives* 1(2): 131-144.

Kuo, Shirley W. Y. 1983. *The Taiwan Economy in Transition*. Boulder: Westview Press.

Lary, Hal B. 1968. *Imports of Manufactures from Less Developed Countries*. New York: N.B.E.R.
Leamer, Edward E. 1980. "The Leontief Paradox Reconsidered." *Journal of Political Economy* 88: 495-503.
Leamer, E. E., and R. M. Stern. 1965. *Quantitative International Economics*. Boston: Allyn and Bacon.
Leontief, Wassily. 1953. "Domestic Production and Foreign Trade: The American Capital Position Re-Examined." *Proceedings of the American Philosophical Society* 97: 332-349.
Liebeler, Susan W. 1990. "The Importance of Intellectual Property Issues in U.S.-Republic of China Relations." Presented at Conference on *U.S.-R.O.C. Relations Since 1979*, Taipei, January, 1990.
Liu, Paul K. C., Ying-Chuan Liu, and Hui-Lin Wu. 1989. "New Technologies, Industry and Trade -- The Taiwan Experience." *Industry of Free China* 72(5): 7-29 and 72(6): 23-36.
Liu, Lawrence S. 1989. "Legal and Policy Perspectives on United States Trade Initiatives and Economic Liberalization in Taiwan, Republic of China." (unpublished mimeo)
Liang, Kuo-shu, and Ching-ing Hou Liang. 1982. "Trade and Incentive Policies in Taiwan," in Kwoh-ting Li and Tzong-shian Yu, eds., *Experiences and Lessons of Economic Development in Taiwan*. Pp. 337-390. Taipei: Academia Sinica.
Riedel, James. 1975a. "Factor Proportions, Linkages and the Open Developing Economy." *Review of Economics and Statistics* 57(4): 487-494.
_____. 1975b. "The Nature and Determinants of Export-Oriented Direct Foreign Investment in a Developing Country: A Case Study of Taiwan." *Weltwirtschaftliches Archiv* 3(3): 58-87.
_____. 1988. "Economic Development in East Asia: Doing What Comes Naturally?" in H. Hughes, ed., *Achieving Industrialization in East Asia*. Cambridge: Pp. 1-38. Cambridge University Press.
Schive, Chi. 1987. "Trade Patterns and Trends of Taiwan," in Colin I. Bradford and William H. Branson, eds., *Trade and Structural Change in Pacific Asia*. Chicago: University of Chicago Press.
_____. 1988. "Foreign Investment and Technology Transfer in Taiwan: Past Experience and Future Potentials," in *Conference on Economic Development Experience of Taiwan and Its New Role in an Emerging Asia-Pacific Area*. Pp.345-385.
_____. 1989. "Restructuring Taiwan's Economy in the 1980's and Its Future Developments." Presented at the Fourth Sino-South African Conference. January, 1984. Taipei, Taiwan.
Takeuchi, Kenji. 1989. "Does Japan Import Less Than It Should? A Review of the Econometric Literature." *Asian Economic Journal* 3(2): 138-170.

Tu, Chaw-shia, and Wen-thuen Wang. 1988. "Trade Liberalization in the Republic of China and the Economic Effects of Tariff Reductions," in *Industrial Policies of Korea and the Republic of China*, pp. 42-102.

Tsiang, S. C., W. L. Chen, and A. Hsieh. 1985. *Developments Towards Trade Liberalization in Taiwan, Republic of China.* Proceedings of Conference on U.S.-Taiwan Economic Relations, Taipei, March 1985.

United States Trade Representative. 1990. *National Trade Estimate Report on Foreign Trade Barriers*, p. 216.

Yeats, Alexander J. 1985. "On the Appropriate Interpretation of the Revealed Comparative Advantage Index: Implications of a Methodology Based on Industry Sector Analysis." *Weltwirtschaftliches Archiv* 121(1): 61-73.

_____. 1989. "Shifting Patterns of Comparative Advantage: Manufactured Exports of Developing Countries." World Bank PPR Working Paper No. 165. (unpublished)

8

Capital and Labor Mobility in Taiwan

Joseph S. Lee

1. Introduction

Having maintained a high rate of economic growth for forty years, Taiwan has graduated from the group of newly industrialized economies (NIEs) and is on its way to joining the ranks of the major industrial countries by the year 2000. At that time, its per capita income is expected to be US$17,000 and its trade position should improve from the current rank of thirteenth to tenth in the world. Its comparative advantage will be in the technology intensive areas and its social security and national health insurance system will have been established (Yu 1990). In short, by the year 2000 Taiwan's economic structure should look a lot more like that of the developed market economies (see Table 8.1).

During the process of development, the government of Taiwan has gradually liberalized its economy. The first liberalization occurred in the commodity markets and has more recently moved to the financial markets. The rate of liberalization has quickened in recent years. For example, in 1987 the government lifted the limitations that had been placed on capital inflow and outflow, reduced the average effective tariff tax rate to about 5.7 percent, and opened the service, fast-food, supermarket, banking, insurance, leasing, and transportation industries to foreigners. As a result, in 1989 two-way trade accounted for as much as 85 percent of Taiwan's GDP. The outflow of capital was US$8.5 billion; in the same year, direct foreign investment (DFI) inflow amounted to US$1,604 million, and approved DFI outflow reached US$931 million (Investment Commission 1990).

The labor market has not been globalized to the extent of the commodity and the financial markets, however. This is largely because since the 1950s, after the large-scale migration of Mainlanders to Taiwan with the Nationalist Government, there has not been any large scale immigration or emigration due to strict governmental restrictions (Hsieh *et al.* 1989). The

TABLE 8.1 Structure of GDP for Selected Countries: 1986 (unit: %)

Country	Agriculture	Industry	Manufacturing	Services
ROC (1986)	6	51	43	43
(1996)	3	42	33	56
United States	2	31	20	67
(West) Germany	2	40	32	58
Japan	3	41	30	56
United Kingdom	2	43	26	55
France	4	34	--	63
Canada	3	36	--	61
Singapore	1	38	27	62
South Korea	12	42	30	45
Hong Kong	0	29	21	71

Source: *National Development Plan: 1991-96*, Council for Economic Development and Planning, January 1991, p. 13, and *The Long-Term Prospect of Economic Development in Taiwan: 1986-2000*, Council for Economic Development and Planning, Executive Yuan, May 1986.

government wanted to control emigration because it feared wanton emigration could lead to an exodus of people from the island which could affect the country's stability, one of the most essential conditions for economic development. The government's tight control of immigration also stemmed from its fear of infiltration by Communist Chinese agents. The only exemption from these restrictions was given to the several thousand students who wanted to go to foreign countries for advanced study and who quite often remained abroad after the completion of their studies. However, the increasing internationalization of the financial markets in Taiwan has put pressure on the government to open up its labor market as well. This pressure exists because, as more DFI flows into the island, the transnational corporations (TNCs) based in foreign countries also send an increasingly large number of management personnel, engineers, and technicians (professional transients) to Taiwan. At the same time, more companies from Taiwan have been investing in Southeast Asian countries and in other areas, and they also send Chinese professional transients abroad. The increased DFI outflow from Taiwan to other Southeast Asian countries and Mainland China has also attracted a large number of guest workers from these countries to Taiwan. Most of these guest workers coming into Taiwan do so on tourist visas (except those from Mainland China who are strictly illegal immigrants). When the visas expire, they become illegal immigrants. Although there are no official records of these guest workers, estimates range from 40,000 to 120,000 (Chang 1989; *China Times* August 13, 1990). The Legislative Yuan is considering the passage of the Employment Services Law which will open up Taiwan's labor market partially to the guest workers from Southeast Asian countries but not to those from Mainland China. The Law will also allow for the importation of professional and technical workers from foreign countries.

The crucial questions at this point in time are: As Taiwan pushes towards a mature economy, to what extent must it continue to open up its commodity, financial, and labor markets to the world? What would be the directions and patterns of these flows of capital and labor? What problems will Taiwan encounter as the capital and labor markets continue to be opened up? What problems will arise as the international flows of capital and labor into, and out of, Taiwan continue to rise? What actions must the government take in order to cope with these problems and to assure a smooth transition to a mature economy?

This paper will address these questions and is divided by section as follows: 2. Capital and labor mobility and the stages of economic development; 3. Directions and patterns of capital flows; 4. The roles of capital flows in Taiwan's push towards becoming a mature economy; 5. DFI inflow and Taiwan's push towards a mature economy; 6. Professional transient inflow and Taiwan's push towards a mature economy; 7. The roles of DFI outflow in Taiwan's push towards a mature economy; 8. DFI outflow, professional transients, guest workers, and Taiwan's pursuit of a mature economy; 9. Summary and conclusions.

Capital flows can take many different forms: portfolio investments, direct foreign investments, and export credits. In this paper more attention is given to direct investment because of its close link with international labor mobility and because, until very recently, portfolio capital outflow was prohibited by the government of Taiwan.

2. Capital and Labor Mobility and the Stages of Economic Development

According to Kindleberger and others, there is a correlation between economic development and the different stages of the balance of payments and hence in the directions, patterns, and composition of international capital flows. A country normally starts at the stage of "young debtor," where it is capital-poor and lacks foreign trade. The direction of capital flows during this stage is inward, and mostly in the form of official development assistance (ODA), either as grants or loans. Private loans are few, and usually difficult to obtain at this stage of development. The second stage is the "mature debtor," where the country displays considerable success in economic development and trade, and possesses the ability to obtain private loans and direct investment. At this stage, due to its success in foreign trade, the country's current account gradually turns into a surplus, and consequently the country begins to pay back its debts and even accumulate wealth of its own. The third stage is the "young creditor," where the country becomes industrialized; its assets begin to exceed its liabilities, and it even becomes a capital exporter. The final stage is that of the "mature creditor," where the country lives off the interest and dividends on its net claims, and may even consume some of its capital (Kindleberger 1988, pp. 34-35). The United States went through these stages rapidly during World War I, and is now in the mature creditor stage. Britain and France are a few years ahead of the United States in economic maturity and have consumed a great deal of their foreign wealth already. TNCs from these European countries invested in the United States because of their economic pessimism towards the future of Europe, not because of their countries' stage of economic development (Kindleberger 1988, p. 34). However, as the twelve European countries move towards one single market by 1992, more capital will flow to Europe. In fact, this is already happening because not only has Japan been heavily investing into Europe during the last two years, but TNCs from Europe and the United States are busy joining hands in an attempt to prevent the Japanese from taking over the European industries as they have done in the United States during the late 1980s (*Business Week* July 3, 1991, p. 21).

On the other hand, the outflow of Japanese capital to the United States arises out of the stages of economic development that the two countries have reached: the U.S. is in the mature creditor stage and Japan is in the young creditor stage. Thus, the flow of long-term capital to the United States from the Pacific area will not be readily reversed regardless of efforts taken by the two governments (Kindleberger 1988, p. 35; Akiyama and Onitsuka 1985).

This theory not only accurately describes the development process of the western industrial countries, but also that of the Asian developing countries. For example, as the figures in Table 8.2 show, the low-income South Pacific, South Asian, and Southeast Asian countries are capital importers, and the four high income Asian newly industrializing economies (ANIEs) have just recently entered the capital exporting stage.

Table 8.3 shows Taiwan's international current account between 1951 and 1989. Since the accounts fluctuate erratically from year to year, they are presented in the form of five-year averages. The figures from the table reveal that Taiwan's balance of payments recorded deficits until 1975, then changed into a surplus which rose sharply after 1985. These figures seem

TABLE 8.2 Capital Flows in Asian and Pacific Countries
(unit: in millions of U.S. dollars)

	1970	1980	1985	1986	1987
South Pacific countries[a]					
Official flows	172	437	302	295	400
Private flows	157	63	73	-23	-38
Direct investments	130	55	45	63	10
Portfolio investments[e]	12	6	41	0	11
Export credits	15	10	-13	-85	-16
Total	329	500	375	272	362
South Asian countries[b]					
Official flows	1394	5506	5085	6353	6303
Private flows	53	374	622	1115	883
Direct investments	49	121	120	97	143
Portfolio investments	-24	-15	222	259	353
Export credits	28	267	280	758	387
Total	1446	5871	5707	7468	7186
Southeast Asian countries[c]					
Official flows	729	2803	3414	3382	4763
Private flows	407	1754	148	-140	198
Direct investments	196	887	-519	-588	355
Portfolio investments	56	145	506	831	99
Export credits	156	722	161	-382	-257
Total	1137	4557	3562	3243	4961
Newly industrializing countries[d]					
Official flows	535	1050	-192	-699	-3364
Private flows	357	1875	-207	-897	4784
Direct investments	80	979	389	2236	5142
Portfolio investments	-32	-338	-499	-2921	-468
Export credits	308	1234	-97	-212	109
Total	892	2925	-399	-1597	1420

[a]Fiji, Papua New Guinea, and West Samoa.
[b]Bangladesh, Burma, India, Nepal, Pakistan, and Sri Lanka.
[c]Indonesia, Malaysia, Philippines, and Thailand.
[d]Hong Kong, Korea, Singapore, and Taiwan, ROC.
[e]Includes bank lending and bond lending and excludes export credits.

Source: Lee and David, 1989.

TABLE 8.3 Balance of Payments of ROC: 1951-1989 (5-year average)

Year	Current account
1951-55	-13
1956-60	-1,116
1961-65	-187
1966-70	-41
1971-75	-91
1976-80	422
1981-85	4,670
1986-89	13,864

Unit: 1951-1965 figures are in millions of NT dollars, and 1966-1989 are figures in millions of U.S. dollars.

Source: Chen (1990, pp. 54-55).

to indicate that prior to 1975, Taiwan was in the young debtor stage and reached the mature debtor stage between 1975 and 1985, when Taiwan began to pay back its debts and started to accumulate some foreign assets. Since 1985, Taiwan's trade surplus has increased rapidly, marking the economy's arrival at the young creditor stage (see also Lee 1978). Based on the theory of this stage of balance of payments, one can expect capital outflow from Taiwan to continue to rise as it moves towards a mature economy, just as those of Japan and Germany did when they reached the same stage of development.

Links between Capital and Labor Mobility

Along with the flow of capital, the international mobility of labor is also related to the different stages of economic development. In general, the mobility of two types of international labor is related to the international flows of capital and the stages of economic development. These two types are professional transients and low-skilled guest workers.

Professional transients are those highly trained professional, managerial, or technical employees who are assigned by their TNCs to work for their subsidiaries in a foreign country for a period of time, ranging from several months to several years (Salt and Findlay 1989, p. 161). They are sent to foreign countries because when TNCs invest in foreign countries, they usually have difficulties in getting qualified professional, managerial, and technical workers in the local markets. Thus, for example in 1985, Japan sent 5,000 business executives, 2,000 office workers, and 1,000 engineers and technicians to Australia to work with their investments there (Price 1989, p. 144). In 1984 approximately 105,750 professional transients were admitted into the United States (Salt and Findlay 1989, p. 161).

There is no direct relationship between the stage of economic development and the direction of the flow of professional transients, but there is a direct relationship between the direction of the flow of professional transients and the direction of DFI flow; thus, indirectly, the flow of professional transients and the stages of economic development are related. Therefore, during the young debtor stage there is little DFI inflow and outflow; consequently there is no inflow and outflow of professional transients; as a country enters the mature debtor stage there is DFI inflow, hence there is also professional transient inflow. When a country reaches the stage of young creditor and the stage of mature creditor, there is both DFI inflow and outflow and hence, inflow and outflow of professional transients.

Guest workers, on the other hand, consist mostly of less-educated and low-skilled workers who are attracted by the higher wage rates and better employment opportunities of the more developed countries; they therefore work in these countries for a period of time, though some may eventually become permanent immigrants. Although the motive of guest workers going abroad may or may not relate to international capital flows, their presence in foreign countries does. This is partly because the remittances that they send home can become a large share of foreign exchange for their home countries. For example, during the early 1980s the amount of remittance that Korean guest workers sent home amounted to US$1,939 million, or 2.7 percent of Korea's GNP. In 1988, the amount of remittances that the 118,957 Thai guest workers sent home amounted to 5.8 percent of total export earnings, and at one time (1985) it reached 12.4 percent of total export earnings (Kusol and Soonthorndhada 1991). The direction of the flow of guest workers is related to the stage of economic development: the outflow of guest workers normally starts sometime during the take-off stage and reverses to an inflow when the country reaches the stage of a mature economy. Thus, the United States and many of the western European countries were in the guest-workers-importing stage shortly after World War II; meanwhile, Japan was in the guest-worker-exporting stage. Ever since Japan entered the mature economy stage in the 1970s it has been a guest-worker-importing country (Kuwahara 1988; Kuo *et al.* 1989, pp. 30-43). There is very little outflow of guest workers from the South Pacific countries, some outflow from South Asian countries, and a substantial outflow of guest workers from Southeast Asian countries and Mainland China. In contrast, the mature ANIEs are in the guest-worker-importing stage. This assertion is also supported by the figures in Table 8.2. For a more detailed discussion of the link between DFI and the inflow of guest workers, see Section 8 of this chapter. A summary of these relationships between capital and labor mobility and the stage of economic development is presented in Table 8.4.

TABLE 8.4 Stages of Economic Development and Directions and Patterns of Capital and Labor Mobility

Stages of economic development	Capital — Types of capital	Capital — Directions of flows	Labor — Types of labor	Labor — Directions of flows
Young debtor	1. Official (aid, loans & grants)	1. Inflows	1. Low-skilled guest workers	1. Limited outflows
	2. Private loans	2. Limited inflows	2. Professional transients	2. No flows
	3. DFI	3. Limited inflows		
Mature debtor	1. Official (aid, loans & grants)	1. Inflows & outflows for paying back their loans	1. Low-skilled guest workers	1. Outflows
	2. Private loans	2. Inflows	2. Professional transients	2. Inflows
	3. DFI	3. Inflows & some outflows		
Young creditor	1. Official (aid, loans & grants)	1. Outflows	1. Low-skilled guest workers	1. Inflows
	2. Private loans	2. In & outflows	2. Professional transients	2. In & outflows (brain exchange)
	3. DFI	3. In & outflows		
Mature creditor	1. Official (aid, loans & grants)	1. In & outflows	1. Low-skilled guest workers	1. Inflows
	2. Private loans	2. In & outflows	2. Professional transients	2. In & outflows (brain exchange)
	3. DFI	3. In & outflows		

3. Directions and Patterns of Capital Flows

Not only are the directions of capital and labor flows influenced by a country's stage of economic development, but so are the patterns of capital flows. In the early stage of development, the inflow of capital is mostly from multilateral agencies, such as the World Bank; this is because the country is unable to raise capital through private arrangements. As the country becomes more developed, its ability to raise money through private sources improves; consequently, it starts to pay back some of the loans borrowed previously from the multilateral agencies. When a country reaches the young creditor stage, it not only begins to repay its loans to the multilateral agencies but is expected to aid these international organizations in helping other LDCs. As the figures in Table 8.2 show, the low income South Asian countries rely mostly on official sources for their capital inflow, i.e., development assistance grants and loans (87.7 percent of the total capital inflow), and private or direct investment is rare (2 percent). Southeast Asian countries and Mainland China, which are in the second tier of NIEs, enjoy more private flows; in fact, they are at the stage where they can attract a large amount of DFI. The majority of capital flows of the four ANIEs came through private sources (63 percent of the total US$9,084 million of inflow and outflow).

Table 8.5 presents the patterns of capital flow into Taiwan. In the table, the flow of capital is classified in two ways: by origin, i.e., multilateral versus bilateral; and by source, i.e., official versus private.

Multilateral v. Bilateral Flows

The figures in Table 8.5 reveal that multilateral loans and grants have not been an important source of capital inflow to Taiwan in the past, while the bilateral flows have been. For example, in 1970, only 19 percent of the total capital inflow to Taiwan came from multilateral sources; this figure further declined to less than 1 percent in 1975, and turned negative beginning in the 1980s. If one looks at the total amount of loans that Taiwan has received from these international organizations, the picture is even clearer. As of December 31, 1989, the total amount of loans that Taiwan had received from these organizations was as follows: US$309.7 million from the International Bank of Reconstruction and Development (IBRD); US$15.7 million from the International Development Association (IDA); US$91.1 million from the Asian Development Bank (ADB); and US$1,979 million from the Export-Import Bank of the United States. The outstanding balance of these loans as of December 1989 was US$4.03 million for those from the IBRD, US$10.4 million for those from the IDA, and US$4.9 million for those from the ADB (*Taiwan Statistical Data Book* 1990, p. 263).

TABLE 8.5 Financial Flows to Taiwan: 1970-1988
(unit: in millions of U.S. dollars)

	1970	1975	1980	1982	1984	1986	1987	1988
Total receipts[a]	191	373	439	428	-74	-476	-304	-139
a. Bilateral	155	370	456	444	-63	-446	-164	-123
Japan	119	--	111	117	161	-20	-325	446
U.S.A.	5	286	388	100	-105	-281	-454	-55
Europe	32	84	-44	227	-119	-146	-45	-513
Others	1	0	1	0	0	0	0	0
b. Multilateral[b]	36	3	-18	-18	-18	-21	-131	-7
ADB	0	1	--	--	--	--	--	-6
IBRD	24	3	-17	-18	-17	-21	-131	-1
IDA	0	0	0	-1	-1	-1	-1	--
Others	11	-1	-1	0	0	1	1	--
c. OPEC countries	--	--	1	2	7	-9	-9	-9
d. Total official	76	138	389	109	-145	-316	-1021	-18
ODA grants	5	-2	2	0	3	0	3	3
ODA loans	4	-18	-6	-6	2	-10	-11	-10
Others	66	158	392	116	-151	-306	-1013	-11
e. Private flows	116	236	50	318	72	-160	717	-121
Direct investment	23	20	163	57	208	278	767	-132
Portfolio investment[c]	13	61	-125	185	-89	-151	91	-270
Export credits	80	155	13	77	-47	-287	-141	17

[a]Total receipts are divided into bilateral flows, multilateral flows and flows from OPEC countries. Therefore the sum of items a, b and c is equal to total receipts. Total receipts are also classified into official and private flows. The sum of items d and e is equal to the total receipts.

[b]ADB, Asian Development Bank; IBRD, International Bank for Reconstruction and Development; IDA, International Development Association.

[c]Includes bank lending and bond lending and excludes export credits.

Source: 1970-1986, Lee and David, 1989; 1987-1988, OECD, *Geographical Distribution of Financial Flows to Developing Countries*, Paris, 1990.

The negative outflow of capital from these international organizations to Taiwan since the mid-1980s is precisely because there have been only loan repayments and no additional loan disbursements from these multilateral agencies. In 1972, the ROC lost its seat in the United Nations and is no longer qualified to receive loans from these organizations (Yeh 1980).

On the other hand, bilateral flows were an important source of capital inflow. Among all the capital suppliers, the United States was the most important; between 1970 and 1975 it supplied 55.5 percent of the total bilateral inflow to Taiwan while Japan and the European countries supplied 22.7 and 22.1 percent, respectively. Between 1976-1980 America's share of capital inflow to Taiwan further increased to 77.6 percent while Japan's and the European countries' shares dropped to 14 and 8.4 percent. However, America's role as a capital supplier started to decline in the 1980s, and it ceased to be a capital supplier by the mid-1980s. Instead, it became an importer of Taiwan's capital. In fact, by 1980, the United States had ceased to be a major capital supplier to the world and became a major capital importer (OECD 1987, p. 9). Figures from the same table also show that the outflow of capital from Taiwan to the United States increased rapidly, from an average of US$96 million per year between 1981-1985 to US$735 million per year between 1986-1987 (Lee and David 1989, Appendix 23). As the United States lost its position as a capital supplier to Taiwan, Japan's position became more important. However, the absolute amount of capital inflow from Japan to Taiwan has been small; it was US$100 million per year between 1981-1985, and US$103 million per year between 1986-1987 (Lee and David 1989, Appendix 23). By contrast, Japan's capital outflow to Singapore and Hong Kong was much larger, relative to their populations. For example, between 1986-1987 Japan's average capital outflow to these areas was as follows: US$5.7 million per capita to Taiwan; US$170 million per capita to Hong Kong; US$106.6 million per capita to Singapore (OECD 1989). The European countries have never been important capital suppliers to Taiwan; on the contrary, since the mid-1980s they have been importers of Taiwan's capital.

In summary, in the past most of Taiwan's capital flows were inward, and the majority of the inflow were through bilateral, not multilateral sources. The United States and Japan were the two major capital suppliers to Taiwan; however, compared to other countries, the amount of Taiwan's capital inflow is rather small.

Official Versus Private Flows

The figures from Table 8.5 reveal that the official flows have never been a major source of capital for Taiwan, except for U.S. aid during the 1950s and early 1960s (see also Lee 1978, p. 117). Throughout the 1970s, only 40 percent of capital inflow came from official sources, and by the mid-1980s, the figures turned negative. In recent years, official sources became major avenues for capital outflow; in fact, in 1987 the official outflow recorded by the government reached US$1.021 billion.

Private flows, however, have been an important source of capital inflow to Taiwan. During earlier years, export credits were an important source of capital inflow, while direct investments and portfolio investments were not. However, the importance of direct investment as a source of capital inflow gradually increased in the 1980s, and by 1987 reached US$767 million. Portfolio investments have never been an important source of capital inflow due to the government's tight regulation of the financial market. However, portfolio investment became an important avenue for capital outflow when the government relaxed its regulations in 1986.

4. The Roles of Capital Flows in Taiwan's Push Toward a Mature Economy

Efforts in Liberalizing the Capital Market

Thus far, Taiwan's economic development has relied more on domestic capital and less on the inflow of foreign capital, except for U.S. aid during the 1950s and early 1960s. This assertion is supported by the figures presented in Table 8.6. As the figures in the table show, from 1970 to 1987 the net flow of capital as a percentage of GNP was consistently smaller for Taiwan than for the other ANIEs. Between 1980 and 1987, Taiwan's average net flow was only 0.2 percent of its GNP, while it was 4.1 percent for Singapore, 2.7 percent for Hong Kong, and 1.3 percent for Korea. The lack of capital inflow was due to the government's policy of permitting only DFI inflow and prohibiting portfolio capital movement, a policy which stemmed from the government's fear of capital flight. But the results were a fragmentation of the capital market and the absence of all inflow of foreign capital except DFI. The lack of foreign capital may have been one of the contributing factors in limiting Taiwan's economic development to labor intensive and small scale businesses, while other countries with free capital markets and access to large sums of foreign capital, Singapore for example, have developed more capital and technology intensive industries. As Taiwan moves towards becoming a mature economy and developing its capital and technology intensive industries, it will require a much larger amount of capital. Thus, while the government has previously ignored the important role of the international mobility of capital in the development process, it can no longer afford to do so. In other words, the government must deregulate the capital market, develop the stock market, encourage

TABLE 8.6 Capital Flows among Developing Countries (total net flows as percent of GNP)

Country	1970	1975	1980	1985	1987	1980-1987 average
ANIEs	4.5	3.4	2.1	-0.2	0.5	1.4
Hong Kong	5.5	1.8	3.3	-3.6	7.8	2.7
Korea	4.6	5.2	1.4	1.9	-2.1	1.3
Singapore	6.0	2.1	6.7	-1.5	3.5	4.1
ROC (Taiwan)	3.4	2.4	1.1	-0.9	-0.4	0.2
Southeast Asia	4.1	4.9	2.8	2.0	2.8	3.2
Indonesia	5.5	8.4	2.4	2.2	4.7	3.5
Malaysia	2.2	3.3	2.9	0.8	0.8	2.8
Philippines	4.5	2.5	2.8	2.0	2.0	2.9
Thailand	2.8	1.3	3.5	2.4	2.0	3.0
South Asia	1.9	3.2	2.7	2.1	2.3	2.3
Bangladesh	0.0	7.5	9.8	7.0	9.3	8.9
India	1.6	2.0	1.4	1.2	1.4	1.3
Pakistan	4.9	7.5	5.2	3.0	2.7	3.2
Sri Lanka	3.0	5.1	10.9	10.0	7.9	9.8
PRC	0.0	0.0	0.1	0.8	1.5	0.7
Total	1.8	2.4	1.7	1.2	1.7	1.8

Source: Lee and David, 1989.

the development of new financial instruments, and make Taipei an international financial center. When this happens, Taiwan will be in a better position to attract the inflow of large sums of capital and to finance its long-term investment projects (see also Hsu and Liu 1990).

Recently recognizing the important role of the capital market in the development process, the government has taken a series of actions since 1987 to deregulate both the capital and financial markets. These actions include:

1. Lifting the restrictions on interest rates. The Banking Law which was amended in 1989 ended all interest rate controls.

2. Deregulating exchange rates. Up until 1978 the NT dollar was pegged to the US dollar, and the inflexible exchange rate hindered the automatic adjustment of currency values needed for balance of payments

equilibrium. The restrictions were modified in 1979 and 1989. Recently the Central Bank announced that it would end all foreign exchange control by the end of September 1991. In other words, from September 1991 on foreign exchange rates will be fully determined by market forces, except in emergency cases (*Economic Daily* July 14, 1991).

3. Deregulating the banking industry. To increase competition and efficiency in the banking industry, the government of Taiwan has deregulated the restrictions on the number of branches that can be established by existing banks. In May 1991, fifteen private banks were granted permission by the government to operate, and several government owned banks will soon be privatized. The restrictions on foreign banks have also been relaxed. They are now allowed to set up branch-offices and accept long-term saving deposits, to conduct underwriting, and to trade in securities on behalf of their clients. To meet the challenge of the foreign banks and to help local business to invest abroad, local commercial banks are encouraged to establish branches in the world's leading financial centers.

4. Deregulating capital flows. In 1987 the Central Bank was directed by the government to lift the controls on its trade relations account, and to allow ROC residents to freely hold and use foreign currencies. At present, the outward and inward remittance of foreign exchange is allowed up to three million US dollars for each adult per year. For people to invest outside of the country, the government has set up the so-called "Designated-Purpose Trust Program." Under this program, twelve local banks and trust companies have been authorized to acquire shares in mutual funds issued by foreign securities institutions such as Jardine Fleming, Fidelity, Citicorp, and Daiwa. Private investors can either invest in these mutual funds or entrust them to purchase other foreign securities on their behalf. Another way to invest abroad is to purchase investment fund beneficiary certificates. Currently four funds have been created under this program. The government has also recently granted permission to seven leading security firms from Hong Kong, Japan, the United States, and England to invest directly in domestic securities (*Economic Daily* July 13, 1991, p. 6).

Although the high savings rate and the large foreign exchange surplus put Taiwan in an excellent position to be a major capital supplier to Asian countries in the twenty-first century, most experts agree that unless the financial market is liberalized quickly Taiwan will not become a world financial center (*Economic Daily* July 11, 1991, p. 4). Therefore the government must immediately do the following:

1. build a modern financial tower, keeping all financial institutions centrally located;

2. improve and develop modern telecommunication facilities so that reliable electronic banking services can be provided and cross-country capital flows and global investment activities are possible;

3. import international money brokers to Taiwan;
4. expand the current financial training center in order to train a very large number of financial professionals;
5. establish a gold market;
6. continue to remove barriers restricting the NT dollar's international flows, allow the creation of Euro-NT dollar markets, and promote offshore financial transactions denominated in NT dollars;
7. renovate local financial institutions, enact up-to-date laws and regulations and enforce them strictly and consistently. A sound monitoring and supervisory system is urgently needed to ensure the safety and proper performance of all financial institutions.

The Patterns and Directions of Future Capital Flows

In terms of multilateral versus bilateral flows, one would expect a rise in capital outflow from Taiwan to multilateral agencies. This is because when Taiwan joins the industrial countries it is expected to share the responsibilities of helping other LDCs by making contributions to the international development assistance agencies. In fact, the government of Taiwan recently made some contributions to the Asian Development Bank, and has established an International Economic Cooperation and Development Fund (IECDF) for providing development grants and loans to LDCs. The Taiwan government recently pledged to allocate US$200 million annually to this fund, which is 0.15 percent of Taiwan's GNP. The government's plan is to allocate US$400 million annually to the fund by the year 2000 which is estimated to be 0.25 percent of Taiwan's GNP (*Economic Daily* July 20, 1991, p. 1).

As for bilateral flows, one can expect the trends of capital outflow to the United States and European countries to continue increasing. This is because the United States has a sizable budget deficit and needs foreign capital to finance it, and the European countries will need a large amount of investment funds as they merge into a single market in 1992. The newly opened eastern European countries are also in need of a large amount of investment funds. If President Bush's plan for revitalizing Latin American countries works, the flow of Taiwan's capital to these countries will increase also. However, the level of outflow will increase at a moderate rate due to two conflicting factors working simultaneously. First, the rise of regionalism around the world will make it necessary for Taiwan to invest in these areas in order to bypass trade barriers. For example, the twelve European countries will become a single market by 1992, and Canada and the United States signed a Free Trade Agreement in 1989 which will probably include Mexico by 1992. The other factor which will work against the outflow of capital is the Six-Year National Development Plan. Under this Plan,

Taiwan is scheduled to spend US$300 billion on infrastructure construction, environmental clean-up, education, etc., and will therefore not have much capital available for outflow until after the Plan's completion in 1996.

On the other hand, the inflow of capital to Taiwan from the United States and major European countries is expected to increase, mainly due to the liberalization of Taiwan's financial market. Japan will increase its capital outflow to Taiwan also, since it currently has a large surplus in its current account. But the level of capital inflow from Japan will remain low since Japan has its eye on other areas such as North America, Mainland China, and the European countries, due to their large-sized markets. For example, between 1988-1990 Japan's investment in Europe increased from US$25 billion to US$55 billion (*Business Week* July 3, 1991, p. 21). Thus, if Taiwan wants Japan's capital to finance its long-term projects, it will have to provide more favorable conditions in order to compete with other areas.

5. The Roles of DFI Inflow in Taiwan's Push Toward a Mature Economy

DFI Inflow

DFI inflow was at a negligible level during the 1950s; the average annual amount of DFI inflow was only US$4.1 million between 1952-1960. The situation improved in the 1960s and 1970s as the average annual amount of DFI inflow increased to US$52.6 million between 1961-1970, and US$215.9 million between 1971-1979. The greatest increases, however, occurred in the 1980s. The average annual DFI inflow amounted to US$914.7 million between 1981-1989 (see Table 8.8). Some scholars argue that the level of DFI inflow to Taiwan was low in that the amount never exceeded 10 percent of Taiwan's private fixed investment and it hired no more than 6 percent of Taiwan's total workforce (Tu 1990, p. 2). Even so, when measuring the total cumulative DFI inflow as a percentage of GDP, Taiwan did well. It was ahead of most non-African countries in 1975, and was behind only the African and Latin American countries in 1985 (see Table 8.7).

Prior to 1970, the United States and overseas Chinese were the major sources of DFI inflow in Taiwan. Overseas Chinese provided 30 percent and the U.S. provided 62 percent of DFI inflow between 1952 and 1960; and 29 percent and 42 percent, respectively, of the DFI inflow between 1961 and 1970. However, their importance as sources of DFI inflow declined in the 1970s and 1980s, and gradually was replaced by the Japanese. For example, during the 1980s the Japanese share of DFI rose to 29 percent,

TABLE 8.7 Stocks of DFI Inflow as a Percentage of GDP (unit: %)

Country	1975	1985
Developed market economies	4.5	5.5
Western Europe	5.8	6.6
U.S.A.	1.8	4.7
Others	7.0	5.7
Japan	0.3	0.5
Developing countries	6.4	8.5
ROC (Taiwan)	9.0	8.3
ROC (Taiwan) 1989		7.4
Africa	15.7	10.8
Asia	3.2	5.7
Latin America & Caribbean	8.9	13.6
Others	2.1	3.4
Total	4.9	6.1

Source: UNCTC, 1988, p. 25, and *Taiwan Statistical Data Book 1990*.

while the American share, despite absolute increases, dropped by 23 percent and the overseas Chinese to less than 10 percent. DFI from European countries, unheard of during the 1950s, gradually increased to US$1,419 million in the 1980s, accounting for 17 percent of total DFI.

In terms of industrial distributions, DFI inflow has been concentrated in the manufacturing industries: prior to 1980, more than 90 percent was destined for manufacturing. However, as the economy developed, DFI inflow gradually shifted away from the manufacturing sector and into the trade, finance, and service industries. As the figures in Table 8.9 show, the share of DFI inflow into the trade, finance, and service industries rose from 5.8 percent between 1952-1979 to 17.9 percent between 1980-1985, and 25.3 percent between 1986-1990. Within the manufacturing industries, the electronics and electrical industry received the largest share of DFI (48 percent of DFI inflow between 1952-1979). However, its importance has been declining steadily: in 1986-1990 its share dropped to 21.2 percent. The declining importance of the electronics industry as a recipient of DFI is a trend found in all ANIEs. As the wage rates in these ANIEs rise, investors are redirecting their investments into the second tier of NIEs where the wage rates are lower and the supply of labor is abundant (*Electronic Business* August 7, 1989, p. 69). The other important recipient of DFI has been

TABLE 8.8 DFI Inflow to Taiwan: By Source (unit: millions of U.S. dollars)

Source	1952-1960	1961-1970	1971-1980	1981-1989	1952-1989
Overseas Chinese	10 (30)	153 (29)	801 (37)	768 (9)	1734 (16)
Non-Chinese	23 (70)	373 (71)	1358 (63)	7462 (91)	9216 (84)
U.S.A.	21 (62)	221 (42)	534 (25)	1970 (23)	2746 (25)
Japan	2 (8)	87 (16)	369 (17)	2398 (29)	2856 (26)
Europe	--	36 (7)	225 (10)	1419 (17)	1680 (15)
Others	0 (0)	29 (6)	230 (11)	1676 (20)	1935 (18)
Total	33 (100)	526 (100)	2159 (100)	8232 (100)	10950 (100)
Average	4.1 [4.6]	52.6 [23.9]	215.9 [73.7]	914.7 [514.6]	295.9 [148.6]

Note: Figures in parentheses are the percentage distribution of the DFI inflow. Figures in brackets are the figures for arrived investment.

Source: 1952-1987: Schive (1988, Table 1); 1988 and 1989: *Industry of Free China*, January issues of 1989 and 1990.

TABLE 8.9 DFI Inflow: By Industry (unit: thousands of U.S. dollars)

Industry	1952-1979 $	1952-1979 %	1980-1985 $	1980-1985 %	1986-1990 $	1986-1990 %
Agriculture	1,895	0.1	5,278	0.2	5705	0.1
Manufacturing	1,371,481	90.8	1,988,385	80.3	5,106,094	69.8
Food	13,702	0.9	71,660	2.9	458,546	6.3
Textiles	31,947	2.1	7,166	0.3	86,540	1.2
Garment	15,328	1.0	8,625	0.3	16,470	0.2
Lumber	5,233	0.3	2,921	0.1	36,157	0.5
Paper	4,400	0.3	11,245	0.5	35,900	0.5
Leather	2,991	0.2	3,875	0.2	5,687	0.1
Plastics	35,655	2.4	66,236	2.7	243,290	3.3
Chemicals	228,523	15.1	496,855	20.1	1,420,525	19.4
Non-metal	36,603	2.4	34,189	1.4	155,975	2.1
Basic metal	132,101	8.7	197,847	8.0	562,454	7.7
Machinery	139,690	9.3	331,736	13.4	535,953	7.3
Electronics	725,308	48.0	756,030	30.5	1,548,598	21.2
Construction	9,954	0.7	1,034	0.0	43,809	0.6
Trade	2,003	0.1	10,397	0.4	607,297	8.3
Finance	47,468	3.1	103,143	4.2	435,275	6.0
Transportation	7,387	0.5	228	0.0	217,932	3.0
Services	39,052	2.6	329,391	13.3	803,770	11.0
Others	30,646	2.0	37,160	1.5	92,558	1.3
Total	1,509,886	100.0	2,475,016	100.0	7,312,441	100.0

Sources: *Statistics on Overseas Chinese and Foreign Investment.* Investment Commission, Ministry of Economic Affairs, July 1990.

been the chemicals industry. During the early years, its share of DFI inflow was 15.1 percent; it rose to 20.1 percent in the early 1980s and remained stable between 1986-1990.

DFI Inflow and Taiwan's Push Toward Becoming a Mature Economy

In order to see the roles of DFI inflow in Taiwan's push towards becoming a mature economy, one needs to review its contributions in the past. In general, DFI inflow can play the following roles in a country's economic development process:

1. It can increase the level of investment in the host country and, as a consequence, its level of growth and employment;
2. It stimulates a demand for local inputs and, hence, increases wages and revenue;
3. It improves the productivity of the host country by transferring advanced technology and training skilled workers and managers, thus increasing the competitiveness of the host country's products (OECD 1987, p. 43).

DFI and Employment Opportunities. It is generally agreed upon by most scholars in Taiwan that DFI inflow has made an important contribution to the creation of employment opportunities in Taiwan (Chou 1988; Liu 1985; Schive 1988; Tu 1990; Wu 1986). In a recent study, Schive estimated that about 15 percent of the jobs in the manufacturing sector were created by foreign firms. He cited that foreign firms tended to concentrate more on exporting and used more labor intensive technology, thus creating more employment opportunities than domestic firms. For example, exporting firms created, on average, 120 jobs for every million US dollars in sales, while each million US dollars in domestic sales created only fifty jobs (Schive 1988, Pt. 2, p. 18). In another study Wu estimated that the DFI inflow from the United States in 1981 created 131,917 jobs, which accounted for 7.1 percent of the total employment in the manufacturing sector (Wu 1986, p. 9). In 1990 Tu constructed a macroeconomic model to estimate DFI's direct and indirect effects on employment, and found that DFI accounted for a range of 13.1 to 19.4 percent of the jobs in the manufacturing industries, or 4.1 to 5.7 percent of the jobs in the entire economy (Tu 1990, p. 128).

DFI and the Transfer of Advanced Technology. Most scholars in Taiwan agree that DFI has played a significant role in the transmission of new methods of production and managerial skills to Taiwan. DFI inflow has been concentrated in the electronics and electrical, chemicals, petroleum, machinery and technical instruments, basic metal, and nonferrous metal industries, which are technology-intensive (Tsiang and Wu 1985, p. 328). Schive also points out that DFI inflow has served as an intermediary in transferring advanced technology to Taiwan because DFI firms tend to apply foreign technology more than domestic firms (Schive 1988). Kuo (1972) and Hsu (1989) also found that DFI inflow transferred advanced technology to Taiwan.

DFI and Exports. There is a consensus in Taiwan that DFI inflow has made an important contribution in helping Taiwan to export its products. As a developing country, Taiwan was very primitive in its marketing techniques and had no marketing network at all. DFI firms helped to remedy these deficiencies by selling Taiwan-made products through their parent companies' marketing channels. The results of a government survey support this assertion, showing that three-fourths of the 127 foreign exporting firms participating in the survey utilized their parent company's marketing facilities, either exclusively or in conjunction with other marketing channels (Schive 1988, p. 19). As Amsden points out, without these foreign firms, the ANIEs would never have been able to penetrate into the industrialized countries' markets so quickly and so successfully (Amsden 1989). In other words, DFI inflow has played an important role in Taiwan's successful implementation of its export-led development policy.

DFI and Domestic Investment. DFI inflow can have positive or negative effects on domestic investment. It can have a negative effect by replacing domestic investment, or a positive effect by stimulating domestic investment through its forward and backward linkage effects. DFI inflow can also be channeled into frontier industries, thus stimulating new domestic investment. What was the impact of DFI inflow on Taiwan's domestic investment? Tu, in his 1990 study, found that one NT dollar of DFI inflow into Taiwan between 1960 and 1987 directly induced NT$0.904 of new domestic private fixed investment. The inducement effect was greater in nonmanufacturing than in manufacturing industries (Tu 1990, p. 105). Technologies in the nonmanufacturing industries tend to be less complicated and easier to master, and are thus more inviting for local capital owners to invest in the same industries (Tu 1990, p. 105; UNCTC 1988, p. 176). The investments by McDonalds and 7-Eleven are vivid examples of DFI's impact on domestic fast-food and chain stores.

What roles will DFI inflow play in Taiwan's push towards becoming a mature economy? As Taiwan enters a new developmental stage, DFI inflow will accordingly play different roles. For example, the role of generating employment opportunities will no longer be important, both because Taiwan is currently experiencing a labor shortage and because generating a large number of low-skill jobs is not on the government's high priority list. Moreover, the type of DFI inflow that Taiwan is trying to attract at this stage is in capital- and technology-intensive industries, and therefore will not have an important impact on employment. The increasing inflow of DFI in the service sector will be directed towards upgrading the quality of the industries, not generating a large number of employment opportunities. Promoting exports will not be an important role for DFI inflow either, because, as the country moves towards a mature economy, it will be producing customer-designed products and industrial materials. Close and long-term relationships with customers are important at this stage. Taiwan will have to develop its own marketing channels for accomplishing these goals.

On the other hand, DFI inflow will play a much more important role in transferring technology and stimulating domestic investment at this stage. Taiwan is currently shifting towards a high-tech economy where DFI can play a very important role and will be even more important than in the past. The lack of domestic investment opportunities is also currently a real problem for Taiwan, and DFI inflow can play an important role in this area as well.

Given that DFI inflow has an important role to play in the future, what will be the level of DFI inflow? The figures in Table 8.7 show that DFI inflow as a percentage of GDP steadily declined from 9 percent in 1975 to 8.3 percent in 1985, and 7.4 percent in 1989. Will it continue to decline? What can the government do to bring DFI inflow to a desirable level? The answer to these questions can be found in Professor Tu's DFI inflow equation:

$$DFI = 15647.87 + 0.019\Delta Y(t-1) + 0.267 Pcy - 21.984 WD$$
$$+ 0.002 WDFI + 192.1\Delta E - 1.888 W + 1254.8 D6770$$

According to Tu's findings, the level of DFI inflow is affected positively by the last period's output changes $Y(t-1)$, the level of per capita income (Pcy), the volume of the world DFI outflow ($WDFI$), the appreciation of NT\$ against the US\$(E), and major infrastructure construction ($D6770$). DFI inflow is negatively affected by wage differentials, i.e., the difference between wages paid by foreign firms and domestic firms (WD), and the wage level of the domestic firms (W). From this equation one can tell that the future level of DFI inflow into Taiwan will increase because the economic growth rate is expected to increase at a rate of 7 percent from now to the year 2000; per capita income is also expected to increase from the current US\$8,000 level of US\$17,000 by the year 2000 (Yu 1990). The volume of the world's DFI outflow will certainly increase in the future due to the continuous integration of the world's economies (UNCTC 1988; Wallace 1990). The value of the NT dollar is expected to be stable or to appreciate slightly since the government has done well in diversifying Taiwan's foreign trade, and its trade surplus with the U.S. is on the decline. With the majority of the US$300 billion in the Six-Year National Development Plan to be spent on infrastructure construction and environmental clean-up projects, the variable $D6770$, which represents the improvement of infrastructure, should have a very significant effect on DFI inflow. In fact, high ranking government officials and executive officers of large firms from France, Italy, America, and Japan are all currently trying to get a piece of the National Development Plan's pie. The variables WD and W are the two most interesting variables in the equation. Why would a narrowing of the wage differentials between foreign and domestic firms have a positive effect on the level of DFI? This association holds because the narrower the wage gap between foreign and domestic firms, the narrower the productivity gap between these two groups. If the domestic firms' wages are not far away from those of the foreign firms, it means they have a greater ability to learn the advanced technology used by the foreign firms. To put it in a different way, the advanced technology brought in by the foreign firms will be able to spread to other parts of the economy faster if the difference in wages between the foreign and domestic firms is small. Faster diffusion of the advanced technology speeds the rate of economic growth and induces even greater DFI inflow. This relationship has an important policy implication for the government, i.e., in order to attract more DFI to Taiwan and to have the economy benefit more from the DFI inflow, the government must invest more in education. A better educated workforce has a greater ability to learn advanced technologies from foreign firms, thus enhancing the dissemination of the advanced technology. The net result will be a higher rate of economic growth and greater DFI inflow. The government, in fact, appears fully aware of this relationship because the Six-Year National Development Plan calls for the construction of another twenty-five colleges and universities on top of the 121 colleges and universities that already exist. By 1996 there will be twenty-six college graduates per 1,000 individuals, a ratio higher than in any other country except the United States, Germany and Japan (*Six-Year National Development Plan*, Book 2, p. 152). Another policy that the government of Taiwan needs to follow is that of keeping its labor market free from any institutional interference. Any factors which hinder the mobility of labor will have a negative effect on the diffusion of advanced technology from the DFI firms. As Taiwan's past experience shows, when the mobility of labor is unhindered, people who learn their skills in foreign firms can return to domestic firms or set up their own businesses, hence quickly spreading the advanced knowledge or technology.

6. Professional Transient Inflow and Taiwan's Push Toward a Mature Economy

As was mentioned previously, there is a close relationship between the level of DFI inflow and the level of professional transient inflow. Japan and the United States are the two major DFI investors in Taiwan; one can, therefore, expect that most of the professional transients in Taiwan are from these two countries. Exactly how many professional transients have Japan and the United States sent to Taiwan? Accurate data is not available in Taiwan, but limited information from the Investment Commission of the Ministry of Economic Affairs shows that the number of professional transients related to DFI activities is not large. In 1988, the 1,088 foreign-country-based TNCs sent 960 Japanese managers, 181 American managers, and fifty-nine European managers to Taiwan. There were also 742 Japanese, 114 American, and fifteen European engineers/technicians in these companies. On average, Japanese TNCs had a higher percentage of professional transients than American and European TNCs. As the figures in Table 8.10 show, in 1988 the Japanese companies brought in 4.8 Japanese managers for every 100 managers hired locally, while American and European TNCs imported 1.7 and 1.8 persons, respectively. The Japanese also had the highest ratio of foreign to native engineers and technicians. For every 100 Chinese engineers and technicians, they brought in 4.9 Japanese. American companies were next with 1.3, and the European TNCs were third with 0.6 persons (see also Chen 1986).

Why did Japanese TNCs bring in more professional transients to Taiwan than the Americans and Europeans? This was largely due to cultural differences. Japanese tend not to trust outsiders and hence import more of their own people. Additionally, the Japanese are known for being protective of their technologies, much more so than the Americans and Europeans. They send their own engineers and technicians to other countries in order to keep the advanced knowledge and technology to themselves. The social and living conditions of the host countries are also important determining factors. The Japanese and Chinese share a similar culture; in fact, Taiwan was at one time a Japanese colony. Thus, the Japanese feel more at home in Taiwan than Westerners do. Besides cultural and social factors, the industry in question also makes a difference. TNCs engaged in capital and technology intensive industries tend to send a higher percentage of professional transients to the host country than those in labor intensive industries. For example, the ratios of foreign professional transients to local employees are higher in the chemicals, basic metals, machinery, and non-metallic minerals industries than in the clothing, food, and other labor intensive industries. (The only exceptions are the wood and electronics industries.) The ratios of foreign professional

TABLE 8.10 Professional Transilients in Taiwan
(unit: persons and percent)

	Management				Engineers & technicians			
Industry	N 1984	N 1988	FM/TM 1984	FM/TM 1988	N 1984	N 1988	FE/TE 1984	FE/TE 1988
Japanese companies								
Manufacturing	508	844	3.0%	4.7%	595	665	3.0%	4.6%
Food	8	15	2.5%	2.7%	15	11	7.3%	7.6%
Textiles	2	6	0.4%	1.3%	8	4	1.1%	1.2%
Clothing	5	4	3.1%	1.5%	4	0	4.2%	0.0%
Wood	3	4	4.4%	10.8%	6	1	33.3%	16.7%
Paper	1	0	3.3%	0.0%	1	1	1.1%	1.3%
Leather	2	1	3.8%	1.6%	2	0	5.9%	0.0%
Plastics	37	48	3.7%	4.3%	47	125	8.2%	22.6%
Chemicals	54	149	4.1%	7.5%	36	69	6.4%	6.7%
Non-metallic	11	20	6.3%	5.1%	9	16	7.8%	7.9%
Basic metals	61	100	3.9%	6.0%	96	81	6.7%	6.9%
Machinery	94	153	5.0%	4.3%	120	121	4.8%	3.3%
Electronics	230	344	2.3%	4.5%	251	236	1.9%	3.4%
Non-manufacturing	45	116	2.6%	5.3%	48	77	5.9%	7.9%
Services	2	66	0.2%	4.4%	7	20	1.6%	3.3%
Others	43	50	5.5%	7.4%	41	57	11.4%	15.7%
Total	553	960	2.9%	4.8%	643	742	3.1%	4.9%
American companies								
Manufacturing	146	129	1.2%	1.5%	54	83	0.7%	1.0%
Food	4	8	1.0%	0.9%	0	1	0.0%	0.9%
Textiles	8	2	0.3%	0.4%	1	0	0.0%	0.0%
Clothing	1	0	0.2%	0.0%	1	1	1.7%	0.0%
Wood	0	0	0.0%	0.0%	0	0	0.0%	0.0%
Paper	4	2	1.6%	1.1%	2	0	7.4%	0.0%
Leather	0	0	0.0%	0.0%	0	0	0.0%	0.0%
Plastics	2	0	1.3%	0.0%	1	1	4.8%	6.7%
Chemicals	23	25	1.9%	1.8%	16	3	5.7%	0.9%
Non-metallic	2	0	0.7%	0.0%	1	0	9.1%	0.0%
Basic metals	10	5	4.9%	1.0%	4	1	2.3%	0.6%
Machinery	7	10	0.6%	0.7%	4	3	0.2%	0.2%
Electronics	85	77	1.8%	2.4%	25	73	0.5%	2.1%
Non-manufacturing	31	52	2.3%	2.6%	39	61	0.7%	1.0%
Services	18	45	2.1%	2.4%	37	52	2.6%	1.9%
Others	13	7	2.5	5.6%	2	9	2.7%	20.5%
Total	177	181	1.3%	1.7%	93	144	1.0%	1.3%

(continues)

TABLE 8.10 (continued)

	Management				Engineers & technicians			
Industry	N 1984	N 1988	FM/TM 1984	FM/TM 1988	N 1984	N 1988	FE/TE 1984	FE/TE 1988
				European companies				
Manufacturing	41	21	1.5%	0.9%	20	12	2.7%	0.5%
Food	7	2	10.8%	8.0%	2	3	9.5%	16.7%
Textiles	2	3	20.0%	10.7%	0	1	0.0%	20.0%
Clothing	1	0	5.9%	0.0%	1	0	20.0%	0.0%
Wood	0	0	0.0%	0.0%	0	0	0.0%	0.0%
Paper	0	0	0.0%	0.0%	0	0	0.0%	0.0%
Leather	0	0	0.0%	0.0%	1	1	14.3%	11.1%
Plastics	1	0	16.7%	0.0%	2	0	100.0%	0.0%
Chemicals	7	8	0.8%	1.7%	4	4	3.3%	1.4%
Non-metallic	1	0	1.2%	0.0%	7	0	9.0%	0.0%
Basic metals	0	2	0.0%	3.9%	0	1	0.0%	3.2%
Machinery	3	1	3.1%	1.6%	2	1	4.8%	1.6%
Electronics	19	5	1.2%	0.4%	1	1	24.5%	0.1%
Non-manufacturing	0	38	0.0%	4.1%	0	3	0.0%	0.9%
Services	0	37	0.0%	4.6%	0	3	0.0%	0.9%
Others	0	1	0.0%	0.8%	0	0	0.0%	0.0%
Total	41	59	1.5%	1.8%	20	15	2.7%	0.6%

FM/TM: Foreign management/total management.
FE/TE: Foreign engineers and technicians/total engineers and technicians.

Source: Report on the Operations of the Foreign and Overseas Chinese Investments and Their Contributions to Our National Economic Development, Investment Commission, Ministry of Economic Affairs, ROC, 1985, 1989.

transients are also higher in the trade and services industries than in the manufacturing industries, perhaps because there is a higher percentage of white collar workers in the former. It is also interesting to note that in the trade and service industries the professional transient ratio is higher for the American and European TNCs than for the Japanese TNCs. This reversal could be due to the fact that in these industries the Japanese concentrate on department stores and supermarkets, while Americans and Europeans focus on the banking industry where the professional transient ratio is higher.

The Roles of Professional Transients in Taiwan's Push towards Mature Economy. What role will these foreign professional transients play as Taiwan enters the stage of mature economy? They will play an important role in transferring advanced technology to Taiwan because the technology Taiwan needs from other countries will be more advanced and complex than before. Locals will have to work with these professional transients side by side in order to learn the advanced technologies. Employers in the textile and dyeing industries now complain of being unable to entice foreign experts to Taiwan because of the government's restrictive and cumbersome procedures in admitting foreigners to work there.

One can expect the number of professional transients in Taiwan to increase in the future for the following three reasons: 1. the rate of DFI inflow into Taiwan is expected to increase; 2. Taiwan's economic structure is shifting from labor intensive industries to capital and technology intensive industries, and from manufacturing to nonmanufacturing industries where the professional transient ratios are higher; 3. the U.S. share of DFI inflow into Taiwan is declining while the Japanese share of DFI inflow is increasing. As mentioned before, the ratio of professional transients in the Japanese TNCs is 2.8 times higher than in the American and European TNCs, so the future should witness an influx of professional transients, the majority of whom will be Japanese.

In view of the reluctance of the Japanese professional transients to transfer their technologies to the host country, and to promote local management to top positions, a recent report shows that young and able Chinese refuse to work for Japanese TNCs since they do not promote non-Japanese to top management positions (*United Daily* September 4, 1990, p. 9), the government of Taiwan should encourage greater DFI from western countries and improve their services to western and non-Japanese professional transients. For example, the government could expand the capacity of, and increase accessibility to, English primary and secondary schools, and it could provide more orientation programs for the newly appointed western professional transients, their spouses, and their dependents. Orientation services should be provided not only when they arrive in Taiwan. Such services should be the job of the Taiwan trade offices located in the foreign countries. These measures can make the western professional transients feel more comfortable and thus more willing to come to Taiwan. Simplifying the current visa application and other entrance procedures for western and overseas Chinese professional transients would be helpful also. The current proposal of the Bureau of Industry Development in simplifying procedures for introducing western and overseas Chinese professional and managerial workers into Taiwan is a move in the right direction (*China Times* November 6, 1989). By improving communication, transportation, and environment conditions, the Six-Year

National Development Plan will also be helpful in narrowing the gap between the living standards in Taiwan and in the western countries. All these are very helpful in attracting western managers, engineers, and technicians to Taiwan. Greater inflow of professional transients, especially from the West, will mean a faster rate of transfer of advanced technology to Taiwan, hence, a shorter period of time for Taiwan in reaching the stage of a mature economy.

7. The Roles of DFI Outflow in Taiwan's Push Toward a Mature Economy

DFI Outflow

The data pertaining to DFI outflow from Taiwan is inaccurate and grossly understates the actual amount of foreign investment. First, prior to 1989, the government had a policy of tight control on outward investment which caused many businessmen to bypass the government and directly invest in foreign countries through underground channels. Second, the DFI outflow figures to Mainland China are not included in the government's records since the two governments are officially still at "at war" and direct investment in Mainland China is "illegal." The third reason for this inaccuracy is the differential tax treatment of foreign income received by private citizens and corporations. According to the current tax regulations, foreign income received by private citizens is not subject to Taiwan's income tax, but such corporate income is. Therefore, many businessmen do not report their foreign investment in order to avoid income taxes. It has been estimated by many that the actual DFI outflow is probably twenty times more than the official figures show (Schive 1989). Regardless of their gross underreporting, the official figures which are presented in Table 8.11 can provide us with some sense of direction, trends, and the patterns of Taiwan's DFI outflow.

In Table 8.11, DFI outflow is broken into four periods: 1. from 1959 to 1981 the amount of DFI outflow was negligible due to the government's tight restriction on capital outflow and the shortage of foreign exchange. The average amount of DFI outflow during this period was only US$5 million per year; 2. the period from 1982-1985 was the eve of the rapid appreciation of the NT dollar. During this period DFI outflow from Taiwan increased from US$25.7 million per year, but was still at a relatively low level; 3. 1986-1988 was a period of DFI outflow expansion where average outflow rose to US$124 million per year; 4. 1989-1990 was a period of rapid DFI expansion. The average amount of DFI outflow during these two years jumped to US$1.2 billion per year. In fact, the amount of investment for these last two years accounted for 77 percent of the total amount of accumulated DFI outflow between 1959-1990. DFI outflow to Mainland China was not included in Table 8.11 due to the lack of reliable data. Although there are many diffeent estimations, the general consensus puts the total cumulative DFI outflow to Mainland China, as of December 1990, at US$1.8 billion (*Taiwan Economic Studies Monthly* June 1991, p. 39). In other words, the total recorded cumulative DFI outflow from Taiwan to the entire world, as of December 1990, was US$4.87 billion. The actual amount of DFI outflow could be several times this figure due to the documentation problems cited above.

The rapid increase of DFI outflow during the last few years has been due to a combination of factors: 1. the rapidly increasing surplus of foreign exchange; 2. the deregulation of the capital market whereby each citizen is permitted to send up to US$3 million abroad annually without the government's explicit approval; 3. the worsening of the domestic investment climate due to the increasing political and social unrest on the island; 4. the loss of competitiveness in many labor intensive industries due to the increase in wage rates and the shortage of unskilled labor; 5. the rapid appreciation of the NT dollar from one US dollar to NT$39.85 in 1985, to NT$35.50 in 1986, NT$28.55 in 1987, and NT$26.17 in 1989. This rapid appreciation of the NT dollar made many of the exporting labor-intensive industries no longer competitive and created a need for their relocation to Southeast Asian countries and Mainland China, where labor is cheaper and more abundant.

Figures from Table 8.11 also show that DFI outflow was heavily concentrated in the manufacturing industries (86 percent of the total DFI outflow between 1959-1981 and 1982-1985), and were almost non-existent in the agriculture, fishery, and mining industries. Again, the amounts of DFI outflow to Mainland China are not included in Table 8.11, but our conclusions will not be affected if DFI outflow to Mainland China is included because it is also heavily concentrated in the manufacturing industries. For example, the top five recipients of Taiwan's DFI are: electronics (US$102 million); transportation (US$78.9 million); shoes (US$58.7 million); services (US$56.5 million); and the plastics industry (US$44.5 million) (*Economic Outlook* July 1991, p. 59).

The absence of DFI outflow in the agriculture and mining industries implies that, unlike other countries, Taiwan did not use DFI outflow as a means to assure its supply of raw materials, except lumber from Indonesia. Although the importance of DFI outflow in raw materials industries has been declining in recent years, it should not be totally ignored. For example, in 1985 the share of the accumulated DFI outflow in the agriculture and mining industries was 15.5 percent for Japan, 55.0 percent for the Netherlands, 33.3 percent for the U.K., and 23.1 percent for the United

TABLE 8.11 DFI Outflow by Industrial and Geographical Distribution: 1959-1990
(unit: thousands of U.S. dollars and %)

Industry	Japan 1959-1981	Japan 1982-1985	Japan 1986-1988	Japan 1989-1990	Hong Kong & Singapore 1959-1981	Hong Kong & Singapore 1982-1985	Hong Kong & Singapore 1986-1988	Hong Kong & Singapore 1989-1990	Southeast Asian countries 1959-1981	Southeast Asian countries 1982-1985	Southeast Asian countries 1986-1988	Southeast Asian countries 1989-1990
Agriculture, fishery, mining	--	--	--	--	--	--	--	--	10.4	34.6	33.3	100
Manufacturing	--	--	--	0.1	8.0	1.4	2.4	3.0	29.6	26.8	34.9	48.5
Food & beverage	--	--	--	--	--	--	--	0.0	41.8	--	27.7	6.5
Textiles	--	--	--	--	18.2	--	66.8	--	32.6	97.6	33.2	92.2
Garments	--	--	--	--	75.4	--	--	--	8.0	--	--	25.5
Lumber	--	--	--	--	--	--	--	--	74.8	100	40.0	95.4
Plastic & rubber	--	--	--	--	13.6	--	--	2.2	5.2	--	37.0	38.1
Leather	--	--	--	--	--	--	10.1	--	--	--	74.6	100
Pulp paper	--	--	--	--	--	--	--	--	100	95.7	67.1	83.4
Chemicals	--	--	--	--	2.2	5.9	--	--	34.2	--	76.6	31.0
Non-metallic minerals	--	--	--	--	13.6	29.4	14.4	--	2.1	32.7	39.3	100
Basic metals	--	--	--	--	24.9	2.6	0.3	--	47.9	81.8	94.0	59.6
Machinery equipment	--	--	--	--	--	--	6.8	--	32.8	--	10.2	91.0
Electronics	--	--	--	0.2	15.5	0.0	0.5	8.4	9.8	2.7	15.4	55.2
Trade	--	--	--	1.1	2.4	4.4	3.1	20.3	3.3	--	11.9	8.2
Finance	--	--	--	--	--	--	--	2.5	--	--	--	0.4
Services	--	--	--	--	--	--	2.4	3.2	--	--	1.4	1.1
Others	--	--	--	--	--	--	--	--	--	--	20.1	94.8
Distribution by areas	--	--	--	0.1	7.1	1.4	2.2	3.4	26.1	23.2	20.1	32.3

Industry	U.S.A. 1959-1981	U.S.A. 1982-1985	U.S.A. 1986-1988	U.S.A. 1989-1990	Other American areas 1959-1981	Other American areas 1982-1985	Other American areas 1986-1988	Other American areas 1989-1990	European countries 1959-1981	European countries 1982-1985	European countries 1986-1988	European countries 1989-1990
Agriculture, fishery, mining	--	--	--	--	--	--	--	--	--	--	--	--
Manufacturing	39.6	67.0	57.5	43.8	--	--	--	2.6	--	--	--	0.9
Food & beverage	3.2	88.9	72.3	93.5	--	--	--	--	--	--	--	--
Textiles	--	--	--	--	--	--	--	--	--	--	--	5.5
Garments	--	--	--	29.1	--	--	--	45.4	--	--	--	--
Lumber	--	--	60.0	--	--	--	--	--	--	--	--	--
Plastic & rubber	65.1	100	41.5	59.7	--	--	--	--	--	--	--	--
Leather	--	--	12.7	--	--	--	--	--	--	--	--	--
Pulp paper	--	4.3	32.9	16.6	--	--	--	--	--	--	--	--
Chemicals	63.0	94.1	22.9	69.0	--	--	--	--	--	--	--	--
Non-metallic minerals	4.4	14.7	--	--	--	--	--	--	--	--	--	--
Basic metals	6.3	15.0	--	16.4	--	--	--	--	--	--	--	--
Machinery equipment	67.2	100	54.1	8.5	--	--	--	--	--	--	--	--
Electronics	47.4	93.4	82.9	26.8	--	--	--	7.3	--	--	--	1.7
Trade	79.8	69.4	28.5	41.3	--	--	--	--	--	--	--	22.4
Finance	--	--	100	23.0	--	--	--	29.3	--	--	--	33.8
Services	--	100	77.7	53.5	--	--	--	2.6	--	--	--	9.0
Others	36.7	100	13.1	4.8	--	--	--	--	--	--	--	--
Distribution by areas	41.4	69.6	62.8	38.1	--	--	--	9.9	--	--	--	11.0

(continues)

335

TABLE 8.11 (continued)

Industry	African & Oceanic countries				Total				Distribution by industries			
	1959-1981	1982-1985	1986-1988	1989-1990	1959-1981	1982-1985	1986-1988	1989-1990	1959-1981	1982-1985	1986-1988	1989-1990
Agriculture, fishery, mining	89.6	65.4	66.7	--	$4,219	$578	$1,200	$5,338	3.8	0.6	0.3	0.2
Manufacturing	22.8	4.8	5.2	1.1	94,389	88,348	193,490	1,565,126	85.7	85.9	51.8	64.7
Food & beverage	55.1	11.1	--	--	7,544	2,250	6,911	163,704	6.8	2.2	1.9	6.8
Textiles	49.2	2.4	--	2.3	3,884	7,170	4,422	87,782	3.5	7.0	1.2	3.6
Garments	16.6	100	100	--	749	826	1,992	2,753	0.7	0.8	0.5	0.1
Lumber	25.2	--	--	4.6	3,965	33	834	6,254	3.6	0.0	0.2	0.3
Plastic & rubber	16.1	--	21.5	--	9,221	701	16,497	51,933	8.4	0.7	4.4	2.1
Leather	--	100	2.6	--	--	140	2,843	947	--	0.1	0.8	0.0
Pulp paper	--	--	--	--	3,920	11,729	7,604	25,338	3.6	11.4	2.0	1.0
Chemicals	0.5	--	0.5	--	38,076	4,253	38,010	492,862	34.6	4.1	10.2	20.4
Non-metallic minerals	79.9	23.2	46.3	--	10,516	3,058	5,011	123,140	9.5	3.0	1.3	5.1
Basic metals	20.9	0.6	5.6	24.0	3,002	3,669	3,426	52,894	2.7	3.6	0.9	2.2
Machinery equipment	--	--	29.0	0.5	372	600	1,553	11,746	0.3	0.6	0.4	0.5
Electronics	27.3	3.9	1.3	0.4	13,140	53,919	104,387	545,773	11.9	52.5	28.0	22.6
Trade	14.4	26.2	56.5	6.7	9,831	4,781	20,527	72,484	8.9	4.7	5.5	3.0
Finance	100	--	--	11.0	1,050	--	19,267	670,853	1.0	--	5.2	27.7
Services	27.9	--	18.5	30.6	416	8,605	123,461	97,664	0.4	8.4	33.1	4.0
Others	63.3	--	66.8	0.4	245	480	15,257	7,319	0.2	0.5	4.1	0.3
Distribution by areas	25.4	5.7	14.9	5.2	110,150	102,792	373,202	2,418,784	100	100	100	100

Sources: *Statistics of Overseas Chinese and Foreign Investment The Republic of China Investment Commission, Ministry of Economic Affairs, R.O.C., December 1981-90.*

States (UNCTC 1988, p. 86). South Korea in 1984 kept 38 percent of its stock in DFI outflow in the mining industry and 13 percent in forestry (Euh and Min 1986).

The trend of DFI outflow in Taiwan is now away from manufacturing and towards the trade, finance, and services industries. As one can see from the figures in Table 8.11, manufacturing's share of total DFI outflow dropped from 86 percent during the 1982-1985 period to 65 percent in 1989-1990, while the finance and banking industry's share jumped from 1 percent prior to 1985 to 27 percent in 1989-1990. DFI outflow in the services industries also jumped rapidly between 1986-1988 period but slowed down in 1989-1990. Shifting away from manufacturing into trade, finance, and services industries has been an international trend for DFI outflow in the 1980s (UNCTC 1988, pp. 86, 375). The shift towards banking, insurance, and other financial services industries has come in response to the worldwide liberalization of financial markets and the development of transnational banks (UNCTC 1988, pp. 382-83). The upsurge in Taiwan's DFI outflow into financial industries is also a response to the recent deregulation of the financial markets in Taiwan.

Geographically, the trend in DFI outflow is towards diversification. Prior to 1982, DFI from Taiwan was spread among the neighboring Asian countries (33 percent), the United States (41 percent), and African and Oceanic countries (25 percent), and excluded European countries (0 percent). By the early 1980s, Taiwan's DFI outflow became heavily concentrated in the United States (70 percent of the total DFI outflow in 1982-1985). However, the situation has been corrected recently, as the Untied States' share of Taiwan's DFI dropped to 38 percent in 1989-1990, while the Asian countries' share increased to 32 percent and the shares of the European countries and countries in the Americas other than the United States rose to 10 and 11 percent of Taiwan's DFI, respectively. When DFI outflow to Mainland China is included, the trend towards diversification is even more pronounced.

As one looks at the detailed breakdown of DFI outflow by industry in Table 8.11, one might wonder what the factors were which motivated some to invest in the United States and others to invest in Southeast Asian countries, Mainland China, or Panama: Why was DFI outflow from Taiwan so heavily concentrated in the electronics industry and in the United States during the 1982-1985 period? What caused this switch to Southeast Asian countries? What made some employers in the textile and garment industries invest in Europe in 1989-1990, while others invested in Southeast Asian countries or Mainland China? The answer to these questions can be found by investigating the motive of employers investing abroad. Chen in a 1986 study surveyed sixty-five Taiwanese TNCs around the world. He found that expansion of the local market was the most important factor motivating

TABLE 8.12 Motivating Factors for DFI Outflow: By Areas
(unit: rank)

Country	Factors[a]							
	1	2	3	4	5	6	7	8
	Rank							
MDCs	2	1	3	5	6	7	4	8
NICs	2	3	1	6	4	7	8	5
LDCs	3	2	1	6	5	7	8	4
Total	3	1	2	4	5	8	7	6

[a]1. Assurance of the local market; 2. expansion of the local market; 3. facilitating the export to other countries; 4. securing raw-material supply; 5. diversifying investment risk; 6. loss of competition; 7. gaining access to advanced technology; and 8. others.

Source: Chen, 1986, p. 44.

employers to invest in advanced countries, while protecting the share of the local market, facilitating exports to other countries (MDCs), and gaining access to advanced technologies were respectively the second, third, and fourth most important factors (see Table 8.12). For the upper tier of developing countries (NICs), facilitating the export of their products to other countries was the most important factor in investing abroad. Employers wanted to use DFI outflow to these areas for three reasons: to enjoy GSP tax benefits which are no longer available to Taiwan; to bypass the discriminatory tariffs set by the European countries against "outsiders"; and to circumvent import quotas set by the United States and other countries. The most important factors motivating employers to invest in less developed areas (LDCs) were the expansion of the local market into the host country and the protection of their market share in the local area (Table 8.12). In the same study Chen also found that employers in different industries were motivated by different factors in investing abroad. For example, facilitating exports to other countries (circumventing the quota) was the most important factor for motivating employers in the textile and garment industries while assurance of the supply of industrial materials was the most important motive for employers in the lumber and chemicals industries. None of the employers in the labor intensive industries indicated gaining access to advanced technologies as their motive, but it was a motivating factor for employers in the chemicals, basic metals, and machinery industries (Table 8.13). More recent studies of Taiwan's DFI outflows to Southeast Asia and Mainland China found low labor cost as the most important determinant for employers investing in these countries; market factors, including the facilitation of exports to other countries ranked second (see Chen and Wang 1991; Yen 1990; and Kuo 1989). These findings are very similar to the motives of the Japanese TNCs investing abroad: Yonekura found in his study of Japan's global investment in the electronics and electrical products industry that market-expansion was the most important motive for the Japanese to invest in North America and Europe; low-labor-cost was the most important factor for them to invest in Taiwan and other Asian countries (Yonekura 1988; see also Chen and Wang 1991, p. 10).

TABLE 8.13 Motivating Factors for DFI Outflow: By Industry (unit: rank)

Industry	Factors[a]							
	1	2	3	4	5	6	7	8
	Rank							
Food & beverage	1	2	3	–	4	5	–	–
Textiles	–	3	1	–	–	3	–	2
Garments	2	2	1	–	–	–	–	4
Lumber	2	–	3	1	4	–	–	–
Pulp paper	1	3	4	2	–	–	–	–
Plastic & rubber	3	1	2	–	4	–	6	4
Chemicals	2	3	–	1	–	–	4	–
Non-metallic minerals	3	1	2	–	4	–	6	5
Basic metals	2	1	3	7	6	8	4	5
Machinery equipment	1	2	6	3	5	7	4	8
Electronics	3	1	2	8	4	5	–	7
Manufacturing	2	1	3	4	6	8	7	5
Construction	2	1	2	–	–	–	–	4
Trade	3	2	1	–	4	–	5	–
Other	1	1	3	4	5	7	8	5
Total	3	1	2	4	5	8	7	6

[a]1. Assurance of the local market; 2. expansion of the local market; 3. facilitating the export to other countries; 4. securing raw material supply; 5. diversifying investment risk; 6. loss of competition; 7. gaining access to advanced technology; and 8. others.

Source: Chen, 1986, p. 45.

*DFI Outflow in Taiwan's Push Toward
a Mature Economy*

Since DFI outflow is such a recent phenomenon in Taiwan, it has obviously played a small role in Taiwan's economic development thus far. But what about its current and future roles as Taiwan moves towards a mature economy? Generally speaking, DFI outflow can play the following roles:

1. Market penetration and trade replacement. As Taiwan moves towards a mature economy, its foreign trade will expand further. But many countries are now in the process of forming their own regional markets and trying to keep others out; for example, the free trade agreements between the U.S., Canada, and Mexico; the merger of the twelve European countries into a single market in 1992; and the formation of the Asian Pacific Economic Corporation (APEC), which is comprised of Japan, Australia, New Zealand, South Korea, and the six countries in the Association of Southeast Asian Nations (ASEAN). All of these developments point to the urgent need for Taiwan to invest in these markets quickly before they are closed out entirely. By investing in these countries, Taiwan can also reduce its current trade friction with the United States and any potential trade friction with other countries. The rise of international protectionism also points to the importance for Taiwan of investing in other countries to avoid tariff barriers. In other words, as Taiwan evolves into a mature economy it needs to use DFI outflow as a "trade replacement," just as Japan did in the 1980s to soften its trade frictions with the United States, and as Taiwan itself has done to the European countries during the last few years.

2. Acquisition of advanced technology. Taiwan is in the process of upgrading its economic structure by shifting to technology- and capital-intensive industries. Thus, it is important for Taiwan, through the process of DFI, joint ventures, and acquisitions, to gain access to industrialized countries' advanced technologies. Recently, many industrialized countries have become more protective of their new technologies; therefore, DFI has become one of the most effective ways of gaining access to them (UNCTC 1988).

3. Utilization of the cheap labor of the second-tier NICs. As Taiwan moves into high tech industries, it needs to develop vertical integration of its labor intensive industries with the Southeast Asian countries. Taiwan would specialize in the more sophisticated components, while the Southeast Asian countries and Mainland China would concentrate on the primary stages of production. To restructure its economy quickly Taiwan also needs to relocate its obsolete and no longer competitive labor intensive industries to Southeast Asia, Mainland China, and even South America.

4. Recycling Taiwan's capital surplus. Taiwan currently has a US$70 billion plus foreign exchange reserve and some of this needs to be recycled. DFI outflow can help to accomplish this.

5. Breaking Taiwan's diplomatic isolation. The "one China" principle held by both the Mainland China and ROC governments has caused those countries which recognize Mainland China to sever formal diplomatic relations with the ROC. Recently, even Taiwan's closest ally, Singapore, was attracted by the enormous market in Mainland China, broke its formal diplomatic relations with Taiwan and recognized Mainland China. With a substantial amount of DFI outflow going to countries with no diplomatic ties with Taiwan, the governments of the recipient countries will be forced to deal with the government of Taiwan for business reasons. Taiwan's trade offices in these countries can actually enjoy not only quasi-governmental status, but in some cases diplomatic privileges and immunities as well. Currently forty-one of Taiwan's trade offices around the world have been granted such privileges (Chow 1990).

6. Improving Taiwan's economic position and international status around the world, and especially among the Asian countries. A substantial amount of DFI outflow to the labor-intensive industries in Southeast Asia and Mainland China will not only accelerate the restructuring of Taiwan's economy but will also hasten the process of industrialization in these countries. The improved economic position of these countries will then have a "boomerang effect" whereby their demand for capital goods from Taiwan and other NICs will increase. Although this increased demand for capital goods would go to other industrialized countries as well, the lower wage rates of skilled labor in Taiwan, relative to Japan and the United States, will put Taiwan in an excellent position to serve as an intermediary in transferring technology to the Southeast Asian countries. Such a relationship is likely to improve not only Taiwan's economic position, but its international status as well.

In short, while DFI outflow has played a very limited role in Taiwan's process of economic development thus far, it will play a decisive role in Taiwan's push towards a mature economy and beyond. However, in order for DFI outflow to play the roles listed above the government must correct the following deficiencies:

1. More geographical diversification of Taiwan's DFI outflow, especially to Latin America, Mexico, and the Caribbean. DFI outflow to Mexico and the Caribbean countries is essential for Taiwan to obtain access to the enormous U.S. market at low cost in the future, as the United States, Canada and Mexico form their economic alliance in 1992. In fact, many employers from Hong Kong were investing heavily in Mexico during 1990 in preparation for the creation of the North American economic region.

TABLE 8.14   Stocks of DFI Outflow: By Country
(unit: percent)

Country	Stocks of DFI outflow as a percentage of GDP (1985)	
ROC (Taiwan)	0.3	1.0 (1989)
U.S.	6.4	
U.K.	23.3	
Japan	6.3	
Germany	9.6	
Switzerland	48.9	
Netherlands	35.1	
Canada	10.5	
France	4.2	
Italy	3.4	
Sweden	9.0	
Others	3.3	

Source: UNCTC, 1988, p. 24.

2. The current amount of DFI outflow from Taiwan is too small by international standards. Taiwan's official stock of DFI outflow was only 1 percent of its GDP in 1989, while the same figure in other countries ranged from 3.4 to 48.9 percent (see Table 8.14). The government of Taiwan must take actions to encourage DFI outflow. These actions include the following: change and update the current tax law; quicken the process of financial liberalization so that Taiwanese banks in foreign countries can provide investment information, loans, and investment consulting services to employers from Taiwan intending to invest abroad; negotiate with other governments to protect Taiwan's businessmen from paying double taxes (income tax from the host country and from the home country). Taiwan needs to increase the amount of DFI outflow substantially so that it can have a meaningful impact and accomplish the functions listed above.

3. The government needs to have clear guidelines as to what types of DFI outflow will be encouraged due to their ability to bring maximum benefit to the country, and what types of DFI outflow will be discouraged because they compete with employers in the home country who export similar products to the same markets. Such guidelines are important because improper DFI could cause a suffocation of industry in Taiwan. It is important to have DFI outflow complementing domestic industries.

8. DFI Outflow, Professional Transients, Guest Workers and Taiwan's Pursuit of a Mature Economy

DFI Outflow and the Outflow of Professional Transients

As companies from Taiwan invest in other countries, they send managerial, professional, and technical employees to the host countries. Therefore, when Taiwan's DFI outflow increases, more Chinese professional transients are sent abroad. The outflow of these highly trained professionals and managerial workers should not be mistaken as a brain drain. For a brain drain to occur, these highly trained professionals must leave the country permanently; instead, professional transients are highly trained professionals who leave the country temporarily and work for Chinese firms making contributions to Taiwan's economy. Instead of a brain drain, this process should actually be considered a brain exchange.

How many professional transients does Taiwan have and where are they located? Thus far, there is no available data. One report estimates that in 1987, 45,000 ROC professional transients were in the United States (Weiss 1988, p. 27). Another survey found that, in 1984, TNCs based in Taiwan sent abroad an average of 17.6 professional transients for each investment project. The average was 6.2 persons in 1981, 7.7 persons in 1982, and 14.4 persons in 1983 (Chen 1986, p. 66). This rapid increase in the professional transient ratio in 1983 and 1984 is somewhat misleading. In those two years, some of the investment projects were in the construction industry, where the investors needed to bring their own construction crews from Taiwan. These workers were blue collar workers and not professional staff members. Thus, taking the average between 1981 and 1982, the average number of professional transients sent to foreign countries by TNCs in Taiwan was seven persons. Using this ratio, one could estimate that in 1990 there should have been 6,125 ROC professional transients abroad ($7 \times 875 = 6,125$, where 875 is the cumulative number of DFI projects; Investment Commission 1990). Since the actual DFI outflow figures are probably twenty times higher than the official figures (Schive 1988), the actual number of Chinese professional transients abroad could be as high as 122,500 persons.

The ratio of professional transients differs according to the industry and location of the project. For example, the ratio was higher for projects located in the industrialized countries than those in the LDCs and NICs. According to a 1984 survey, for projects in the manufacturing industries, Taiwan TNCs sent an average of 19.3 persons per investment project to the industrialized countries, and 2.9 persons and 11.3 persons to NICs and

LDCs respectively (Chen 1986, p. 67). In another study of TNCs in electronic and electrical industries in Mainland China, Chen and her associates found the ratio of professional transients to be 8.5 persons for every 100 local technicians, and 10.5 persons for each 100 middle level supervisors and managerial employees (Chen and Wang 1991, pp. 10-14). TNCs in the manufacturing industries tend to send more professional transients (11.6 persons) to the host countries than those in the trade and service industries (0.5 persons) (Chen 1986). A higher ratio of professional transients go to the industrialized countries because employees are willing and eager to go to these countries, where they find better living environments and better educational opportunities for their children. Some of them even emigrate to the host country permanently. The lower ratio of professional transients going to the LDCs is primarily due to the poorer living environment and the lack of quality education for their children in those countries. Employers often complain about their difficulties in getting anybody to accept an assignment for longer than six months in Thailand, Malaysia, or Mainland China. In view of the important function of DFI outflows to Southeast Asian countries and the reluctance of Chinese to be assigned to these countries, trade offices and the Ministry of Foreign Affairs in Taiwan should work together in providing orientation programs, such as those geared towards basic language ability, customs, housing, schools and hospitals for the newly arrived Chinese professional transients in these countries. The government of Taiwan can also set up cultural activity centers in the major cities of these countries. These centers can lend Chinese videos, books, and magazines to the professional transients and their family members. They can also form Taiwanese businessmen's associations where they can share information and engage in social activities. In some cases, where the number of professional transients is large and concentrated, the government of Taiwan can even consider offering Chinese language schools. With these facilities, Chinese professional transients can bring their children to these LDCs and be able to stay a longer period of time. When they come back to Taiwan a year or two later their youngsters will easily be able to integrate back into Taiwan's school system. In helping Taiwan-based TNCs to meet their need for professional transients, the government manpower offices on Taiwan should also provide recruiting services or consulting services to these TNCs. Another way to resolve the shortage of professional transients for TNCs based in Taiwan is to have Taiwan's overseas trade offices recruit locals with qualified backgrounds and place them in TNCs based in Taiwan to receive the appropriate training. Upon completion of the training the overseas workers can return home and work for TNCs from Taiwan. Such programs have been implemented by the Irish government in order to attract Japanese investment.

DFI Outflow and the Inflow of Guest Workers

In recent years, there has been a rapid increase in legal and illegal foreign guest workers in Taiwan. These workers come from the Philippines, Thailand, Malaysia, Indonesia, and Mainland China. They primarily work in the construction, manufacturing, and restaurant industries and some of them, mostly those from the Philippines, find work as private household maids. Although there is no accurate record of how many guest workers have come to Taiwan, estimates range from 40,000 to 120,000 (Chang 1989, p. 402; *China Times* August 13, 1990; Tsai 1990). These workers enter Taiwan on tourist visas; when the visas expire, the workers become illegal immigrants. The guest workers from Mainland China are almost all illegal immigrants, having entered Taiwan in fishing boats at night.

The causes for the rapid increase of guest workers in Taiwan are many. Most people point to the recent labor shortage in Taiwan as creating a demand for guest workers, and to the low wage rates and high unemployment in the home countries of the guest workers, along with cheap transportation costs to Taiwan. However, such a simple neoclassical model is incomplete because it fails to explain: 1. why there were no guest workers in Taiwan during the early 1970s when the island was experiencing a serious shortage of female workers (i.e., why didn't we see a large number of female guest workers moving into Taiwan at the time; Lee 1975)? 2. Why are guest workers not from other Asian LDCs where the unemployment rates are higher and the wage rates are lower than in the home countries of the current guest workers in Taiwan, namely the Philippines, Malaysia, and Thailand? People who accept the labor shortage and wage differential model would also have difficulties in explaining why there are Malaysian guest workers in Taiwan at a time when there is such a labor shortage back in their home country that employers in Malaysia are importing guest workers from Indonesia. What is missing in the neoclassical labor shortage and wage differentials models is the DFI variable (see also Sassen 1989).

The link between guest workers and DFI can be seen from the figures in Table 8.11 and Table 8.15. As we recall from the figures in Table 8.11, the majority of Taiwan's DFI outflow to Asian countries goes to the Philippines, Thailand, Malaysia, and Indonesia. Less than 1 percent of Taiwan's DFI outflow goes to the other Asian countries. Figures from Japan, the United States, European countries and Korea also show that a majority of their DFI outflow to the Asian region, besides ANIEs, is concentrated in the second tier of the Asian NICs. The figures from Table 8.15 show that there is a correlation between the amount of DFI outflow and the number of guest workers in Taiwan.

TABLE 8.15 DFI Outflow and Guest Workers (unit: millions of U.S. dollars and number of persons)

	DFI outflow (1986-89)	Number of guest workers (1988)
Malaysia	$167185	21,011
Philippines	105,235	5,698
Thailand	74,666	9,984
Indonesia	4,964	3,851

Source: Table 8.11 and Chang, 1989.

Why is there an association between DFI outflow and guest workers? DFI outflow to these countries does not actually cause the outflow of guest workers to Taiwan, but it affects the guest workers' decision to come to Taiwan in the following three ways:

1. Demonstration effect. When businessmen from Taiwan invest in other Southeast Asian countries, their workers become familiar with the conditions in Taiwan, especially when some of them are brought to Taiwan for training (Chang 1989, p. 407). These trainees see and envy the high standards of living in Taiwan.

2. Displacement effect. Most of the DFI outflow from Taiwan and from other countries to these Southeast Asian countries is concentrated in labor intensive exporting industries, which employ primarily young female workers. A large percentage of these young female workers come from rural areas and replace many of the male workers in the urban areas. The displaced young male workers are influenced by the "demonstration effect," which leads them to go to Taiwan as guest workers. In 1990, 81 percent of the Malaysian guest workers, 58 percent of the Filipinos, 82 percent of the Thais, and 68 percent of the Indonesians were males (Tsai 1990, p. 10). Also female workers who leave the rural areas to work in the urban areas become accustomed to urban life quickly, and find it difficult, if not impossible, to readjust to the rural environment once they lose their factory jobs. Again the DFI "demonstration effect" works to lead these girls to Taiwan.

One might ask why a large number of Chinese males did not migrate to Japan or other more industrialized countries when Taiwan was in the lower stages of economic development. They did not, partly because of the government's tight control on emigration, and partly because of the cultural and social backgrounds that prevailed in Taiwan. In Taiwan, young female workers who work in factories, on average, save one-third of their monthly income and send it to their parents. The parents, who are influenced heavily by the Confucian principle of placing a high value on education, then use their daughters' savings to send their sons to schools. These young female workers have made a great contribution towards the formation of skilled labor in Taiwan (Liu 1984). In other words, the young Chinese female and male workers did not compete with each other for the same jobs: the males took the majority of the skilled jobs and the females took the majority of the semi-skilled and unskilled assembly jobs. In the Philippines, Malaysia, and Indonesia, the family relationships are not as close as they are among the Chinese and the families are not influenced by Confucianism, so they do not value education as much as Chinese parents. Therefore, when the males are replaced by females the young males do not go to school; instead they become unemployed and are recruited by employment agencies and become guest workers in Taiwan or in Arab countries.

3. Income effect. When a country is very poor, a person does not have any money to go abroad. DFI outflows help these Southeast Asian countries get their economies off the ground. Once the income level has been improved people have the savings and the ability to travel abroad and become guest workers.

In summary, while labor shortage and wage differentials are necessary conditions for the appearance of guest workers in Taiwan, they alone are not sufficient conditions. DFI outflow provides the missing ingredient by linking the guest workers' home countries and Taiwan. The absence of guest workers from other Asian LDCs is precisely because there is a lack of Taiwan DFI outflow to these countries.

What are the possible policy implications of these findings?

1. To regulate but not to eliminate the flow of guest workers. Currently there is a group of people in Taiwan advocating the prohibition of guest workers entering Taiwan. They argue that guest workers can cause unemployment for local workers, lower wage rates, and slow down the progress of automation and thus the upgrading of the economy. Guest workers can also cause many social problems such as racial tension, crime, etc. (for a good discussion of social costs of guest workers, see Chang 1989). However, as Taiwan becomes more internationalized and more integrated into the global economy, it is unfeasible for Taiwan to try to maintain a closed door policy. The experience of the United States, Japan, and other countries has shown, except for the small city states such as Singapore, that it is impossible for a country to close its doors to guest workers because they enter either as legal guest workers, if they are allowed to do so, or as illegal immigrants, if they are prohibited to enter legally. Thus, for example, according to one estimation, in 1990 there were more than 10,000 illegal immigrants from Mainland China and more than 40,000 illegal immigrants from Southeast Asian countries in Taiwan (*United Daily* March 1, 1991, p. 7). Furthermore, as Taiwan expands its DFI outflow to other Asian countries, e.g., Vietnam and Cambodia, workers from these countries

will also want to come to Taiwan. Thus, the current debate of whether to admit guest workers into Taiwan is a moot one. The real question is how to regulate the flow of these guest workers, i.e., how many, what type, for how long, from what countries, which industry, and which employers?

2. To take the flow of guest workers into consideration when the government formulates DFI outflow policy. The pattern of the inflow of guest workers is related to the pattern of DFI outflow. For example, Taiwan's current DFI outflow to Mainland China is heavily concentrated in the coastal cities immediately across the Taiwan Strait (90 percent of Taiwan's DFI outflow is found in Fukien Province, Yen 1990, p. 55), and in shoes, electronics, clothing, textiles, toys, leather, and plastics industries (Yen 1990, p. 57) where a large percentage of the workforce is women. Heavy DFI in labor intensive industries creates a large number of jobs and consequently attracts many families to migrate to these cities. When the wives and daughters find jobs in these industries and the males of the household do not, these unemployed persons venture out across the Taiwan Strait hoping to find jobs there. In Taiwan, they often find jobs in construction or manual work in restaurants and factories. Since they are also Chinese, it is difficult for the police in Taiwan to identify who are the natives and who are the illegal immigrants from Mainland China. Thus, available data show that more than 90 percent of the illegal immigrants caught were citizens from the coastal cities immediately across the Taiwan Strait. In short, Taiwan's current pattern of DFI outflow could encourage the increase of illegal immigrants from Mainland China to Taiwan. Thus, in formulating DFI outflow policy the government should take this factor into consideration. For example, the government may want to encourage the diversification of DFI outflow to Mainland China either geographically or industrially. It is in this sense that the recent move of Taiwan's DFI outflow into the male-dominated chemicals and machinery industries in the coastal cities across the Taiwan Strait is a move in the right direction.

3. To import quality labor, not cheap labor. Currently employers in Taiwan use guest workers because they are cheap and abundant. Guest workers here earn on the average about half of the native workers' wages with no fringe benefits (*China Times* August 13, 1990). However, Taiwan is on its way towards a mature economy and the concept of cheap labor is becoming outmoded. Today Taiwan needs quality labor, not cheap labor. Taiwan is only one of the many labor markets in the world receiving guest workers from the Southeast Asian countries. For instance, in 1988 Taiwan employed 9,984 Thai workers which consisted of only 8 percent of the total Thai guest workers abroad (Kusol and Soonthorndhada 1991, p. 5). In 1987 Taiwan employed only 1.3 percent of all the Filipino workers abroad (Carino 1991). These workers are not identical in quality; instead, they

vary greatly, from inexperienced, poorly educated rural workers to well educated and experienced semi-skilled or skilled factory workers. In the case of Filipino maids some of them are even college graduates. In other words, the quality of the guest workers that Taiwan receives depends on the relative attractiveness of the local labor market as compared with those in other parts of the world. Thus, if employers in Taiwan pay guest workers slightly higher than the prevailing wages in the international markets, with some fringe benefits, and treat them with dignity and respect, they can attract high quality guest workers to Taiwan. Better educated and experienced workers require less training, have higher productivity, and generally lower social costs.

The roles of guest workers in Taiwan's drive towards a mature economy should include:

1. To supply the labor needed for major infrastructural construction projects. In the past, the progress of the fourteen major construction projects was delayed due to the shortage of labor. As the government started to implement its ambitious US$300 billion Six-Year National Development Plan in July 1991, with most of the projects in infrastructure construction, the need for guest workers was greater than ever. Without the required labor the progress of the Six-Year National Development Plan will be delayed, as will the timetable for moving towards a mature economy (*Economy Daily* June 22, 1991).

2. To supply labor to industries with severe labor shortage. The government has decided that industries which have experienced severe labor shortages may apply for the importation of guest workers. Thus far the government has identified six industries in which the employers are qualified to import guest workers. They are textiles, basic metals, metal products, machinery, electronics and electrical products, and construction industries (*Economic Daily* June 22, 1991). To limit the undesirable social effect of the guest workers, the Council on Labor Affairs has decided to import only 15,000 guest workers and not the number which the employers requested. However, the allocation of guest workers should not be based on the employers' needs; instead, it should be based on the following criteria.

The economy should be divided into nontraded goods, e.g., services, transportation and communication, and traded goods, e.g., manufacturing. The traded goods industries should be further divided into high ratio of import versus low ratio of import, and high ratio of export versus low ratio of export categories. Among these categories, the nontraded goods industries should have top priority in the allocation of imported guest workers. Therefore, all the public infrastructure construction projects have top priority, since they have such a significant impact on the investment environment in Taiwan and on other private investment projects as well. Other private construction projects and transportation services are also in this category. The reason for doing so is simple: these goods and services can not be purchased from outside and they must be produced locally. Thus, it is reasonable for the citizen who enjoys these products to bear the social costs of using guest workers.

The second priority should go to the industries in traded goods with high ratios in importing, especially key component industries, such as the machinery, auto parts, and certain electronic and electrical product industries. The reason for doing so is that Taiwan needs to develop these industries, and lower labor costs and adequate labor supply can increase their competitiveness. The social costs of using guest workers borne by the citizen are justifiable on the grounds that Taiwan needs to develop these industries in order to move into the mature economy stage. The third priority should go to industries in traded goods in the high-tech area and with high export ratios, e.g., certain electronic industries. These are the industries that Taiwan wants to develop as it enters the mature economy stage. The rest of the industries should not be allowed to import guest workers, or at least have a low priority, especially industries in the traded goods area with high exporting ratios, but low technology intensities. These should receive the lowest priority in allocating guest workers because, while the social costs of using guest workers are borne by the citizens of Taiwan, the products are actually enjoyed by the citizens of other countries.

3. To release females from household work, increase their labor force participation rates (especially the better educated women), and hence increase the supply of high quality labor. However, this should be done carefully. To avoid the charge of creating a special privilege group, guest workers should not be employed in private households as maids, instead, they should be employed by temporary agencies such as janitorial services, or as helpers in child-care centers, day-care centers for the elderly, and nursing homes.

4. To provide leverage for the government in negotiating with foreign governments. Currently none of the Southeast Asian countries have formal diplomatic relations with Taiwan. With the presence of a large number of guest workers from these countries in Taiwan, these governments will be forced to deal with the government of Taiwan either formally or informally for the purpose of protecting their citizens. When this happens, the ROC government will have the leverage to negotiate agreements with these governments to in turn protect the safety of Taiwan businesses and citizens abroad.

5. Internationalization of the labor market in Taiwan. By admitting guest workers to Taiwan the labor market will be much more internationalized and diversified in terms of race, color, and religion. People in Taiwan can learn to work and live with people of different backgrounds and to be

more open-minded. When Taiwan's labor market is internationalized, some of the skilled and professional workers from other countries, especially from Southeast Asian countries, will probably also want to come to work in Taiwan. Thus, like other industrialized countries, Taiwan could benefit from the human capital inflow from other countries to meet its needs for skilled manpower in the mid-1990s.

9. Conclusions

After forty years of rapid development Taiwan is ready to enter the mature economy stage and join the rest of the industrialized countries. As Taiwan enters this stage, it must open its capital and labor markets internationally. It is in this way that Taiwan can enjoy the inflow of capital and professional transients from other countries, which can help Taiwan transform its economy into a high-tech one at a much faster rate. The outflow of capital and professionals from Taiwan can also assure that it plays a prominent role in the world economy and becomes a world-class country.

Note

The author would like to thank Professor Gustav Ranis, Tzong-Shian Yu, and Paul K. C. Liu for their help at various stages in the preparation of this chapter. He would also like to thank Professor Jenn-Hwa Tu for making available his dissertation and Professor Chi Schive and other members of the "Workshop on Labor Flows to Taiwan" for their constructive comments. The help of the Institute of Economics at Academia Sinica, which provided space and facilities for the research, is also greatly appreciated. The project was partially supported by a grant from the Faculty Research Council at Mankato State University. As usual the author bears the responsibility for any errors.

References

Aliber, Robert Z. 1970. "A Theory of Direct Foreign Investment," in C. P. Kindleberger, ed., *The International Corporation*. Pp. 17-34. Cambridge, Mass.: M.I.T. Press.

Akiyama, Taro, and Yusuke Onitsuka. 1985. "Current Account, Capital Exports and Optimal Patterns of Development Stages of Balances of Payments." Discussion paper series 85-7, Center for International Trade Studies, Faculty of Economics, Yokohoma National University, Japan.

Amsden, Alice. 1989. *Asia's Next Giant: South Korea and Late Industrialization*. Oxford: Oxford University Press.

Baldwin, Robert E. 1988. "U.S. and Foreign Competition in the Developing Countries of the Asian Pacific Rim," in Martin Feldstein, ed., *The United States in the World Economy*. Pp. 79-140. Chicago: University of Chicago Press.

Business Week. July 3, 1991. New York: McGraw-Hill Publication.

Carino, Benjamin V. 1991. "Philippine Labor Flows to Taiwan: A Research Concept." Paper presented at Workshop on Labor Flows to Taiwan, the Institute of Economics, Academia Sinica, June 6-8, Taipei.

Chang, Ching Hsi. 1989. "The Problems of Foreign Workers in Taiwan," in *Proceedings of the Conference on Trade and Foreign Exchange*. Pp. 401-434. Taipei: Institute of Economics, Academia Sinica.

Chen, Chun-Shun. 1990. "Economic Development and Foreign Direct Investment of Taiwan," in Koji Taniguchi, ed., *Development of Taiwanese and Korean Overseas Investment*. Pp. 41-75. Tokyo: The Institute of Developing Economies. (in Japanese)

Chen, Pao-Yui. 1986. *A Study of Taiwan's Private Investment Overseas*. Taipei: Economic Planning and Development Council.

Chen, Tain-Jy. 1987. *An Evaluation of the Policies on Promoting Foreign Investment*. Taipei: Chung-Hua Institution for Economic Research.

Chen, Tain-Jy, and Wen-Thuen Wang. 1991. "Globalization of Taiwan's Electronics Industry." Paper presented at the 1991 Sino-European Conference on Economic Development: Globalization and Regionalization, May 23-24, Taipei.

China Times. November 6, 1989 and August 13, 1990. Taipei, Taiwan.

Chou, Tein-Chen. 1988. "American and Japanese Direct Foreign Investment in Taiwan: A Comparative Study." *Hitotsubashi Journal of Economics* 29: 165-179.

Chow, Peter C. Y. 1990. "The Political Role of the ROC in Asia Pacific Region." *Proceedings of the National Development Seminar*. Pp. 556-570. New York.

Council for Economic Development and Planning. 1986. *The Long-Term Prospect of Economic Development in Taiwan: 1986-2000*. Taipei: Council for Economic Development and Planning, Executive Yuan.

──────. 1991. *Six-Year National Development Plan: 1991-96*. January. Taipei: Council for Economic Development and Planning, Executive Yuan.

Economic Daily. June 22, July 11, July 13, July 14 and July 20, 1991. Taipei, Taiwan.

Economic Outlook. July 1991. Taipei, Taiwan.

Electronic Business. August 7, 1989. Boston, MA.

Euh, Yoon-Doe, and Sang H. Min. 1986. "Foreign Direct Investment from Developing Countries: The Case of Korean Firms." *The Developing Economies*, vol. 24.
Hill, Hal. 1990. "Foreign Investment and East Asian Economic Development." *Asian-Pacific Economic Literature* 4: 21-58.
Hsieh, Kao-Chiao, et al. 1989. *An Investigation of the Present Situation and Problems of Emigration*. Taipei: Executive Yuan, Research and Development Council. (in Chinese)
Hsu, Paul. 1990. "Strategy for Globalization of Taiwan's Economy." *Proceedings of the National Development Seminar*. Pp. 369-372. New York.
Hsu, Paul, and Lawrence S. Liu. 1990. "Recent Developments in Taiwan's Capital Market." *Industry of Free China* 74(2): 1-16.
Hsu, Y. Y. 1989. "Studies on the Foreign Investment and Technology Transfer: The Case of Taiwan." Ph.D Dissertation, Chinese Culture University. (in Chinese)
Investment Commission. 1990. *Statistics on Overseas Chinese and Foreign Investment*. Taipei: Ministry of Economic Affairs.
Kindleberger, Charles P. 1988. *International Capital Movements*. Cambridge: Cambridge University Press.
Kuo, W. Y. 1972. "Technical Change, Foreign Investment, and Growth in Taiwan's Manufacturing Industries, 1952-70." *Economic Essays* 2: 197-224.
Kuo, Wen-Cheng, et al. 1989. *A Study of the Relationship Between Emigration Policy and Economic Development in Taiwan*. Taipei: Chung-Hua Institution for Economic Research. (in Chinese)
Kusol, Vatchareeya Orathal, and T. A. Soonthorndhada. 1991. "International Labor Migration: Thailand." Paper presented at the Workshop on Labor Flows to Taiwan, June 6-8, the Institute of Economics, Academia Sinica, Taipei.
Kuwahara, Yasuo. 1988. "Towards Reestablishing a Foreign Worker's Policy." *Japan Labour Bulletin* 27(11): 4-8.
Lee, Jevons. 1978. "Capital Movement in Taiwan: A Stock Adjustment Approach." *Academia Economic Papers* 6(2): 113-129.
Lee, Joseph S. 1975. "A Study of the Labor Shortage in Taiwan," in Joseph S. Lee, ed., *Essays on Manpower Resources in Taiwan*. Pp. 153-192. Taipei: Li Chien Publishing Company. (in Chinese)
Lee, Jungsoo, and I. P. David. 1989. *Changing Pattern of Financial Flows to Asian Pacific Developing Countries*. Manila: Asian Development Bank.
Liu, Paul K. C. 1984. "Trends in Female Labor Force Participation in Taiwan: The Transition towards Higher Technology Activities," in Gavin W. Jones, ed., *Women in the Urban and Industrial Workforce: Southeast and East Asia*. Canberra: The Australian National University Press.

Liu, T. I. 1985. *Japanese Foreign Investment and Its Effects on Our National Economy*. Taipei: Council for Research, Development and Evaluation, Executive Yuan. (in Chinese)

Nelson, Phillip. 1959. "Migration, Real Income, and Information." *Journal of Regional Science* 1: 43-74.

Organization for Economic Cooperation and Development (OECD). 1987. *International Investment and Multinational Enterprises: Recent Trends of Foreign Direct Investment*. Paris: OECD.

_____. 1989. *Geographical Distribution of Financial Flows to Developing Countries*. Paris: OECD.

Oman, Charles. 1989. "Investing Development." *OECD Observer* 157: 23-27.

Oman, Charles et al. 1989. *New Forms of Investment in Developing Country Industries: Mining, Petrochemicals, Automobiles, Textiles, and Food*. Paris: Development Center, OECD.

Price, Charles. 1989. "Long-term Immigration and Emigration: Its Contribution to the Developing World," in Reginald Appleyard, ed., *The Impact of International Migration on Developing Countries*. Paris: OECD.

Ranis, G., and C. Schive. 1985. "Direct Foreign Investment in Taiwan's Economic Development," in Walter Galenson, ed., *Foreign Trade and Investment: Economic Development in the Newly Industrializing Countries*. Madison: University of Wisconsin Press.

Ricketts, Erol R. 1983. "Periphery to Core Migration: Specifying a Model." Ph.D. Dissertation, University of Chicago.

Salt, John, and Allen Findlay. 1989. "International Migration of High-Skilled Manpower: Theoretical and Development Issues," in Reginald Appleyard, ed., *The Impact of International Migration on Developing Countries*. Paris: OECD.

Sassen, Saskia. 1989. *The Mobility of Labor and Capital*. Cambridge: Cambridge University Press.

Schive, Chi. 1988. "Foreign Investment and Technology Transfer in Taiwan: Past Experience and Future Potential," in *Industry of Free China*. 70(2): 13-24 and 70(3): 13-30.

_____. 1989. "Restructuring Taiwan's Economy in the 1980s and Beyond." *Industry of Free China* 72(3): 13-28.

Shieh, Samuel C. 1989. "Financial Liberalization and Internationalization in ROC: Current Status and Future Policy Directions." *Industry of Free China* 72(6): 9-18.

Taiwan Economic Studies Monthly. June 1991. Taipei, Taiwan.

Taiwan Statistical Data Book: 1990. Taipei: Council for Economic Planning and Development.

Tsai, Ching Lung. 1990. "A Preliminary Study of Foreign Workers in Taiwan: Quantity and Characteristics." Paper presented at the Conference of Population and Social and Economic Changes in Taiwan, Institute of Economics, Academia Sinica, Taipei. (in Chinese)

Tsiang, S. C., and Rong-I. Wu. 1985. "Foreign Trade and Investment as Boosters for Take-off: The Experiences of the Four Asian Newly Industrialized Countries," in Walter Galenson, ed., *Foreign Trade and Investment: Economic Development in the Newly Industrializing Countries*. Madison: University of Wisconsin Press.

Tu, Jenn-Hwa. 1990. "Direct Foreign Investment and Economic Growth: A Case Study of Taiwan." Ph.D. Dissertation, Johns Hopkins University.

United Daily. September 4, 1990 and March 1, 1991. Taipei, Taiwan.

United Nations Center on Transnational Corporations. 1988. *Transnational Corporations in World Development: Trends and Prospects*. New York: United Nations.

Wallace, Cynthia Day. 1990. *Foreign Direct Investment in the 1990s*. Boston: Martinus Nijhoff Publishers.

Weiss, Julian. 1988. "Establishing Offshore Partnership." *Investment* 38(4): 24-27.

Wu, Rong-I. 1986. "U.S. Direct Investment in Taiwan: An Economic Appraisal." *Economic Review* 229: 1-12.

Wu, Hui-Ling. 1990. "Labor Shortage in Taiwan." Paper presented at the Conference on Population, Social and Economic Changes, Academia Sinica, Taipei.

Yeh, Hsueh Tse. 1980. *International Capital Inflows*. Taipei: Lien-Chin Publishers. (in Chinese)

Yen, Chung-Tai. 1990. *Investment in Mainland China and Its Impact on the Industry in Taiwan*. Taipei: Chung-Hua Institution for Economic Research. (in Chinese)

Yonekura, Minoro. 1988. "Overseas Operations of Medium and Medium-Small Electronic Firms." *Sekai Keizai Hyoron* 32(4). (in Japanese)

Yu, K. H. 1990. "Economic Prospects of the Republic of China on Taiwan at the Turn of the 21st Century." *Economic Review* 253: 1-6.

9

Science, Technology and Human Capital Formation

Paul K.C. Liu

1. Introduction

Science and technology development is now generally recognized as one of the basic dynamic forces in the process of economic development. While such development is partially determined by the availability of natural and physical resources, it is to a large extent governed by a society's capacity for generating, assimilating, and utilizing advances in science and technology. Investment in the development of human resources is therefore a prerequisite for the development of science and technology.

Human resource development has both quantitative and qualitative dimensions. The quantitative components consist of population size, sex, age, location, population growth rate, worker participation rate, and number of working hours. The process of increasing the knowledge, skill, and capabilities of the workforce in a society are essentially the qualitative characteristics of human resource development. The two dimensions can be separately identified, but they are also closely interwoven and their components interact. Moreover, the relative importance of the two changes in the process of economic development. Studies in the history of developed countries reveal that the qualitative dimension became increasingly important during their transition from traditional agrarian societies to societies exhibiting modern economic growth. This modern growth, which, as defined by Simon Kuznets, started in England in the late eighteenth century and spread to Western Europe, North America and then Japan in the nineteenth century, is characterized by sustained high rates of economic growth based on advancing science and technology and the institutional and ideological adjustments that they demand.

Since the end of World War II, Taiwan has been among the few so-called newly industrializing countries to successfully catch up with its forerunners. As discussed in other chapters of this book, this success is attributable to many factors, but government policies stimulating the development of science, technology and human resources at different stages of growth are among the most instrumental.

In the catch-up process, there exists a basic family affinity between nineteenth-century Japan and Taiwan during the postwar period (Ranis 1981). Taiwan, of course, has some unique transition experiences in accordance with her own geographic, historical and cultural background, and naturally her experiences in human capital formation and the development of science and technology have characteristics which conform to her typological family as well as being peculiar to her alone. But in guiding Taiwan's economy to maturity, it is helpful to draw upon experiences and lessons from the history of developed countries.

This chapter attempts to examine the status and development of human capital formation and science and technology in Taiwan in both its quantitative and qualitative aspects. It also attempts to highlight challenges that Taiwan will face in the future. Section 2 describes the geographic, historical and cultural background of Taiwan. In Section 3, the population trends and demographic aspects of labor are examined. The completion of the demographic transition in the postwar period has led to slower growth and an aging of the population and labor force. Section 4 looks at the educational performance of Taiwan in relation to the structure of the labor market. Compared to the developed countries, Taiwan, while expanding enrollment at all levels, seems to have more difficulty in improving the quality of education. Section 5 examines the development of science and technology. The conclusion will then highlight some of the major challenges that lie ahead.

2. Geographic, Historical and Cultural Background

Taiwan, a mountainous island of 36,000 square kilometers, is situated in the Pacific Ocean about 160 kilometers off the southeastern coast of mainland China. The economic value of its mineral deposits is negligible. Only one-fourth of the island's total area comprises arable land, although it ranks as the best natural resource of the island. Furthermore, the quality of the land is poor and rainfall is unevenly distributed throughout the year. Because of the absence of natural resources, the development of Taiwan has had to rely on the mobilization of its human resources and on the accumulation of material capital.

Prior to 1600, Taiwan was a sparsely populated frontier island. Thereafter, farmers, accompanied by a small number of merchants and artisans from nearby Provinces (Fukien and Kwangtung), gradually began to settle on the western plain of the island. The influx of people from the commoner strata brought with them Chinese folk culture and values which placed special emphasis on the traditions of family, kinship and communal cooperation. It was not until the establishment of Taiwan as a prefecture of Fukien in 1875, however, that people of the elite social class became influential, a result of the increasing inflow of the scholar-gentry.

When Japan took control of Taiwan from China in 1895, the Japanese authorities decided to develop the island as a supplier of agricultural products to aid Japan in her industrial development. In order to maintain peace and order, traditional Confucian values and the small-scale family farming system of Taiwan were preserved. Farm labor was composed of Chinese immigrants from the mainland who migrated to Taiwan before 1895 and their descendants. In order to raise agricultural productivity through the application of modern techniques, primary education aimed at teaching the population elementary science and practical knowledge was vigorously promoted.

Opportunities for administrative and industrial jobs were virtually all reserved for Japanese nationals. Social mobility of the indigenous population was thus limited to the following classes: landed gentry, landlords, peasants, artisans, and merchants. The social and economic status of individuals was based largely on the achievements and failures of their families; hence, the head of the family had great power in the management of individuals within the family unit.

From the point of view of the development of human resources, traditional Chinese culture, which has been dominated by Confucian teaching for more than two thousand years, has bred a favorable milieu for economic growth. Confucianism advocates diligence, frugality, and universal non-discrimination in education. All of these are beneficial in the accumulation of human and physical capital. Its emphasis on the role of family and clan has resulted in a social system organized around the extended family. This type of society, as compared with that based on the nuclear family unit, was once considered to be a hindrance to modern economic development, but is now considered to be conducive to the promotion of rapid growth and the integration of such societies/economies into the global economy (Kahn 1979; Myers 1984; Greenhalgh 1988).

The fact that the Chinese society on the Mainland -- the source of Confucian culture -- has long been stagnant economically, as evidenced by its low-income agrarian economy, while Chinese societies in Taiwan, Hong Kong and Singapore and their Confucian-influenced neighbors, Japan and South Korea, have been able to make the transition from agrarian to modern industrial economies with substantially higher incomes, has recently revived the interest of economists in reassessing the role of traditional Chinese culture in the process of modern economic growth.

One of the widely accepted explanations of the failure of industrialization in China's history is the lack of a flexible social and economic order that provides sufficient incentives to promote the application of science-based technology to the development of industry and trade (Cheng 1989). Historically, the Confucian influence in education can be seen in the competitive imperial examinations, the means of entrance into officialdom. The knowledge required to pass the examinations, at all levels, was limited to Confucian classics, stereotyped theories of administration, and literature. Those who passed the examinations were elevated to the government class -- the gentry. Those who did not remained commoners but enjoyed a higher social status than the other major functional classes among the commoners, i.e., peasants, artisans, and merchants.

Since agriculture was predominant in traditional China, the state regarded peasants as primary producers of wealth on whose labor the nation depended for sustenance, whereas artisans and merchants were considered as secondary producers of wealth or middlemen. Consequently, the privilege of taking the civil service examinations was reserved for the gentry and the peasants only. This competitive examination system, which was a permanent institution from the T'ang to the Ch'ing dynasty (618-1911), had established a gentry-peasant society based on individual merit rather than family status (Ho 1962). In this Confucian-oriented society, agricultural productivity per acre rose to the limit of traditional farming techniques. The population increased so rapidly that a level of subsistence was obtained where all of the agricultural surplus which could otherwise have been produced, either by an expansion of cultivated land or increased usage of traditional technology, was exhausted (Elvin 1973). This lack of agricultural surplus, which dampened the demand for manufactured goods and services, and the Confucian legal bias against artisans and merchants discouraged the development of science and technology, and hence that of industry and trade (Elvin 1973; Ho 1964).

Beginning in 1902, Taiwan's traditional Confucian examinations system and its educational system were gradually remodeled into the Japanese version of the Western model. Given that primary education was limited to six years for virtually all of the Taiwanese population, the curriculum was revised to include elementary science and practical knowledge, in addition to Confucian ethics. More important is that formal education for girls was equally encouraged. The percentage of Taiwanese school-aged children enrolled in primary school increased rapidly from 3.21 in 1902 to 71.31 (80.86 for boys and 60.94 for girls) in 1944.

In spite of the fact that the Japanese used education as a servant of the state, charged with the purpose of instilling loyalty in the people and teaching the Taiwanese new skills, habits and the discipline to take up the occupations of their parents, Japanese-style modern primary schools remolded the traditional attitude which favored intellectuals over manual laborers. It also exposed them to scientific techniques, machine technology, and modern business practices (Tsurumi 1977). As a result, an increasingly larger proportion of the working force was able to read and write, calculate, and conduct scientific research and development (R&D), applying technology to the production process and managing their businesses with more emphasis on economic factors. The manifestation of the effect of colonial education was that even in the absence of indigenous industrial development, the labor productivity of farmers doubled between 1913 and 1937 (Lee and Chen 1975).

These results are consistent with Simon Kuznets' conclusion in his study on Taiwan's postwar growth and structural changes that the contexts within which high growth rates become feasible include those in which a country has a backlog of applicable useful knowledge. This knowledge is usually more powerful in stimulating growth (proportionally) in countries that lag behind the developed countries, or in countries which lag behind and have historically inherited resources. These resources can be converted to new and much more productive uses; however, elements of the inherited economic and social institutions must be modified to allow for a shift in the uses of resources for more advanced opportunities, and at a moderately high rate. Of the historically inherited resources, Kuznets alleges that human resources are of great importance (Kuznets 1979). But under colonial control, the inherited economic and social institutions in Taiwan were not modified to maximize the welfare of the indigenous population of the island. Similarly, the rigid economic and social structures of the Chinese Communists explain why China is currently lagging behind in the race for modern economic growth.

3. Demographic Transition and Labor Supply

In order to develop Taiwan as an agricultural supplier to Japan, the colonial authorities, after failing to bring Japanese farmers to Taiwan, resorted to depending on the natural increase of the Chinese population on the island as the only supply of primary labor. The Confucian-oriented social system in Taiwan has long supported a high fertility rate; thus, under the traditional family and clan institutions, measures for improving health conditions alone could help accelerate population growth through an increase in the rate of fertility and a decrease in the rate of mortality. Instead of increasing spending on health programs as the population increased, the colonial government started to rely mainly on the use of administrative and policy forces to eradicate epidemics and endemic diseases (Barclay 1954).

By 1920, epidemics, mainly plague and cholera, were brought under control. In later years, efforts were directed towards installing medical facilities and training medical personnel to deliver primary health care. As a result, the birth rate rose moderately, from an average of forty births per 1,000 people during 1906-1909 to forty-five per 1,000 during 1940-1943, while the death rate declined from thirty-three to nineteen per 1,000 during the same periods. The combination of a high and slightly rising birth rate and a substantially declining death rate thus produced an acceleration in the rate of natural increase from seven per 1,000 to twenty-three per 1,000. The population of Taiwan doubled in thirty-five years, from three million in 1905 to six million in 1940. The labor force, owing to the population boom and changes in the rates of labor force participation, increased only from 1.4 million in 1905 to 2.2 million in 1940. This, however, was compensated by a gain in the length of a person's average working life from thirty years in 1915 to thirty-six years in 1940 (Table 9.1).

Social and economic development brought a slight decline in the participation rate of active males, from 94 percent in 1905 to 87 percent in 1940 (Table 9.1). As a rule, the male participation rate of those in the prime age group, 25-54 years old, stayed high and stable. The decline occurred largely among elderly males over 55 years old, and, to a small degree, among young men, 15-19 years old, during the colonial period (Figure 9.1a).

Female participation in the labor force was especially sensitive to changes in the economic environment. The rate for women of all working ages increased from 31 percent in 1905 to 42 percent in 1915 in response to a need for agricultural laborers, but decreased continuously thereafter to 29 percent in 1930 as the burden of childcare became greater. Participation rose again to 35 percent when war broke out in 1940 (Table 9.1). The differences in female participation among the age groups follow a descending pattern, going from the young to the old, with the old obviously having the lowest rate of participation (Figure 9.1b).

All these changes reflect Chinese tradition wherein women could join in direct agricultural production if their responsibility for raising children did not fully occupy their time. While both activities were viewed as productive by the Japanese authorities, the shift from direct production to childcare during 1905-1930 was economically more desirable. This was one of the Japanese policies to promote Taiwan's human resource development that proved to be highly efficient in helping to achieve the goal of establishing the colony as a grain producer for the mother country.

After the war, positions were left vacant by about half a million repatriating Japanese officials, technical personnel, skilled workers and their dependents. These positions were not fully filled until the sudden inflow of Chinese civilian and military forces from mainland China during 1948-1950, totalling over one million. In 1950, the population register reported that

TABLE 9.1 Comparison of Civilian Population and Labor Force, 1905-1990, Taiwan (1000 persons)

	1905	1915	1920	1930	1940	1950	1960	1970	1980	1990
					Male					
Total population	1611	1813	1894	2353	2777	3854	5525	7324	8845	10149
Population aged 12 (15) and over	1160	1264	1328	1553	1736	2530	3337	4093	5714	7116
Population aged 12 (15) + as % of total population	72.0	69.7	70.1	66.0	62.5	65.6	60.4	55.9	64.6	70.1
Labor force	1090	1165	1181	1372	1491	2084	2623	3228	4406	5263
Labor force as % of pop. aged 12 (15) + and over	94.0	92.2	88.9	88.3	85.9	82.4	78.6	78.9	77.1	74.0
Net years of working life at 15 years old	–	29.5	30.9	35.2	36.3	39.0	39.5	40.4	41.0	–
					Female					
Total population	1429	1667	1762	2239	2733	3701	5267	7252	8796	10086
Population aged 12 (15) and over	1028	1149	1225	1466	1724	2437	3192	4022	5664	7102
Population aged 12 (15) + as % of total population	71.9	68.9	69.5	65.5	63.1	65.8	60.6	55.5	64.4	70.4
Labor force	314	478	456	418	608	764	721	1244	2191	3160
Labor force as % of pop. aged 12 (15) + and over	30.5	41.6	37.2	28.5	35.3	31.4	22.6	30.9	38.7	44.5

Note: Figures for 1905 to 1960 are population aged 12 and over; the rest are aged 15 and over. Taiwanese population only.

Source: Data for 1905 to 1940 taken from the *Population Census Reports* for the respective years; data for 1950 to 1960 taken from *Population Registration Reports* for the respective years; and data for 1970 to 1990 taken from *Labor Force Survey Reports* for the respective years.

FIGURE 9.1a Male Labor Force Participation by Age Group, 1905-1990

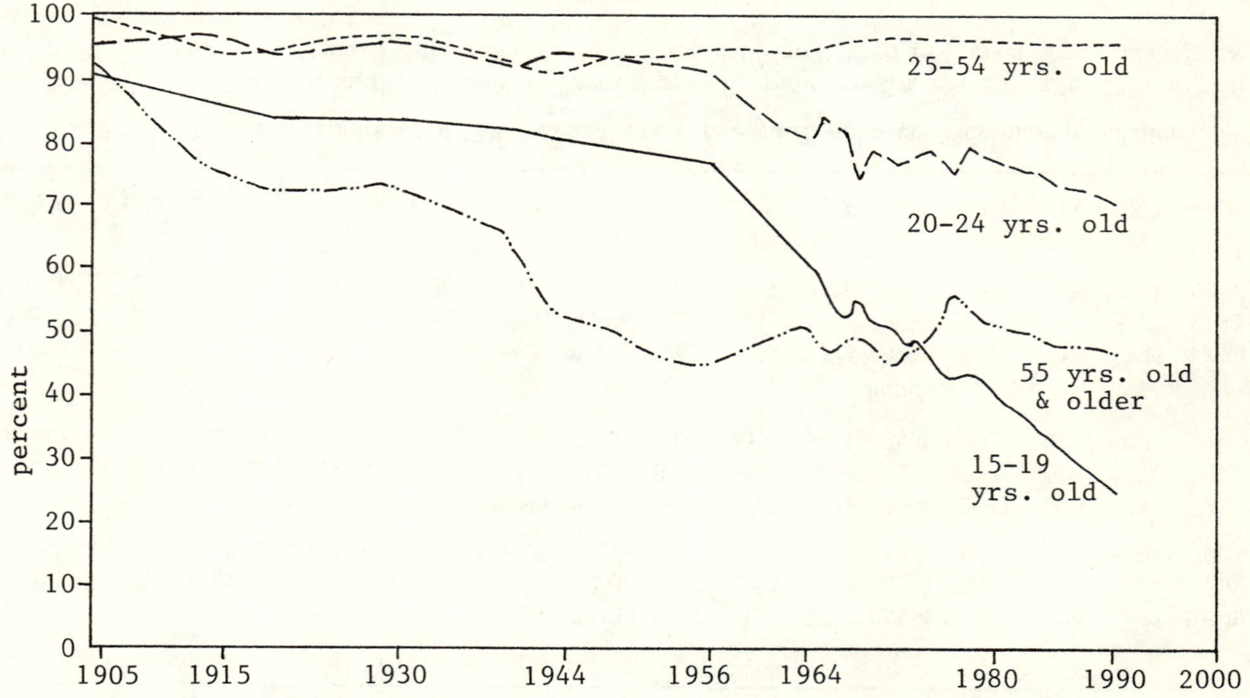

Sources: **Data for** 1905 to 1940 taken from the Population Census Reports for the respective years; data for 1950 to 1960 taken from Population Registration Reports for the respective years; and data for 1970 to 1990 taken from Labor Force Survey Reports for the respective years.

FIGURE 9.1b Female Labor Force Participation by Age Group, 1905-1990

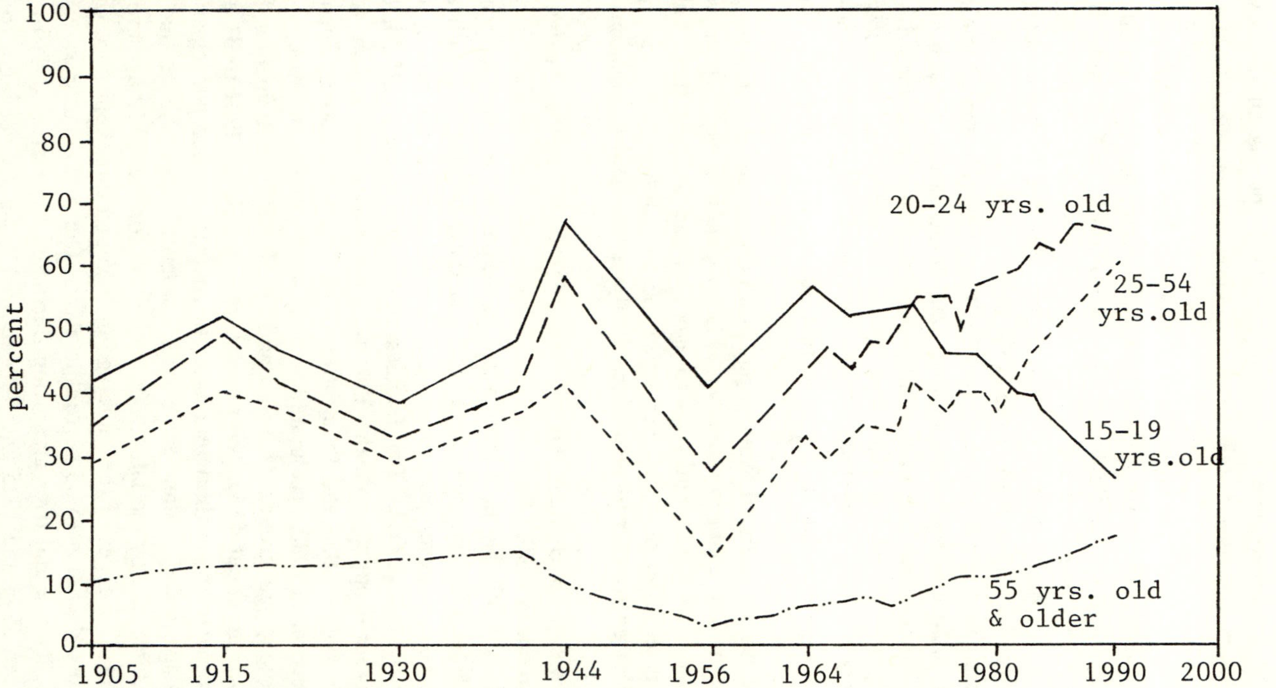

Sources: Data for 1905 to 1940 taken from the Population Census Reports for the respective years; data for 1950 to 1960 taken from Population Registration Reports for the respective years; and data for 1970 to 1990 taken from Labor Force Survey Reports for the respective years.

there were 7.6 million people in Taiwan, an island poorly endowed with natural resources and only 36,000 square kilometers in area. Despite the overcrowded conditions, the population continued to increase, to 14.6 million in 1970 and then to twenty million in 1990, an increase of 260 percent over the 1950 level. In contrast, the labor force increased, from 2.8 million in 1950 to 4.5 million in 1970 and then to 8.4 million in 1990, tripling from 1950 to 1990. The huge increase in the labor supply, while in part due to the increase in the population, was more importantly due to the increase in the participation rate of women in the labor force.

The increase in the population from 1950 on resulted almost entirely from the net balance of births and deaths, namely the natural growth of the population. The annual rate of natural growth started with a record high of thirty-six per 1,000 during 1950-1954 and steadily declined to a low of eleven per 1,000 during 1985-1990. The underlying factor for this drastic decline was a rapid decline in the birth rate accompanied by only a slight decline in the death rate.

As a consequence of the slowing population growth, the age structure of Taiwan's population changed quickly. The population went from very young to moderately young and then to aged. It can be seen from Table 9.1 that the proportion of young people in the age group of 12 years old and over (changed to 15 and over since 1970) in the total population for both sexes followed the prewar declining trend and fell to about 55 percent in 1970. However, since then this trend has reversed direction, rising to almost 70 percent in 1990.

From 1950 to 1990, the male labor force participation rate for the prime age group, 25-54 years old, remained high and fairly constant. Significant changes occurred, however, in the participation of females, the young and the aged during this period. For females at the prime age of 25-54, the participation rate dropped from the 1944 wartime peak of 41 percent to a low of 15 percent in 1956 and then, after climbing up with some fluctuations to 37 percent in 1980, accelerated steadily to 55 percent in 1990.

For the young age groups of 15-19 and 20-24, male participation fell fairly steadily from about 40 and 80 percent, respectively, in 1944 to 31 and 72 percent, respectively, in the late 1980s. In contrast, female participation for the 20-24 age group attained a participation level comparable to that of males of the same age by the late 1980s, while that for the 15-19 age group reached the level of males of the same age in 1965 and then kept pace with the latter before declining to 33 percent in 1989. The participation rate for males in the fifty-five and over age group fluctuated from around 44 to 56 percent between 1944 and 1975 and then showed a slightly declining trend in more recent years. The participation rate of aged females fell from 10 percent in the prewar period to less than 3 percent in 1956 and then increased steadily to 15 percent in 1990.

In sum, since the end of the Second World War Taiwan has experienced a profound demographic transformation. Fertility and mortality have fallen rapidly to a low level comparable to that of the developed countries, and the pace of population and labor force growth has moderated. As a result, the proportion of persons in the working age groups has increased steadily, and hence the burden of the young and aged has been diminished. If, however, the declining trends in fertility and mortality continue, or are even maintained at the present level, Taiwan will inevitably be confronted with a slowly growing but rapidly aging population and labor force. Nearly all able-bodied working-age males and about a third of working-age females participated in direct production before the war. Significant changes in the participation rate of the young and of females of all ages has occurred since the war. The participation rates of young males in the 15-19 age group and the 20-24 age group have fallen persistently, while those of females first rose to the same level as their male counterparts and then decreased, as in the case of males of the same ages. The female participation rate for the 25-54 age group increased rapidly to record high levels. All these changes indicate that the economy in Taiwan is increasingly relying on the prime age group of both sexes (24-54 years old) to supply labor.

The growth of the work force in the last four decades in Taiwan constituted one of the greatest challenges as well as one of the greatest opportunities to the economy. It was a challenge in the sense that a serious unemployment problem arose in the 1950s as the limited amount of arable land and water were all brought into full use, while alternative job opportunities had not yet been sufficiently created to absorb the increase in the size of the work force. The estimated unemployment rate, adjusted for unutilized man-days in agriculture, rose to 12-14 percent in the early 1950s. This pool of surplus labor, however, allowed the government to pursue policies that promoted labor-intensive technologies in the primary import and export substitution subphases (1953-1961 and 1961-1975) in the process of modern transition growth, until the pool of surplus labor gradually became exhausted in about 1968. The continuing reliance on labor-intensive technology thereafter, however, led the labor market to one of under-utilization in terms of the income and education mismatch in the 1970s (Liu 1985). Furthermore, continuous rapid export growth and low rates of increase in the population and labor force combined to produce rising wages and, more importantly, a brisk demand for well-educated workers. The need to restructure the economy and upgrade levels of technology in order to replace the work force, which possessed a low-level of education and often outmoded skills, with better-educated and trained workers became increasingly urgent in the 1980s. The replacement process will be slow as the rapid decline in fertility slows the growth of the younger age groups now entering the labor force, on the one hand, and the process of acquiring education and training delays their entry into the work force, on the other.

4. Acquisition of Knowledge and Skills

As discussed in Section 2, an effective and modern primary education system was established during the period of Japanese occupation. At the time of the restoration of Taiwan to the Republic of China in 1945, the primary school enrollment rate had already reached 81 percent for boys and 61 percent for girls. This achievement undoubtedly provided Taiwan's economy with a positive human capital asset during its initial stage of modern economic growth. To sustain further growth, Taiwan must not only maintain the existing primary education system, but, more importantly, must improve and expand higher education. Rapid increase in the school age population and urban growth have made the task difficult in the postwar period. Under the government's stringent financial constraints in the early stage of its development, the spread of education was promoted at the cost of a great decline in its quality.

In the postwar period, about 98 percent of primary schools, 75 percent of secondary schools, and 60 percent of colleges and universities were public, and the overall performance of the system was heavily influenced by the amount of public resources devoted to it. Government expenditure for public education increased quickly in real terms (in 1986 NT dollars) from NT$4.4 billion in 1952 (1.7 percent of the GNP), to $42.3 billion in 1972 (3.6 percent of the GNP), to $100 billion in 1982 (5.0 percent of the GNP), and then to $162 billion in 1988 (5.2 percent of the GNP). The allocation of funds between primary, secondary, and higher education differed depending on the process of development. In the 1950s, about half of the expenditures were allocated to support primary education to handle the rapidly increasing school-age population resulting from the postwar baby boom. Secondary and higher education's share of the expenditures were only about 35 and 15 percent, respectively. As the primary school-age population leveled off in the late 1960s, the government extended compulsory education from six to nine years in 1968, and thus the share for secondary schooling increased to slightly more than 40 percent and has remained about the same since. In response to the sharp reduction in births, the share of the government education budget allocated to primary education declined to 30 percent by the late 1980s and the share of higher education increased to 30 percent. The change in the distribution of public education expenditures in the postwar period reflects the fact that Taiwan's government, in contrast to most governments of developing countries, followed the classic educational pyramid pattern, building a strong base and only thereafter allowing the pyramid system to grow in the middle and then at its apex (Blaug 1979). Such a distribution favored lower-income groups and enabled socio-economic development programs, such as population control, health maintenance, nutrition and technology diffusion, to work more efficiently. It also avoided unemployment of the educated as long as a low level of technology prevailed in the primary import substitution subphase (1950-1961).

The growth of enrollment at the various levels of the educational system, for both sexes, was strongly affected by the flow of expenditures. Figure 9.2 shows that in 1950 the primary school enrollment rates for both boys and girls were well over 80 percent -- the critical point for sustaining development. These rates grew rapidly to complete enrollment, with a negligible number of dropouts, by 1960. The secondary enrollment rates were low and their sex differences were remarkable in the 1950s. By 1980, these differentials had disappeared as growth in enrollment reached the high levels of about 94 percent of those eligible for junior high school and 75 percent of those eligible for senior high school. Impressive gains were also made in the enrollment rates of colleges and universities, including junior colleges. By 1989, the rate of high school students entering college rose to 30 percent for both sexes, a figure comparable to that of the developed countries.

Despite rapid increases in the enrollment rate over the period 1952-1989, the quality of education as measured by the level of public expenditure per student improved substantially. With the exception of a few setbacks caused by world-wide upheavals in the 1970s, public expenditure per student in real 1986 prices rose markedly from NT$2,100 to NT$16,000 at the primary level, from NT$9,500 to NT$26,600 at the secondary level, and from NT$46,100 to NT$110,000 at the tertiary level over this period.

In spite of all these accomplishments, Taiwan's educational system has been confronted with some fundamental problems and new challenges during the last few decades. As previously discussed, the Chinese people are traditionally highly education-oriented. However, the dream became a reality only after a sufficient number of job opportunities was created for the educated in the process of postwar industrialization and modernization. As a result, the demand for more and better education by the people has exceeded the supply that the government can adequately afford to provide. To be fair to the applicants for admission, joint entrance examinations at all levels beyond the compulsory or free national educational levels are held once a year. In order to allow for efficient and unbiased grading, tests are constructed to secure objective, rather than creative, responses. This type of selection method leads to the overemphasis of academic achievement and the neglect of social, emotional, and physical development of the children in both primary and secondary schools. More seriously, the learning process

FIGURE 9.2 Enrollment Ratio by Sex, 1906–2000

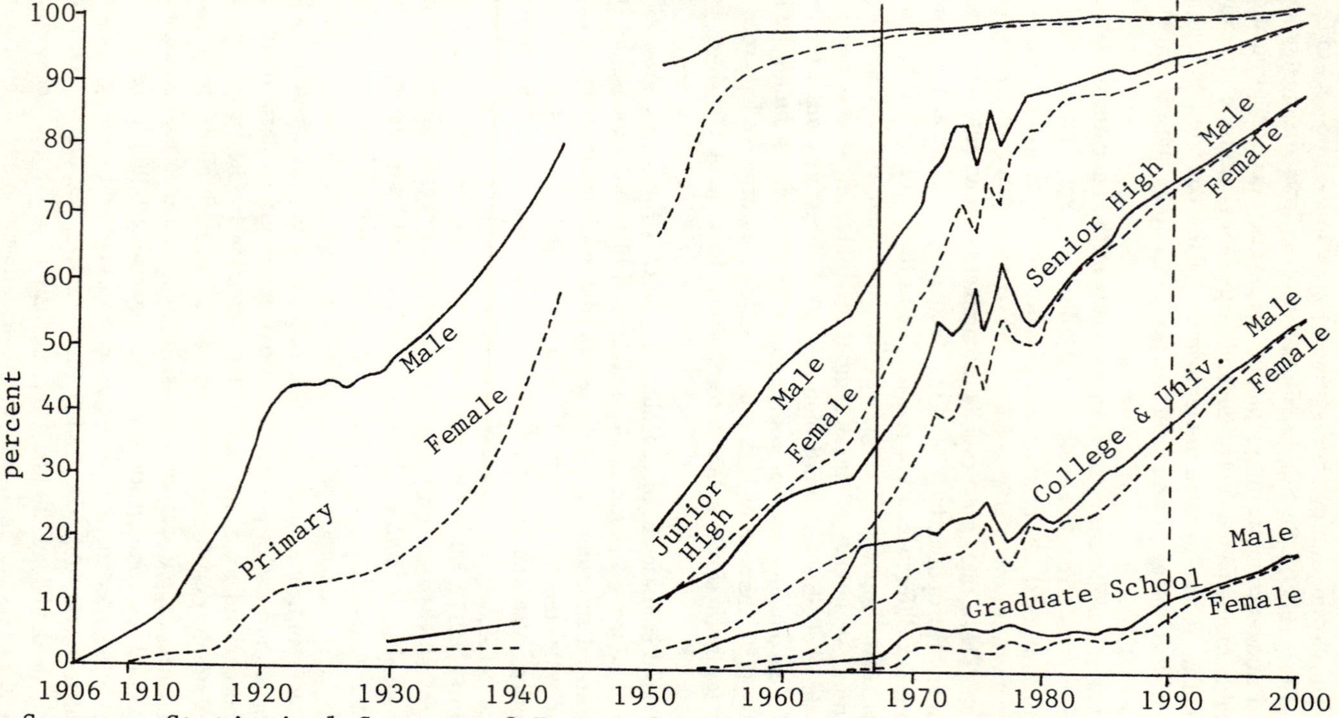

Sources: Statistical Summary of Taiwan for the Past 51 Years, Taiwan Provincial Department of Statistics, 1946; Educational Statistics of the Republic of China, Taipei, Ministry of Education, 1981.

tends to discourage creative and critical thinking and thereby hinders intellectual development. Also, the well-established goal of inculcating the traditional Confucian values in the younger generation has often been neglected. Consequently, the younger generation has lost a great deal of the good values of tradition but has acquired few of the rational values of the West that are inherent in industrialized society.

Academic achievement is overemphasized, i.e., the curriculum is almost exclusively geared to the next stage of education and tends to ignore those who intend to enter the labor market after completing the current level of schooling. Graduates from the so-called 'cowboy class' at the primary or junior high level are not adequately prepared for employment in the modern economy. An immediate remedy that was implemented in the 1960s was the introduction of a program allowing private enterprises to offer vocational training in schools and universities for recruited students as part of the formal education system. This program indeed alleviated the urgent need for factory workers, particularly female workers, in the development of labor-intensive industries during the 1960s.

The long-term remedy is vocationalization of the educational system. Prior to 1967 over 60 percent of the students at the senior high school level were enrolled in academic schools and only 40 percent in technical and vocational schools. The imbalance in the education system has been corrected; the government has adopted policies for diversifying secondary education to provide technical and vocational education in response to the manpower needs of the late stage of industrialization. By 1989, the proportions had been reversed to 30 percent and 70 percent, respectively. Technical and vocational senior high schools have an equal share of the students. It is worth noting that 85 percent of male students are enrolled at technical (industrial) schools, whereas 90 percent of female students are at vocational (commerce and nursing) schools.

Attending college or graduate school is the ultimate goal of the majority of the Chinese on Taiwan. Between 1952 and 1988, the total number of college students rose rapidly, from 10,000 to 496,000. The number of graduate students grew from 0.1 to 4.5 percent of this total. The breakdown of university students by discipline during this period shows that there was a shift towards the social sciences, engineering and the medical sciences and away from the humanities and agriculture (Table 9.2).

The small proportion of graduate students in Taiwan is in part due to the difficulties in the expansion of qualified graduate institutes, but also in part is due to the fact that the government has given permission to college and university graduates to go abroad for graduate school since 1951, while permission to senior high school graduates to study abroad was not granted until 1987. The number of college and university graduates from Taiwan going abroad increased rapidly from 558 in 1951-1961 to 1,833 in 1962, and

TABLE 9.2 University Students among Groups of Disciplines

	Total	Humanities	Social Sciences	Natural Sciences	Agriculture	Engineering	Medical
\multicolumn{8}{c}{Number of university students}
1952	10,037	2,207	2,991	693	1,231	2,590	325
1955	18,174	2,882	6,946	1,129	2,038	4,467	712
1960	35,060	7,355	11,730	3,243	3,049	6,958	2,725
1965	85,346	13,071	41,248	5,511	5,447	12,920	7,149
1970	203,473	24,834	86,123	10,464	11,477	49,886	20,689
1975	289,435	39,273	116,866	13,796	10,341	87,823	21,336
1980	342,528	39,562	133,843	15,336	11,960	115,186	26,641
1985	428,576	38,764	172,567	26,903	13,171	141,555	35,616
1988	496,530	42,667	194,802	34,071	15,119	167,358	42,513
\multicolumn{8}{c}{Percent}
1952	100.0	22.0	29.8	6.9	12.3	25.8	3.2
1955	100.0	15.9	38.2	6.2	11.2	24.6	3.9
1960	100.0	21.0	33.5	9.2	8.7	19.8	7.8
1965	100.0	15.3	48.3	6.5	6.4	15.1	8.4
1970	100.0	12.2	42.3	5.1	5.6	24.5	10.2
1975	100.0	13.6	40.4	4.8	3.6	30.3	7.4
1980	100.0	11.6	39.1	4.5	3.5	33.6	7.8
1985	100.0	9.0	40.3	6.3	3.1	33.0	8.3
1988	100.0	8.6	39.2	6.9	3.0	33.7	8.6

Source: Ministry of Education, 1989. *Educational Statistics of the Republic of China*, Taipei.

from then grew steadily to 5,933 in 1980 and to 7,122 in 1988 for a total of 106,500 students. Of these students, 57,000 majored in the natural sciences, medicine or engineering, and 49,500 majored in the humanities and social sciences. The majority of them, slightly over 90 percent, went to the U.S. and remained there after the completion of their schooling. Between 1951 and 1988, the accumulated number of returning students was only 18,500. There were forty-eight in 1951-1961. This number increased to sixty-three in 1962, to 640 in 1980, and then to 2,296 in 1988.

On the negative side, the loss of highly educated manpower -- the so-called "brain drain" -- has reduced the supply of vital professional people available within Taiwan. On the positive side, since the primary cause of the brain drain problem originated in the lack of opportunities for university graduates in the job market, the emigration of these people has alleviated and reduced the pressure on the labor market to find jobs for highly educated workers in Taiwan. More importantly, family and social connections between people in Taiwan and those who remain abroad enhance academic and technological communication and international understanding.

In fact, rapid economic restructuring on Taiwan in the 1980s has provided higher status, opportunities and resources, particularly in the science and engineering fields which have attracted an increasingly large number of students abroad. Survey findings, however, reveal that among the returnees, non-engineers were significantly more satisfied with their life environment than engineers (Pedersen, Hu and Hwang 1989). The first priority in developing the resources of Taiwan at the current moment should be to strengthen the coordination of educational resources at home and abroad by giving incentives to the foreign educated students to return and stay in Taiwan.

The growth of educational opportunities has significantly improved the level of educational attainment of the labor force. On average, the number of years of formal education of employed males persons rose from 6.2 in 1964 to 10.8 in 1988 and that of employed females from 4.2 to 10.4 during the same period. Rapid reductions in the proportion of those with no formal education and those attending only primary school, vis-a-vis the increase in the proportion of junior high graduates and above, were the underlying cause of the increase in the educational attainment level of the labor force in this period. Judging from the trends in enrollment rates, a decline in the proportion of junior high graduates will occur in the 1990s. It is worth noting that between 1964 and 1988, the proportion of female technical and vocational graduates in the labor force rose from 2.2 to 23.5 percent, while, for males, this proportion rose from 4.4 to 17.9 percent. In contrast, the proportion of students at college level or above increased from 3.8 to 15.3 percent for males and from 0.8 to 13.8 for females during the same period.

The impressive improvement in the quality of human resources obtained through increased investment in education has provided general human capital for the economy on the whole. Specific human capital -- job-related knowledge and skills -- needed by individual firms depends, however, largely on training programs offered by employers. Prior to 1966, there were no government policies dealing with in-service training. Most of the training was conducted by public and large private enterprises for specific purposes. As labor-intensive industries thrived, the shortages of semi-skilled and skilled labor became increasingly obvious. To cope with this problem, the first manpower development plan was formulated and implemented in

1966. Later, this plan was integrated into the Fifth Four-Year Economic Plan (1969-72). Between 1966 and 1976, nine public training centers were established throughout Taiwan to facilitate the training of vocational training instructors and workers (San and Chen 1988).

Figure 9.3 shows that the total number of in-service trainees increased steadily, from 54,000 persons in 1966, to 203,000 in 1980, and then to 223,000 in 1988. Of the trainees, the proportion of those who were sponsored by private enterprises and institutions increased from 27 percent in 1966 to a peak of 65 percent in 1974. Since then the proportion has gradually slid back down to 50 percent. The surge of trainees in the private sector was largely a result of the implementation of the Vocational Training Fund Statute of 1972. According to this statute, employers with forty or more employees have to appropriate an amount equal to 1.5 percent of their total wage bill to an in-service training fund for the training of their employees. This statute, however, was suspended in 1974, in part because the contributions did not benefit firms on an equal basis, and in large part because employers' ability to supply funds was severely decreased by the first oil shock. In 1982, the Employment and Vocational Training Administration within the Council of Labor Affairs was established to unify and strengthen employment services, vocational training and trade-skill tests.

It is worth noting that when consecutive external shocks hit the economy, most of the domestic-owned enterprises, instead of laying off workers, kept their employees and sent them to programs sponsored by the Vocational Training Fund to gain job-related knowledge and skills. To keep businesses running, an agreement was reached on a cut in wages and salaries, with an average reduction in 1974 of 20 percent of the previous year's real earnings, and of another 10 percent soon thereafter. This practice, which in fact is an extension of Confucian traditions and which was applied to family businesses in the modern sector, proved to be one of the more efficient approaches in developing employees' potential for future utilization as well as in ensuring harmonious labor-management relations even during periods of slack business.

Despite recent progress, training of the work force in Taiwan is both quantitatively and qualitatively deficient, and a particularly well-planned system of training has yet to be established. The Nation-wide Labor Force Survey shows that in 1988 only 18.6 percent of the population eligible for training (defined as those aged fifteen and over, excluding students and the disabled) had received in-service training for a month or more. Differences in in-service training among the sexes and age groups were significant. About one-third of all male workers under forty-five years old, in contrast to one-tenth for females under forty-five, had received training, whereas only 15 percent of males over 54 years old and 1.5 percent of females over 45 had received training. Training tended to concentrate on workers with a

FIGURE 9.3 Accumulated Number of In-service Trainees, 1966-1988

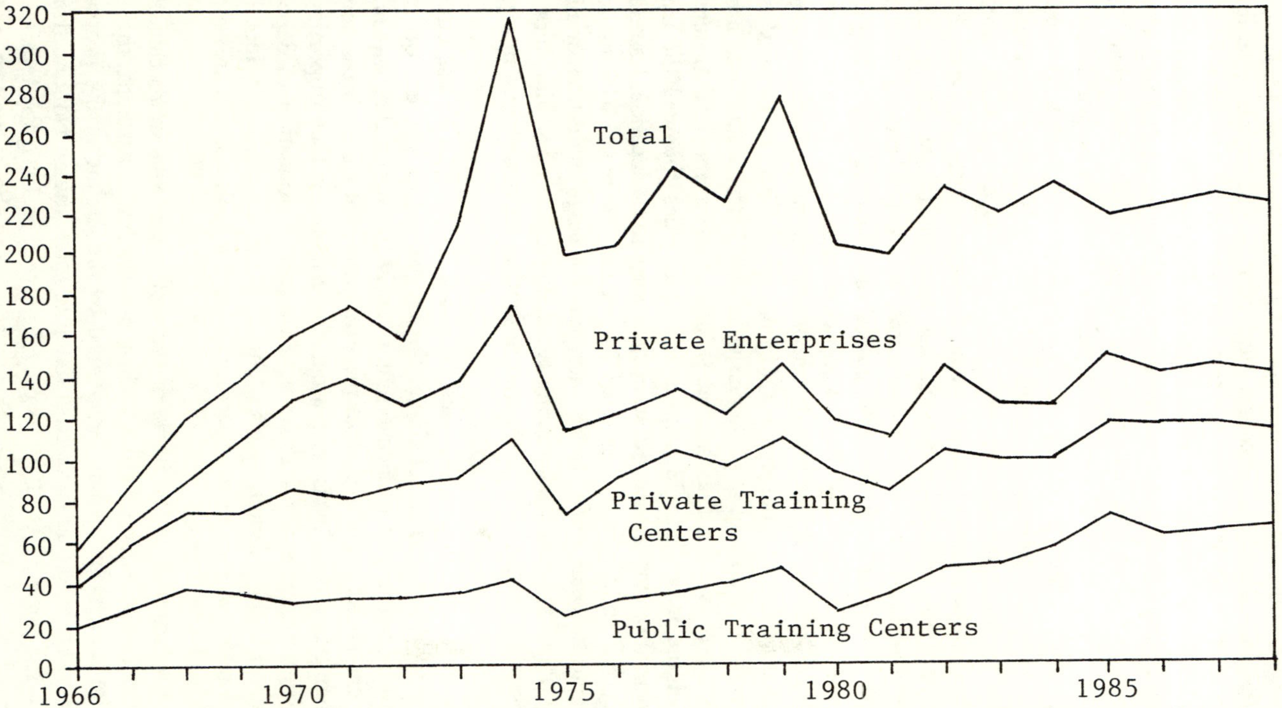

Source: The Statistics of Vocational Training, Skill Test and Employment Service in Taiwan Area of the Republic of China, Employment and Vocational Training Administration Council of Labor Affairs, Executive Yuan, 1989.

375

junior high school education -- 38 percent for males and 13 percent for females in this category. Those with less or more education were likely to have had moderately less in-service training (Tables 9.3 and 9.4).

Table 9.3 shows that in 1988 the proportion of the population eligible for training with the intention to receive more training amounted to 2.3 percent for those who had received training and 4.3 percent for those who had not received training. Both of these proportions tended to be positively associated with their educational attainments. Those who had no intention of participating in the training programs were partly frustrated by the lack of opportunities for advancement, but were also burdened with household work. The policy implication of these findings clearly suggests that improvement in the internal labor market and the raising of the level of productivity of household production activities are fundamental to increasing the technological level of human capital in Taiwan today.

A closer examination of the major characteristics of those who had received vocational training reveals important insights into the weaknesses of Taiwan's domestic labor market (Table 9.4). First, employers' investments in their employees, particularly in the better educated, are still insufficient. It is seen that among those who had received training, 41 percent of the males and 73 percent of the females financed the training themselves. Looking at the differences among the educational strata, the percentage of training increases from 29 percent for males with no formal education to 83 percent for those with junior college education or higher. The majority of self-financed training is not to gain new knowledge or skills to improve their current job performance, but rather to obtain a new job or a transfer.

Second, most training is provided by small enterprises to less educated workers over short periods of time. On the whole, 61 percent of trained males and 67 percent of trained females received training that was offered by small enterprises. As expected, the proportions of the trainees decreased as their education levels increased; i.e., for males the proportion decreased from 84 percent for those with no formal education to 8 percent for those with an education level above university, and for females it decreased from 93 percent to 4 percent. The duration of training averaged from four to twelve weeks.

Third, the majority of the workers acquired their skills more than seven years prior to the survey, and the less educated the workers, the more obsolescent their skills. This is evidenced by the decline in the proportion of male workers who had received training to total trained workers from 30 percent in the period 1982-1986 to only 7 percent in 1987; for females, the proportion declined from 38 to 11 percent. For the same two periods, males with primary education accounted for only 10 and 1 percent of those trained, and females, 16 and 2 percent, respectively. Although the propor-

TABLE 9.3 Population Eligible for Training by Status and Intention of Training: 1988

	Total	No Formal	Primary School	Junior High School	Senior High School	Vocational School	Junior College	University and Graduate
Population eligible for training (1000 persons)	11,086	1,094	3,816	2,134	766	2042	697	537
	Percent of population eligible for training							
Have received vocational training	18.6	3.9	17.2	26.5	18.3	19.1	20.7	22.3
With intention of training	2.3	0.0	0.7	2.6	3.0	3.8	5.5	6.4
Professional and managerial	0.6	0.0	0.1	0.2	0.4	0.7	3.0	3.8
Clerical workers	0.5	0.0	0.0	0.1	0.3	1.1	1.3	2.0
Production and sales workers	1.2	0.0	0.7	2.3	1.2	2.0	1.2	0.6
Without intention of training	16.3	3.9	16.4	23.9	15.3	15.4	15.2	15.9
Intended to if upgrading possible	2.4	1.2	2.1	3.5	2.6	2.4	1.9	2.5
Need no more training	6.2	1.4	5.8	9.3	6.3	5.6	6.3	7.2
Fully occupied with work	3.2	0.7	3.7	5.4	2.4	2.7	1.4	0.5
Fully occupied with housework	0.7	0.3	1.0	0.8	0.3	0.4	0.3	0.2

(*continues*)

TABLE 9.3 (continued)

	Total	No Formal	Primary School	Junior High School	Senior High School	Vocational School	Junior College	University and Graduate
Have no received vocational training	81.4	96.1	82.8	73.5	81.7	80.9	79.3	77.7
With intention of training	4.3	0.3	1.3	3.7	6.6	7.9	10.6	9.9
Professional and managerial	1.1	0.0	0.1	0.3	1.3	1.6	5.0	5.6
Clerical workers	1.1	0.0	0.0	0.2	2.1	3.0	3.2	3.5
Production and sales workers	2.1	0.3	1.2	3.2	3.1	3.3	2.4	0.7
Without intention of training	77.2	95.8	81.5	69.8	75.2	72.9	68.6	67.8
Intending to if upgrading possible	13.4	18.0	12.0	13.5	14.8	13.8	12.7	11.1
Need no more training	18.0	15.9	16.2	14.1	19.6	19.9	26.3	30.8
Fully occupied with work	23.5	17.1	23.6	23.3	26.5	26.2	22.8	21.7
Fully occupied with housework	21.8	44.7	28.3	18.9	14.3	13.0	6.8	4.3

Note: Population eligible for training is defined as population aged 15 and over, excluding student and disabled.

Source: Directorate-General of Budget, Accounting and Statistics, 1988. *Report on the Vocational Training Survey, Taiwan Area, Republic of China, Taipei.*

TABLE 9.4 Major Characteristics of Population Eligible for Training Who Have Received Vocational Training, 1988

	Total	No Formal	Primary School	Junior High School	Senior High School	Vocational School	Junior College	University and Graduate
MALES								
Population eligible for training	5,477	267	1,835	1,180	451	989	406	349
Population who have received training	1,609	32	507	446	110	303	118	94
% in population eligible for training	29.4	12.1	27.6	37.8	24.4	30.6	29.0	26.8
		Percent in population who have received training						
Sponsorship and purpose of training								
Sponsored by employer	59.1	71.2	69.0	69.7	45.9	41.6	16.7	16.8
Preemployment training	33.5	38.6	36.6	40.8	27.3	26.3	9.9	10.7
Advanced training for in-service worker	25.5	32.6	32.4	29.0	18.5	15.2	6.8	6.1
Self-financed	40.9	28.8	31.0	30.3	54.1	58.4	83.3	83.2
Preemployment training	7.2	11.1	5.0	7.8	9.2	9.1	9.9	7.2
Facilitating job seeking or transfer	22.4	15.4	11.6	14.9	35.6	35.3	66.3	67.0
Training for internal upgrading	20.5	2.3	25.4	19.3	12.2	21.3	8.8	10.0
Trainees' occupation								
Professional and managerial	6.3	1.7	2.0	1.7	9.6	7.6	31.5	13.4
Clerical workers	6.3	0.0	0.9	1.0	12.0	6.7	23.6	33.9
Production and sales workers	85.5	98.3	97.1	97.2	78.9	85.7	45.0	20.6
Type of training institute								
Vocational training institutions	8.5	2.1	2.2	2.2	15.8	10.4	27.5	36.5
Large enterprises	9.4	2.6	3.5	3.4	19.0	14.9	24.0	24.5
Small enterprises	60.8	83.8	75.8	78.6	33.9	48.1	23.4	7.5
School affiliated training institutions	21.3	11.5	18.5	15.8	31.4	26.7	25.0	31.6

(continues)

TABLE 9.4 (continued)

	Total	No Formal	Primary School	Junior High School	Senior High School	Vocational School	Junior College	University and Graduate
Duration of training								
4-12 weeks	38.4	32.3	29.5	27.4	52.2	46.0	65.9	65.1
13-52 weeks	30.8	27.5	25.7	34.4	29.3	35.4	30.2	29.4
53-104 weeks	14.7	13.0	19.1	19.3	9.8	11.0	2.1	2.8
105-156 weeks	11.3	15.1	17.2	13.7	6.7	6.3	1.3	1.6
157 weeks and more	4.8	12.1	8.5	5.2	2.0	1.3	0.5	1.1
Years of training								
Before 1966	9.6	49.4	20.1	4.3	6.7	1.5	1.7	3.0
1962-1971	15.6	31.7	30.4	10.0	7.8	7.3	4.0	6.4
1972-1981	38.4	15.9	38.2	45.4	38.4	36.5	33.6	26.4
1982-1986	29.7	3.1	10.3	32.5	39.7	43.1	48.6	51.9
1987	6.7	0.0	0.9	7.8	7.5	11.6	12.1	12.4
FEMALES								
Population eligible for training	5,607	825	1,981	954	315	1,053	291	188
Population who have received training	451	11	149	120	30	88	27	26
% in population eligible for training	8.0	1.3	7.5	12.6	9.6	8.4	9.3	14.0
	Percent in population who have received training							
Sponsorship and purpose of training								
Sponsored by employer	26.7	21.7	18.9	30.6	30.2	22.2	32.5	30.5
Preemployment training	15.3	21.7	10.9	10.1	18.4	10.4	18.0	16.9
Advanced training for in-service worker	11.4	0.0	8.0	20.5	11.8	11.8	14.5	13.7
Self-financed	73.3	78.3	81.1	69.4	69.8	77.8	67.5	69.5

Preemployment training	16.7	27.0	14.9	10.9	14.4	19.4	12.7	17.5
Facilitating job seeking or transfer	30.3	51.3	33.6	21.0	32.3	30.3	24.0	19.5
Training for internal upgrading	26.3	0.0	32.6	37.5	23.1	28.0	30.8	32.5
Trainees' occupation								
Professional and managerial	12.1	1.5	2.7	3.4	19.2	16.8	46.1	49.3
Clerical workers	11.8	0.0	0.2	3.6	23.2	22.7	41.1	40.3
Production and sales workers	76.1	98.5	96.9	93.0	57.6	60.5	12.8	10.3
Type of training institute								
Vocational training institutions	6.7	0.0	0.1	1.4	13.4	8.6	31.7	31.5
Large enterprises	8.6	0.0	3.1	4.8	12.3	12.0	27.9	24.2
Small enterprises	67.1	92.8	86.1	84.6	49.2	51.5	6.1	4.2
School affiliated training institutions	17.6	7.2	10.6	9.2	25.1	27.9	34.3	40.1
Duration of training								
4-12 weeks	37.0	12.7	20.8	26.1	46.6	51.3	83.1	82.4
13-52 weeks	33.1	25.5	33.9	41.1	35.2	32.9	13.3	14.3
53-104 weeks	16.1	25.7	20.6	20.5	13.7	10.2	3.1	2.0
105-156 weeks	9.3	22.4	16.0	9.1	3.6	3.7	0.6	1.3
157 weeks and more	4.4	13.6	8.6	3.2	0.9	1.8	0.0	0.0
Years of training								
Before 1966	5.2	28.8	11.8	2.5	1.7	0.3	1.4	0.0
1962-1971	15.8	49.2	33.4	6.2	8.2	4.4	6.9	2.8
1972-1981	30.8	13.8	37.1	30.5	27.4	22.8	26.8	27.3
1982-1986	37.6	8.2	15.9	47.5	50.6	53.0	47.9	49.0
1987	10.7	0.0	1.8	13.4	12.1	19.6	17.0	20.9

Population eligible for training is defined as population aged 15 and over, excluding students and disabled.

Source: Directorate-General of Budget, Accounting and Statistics, 1988. *Report on the Vocational Training Survey, Taiwan Area, Republic of China, Taipei.*

tion of better educated people receiving training has increased in more recent years, over 40 percent of the males and 30 percent of the females received their training more than seven years ago.

Basically, the share of the cost of training borne by employers and that borne by employees depends upon the returns on their respective investments. The returns are composed not only of wage increases and growth in productivity but also of the chance of being promoted to higher job levels. Moreover, internal promotion, when used as the principal means of filling higher-level vacancies, assures employers of reaping returns on their training investments. There is a prevalence of small family businesses in Taiwan, and, despite the traditional preference for long-term paternalistic relations between employers and employees, the limited number of job vacancies at the higher levels tends to encourage highly educated employees to invest in training for the external rather than the internal labor market. In addition, the strong inclination for people to be a small boss rather than an esteemed employee, as expressed in the proverb, "prefer to be a chicken head than the tail of a cow," reinforces the growth of small businesses. Consequently, most workers consider their jobs as a place to gain work experience to aid in seeking better jobs or for preparing to set up their own businesses.

In summary, in the early development stage, a surplus of unskilled human resources was available in Taiwan and the labor-intensive small-scale family firms were competitive in world markets. However, as industrialization progressed, this surplus of labor was quickly exhausted and competition from other developing countries became fierce. To cope with these adverse changes, the traditional business organizations had to switch from unskilled labor-intensive manufacturing to technology- and capital-intensive industries. Government efforts towards human resources investment and the development of science and technology became crucial during this transitional stage.

5. Science and Technology Development

As one of the latecomers to economic development, Taiwan has enjoyed a large array of opportunities for high growth. These opportunities, which exist in the form of useful technology both from home and abroad, are accessible to all but can only be exploited by those who are prepared. In Taiwan, the key to the exploitation of technology has been the adoption of strategies and policies by the government and firms to gradually reduce price distortions and barriers to competition, with the purpose of achieving a better functioning market economy, on the one hand, and improving the quality of human resources to increase the efficiency of the work force (in particular, private entrepreneurs), on the other. As a result, sustained economic growth along with equity in distribution has been attained with the continuous absorption of new technologies.

As simple technologies have been exploited, enterprises in Taiwan have had to rely on the acquisition of more complex and sophisticated technologies. In addition to imported technologies, Taiwan has had to depend increasingly on indigenous science and technology development. The prevalence of small and medium-size enterprises in Taiwan, however, limits industry's R&D capacity; the role of government in promoting science and technology development for industry has therefore become increasingly crucial to economic growth and export competitiveness.

In response to this need, the Executive Yuan (Cabinet) convened the First National Conference on Science and Technology Development. This conference, held in 1978, was attended by some 400 top scientists, engineers, business leaders and government administrators, who deliberated on the directions and strategies of science and technology development. Based on the recommendations of the Conference, the first Science and Technology Development Program was drafted and finalized in 1979 by the National Science Council of the Executive Yuan and was critically reviewed by the government agencies responsible for its implementation. Later, this program was integrated into the Eighth Four-Year Economic Plan (1982-1985). Conferences of this nature were held every four years to review and evaluate the performance of the economy and to make recommendations for future development. The second (1982) Conference recommended the selection of eight strategic areas for technology development: energy, materials, automation, information, electro-optics, biotechnology, food and hepatitis control. The recommendations of the third (1984) Conference led to the formulation of the Ten-Year National Science and Technology Development Plan (1986-1995), a major goal of which is the improvement of the general environment for science and technology development. The strategic priorities in the long-range plan have been expanded from those concerned only with the acceleration of economic growth to also cover improvements in the quality of life (environmental protection and the prevention of diseases and natural disasters) and the upgrading of academic standards (synchrotron radiation and oceanography).

At the recommendation of the first National Conference, a Science and Technology Advisory Committee was established under the Cabinet. The science and technology board, comprised of distinguished scientists from both Taiwan and the U.S., meets annually with relevant experts and officials to review and evaluate performance and perspectives. Recommendations made by the Advisory Committee are submitted to a planning, control, and evaluation department within the Executive Yuan for implementation. By 1988, ten board meetings had been held. On the whole, this process of decision-making, planning and implementation provides a timely, flexible, and pragmatic system for science and technology development. The fourth National Conference on Science and Technology Development was held in early 1991. The main theme of this conference was the management of science and technology development and its interaction with cultural, social and economic dimensions.

In a mixed-market economic system, this decision-making process, which is characterized by broad participation and constant modifications to accommodate the current status of progress, is inclined to forge a "diffusion oriented" science and technology policy. As Ergas describes it, this kind of policy is "closely bound up with the provision of public goods" and "its principal purpose is to diffuse technological capabilities throughout the industrial structure, thus facilitating the ongoing and mainly incremental adaptation to change" (1986). The central government agencies in Taiwan play a dominant role in developing basic and applied science and in promoting science and technology research, the implementation of which they delegate to industrial associations and research organizations in both public and private sectors.

The implementation of the Four-Year Plan (1982-85) and the subsequent Ten-Year Plan (1986-95) may be evaluated in terms of the trends and patterns of R&D expenditures and manpower inputs. According to the annual National Science and Technology Activities Surveys, a project begun in 1979 at the recommendation of the board of the Advisory Committee, total R&D expenditure increased from 0.7-0.8 percent of the GNP immediately before the implementation of the first Plan to 1.06 percent by the end of 1985. Due to the 1985 economic recession, the proportion fell slightly to 1.04 percent in 1986, but rose again to 1.22 percent in 1988 as the economy recovered. Despite significant proportional increases in R&D expenditure during the period 1979-88, the current level is still much too low in comparison with the levels ranging from 2.3 to 3.8 percent for other industrialized countries.

As regards the sources of R&D financing, between 1977 and 1988, about 50 to 65 percent of total R&D spending was undertaken by the government (35 to 46 percent by government agencies, 10 to 25 percent by public enterprises), 32 to 47 percent by private enterprises, and, beginning in 1980, less than 1 percent by the foreign sector (Table 9.5). The heavy dependence on the government to finance R&D activities is obviously due to the lack of research capabilities of the prevailing small- and medium-sized manufacturing enterprises. To realize the planned targets of raising R&D expenditure to 2 percent of the GNP -- 40 percent from government (including public enterprises) and 60 percent from private enterprises -- by 1995, policies to improve the environment for technological innovation and industrial organization of small- and medium-sized enterprises should be stressed.

TABLE 9.5 R&D Expenditure by Types of R&D Organization, 1978-1986

Period	Total Expenditures (Mn.NT$)	R&D Expenditures/GNP (%)	Government (%)	Public Enterprises (%)	Private Enterprises (%)	Private Foundations (%)	Foreign Enterprises (%)
1978	6,407	0.66	44.2	24.3	21.8	4.9	4.8
1979	9,908	0.84	45.5	19.3	26.5	5.2	3.5
1980	10,563	0.72	35.7	24.7	34.4	5.1	0.1
1981	16,414	0.94	35.4	17.3	41.9	5.2	0.2
1982	16,864	0.91	43.5	14.7	38.4	3.0	0.4
1983	19,200	0.94	45.5	15.8	36.9	1.7	0.1
1984	22,444	0.99	45.7	16.5	35.6	1.3	0.9
1985	25,397	1.06	46.3	14.0	36.7	1.9	1.1
1986	28,702	1.04	45.6	14.5	38.7	0.7	0.5
1987	36,780	1.16	38.3	12.6	47.6	0.9	0.6
1988	43,839	1.22	47.1	9.5	43.4	-	-

Source: National Science Council, Taipei, 1989. *Science and Technology Yearbook*.

A breakdown of the types of R&D expenditure shows that spending on basic research increased steadily, from 5.6 percent of the total R&D expenditure in 1979 to 12.4 in 1988, while spending on product development decreased from 66.5 to 40.2 percent. It is apparent from these figures that the government has reallocated R&D resources to higher levels of research with the intention of leaving product development research to the private sector.

With respect to different fields of research, engineering took the lion's share of total R&D expenditure, accounting for 65 percent in 1979 and more than 70 percent in the period of 1984-1988. Agriculture ranked next; its share declined from about 20 percent in the early 1980s to 12 percent in more recent years. The natural and medical sciences maintained their levels of expenditure at 5 to 8 percent, respectively. R&D has clearly been mainly concentrated in areas supporting industrialization.

The integration of science and technology plans into economic plans has shifted emphasis towards promoting innovations in higher education and research institutions. Higher education and research institutions receive funds for basic research from two government sources: the Ministry of Education and the National Science Council. The Ministry provides basic research funding for the graduate schools of the national universities, while the National Science Council distributes grants for basic and applied research to all universities and research institutes on a project-by-project basis.

The promulgation of the Act for Recruitment of High-Caliber Scientists in 1983, which has been vigorously implemented by the National Science Council, has attracted the most talented scientists, both from the indigenous population and overseas Chinese, to do research in the eight priority areas specified by the science and technology plan. The results are clearly reflected in Tables 9.6 and 9.7. From Table 9.6, it can be seen that between 1979 and 1982, R&D manpower more than doubled, from 8,345 to 18,386 persons. Among the then newly recruited personnel, 6.6 percent held a Ph.D. degree, 16.8 percent an M.S. or an M.A. and 76.6 had a bachelor's or junior college degree. Between 1982 and 1988, despite the moderating rate of growth, the percentage of R&D manpower holding a higher degree was significantly larger. Of the 17,051 newly recruited persons, 14.3 percent held a Ph.D. degree, 26.2 percent an M.S. or M.A., and 59.5 percent held a bachelor or junior college degree.

Table 9.7 shows that the share of R&D manpower devoted to the eight priorities increased from 37 percent in 1982 to 52 percent in 1986. Of the R&D manpower in the eight strategic priority areas, more than one-third was allocated to information science and about one-fifth to each of automation and materials science, while the rest was thinly spread among the other five strategic priority areas. Evidently, R&D activities were directed mainly towards accomplishing the planned goal of accelerating economic growth. Taking into account the fact that Taiwan suffers from a scarcity of both natural resources and high-level engineers and scientists, the selected priorities focus on projects dealing with resource-conservation and attainable technology. In information science, efforts are being concentrated on the development of micro and minicomputers, peripheral and interface devices, and software utilizing the Chinese language. Efforts towards automation are devoted to the development of CAD and CAM systems that can be adapted to Taiwan's industrial mode. The development of materials and energy technology emphasizes new materials and conservation. Based on the foundation laid by the First Science and Technology Plan (1982-85), the priorities set in the Second Long-Term Plan (1986-95) are shifting to areas related to the improvement of the quality of life and research capability.

It is evident from the above discussion that Taiwan has allocated increasingly larger amounts of resources to science and technology development since 1980. As a result, a notable increase in the national level of research and development activity has been manifested in major 'output' measures for science and technology -- patents, publications and citations. The number of patents issued to Chinese nationals in Taiwan increased from 2,770

TABLE 9.6 National R&D Manpower by Educational Attainment, 1979-1988

Period	Total	Persons Doctor's	Master's	Bachelor's	Junior College	Doctor's	Master's	Bachelor's	Junior College
1979	8,345	1,074	2,058	4,327	886	12.9	24.7	51.8	10.6
1980	13,656	1,334	3,261	7,706	1,355	9.8	23.9	56.4	9.9
1981	15,633	1,568	3,198	9,279	1,588	10.0	20.5	59.3	10.2
1982	18,386	1,733	3,745	10,806	2,102	9.4	20.4	58.8	11.4
1983	18,580	1,965	3,617	9,324	3,674	10.6	19.5	50.2	19.7
1984	22,354	2,887	4,928	9,983	4,556	12.9	22.0	44.7	20.4
1985	24,600	2,889	5,465	11,258	4,988	11.7	22.2	45.8	20.3
1986	27,747	3,146	6,514	12,485	5,602	11.3	23.5	45.0	20.2
1987	34,055	3,807	7,722	15,740	6,786	11.2	22.7	46.2	19.7
1988	35,437	4,163	8,220	13,231	9,823	11.7	23.3	37.3	27.7
Increment									
1979-82	10,041	659	1,687	6,479	1,216	6.6	16.8	64.5	12.1
1982-88	17,051	2,430	4,475	2,425	7,721	14.3	26.2	14.2	45.3

Source: National Science Council, Taipei, 1989. *Science and Technology Yearbook.*

TABLE 9.7 R&D Manpower and Expenditure in Eight Strategic Priority Areas

| Areas | Manpower (Researcher FTE[a]) ||||| Expenditure (NT$ million) |||||
	1982	1983	1984	1985	1986	1982	1983	1984	1985	1986
Total	18,386	18,580	22,354	24,600	27,747	4,752	6,615	7,740	9,026	12,288
	Percent shares of eight strategic priorities in total R&D									
	36.95	45.57	45.45	44.69	52.21	19.18	28.71	30.35	30.80	31.94
	Percentage shares in eight strategic priorities									
Information	33.81	31.50	41.02	39.29	31.21	29.97	29.15	41.90	35.31	28.30
Automation	19.03	23.34	17.33	18.95	19.57	21.15	21.44	19.16	21.81	17.19
Materials	16.28	18.84	10.01	13.99	18.36	16.90	16.73	11.02	15.36	26.42
Energy	7.94	6.47	7.27	7.31	9.30	11.41	10.61	6.10	8.82	9.97
Electro-optics	5.96	5.89	5.25	5.94	7.68	11.05	10.67	7.56	7.04	5.66
Food technology	9.10	5.89	5.90	6.76	8.28	5.49	4.97	3.85	5.43	6.04
Biotechnology	6.32	7.09	12.23	6.22	4.78	2.44	4.78	7.05	4.93	5.52
Hepatitis control	1.56	0.99	2.33	1.54	0.68	1.60	1.65	3.36	1.31	0.92

[a]FTE = Full Time Equivalent.

Source: National Science Council, Taipei, 1989. *Science and Technology Yearbook.*

in 1980 to 7,448 in 1989, an increase of almost 300 percent in nine years. The number of papers published by Taiwanese researchers in a consistent set of 2,300 journals covered by the *Science Citation Index* rose from 230 papers in 1974 to 1,098 papers in 1985 and then jumped to 2,141 papers in 1988. The high rate of increase in citations may reflect a rapid catching-up in science and technology development.

The effects on the economy of the government's effort to inject scientific and technical resources into the development of new technology can be seen in the rapid growth of export value of technology-intensive electronic and information products, which has surpassed that of labor-intensive textile products and garments to become the largest single industry by 1987. More specifically, the export value of electronic and information products increased from US$3.1 billion in 1981 to US$12.5 billion in 1989, as against that of textile products and garments, which increased from US$4.8 billion to US$10.3 billion over the same period. This rapid development of electronic and information industries has had repercussions on many aspects of the economy. It has not only raised the productivity of all domestic industries but also affected the mode of life and work and, finally, the direction of science and technology development. Most importantly, it inspires hopes and fears and brings large new challenges to the prospects for modern economic growth in Taiwan.

6. Meeting the Future Challenges of Taiwan

The preceding sections have shown that, within the spheres of science, technology and human resource development in Taiwan, rapid and important changes are underway. All these changes have been concentrated in a short time period after the Second World War. One of the most critical features of these changes in the recent decade has been the shift of emphasis to developing indigenous science and technological capacity among a slowly growing but rapidly aging population and labor force. This shift is an inevitably necessary response to changing social, economic and demographic conditions. The challenges brought by this shift interact in complex ways and are different in nature from those that faced Taiwan in the past. Analyses in this study suggest that three major challenges are critical to Taiwan during the next few decades. The success or lack of success in meeting these challenges will have a profound impact on Taiwan's catching-up with the industrialized countries, and hence on the progress towards a mature economy.

The first major challenge facing Taiwan is the slowly growing but rapidly aging population and labor force of the future. The drastic decline in fertility during the past three decades will bring about dramatic changes in age distribution and a decrease in the absolute number of entrants into the labor force in the immediate future. Furthermore, growing affluence is eroding the traditional work ethic in Taiwan. An increasingly larger proportion of workers demands more leisure and fewer hours of work. The postwar upward trend in the labor force participation rates of women above 25 years of age is likely to continue to be a potential source of labor supply. But because of the tendency for women laborers to concentrate mainly in traditionally feminine professions, such as teaching, nursing, social work and clerical work, they would only meet part of the need for future development. All these trends have far-reaching implications for employment planning and economic development. The strategy of raising skills and the technological level of the economy and relocating the labor-intensive industries to other developing countries would, to some extent, reduce the need for labor but not eliminate all unskilled jobs. At the present time, a shortage of local unskilled laborers is already badly felt in the labor-intensive manufacturing and construction industries. The labor market will be even more pressed, particularly for low-skilled construction workers, if the long-term projects for construction of the nation-wide transportation system begin full-swing. Importing foreign workers is one of the possible ways to meet labor shortages. The difficulty will be in coping with the profound social costs involved.

The second challenge is to provide the younger generation with a sound modern education based on Confucian morals. As discussed before, education has been highly valued in Chinese tradition, and the postwar success in economic growth in Taiwan reinforces the demand for more higher education. The growing competition for opportunities in higher education has already forged a rigid entrance examination system that erodes the quality of education in schools at all levels. Furthermore, overemphasis on academic achievement leads to the neglect of social, emotional, moral, and physical development. As a consequence, the current education system would not efficiently inculcate in the younger generation the traditional Confucian values and norms that are appropriate for this rapidly changing society. With Taiwan facing a trend of accelerating educational demand in the future, the implementation of an educational plan to expand the examination system beyond rote memorization will be the most critical to producing a high-quality work force for future modern economic growth.

As Taiwan continues on the path towards industrialization, the science and technology gap between the technologically advanced countries and Taiwan is gradually narrowing. Know-how that may be obtained free or at a low cost from either textbooks or the importation of capital equipment has also quickly been assimilated. Further advances in science and technology will depend much on Taiwan's own ability in research and innovation. Analyses of the previous sections, however, indicate that the recent progress in this respect is largely attributable to the government's direct involvement. The small- and medium-scale entrepreneurs are still reluctant to invest in their human resource and develop R&D capacity because of size constraints. The last, but not least, challenge is, therefore, to improve the economic environment for private entrepreneurs to compete fairly in technological adaptation and innovation. Only in this way, through the development of a more strictly disciplined economy, can Taiwan achieve its goal of joining the ranks of the industrialized nations.

References

Barclay, George W. 1954. *Colonial Development and Population in Taiwan*. Princeton: Princeton University Press.

Blaug, Mark. 1979. "The Quality of Population in Developing, with Particular Reference to Education and Training," in Philip M. Hauser, ed., *World Population and Development, Challenges and Prospects*. New York: Syracuse University Press.

Cheng, Hang-sheng. 1989. "Historical Factors Affecting China's Economic Underdevelopment," in Hung-chao Tai, ed., *Confucianism and Economic Development: An Oriental Alternative*. Washington, D.C.: The Washington Institute Press.

Elvin, Mark. 1973. *The Pattern of the Chinese Past*. Stanford: Stanford University Press.

Ergas, Henry. 1986. "The Importance of Technology Policy," in Partha Dasgupta and Paul Stoneman, eds., *Economic Policy and Technological Performance*. Cambridge: Cambridge University Press.

Greenhalgh, Susan. 1988. "Families and Networks in Taiwan's Economic Development," in Edwin A. Winckler and Susan Greenhalgh, eds., *Contending Approaches to the Political Economy of Taiwan*. New York: Sharpe.

Ho, Pig-Ti. 1962. *The Ladder of Success in Imperial China*. New York: John Wiley & Sons.

Kahn, Herman. 1979. *World Economic Development: 1979 and Beyond*, New York: Morrow Quill.

Kuznets, Simon. 1979. "Growth and Structural Shifts," in Walter Galenson, ed., *Economic Growth and Structural Change in Taiwan: The Postwar Experience of the Republic of China*. Ithaca: Cornell University Press.

Lee, Teng-hui, and Yueh-eh Chen. 1975. *Growth Rates of Taiwan Agriculture 1911-1972*. Taipei: Chinese-American Joint Commission on Rural Reconstruction.

Liu, Paul K. C. 1985. "Human Resource Development and Modern Economic Growth in Taiwan." *Academia Economic Papers* 13: 367-406.

Myers, Ramon H. 1984. "The Economic Transformation of the Republic of China on Taiwan." *The China Quarterly* 99: 500-528.

Pedersen, P. B., L. T. Hu, K. K. Hwang, A. B. Pedersen, P. J. Grey, J. N. Martin, and B. Florini. 1988. *The Reentry of U.S. Educated Scientists and Engineers to Taiwan: An International Cooperative Research Project*. Presented at the International Congress of Psychology, Syndey, Australia, September 1.

Ranis, Gustav. 1981. "Prospects of Taiwan's Economic Development," in Kwoh-ting Li and Tzong-shian Yu, eds., *Experiences and Lessons of Economic Development in Taiwan*. Taipei: Academia Sinica.

San, Gee, and Chen Chao-nan. 1988. *In-service Training in Taiwan, R.O.C.* CIER Economic Monograph Series No. 20. Taipei: Chung-Hua Institution for Economic Research.

Tsurumi, E. Patricia. 1977. *Japanese Colonial Education in Taiwan, 1895-1945*. Cambridge: Harvard University.

10

Living Standards, Labor Markets and Human Resources in Taiwan

Gary S. Fields

1. Introduction

This paper has three general aims: to demonstrate that standards of living have continued to improve during Taiwan's recent economic growth, to analyze the causes of improvements in the 1980s and before, and to discuss some specific issues which are likely to arise and which will need to be resolved in the years ahead.

Section 2 presents evidence on standards of living and economic growth in Taiwan. It is shown that the improvements registered in the 1960s and 1970s continued in the 1980s. As a result, social indicators have improved and poverty rates have fallen. Inequality in Taiwan remains the lowest of any country in the world for which we have data. These improvements are explained by the choice of appropriate development policies, the resultant intersectoral shifts of production, and the consequent growth of demand for labor. The section concludes by speculating on the possibilities for Taiwan to sustain export-led growth in the future.

Section 3 turns to an analysis of the Taiwanese labor market, for it is there that standards of living are to a large degree determined. It is shown that differences in income among households are accounted for in the first instance by differences in the amounts of their labor incomes. This finding directs our attention to the functioning of labor markets and the determination of labor market rewards. I present alternative models of labor markets and conclude that Taiwan's is best characterized as an integrated, well-functioning one rather than a segmented one. Consequently, I see the economic growth that has taken place in Taiwan as having been transmitted throughout the economy by an integrated labor market, with the results that full employment has been maintained, the mix of jobs has improved, and real labor earnings have risen in all major sectors. Section 3 concludes with a look at the future functioning of Taiwan's labor market in the context of the recently-legislated Basic Labor Standards Law and other attempts to regulate the terms and conditions of employment.

Conditions on the supply side of the labor market will also change in the future. Section 4 deals with three of these human resource issues: the supply and demand of skills, the supply and utilization of female labor, and the aging of Taiwan's work force and population. These issues are unified by a common feature: the fact that future changes in living standards in Taiwan are constrained by the economy's ability to mobilize and deploy a sufficient quantity and quality of human resources. Section 4 also analyzes one key government program -- regulations regarding pensions and old-age benefits -- which, though still in flux, is certain to become a leading issue for public policy in the coming years.

A concluding section summarizes the main findings.

2. Poverty, Inequality, Living Standards and Economic Growth

Continued Improvements

Taiwan's record of improving standards of living is an enviable one. This section documents these changes in some detail.

As is well-known, Taiwan's economy has enjoyed sustained economic growth since the 1950s. Per capita national income increased in real terms by approximately a factor of seven from 1952 to 1987 (Tsiang 1986; *Statistical Yearbook of the Republic of China*, various issues).

The benefits of this growth in the 1960s and 1970s were widespread. During that time, full employment was attained, the mix of jobs improved, real wages increased several-fold, absolute poverty fell, and income inequality fell to the lowest level of any economy in the world. See Fei, Ranis, and Kuo (1979), Kuo (1983), and Fields (1984, 1985) for details regarding this earlier period.

In the 1980s, the record remained an enviable one (Table 10.1). In the early 1980s, growth nearly halted in the aftermath of the second OPEC oil-price shock, growth of wages in excess of productivity increases, and decreased investment rates in light of uncertainties brought about by the agreement on Hong Kong between the PRC and the UK. But then, in 1983, the rate of growth accelerated, reaching double digits in 1986 and 1987. GNP per capita was 60 percent higher in real terms by the end of the decade than it was at the beginning.

Growth of this magnitude would be expected to reduce poverty and raise standards of living. Indeed it did. Taiwan has no official poverty line; the

TABLE 10.1 Rate of Growth of GNP Per Capita (in 1981 constant prices)

Year	Growth (%)	Per Capita GNP, in 1981 prices (NT$)
1980	5.1	94,580
1981	3.8	98,179
1982	1.5	99,687
1983	6.2	105,893
1984	8.9	115,356
1985	3.7	119,606
1986	10.4	132,019
1987	10.7	146,111
1988 (preliminary)	5.9	154,783

Source: *National Income in Taiwan Area, the R.O.C. 1988*, Table 2, p. 13.

TABLE 10.2 Proportion of Households With Income Below Specified Amounts in Specified Year (at 1981 constant prices in percentages)

Year	Less than 100 thousand NT dollars	Less than 200 thousand NT dollars	Less than 300 thousand NT dollars
1980	6	35	68
1981	6	37	69
1982	7	36	69
1983	6	33	65
1984	5	28	60
1985	5	27	59
1986	5	24	55
1987	4	21	49

Sources: For Income Data: *Report on the Survey of Personal Income Distribution in Taiwan Area of the R.O.C.*, various years. For Consumer Price Index: *Statistical Yearbook of R.O.C. 1988*, Supplementary Table 32, p. 157.

closest it has is an income cut-off for public assistance of approximately NT$3,000 per household member per month. But because only about 1.5 percent of households are below this line (Chu 1987), a higher poverty line might be preferable. A plot of the income distributions shows that the fraction of poor fell from 1980 to 1987 for *all* poverty lines. To illustrate for three poverty lines (annual household incomes of NT$100,000, 200,000, and 300,000, in 1981 prices), we find that poverty fell from 6 percent of households to 4 percent using the first line, from 35 percent to 21 percent using the second, and from 68 percent to 49 percent using the third (Table 10.2). Thus, Taiwan's already impressive record of poverty reduction continued unabated through the 1980s.[1]

Poverty did not decline uniformly, however. Between 1980 and 1982, when the economy was barely growing, the rate of poverty *increased*. An important point to note, though, is that the slowdown in economic growth in Taiwan in 1980-1982 and the concomitant increase in poverty were much milder than the declines that took place in many other economies at that time. But since 1982 poverty rates have fallen steadily.

Using other social indicators, the data presented in Table 10.3 also show that standards of living continued to improve from 1980 until 1987, the most recent year for which information is available. The infant mortality rate fell from 11.0 per thousand to 5.6. Life expectancy at birth increased from 69.6 to 71.1 for males and from 74.5 to 76.3 for females. The number of hospital beds per person doubled. School enrollment rates remained at virtually 100 percent for children aged 6-14 and increased from 27.0 percent to 35.7 percent for young people aged 15-24. As a result, by 1985, the adult literacy rate had reached 85 percent for females and 96 percent for males (UNICEF 1989). These improvements reflect Taiwan's continued investment in health and human resources.

In sum, by all these measures -- poverty rate, infant mortality rate, life expectancy, hospital beds per capita, school enrollment rates and adult literacy rates -- living standards have continued to improve in Taiwan in the 1980s.

Turning now to income inequality, Taiwan has now, and has had in the past, an extraordinarily equal distribution of income. In fact, among the countries for which we have data from household surveys or censuses, Taiwan's distribution is the *most* equal of any. Measuring inequality by the Gini coefficient, we find that Taiwan's Gini was 0.30 in 1987. No other non-socialist country, developed or developing, has a Gini coefficient that low. To put Taiwan's inequality in perspective, the Gini coefficient for household income is 0.42 in Singapore, 0.50 in Mexico, 0.51 in Malaysia, and 0.57 in Brazil. It should be noted that Taiwan's inequality remains lower than in any other country, even though inequality has been increasing slowly but steadily throughout the 1980s (from 0.277 in 1980 to 0.299 by 1987) (Table 10.4).

TABLE 10.3 Changes in Social Indicators in the 1980s

	Infant mortality (per thousand)	Life expectancy at birth Male	Life expectancy at birth Female	Population per hospital bed	School enrollment rates 6-14 yrs.	School enrollment rates 15-24 yrs.
1980	11.0	69.6	74.5	450	99.5	27.0
1981	10.1	69.7	74.5	412	99.7	30.3
1982	9.0	69.9	74.9	345	99.7	29.5
1983	8.3	69.9	75.1	326	99.9	30.6
1984	7.5	70.5	75.5	304	99.9	31.4
1985	7.4	70.8	75.8	260	99.9	32.5
1986	6.6	71.0	75.9	240	99.9	34.5
1987	5.6	71.1	76.3	228	99.7	35.7

Source: *Statistical Yearbook of R.O.C. 1988*, Tables 19 and 53 and Supplementary Table 7.

TABLE 10.4 Gini Coefficient of Income Among Households

Year	Value
1980	0.277
1981	0.281
1982	0.283
1983	0.287
1984	0.287
1985	0.290
1986	0.296
1987	0.299

Source: *Report of the Survey of Personal Income Distribution in Taiwan Area of the R.O.C. 1987*, Table 4, p. 15.

Improvements in Standards of Living Through Policies Promoting Intersectoral Shifts

Taiwan's development policies have fostered rapid economic growth of a type that has engendered large-scale, broad-based improvements in standards of living. Among the policies responsible for these improvements are Taiwan's extensive land reform from 1949 to 1953, and the consequent equalizing of initial incomes; the labor intensity of growth in both agriculture and industry; and the decentralization of industry. Noteworthy in the history of Taiwan's development policy is the adaptiveness of both planners and entrepreneurs to changing economic circumstances.

When Taiwan's modern growth epoch began in the 1950s, the dominant strategy chosen was import substitution. Policies to achieve this included high tariffs and quantitative restrictions to protect domestic industries, overvalued exchange rates to encourage the use of imported raw materials and intermediate goods, artificially low domestic interest rates to encourage capital deepening, and other measures aimed at increasing production at home of goods that had been previously imported. By around 1960, these policies had succeeded, domestic markets had been satisfied for many products, and the prospects for further import substitution were considerably less rosy. Taiwan's policy makers had thus reached a critical decision point: were they going to continue into "secondary import substitution" or switch to a more export-oriented strategy? The latter was chosen. Fei (1989, pp. 36-37) cites two reasons for this: the negative reason that "secondary import substitution" was not seen as promising, and the positive reason that learning-by-doing by both entrepreneurs and workers rendered economically viable the transition to an external orientation. To effectuate outward-oriented growth, around 1962 exchange rates were made more realistic, interest rates were reformed, and barriers to trade were reduced. Export-led growth took off rapidly and has continued ever since.

The growth phase from 1962 to 1980 is seen differently by different groups of observers. Some (e.g., Ranis 1974, 1979, 1989; Kuo 1983; Krause 1985; Fei 1989) stress that 1962-1980 marked a period of export-led growth with new industries emerging to compete in world markets. These authors emphasize the outward-oriented policies used to achieve these results. Others (e.g., Schive 1985; Bradford 1986; Wu 1986, 1989; and Gereffi 1988) stress that policy measures for import substitution and export promotion existed concurrently. Wu (1989, pp. 71-79) cites import restrictions and tariffs on the import substitution side and rebates of tariffs, low-interest export loans, and the establishment of export processing zones on the export promotion side. To this second group of authors, this policy mix facilitated development by providing domestic entrepreneurs with the opportunities of learning how to export while operating behind protective barriers.

However, by the 1980s, as liberalization proceeded and protection waned, the life cycle of transition to modern economic growth has been largely completed. In the words of Ranis (1989, p. 19): "By 1983, [the government of Taiwan] could take on an entirely new and unprecedentedly ideological appeal by accepting the principle of the survival of the fittest and the discipline of international competition in the domestic market -- a far cry from the xenophobia and autarkic appeal of the early import substitution era." The problems of modern economic growth in a mature economy must now be faced.

The success of these development policies over the years has brought about major intersectoral shifts of production and employment which have been ongoing for the last three decades. Data for the 1980s appear in Table 10.5. For earlier data, see, for instance, Kuznets (1979) and Kuo (1983).

Let us look first at broad sectoral aggregates. One change we observe is a shift from agriculture to manufacturing. Between 1980 and 1987, real GDP in the economy as a whole grew by 69.6 percent. Manufacturing GDP grew at a disproportionately high rate, 88.3 percent. Meanwhile, agricultural production has increased, but barely (8.5 percent increase in seven years). Employment has shifted accordingly. Overall, employment grew by 22.5 percent. But manufacturing employment grew by 32.0 percent, while agricultural employment fell by 0.9 percent. Thus, the rapid economic growth in manufacturing continued to draw labor away from agriculture.

Another structural shift that has taken place is the growth of services and commerce. In both sectors, we find that output and employment both grew at above-average rates: output and employment in commerce grew by 78.1 percent and 37.2 percent, respectively; output and employment in financial and related services grew by 66.2 percent and 64.7 percent, and output and employment in public administration and personal services grew by 81.1 percent and 37.8 percent.

Within manufacturing, major substitutions are taking place. Most pronounced are the decline of textiles and the growth of electronics and electrical products. In 1975, the five two-digit industries with the highest employment levels were textile mill products (20.2 percent of manufacturing employment), electrical and electronic equipment (11.2 percent), plastic products (8.7 percent), food and kindred products (6.3 percent), and apparel and other textile products (6.3 percent). Between 1975 and 1987, the manufacturing sector experienced major shifts: employment in electrical and electronic equipment grew by 5.6 percentage points and plastic products by 2.8 points, while employment fell in apparel and other textile products by 0.1 points, in food and kindred products by 2.0 points, and in textile mill products by 7.7 points. Taiwan's comparative advantage is thus shifting toward more high-tech and less basic manufactured production.

What characterizes these intersectoral shifts in production is that they induce changes in the mix of employment opportunities, enabling workers to leave the lower-paying sectors of the economy and move into better-paying jobs and thereby improve their standards of living. Of the five manufacturing industries, textiles and apparel were the lowest-paying sectors in 1975 (average earnings levels of NT$2,785 and NT$2,357 respectively) and electrical and electronic equipment the highest (average earnings of

TABLE 10.5 Changes in Output and Employment by One-digit Industry

	Real GDP[a] (NT millions) 1980	1987	Growth rate (%)	Employment[b] (thousands) 1980	1987	Growth rate (%)	Monthly earnings[c] (NT dollars) 1980	1987	Growth rate (%)
Agriculture, forestry, fishing	129,974	141,074	8.5	1,277	1,266	-0.9	---	---	---
Mining & quarrying	15,196	14,359	-5.5	65	31	-52.3	11,549	17,940	55.3
Manufacturing	582,802	1,097,584	88.3	2,129	2,810	32.0	8,040	15,220	89.3
Electricity, gas & water	57,075	108,414	90.0	27	35	29.6	13,451	27,437	104.0
Construction	98,634	112,565	14.1	553	554	0.2	8,325	15,942	91.5
Commerce	220,677	392,967	78.1	1,046	1,435	37.2	9,033	16,451	82.1
Transport, storage & communication	95,632	167,281	74.9	387	429	10.9	9,905	17,729	79.0
Finance, insurance, real estate & business service	184,020	305,888	66.2	139	229	64.7	13,529	25,907	91.5
Community, social & personal service	67,539	122,326	81.1	925	1,275	37.8	9,951	15,452	55.3
Overall	1,451,549	2,462,548	69.6	6,547	8,022	22.5	8,957	16,276	81.7

[a]In 1981 constant prices.
[b]"Employment" includes wage and salaried workers, the self-employed, and unpaid family workers.
[c]Nominal earnings.

Source: Real GDP: *Statistical Yearbook of the Republic of China, 1988*, Supplementary Table 9; Table 20, Table 29-30.

NT$3,701). The movement of workers from textiles and apparel to electrical and electronic equipment thus represents an improvement in earning opportunities for workers.

As for services, the major growth areas are expected to be financial, insurance, real estate, and business services, as well as transportation, storage, and communications (CEPD 1986). This is a welcome development, for these sectors offer higher earnings and shorter work hours. Labor in the service sector is disproportionately well-educated and female, which presents both challenges and opportunities; see Section 4.

These processes of structural change are expected to continue, even accelerate, in the future. I would thus forecast the persistence of an intersectoral shift process which elsewhere I have called "high-income sector enlargement" (Fields 1980).

To bring about these changes, Taiwan's planners have been required to face new problems and challenges for development policy. Labor market conditions have become so tight that it is no longer economically attractive for Taiwan to continue to seek to expand production through labor-intensive methods. Making more effective use of the labor force is now the prime necessity of the economy's growth strategy. The main mechanisms for achieving this are the upgrading of skills, capital-deepening, and research and development (Kuo 1983; Ranis 1989; Li 1989). In addition, excess savings have appeared, which needed to be channeled into investment. And then, on the international front, Taiwan has been recording such large trade surpluses that the NT dollar is appreciating, discouraging exports and posing the risk of inflation.

Taiwan's policy-makers have responded to these changed conditions by a three-pronged strategy of "liberalization, internationalization, and systemization." Trade liberalization is being pursued by opening the domestic market through decontrol of imports and lowering of import tariffs. Foreign exchange controls are being relaxed. Relative prices are being freed up. Investment is being liberalized so that the flow of private investment will be guided completely by market forces free of government intervention. State-run firms are being privatized. The export performance requirement and the domestic content requirement which had previously applied to direct foreign investment in Taiwan have been completely abolished. Large-scale public infrastructure projects are under way. In general, the economic system is being depoliticized.

The government of Taiwan has encouraged capital-deepening as a means of raising the productivity of labor and thereby maintaining international competitiveness. This has indeed happened. High rates of physical capital formation and human capital formation have been registered. As a result, in the 1980s, real wages and productivity grew apace of one another.

Continuing investments in physical and human capital, encouraging research and development, and constantly probing for new markets domestically and abroad, hold out great hope for Taiwan's future economic development and continued improvements in standards of living for its people.

The point to be made from this review is that Taiwan's development policies have been changed repeatedly to fit changing circumstances, facilitating intersectoral shifts and permitting improvements in standards of living. The switch from import substitution to export-led growth, intensive in unskilled labor, and then to export substitution favoring more capital- and technology-intensive development has reflected the policy response to changing domestic and world economic conditions. Taiwan's policy-makers, more so than those in most other countries, have been extraordinarily responsive to new events and changing comparative advantage.

Sustaining a Growing Demand for Labor Through Export-Led Growth in the 1990s

For nearly three decades, living standards in Taiwan have been improved through export-led growth. At first, this benefitted workers by increasing the number of manufacturing jobs. Afterwards, once full employment was attained, workers benefitted from rapidly-rising real wages. I am convinced that an export-oriented development strategy remains a viable option for the future.

An outward-oriented trade strategy is predicated on the continued openness of world markets to Taiwan's products. I am quite optimistic about this. Markets for industrial products and consumer electronics have been kept open to Taiwan's goods. In most of the world's markets, the constraints to Taiwan's exports have been not because of barriers to trade in the recipient country (tariffs and quotas) but rather because of limitations on the supply side, that is, in Taiwan's ability to produce products of suitable quality and lower price than the competition. When Taiwan has done this in the past, world markets have proved to be open. Should Taiwan's manufacturers continue in this direction with new product lines in the future, I predict comparable success.

Take the case of automobiles, which Taiwan is now trying to develop for export to North America. I see no reason why Taiwanese manufacturers in the future should not be able to repeat the successes of Toyota, Nissan, and Honda before them, provided that they build an automobile which is truly better than the competition's. And the same is true in a great many other product areas as well.

Given the importance of exports to Taiwan's economic growth, the government is ever-vigilant about the possible closure of overseas markets. At the time Taiwan passed its Basic Labor Standards Law (discussed further below), the then-Minister of Interior, Mr. Po-Hsiung Wu, stated that among the reasons for passing the law were the preservation of American preferential tariff treatment and the winning of the approval of the U.S. media.

A more serious concern, I think, than the closure of developed country markets is competition from below from the "next-NIEs" (or "near-NIEs"). The Philippines, Malaysia, Indonesia, Thailand and many other countries have tried to get into markets which Taiwan once held, and in many cases are succeeding. The reverse side of full employment and rising real wages in Taiwan is labor abundance and lower real wages elsewhere. These other countries are coming to dominate markets in which Taiwan can no longer compete efficiently, such as garments and low-quality, low-tech manufactures. In these product areas, comparative advantage is changing, and Taiwan's manufacturers will have to change with it.

Looking ahead, I would predict that, although economic growth in Taiwan will surely continue, Taiwan will not be able to maintain as high a level of economic growth in the future as was the case in the past. The engine of growth in the Taiwan economy has been the export sector. Certain important industries -- among them textiles, assembly, and light manufacturing -- face increasing competition from other Asian countries aspiring to emulate Taiwan's success. To the extent that the next-NIEs succeed in penetrating these export markets -- and I think they will -- Taiwan's growth will be slowed. It will not, however, be halted. There is every reason to believe that Taiwan's entrepreneurs and planners will continue to do in the future what they have done so well in the past: examine markets for possible new niches and seek to do better than others are now doing.

The ability to adjust rapidly -- getting into profitable markets at the right time and, equally, getting out at the right time -- is essential. Both the government of Taiwan and its industrialists have recognized this and are seeking to respond as quickly and flexibly as possible.

3. Labor Market Issues

The Primary Importance of Labor Incomes

The sources of income inequality in Taiwan have been examined in depth by past researchers. Decomposition studies have been conducted by Fei, Ranis, and Kuo (1978) and by Pyatt, Chen, and Fei (1980). These authors have decomposed the Gini coefficient into "factor inequality weights" associated with wage income, profit income, agricultural income, and all other income.[2]

Table 10.6 presents the results of the decomposition using Taiwan household survey data for 1976. We see that the bulk of inequality of household

TABLE 10.6 Decomposition of Income Inequality in Taiwan, 1976

Income source	Share of total income (1)	Pseudo-Gini coefficient (2)	Factor inequality weight (3)
Wage	.591	.269	.55
Profit	.107	.418	.05
Agriculture	.09	.097	.03
All other (including mixed)	.211	.362	.26
	100%		100%

Sources: Column (1): Pyatt, Chen, and Fei, 1980, Table II. Column (2): Pyatt, Chen, and Fei, 1980, Table III. Column (3): My calculations, using equation (4) in footnote 2.

incomes in Taiwan is accounted for by labor income inequality. The reason for this is that most households in Taiwan receive most if not all of their income from the work they do. These findings direct our attention to the labor market to understand the sources of improvements in economic well-being. This is the subject of the next section.

Improvements in Labor Market Conditions with Economic Growth

What stands out about Taiwan's labor market is how well the economy has done in generating improved labor market opportunities. Nearly full employment has been maintained since the late 1960s -- the unemployment rate has hovered between one and two percent. But with the recession of 1982, the unemployment rate rose, approaching 3 percent by 1985 (Table 10.7). It has since come down, to 1.3 percent by mid-1989. The labor force participation rate has increased as more workers have been drawn into the labor market in response to persistent labor shortages and the opening up of employment opportunities to women. This means that the economy has succeeded not only in creating enough jobs for all who were already seeking employment but in going beyond that to create new job opportunities for an expanding labor force.

Real labor earnings have risen throughout Taiwan's economy. The engine of growth in Taiwan's recent economic development has, of course, been the manufacturing sector. Real earnings of manufacturing workers have doubled approximately every decade. The data show that between 1980 and 1987, real earnings of manufacturing workers in Taiwan increased by more than 50 percent, continuing a prior trend dating back to the 1960s (Table 10.8). Overall, real earnings of manufacturing workers are six times higher now than they were in 1961. Since then, employment in manufacturing has more than tripled. This implies that manufacturing earnings were not pushed up artificially at the expense of employment. Rather, wages in manu-

TABLE 10.7   Unemployment Rate (in percentages)

Year	Value
1980	1.2
1981	1.4
1982	2.1
1983	2.7
1984	2.4
1985	2.9
1986	2.7
1987	2.0

Source: *Statistical Yearbook of R.O.C. 1988*, Table 21, p. 5.

TABLE 10.8   Real Average Monthly Earnings in Manufacturing (in 1986 NT dollars)

Year	Value (NT dollars)
1980	9811
1981	10007
1982	10659
1983	11182
1984	12912
1985	12697
1986	13874
1987	15141

Source: For Nominal Average Monthly Earnings: *Statistical Yearbook of R.O.C. 1988*, Supplementary Table 29-30, p. 156.   For Consumer Price Index: *Statistical Yearbook of R.O.C. 1988*, Supplementary Table 32, p. 157.

facturing were pulled up in response to increased demand in the labor market.

Besides rising real wages, Taiwan's labor market shows improvements in the types of jobs workers were engaged in. The lowest-paying sector in Taiwan's economy is agriculture. Because agricultural jobs pay the least, a fall in agriculture's share of total employment can be regarded as an improvement in employment opportunities. In the 1980s, the share of agriculture in total employment continued its long term decline, decreasing from 20 percent to 15 percent (Table 10.9).

During this same time, the labor force came to be employed in better occupations. The top occupations are professional and technical, administrative and managerial, clerical, and sales. Whereas 32 percent of employed persons were found in these occupations in 1980, by 1987 the share had increased to 35 percent (Table 10.10).

We find too that workers have been employed in better occupational positions. Paid employees earn more than own-account workers and unpaid family workers do. We may therefore regard an expansion of the share of paid employees in total employment as an improvement in labor market conditions. Indeed, such an expansion has occurred, albeit slowly (Table 10.11).

In sum, Taiwan's economy has done extraordinarily well in generating improved employment opportunities, thereby relaxing some of the previous constraints on living standards. In the 1980s, as before, economic growth has increased the derived demand for labor. The continued increase in demand for labor in growing sectors and increased competition for workers throughout the labor market has maintained full employment, raised earnings, and improved standards of living overall.

TABLE 10.9 Agriculture as a Percentage of Total Employment

Year	Percentage
1980	19.5
1981	18.8
1982	18.9
1983	18.6
1984	17.6
1985	17.5
1986	17.0
1987	15.3

Source: Calculated from *Statistical Yearbook of R.O.C. 1988*, Table 20, p. 4.

TABLE 10.10 Professional and Technical, Administrative and Managerial, Clerical, and Sales Occupations as a Percentage of Total Employment[a]

Year	Value (%)
1980	31.8
1981	32.7
1982	33.1
1983	33.4
1984	33.7
1985	34.2
1986	34.3
1987	35.1

[a]"Sales" is listed as "trades."
Source: Statistical Yearbook of R.O.C. 1988, Supplementary Table 23, p. 57.

TABLE 10.11 Paid Employees as a Percentage of Total Employment

Year	Value (%)
1980	64.4
1981	64.3
1982	64.1
1983	63.8
1984	64.4
1985	64.1
1986	64.7
1987	66.7

Source: Calculated from *Statistical Yearbook of R.O.C. 1988*, Supplementary Table 25, p. 58.

Taiwan's Integrated Labor Market: Theory and Evidence

The Taiwan economy has achieved its enviable labor market record by establishing policies conducive to the smooth functioning of labor markets. Supply and demand have largely been allowed to set wages and working conditions for Taiwan's work force. To quote at length from a recent study by Fields and Wan (1989):

The four East Asian NIEs [Hong Kong, Korea, Singapore, and Taiwan] are frequently grouped together in the literature. Indeed, we would note certain similarities about wage-setting institutions among these four economies. Minimum wages exist in some of the countries, but their levels are so low as to be meaningless (Starr 1981). Only in Hong Kong does trade union bargaining over wages take place free of government restraint. Public employees receive wages comparable to those in the private sector, but not higher. Multinational corporations also follow market forces. Labor codes have not prevented employers from making desired labor market adjustments. Thus, at the risk of overgeneralizing, we would conclude that market wage determination has generally prevailed in the East Asian NIEs.[3]

Similar conclusions have been voiced by Kuo (1983, Chapter 4), Hou and Wu (1985, p. 6), Wu (1986, p. 51), Kuznets (1988, pp. S27-29), Deyo (1989), and Li (1989, p. 143), among others.

What these labor market policies have done is to facilitate full employment, followed by a many-fold increase in real earnings among a fully-employed labor force. Real earnings of manufacturing workers are now six times higher in Taiwan than they were in the early 1960s.

Wage differentials between sectors are also smaller in Taiwan than elsewhere. Workers in manufacturing earn about 20 percent more in Taiwan than do workers in agriculture. This contrasts with a manufacturing-agriculture differential of approximately 100 percent in much of Latin America and Africa. Taiwan's labor market is thus much more balanced than are labor markets in these other regions.

The improvements in labor market conditions in Taiwan have taken place in an environment in which supply and demand have generally been free to reign. In this subsection, I demonstrate why Taiwan's labor market is best characterized as an integrated, well-functioning one.

The empirical basis for this claim comes from an examination of intertemporal data on various sectors' growth performances. For simplicity, I shall talk about two productive sectors: a "growing sector" and a "stagnant sector." This dualistic characterization is a stylized version of the pattern of intersectoral shifts described above, with industry in Taiwan expanding rapidly while the agricultural sector grew only slowly in output terms and contracted in employment terms. The growth of the "growing sector" in terms of output generated an outward shift in that sector's demand for labor. The effects of such shifts are analyzed below in three alternative labor market models. The three models are of a segmented labor market, a Harris-Todaro-type labor market, and an unsegmented labor market.

A segmented labor market has two defining characteristics: (1) Real earnings levels differ between segments, and (2) Barriers to mobility prevent earnings levels from equalizing. There may be institutional forces such as minimum wages or collective bargaining keeping earnings levels in some sectors above market-clearing levels. Firms might pay higher-than-market-clearing levels (so-called "efficiency wages") in order to induce employees to work harder, quit less, or be more careful with equipment. Or the mobility of labor from the relatively low-paying sectors to the relatively high-paying ones may itself be restricted by direct migration restrictions, housing limitations, transportation costs, or discrimination.

One version of a segmented labor market model is illustrated in Figure 10.1. The "growing sector" (which may be thought of as "industry") is assumed to have experienced economic growth, which has resulted in the supply and demand for labor intersecting at a relatively high earnings level. By contrast, earnings are lower in the other sector, called the "stagnant sector" (which may be thought of as "agriculture"). Model 1 is constructed on the following assumptions: (1) Each sector has its own market-clearing earnings level, (2) There exist barriers to intermarket mobility so that this earnings differential is not competed away, and (3) Any worker not employed in the high-paying sector takes up employment in the lower-paying sector.

Suppose now that the high-paying sector continues to achieve growth of output, some fraction of which is exported, and that the stagnant sector continues not to. In the sector that experiences economic growth, the demand for labor curve shifts from D to D'. Employment and earnings within that sector both increase, as shown in Figure 10.1. In this way, the growth of output, exports, employment, and wages all coexist in the growing sector, whereas in the stagnant sector, all of these remain constant.

If the segmented labor market model just described is an accurate characterization of how Taiwan's labor market has functioned in the course of economic growth, it would lead to the following empirical prediction: we would expect to find that sectoral output, exports, employment, and wages would grow together at high rates in some sectors and all grow at low or negligible rates in others.

To test the empirical validity of this hypothesis, I have assembled data at the one-digit level for eight economic sectors: mining and quarrying; manufacturing; electricity, gas, and water; construction; commerce; transport, storage, and communication; finance, insurance, real estate, and business services; and public administration, social and personal services.[4]

I have also assembled data at the two-digit level for seventeen manufacturing industries (examples are textile mill products, plastic products, and electrical and electronic equipment).[5]

Growth rates of output, employment, and earnings over the period 1980-1987 are available at the one-digit level; at the two-digit level, we have this information plus the growth rate of exports.[6]

FIGURE 10.1 A Segmented Labor Market with Market-Clearing Earnings Within Sectors

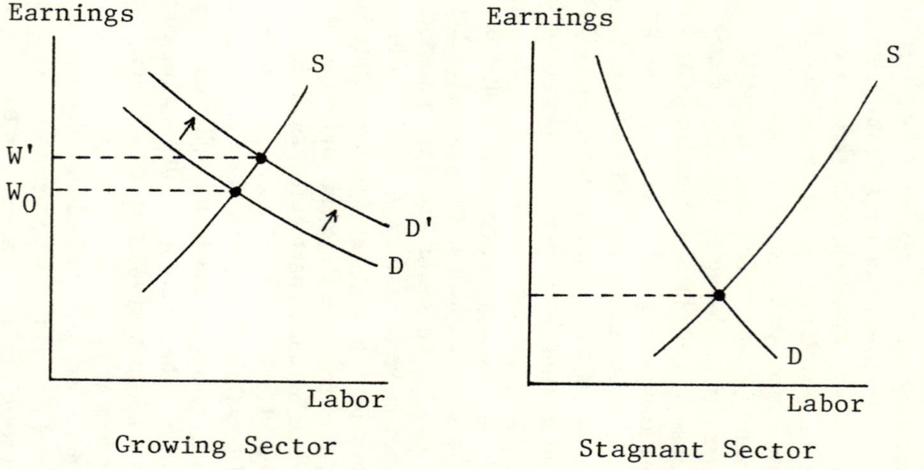

At both the one-digit and two-digit levels, the data do *not* support the segmented labor market hypothesis. The correlation coefficients and the associated statistical significance levels are shown in Table 10.12. The only relationship found to be statistically significant is between output growth and employment growth (statistical significance level = .001 in the one-digit analysis and .007 in the two-digit analysis). This means that labor is a normal input in the productive process, so that when output increases, so too does labor usage. However, the rate of growth of earnings exhibits *no* statistically significant relationship with either the rate of growth of output, the rate of growth of exports, or the rate of growth of employment.

In sum, the correlations predicted from Model 1 are *not* found. This suggests that the particular segmented labor market model posited in Figure 10.1 is not the correct one for Taiwan.

Why? One possibility is that Taiwan's labor market is segmented but in a different way. An alternative segmented labor market model is shown in Figure 10.2. (This is essentially the model of Harris and Todaro, 1970.) In this model, earnings in the growing sector are set at higher-than-market-clearing levels by a union, a minimum wage authority, or some other institutional force. Given the high wage, workers queue up for the available jobs, resulting in search unemployment.[7]

If an economy with these characteristics experiences export-led economic growth of a labor-intensive type, the demand curve for labor in the growing sector will shift from D to D'. Employment will increase directly with faster output growth, but earnings levels within that sector will remain unchanged. Thus, in this model, higher output growth will lead to higher employment growth but not to higher earnings growth.

The empirical evidence presented in Table 10.12 is consistent with this, so the problem encountered with Model 1 is overcome by Model 2. However, another problem remains: Model 2 predicts rising unemployment rates in the growing sectors, and this has not happened in Taiwan. As noted above,

TABLE 10.12 Economic Growth and Changing Labor Market Conditions, 1980-1987

Correlation between	One digit analysis Correlation coefficient	Significance level	Two-digit analysis Correlation coefficient	Significance level
Output growth and employment growth	+.92	.001	+.63	.007
Output growth and earnings growth	+.37	.37	+.18	.50
Earnings growth and employment growth	+.42	.30	+.03	.89
Export growth and employment growth			+.21	.40
Export growth and earnings growth			-.02	.95

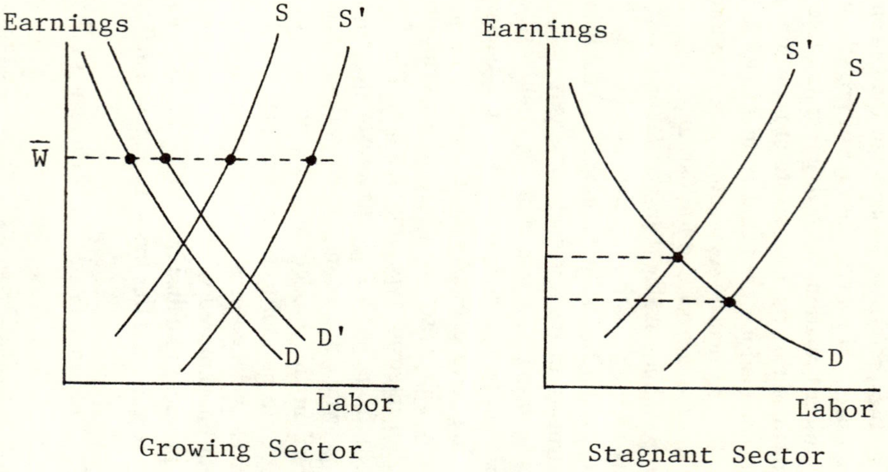

FIGURE 10.2 A Segmented Labor Market with Search Unemployment

except for a brief recession, open unemployment has been very low throughout the course of Taiwan's economic development. Model 2 cannot be the correct empirical characterization either. A different model is needed.

The model of Figure 10.3 is constructed on the assumption of the absence of labor market segmentation. In such an integrated labor market, earnings are determined by supply and demand in both sectors and earnings are equalized across the two (at level W^*).

Using this model, suppose that the economy continues to grow and that as a result the growing sector's labor demand curve shifts from D to D'. If the labor market is very tight, employers will be in keen competition with one another for labor. Firms in the growing sector will offer higher earnings to try to increase employment.

In an integrated and well-functioning labor market, the demands expressed for workers in one sector of the economy will have effects in other sectors. What happens in this case is that the supply curve of labor to the stagnant sector shifts leftward from S to S', because some workers are induced to leave that sector and take up jobs in the growing sector. Employers in the stagnant sector have to pay more if they are to retain their work forces. Those firms which are unwilling or unable to do this must either contract in size or go out of business entirely.

In this way, heightened competition for workers in an integrated labor market leads to a generalized increase in earnings *throughout* the economy. These sectoral earnings growth rates would be found to be *uncorrelated* with sectoral employment, output, or export growth. This is exactly what has happened in Taiwan -- which is why the integrated labor market model (Model 3) is arguably the better characterization of how Taiwan's labor market evolved in the 1980s.[8]

Summing up, the Taiwanese labor market is better characterized as integrated and well-functioning rather than segmented and pathological. The major institutional interventions that segment labor markets in other countries -- minimum wages, unions, public sector pay policies, multinational corporations, and labor codes -- have little distortionary effect in Taiwan. The Taiwan labor market is almost a textbook case of a smoothly-operating labor market in which employment and earnings reflect the scarcity value of labor.

The Future of Taiwan's Labor Market

Will the smooth functioning of labor markets in Taiwan continue into the future? There is good reason to expect that the labor market will remain tight in the 1990s and that improvements in labor market conditions will therefore continue, provided that present policies are continued. This

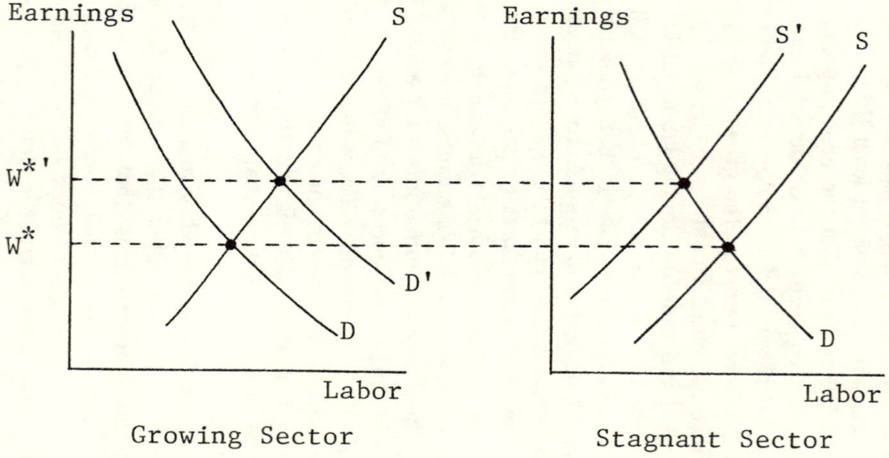

FIGURE 10.3 An Integrated Labor Market with Market-Clearing Earnings

presupposes that no major change in labor market policy takes place in Taiwan. If it does, and there is some risk that it might, labor market conditions might slacken. In 1984 the Taiwan government passed a far-reaching Basic Labor Standards Law, modifying or superseding several earlier laws.

The stated purposes of the new law were "to provide minimum standards of labor conditions, protect workers' rights and interests, strengthen labor-management relationship, and to promote social and economic development." These are laudable goals. They are also issues which the government of Taiwan takes extremely seriously.

At issue are whether the law will be enforced and, if so, if it will help achieve its stated goals. Provisions regarding labor relations and protective labor legislation are taken up now; discussion of the economic security aspects of the law is deferred until Section 4.

The percentage of employees who are members of unions in Taiwan is 34 percent, compared to less than 20 percent in the United States. Moreover, the rate of unionization in Taiwan is rising (it is now two-thirds higher than it was in 1970), whereas union membership in the United States has fallen over the same period of time (by about one-fourth). Labor unions in Taiwan are coordinated by the Chinese Federation of Labor, to which all unions must belong. Only 24 unions (out of 3,076 in all) belong to the Taiwanese Association for Labor Movement, which is an independent association of unions. Those in the Chinese Federation of Labor receive most of their funding from government grants and hardly ever call strikes. Consequently, labor actions in Taiwan, although now more numerous by Taiwan standards, are by no means serious by international standards (Deyo, 1989, Chap. 2).

An industrial or craft union is required in any factory or geographic area with more than thirty adult workers (Union Act of 1929, as amended). In addition, all workers over the age of 16, male or female, have the right and obligation to join the labor union for the industry or craft in which they work, except in the public or quasi-public sector. However, the law provides no penalty for non-adherence, and in fact the law is not adhered to. If it were, we would find unionization rates approaching 100 percent, which we do not.

Why do workers not form unions or join existing ones? The simplest plausible answer is that they do not find it worthwhile to do so. The underlying economic forces in Taiwan assuredly work against strong unions. Well-known in labor economics (e.g., Ehrenberg and Smith 1988) are the four "Hicks-Marshall Laws of Derived Demand" which determine when the own-wage elasticity of demand for a category of labor is apt to be high and consequently when the bargaining power of a union is apt to be low:

1. When the price elasticity of demand for the product being produced is high;
2. When other factors of production can be easily substituted for that particular category of labor;
3. When the supply of other factors of production is highly elastic; and
4. When the cost of employing that category of labor is a large share of the total costs of production.

In a highly-open economy such as Taiwan's, which relies on labor-intensive production methods for a large fraction of output, these conditions are likely to hold. It would be expected, therefore, that unions would have only limited ability to raise wages much above market levels without inducing substantial unemployment among union members.

Another reason that the labor movement is not strong in Taiwan is that the unions are covered by exclusive jurisdiction clauses; that is, only one union has jurisdiction over workers in a particular work place, industry, or geographic area. Given the lack of competition among unions for the right to represent a particular group of workers, and given that most union leaders are appointed by the government, the exclusive jurisdiction clause can become a tool for enterprises to establish docile unions rather than a means by which workers can choose to be represented by the strongest possible organization.

Yet another reason for weak unions in Taiwan is that unions have very limited means for improving the wages and working conditions of their members. The Chinese Federation of Labor does not enter into bargaining on behalf of workers, which implies that individual unions are on their own. This is one of the reasons that only 0.2 percent of firms have signed collective bargaining agreements with their unions. In addition, the threat of a strike -- the major weapon of unions -- is all but absent. This is despite the fact that previous limitations on strikes appear to have been revoked. (The prohibition of strikes under martial law was lifted in 1987 and restrictions on strikes under the National Mobilization Act are seldom applied.) However, mediation is required in the event of a labor dispute. If this breaks down, the authority in charge can refer the dispute to compulsory arbitration, the decision of which cannot subsequently be appealed. Lockouts and strikes are outlawed during arbitration.

A somewhat different list of reasons for weak unions is given by San (1989). He cites suppression of the labor movement by the ruling KMT party, the impassiveness of the worker toward unionization, the prevalence of small and medium size enterprises, the high rate of labor turnover, and the competitiveness of the labor market.

Because of these various economic forces and institutional limitations on union power, it would not be surprising to find that unions have had little effect on the wages and conditions of employment of workers in Taiwan.

Econometric evidence shows that indeed this is the case. One study by Lin (1989) found that union employees in Taiwan earn only 0.3 percent to 1.9 percent more than do non-union employees. Another study by Lin (1988) found that the Basic Labor Standards Law had no effect on wages or working hours during the period 1980-1988. Thus far, unions have made little difference to labor market conditions, and the same is true of the Basic Labor Standards Law.

There are signs, though, that the labor movement is becoming more militant. Strikes have occurred in the Taiwan Railroad Company, in many local bus companies, in some utility industries, and in certain public enterprises. Typically, these have been over worker rights issues rather than wages. For example, workers have struck over whether companies have the right to transfer them unilaterally from one location to another. These work disruptions are noteworthy precisely because they have been so infrequent. Whether they will grow into something more substantial is hard to foretell. But if the experience of the Republic of Korea is any guide, the probability is high that labor relations in Taiwan will become more confrontational and less stable.

Overall, one observer has concluded thus: "The termination of the martial law and the revision of the Labor Dispute Law [in Taiwan] have done little to change the legality of unionization and strikes. We are therefore forced to search for the true cause of the recent labor movement. The best reason that we can find is the political democratization that started in 1987 and the ending of authoritarian rule in 1988. What we are less certain about is the impact of the labor movement on the function of the labor market and eventually on economic development." (Chang 1989, p. 17).

Looking ahead, one can imagine a number of possible scenarios. One is a scenario of escalating conflict, growing union militancy, increasingly frequent work disruptions, more employer lockouts, and repression of the labor movement by the State -- in short, a highly confrontational pattern. Another is a more harmonious relationship, with employers, workers, and the State continuing to regard themselves as partners in the economic development effort but adapting their behavior to changed circumstances. In my view, the harmonious approach in a highly competitive labor market has served the people of Taiwan extremely well in the past -- which is the best reason to stay the present labor relations course in the future. Will it happen? Labor unrest in Taiwan reportedly is on the wane, which augurs well for the future.

Turning now to protective labor legislation and workers' rights issues, we find that the 1984 Basic Labor Standards Law has come under attack, not only from industrialists but also from independent economists in think-tanks and universities. Maintaining a flexible, competitive labor market is essential to facilitating the kinds of adjustments Taiwan's economy will be called upon to make in the years ahead. If regulations regarding layoffs, dismissals, severance pay, and other workplace issues impede the economy's ability to respond to overseas challenges and opportunities, Taiwan will suffer. The last thing Taiwan wants to do is to introduce rigidities of the type that have produced hysteresis in Europe.

Whether this will happen is an open question, in part because of widely variable enforcement of the programs and protections under the Basic Labor Standards Law. For some, there is little problem. For example, the injury compensation provisions under the law appear to be complied with. According to a study by Lin (1989), only 0.14 percent of collective labor-management disputes were caused by injury compensation cases. For other programs, though, non-enforcement is a serious issues. Minimum wages (in the form of a Basic Wage Scale) have been declared. Their amounts have become more sizeable than in the past, and now amount to nearly half the average wage. Yet minimum wages do not receive attention in public discourse in Taiwan, for the simple reason that they are a non-issue: no employer has ever been reported to have been punished for violating the scale (Chang 1989, p. 20).

Mention may be made as well of an obvious loophole in the guaranteeing of workers' rights. Workers become eligible for benefits and protections only after a certain length of time on the job. Firms apparently are dismissing workers just before they become eligible for benefits and then rehiring them afresh, still without benefits. Out-sourcing is another commonly-practiced method of evading the law.

Taiwan will have to strike a balance between adversarial or cooperative structures, between regulatory or market approaches, and between protective or flexible arrangements. A healthy debate on these issues lies ahead.

4. Human Resource Issues for the 1990s

The continued improvement of standards of living in Taiwan in the 1990s will depend importantly on the economy's ability to supply adequate human resources to meet the demands of employers. By all accounts, the labor force will have to be increasingly skilled; labor shortages will have to be met by inducing women to enter the labor force and by discouraging employers from exercising some of their traditional discriminatory practices against women; and provisions will have to be made to lure more prime-age persons into the work force to support an ever-aging population. These issues, along with the related question of how to fund adequate living standards for retirees, are treated in turn in the balance of this section.

Supply of and Demand for Skills

Taiwan has invested heavily in human capital throughout the post-World War II period. These investments have facilitated improvements in standards of living in two major ways: by assuring functional literacy and numeracy at the lower end of the distribution and by expanding the supply of educated and technically-trained personnel at the upper end.

According to the Constitution of the Republic of China, all children from 6 to 12 years of age are required to receive free elementary education. In 1968, the period of free education was extended from 6 years to 9 years, including elementary school and junior high school. Although junior high school is not compulsory, the school enrollment rate is 93.8 percent in the 12-17 year age category. Beginning in 1993, the period of free education will be extended from 9 years to 12.

Along with this numerical expansion is attention to educational quality. The average number of students per teacher in elementary school fell from 42 in 1968 to 31 in 1987. At the junior high level, the reduction has been from 33 students per teacher in 1968 to 22 in 1987.

The result of these investments in education has been a marked improvement in the quality of Taiwan's labor force at the lower end. The percentage of employed workers with no schooling decreased in the 1980s from 10 percent to 7 percent, and the percentage illiterate from 7 percent to 5 percent (Table 10.13).

TABLE 10.13 Percentage of Employed Workers With No Schooling[a] (percentage illiterates in parentheses)

Year	Value (%)
1980	9.8 (6.7)
1981	9.4 (6.5)
1982	8.9 (6.3)
1983	8.9 (6.5)
1984	8.6 (6.2)
1985	8.2 (6.0)
1986	8.0 (5.6)
1987	7.1 (5.1)

[a]Includes illiterates and self-educated.

Source: *Statistical Yearbook of R.O.C. 1988*, Supplementary Table 25, p. 61.

At the upper end, the government aims to meet the seemingly insatiable demand of private employers for well-educated labor with vocationally-useful skills. Taiwan has rapidly increased the numbers of vocational schools and junior colleges. Two-thirds of students are in vocational schools. The emphasis on vocational education is also indicated by the growth of the share of secondary vocational education in the government's budget. Interestingly, although the higher education system has been expanded, it has been at a below-average rate. The share of higher education in total educational expenditures has fallen, from 27.3 percent of the education budget in 1971 to 21.4 percent in 1986.

These investments in education have entailed an extraordinary commitment of resources. Taiwan spent 5.1 percent of its GNP on education in 1988, much higher than the average for middle-income countries. More than 80 percent of Taiwan's education expenditures were made by the public sector. Moreover, international comparisons of student achievement show that the students in Taiwan perform much better on standardized tests than do students in the United States (Stevenson *et al.* 1986). This shows that Taiwan is genuinely succeeding in educating its people, which bodes well for improvements in standards of living in the future.

At present, Taiwan is encountering an imbalance between the skills offered by workers and employers' demands for them. The *Report on the Manpower Utilization Survey, Taiwan Area, R.O.C., 1988* has defined labor as underutilized if a worker falls into one of the following categories: (i) unemployed; (ii) employed but working under 40 hours and willing to increase working hours; (iii) employed below a certain income level; (iv) employed in an occupation not matching the worker's educational attainment. According to this survey, the underutilization rates by level of education were: primary school, 17.1 percent; junior high school, 11.9 percent; senior high school, 18.8 percent; vocational school, 32.2 percent; junior college, 37.1 percent; college and graduate school, 28.8 percent. The reason for the higher reported rates of underutilization among those with greater educational attainments is that their employment is judged to be in occupations below those for which they are qualified. Within this group, there is a clear distinction between graduates in scientific and technical subjects, for whom the demand is very great, and graduates in the arts and the humanities, for whom job opportunities are much more limited.

According to a DGBAS survey in 1987, 66 percent of manufacturing firms reported having labor shortages. Those manufacturing industries with the most acute shortage rates are textiles, apparel and other textile products, plastic products, and electrical and electronic equipment. In construction, 86 percent of firms report labor shortages.

According to a Ministry of Economy survey in 1988, the main labor shortages are in the unskilled labor market. Junior high school, senior high school, and vocational school graduates are reported to be in the shortest supply.

This suggests that three groups be distinguished: highly-educated labor with general skills, highly-educated labor with technical skills, and unskilled labor. At present, those in the first category are in excess supply, whereas those in the latter two categories are in excess demand.

Looking ahead, this structural mismatch will probably become a more severe problem unless steps are taken soon to deal with it. One way of resolving the shortage of educated labor with needed skills is through domestic educational policy and further expansion of scientific and technical faculties in universities, colleges and junior colleges, and secondary vocational schools. Another is by encouraging the return of overseas Chinese with the desired qualifications. Countries such as the United States are now the beneficiaries of large influxes of Taiwanese with valuable skills in such areas as engineering, computer science, and economics. Many of these people study in the United States and remain after graduation because labor market opportunities are so favorable for them. But if Taiwan's economy continues to grow by expanding those activities which make intensive use of highly-skilled and technical personnel, earnings and other conditions of employment in Taiwan might rise to the point where many of these overseas Chinese might return home. Indeed, there are already signs that such a "reverse brain drain" has begun.

Mention should also be made of possible immigration from Hong Kong. Events in Tiananmen Square in the summer of 1989 have cast doubt on the security of Hong Kong after 1997. If Hong Kong's best-educated and best-skilled people cast about for a secure home, Taiwan will face a unique opportunity to receive an exceptionally-talented group of people. Only time will tell whether this eventuality actually comes to pass.

At the lower end of the skill ladder, changes are needed. Taiwan may need to revise its immigration policy. It is illegal now for employers to hire immigrants, whether from mainland China or from other countries. In fact, though, immigrants from other Asian countries are known to be working in Taiwan in large numbers. The Council of Labor Affairs estimates that there exist somewhere between 10,000 to 30,000 foreigners, mostly from Southeast Asia, working illegally in Taiwan at the present time. Newspaper reports place the number of illegal foreign workers at about ten times that number. Regularizing these workers' immigration statuses and regulating the flow would be preferable to pretending that immigration is not going on. Taiwan's immigration policy needs to be seriously revised in light of labor market realities, now and in the years ahead. For some theoretical speculations on the subject (but little data), see Chang (1988).

Utilization of Female Labor

One factor responsible for continued economic growth and improved standards of living is the rising rate of utilization of women in the Taiwan economy. From 1980 to 1988, the total labor force participation rate increased from 58.3 percent to 60.2 percent. During this time, the male labor force participation rate decreased from 77.1 percent to 74.8 percent, whereas the female labor force participation rate increased from 39.3 percent to 45.4 percent. Therefore, the increase in the rate of labor force participation in the 1980s was due entirely to an increase in the labor force participation of women.[9]

Among the reasons cited in the literature for decreasing labor force participation of males in Taiwan are the continued expansion of educational opportunities, which increases the share of young men in school, thereby postponing males' age of entry into the labor force, and continued improvements in life expectancy, which increases the 65+ population. Both push-side and pull-side factors have caused the increase in females' labor force participation. On the push-side are the decrease in the fertility rate, changing social attitudes toward women's work, improvements in home-production technology, and the increase in females' educational attainment. On the pull-side are the labor-intensity of economic development (for both sexes) and the rapid growth of female-intensive industries.

This last point merits further attention. Studies by Liu (1984) and Wu (1988) have shown that those sectors of the economy which traditionally have employed large numbers of women have expanded most rapidly. Those sectors include manufacturing industry, commerce, business services, and other services.

In the future, rising female labor force participation can facilitate the growth of the economy by alleviating labor shortages. The recent trend toward greater female labor force participation may be coming to an end, though. Between 1987 and 1988, the rate of female labor force participation fell from 45.8 percent to 44.5 percent, reversing the previous secular increase. It is not clear at present whether the recent trend toward greater equality between the sexes will continue in the decade ahead.

Population Aging and Retirement Income Policy

Taiwan's population has been aging. Whereas the ratio of elderly (65 years and over) to prime-age people (15-64) was 4.8 percent in 1961, that ratio has risen to 5.2 percent in 1971, 6.9 percent in 1981, and 8.4 percent in 1987. Demographers expect that the rate of population aging will accelerate in the future.

Population aging has important implications for Taiwan's retirement income system which, in the last few years, has been very much in flux. Until 1984, the most important source of retirement income was the Labor Insurance Law. This law requires that pensions be provided to workers in covered employment. In 1988, six million workers were in jobs covered by labor insurance, out of a labor force of somewhat more than eight million. Approximately 60 percent of persons aged 65 and over received old-age benefits under the Labor Insurance Law.

Old-age benefits consist of medical insurance and a retirement benefit, paid on a lump-sum basis. The retirement benefit amounts to one month's earnings for each of the first 15 years of service, plus two months' earnings for each additional year of service, up to a maximum benefit of 45 months' earnings. Employers pay 80 percent of the premium for this insurance and workers 20 percent. For the self-employed, the insured pays 60 percent of the premium and the government the remaining 40 percent.

The Basic Labor Standards Law of 1984 stipulated that employers provide an additional retirement pension to any worker who has served in the same enterprise unit for fifteen years or more, who has worked twenty-five years or more overall, and who has reached age 55. This pension is payable on a lump-sum basis. The amount of the benefit is equal to the worker's final-year monthly wage multiplied by the number of pension points, defined as follows. A worker who retires with exactly fifteen years of service receives thirty pension points. He or she receives one additional pension point for each additional year of service, up to a maximum of forty-five points (i.e., a cash retirement benefit of forty-five months' wage).

To finance these pensions, employers are required to contribute reserves to a retirement fund. There is some question, though, as to whether firms are actually complying. San (1987) collected data from ninety-nine firms, mostly in manufacturing. His survey showed that only nineteen firms have made the full contributions required of them. Ko (1989) reports that only 11 percent of firms made the required contributions under the Basic Labor Standards Law in 1988.

This pension system has a number of defects. One is that pensions are lump-sum payments rather than annuities. An annuity is a promise to make regular payments to a retiree for as long as he or she lives. Annuities provide retirees with insurance against the economic risk of living too long and thereby outliving their resources. Replacing lump-sum payments by actuarially-fair annuities with the same expected present value would have the same total cost while at the same time providing retirees with insurance against the economic consequences of living too long. Such a change in Taiwan's retirement income system merits serious attention.

Other problems with the present system are touched upon in two other papers by San (1988, 1989). One concern is that workers receive pensions only after fifteen years in the firm. In Taiwan, 98 percent of enterprises are small or medium size. The expected life of these enterprises is well under fifteen years. Therefore, the requirement that pensions be paid only after fifteen years of service leaves a large fraction of Taiwan's workers without pension coverage. Another problem is that the fifteen year stipulation imposes the heaviest pension obligations on firms with the most stable work forces -- in all likelihood, precisely those firms that offer the highest wages and best working conditions to begin with. Yet another problem is that the required contributions take no account of the firm's past pension funding. Consequently, some firms will overfund their pension funds and some underfund them. Another concern is that pension obligations are being imposed upon firms retroactively; that is, workers already on the payroll who subsequently retire are entitled to receive pension benefits based on their years of service since joining the firm, not the years of service since the enactment of the Basic Labor Standards Law. Finally, because pension benefits are calculated as a fraction of the last year's earnings, firms cannot forecast their obligations accurately and set aside actuarially-appropriate contributions.

The type of pension plan which Taiwan has set up is called a defined benefit pension -- that is, the benefits are determined according to a defined formula. These benefits are financed by employer contributions. The possible disparity between promised benefits and required contributions is enormous. Indeed, by 1985, the Old Age, Survivors', and Disability Benefit Payments Fund was already paying out more than it took in, leading to predictions that the fund will soon be depleted (Cheng 1987, p. 532). For this reason, it might be better for Taiwan to move to a so-called defined contribution pension scheme. This is where the contribution rate is specified, and the subsequent pension benefit is determined on an actuarial basis from the amount contributed, after allowing for interest accumulations. One advantage of this would be to assure that future pension benefits will be fully funded. Also, this would internalize the costs and benefits of pensions into a single decision, and perhaps help avoid the mistake the United States has made in giving older people the false impression that because they have contributed to the Social Security system, they have paid fully for all of the old-age benefits they are receiving.

The aging of Taiwan's labor force will accelerate in the future. For this reason, serious attention should be given now to the specific benefit and financing provisions of the pension law, since they will gain in importance as a larger fraction of Taiwan's population reaches retirement age and qualifies for these benefits.

5. Conclusions

Taiwan's economy has continued to raise standards of living. Social indicators have improved. Poverty has continued to fall. Inequality has remained low.

These improvements have continued even through the difficult times of the 1980s, during which many newly-industrializing economies have fared much less well. Proximate determinants for Taiwan's success include the economy's ability to sustain macroeconomic growth with only a minimal recession and the continued participation of the poor in the growth process, primarily through the labor market. Underlying determinants include appropriate policies with respect to development strategies, labor market institutions and human resource utilization.

Taiwan's macroeconomic policies have continued to foster rapid economic growth. Past phases of import substitution industrialization and promotion of labor-intensive exports have given way to an increasingly skill-, capital-, and technology-intensive development path. While there is no good reason to expect that economic growth will halt, I would forecast that because of competition from the next-NIEs, Taiwan will not be able to maintain as high a level of economic growth in the future as was the case in the past.

In the 1980s, as before, economic growth has increased the derived demand for labor. The continued increase in demand for labor in growing sectors and increased competition for workers throughout the labor market have maintained full employment, raised real earnings, improved standards of living, and lessened poverty. Taiwan's labor market is better characterized as integrated and well-functioning rather than segmented and pathological. In all likelihood, the labor market will remain tight in the 1990s and improvements in labor market conditions will therefore continue. However, there is now considerable pressure for additional protective labor legislation and greater call for attention to workers' rights. It is possible, therefore, that the labor market regulations now being promulgated under the 1984 Basic Labor Standards Law may be pushed further than is warranted by competitive forces, jeopardizing both labor market progress and industrial peace.

Intersectoral shifts of production and employment have been sustained in the 1980s and will continue in the years ahead. As manufacturing exports grow and agricultural production increases but at a slower rate than total production, employment will continue to shift away from agriculture and toward manufacturing and services. Within manufacturing, major substitutions are taking place. Taiwan's comparative advantage is shifting toward more high-tech and less basic manufactured goods production. These intersectoral shifts induce changes in the pattern of employment, enabling workers to leave the lower-paying sectors of the economy and move into better-paying jobs, thereby improving their standards of living. Such shifts should be facilitated to the maximum extent possible in the years ahead.

Educational policy has facilitated improvements in standards of living, both by assuring functional literacy and numeracy at the lower end of the distribution and by expanding the supply of educated and technically-trained personnel at the upper end. Graduates of higher education with training in the arts and the humanities are experiencing difficulties in finding jobs commensurate with their training. On the other hand, graduates in technical areas find fierce competition for their services. Perhaps the mix of subject areas should be changed accordingly. At the lower end of the job ladder, shortages of unskilled workers at prevailing wage rates are widely reported. Either wages will have to rise, or the supply of unskilled labor will have to be expanded, or both. Policies for the 1990s with respect to immigrants, female labor, and older persons will have to be carefully considered to assure that labor market opportunities are maximized and bottlenecks to economic expansion minimized.

As the population continues to age, increasing demands will be placed on Taiwan's retirement income system. Social insurance programs are sure to acquire ever-greater importance in the future as the economy gets richer and these programs become more affordable. The pension system established thus far has some serious design problems. If these are not rectified in the near future, old-age economic security may be more a mirage than a reality. In other areas of social insurance, Taiwan would do well to study other countries' programs, borrow their best features, and avoid others', and its own, mistakes.

For nearly three decades, Taiwan has prospered through export-led growth. Such a strategy will probably be appropriate for the future. But an outward-oriented trade strategy is predicated on the continued openness of world markets to Taiwan's products (about which I am quite optimistic) and the continued competitiveness of Taiwan's products vis-a-vis other producers (which will probably suffer erosion in certain sectors from the next-NIEs). Shifting in accordance with changing comparative advantage is and will continue to be essential.

Notes

I am deeply indebted to Gustav Ranis for helpful comments, to Henry Wan for many insightful discussions, and to Ping-Lung Hsin for invaluable research assistance.

1. Unfortunately, the data are not presented in disaggregated enough fashion to permit calculation of other, more comprehensive, poverty meas-

ures such as the Sen index or the P_α class. These two measures include, in addition to the fraction of the population which is poor, the average income shortfall of the poor, and the extent of income inequality among the poor. These latter two components cannot be calculated reliably from published tabulations.

2. The decomposition formula used is:

$$G = G_1^* \Phi_1 + G_2^* \Phi_2 + G_3^* \Phi_3 + G_4^* \Phi_4, \tag{1}$$

where G is the Gini coefficient, G_i^* is the "pseudo-Gini" (F-R-K terminology) or "concentration ratio" (P-C-F terminology) of the i-th income source, and Φ_i is the share of that income source in total income. The "pseudo-Gini" or "concentration ratio" is equal to the product of the true Gini for that income source (G_i) and a relative correlation coefficient R_i

$$G_i^* = G_i R_i. \tag{2}$$

For each income source, the relative correlation coefficient R_i is the ratio of two other correlations:

$$R_i = \text{cor}(Y_i, \rho)/\text{cor}(Y_i, \rho_i), \tag{3}$$

where $\text{cor}(Y_i, \rho)$ is the coefficient of correlation between a household's income from the i-th source and its rank in the total income distribution and $\text{cor}(Y_i, \rho_i)$ is the coefficient of correlation between a household's income from the i-th source and its rank in the distribution of income from that same source. Substituting (2) and (3) into (1) and dividing through by G, we obtain

$$100\% = FIW_1 + FIW_2 + FIW_3 + FIW_4, \tag{4}$$

where $FIW_i = \Phi_i G_i [\text{cor}(Y_i, \rho)/\text{cor}(Y_i, \rho_i)]/G$. The FIWs are the so-called "factor inequality weights" of wage income, profit income, agricultural income, and all other income respectively.

3. Reprinted with permission from *World Development* 17(9), "Wage-Setting Institutions and Economic Growth," 1989, Pergamon Press plc.

4. Sources: *Statistical Yearbook of R.O.C.*, 1988, Tables 20, 29, and 30 and Supplementary Table 9. *Monthly Statistics of R.O.C.*, No. 268, 1988, Table 11. *Monthly Statistics of Exports and Imports, Taiwan Area, the R.O.C.*, April, 1988, Table 10.

5. Sources: *National Income of R.O.C.*, 1987, Chap. 4, Table 2. *Monthly Statistics of Exports and Imports, Taiwan Area, the R.O.C.*, April, 1988, Table 10. *Statistical Yearbook of R.O.C.*, 1988, Supplementary Tables 2 and 31.

6. Because these variables are jointly determined, and therefore no one variable is obviously a dependent variable and another an exogenous variable, correlative rather than causal analysis is used to analyze the data.

Ideally, this analysis would use multivariate methods to control for differences in productivity among workers. The data sets presently available to me do not permit such an analysis.

7. When job aspirants leave low-wage sectors in which jobs are available in order to search for jobs in higher-paying sectors elsewhere, those who cannot find such jobs and end up unemployed are said to be experiencing "search unemployment."

8. It would be interesting to know whether the integrated labor market characterization also applies to the pre-1970 period (before full employment was reached), but data are lacking with which to determine this.

9. On the labor supply decisions of women, see the papers by Su-Mei Chang, Ying-Chuan Liu, Gee San, and Ching-Lung Tsay in the *Taiwan Economic Review*, June, 1988 and the references cited therein.

References

Bradford, Colin. 1986. "East Asian 'Models': Myths and Lessons," in John P. Lewis and Valeriana Kallab, eds., *Development Strategies Reconsidered*. Washington: Overseas Development Council.

Chang, Ching-Hsi. 1988. "An Economic Analysis of Guest Workers in Taiwan." Paper presented at the Conference on Labor and Economic Development, December. Taipei, Taiwan.

Chang, Ching-Hsi. 1989. "A Study on the Labor Market in Taiwan." Paper presented at the 1989 Joint Conference on the Industrial Policies of the R.O.C. and the R.O.K., Taipei, Taiwan. Sponsored by Chung-Hua Institution for Economic Research and Korea Development Institute.

Cheng, Peter Wen-Hui. 1987. "Financing Social Insurance in Taiwan." Paper presented at the Conference on Economic Development and Social Welfare in Taiwan, Institute of Economics, Academia Sinica, January.

Chu, Yun-Peng. 1987. "Taiwan's Poverty: Decomposition and Policy Simulation." Paper presented at the Conference on Economic Development and Social Welfare in Taiwan, Institute of Economics, Academia Sinica, January.

Council for Economic Development and Planning. 1986. *The Long-Term Prospect of the Economy in Taiwan, R.O.C., 1986-2000*.

Deyo, Frederic C. 1989. *Beneath the Miracle: Labor Subordination in the New Asian Industrialism*. Berkeley: University of California Press.

Ehrenberg, Ronald G., and Robert S. Smith. 1988. *Modern Labor Economics*, Third Edition. Glenview, IL: Scott Foresman.

Fei, John C.H. 1989. "A Bird's Eye View of Policy Evolution on Taiwan: An Introductory Essay," in K. T. Li, *The Evolution of Policy Behind Taiwan's Development Success*. New Haven: Yale University Press.

Fei, John C. H., Gustav Ranis, and Shirley W. Y. Kuo. 1978. "Growth and the Family Distribution of Income by Factor Components." *Quarterly Journal of Economics*, February.

Fei, John C. H., Gustav Ranis, and Shirley W. Y. Kuo. 1979. *Growth with Equity: The Taiwan Case*. New York: Oxford.

Fields, Gary S. 1980. *Poverty, Inequality, and Development*. New York: Cambridge University Press.

―――. 1984. "Employment, Income Distribution, and Economic Growth in Seven Small Open Economies." *The Economic Journal*, March.

―――. 1985. "Industrialization and Employment in Hong Kong, Korea, Singapore, and Taiwan," in Walter Galenson, ed., *Foreign Trade and Investment: Economic Growth in the Newly Industrializing Asian Countries*. Madison: University of Wisconsin Press.

Fields, Gary S., and Henry Wan, Jr. 1989. "Wage-Setting Institutions and Economic Growth." *World Development*, September.

Galenson, Walter. 1979. *Economic Growth and Structural Change in Taiwan*. Ithaca, NY: Cornell University Press.

Gereffi, Gary. 1988. "Industrial Restructuring in Latin America and East Asia." Paper presented at the 83rd annual meeting of the American Sociological Association, August. Atlanta, GA.

Harris, John R., and Michael P. Todaro. 1970. "Migration, Unemployment, and Development: A Two-Sector Analysis." *American Economic Review*, March.

Hou, Chi-Ming, and Hui-Lin Wu. 1985. "Wages and Labor Productivity in Taiwan." *Industry of Free China*, May.

Ko, Mu-shing. 1989. *A Study on Taiwan's Retirement and Layoff Policy*. Taipei: Council for Labor Affairs.

Krause, Lawrence B. 1985. "Introduction," in Walter Galenson, ed., *Foreign Trade and Investment: Economic Growth in the Newly Industrializing Asian Countries*. Madison: University of Wisconsin Press.

Kuo, Shirley W. Y. 1983. *The Taiwan Economy in Transition*. Boulder, CO: Westview.

Kuznets, Paul. 1988. "An East Asian Model of Economic Development: Japan, Taiwan, and South Korea," *Economic Development and Cultural Change*, Supplement.

Kuznets, Simon. 1979. "Growth and Structural Shifts," in Walter Galenson, ed., *Economic Growth and Structural Change in Taiwan*. Ithaca, NY: Cornell University Press.

Li, K.T. 1989. *The Evolution of Policy Behind Taiwan's Development Success*. New Haven: Yale University Press.

Lin, Chung-Cheng. 1988. "The Basic Labor Standards Law and Operation of Labor Market: Theory and Partial Empirical Results," working paper. Taipei: Academia Sinica.

Lin, Chung-Cheng. 1989. "Economics of Unions: Taiwan's Case Study." (self-published)

Liu, Paul K. C. 1984. "The Relationship between Female Labor Force and Industry Development." Paper presented at Conference of Taiwan's Industry Development. Taipei, Taiwan.

Pyatt, Graham, Chau-Nan Chen, and John Fei. 1980. "The Distribution of Income by Factor Components." *Quarterly Journal of Economics*, November.

Ranis, Gustav. 1974. "Taiwan," in Hollis B. Chenery *et al.*, eds., *Redistribution with Growth*. New York: Oxford University Press.

_____. 1979. "Industrial Development," in Walter Galenson, ed., *Economic Growth and Structural Change in Taiwan*. Ithaca, NY: Cornell University Press.

_____. 1989. "The Evolution of Policy in a Comparative Perspective: An Introductory Essay," in K. T. Li, *The Evolution of Policy Behind Taiwan's Development Success*. New Haven: Yale University Press.

San, Gee. 1987. "A Study and Survey on the Pension Fund Contribution Rate in the Labor Standards Law in Taiwan." Economic Papers No. 110, Chung-Hua Institution for Economic Research, Taipei, May, 1987.

_____. 1988. "A Critical Review of the Labor Standards Law in Taiwan, R.O.C. -- With Emphasis on the Pension and Severance System." Paper presented at the Conference on Labor and Economic Development, December 21-23.

_____. 1989. "The Emerging Issues of Industrial Relations and Labor Markets in Taiwan." Paper presented at the Conference on Emerging Issues of Labor Markets and Industrial Relations in Developing Asian Countries, Seoul, Korea, December 7-8.

Schive, Chi. 1985. "A Measure of Secondary Import Substitution in Taiwan." Taipei: Harvard-Yenching Institute.

Stevenson, Harold W., Shin-Yeng Lee, and James W. Stigler. 1986. "Mathematics Achievement of Chinese, Japanese, and American Children." *Science*, February: 93-699.

Tsiang, S. C. 1986. "Reasons for Taiwan's Economic Takeoff," in Institute of Strategic and International Studies, ed., *Lessons from Taiwan: Pathways to Follow and Pitfalls to Avoid*. ISIS: Kuala Lumpur.

UNICEF. 1989. *State of the World's Children*.

Wu, Chung-Chi. 1988. "A Preliminary Study on the Structure of Industrial Employment Between Sexes." *Taiwan Economic Review* 16(3): 439-457.

Wu, Rong-I. 1986. "Taiwan's Industrialization," in Institute of Strategic and International Studies, ed., *Lessons from Taiwan: Pathways to Follow and Pitfalls to Avoid*. ISIS: Kuala Lumpur.

_____. 1989. "Economic Development Strategies and the Role of Direct Foreign Investment in Taiwan," in Cheng F. Lee and Sheng-Cheng Hu, *Advances in Financial Planning and Forecasting, Supplement 1: Taiwan's Foreign Investment, Exports and Financial Analysis*. Greenwich, CT: JAI Press.

About the Contributors

Ching-huei Chang was born in Taiwan and completed his Ph.D. dissertation in economics at Pennsylvania State University in 1978. He was a Fulbright-Hays Visiting Scholar at Harvard University from September 1986 to July 1987. He is presently Research Fellow at the Sun Yat-Sen Institute for Social Sciences and Philosophy, Academia Sinica, and Professor of Economics at National Chung-Hsing University in Taiwan. He has published numerous articles in professional journals, such as the *Journal of Public Economics*, and contributed papers to books related to topics in taxation and development.

Paul C.H. Chiu is Deputy Governor of the Central Bank of China in Taiwan and Adjunct Professor of Economics at National Taiwan University. He was previously President of the Hua-Nan Commercial Bank and has held various other senior positions in the Central Bank of China. He was the recipient of the 1983 Best Government Service Award and was an Eisenhower Fellow in the United States in 1988. Dr. Chiu holds a Ph.D. from Ohio State University and has written extensively on the workings of financial markets.

Gary S. Fields is Professor of Labor Economics and Economic Development at Cornell University. He is the author of over sixty articles and two books, *Poverty, Inequality, and Development* (Cambridge University Press) and *Retirement, Pensions, and Social Security* (MIT Press). His fields of specialization are the theory and empirical functioning of labor markets and changes in poverty and inequality in developing countries.

Joseph S. Lee is Professor of Economics and Director of the Center for International Labor Studies at Mankato State University, Mankato, Minnesota. He received his B.A. from National Taiwan University and his M.S. and Ph.D. from the University of Massachusetts, Amherst, Massachusetts. His research interests and publications are mainly in the areas of manpower and labor relations.

Christina Y. Liu has been an assistant professor in the Department of Economics and Finance at the City University of New York since 1987. She received her B.A. degree in Political Science from National Taiwan University, an MBA in Finance from the University of Chicago, and a Ph.D. in Economics from the University of Chicago. She has published several articles in a number of professional journals, including the *Journal of Finance*, the *International Economic Journal*, and *Economics Letters*. She is now a visiting associate professor in Finance at National Taiwan University.

Paul K.C. Liu is a Research Fellow at the Institute of Economics, Academia Sinica, and concurrently Professor of Economics at National Taiwan University. He holds a doctorate in Economics from Michigan State University, specializing in population economics and economic development. Professor Liu is the author of many publications on population issues related to Taiwan, including fertility, migration, and human resource development.

Howard Pack is Professor of City and Regional Planning, Economics, and Public Policy and Management at the University of Pennsylvania and Director of the Program in International Development and Appropriate Technology. He previously taught at Yale University and Swarthmore College and holds a Ph.D. in economics from M.I.T. He has been a Research Associate of the Falk Institute for Economic Research in Israel and the Department of Economics of the Hebrew University. Professor Pack has been a consultant to the World Bank, the U.S. Agency for International Development, the Interamerican Development Bank, The Asian Development Bank, the OECD, UNCTAD, and other international aid agencies. He has written extensively on industrial development problems and policies of developing countries. His recent work includes *Productivity, Technology, and Industrial Development* (Oxford University Press, 1987).

Gustav Ranis is the Frank Altschul Professor of International Economics at Yale University. He was Director of the Pakistan Institute of Development Economics (1959-1961) and Director of the Economic Growth Center at Yale (1967-1975). Between 1965 and 1967 he served as Assistant Administrator for Program and Policy in the U.S. Agency for International Development. He has been a consultant to the World Bank, ADB, AID, OECD, UNIDO, FAO, UNDP, the Ford and Rockefeller Foundations, among others, and currently serves as a member of the advisory board of a number of third world research institutions. He was Chief of the ILO Comprehensive Employment Strategy Mission to the Philippines in 1973 and Chief of the World Bank/Caricom Mission on Production and Investment Incentives in the Caribbean in 1981. In 1976 he organized the U.S. National Academy of Sciences' Bicentennial Symposium on the Role of Science and Technology in Economic Development. Professor Ranis has written extensively on theoretical and policy-related issues of development. His major book-length publications include *Development of the Labor Surplus Economy: Theory and Policy* 1964 (with John Fei), *Growth with Equity: the Taiwan Case* 1979 (with John Fei and Shirley Kuo), *Japan and the Developing Countries* 1988 (with K. Ohkawa), *Comparative Technology*

Choice 1988 (with K. Otsuka and G. Saxonhouse), *The State of Development Economics: Progress and Perspectives* 1988 (with T. Paul Schultz), and *Science and Technology: Lessons for Development Policy* 1990 (with Robert Evenson).

James Riedel is a Professor of International Economics at the Paul H. Nitze School of Advanced International Studies of the Johns Hopkins University and a consultant to the World Bank. He has been a visiting scholar at Nuffield College, Oxford and the Australian National University. His publications are in the fields of international trade theory and policy, international finance, and economic development. Among his recent publications are *The Direction of Trade Policy* (Blackwell, 1990) and "The Small Country Assumption: A Reassessment with Evidence from Korea," *Weltwirtschaftliches Archiv*, 1991.

Erik Thorbecke is the H.E. Babcock Professor of Economics and Food Economics and Director of the Program on Comparative Economic Development at Cornell University. His past positions include Chairman of the Department of Economics at Cornell, a Professorship at Iowa State University, and Associate Assistant Administrator for Program and Policy at the Agency for International Development. He was awarded an honorary degree by the University of Ghent in 1981. He is a Senior Research Fellow of the Institute for Policy Reform in Washington, D.C. He has worked extensively in the areas of economic and agricultural development, the measurement and analysis of poverty and malnutrition, the Social Accounting Matrix and general equilibrium modelling, and international economic policy. Recent publications include *Adjustment, Growth and Income Distribution in Indonesia*; *Economic Policies and Agricultural Performance in Low-Income Countries*; *The Role of Institutions in Economic Development* (coeditor with I. Adelman). He is the author and coauthor of about twenty books and ninety articles. He has been an economic adviser to numerous U.S. and international agencies, and foreign governments, including USAID, the Food and Agricultural Organization, the International Labor Organization, the World Bank and the OECD.

About the Book and Editor

Policymakers and academicians in both rich and poor countries have observed the postwar development of Taiwan with a mixture of wonder and amazement. Characterized in the 1950s by per capita incomes of less than $50, hyper-inflation, and complete dependence on outside aid, tiny Taiwan has emerged as the 13th strongest trading nation in the world, moving steadily toward equitable distribution of income and the alleviation of poverty. Observers throughout Asia, in Latin America, and in Africa seek to understand how this "economic miracle" has been accomplished and ask whether the experience is transferable, in whole or in part, and whether the economic gains will continue.

What must Taiwan do in order to fully join the charmed circle of mature capitalist countries? Looking at the island's economic and social system as a whole and on a sector-by-sector and market-by-market basis, the contributors to this volume reveal the path of structural changes that made existing gains possible and analyze current conditions and specific requirements for organizational and policy changes in the future.

Gustav Ranis is the Frank Altschul Professor of International Economics, Economic Growth Center, Yale University.

Index

Accelerated Rural Development Program (ARDP), 33, 35, 37
Act for Recruitment of High-Caliber Scientists, 386
ADB. *See* Asian Development Bank
Africa, 336(table)
Agricultural Development Act (1973), 35, 68(n21)
Agriculture, 1, 399–400, 401
  capital substitution, 48, 53
  consumption rates, 69(n32)
  cooperative, 33, 37–38
  development stages, 17
  diversification of, 47, 49, 50–52, 54, 59
  entrusted, 37, 53
  export, 16(table), 17, 49, 50(table), 50–51, 52(table), 52–53
  farm crops, 18, 19–21(tables), 26–29, 34, 47, 49, 50–54
  industrialization and, 155
  inputs, 22–23(table), 24, 34, 48(&table). *See also* Labor, agricultural
  under Japanese, 359, 361, 362
  liberalization phase, 46–55
  marketing and distribution, 65
  1975–1978, 33–46
  part-time, 34, 36, 49
  performance, 17–25, 27, 28, 33–35, 46–49, 50(table), 59, 69(n31)
  post-1978, 46–55
  pre-1973, 25–33
  price supports, 31, 38–39, 43–46
  protection of, 12, 43–46, 51, 55–56, 70(n43)
  R&D in, 61, 62(fig), 65–66, 385
  reform of, 35–43, 46
  role of, 12–13, 15–17
  subsidies, 12, 34
  taxation of, 38
  technology and, 8, 24–25, 29, 36, 46, 67(n13)
Amsden, Alice, 325
Anderson, Kym, 55–56
APEC. *See* Asian Pacific Economic Corporation
ARDP. *See* Accelerated Rural Development Program
ASEAN. *See* Association of Southeast Asian Nations
Asian Development Bank (ADB), 313, 314(table), 319
Asian Pacific Economic Corporation (APEC), 340
Association of Southeast Asian Nations (ASEAN), 4, 5–6, 11, 294, 340
Astley & Pearce, Inc., 212
Australia, 57(table), 257(table), 311, 340
Austria, 257(table)
Automobile industry, 404
Aw, Bee Yan, 288

Balance of payments, 308, 309(table), 310(table). *See also* Trade
Balassa, Bela, 270
Baldwin, Robert E., 299
Bangladesh, 317(table)
Bankers' acceptances, 175, 176(table), 197, 199
Banking Law, 125, 128, 133, 169, 186, 197, 200, 210, 218(n3), 317(table)

Bank of Taiwan, 184
Banks, 7, 125, 126(table), 129–130(table), 131, 132–133, 186, 210–211, 213
  deregulation of, 318
  foreign, 126(table), 128, 129–130(table), 164, 210, 318
  loans from, 162–164, 199
  off-shore, 187, 212
  open-market operations, 150
  privatization of, 128
  savings plans, 159
Barter system, 27, 28, 29, 31, 35, 38
Base metals industry, 338
Base money, 148–154. *See also* Monetary policy
Basic Labor Standards Law, 404–405, 417, 419–420, 425, 426, 427
Basic Wage Scale, 420
Becker, 236
Belgium, 257(table)
Bhagwati, Jagdish, 295, 299
BIT. *See* Taxes, business income
"Blueprint for the Outlook of New Rural Villages in Taiwan," 53–55, 61, 70(n41)
Bonds, 177, 178(table), 187, 240–241, 249, 250(n15)
Brain drain, 343–344, 372–373, 423
Brazil, 291, 398
Budget surplus, 238–241
Bush, George, 319

Cambodia, 347
Canada, 57(table), 249(n3), 257(table), 306(table), 319, 340, 341, 342(table)
CAPD. *See* Council for Agricultural Planning and Development
Capital
  formation, 159–162, 228, 232–235, 403
  surplus, 341
  See also Capital flows; Financial markets; Foreign exchange; Monetary policy

Capital flows, 169, 173, 175, 185, 204, 207–209, 213–216, 305
  in Asian Pacific nations, 309(table)
  deregulation of, 318
  development and, 307–308, 316–320
  labor mobility and, 310–312
  official, 314(&table), 315–316
  patterns of, 313–316, 317(table), 319–320
  private, 314(table), 315–316
Capital market. *See* Financial markets
CBC. *See* Central Bank of China
CDIC. *See* Central Deposits Insurance Company
CDs. *See* Certificates of Deposit
Central Bank of China (CBC), 125, 127(table), 129–130(table), 131, 133, 140, 145, 148, 150, 153, 165, 168, 169, 186, 197, 209, 241, 250(n15), 318
Central Deposits Insurance Company (CDIC), 125
"Central Inter-bank Call Rate System," 199
CEPD. *See* Council for Economic Planning and Development
Certificates of deposit (CDs), 165, 175, 176(table), 177, 197, 199
Chang, C., 237
Chang, Ching-Hsi, 423
Chemicals industry, 323(table), 324, 338
Chen, Chau-Nan, 405
Chen, Pao-Yui, 337–338
Chen, Tain-Jy, 99–100, 103–104, 106, 344
Chenery, Hollis B., 83, 95, 107, 256
Childcare, 362
China, 320, 328, 396
  capital flows, 317(table)
  DFI to, 332, 333, 348
  diplomatic relations with, 13, 341
  economic relations with, 13, 240
  economy of, 294, 359–360
  education in, 360
  immigration from, 347, 348
  labor from, 331, 344, 345

Index

China Development Corporation, 132
China Petrochemicals, 7
China Petroleum Corporation, 164, 239
China Steel, 7
Chinese Federation of Labor, 417, 418
Citicorp, 318
Clark, 107
Commerce, 107, 401. *See also* Trade
Commercial paper, 175, 176(table), 197
Compact disk players, 111
Company Law, 177
Computer chips, 111–112
Confucianism, 359–360, 361, 371, 374
Cooperative Bank of Taiwan, 125, 131
Corn, 48, 51
Council for Agricultural Planning and Development (CAPD), 53–54
Council for Economic Planning and Development (CEPD), 240
Council of Labor Affairs, 374, 423
Credit
  cooperatives, 126(table), 128, 129–130(table), 131
  growth and, 162–164
  tsouh-wih, 6
  See also Banks
CRP. *See* United States, Conservation Reserve Program
Currency valuation, 85, 200, 201(fig), 203–204, 209, 219(n5), 258, 265, 295
Current accounts, 308, 309(table), 310(table). *See also* Trade

Dai-Ichi Kangyo, 128
Daiwa, 318
Debt
  domestic, 7–8
  foreign, 313, 314(table)
  public, 249
  See also Credit
Defense spending, 225
Demand
  domestic, 5, 83(table), 84, 85–86, 133

growth of, 73
income elasticities, 107
monetary, 143–144
for services, 107
Demarcation Law of the Central and Local Governments' Revenues and Expenditures, 241, 243
deMelo, Jaime, 83–84
Demographics, 361–368, 389–390, 424–426, 428
Denmark, 57(table), 257(table)
Designated-Purpose Trust Program, 318
Development
  assistance (ODA), 307, 314(&table), 315–316
  capital flows and, 307–308, 316–320
  DFI and, 320–327, 340–342
  human resources and, 361
  political economy approach, 74
  science & technology and, 357
  stages of, 307–308, 312(table)
  See also Growth; Industrialization
Deyo, Frederic C., 410
DFI. *See* Investment, foreign
Domestic assets, 150, 151(table), 152(table)
Dyeing industry, 331

Education, 10, 102(table), 102–103, 109, 235–237, 248, 285, 346–347, 428
  agriculture and, 66
  compulsory, 421
  Confucian values in, 371, 390
  DFI and, 327
  elasticity and, 106
  enrollment rates, 369, 370(fig), 373, 398, 399(table)
  farm-land surtax, 35
  government spending on, 368, 369, 422
  income and, 236, 237–238
  under Japanese, 360–361
  labor market and, 421(table), 423
  labor quality and, 368–382

post-secondary, 371–372, 372(table)
vocational, 371, 373, 422–423
EEC. *See* European Economic Community
Effective protection coefficients (EPCs), 43, 46, 69(n30)
Elasticity of substitution, 100, 103
Electrical machinery, 288(table)
Electronics industry, 294, 321, 323(table), 389, 401
Emigration, 305–306. *See also* Brain drain
Employment, 97, 98(table)
 full, 410
 in manufacturing, 104(table), 104–105
 sectoral structure of, 87(table), 88, 401, 402(table), 403
 in service sector, 108(&table)
 See also Unemployment
Employment and Vocational Training Administration, 374
Employment Services Law, 307
Engineering, 385
Engineers, 373
Entrusted farming, 37, 53
EPCs. *See* Effective protection coefficients
Ergas, Henry, 384
"Essentials of Interest Rate Adjustment," 165, 197, 199
Eurobonds, 213
Eurocurrency, 212, 213
Europe
 capital from, 314(table), 315, 320, 321(table), 322(table)
 DFI to, 335(table), 336
 economic unification of, 319, 340
 labor from, 328, 330(&table), 331, 345
 trade with, 110
European Common Market, 212
European Economic Community (EEC), 12, 56, 57(table), 63, 296(table), 298
Exchange rates. *See* Foreign exchange

Export-Import Bank of China, 125, 127(table)
Export processing zones, 292
Exports, 110
 agricultural, 16(table), 17, 49, 50(table), 50–51, 52(table), 52–53
 composition of, 3, 81–83, 260, 261(fig), 279
 credits, 314(table)
 demand and, 85–86
 dependence on, 256
 deregulation of, 403
 DFI and, 325
 geographic pattern of, 263(fig), 266(fig)
 growth in, 13, 75–76, 155, 156, 255(fig)
 manufactured, 3–4, 4(table)
 productivity growth, 81, 86–92
 promotion of, 295, 400, 404–405
 quality of, 287–291
 ratios, 3
 surplus, 84(table), 84–85
 See also Trade

Farm crops, 18, 19–21(tables), 26–29, 34, 53
 diversification of, 47, 49, 50–52, 54
 See also Agriculture
Farmers' Associations, 126(table), 128, 129–130(table), 131
Farms
 entrusted, 37, 53
 group, 37–38
 large, 35–37
 management forms, 37–38
 part-time, 59–60, 60(table), 64
 size of, 53–54, 61, 68(n24)
Feder, Gershon, 159
Fei, John C.H., 85, 396, 400, 405
Feldstein, M., 246
Fertilizer, 22–23(table), 24, 27
Fidelity, 318
Fields, Gary S., 396
Finance companies, 127(table), 132
Financial institutions, 122–133. *See also* Banks

Index

Financial markets, 6, 175–184, 212–213
  domestic, 197–200
  government intervention in, 93
  international, 200–210, 213
  internationalization of, 5, 210–212
  liberalization of, 122, 195, 196–210, 213, 316–320
  See also Interest rates
Finland, 257(table)
Fiscal budget, 196
Fiscal policy
  capital formation and, 232–235
  human capital and, 235–238
  reform of, 8
  savings and, 228–232
Fishermen's Associations, 126(table), 128, 129–130(table), 131
Fishery, 18, 19–21(tables), 27, 28, 53
Food crops, 59, 66. *See also* Agriculture
Food Stabilization Fund, 51
Footwear industry, 290(fig), 291
Foreign assets, 150, 151(table), 153
"Foreign Currency Call Loan Market," 212, 213
"Foreign Currency Loan Market," 195
Foreign exchange, 169, 173, 175, 185, 186–187, 198(table), 200–210
  borrowed, 216–218
  controls, 209
  deregulation of, 317, 318, 319, 403
  growth and, 101–102
  rates, 123–124(table), 209–210, 213, 258, 260, 267(fig), 268(fig), 269, 295, 300(nn 2–4)
  remittances and, 311
  reserves, 1, 5, 85, 144, 185, 200, 202(fig), 203(table)
Forestry, 18, 19–21(tables), 27
France, 57(table), 249(n3), 257(table), 306(table), 308, 327, 342(table)
Friedman, Milton, 143
Fry, Maxwell J., 155, 159
Fukien Province, 6

GATT. *See* General Agreement on Tariffs and Trade
General Agreement on Tariffs and Trade (GATT), 5, 296, 298, 299
Geography, 358
Germany, 57(table), 249(n3), 257(table), 306(table), 310, 327, 342(table)
Gerschenkron, Alexander, 73–74, 79
Government, local, 241–244
Government enterprises, 94, 95(table)
Government spending, 224–226, 239, 241–243, 247–248, 249, 320, 327
  on defense, 225
  on education, 368, 369, 422
  on infrastructure, 35, 185, 248, 349, 403
  on R&D, 384, 385(&table), 388(table), 404
  See also Investment, public
Great Britain. *See* United Kingdom
Green Revolution, 8
Gross national product, 186, 223(table), 239, 396, 397(table)
Growth, 86, 427, 428
  capital formation and, 78(table), 79, 159–162
  credit and, 162–164
  exports and, 155
  government intervention and, 99–100
  industrial, 97–98
  labor market and, 406–408, 413(&table)
  monetary policy and, 144, 145
  rate of, 73–74, 185, 196, 396
  sectoral, 97–100
  sources of, 77–79, 83(table), 83–84, 100–101
  technology and, 8–9, 383
  in value added, 78(&table)
  See also Total factor productivity
Guest workers, 311, 312(table)
  allocation of, 349–350
  DFI and, 345–351
  infrastructure and, 349
  quality of, 348–349

Hall, R., 234
Hayami, Yujiro, 55–56
Health care, 398, 399(table)
Heckscher-Ohlin model, 81, 277, 278
Hicks-Marshall Laws of Derived Demand, 417–418
Hirschman, 92
History, 358–359
Ho, P. S., 15, 26, 82
Hog Stabilization Fund, 43
Holland, 111
Homma, M., 56
Honda, 404
Hong Kong, 396, 410
  brain drain, 423
  capital flows, 316, 317(table)
  development in, 253, 285, 306(table)
  DFI from, 318, 341
  DFI to, 315, 334(table)
  industrialization of, 291, 359
  trade practices, 299, 301(n12)
  trade through, 4, 6
Hou, C., 236, 237
Hou, Chi-Ming, 410
Hsinchu Science-based Industrial Park, 292
Hsing, Mo-huan, 155, 162
Hsu, S., 243
Hsu, Y., 236
Hsu, Y. Y., 325
Hulten, Charles, Jr., 80
Human capital. *See* Labor
Hyundai, 112

IBM, 111
IBRD. *See* International Bank of Reconstruction and Development
ICBC, 210
IDA. *See* International Development Association
IECDF. *See* International Economic Cooperation and Development Fund
IIT. *See* Taxes, household income
Immigration, 306. *See also* Guest workers; Professional transients

Imports
  agricultural, 59, 67(n4)
  composition of, 260, 262(fig)
  geographic pattern of, 264(fig)
  growth of, 255(fig)
  licensing, 296
Import substitution, 79, 83(table), 84, 400, 404
Income
  DFI and, 347
  distribution, 238, 398, 399(table), 405–406, 406(table), 429(n2)
  education and, 236, 237–238
  in exports, 114–115(n20)
  farm, 29, 30(table), 32(table), 33, 34, 35, 49, 59–60, 60(table), 61, 64–65, 67(nn 12, 16), 67–68(n17)
  foreign, 332
  per capita, 1, 15, 29, 30(table), 35, 49, 121, 196, 253, 254, 305, 396, 397(table)
  retirement, 424–426
  rising, 89
  tax-exempt, 244–245
  See also Wages
India, 88, 317(table)
Indonesia, 6, 317(table), 333, 345, 346(table), 347, 405
Industrialization, 8–9, 15, 27, 74, 75–76, 83, 260, 359, 401
  agriculture and, 155
  import substituting (ISI), 79, 83(table), 84, 400, 404
  incentives, 84
  political process of, 115(n22)
  technology and, 390–391
Industrial policy, 92–103, 114(n19)
  growth sources and, 100
  impact of, 94–100
Industry, 427–428
  comparative advantage in, 269–275
  decentralization of, 400
  DFI and, 321, 323(table), 324–325, 331, 334–336(table), 338, 339(table)
  employment shifts in, 401, 402(table)

Index

firm size, 105-106, 110-111, 113(n7), 115(n28)
guest workers in, 349-350
monetary policy and, 134, 138, 139(fig), 140
production structure, 95-98
professional transients in, 329-330(table)
rates of, 121, 141, 165, 185
Information hardware, 292, 293(fig), 294
Information science, 386
Infrastructure, 35, 185, 248, 349, 403
Insurance, 127(table), 129-130(table), 132, 211-212
Intellectual property rights, 296, 298, 301(n11)
Interest rates, 123-124(table), 133-141, 146-147(table), 184
 on bills of exchange, 165
 capital flow controls and, 169, 173, 175
 on deposits, 165, 166(fig), 167(fig), 168-169, 170(fig), 171(fig), 172(fig), 174(fig)
 floating, 164, 213
 inflation and, 145
 liberalization of, 164-175, 185, 197, 199-200, 213
 on loans, 165, 166(fig), 167(fig), 168, 171(fig), 172(fig), 189(n6)
 parity condition, 204, 213-216, 219(n7)
 prices and, 142(fig), 144-145
 See also Financial markets
Intermediation network, 6-7
International Bank of Reconstruction and Development (IBRD), 313, 314(table)
International Development Association (IDA), 313, 314(table)
International Economic Cooperation and Development Fund (IECDF), 319
Investment, 4, 5-6, 228, 229(table), 232(table), 232-233, 403
 DFI outflow, 239, 332-351

 domestic, 5, 6, 325-327
 in exports, 83
 foreign, 83, 183, 211, 213, 291-294, 305, 306, 311, 313, 316, 320-327
 industrial, 80
 portfolio, 314(table)
 production structure and, 103
 public, 7, 232(table), 232-233, 239-240, 247-248, 249, 403
 rates, 155-156, 157(fig), 198(table)
 savings and, 93
 structures, 182-183
 taxes and, 233, 234-235, 250(n8)
Ireland, 257(table), 344
ISI. *See* Industrialization, import substituting
Italy, 56, 57(table), 257(table), 291, 327, 342(table)

Japan, 2, 12, 75, 111, 210, 310, 327, 340, 347
 capital from, 308, 314(table), 315, 318, 320-321, 321(table), 322(table), 327, 328, 342(table)
 capital markets in, 212
 comparative advantage, 291
 DFI to, 333, 334(table)
 exports, 257(table)
 financial institutions, 132
 GDP structure, 306(table)
 industrialization of, 359
 investment by, 9
 labor from, 310-311, 328, 329(table), 330, 331, 344, 345
 occupation by, 82, 359, 360-361, 362, 368
 protectionism in, 56, 57(table), 256
 "Sunset" sectors in, 87
 taxes in, 249(n3)
 trade with, 3, 260, 263(fig), 264(fig), 265, 296(table)
Jardine Fleming, 318
JCRR. *See* Joint Commission on Rural Reconstruction
Joint Commission on Rural Reconstruction (JCRR), 26, 27, 28, 33

Joint ventures, 112
Jorgenson, K., 234

Kindleberger, Charles P., 307
Kmenta, J., 162
KMT. *See* Kuomintang
Knowledge transfers
  exports and, 88–89, 91
  from foreign purchasers, 88–89
  purchased, 90–92
  from returning nationals, 89–90
  royalty payments, 82, 90
  TNCs and, 91
Ko, Mu-shing, 425
Kravis, 92
Kuangdung Province, 6
Kubo, Yuji, 95
Kuo, 396, 405
Kuo, S., 238
Kuo, Shirley W.Y., 28, 240, 396, 410
Kuo, W. Y., 325
Kuomintang (KMT), 418
Kuznets, Paul, 410
Kuznets, Simon, 1, 8, 74, 79, 107, 357, 361

Labor
  agricultural, 22–23(table), 24–25, 27, 28–29, 31, 32(table), 33, 48(&table), 66–67(n3), 408(&table), 410
  brain drain, 343–344, 372–373, 423
  capital formation, 357
  comparative advantage and, 279, 284(fig), 285
  displacements, 346
  employment standards, 417, 419–420
  female, 346–347, 350, 362, 365(fig), 366, 367, 390, 406, 424
  force changes, 78(table), 79, 80, 83
  foreign, 11, 306–307, 311, 312(table), 328–332, 345–351, 390, 423
  integrated market, 415, 416(fig)
  intensity, 285, 286(fig), 287(&table)
  international division of, 340, 350–351
  manufacturing, 104(table), 104–105
  markets, 27, 305, 341, 390, 403, 404–420, 421(&table), 423, 427
  mobility, 236–237, 310–312, 312(table), 327
  organized, 417–419
  participation, 237, 357, 362, 363(table), 364(fig), 365(fig), 366, 367, 390, 406
  productivity, 155
  professional, 328–332, 343–344, 351, 408, 409(table)
  remittances by, 311
  sectoral shifts, 70(n44), 103
  segmented market, 410–415
  separation rates, 90–91, 91(table)
  in service sector, 108(&table)
  shortages, 10–11, 349, 422–423
  surplus, 367
  trade and, 280(fig), 284(fig), 285, 286(fig)
  underutilization of, 422
  unions, 11, 417–419
  unit costs, 109, 110
  unrest, 419
Labor Dispute Law, 419
Labor Insurance Law, 425
Lall, Sanjaya, 88
Land
  reform, 25–26, 38, 53, 155, 399
  trade requirement, 282–283(figs)
  value increment taxes (LVIT), 226, 243, 244
  values, 63
Land-aside programs, 63–64
Land-to-the-Tiller Program, 25, 26
Lary, Hal B., 285
LDCs. *See* Less-developed countries
Lee, Teng-Hui, 15, 84
Leontief, Wassily, 277, 278, 287
Less-developed countries (LDCs)
  industrialization of, 76
  productivity, 78, 80
  technology adoption in, 74
Levy, Brian, 105, 106
Lewis, 85
Lewis, Arthur, 1

Index

Li, I., 230, 231
Li, K. T., 410
Liang, Kuo-shu, 84
Liang, Ming-yi, 156
Liberalization, 305, 400–401, 403
  of agriculture, 46–55
  of financial markets, 122, 195, 196–210, 213, 316–320
  of interest rates, 164–175, 185, 197, 199–200, 213
  of trade, 143, 196–197, 295–296, 403
LIBOR. *See* London inter-bank offer rate
Life expectancy, 1
Life insurance companies, 127(table), 129–130(table), 132
Lin, Chung-Cheng, 419, 420
Literacy, 398
Little, Ian, 14
Little, I.M.D., 76
Liu, Alan P.L., 89, 94
Liu, Paul K.C., 424
Livestock, 18, 19–21(tables), 26, 27, 28, 29, 34, 48, 51, 53, 59
Loans, 199
  foreign, 313, 314(table)
  interest on, 165–168, 171(fig), 172(fig), 189(n6)
  structure of, 163(table), 163–164
Local governments, 241–244
London inter-bank offer rate (LIBOR), 212
Lumber industry, 338
Lundberg, Erik, 133, 134
LVIT. *See* Taxes, land value increment

McDonalds Corporation, 325
Machinery industry, 338
Mainland China. *See* China
Malaysia, 6, 317(table), 344, 345, 346(&table), 347, 398, 405
Mao Zedong, 64
Marine Transport, 7
Market lending, 183–184
Medical sciences, 385
Medium Business Bank of Taiwan, 125

Merrill Lynch, 211
Mexico, 319, 340, 341, 398
Mill-Bastable criterion, 93
Ministry of Economic Affairs, 296
  Investment Commission, 173
Ministry of Education, 385
Ministry of Finance (MOF), 125, 126(table), 133, 186
MNCs. *See* Transnational corporations
MOF. *See* Ministry of Finance
Monetary authorities, 125, 126–127(table)
Monetary policy, 133–154, 177, 184–185, 204, 205(fig)
Money markets, 185, 187, 197, 198(table), 199
Mortality rates, 361–362, 367, 398, 399(table)
Multi-national corporations (MNCs). *See* Transnational corporations

National Conferences on Science and Technology Development, 383–384
National Financial Conference (1991), 186
National Health Insurance Program (NHIP), 247
National Mobilization Act, 418
National Science Council, 385–386
Natural sciences, 385
Nelson, Richard R., 79–80
Netherlands, 257(table), 333, 342(table)
New Zealand, 57(table), 257(table), 340
NHIP. *See* National Health Insurance Program
19 Points policy, 13
Nissan, 404
Nominal protection coefficients (NPCs), 43, 46, 69(n29)
NPCs. *See* Nominal protection coefficients

OBUs. *See* Banks, off-shore
ODA. *See* Official development assistance

OECD. *See* Organization for Economic Cooperation and Development
OEM. *See* Original equipment manufacturers
Official development assistance (ODA), 307, 314(&table), 315–316
Oil prices, 145, 228, 238, 396
Old Age, Survivors', and Disability Benefit Payments Fund, 426
Olson, Mancur, 86
Ong, Shao-Er, 54
OPEC. *See* Organization of Petroleum Exporting Countries
Organization for Economic Cooperation and Development (OECD), 75, 76, 78, 79, 98, 110, 112, 113, 253, 296
Organization of Petroleum Exporting Countries (OPEC), 314(table), 396
Original equipment manufacturers (OEMs), 294

Pakistan, 7, 317(table)
Patents, 386, 389
Pensions, 425–426
People's Republic of China. *See* China
PEs. *See* Productive enterprises
Philippines, 6, 317(table), 345, 346(&table), 349, 405
PIRD. *See* Preferential Interest Rate Deposit
"Plan for Introduction of Foreign and Overseas Chinese Capital into Securities," 211
Planned Adjustment in Acreage Allocation, 51
Plastics, 401
Population growth, 366
Postal savings system, 126(table), 129–130(table), 131, 152(table), 153, 159, 165, 168
Poterba, J., 231
Poverty, 396, 398, 428–429(n1)
Preferential interest rate deposit (PIRD), 133–141
Price indices, 123–124(table), 288

Prices, 189(table), 403
  agricultural, 31, 38–39, 43–46
  exchange rates and, 258, 265
  import, 143
  interest rates and, 142(fig), 144–145
  monetary policy and, 134, 135(fig), 136, 139(fig), 141–154
  stability of, 196
  supports, 31, 38–39, 43–46, 53, 68(n27), 69(n35)
Privatization, 403
Product cycles, 111
Production structure, 95–98
Productive enterprises (PEs), 233
Productivity, 198(table)
  growth of, 75, 77–80, 86–92
  total factor (TFP), 74, 75, 77–79, 80–81, 86–92, 99(&table), 103–106, 108–109, 112–113
Product quality, 287–291
Professional transients, 328–332, 343–344, 351
"Program on Basic Infrastructure Development," 53
"Program on Enhancing Farm Income and Strengthening Rural Reconstruction," 53
"Program on Strengthening Basic Infrastructure and Enhancing Farm Income," 53
Protectionism, 5, 294–295, 296, 299
  agricultural, 12, 43–46, 51, 55–66, 70(n43)
  industrial, 76, 84
  political economy of, 55–56
Pursell, Garry, 88
Pyatt, Graham, 405

R&D. *See* Research and Development
Ranis, Gustav, 85, 90, 91, 92, 396, 400, 405
RCA. *See* Trade, comparative advantage
Real estate market, 204
"Regulations for Interest Rate Management," 199

Index

"Regulations Governing Securities Investment by Overseas Chinese and Foreign Investors and Procedures for Remittance," 212
Remittances, 311
Report on the Manpower Utilization Survey, Taiwan Area, R.O.C., 1988, 422
Research and development (R&D), 383–389
　agricultural, 61, 62(fig), 65–66, 385
　capacities, 384–385
　expenditures, 384, 385(&table), 388(table), 404
　institutions, 384, 385
　manpower, 386, 387(table), 388(table)
　See also Monetary policy
Resource allocation, 204
Retirement benefits, 424–426, 428
Rhee, Young, 88
Rice
　as feed, 69(n34)
　indicators, 39, 40(table)
　price supports, 50
　reserve program, 64
　stock formation, 40, 41(fig), 42(table), 43, 50–51, 59
Rice-fertilizer barter program, 27, 28, 29, 31, 35, 38
Rice Nursery Centers (RNCs), 39
Rice Stabilization Board (RSB), 39, 50, 51
Rice Stabilization Fund, 33, 39
RNCs. *See* Rice Nursery Centers
Roberts, Mark J., 288
ROC Taiwan Fund, 211
RSB. *See* Rice Stabilization Board

SAAs. *See* Specialized agricultural areas
San, Gee, 418, 425, 426
Savings, 403
　fiscal policy and, 228–232
　"forced," 159
　institutions, 125, 126(table), 128, 131
　　rate of, 1, 4–5, 83, 93(&table), 121, 140, 146–147(table), 156, 157(fig), 158(table), 159, 198(table)
　sources of, 229(table), 229–230
Schive, Chi, 90, 91, 294
Schultz, 236
Science and Technology Advisory Committee, 383, 384
Scientists, 386
Scott, Maurice, 76, 88, 90
Second Stage of the Agricultural Land Reform (SSALR), 53
Sectoral linkages, 96(&table)
Securities and Exchange Law, 211
Securities industry, 132–133, 185, 211, 213
Securities investment consulting enterprises (SICEs), 211
SEI. *See* Statute for the Encouragement of Investment
Service sector, 107–109, 326, 401, 403
7-Eleven, 325
Shearson Lehman, 211
Shih, Yen, 144
Short-term bills, 175, 176(table), 177
SIBOR. *See* Singapore inter-bank offer rate
SICEs. *See* Securities investment consulting enterprises
Siemens, 111
Singapore, 306(table), 315, 317(table), 347, 410
　DFI to, 334(table)
　diplomatic relations with, 341
　income in, 398
　industrialization of, 253, 359
Singapore inter-bank offer rate (SIBOR), 212
Singer Sewing Machine Company, 91
Small- and medium-sized enterprises (SMEs), 155–156, 159, 179, 180–181(table), 182, 183–184, 185
Small Grains Deficiency Scheme, 43, 46, 50, 51
Small-scale enterprises (SSEs), 76, 82, 103–106, 376

SMEs. *See* Small- and medium-sized enterprises
Smith, Adam, 85
Social indicators, 398, 399(table)
Solow, 237
Sony, 9
Sorghum, 48, 51
South Korea, 13, 58, 76, 112, 210, 291, 306(table), 311, 316, 317(table), 340, 410, 419
  DFI to, 337(table)
  guest workers from, 345
  industrialization of, 75, 88, 89, 109–110, 111, 253, 359
  labor in, 11, 109
  protectionism in, 56, 57(table), 75
Spain, 257(table), 291
Specialized agricultural areas (SAAs), 37–38
Sri Lanka, 317(table)
SSALR. *See* Second Stage of the Agricultural Land Reform
SSEs. *See* Small-scale enterprises
Standards of living, 396–404, 420, 421, 427–428
Statute for the Encouragement of Investment (SEI), 159, 233
Stock market, 177–179, 182–183, 187, 204, 206(fig)
Subcontracting, 9, 106
Sugar Stabilization Fund, 43
Sun, Chen, 156
Sweden, 56, 57(table), 257(table), 342(table)
Switzerland, 56, 57(table), 249(n3), 257(table), 342(table)
Syrquin, Moshe, 95

Taipei inter-bank offer rate (TIBOR), 212
Taiwanese Association for Labor Movement, 417
Taiwan Food Bureau, 51
Taiwan Fund, 211
Taiwan Power Company, 164
Taiwan Railroad Company, 419

Taiwan Stock Exchange (TSE), 183
Taiwan Sugar Corporation (TSC), 68(n25)
Tang, De-Piao, 99–100, 103–104, 106
Tariffs, 143, 296(table), 297(fig), 305.
  See also Protectionism; Trade
Taxes, 187
  agricultural, 38
  business income (BIT), 230, 233, 243, 244, 248
  corporate, 184
  deductions from 245–246
  exemptions from, 250(n6)
  on foreign income, 332
  household income, 226, 228, 243, 244–246, 248
  investment and, 233, 234–235, 250(n8)
  investment credits, 233, 234–235
  land value increment (LVIT), 226, 243, 244
  reform of, 231–232, 246, 248, 249
  savings rates and, 230
  structure of, 226, 227(table)
Technology, 109, 110, 111–112
  agricultural, 8, 24–25, 29, 36, 46, 67(n13)
  best practice gap, 74, 75
  employment and, 367
  growth and, 8–9, 383
  growth of, 382–389, 391
  industrial, 155
  industrialization and, 390–391
  property rights, 10
  R&D, 9, 10, 383–389
Technology transfer, 79–81, 82–83, 291–294, 383
  DFI and, 324–325, 326, 327, 340
  education and, 102–103
  professional transients and, 331
Telecommunications, 187, 318
Televisions, 111
Tenancy, 68(n21)
"Ten Big Construction Projects," 226
"Tenth Trust Cooperative (financial) scandal," 228
Textile industry, 331, 389, 401

Index

TFP. *See* Total factor productivity
Thailand, 6, 317(table), 344, 345, 346(table), 348, 405
Tiananmen Square incident, 423
TIBOR. *See* Taipei inter-bank offer rate
Tiller Act, 26
Tobacco industry, 7
Total factor productivity (TFP), 74, 75, 77–79, 80–81, 86–92, 99(&table), 103–106, 108–109, 112–113
Toyota, 404
Trade
  account balance, 198(table), 259(fig), 308, 309(table), 310(table)
  agricultural, 16(table), 17, 49, 50(table), 50–51, 52(table), 52–53, 59, 67(n4), 69(n36)
  comparative advantage, 269–275, 276(fig), 277–291
  composition, 260, 261(fig), 262(fig)
  factor content, 277–287
  geographic pattern, 260, 263(fig), 264(fig), 265
  growth and, 254–260
  growth of, 121, 144, 155, 228–229, 255(fig)
  indirect, 4, 6
  inputs, 280–283(figs)
  liberalization of, 143, 196–197, 295–296, 403
  policy, 294–299
  surplus, 207, 296
  See also Exports
Training, 373–374, 375(fig), 376, 377–378(table), 379–381(table), 382.
  See also Education
Transnational corporations (TNCs), 90–92, 306, 308, 310, 339
  brain drain and, 343–344
  foreign labor and, 328, 331
Treasury bills, 152(table), 153, 174(fig), 175, 176(table), 197
Trust funds, 127(table), 129–130(table), 132
TSC. *See* Taiwan Sugar Corporation
TSE. *See* Taiwan stock exchange

Tsiang, S. C., 134, 162
Tu, Jenn-Hwa, 325, 326
Tzeng, Y., 230

Underground economy, 245
Unemployment, 198(table), 223(table), 254, 367, 406, 407(table)
  DFI and, 324, 325–326
  "search," 430(n7)
Unions, 11, 417–419
United Kingdom, 257(table), 306(table), 308, 318, 333, 396
  DFI from, 342(table)
  land-aside programs, 63, 64
  Ministry of Agriculture, 63
United Nations, 315
United States, 12, 299, 308, 327, 347
  agricultural assistance from, 27–28
  capital from, 27–28, 314(table), 315, 318, 319, 320–321, 321(table), 322(table), 324, 327, 328, 342(table)
  capital markets, 212
  Conservation Reserve Program (CRP), 63, 64
  DFI to, 333, 335(table), 336, 337
  Export-Import Bank, 313
  exports, 257(table)
  financial institutions, 132
  Food Security Act, 63
  foreign workers in, 311
  GDP structure, 306(table)
  labor from, 328, 329(table), 330, 331, 345
  land-aside programs, 63, 64
  protectionism in, 57(table)
  relations with, 10, 296, 298
  Social Security system, 426
  Taiwanese students in, 423
  taxes in, 249(n3)
  trade policy, 298
  trade relations, 319, 340, 341
  trade with, 3, 5, 110, 263(fig), 264(fig), 265, 266(fig), 296(table), 327, 405

Valuation, 85, 91, 200, 201(fig), 203–204, 209, 219(n5), 258, 265, 295
Value added, 97, 98(table)
  in government enterprises, 94, 95(table)
  growth in, 78(&table)
  knowledge transfer and, 89
  sectoral structure of, 87(table), 88
  in service sector, 107(&table)
Vietnam, 347
Vocational Training Fund, 374
von Furstenberg, G., 231

Wade, Robert, 75, 76, 84, 94
Wages, 185, 279, 284(fig), 327, 428
  DFI and, 321
  industrial, 401, 402(table), 403, 406–408, 410, 411
  minimum, 410, 411, 420
  product quality and, 291
  remittance of, 311
  See also Income
Westphal, Larry E., 88
Wine industry, 7
Women
  education of, 370(fig), 373
  in labor force, 346–347, 350, 362, 365(fig), 366, 367, 390, 406, 424
  training of, 374, 376, 380–381(table), 382
World Bank, 313
Wu, Chung-Chi, 424
Wu, Hui-Lin, 410
Wu, Po-Hsiung, 404–405
Wu, Rong-I., 324, 400, 410

Yonekura, Minoro, 339